THE CITY AS COMEDY

EDITED BY GREGORY W. DOBROV

THE CITY AS COMEDY

Society and
Representation in
Athenian Drama

The University of
North Carolina Press

Chapel Hill & London

© 1997 The University of North Carolina Press

All rights reserved

Designed by April Leidig-Higgins

Set in Berkeley Book and Kadmos Greek

by Keystone Typesetting, Inc.

Manufactured in the United States of America

The paper in this book meets the guidelines for
permanence and durability of the Committee on
Production Guidelines for Book Longevity of the
Council on Library Resources.

Library of Congress Cataloging-in-Publication Data

The city as comedy: society and representation
in Athenian drama / edited by Gregory W. Dobrov.
p. cm. Includes bibliographical references and index.
ISBN 0-8078-2337-6 (cloth: alk. paper)
ISBN 0-8078-4645-7 (pbk.: alk. paper)
1. Greek drama (Comedy)—History and criticism.
2. Literature and society—Greece—Athens.
3. City and town life in literature. 4. Cities and
towns in literature. 5. Athens (Greece)—In
literature. 6. Mimesis in literature. I. Dobrov,
Gregory W., 1957– .
PA3875.A8D63   1998   97-9888
882′.019091732—dc21   CIP

01 00 99 98 97   5 4 3 2 1

FOR JONI,

who hatched with our
San Francisco *Birds*

Why behave in public if
you're living on a playground?
—David Lee Roth

CONTENTS

INTRODUCTION

In late March of the year 414 B.C. (Elaphebolion 11, archonship of Charias), a representative subset of the Athenian body politic—upward of sixteen thousand—gathered on the south slope of the Acropolis for the second official day of the City Dionysia. The next portion of the festival would be devoted to the dramatic competitions played before this polis-in-microcosm arranged, perhaps, by tribe in the sections of the Theater of Dionysus. Among the announcements made several days earlier in the Odeon were the comic titles *Revelers* by Ameipsias, *The Solitary* by Phrynichus, and *Birds* by Callistratus, Aristophanes' "assistant" under whose name the playwright had launched his career in the early 420s. Comedy and tragedy were important, if not dominant, components of this national festival, which involved much else besides: first a day of preliminary ceremonies in honor of Dionysus, followed by the official inauguration on Elaphebolion 10 by a great procession and other solemn business, culminating in the dithyramb, the premier event in which the Athenian tribes competed for prestigious prizes. Significantly, this first day was honored by a law that prohibited the holding of assemblies and the initiation of any legal business (even prisoners were released on bail in order to attend). On the morning of the second day, the demos would see an impressive sequence of public displays in which Athens dramatized itself as a community and imperial power: the ritual purification of the theater, the pouring of libations by civic leaders, the solemn naming of eminent citizens and state benefactors, the display of allied tribute, and the presentation of honors to (male) war orphans. Finally, toward noon, the herald would cry out "Bring on your chorus!" signaling that the show had begun. We cannot know which day of the festival saw the performance of Aristophanes' *Birds*, but we can be certain that, with over twenty speaking parts, unusually beautiful and varied costumes, and a heady mixture of poetry, music, and fantasy, it was a memorable performance. No one could have guessed, however, that this second-prize winner would survive for millennia as one of *the* masterpieces of Greek comedy, famous for sustaining an outlandish city hovering aloft in brazen defiance of Heaven itself.

Even from our cultural and temporal distance, we can appreciate how profoundly Cloudcuckooland must have been determined by the contexts of its production, and it is telling that the name lingers in English usage as a rare trace of ancient utopianism. Current work on tragedy, satyr play, and dithyramb reveals how much the literary critic, philologist, and historian have to gain from an awareness of these contexts. Drama's "mental venture of politics," to use Christian Meier's phrase, both drew upon and influenced the pervasive theatricality of Athenian public life. We submit that neither aspect—"purely political" or "purely theatrical"—can be assigned priority and that each must be viewed with the other as evolving in a hermeneutic circle. In the case of comedy we are dealing with an immanently political genre that *directly* transformed its environment, and its contexts into a fictional scenario played to the demos by its own members. "Only at the comic festivals," Jeffrey Henderson has noted in his essay "Comic Hero versus Political Elite," "could the mass of ordinary citizens see one of their own in the limelight, speaking their own language, and voicing their own complaints and desires in a contemporary context." The polis—as a place, a political entity, a system of social organization, and a set of ideological representations—was featured on the stage from Cratinus to Menander in a remarkable and changing series of cityscapes that were striking as explicit self-representations with a twist—that is, reflections complicated by distortion in the curved mirror of comedy. The extant plays of Aristophanes and the rich fragmentary remains of works by other composers have long been plundered as a source book of Athenian social and political history. Until recently, however, there has been little interest in reversing this process—studying how, for at least two centuries, Athens itself was transformed, staged as comedy, shaped at each point by current thematic, social, and ideological forces. This aspect of the "Greek imaginary"—the complex of representations through which a civilization articulates itself and its world—is the subject of our collective inquiry.

The City as Comedy is situated at the crossroads of several discourses. In the precinct of classical studies we find abiding interest in theatrical production and its material circumstances (with the works of A. W. Pickard-Cambridge as the cornerstone), and the question of "Aristophanes and politics," which has engaged historians such as A. W. Gomme, G. E. M. de Ste. Croix and W. Kraus. In a more exploratory "crossover" sector, P. Pucci, C. Segal, F. Zeitlin, and others have broken new ground by bringing the perspectives of cultural anthropology, psychoanalysis, feminism, and poststructuralist theory to bear on the ancient material. Recent publications in a variety of fields outside classics such as T. Leinwand's *The City Staged* (Jacobean comedy), M. Carlson's *Places of Performance* (theater architecture and semiotics), and C. Wick-Sizemore's *A Female Vision of the City* (nineteenth-century novel) attest to a growing interest in the urban contexts of literary production. The "literary city" has emerged as an organizing principle, a repository of cultural vectors, and a construct whose relationship to the "real world" is oblique and unstable. From a given scenario with a specific topography—Philocleon's house, for example—we work our way mentally outward to the wider, imagined city environment, the "theatrical space without," in which every play, scene, and gesture is embedded and by which everything that happens on stage is determined. We begin, then, by avoiding the extremes of approaching the comic polis either as a mere fantasy evoked by an autonomous text or as a simple mirror of contemporary politics. To this we must add that the striking differences between the political organization of Athens and that of later European states and between the Athenian festivals and later modes of theatrical production render cross-cultural generalizations about "theater" and "city" problematic, not to say misleading. We can only do justice to a genre as so long-lived, sophisticated, and engagé by striving for depth and detail.

Athenian comedy has long struggled to escape the overpowering gravity of its more prestigious and (deceptively) accessible sister genre. For generations, in all areas from metrics to exegesis, tragedy has claimed the lion's share of scholarly attention. Comedy's very resistance to inquiries from the fields of literary and cultural studies has everything to do with its value for historians. The intense engagement with society and the circumstances of its production imparts to the language, subjects, and design of the genre a special degree of difficulty and specificity that can be enormously informative but frustrating. In other words, comedy is very "live" and very "other." To begin with, we know very little about the first sixty years of comedy in festival competition between Chionides' first recorded victory (486 B.C.) and *Acharnians*, the earliest surviving script. The extant plays of Aristophanes, moreover, are baffling even in a narrow comparison with tragedy. Absurd fantasy, ubiquitous topicality, difficult play with an already difficult language, uniquely elaborate *Bauformen* (epirrhematic syzygy and parabasis), and a peculiar lyric style conspire against the casual reader/viewer. To this we must add the complexity of comedy's reflexive subject, the polis itself. Neither the audience at the festivals nor the polis at large was in any way unitary, and we must acknowledge the existence of many coexisting communities: citizen-males in their "executive" sphere; visiting and resident foreigners; women, as a potential "female body politic" (δῆμος τῶν γυναικῶν, *Thesm.* 309, 336), as members of the oikos (with children, slaves, etc.), and as participants in cults where various social strata mingled. Our understanding of the complexities and nuances of the comic polis will always be a function of our grasp of the historical and cultural realia. Equally important, however, is an understanding of the comic forces by which these realia are shaped, distorted, and transformed. The present volume, then, finds its raison d'être in comedy's relative neglect and the lack of a readily available and up-to-date collection devoted exclusively to the genre that integrates new and diverse critical approaches.

In focusing on one theme in a single genre, this symposium nevertheless comprehends an unusual variety—from Eupolis to Menander, fantasy to mannerism, food to ideology—through a plurality of critical approaches: philological, historical, performance, feminist, deconstructive, new historicist. The main sections into which the volume is articulated represent the principal fields of inquiry: fifth-century utopianism, comic transformations of social reality, and the construction of a realistic, if stylized, comic polis in which to play the new comedy of manners. Despite its notoriously social and utopian constitution, Old Comedy has only recently begun to be studied in ways that embrace both its engagement with the polis and its uniqueness as a scenic, linguistic, and literary construct. The first five essays, "The Theory and Practice of Utopia," undertake this project, concentrating on Aristophanes' Nephelokokkugia, the most sustained and enigmatic utopian city in fifth-century drama. The conspicuous lack of effective criticism on *Birds* is symptomatic of a scholarly tradition that has been outclassed and outwitted, so to speak, by its subject. Among the questions addressed in these essays are: How is the comic polis "other"? What criteria inform its departures from reality? How were the comic inventions of Aristophanes, Eupolis, et al. influenced by utopianism and proto-utopianism in discourses outside comedy? Did the "looking-glass" cities in plays such as *Birds* and *Ecclesiazusae* engage the spectators in harmless, carnivalesque fun or were they ironic comedies of ideas whose force was satirical and critical, perhaps even with some power to influence public opinion? How did the manipulative and creative powers of language cultivated by the sophists manifest themselves in the discovery of possible stage-worlds? What is the significance of conspicuous visitors from other genres such as Prometheus and Tereus and what relationship do they establish between the comic fiction and that of their apparent origin? How was the polis played, physically, before its own microcosm assembled in the theatron?

We begin with a lucid anatomy of the utopian polis along ideological lines by David Konstan. Building on a suggestion by Umberto Eco, Konstan sharpens the blunt neologism "utopia" to cut four ways, extending the polysemous cultural determinant *nomos* to negotiate the relationships between the Athenian society and Nephelokokkugia: *anomia*, *eunomia*, *antinomia*, and *megalonomia*. Aristophanes' intersection of the four categories preempts any effort to establish a coherent and sustained allegorical relation between the elements of the play and specific real-world referents. *Birds* is an "interrogative text" that generates an astonishing variety of questions as it traces the career of an *apragmon* without a polis to supreme tyranny and beyond. A metaphor of the intellectual and political climate of the city nearly two decades into the Peloponnesian War, Nephelokokkugia flaunts its contradictory ideology by mingling celebration with misgivings in a sustained political satire.

The exploration of Aristophanic utopianism continues in the next essay, by Thomas Hubbard, who focuses on comic reinvention of the polis in accordance with contemporary theoretical paradigms. First, an "Arcadian" yearning for a past beatitude (the golden age, Eden) is distinguished from utopianism proper which looks to political salvation in a future world, a "New Jerusalem." Seen in this light, the only true utopias in extant Greek comedy are those of *Birds* and *Ecclesiazusae*. Hubbard brings the complexity and fascination of his subject into full view by revealing important connections between Aristophanes' constructed cities and the intellectual programs of sophists such as Hippodamus of Miletus, Prodicus of Ceos, and Phaleas of Chalcedon. Reflecting the idea of an intellectuals' mecca à la Thurii, *Birds* dramatizes the abandonment of democracy and the construction of a relativist tyranny in "sophistic space." This satire, Hubbard suggests, would resonate with current popular outrage against members of the social elite held responsible for recent sacrileges and disturbances. *Ecclesiazusae* receives a similarly ironic reading as a critique of radical social reform. Praxagora's program caricatures the unworkable and coercive utopianism of an intellectual elite who deconstructs its democratic discourse through behavior that perpetuates its own influence and power.

F. E. Romer's contribution synthesizes much recent work on Aristophanes in an original and ambivalent reading of the political myth in *Birds*. Constructed in the developing context of pre-utopian legends and proto-utopian literature, Nephelokokkugia reflects human psychology and development by revealing how cultural innovation betrays its continuity, how the new is the old. The "return to origins" suggested in the prologue with its reversal of contemporary evolutionary thinking results, paradoxically, in the reinvention of a counter-Athens in the air. The wide allusive field of the play incorporates countless texts, motifs, and characters for significant comment. We watch Peisetaerus interact with Aesop, Hesiod, and the tragic Prometheus, for example, to redraw the lines of civilization. His brave new world emerges as shockingly archaic, indeed pre-Olympian, in that it conspicuously lacks (mortal) women and is ruled by an anxious patriarch who roasts his own "children."

In the vivid piece of performance criticism that follows, Niall Slater invites us to the theater of the mind for a view of the comic polis as a series of enactments, both mimetic and self-consciously nonillusory. The language of *Birds* participates in the performance situation to an unprecedented degree. Thus the inspired wordplay and prominent use of theatrical terminology articulate the evolving fable in terms of the physical space available in the theater of Dionysus. In a wider perspective, staging the city involves insistent foregrounding of language in its performative dimension, well beyond the expected contexts of civic and cultic ceremony. Peisetaerus hijacks the dramatic festival, as it were, by doubling as city planner (*didaskalos* of the bird folk) and playwright (*chorodidaskalos*) who flaunts his creative power. Slater moderates between extreme responses to the "riddle of *Birds*"—that is, the extent to which it was politically engagé. Underscoring Old Comedy's generic limitations in this regard, he notes that "the bird city, built in a theatre, becomes . . . a model of Aristophanes' own art. As long as he believed in the comedy that he practiced, he could not make his theatrical city a place of misery."

Gregory W. Dobrov takes up the utopian modalities of language and fiction in an essay concluding "The Theory and Practice of Utopia." Suggesting a context for the entire section, his introductory review of scholarship points up the enduring oscillation between historical and escapist readings of *Birds*. This comedy of language has baffled and eluded critics by innovatively embracing aporia and dramatizing the linguistic process itself, especially the dynamics of metaphor with the man-to-bird transformation at the focus. Peisetaerus' Great Idea, for example, is sparked by a simple pun (πόλος to πόλις) and realized through a series of jokes, specious etymologies, and misreadings. The protagonist supervises the deconstruction of metaphor inspired by Tereus, his living blueprint for a future where birds are gods, men become birds, and therefore (at least one) man can be god. The initial indeterminacy of the play is resolved as Nephelokokkugia arises on a metafictional scaffolding of borrowed material such as Pherecrates' *Savages* and Sophocles' *Tereus*. The last section of the essay is devoted to articulating the ways in which comedy—*Birds* in particular—appropriates material from other festival genres and scripts. These "figures of play" are shown to react with the comedy of language to make a vital contribution to theatrical utopia.

The second section, "Playing along the Fault Lines," explores the sociopolitical and material contexts of comic representation to ask how and why effective enactments of the polis invariably trace fissures in the social fabric. Prominent tensions to emerge here are those of mass versus elite, male versus female, oikos versus polis, and dramatic discourse versus the discourses of assembly and the lawcourts. Interest in the social construction of gender and the elusive persona of the comic playwright (and his characters) vis-à-vis his society inspire particularly difficult confrontations with what used to be thought obvious: Who (what sector of society) are Aristophanes and Eupolis championing in their stage figures? How do we approach fictions of the female such as Lysistrata or Praxagora? What lines within the polis do the transgressive energies of comedy cross, and which are sacrosanct? Where, in the larger context of the polis, do we situate the many particular clashes between private and public, rural and urban, husband and wife, father and son?

Jeffrey Henderson negotiates an effective transition from the comprehensive utopianism of the first section to the focus on dramatic microstructure in the second. His analysis of how the comic hero plays along social fault lines responds to the "theory and practice" outlined in the first section with a defiantly nonironic analysis of Peisetaerus, the highly unusual protagonist of *Birds*. Henderson's stimulating disagreement with "ironists" such as Hubbard and Romer proceeds from his understanding of how the comic hero is socially determined. A fictitious, ordinary, and nonpartisan champion of the collectivity, the typical Aristophanic hero of the 420s negotiated a conflict between the demos and an elite who depends on it for power. Members of the elite, by contrast, are specifically depicted as contemporaries, often named and always impersonated. Desirable aristocratic qualities were extended to the common demos, while the "objectively" elite was aligned with outsiders (foreigners, prostitutes, slaves, criminals). True to form, *Birds* challenges this paradigm by innovatively constructing its protagonist as a member of the intellectual and social elite. In Peisetaerus, who emerges as a complex composite—as opposed to a recognizable character type—Aristophanes explores the relationship of this social stratum to the polis at a time of great excitement, tension, and unrest.

In a stimulating subsection, Ralph Rosen and Elizabeth Bobrick take a close look at configurations of gender in the work of Eupolis and Aristophanes, respectively. Eupolis' *Cities* (*Poleis*, produced ca. 422 B.C.) featured a remarkable, allegorical chorus, with women representing individual city-states allied with Athens. The conspicuously marked gender of this city-chorus offers an unusual and subtle perspective on the ways Athenians conceived of their polity, and on the corporate psychology that gave rise to such choral self-presentation. In a careful review of the fragments of *Cities* and other relevant evidence, Rosen demonstrates the various ways in which an Athenian male citizen body conceptualizes the polis as "feminine." The rare glimpse we get from comic choruses intended to represent subject cities reveals how Athens' uncompromising attitudes to its own political hegemony were shaped by contemporary attitudes toward gender, and modeled on the role of male and female within the Athenian oikos. Even though Athenian males conceptualized a polis as "feminine," insofar as they regarded their own polis as superior in force and moral legitimacy to foreign, subject poleis, they applied a different discourse of gendering to each. Athens, as "mother" city, as manager of an oikos, could be described in metaphors from a social realm in which women played an active (o)economic role equivalent to that of men. Foreign cities, on the other hand, though also "feminized" conceptually, were characterized by metaphors that reflected a subordination of female power.

"When the polis becomes a stage," asks Bobrick, "what part do women get to play?" Taking her cue from Barbara Freedman's recent work, she examines how a theatrical narrative manages to promote the ideology whose arbitrariness it purports to unmask. Her detailed study of Aristophanes' *Thesmophoriazusae* reveals the enactment of power on the part of those who produce culture for a subordinate "consumer class" committed to imitating dominant forms. The action unfolds in a display of how members of various social categories participate in the civic spectacle. Although the male-female conflict of the first half mutates into a different set of oppositions—for example, Greek versus barbarian, pathic versus female—the "tyranny of roles" remains intact. Interactions between Euripides' kinsman and the tragic playwright Agathon, in particular, point up the asymmetry of comic travesty: while the imitation of women by men is relatively easy, indeed *required* at certain moments (e.g., in playing a female role), the reverse is difficult and much more constrained. The female figure is a dramatic catalyst that does not so much *act* as *symbolize* action within the wide scope of the male gaze. In the play world, paradoxically, the instability and permeability of male sexual categories confirm the traditional boundaries of female sexuality. Even the ritual underpinnings of the Thesmophoria conspire in this "tyranny of roles" as the motif of female rescue of female (Demeter and Kore) is transformed into male rescue of female. Comedy, in other words, is a good mirror but bad medicine.

The following essay by Gregory Crane explores the "thickly described" struggle between oikos ("household") and polis arising from material conditions such as the emergence of a monetary economy and the growth of empire in the classical period. Taking Aristophanes' *Wasps* as his focal document, Crane foregrounds the way in which the agora mediates the tension between the individual oikos and the polis that threatens to subsume it. This social satire is viewed, however, in a wide and richly articulated context beginning with a discussion situating the discourse of Old Comedy in the Greek poetic tradition as a whole. In a historical tour de force, Crane defines the fifth-century Athenian agora as a site for monetary exchange and centralized government in contrast to civic centers in other cultures (Persia) and times (e.g., the "empty" agora of Archaic Greece). The oikos/polis tension in Aristophanes is then mapped in relation to various ideals of civic and domestic space from Solon to Aristotle. The polis of comedy, however, is not an abstraction but a "*somatic*, sensible entity, shaped by intellectual forces, yet present in its parts and its grainy particularity." *Wasps* presents a spectacle in which a son with elitist affectations weans his father away from the lawcourts and the agora to refashion the old man in his own image. Crane's reading contributes to the long-standing debate about unity by making natural sense of the second part of *Wasps* in relation to this first movement: thinking this "weaning" a success, Bdelykleon tries to establish his father in the sphere of the oikos. He fails (of course) and Philocleon enacts the irony of impasse by escaping both "oikos" and "polis" to dance in the transgressive space of the comic theater.

The political force of comedy remains in the focus as Malcolm Heath explores the complex relation between the dramatic genre and extratheatrical political discourse. Striving to move beyond recent work on this subject, Heath emphasizes the importance of reading Aristophanes against the broad backdrop of oratory of the fifth *as well as* the fourth centuries. Important points of continuity that emerge include political invective, an interest in justice, and an aggressive claim to benefit the city. Many features commonly identified as unique to comic satire turn out to be standard "democratic" topoi that are not ideologically distinct. To be sure, the polis as evoked in plays such as *Knights* and *Frogs* is striking in its particulars, such as the vivid speech of the characters, the specific "design" of the fictive world, and the presentation of the poet himself as a creative and social agent. Heath argues, however, that a successful comic poet told his audience what they already knew and what they wanted to be told, and in this respect we should be wary of equating the comic competition with other forms of political appeal. Any attempt to draw strict lines of demarcation between the comic and primary worlds will be no more than an irreducibly contingent interpretation. To this we must add the danger of circularity whereby, from a script alone, we hypothesize phenomena outside the text, in "tension" with it, or "negotiating" terms between the script and the contexts of its production.

The section on society and representation concludes in a manner appropriate to comedy, with a banquet! John Wilkins brings a special expertise in the ancient cultures of food and eating to his study of the polis as constructed on the comic stage. Where there is comedy, there is food—from the rich banquets of Old Comedy to the scraps from Athenaeus' table that have been a scholarly staple for generations. In a stimulating series of readings from a wide variety of comic authors, Wilkins explores the diacritical force of food in comic representations—how food was central to the life of the polis as an important marker of social identity and status, a vital element of trade and agriculture, a component of negotiation between cities as well as between humans and gods, and a crucial term in relations between individuals. We eavesdrop on a meal in the Prytaneum, pay a visit to the market, and even step outside Athens for a feast with the gods courtesy of Epicharmus. The centerpiece of the essay is a study of *Knights* that outlines the complex ways in which Aristophanes thematizes food and eating throughout this most incisive of political allegories. The irony of circularity looms large here as we realize how much of what we soberly treasure as history—especially material details of daily life—is attested only in the scripts from comic productions. Countless elements of the "real" polis that we would like to hold as "controls" in our study of drama turn out to be scraps from the comic banquet. The comic polis, in other words, is often the only polis!

The final movement of our collective effort looks beyond the fin de siècle brilliance of Aristophanes and his contemporaries to the comic world of the fourth century when the genre underwent profound transformations. Along with formal changes in language and dramatic structure that took place between *Acharnians* and *Dyscolus*, we note a host of internal shifts in theme, plot, and mood. The principle governing the reconfiguration of the comic universe on its way to New Comedy is implicit in Aristotle's notion of "the probable" (*Poet.* 1451b9). First, the logic of plot construction is grounded in probable sequence, unity of action, and the careful motivation of entrances and exits. Second, the realities of place and time are respected, yielding a much more sober and familiar world inhabited by projections of contemporary types. Finally, the speech and actions of these characters conform to what "probably" would happen in real life or, at any rate, what *could* happen. The emergence of the urbane new world of Alexis and Menander had much to do, no doubt, with the influence of tragic melodrama with its tighter plots and pervasive dramatic illusion. Comedy, moreover, had become an export product from which intense topicality and other "Aristophanic" features such as obscenity, fantasy, and political satire were necessarily attenuated by "market pressures." The ongoing discovery of Menander throughout this century, now complemented by the masterly presentation of the comic fragments in R. Kassel and C. Austin's *Poetae Comici Graeci*, puts us in a superior position to ask important questions about comedy and its evolution: What happened to the theatrical cityscape toward the end of Aristophanes' life? What about politics and satire? Is Middle Comedy as barren and New Comedy as apolitical as the handbooks would have us believe? What sort of imaginary space is constructed around the immediate "neighborhood" of a typical Middle and New Comedy? What do the changes in comic representation tell us about how Athenians saw themselves in the generations between Aegospotami and Crannon?

The two final essays of the volume by Heinz-Günther Nesselrath and Timothy Hofmeister are devoted to Middle Comedy and New Comedy, respectively, with a particular interest in addressing common misunderstandings about the genre as it evolved into its most influential and enduring form. Nesselrath extends the contribution of his authoritative *Die attische Mittlere Komödie* to focus on the comic polis between 380 and 320 B.C. Despite the weakness of the evidence, the world of Middle Comedy has not been entirely erased and we read in the fragmentary record a story rich in political and social detail. With a colorful comic prosopography and some remarkably outspoken poets (e.g., Eubulus), Middle Comedy, on close inspection, does not look at all like Gilbert

Norwood's "trickling void." Where a previous generation saw a desert, Nesselrath finds a polis, one that looks Janus-like back to the satire of Old Comedy and forward to the cityscape of Menander. From the grainy details of everyday life such as the preparation and eating of fish and the personae of various hetairai, we ascend to Olympus for a fascinating glimpse of political allegory by Heniochus in which the Greek poleis gather to celebrate their newly won freedom. "The poets of Middle Comedy," concludes Nesselrath, "seem to have captured all aspects of contemporary public life—political, social, and cultural—of Athens. They combined the various elements of polis life into a sometimes curious mixture, which certainly distorted the picture of this polis, but was nevertheless recognizable by its theatergoing inhabitants and highlighted the more peculiar sides of it for them."

"Where then is the polis in Menander?" asks Timothy Hofmeister in the concluding essay. Taking his cue from Nesselrath's closing comments linking the political failure of Athens and the emergence of an apolitical New Comedy, Hofmeister is intent on subverting accepted generalizations and looking much further into the play worlds of Menander to describe their wider context, the "theatrical space without." Though distinctly nonhegemonic, Menander's polis is still palpably Athenian and articulated into specific factions, spaces, and oppositions (e.g., oikos vs. polis). Nuanced readings of *Samia*, *Sicyonian*, *Epitrepontes*, and other plays reveal a Menander who is far from having given up on the polis in favor of a generalized *oikoumenê* animated by fierce individualism. Time and again we catch a glimpse of the entire polis mapped through a combination of setting, characters, and narrative. Menander's plays, as interrogative texts, differ from earlier comedy less in their situation or topography than in the questions they ask and suggest. It is fitting that our volume conclude by looking toward the Hellenistic Age to grapple with issues every bit as "political" as those with which we began: How did the new generation of comic poets view the inherent problems of the oikos? In what ways was the life of the polis seen as endangered or transformed by the *oikoumenê*, the expanded world of the time? How did drama transform its own matrix, socially, politically, and aesthetically to display the city as comedy?

PART ONE

The Theory and Practice of Utopia

DAVID KONSTAN

The Greek Polis and Its Negations

Versions of Utopia in Aristophanes' *Birds*

In the opening scene of *Birds*, which Aristophanes exhibited at the dramatic festival of the City Dionysia in the year 414 B.C., two Athenian citizens, weary of constant lawsuits back home, take off in search of a better, or at all events less litigious, city in which to take up residence.[1] They seek out first an odd creature, the former king of Thrace named Tereus, who, legend had it, had been transformed for his sins into a hoopoe.[2] The idea is that this hoopoe, knowing what both humans and the soaring birds have seen, is best equipped to point them in the right direction (119). The hoopoe turns out to have established himself as a figure of authority among the birds. Thus Pisthetaerus, the cannier of the two Athenian wanderers, after hearing and rejecting a couple of possible sites for relocation, suddenly hits on a different plan: to found a city among the birds themselves. That will be the new, litigation-free community they seek.

What is more, such a city will be in a position to achieve limitless power, and even challenge the gods themselves for supremacy over the universe. The reason is geopolitical: the birds occupy the air, which is the region between the earth, where humans dwell, and the heavenly abode of the gods. If the birds will fortify this zone by surrounding it with a wall, and declare it off limits to all trade and trespass unless official permission is granted, then the birds can strictly control the passage from earth to heaven of sacrificial aromas—that is, the substance on which the gods depend for their nourishment. In a word, the birds can starve the gods into submission. As for humans, the birds can offer extraordinary benefits—for example, an end to plagues of locusts, but also much finer things, like wings and longevity. Contrariwise, they can inflict dire punishment upon the recalcitrant, such as pecking out the eyes of cattle and their own style of aerial bombardment. Thus, mortals are bound to submit to the new avian regime, and gladly.

And so it happens. Men not only yield to the birds, but they also ape their ways and flock to the new city in order to borrow wings and enjoy its special blessings. The gods, for their part, put up some resistance, but hunger gets the better of them and the final scene shows Pisthetaerus, now king of the omnipotent city of the birds, marrying the goddess Sovereignty and thereby confirming in a sacred celebration the new order of things.

Such, in outline, is the plot of *Birds*. Two problems are apparent even in this brief summary. First, the original impulse behind the venture of the two Athenians (namely, to find a calmer, less contentious place) seems to have been all but forgotten in the new scheme, which is to erect an all-powerful state among the birds and seize control over the universe from the gods, all under the leadership of Pisthetaerus.[3] Second, the birds not only achieve sovereignty over gods and men alike, they also become founders of a kind of model city that mortals seek to join, or imitate. Not only benefits, but wings too are conferred on human beings, beginning with Pisthetaerus and his companion, Euelpides, at the moment when they first persuade the birds to adopt their ambitious plan. Is the city of the birds a different place, an ideal community blessed with all good things? Or is it a caricature of human cities, and more particularly of Athens, so that Pisthetaerus and Euelpides, in their pursuit of a peaceful land, have succeeded only in reproducing the very kind of society they had abandoned, full of struggle and restless desire? On the one hand, the solidarity of the birds is contrasted with the competitive strife that characterizes Athens; on the other hand, a vision of peace and plenty coincides with a reign of limitless imperial desire. These paradoxical intersections are a reflection of tensions in Athenian ideology at the time of the Peloponnesian War, and testify to the contradictory elements of which it is composed—elements that Aristophanes reworks into a novel narrative structure.

In the minds of Athenians, in the years 415–414, there was one event in particular: the launching of the great naval expedition against Sicily, with the aim of conquering the Greek cities on the island. These cities favored the Spartan side in the conflict with Athens, recently suspended in a wary truce between the two powers. The larger object of the campaign was to cut the Peloponnesian peninsula off from its overseas allies. If Athens could gain complete control over the western, as well as the eastern, Mediterranean, it might then isolate the Lacedaemonians and compel their surrender. One need not rehearse the extraordinary excitement that attended the launching. Thucydides has given us a brilliant record of the hopes and ambitions that rode with the armada, the greatest military undertaking, he says, in Greek history (6.31). Some voices, to be sure, were raised against it, notably that of the distinguished general Nicias, who was nevertheless placed in charge of the expedition. Alcibiades was avid for it, but charges of impiety leveled against him by opponents—with what truth it is impossible to say—induced him to abandon the fleet and his native city and join the Spartan cause. The upshot, as we know but the Athenians in the audience at the production of *Birds* did not, was the utter defeat of the armada off Syracuse.

This cursory sketch of the circumstances in which the performance of *Birds* took place will readily indicate why it has been tempting to draw a parallel between Athens' ambition to conquer the seaways and Pisthetaerus' plan by which the birds will take over the sky and place an embargo on sacrificial odors until the gods give in. As Jeffrey Henderson writes, "the resemblance of the plot to the sensational events of the preceding year . . . is close enough that no spectator could fail to see it."[4] Various attempts at an allegorical reading have foundered, however, as systematic identifications between figures in the drama and contemporary political personalities have yielded inconsistent results and contradictory messages.

The practice was launched early in the nineteenth century by J. W. Suevern.[5] I quote from a summary of Suevern's view in an old school edition: "*The Birds* is a kind of allegory to dissuade the Athenians from the Sicilian expedition by exposing its folly. The birds are the Athenians; Cloud-cuckoo-land their visionary empire; the planners of it are certain politicians and orators; Pisthetaerus is Alcibiades with a dash of Gorgias . . . ; the gods are the Lacedaemonians, to be surrounded in the Peloponnese and starved out."[6]

This theory was influential in its time,[7] but by the end of the century W. C. Green, whom I have been quoting, could dismiss it without much argument. Green comments simply that "the Bird-city founded in the play with complete success, a city to which is given all that Aristophanes . . . thought good, and from which is excluded all that he thought bad . . .—this city cannot be held up by the poet as a warning, and as a folly to be avoided" (8–9). For good measure, Green cites the opinion of H. A. T. Köchly, who, while remaining committed to the allegorical method, took a view just the reverse of Suevern's. According to Köchly, the city of the birds is not a warning but an ideal: "It is to be a democracy, but yet to have a head: a Periclean democracy. And the head recommended or hinted at . . . is Alcibiades."[8] Given such fundamental disagreement, Green despaired not only of an allegorical reading of the play, but of a political reading on any terms. The play was written by the poet, he declared, "to relieve and amuse his audience." Here and there may lurk allusions to the contemporary world, but the characters in the comedy are universal, and "they suit all time" (12).

The issues canvassed by Green over a hundred years ago are still very much alive. In a brilliant essay, William Arrowsmith revived the theory that the city of the birds is a warning to the Athenians: it is "Aristophanes' image of what all human *physis* [nature] would be if it truly dared to assert itself against the *nomos* [law, custom] of society and religion."[9] It represents what Arrowsmith calls the "fantasy politics" that bore Athens to its heroic defeat, a politics grounded not in moderation or self-control, but in *erōs*, the fatal passion for empire. Arrowsmith reminds us that Alcibiades, according to Plutarch, carried an image of the winged god Eros on his golden shield as he set sail for Sicily,[10] and that the chorus of birds, in its new vision of cosmic mastery, claim Eros as the ancestor of its race (698–99, 703–4). Passionate desire thus characterizes both the city of the birds and the policy of a specific party in Athens, and such desire, for Arrowsmith and doubtless for some Athenians as well, is marked negatively as excess. At least one critic, moreover, has reasserted the contrary idea that the city of the birds represents the ideal rule of the Athenian demos or people. "The Olympian gods are, in the play, the enemies of human beings; they are, moreover, symbols for the enemies of the democracy."[11] Finally, a number of scholars today flatly reject a political reading. Cedric Whitman, for example, asserts: "The theme of the *Birds* is absurdity itself . . . it is about meaninglessness" and "is strangely free of political concerns."[12]

Interpretations of *Birds* thus continue to gravitate between positive and negative allegories of the new city founded by Pisthetaerus and his companion, or else to abandon a political reading altogether and dismiss the entire adventure as sheer comic extravaganza. In his introduction, Gregory Dobrov sounds a wise caution against the alternatives of treating the comic polis "either as a mere fantasy evoked by an autonomous text or as a simple mirror of contemporary politics."[13] If *Birds* is a political drama, it is nevertheless not an immediate reflection or imitation of conditions in the Athenian city-state in the year 414 B.C. In this sense, there is no actual historical referent, a world "out there" represented in the text.[14] The object of criticism is rather to analyze the elements that enter into the complex and contradictory image of the city of the birds, and display the operations by which they are organized in the narrative and made to cohabit in a single imaginary space.[15] We must recognize at the same time that these elements are themselves given by the culture, and are thus signs of social values, subject in their own right to complex determinations.[16]

In discussing the nature of science fiction, Umberto Eco remarks: "What distinguishes the fantastic narrative from the realistic . . . is the fact that its possible world is *structurally* different from the real one."[17] Eco proceeds to enumerate "several paths that fantastic literature can take," assigning to the various species names such as allotopia, uchronia, metachronia, metatopia, as well as the familiar utopia. Eco's classification invites attention to the ways in which a utopian community stands in relation to a society's conventional representation of itself. Fantastic literature, he says, asks "what would happen if the real world was not similar to itself, if its structure, that is, were different?" Eco chooses the roots of *topos* and *chronos*, "place" and "time," as the basis for his neologisms. For the analysis of Aristophanes' *Birds*, however, it is more useful to attend to relations between Aristophanes' fantasy utopia and prevailing social norms. In this spirit, I offer a technical vocabulary based on the term *nomos* (plural *nomoi*), the meaning of which in classical Greek covers the range of ideas we express by the words "law," "custom," and "rule." It can also refer to a certain type of poem, and, with a different placement of the accent, to a pasture or feeding ground (including that of birds).[18] A Dutch scholar has recently argued for the centrality of this term in all its senses to Aristophanes' *Birds*, in which the song of the birds, "as sweet and holy as the surrounding nature," is contrasted with human "law and morality."[19] I shall exploit the idea of *nomos* in order to discriminate several ways in which a utopian society may be distinguished structurally from an order represented as traditional.

The Greeks perceived human communities to be characterized by specific sets of rules or customs. Herodotus, for example, introduces each major ethnic group in his *Histories* with a description of its *nomoi*.[20] The *nomoi* define a social space, a place or *topos* that is marked out as distinctive by virtue of its organization under laws that differentiate it from other regions.[21] The problem, accordingly, is to understand the ways in which an imaginary space, a No-place or Utopia in the name coined by Thomas More, is defined against the customs of known places. I have identified four broad kinds of relation between a utopia and a given place characterized by *nomoi*, and to each of these I have assigned a name. These types are offered as an aid to the analysis of the city of the birds, and the complexity of its ideological determinations.

First, a utopian society may be defined by absolute negation, that is, as having no rules or *nomoi* at all. Such a form may be posited as an ideal type, even if in practice one may doubt that such a community can be described or imagined. Any form of social differentiation among roles or prescribed behaviors presupposes some code or codes of conduct, and the complete absence of *nomoi* would mean the collapse of all social distinctions. But we may call a community that tends toward such an absolute lawlessness anomian, marked, that is, by the absence of rules, *anomia* or anomy.[22]

A second form of imaginary society we may identify as antinomian. Such a society is marked, not by the absence of *nomoi*, but by their reversal or inversion. This is the world turned upside down, as the renaissance emblem pictured it, the world of the antipodes, where everything is done backward. What is illegal at home is lawful there, and vice versa.[23]

We may distinguish a third kind of utopia with the label *eunomia*, or eunomy. This is a society in which the laws and conventions are imagined as just or excellent, rather than as a mirror image of one's own. Thomas More himself toyed with the name *eutopia*, the "good place," for his ideal polity (in the last verse of the second of the poems from Utopia).[24] Such a conception is evidently an extrapolation from some accepted version of good or just *nomoi*, the model for which will be values or laws immanent within one's own culture and projected as ideal.

Finally, a fantastic place may be characterized by hypertrophy with respect to the laws, a tendency to exceed all limits. The distinction here is quantitative rather than qualitative. The order of things is not better, it is simply grander, a magnified world without boundaries in which the rules give scope for ambition and desire. It is a type particularly hospitable to satire. As a neologism for this sort of exaggeration or inflation of the norms, perhaps megalonomy will do.

None of these four kinds of social otherness is likely to be represented in pure form, if indeed they logically can be. Nevertheless, one can call to mind examples in which one or another type seems to predominate in the characterization of an ideal or distant place. Plato presents his republic as just. Herodotus' Egyptians have customs the reverse of Greek practices. The cyclopes are represented in Homer as lacking *nomoi*. The competitive state of nature imagined by such sophists as Callicles and Thrasymachus (according to Plato) valorizes aggression and the pursuit of power, which are taken to be proper norms for human societies.[25] What is remarkable about the fabulous territory of Nephelokokkugia, or Cloudcuckooland, to adopt the most familiar English version of the name, is the way in which all four of the utopian forms I have identified enter into the image of it. I shall illustrate them in the order in which they have been mentioned.

In their primitive or natural condition, before the birds have experienced the benefits—if they are benefits—of their encounter with humans, the region that they inhabit has an anomian quality. To begin with, the birds carry no purses (157), and so are free from corruption, as Euelpides says, and also from the invidiousness of distinctions based on money or power (apart from the retinue of the hoopoe, who was formerly human, there is also no slavery among them).[26] Such simplicity, while it may be charming, strikes the Athenian visitors as a sign of witlessness, and Pisthetaerus, when he conceives his great plan for the birds, advises the hoopoe that they must, first and foremost, cease flying about everywhere with their jaws gaping. The gaping mouth is a standard Aristophanic image for dumb wonder.[27] But the subtler point in Pisthetaerus' advice lies, I suspect, in the adverb "everywhere" (*pantachêi*, 165). This kind of flightiness, says Pisthetaerus, is a dishonorable business: the Greek word he uses is *atimon*, literally, without *timê*, which means honor but, more concretely, applies to privileges of rank or office, and to the financial compensation for those and other services. To be *atimos*, without *timê*, is the legal status of a citizen who has been deprived of his civic rights, of the distinctions pertaining to membership in the polity of Athens.[28] A person who is unstable, *astathmêtos* (i.e., without a fixed abode or *stathmos*), one who is undefined or unfixed, *atekmartos* (the kind who has no marker or boundary, no *tekmar*)—such a one, according to Pisthetaerus, is called a bird back home in Athens. The hoopoe acknowledges the justice in this, and inquires what the birds can do about it. Pisthetaerus' answer is: build a city.

In this exchange, we may observe how the opposition between nature and culture, between the unconstrained freedom of the birds and the civilized order of human communities, is reduced to an elementary polarity: boundaries versus unboundedness, rest versus motion, a here and a there ("there, among us," says Pisthetaerus, 167) versus an everywhere. The domain of the birds is without termini, without the marks of difference. The birds do not "remain in the same place" (170). The terms of this contrast seem in part derived from a culturally valorized opposition between settled cities and nomadic groups,[29] but Aristophanes gives to the polarity an abstract turn. For the birds, in their perpetual changefulness, nothing is self-identical. The two adventurous Athenians, in their journey to the realm of the birds, have indeed arrived at a nowhere.

At the very beginning of the play, Pisthetaerus and Euelpides cannot decipher the cries of the crow and raven they have been carrying to guide them to the habitation of the birds. One seems to be urging them forward, the other back (1–2). They are in fact at the right spot, except that they are below the residence of the hoopoe. Thus, compass-point directions do not apply.[30] Nor do they know any longer in which direction Athens lies (10–11). Playfully, Aristophanes evokes a mysterious indeterminacy, a kind of metaphysical lostness, about the realm of the birds. Spatial vagueness functions as a sign of a primitive lack of differentiation, like Homer's Aethiopians, dear to the gods, who live near the rising and the setting of the sun.[31]

The hoopoe cannot conceive how the birds can build a city, but Pisthetaerus is quick to instruct him. "Look down," he says, and the hoopoe does. "Now look up," and again the hoopoe obliges. With these commands, I should like to suggest, the lesson on how to build a city is already begun. Pisthetaerus has drawn a line; he has defined the difference between higher and lower—a boundary that, as Pisthetaerus will immediately observe, is of considerable importance if the birds can realize the advantage of their position. "What do you see?" Pisthetaerus asks the hoopoe. "The clouds and the sky," Tereus answers. "Now isn't this in fact the birds' firmament?" "Firmament? How's that?" says the bird. To follow Pisthetaerus' explanation, we shall have to spend a moment with the Greek text.

The word that I have translated as firmament is *polos*, from which is derived the English word "pole," in the sense of the axis of the heavens. Loosely, it means "sky" in Greek. Pisthetaerus remarks that a *polos* is essentially a kind of place or *topos* (180); implicitly, this equation demarcates the region as a bounded space. It is no longer quite an everywhere. Pisthetaerus explains that it is called *polos* because it *poleitai*, that is, because it moves around and about, and everything passes through it. But if the birds will settle it and fence it around, then instead of "pole" or *polos* it will be called a *polis*, a city-state. Pisthetaerus adds that the birds will then be able to rule over mankind and conquer the gods. The reason for this, as has been said, is that the air, which the birds inhabit, is "in the middle" (*en mesôi*, 187), between earth and heaven. That the location is strategic is evident. But the point is that for the birds there is now such a thing as a middle, a locus marked by position. What hitherto was by its nature mobile and permeable is now perceived as a fixed place and potential barrier. Thus the birds, by commanding this intermediate zone, can exact a transit fare from the gods, without which they will refuse permission for the savor of sacrificial animals to pass to heaven. It is not just a question of the wall, but of a different way of conceiving space as territorial, a field marked by limits of property. The hoopoe is immediately sold on the idea, and prepares to summon the other birds to a council, remarking, for the benefit of his Athenian guests, that he has already taken the trouble to instruct the barbarous creatures in Greek (199–200).

While the precivilized condition of the birds may be described as a utopia of the anomian variety, without law or differentiation, the city of Cloudcuckooland that comes into being has a different constitution, based as it is on boundaries that are marked off and an established discipline or order among the birds. The city of the birds is not the regime that Pisthetaerus and Euelpides find; it is a city they invent. But it is not possible to discriminate too exactly between the older dispensation and the new. For the birds preserve, even in their walled city, a kind of natural solidarity among themselves that needs no laws or rules to enforce it. Cloudcuckooland sends packing those emissaries from the real city who come bearing anything that smacks of political structure or contention. The inspector and the decree salesman, like the informer, are unceremoniously banished.[32] So too is the geometer Meton, who offers to measure off the sky into individual plots of land (995–96). The birds do not proceed so far in the process of internal differentiation as to attain to private property and the city-state conception of citizenship that is underwritten by property. Thus, in answer to Meton's question whether there is civil strife, or *stasis*, in the new city, Pisthetaerus answers that all are of one mind among the birds, and that they crush swaggerers (1014–16).

The city of the birds is already a complex affair, containing elements of precivil as well as of civic life. The idea of a naturally harmonious society has roots in several cultural traditions among the Greeks. It is implicit in visions of a golden age preceding the reign of Zeus, free of want and of injustice.[33] Aesopian fables are set in a remote time when animals could still converse with men. Distant tribes, like the Argippaeans, who neighbor upon the Scythians (Herodotus 4.23), might be invested with a blessed peacefulness. One may perceive, in this reconstitution of a city without the inner stresses to which conflicting interests and class tensions give rise, a kind of primitivist nostalgia, a desire for civilization without its discontents, that is conveniently projected by a colonizing population onto what they perceive as simpler beings, whether beasts or native peoples, who dwell at the margins of the world known to history.[34] Thus Ariel Dorfman, who examines the series of children's stories based on the character Babar the elephant, observes how European civilization has required the fantasy of "some island, some shore of the universe which is still uncontaminated, where all the positive aspects of 'progress' can be reconstituted without the attendant flaws and dilemmas."[35] The territory of the barbarous birds assumes this function in Aristophanes' play.

This same contradiction between social structure and an undifferentiated presocial condition pertains also to the prehistory of the birds. Pisthetaerus, as has been said, wins the hoopoe to his grandiose scheme with the promise of limitless power, but with the native birds—those who, unlike Tereus, never had been human—he takes a slightly different approach. Pisthetaerus first arouses in them a desire for universal sovereignty by representing it as something they had formerly possessed, but have since lost. With them, that is, he must first implant a sense of lack, a nostalgia for an originary plenitude, which, until he tells them otherwise, they have never missed. Inscription within human society takes the form of an initiation into desire, which is predicated on the memory—here self-consciously constructed as a myth—of former sufficiency. Thus, the birds are made to project their own plenitude onto a prehistoric past, which thereby constitutes them as fallen creatures, now entered into the realm of desire. In former times, Pisthetaerus tells them, the birds were kings. Upon learning this, the birds inquire, "of what?" (or perhaps, "of whom?" *tinos*, 467).

It is a good question, given that this was before the reign of Cronus and the Titans, before gods, mortals, and the earth itself had come into existence (469–70). Pisthetaerus asserts that the birds, as the earliest beings in creation, are naturally entitled to rule (477), and also that, in earliest times, it was they, rather than the gods, who held sway over mankind (481–82). Conceivably one is to understand here a process with discrete stages, but it is likely that the hierarchical principle of kingship is simply projected back onto an original, undifferentiated state of the cosmos to which it does not logically apply. The image of a pre-Olympian state of nature is thus fused with a vision of power and domination. Precisely this fusion characterizes the new city of the birds that will take shape under the inspiration of Pisthetaerus.[36]

In seeking escape from the pervasive litigation that is characteristic of Athens, as Pisthetaerus and Euelpides represent it, the two Athenians encounter a place that is lacking the differentiations on which law itself depends, or rather, which law installs. Order imagines as its opposite a lack of structure, a dissolution of distinctions, which it projects onto an other, differentiated either by species, as here, or by some other quality, such as gender in the *Ecclesiazusae*, where women inaugurate a regime in which the rules of property and kinship are abolished.[37] But difference is present in the encounter between civilized humans and presocial birds, and from this encounter proceed both structure and desire. I shall examine the logic and the consequences of this new arrangement shortly.

There is more than one way in which to imagine the opposite of structure. One may collapse the distinctions it sustains or, alternatively, reverse the signs of the elements that it orders. Thus, it is no great distance, in comic visions of utopia, from anomy to antinomianism, from the absence of law, that is, with the corresponding ideal of a natural harmony, to an inversion of the law, in which the authority of the old law, not utterly canceled by its negation, remains evident in the selfish delight with which it is violated. Pisthetaerus and Euelpides begin their journey out of a desire to escape the lawsuits of Athens, but they do not on that account stand simply for a commitment to just behavior. They unashamedly reveal to the hoopoe that they, like him, are looking to evade their debts (115–16). The hoopoe, who had been human, retains enough of his former nature to keep a slave, for which the native birds have no use (70–76). Later, when the plan to fortify Cloudcuckooland has been adopted, the birds of the chorus invite the audience in the theater directly (in the formal address known as the parabasis) to join them in the pleasant life, "for all the things that are ruled out, where you are, as shameful according to the law [*nomos*] are the very things that are virtuous among us birds" (755–56). They go on to explain that while beating one's father is deemed disgraceful according to Athenian custom (*nomos*, 757)—the example is commonplace for outrageous behavior— it is entirely respectable conduct in their own realm.[38] Slaves, foreigners, sympathizers of the disenfranchised (*atimois*, 766), all are welcome in the new polity. In this topsy-turvy world, shame and honor, authority and obedience are not so much abolished as turned inside out. There is a certain slide into the anomian vision. Slaves do not reverse places with masters, as in the saturnalian festival, nor do foreigners with native citizens; rather, distinctions in status seem to be suspended in the new realm. But the idea of slaves welcomed as citizens is articulated as a transgression rather than as a social leveling, and so is assimilated to the trope of the "verkehrte Welt," the world upside-down.

Later in the play, a father beater takes up the invitation of the chorus and comes to establish residence among the birds, passionate, as he says, for their *nomoi* (1345).[39] Pisthetaerus acknowledges that it is indeed considered manly among the birds for a nestling to strike its father, but he adds that there is also an ancient custom, inscribed among the tablets of the storks,[40] that when the parent has reared his young so that they may fly from the nest, they are then in turn responsible for his support. Such an obligation was traditional at Athens,[41] and the father beater naturally complains that his voyage was of no great use, if he must also feed his father in Cloudcuckooland. Pisthetaerus then gives him the old-fashioned advice he himself received as a youth: that he had best not strike a parent, but, if he is pugnacious by disposition, let him go off and fight the Thracians, where he can, at the same time, sustain himself on a soldier's pay.

Clearly, there is a shift here from the antinomian image of utopia, in which the violation of conventional rules is endorsed in a spirit of unrestrained freedom, to the vision of a well-ordered polity. Contrariness gives way to a heightened sense of decency, inspired by reasonable persuasion that is marvelously effective in Cloudcuckooland. This is the city in its eunomian aspect, with a ready obedience to custom and the deference due to station and degree. This excellent constitution of the birds is ancestral. It is a product both of good legislation and of a spirit of respect for the law that is associated with the mores of former times. The virtues of the antique constitution were a universal touchstone of good legislation in Athens.[42] It is natural, moreover, that there should be a certain blurring of the lines between the ideal of the well-ordered society associated with the ancestral constitution and the tradition of a precivic golden age before the law. In both versions, the past serves as a screen on which the image of an order free of strife is projected, in contrast to the divisions within the contemporary polity. In this way, too, the solidarity characteristic of the anomian world is made a feature of the rule of law. Aggressive energy is directed outward beyond the perimeter of the city (a perimeter that does not exist in the absence of *nomoi*), toward savage enemies in Thrace. And because the carnivalian spirit of the inversion of custom lies so close to the anomian liberation from the constraints of law, it too may be made to coexist with the image of an ideal constitution, without too keen a note of paradox. The ancient order is not repressive. Thus, there is an air of unconstrained goodness among the birds, which is capable of reconciling virtue and desire and of uniting, in the antique legislation of the storks, social order and the state of nature.

The city of the birds has also a restless, expansionist drive, however, that is at odds with the image of a settled, well-governed polity. It has been seen that Pisthetaerus succeeds in rousing desire among the birds. Having submitted to his leadership (548, 637–38), they are infected by new longings. Where they were once contented, gawking creatures, they are now seized by a violent urge to regain their lordship over the universe by any and every means, for without it, they say, life is not worth living (548–49). The hoopoe declares that there is no longer time for dozing or delay; the birds must act now with all possible speed (639–41).[43] This passionate will to power, which culminates in mastery over gods and mortals, transforms the quiet community of the birds into an efficiently aggressive polity unconstrained by the inhibitions of conventional wisdom.[44] Moderation is out of court. This is the megalonomian dispensation, which gives rein to ambition without limit.

The vision of limitless power is grounded in the former plenitude of the birds, when they both ruled the universe and were alone in it. The idea of complete sufficiency is associated with traditions of the golden age, when the earth, under an earlier dynasty of gods, spontaneously yielded up its bounty. There is a suggestion of this earthly paradise in the benefits that the birds are prepared to confer upon mankind in exchange for recognition of their sovereignty. The birds will eliminate agricultural pests such as locusts and burrowing flies, will announce fair weather for sailing so that merchants will prosper, will reveal the sites of buried treasure and extend the lives of men by granting them longevity from their own store of years. Thus mortals will happily revere them as they do god, life, Earth, Cronus, and Poseidon (586–87), the reference to Cronus evoking the fecundity of the pre-Jovian world.[45] The image is a mixed one, inasmuch as commerce, navigation, and mineral wealth are commonly associated with decline, but the overall sense of ease and plenty belongs to the dream of a pastoral age. The birds, then, represent these blessings in their identity as creatures prior to the law of Zeus, but at the same time their fallen state, as it is established for them in the myth of origins insinuated by Pisthetaerus, relocates this fullness as the object of the birds' desire. The birds thus simultaneously stand for a primeval wholeness and want it. This double character is written into the organization of the birds as a polity. They form a city in order to reclaim their heritage. The very act of marking off its perimeter defines the territory they have to conquer, and projects the ideal of a mythic past as the object of a will to power.[46]

One may see here how the city of the birds can be the subject of inconsistent or contradictory political allegories. As a world of natural bounty, free of contention, it stands for the sufficiency of the golden age. But this plenitude at the same time inspires an ambition for universal conquest or domination, and is thus a figure for Athenian expansionism. The two aspects are simultaneous moments in the constitution of the city of the birds, and they reciprocally condition each other. It is in the eyes of Pisthetaerus and Euelpides that the birds are both the representatives of natural solidarity and witless, gaping creatures, needing to be organized to realize their potential power. The anomian and the megalonomian utopias arise in the same instant.

The source of the remarkable vigor of the city of the birds resides in the birds' solidarity, which, as has been said, appears as a residue of their precivic homogeneity, free of strife and litigation. Their extraordinary energy is harnessed in the marvelous construction of the wall around the city, which the birds, working in unison, complete so quickly that Pisthetaerus himself is astonished (1164–67). No longer, he observes, will anyone wish to hire wage laborers (1152). Internal dissension is represented as the objective limit on the power of the city-state, while the cohesiveness or cooperation characteristic of the anomian community, which is miraculously preserved in the process of incorporation into the new city, renders the city invincible. The birds' use of their power, in turn, is true to the nostalgic image of their archaic unity inasmuch as it inaugurates the return of a golden age.

But the city of the birds is not wholly without division. Pisthetaerus is the leader—he is called archon (1123)—and his role is necessary. In their unorganized condition, the birds are passionate but ineffectual. Angry as they are at the intrusion of humans into their domain, they are easily held at bay by Pisthetaerus and Euelpides, who are armed with skewers for swords and pots for shields (357–61).[47] Early in the play, Euelpides had denied the hoopoe's charge that he aspired to rule as an aristocrat (*aristokrateisthai*, 125). But as the city takes shape, there emerges an elementary hierarchy with Pisthetaerus as king and the birds subject to him. In the end, Pisthetaerus is described as an autocrat (*turannos*, 1708), and the power of Cloudcuckooland is his.[48] We learn also that some of the birds have risen up against the popular party, and Pisthetaerus is seen roasting their flesh for dinner (1583–85; cf. 1688).

It may well be that an allegorical reference to contemporary politics has entered the text here as a subtle hint of dissension in the promised land.[49] The tyranny of Pisthetaerus mirrors the role of Athens as the tyrant city, suppressing domestic opposition to its dream of empire.[50] Amid the commotion of the wedding songs for Pisthetaerus and the goddess Sovereignty,[51] it may pass all but unnoticed that the human being is deified, while the birds are reduced to a chorus of admirers (see esp. 1743). At the moment of the birds' triumph, there seems to be a hint of innocence betrayed.

But the principle of leadership in the city of the birds is also grounded in the union of civic order and natural community that drives the entire vision of Cloudcuckooland. The coexistence of two kinds of community, the one collective, the other political and socially differentiated, is figured in the division between the human leader and the crowd of birds.[52] Pisthetaerus is motivated by the desire for power, and to this extent, perhaps, represents the kind of ambitious individualism associated with a sophistic conception of human nature, which takes advantage of the weakness or credulousness of simpler creatures. But this role may also be a synecdoche for the imperial power of the city of the birds as a whole, the polis as tyrant with a tyrant's grandiose aspirations and untrammeled license. If Pisthetaerus vaunts and struts, it is because he represents here the megalonomian moment of Cloudcuckooland itself, just as, elsewhere, he is characterized in accord with other aspects of the birds' utopia. Thus the rogue who sought a place to evade debts and enjoy lubricious pleasures can, in another context, advise a youth on respect for parents. The inconsistency of characterization is a product of the complex ideological construction of the birds' domain.

The four types of utopia that have been identified as variations on the customary order or *nomoi* intersect with one another, and consequently prohibit an allegorical reading that would associate figures in the drama with specific social referents. In this respect, *Birds* differs from *Wasps*, where the jurors and the courts to which they are devoted signify a recognizable social class and the institutional expression of its power. There too Philocleon and the chorus of jurors are complex and multiply determined. In *Birds*, however, the crisscrossing configurations of Cloudcuckooland scramble the allusive pattern more completely.

But this is not to say that the play is unpolitical. Rather, it is an example of what Catherine Belsey calls an "interrogative text," which "invites an answer or answers to the questions it poses." Belsey argues that "to smooth over the contradictions" in such texts by attributing to them "a non-contradictory ideology . . . is to refuse to enter into the debates about revolution, authority and tyranny initiated in the texts."[53]

The city of the birds is, indeed, a city, but it is a city of natural creatures, who have no need of wealth, slaves, or property.[54] It is thus simultaneously a token of the golden age, in which people lived in harmony and the earth spontaneously yielded its bounty, and a well-ordered civic community from which the tensions and litigiousness of Athens (such as resulted, perhaps, in the accusations against Alcibiades) are banished. Restraints are abolished in a spirit of carnivalian liberty; hence the city may resemble the topsy-turvy world of the antipodes, where the rules are all backward. But the inscription of a retrospective ideal of complete sufficiency into the differentiated and competitive structure of a civic polity offers the promise of fulfilling an unlimited desire for mastery. The megalonomia of the city of the birds is presented as the cross product of lawlessness—anomia—and the rule of law. The city of the birds is contradictory because Aristophanes fashioned out of conventional materials a place both social and presocial, harmonious and divided, benign and aggressive. Cloudcuckooland is not, however, an arbitrary fantasy. It is a complex image of Athens' own contradictions, its communal solidarity and its political and social divisions, the conservatism that looked to the image of an ancestral constitution, and an imperial will to power.

Notes

This essay is reproduced with minor changes, and with permission of the Oxford University Press, from D. Konstan, *Greek Comedy and Ideology* (1995); an earlier version under the title "A City in the Air: Aristophanes' *Birds*" appeared in *Arethusa* 23 (1990): 183–207.

1. It is a city that they are seeking from the beginning: 48, 121, 123, 127, 136. Despite the phrase *topon apragmona*, "trouble-free place," 44, there is no suggestion of a pastoral ideal. When Alink 1983, 317, says that Pisthetaerus and Euelpides "are looking for another, non-city-like place to live," this is so only in the sense that they desire a place free of the litigiousness that accompanies city life, at all events in Athens. Heberlein 1980, 27–37, distinguishes the protagonists of Aristophanes' utopian plays, such as *Birds*, from the farmer-heroes of the peace plays (*Acharnians, Peace*), but the differences seem less compelling than the similarities.

2. For an exhaustive examination of this myth in relation to *Birds*, see Hofmann 1976, 72ff., and, with special reference to Sophocles' *Tereus* (produced ca. 431), Dobrov 1993. Zannini Quirini 1987, 35–37, sees Tereus' Thracian origins as a sign of barbarism—dubious in light of his achievement in teaching the birds to speak Greek. On the ideological construction of Thrace as an emblem of barbarism in Athenian drama, see Hall 1989, 133–38.

3. Cf. Blaydes 1882, xiii: "Now, two things in this play seem above all to indicate [Aristophanes' intentions], that is, the departure of two Athenian citizens on account of the crooked condition of the city in the beginning of the play (30–48), and Peisetaerus' triumph and assumption of universal power in the end." There is an abrupt introduction of a new plan of action near the beginning of several of Aristophanes' plays, e.g., the idea of restoring Plutus' sight in *Wealth*; of installing a communist regime in the *Ecclesiazusae*; and of occupying the acropolis in *Lysistrata*, on which see Vaio 1973.

4. See Henderson's essay below. Sommerstein 1987, 4, remarks more cautiously: "It is tempting, and may not be entirely mistaken, to see some association between this fantasy of total power and the popular mood at Athens in 415/4," though he distinguishes *Birds* from Aristophanes' other surviving fifth-century plays for "having no strong and obvious connection with a topical question of public interest" (1). Hubbard 1991, 159, sees scant evidence in the play for "any systematic allegory concerning the Sicilian expedition"; he suggests instead that the rebellion

against the gods evokes the recent desecration of the herms and profanation of the mysteries, and that the play "explores the consequences as well as the causes of such impiety" (161); cf. also Craik 1987; contra: MacDowell 1995, 223–24.

5. Suevern 1827; for an independent and eccentric interpretation along the lines of Suevern's, see Harman 1920.

6. Green 1879, 8.

7. See Dobrov's essay below, Hofmann 1976, 70, and Alink 1983, 250–57, for overviews of interpretations of *Birds*.

8. Köchly 1857; quoted from the summary in Green 1879, 10.

9. Arrowsmith 1973, 155.

10. Plut. *Alc.* 17.1, cited in Arrowsmith 1973, 141.

11. Schareika 1978, 104; see also Katz 1976.

12. Whitman 1964, 179, 169; Dover 1972, 145 (cited in Schareika 1978, 61–62) remarks that *Birds* does not "direct the attention of the community towards any desirable policy or decision or any reform of its political habits." Cf. also MacDowell 1995, 227; Dunbar 1995, 2–5, indicates various political references.

13. Dobrov 1990, 3–4.

14. Cf. Macherey and Balibar 1978, 4 = 1981, 80: "the *model*, the real referent 'outside' the discourse which both fiction and realism presuppose, has no function here as a non-literary, non-discursive anchoring point predating the text."

15. Edwards 1990, 54, observes that the "mimetic conception . . . obscures the genesis of the text, its production, the process of composition occurring in a social and political context."

16. Cf. Volosinov 1973, 10: "the domain of ideology coincides with the domain of signs," cited in Frow 1986, 64. Frow remarks that the sign "signifies only by virtue of a social consensus, and . . . where this consensus is founded on social relations which are contradictory, the symbolic order is necessarily involved in this contradiction."

17. Eco 1984, 1257; my emphasis.

18. On *nomos*, see Ostwald 1969.

19. Alink 1983, 318.

20. The most conspicuous example is the second book, devoted almost in its entirety to the *nomoi* of the Egyptians.

21. There is a connection here with the nature of textuality as such; cf. Blumenberg 1979, 42: "Reality presents itself now as never before as a sort of text which takes on its particular form by obeying certain rules of internal consistency," cited in Gelley 1987, 28. In reference to the discussion of narrative by Michel de Certeau 1980, 205–27, Gelley remarks: "Narrative practices . . . are conceived as establishing boundaries, creating an accredited 'theater' of action, a 'scene'" (29).

22. This has something in common with the notion of "leveling" proposed by Donaldson 1970, 5–9; in the extreme case, however, an anomian place will be no place at all.

23. See Donaldson 1970 for the pattern of inversion; also Carrière 1979, 89–91, for inversion in connection with the golden age.

24. More 1910, 140: "Wherefore not Utopie, but rather rightly / My name is Eutopie: a place of felicity."

25. In the poem on Eutopia partially cited in the previous note, More writes: "Now am I like to Plato's city." On the customs of the Egyptians as the reverse of those of the Greeks, see Hdt. 2.35; Soph. *OC* 337–43. On the cyclopes, see *Od.* 9.189, *athemistia êidê*; 215, *oute dikas eu eidota oute themistas*, "having no knowledge of just ways or sanctions." For Callicles, see Pl. *Gorg.*; for Thrasymachus, Pl. *Rep.* 1.

26. The reference to a cockfight at 70–71 may suggest that aggression and domination among the birds arise through contact with human society.

27. Cf. 20, 51, etc.; in *Knights*, the sausage seller refers to Athens as "the city of the Gapenians" (*tēi Kekhēnaiōn polei*, 1263); Arrowsmith 1973, 138 n. 10.

28. Cf. *Frogs* 692. In Soph. *Ant.* 1069, the correct interpretation of *atimōs* is "without civic status," as Kells 1963, 57, demonstrates; contra, e.g., Jebb 1928, who translates "ruthlessly" (I owe this reference to Diane Juffras). In general, see Harrison 1971, 82–83.

29. Cf. Toynbee 1981, 40: "The Hellenic and the nomad ways of life were at opposite poles."

30. Cf. Slater 1990, 42–43 (and his essay below), who examines the implications for the staging of the scene.

31. See *Od.* 1.22–24. Gelzer 1976, 2–3, sees the indeterminate locale of the opening scenes as a means of exciting the audience's curiosity and preparing for surprise effects; cf. his analysis of the playful punning on *polos* and *polis* (7).

32. The visitors to Cloudcuckooland in the "exemplificatory" scenes in the latter half of *Birds* appear to fall into three groups of three. The first group consists of the priest (851), the poet (904), and the oracle monger (959); all have or pretend to some role in the foundation of the city. The second group consists of Meton the geometer (992), the inspector (1021), and the decree salesman (1035); they arrive before the city is fully established, and offer laws or principles of order. Finally, after a choral interlude and visits from Iris and messengers, a would-be parricide (1337), a dithyrambic poet (1372), and a sycophant or informer (1410) arrive; by now, the city of the birds has its constitution, and subjects each of these visitors to its own discipline. For a different analysis, which collapses the first six visits (801–1055) into one group focused on the foundation ceremony of the city, see Gelzer 1976, 10; the point of demarcation is 1118: "our sacrifices are favorable, O birds." For the division of Aristophanic comedy into the creation of the utopian dispensation followed by scenes illustrating the consequences of the new conditions, see also Zimmerman 1987, 50.

33. See Carrière 1979, 88.

34. I derive this last expression from Wolf 1982.

35. Dorfman 1983, 26; for a model analysis of colonialist discourse in Shakespeare's *Tempest*, see Brown 1985, 48–71. Zannini Quirini 1987, 87, acknowledges that the city of the birds lacks the negative features of Athens, but he argues that by this very circumstance it is "populated by monstrous and ambiguous figures" who are "worthy denizens" of so ridiculous a place; to reject the life of the polis, even for its vices, entails an escape from history to a universe that is still inchoate and monstrous, a state of origins "that *must* rather be closed off once and for all" (150). I do not see as a major theme in the play the dread of primal formlessness.

36. Romer (1990 and his essay below) shows how the new theogony promulgated in *Birds* reproduces the hierarchical structure of power, and more specifically the inequality between the genders, that is authorized by Hesiod's *Theogony*. For the role of Eros or passionate desire in Orphic cosmogony and its relation to myth expounded in *Birds*, see Calame 1991, 229–31; on the role of myth generally in the play, cf. also Bowie 1993, 151–77. It may be noted also that Pisthetaerus plays with respect to the birds a role like that of Prometheus in the development of human beings, especially as represented in the *Prometheus Bound* attributed to Aeschylus; this may in part explain the appearance of Prometheus in Cloudcuckooland later in the comedy (as Romer and others have observed).

37. On the Parthenon in Athens, four conflicts were represented on the metopes: between gods and giants, Lapiths and centaurs, Greeks and amazons, and Greek and Trojans. Barbarians, women, beasts, and primordial deities stand in as antagonistic others, whose aspiration to power is conceived as a challenge to the order of the city-state; cf. Castriota 1992, 96–183, for a full discussion in the context of Athenian imperialism. Cartledge 1993 provides an elegant discussion of the homology between the different categories of "other" in Greek thought. On the battle between gods and giants as the mythological model for the rebellion of the birds in the latter part of the play, see 1249–52, and cf. Arrowsmith 1973, 139, and esp. Hofmann 1976, 86ff.; also Vidal-Naquet 1986, 216–18, on the structure of the Aristophanic utopia.

38. Cf. also 131–32, 1137–42, on the reversal of sexual mores; 793–97, on wings as perfect equipment for adulterers.

39. Cf. also the reference to the *arkhaioi thesmoi*, "ancient sanctions" (331) among the birds, by which human beings were not to be admitted into their realm.

40. The storks' laws are on *kurbeis* (1354), triangular tablets on which some ancient legislation was inscribed at Athens, as opposed to the *stelai* on which modern laws were normally published. Hubbard 1991, 172, treats Pisthetaerus' allusion to the laws of the storks as the ploy of a practiced sophist.

41. The obligation was protected by law; see Harrison 1968, 77.

42. See Finley 1975, 34–59.

43. The word for "delay" is *mellonikian*, a pun on postponing victory (*nikē*) and the dilatory or reluctant policy of Nicias in the Sicilian campaign. Another direct allusion to the Peloponnesian War is the phrase "Meliaōn famine" (186).

44. On the virtue of *sophrosunē* or moderation, see North 1966; Arrowsmith 1973, 124, 140.

45. See Johnston 1980 for a survey of ancient conceptions of the age of Cronus or Saturn; also Vidal-Naquet 1986, 2–3.

46. There is an analogy here with the development of the individual self, as it is represented in the psychoanalytical theory of Jacques Lacan. As Gallop 1985, 81, puts it, "the self is constituted through anticipating what it will become, and then this anticipatory model is used for gauging what was before."

47. These are probably not the instruments that Pisthetaerus and Euelpides brought with them (43), which are suitable for a party rather than for defense; see Hamilton 1985. At 62, the hoopoe's servant presumes the two men to be bird catchers, an inference, perhaps, from their cooking utensils.

48. On tyranny as a commonplace accusation against the ambitions of the well-to-do, cf. *Wasps* 488–507.

49. Henderson (1990 and his essay below), who defends the benevolence of Pisthetaerus' rule, remarks that he "is not doing anything different than the demos had in fact done on the demagogues' advice shortly before"; Henderson sees Pisthetaerus as a representative of the Athenian elite.

50. See Arrowsmith 1973, 131; Alink 1983, 322. For the metaphor of the tyrant city, see Tuplin 1985, 357–58, on Aristophanes (the present passage is not discussed, since it is not an unambiguous reference to imperial tyranny). Tuplin speculates (374) that the ordinary word for king may also have had something of the derogatory significance attaching to the term "tyrant."

51. On the marriage between Pisthetaerus and Basileia, and possible allegorical references to cult and politics, see Hofmann 1976, 140–60; for a more metaphysical interpretation, Epstein 1981.

52. Contrast Arrowsmith 1973, 139: "the *Birds* . . . is the spectacle of innocent and peaceful *physis* . . . corrupted by superior intelligence whose motive power is man's metaphysical discontent, his lust for divinity—the discontent and *erōs* written into his *physis* and nakedly revealed in this chaotic epiphany of Athenian man and man generally"; see also Carrière 1979, 91–94.

53. Belsey 1980, 94–95; the examples of interrogative texts given by Belsey are Marlowe's *Tamburlaine the Great* and Andrew Marvell's "Horatian Ode" to Cromwell.

54. Cf. Ceccarelli 1992, 30–37.

Bibliography

Alink, M. F. 1983. *De Vogels van Aristophanes: een structuuranalyse en interpretatie*. Amsterdam.

Arrowsmith, W. 1973. "Aristophanes' *Birds*: The Fantasy Politics of Eros." *Arion*, n.s., 1.1.119–67.

Belsey, C. 1980. *Critical Practice*. London.

Blaydes, F. H. M. 1882. *Aristophanis Aves*. Halis Saxonum.

Blumenberg, H. 1979. "The Concept of Reality and the Possibility of the Novel." In *New Perspectives in German Literary Criticism*, edited by R. E. Amacher and V. Lange. Princeton.

Bowie, A. M. 1993. *Aristophanes: Myth, Ritual and Comedy*. Cambridge.

Brown, P. 1985. "'This Thing of Darkness I Acknowledge Mine': *The Tempest* and the Discourse of Colonialism." In *Political Shakespeare: New Essays in Cultural Materialism*, edited by Jonathan Dollimore and Alan Sinfield, 48–71. Ithaca.

Calame, C. 1991. "Eros initiatique et la cosmogonie orphique." *Recherches et Rencontres* 3.227–47.

Carrière, J. C. 1979. *Le carnaval et la politique: Une introduction à la comédie grecque*. Paris.

Cartledge, P. 1993. *The Greeks: A Portrait of Self and Others*. Oxford.

Castriota, D. 1992. *Myth, Ethos, and Actuality: Official Art in Fifth-Century BC Athens*. Madison.

Ceccarelli, P. 1992. "Le monde sauvage et la cité dans la comédie ancienne." *Etudes de lettres. Revue de la Faculté des Lettres, Université de Lausanne*, 23–37.

Certeau, M. de. 1980. *L'Invention du quotidien*. Vol. 1. Paris.

Craik, E. M. 1987. "'One for the Pot': Aristophanes' Birds and the Anthesteria." *Eranos* 85.25–34.

Dobrov, G. W., ed. 1990. *Nephelokokkygia: Charting the Comic Polis*. Papers of the APA Seminar. Privately circulated manuscript. Syracuse, N.Y.

——. 1993. "The Tragic and the Comic Tereus." *AJP* 114.2.189–234.

Donaldson, I. 1970. *The World Upside-Down: Comedy from Jonson to Fielding*. Oxford.

Dorfman, A. 1983. *The Empire's Old Clothes*. New York.

Dover, K. J. 1972. *Aristophanic Comedy*. Berkeley.

Dunbar, N., ed. 1995. *Aristophanes' Birds*. Oxford.

Eco, U. 1984. "Science Fiction and the Art of Conjecture." *TLS* 4257 (2 November).1257–58.

Edwards, A. T. 1990. Commentary. In *Nephelokokkygia*, edited by Dobrov, 53–62.

Epstein, P. D. 1981. "The Marriage of Peisthetairos to *Basileia* in the *Birds* of Aristophanes." *Dionysius* 5.6–28.

Finley, M. I. 1975. "The Ancestral Constitution." In *The Use and Abuse of History*. Harmondsworth. Reprint, 1987.

Frow, J. 1986. *Marxism and Literary History*. Cambridge, Mass.

Gallop, J. 1985. *Reading Lacan*. Ithaca.

Gelley, A. 1987. *Narrative Crossings: Theory and Pragmatics of Prose Fiction*. Baltimore.

Gelzer, T. 1976. "Some Aspects of Aristophanes' Dramatic Art in the *Birds*." *BICS* 23.1–14.

Green, W. C., ed. 1879. *The Birds of Aristophanes*. Cambridge.

Hall, E. 1989. *Inventing the Barbarian: Greek Self-Definition through Tragedy*. Oxford.

Hamilton, R. 1985. "The Well-Equipped Traveller: *Birds* 42." *GRBS* 26.235–39.

Harman, E. G. 1920. *The Birds of Aristophanes Considered in Relation to Athenian Politics*. London.

Harrison, A. R. W. 1968, 1971. *The Law of Athens*. 2 vols. Oxford.

Heberlein, G. 1980. *Pluthygieia: Zum Gegenwelt bei Aristophanes*. Frankfurt am Main.

Henderson, J. 1990. "Peisetairos and the Athenian Elite." In *Nephelokokkygia*, edited by Dobrov, 8–16.

Hofmann, H. 1976. *Mythos und Komödie: Untersuchungen zu den Vögeln des Aristophanes*. Spudasmata 33. Hildesheim.

Hubbard, T. 1991. *The Mask of Comedy: Aristophanes and the Intertextual Parabasis*. Ithaca.

Johnston, P. 1980. *Vergil and the Golden Age: A Study of the Georgics*. Mnemosyne suppl. 60. Cologne.

Jebb, R. 1928. *Sophocles: The Plays and Fragments*. Vol. 3: *The Antigone*. 3d ed. Cambridge.

Katz, B. 1976. "The *Birds* of Aristophanes and Politics." *Athenaeum* 54.353–81.

Kells, J. H. 1963. "Problems of Interpretation in the *Antigone*." *BICS* 10.47–64.

Köchly, H. A. T. 1857. "Über die *Vögel* des Aristophanes." In *Gratulationsschrift . . . August Boeckh*. Zurich.

MacDowell, D. M. 1995. *Aristophanes and Athens: An Introduction to the Plays*. Oxford.

Macherey, P., and E. Balibar. 1978. "Literature as an Ideological Form: Some Marxist Propositions." Translated by Ian McLeod, John Whitehead, and Ann Wordsworth, *Oxford Literary Review* 3.1.4–12. Reprinted in *Untying the Text: A Post-Structuralist Reader*, edited by Robert Young, 79–99. London, 1981.

More, T. 1910. *Utopia*. Edited by John Warrington. New York.

North, H. 1966. *Sophrosyne: Self-Knowledge and Self-Restraint in Greek Literature*. Ithaca.

Ostwald, M. 1969. *Nomos and the Beginnings of Athenian Democracy*. Oxford.

Romer, F. E. 1990. "Good Intentions and the *hodos he es korakas*." In *Nephelokokkygia*, edited by Dobrov, 27–41.

Schareika, H. 1978. *Der Realismus der aristophanischen Komödie: Exemplarische Analysen zur Funktion des Komischen in den Werken des Aristophanes*. Frankfurt am Main.

Slater, N. W. 1990. "Performing the City in the *Birds*." In *Nephelokokkygia*, edited by Dobrov, 42–52.

Sommerstein, A. H., ed. 1987. *The Comedies of Aristophanes*. Vol. 6: *Birds*. Warminster.

Suevern, J. W. 1827. "Über Aristophanes Vögel." *Abh. Akad. der Wissenschaften, Berlin, historisch-philologische Kl.*, 1–109. English translation in W. R. Hamilton, *Essay on "The Birds" of Aristophanes*. London, 1835.

Toynbee, A. 1981. *The Greeks and Their Heritage*. Oxford.

Tuplin, C. 1985. "Imperial Tyranny: Some Reflections on a Classical Greek Political Metaphor." In *Crux: Essays Presented to G. E. M. de Ste. Croix on His 75th Birthday*, edited by Paul A. Cartledge and F. D. Harvey. *History of Political Thought* 6. Exeter.

Vaio, J. 1973. "The Manipulation of Theme and Action in Aristophanes' *Lysistrata*." *GRBS* 14.369–80.

Vidal-Naquet, P. 1986. *The Black Hunter: Forms of Thought and Forms of Society in the Greek World*. Translated by A. Szegedy-Maszak. Baltimore.

Volosinov, V. N. [M. Bakhtin]. 1973. *Marxism and the Philosophy of Language*. Translated by L. Matejka and I. R. Titunik. New York.

Whitman, C. H. 1964. *Aristophanes and the Comic Hero*. Martin Lectures 19. Cambridge, Mass.

Wolf, E. 1982. *Europe and the People without History*. Los Angeles.

Zannini Quirini, B. 1987. *Nephelokokkygia: La prospettiva mitica degli Uccelli di Aristofane*. Rome.

Zimmermann, B. 1987. "L'Organizzazione interna delle commedie di Aristofane." *Dioniso* 57.49–64.

THOMAS K. HUBBARD

Utopianism and the Sophistic
City in Aristophanes

The recent essays of David Konstan (in this collection) and Bernhard Zimmermann, together with the publication of Doyne Dawson's important new monograph on the utopian tradition in Greek philosophy and political thought, indicate a renewed interest in Greek theoretical conceptions of the polis and their reflection in the most immanently "political" of all literary genres—Attic Old Comedy.[1] Zimmermann and Konstan each work from an expansive and inclusive definition of utopia, encompassing both its traditional folkloric and its theoretical forms. Konstan presents a suggestive schema of four types of Aristophanic utopia—the anomian, the antinomian, the eunomian, and the megalonomian; while his analysis concentrates on the *Birds*, his schema can clearly be applied in one form or another to much of the Aristophanic corpus. Konstan's general view of the utopian elements in Aristophanes is as positive and festive gestures of ideological critique directed toward contemporary Athenian society. Zimmermann's view is more ambiguous, emphasizing the ultimate impracticality of some utopian designs. Without diminishing the valuable contributions these two essays have made, I would like to propose a more limited and restrictive definition of utopia, confining the concept to serious philosophical treatments of the ideal state, and then reconsider the position of Aristophanic comedy in relation to such intellectual paradigms.

A useful and relevant distinction is made by W. H. Auden in his essay on Dickens, "Dingley Dell & The Fleet":[2]

Our dream pictures of the Happy Place where suffering and evil are unknown are of two kinds, the Edens and the New Jerusalems. Though it is possible for the same individual to imagine both, it is unlikely that his interest in both will be equal and I suspect that between the Arcadian whose favorite daydream is of Eden, and the Utopian whose favorite daydream is of New Jerusalem there is a characterological gulf as unbridgeable as that between Blake's Prolifics and Devourers.

In their relation to the actual fallen world, the difference between Eden and New Jerusalem is a temporal one. Eden is a past world in which the contradictions of the present world have not yet arisen; New Jerusalem is a future world in which they have at last been resolved. Eden is a place where its inhabitants may do whatever they like to do; the motto over its gate is, "Do what thou wilt is here the Law." New Jerusalem is a place where its inhabitants like to do whatever they ought to do, and its motto is, "In His will is our peace."

The man who seeks Eden is the "Arcadian," the man in pursuit of the New Jerusalem the "Utopian."[3] This distinction between the recreation of a vision of bounty and individual freedom in the past and the creation of a new state promising collective security and happiness in the future is fundamental to the consideration of Old Comedy. Previous discussions have in my opinion gone astray to the extent that they have confused "Arcadian" and "utopian" elements. *Birds* and *Ecclesiazusae* are the only truly "utopian" comedies of Aristophanes when viewed from the standpoint of this dichotomy, in that they are the only plays in which we see the polis as such reinvented in accordance with a theoretical paradigm. Several other plays of Aristophanes which have often been viewed as "utopian" are really better classified as "Arcadian" fantasies, aiming not at the creation of a new Athens so much as at a resurrection of the old.

Acharnians and *Peace* both seek to restore an ideal order of agricultural fertility and sensual gratification which is imagined as having existed prior to the war. Similarly, *Lysistrata* uses the methods of social revolution not to create something new, but to reestablish a preexisting structure of domestic economy in which husbands stayed at home and tended to their families' needs. *Knights* also subverts the contemporary political establishment to return the state to an older ideal of political values, represented in the play by the rejuvenated Demos. In the same spirit, *Wasps* discards the contemporary political structure of jury pay as old-age pension in favor of a return to traditional family values, with the elderly holding a proper position of respect within their own households rather than dependent on the state. In all these plays, we see the ultimate triumph of the oikos and its obligations over the demands of the polis. The political domain is presented as inherently evil and corrupt, and man's withdrawal from it is rewarded with the opportunity for unlimited egoistic self-indulgence.

The ideological framework of these fantasies is unquestionably "Edenic" and "Arcadian" in Auden's terms; in the Greek context of this time, it might be best to appeal to the Hesiodic myth of the golden age as the model, although the theme of a primeval paradise of no want, fear, or constraint is a folklore motif that transcends any one literary source.[4] The return to such an uncorrupted, bounteous past seems almost a generic obsession of Old Comedy, as suggested by plays such as Eupolis' *Golden Race*, Cratinus' *Wealth*, Crates' *Animals*, Pherecrates' *Miners* and *Persians*, or Telecleides' *Amphictyons*.[5] One can readily see comedy's interest in a return to primordial fertility as an outgrowth of its origins as a fertility rite in the Rural Dionysia.[6] A generic identification with the agrarian class has also been cited as an explanation for comedy's bias toward autarkic individualism and hostility to political institutions and power: the Attic landholder was often the citizen least involved in urban politics, due to his remoteness and isolation, but the one most affected by political policies, particularly in the realm of war.[7]

Birds and *Ecclesiazusae* are plays that manipulate the audience's expectations by starting out with conventional "Arcadian" premises: *Birds* opens with a retreat from political life and escape into the primeval, precivilized, even pre-human landscape, and *Ecclesiazusae* opens with a women's revolution recalling that of *Lysistrata*, leading us to anticipate that it too will reassert the primacy of the oikos and its needs. Relying on conventional generic expectations, the audience invests its initial sympathy with the protagonists in each of these plays. But like *Clouds*, Aristophanes' other great problem play, the plot leads us in a different direction from that which we at first envision. The "Arcadian" retreat from civilization in *Birds* turns into a hypercivilized, overstructured totalitarian state, a dystopian nightmare vision of grandiose proportions. The reassertion of traditional family values that we expect from the women's revolution in *Ecclesiazusae* turns into another totalizing statist appropriation of everything that once defined the family, even the sexual bond itself. As in *Clouds*, we see theoretical paradigms gone wild, with the hero's comic quest for Arcadian bliss metamorphosed into a sophistic plan for the ideal city, the ultimate absurdity of which issues in a dystopian catastrophe.[8]

Birds and *Ecclesiazusae* thus work from opening assumptions not unlike traditional golden age wish-fulfillment fantasies, but quickly deviate into satirical attacks on sophistic utopianism. That the audience is invited to initial sympathy with the protagonist's vision in each case, only to realize later that it has been manipulated into sympathy with a sinister system of social control, itself illustrates the dangerous and seductive appeal utopian conceptions can have. That there was a long tradition of sophistic and philosophical thought concerning the ideal polis behind these plays cannot be doubted. Long before Plato's *Republic*, thinkers such as Protagoras, Antisthenes, the Socratics Crito and Simon, Hippodamus of Miletus, and Phaleas of Chalcedon were responsible for treatises concerning constitutional theory.[9] The debate among three Persian nobles on the three possible forms of *politeia* dramatized in Herodotus 3.80–83 suggests a well-developed theoretical tradition already at the time of the historian's writing in the mid-fifth century.

Hippodamus of Miletus is perhaps the most fascinating of these fifth-century political theorists, not a statesman, but an "urban planner" involved in the design of the Peiraeus, Thurii, and Rhodes and thus spanning much of the fifth century with his activity.[10] Aristotle devotes a whole chapter of the *Politics* (2.8) to the discussion of Hippodamus, whose chief claim to originality was not in constitutional theory or urban architecture per se,[11] but in the systematic combination of meteorology,[12] numerology, architectural planning, and constitutional theory in pursuit of a holistic and integrated vision of the ideal city. His proposed city of 10,000 inhabitants was to be equally divided into three parts—artisans, farmers, and warriors.[13] The land was to be divided into three parts—sacred (for sacrificial herds), public (to maintain the warriors), and private (for the farmers). Laws were also to be divided into three parts—insult, injury, and homicide. What Hippodamus proposed was therefore a massively regimented state, with a large standing army, most of the land (the sacred and public thirds) under state control, and what appears to have been a rigid caste system of professions. All this was designed not so much from the standpoint of practicality, as Aristotle's criticisms point out, but in accordance with principles of abstract symmetry corresponding to the geometric grid-structures for which Hippodamus' architectural planning was famous.

The fifth century was also a time of sophistic theories concerning the evolution of human culture[14] and ethnographic writings about other societies antithetical to Greek norms. Some sophistic writings, perhaps including Protagoras' *Antilogica*, idealized strange barbarian practices such as community possession of women and children, presenting them as means for achieving social concord.[15] Other sophists, such as Critias, admired Sparta, the cultural anti-Athens, for its system of ideal equality among citizens.[16] The intellectual environment of the late fifth century was one of ever more radical challenges to traditional Athenian social and moral norms in the sophistic quest for a redesigned social order free of the divisions and inequities characteristic of Athens as it was.

Nor was the quest for the ideal city limited to the realm of pure theoretical speculation. Hippodamus was involved in the design of actual cities: the intention of his grid structures seems to have been a certain uniformity and equality in housing stock, symbolic of a desired social equality in all categories.[17] He also played a key role in the layout and design of the Panhellenic colony of Thurii (founded 443 B.C.), as did Protagoras, who was responsible for designing the city's laws and constitution. Indeed, this new city seems to have been a mecca for Athenian intellectuals of the time, including not only Hippodamus and Protagoras, but the historian Herodotus, the minor sophists Euthydemus and Dionysodorus, and others.[18] The intellectuals' involvement with this not altogether successful colony was a topic for ridicule by comedy, as suggested by the *Thurio-Persians* of Metagenes and the allusion to Θουριομάντιες in Aristophanes *Clouds* 332.[19]

The idea of an intellectuals' colony is clearly the inspiration for the plot of Aristophanes' *Birds*. Critics have tended to see this play either as an escapist fantasy[20] or as a covert satire on Athens' overreaching ambition and optimism in undertaking the massive Sicilian expedition.[21] But by the spring of 414, when *Birds* was performed, little had yet happened in Sicily; later events and Thucydides' searing narrative may condition us to regard this campaign as the pinnacle of Athenian hubris, but this was not yet evident to Athenians early in 414. Apart from a few scattered allusions, Sicily is not explicitly mentioned in the play.[22] More relevant to Athenian interests in the spring of 414 were the continuing prosecutions of prominent citizens from among Athens' intellectual and social elite for the mutilation of the herms and the profanation of the Eleusinian mysteries immediately prior to the departure of the Sicilian expedition.[23] The litigation-prone city which Peisthetaerus and Euelpides flee seems precisely like the witch-hunt-obsessed Athens of the time, from which many prominent citizens were fleeing in droves to escape the ever expanding prosecution. Blame for these sacrileges was generally assigned to oligarchic political clubs (ἑταιρίαι) and young aristocrats like Alcibiades, who were thought to be under the influence of Socrates and the sophists, thus losing their respect for traditional religion and morality.[24] I would therefore propose that we see this play primarily as an expression of popular outrage against those social elites held responsible for the sacrileges, showing the consequences of their theoretical paradigm for an ideal city put into action.

Birds makes direct reference to a wide range of contemporary thinkers whose influence was seen in one way or another as atheistic, such as Prodicus, Diagoras of Melos, Socrates and Chaerephon, Gorgias and Philip, the astronomer Meton, the dithyrambist Cinesias.[25] The very name of Peisthetaerus' new city, "Cloudcuckooland" (Νεφελοκοκκυγία, 819), evokes Aristophanes' other famous play attacking contemporary intellectuals, *Clouds* (Νεφέλαι), as is clear from Tereus' line deriving the name "from the clouds and midair [μετεώρων] places" (818).[26] The recent actions of Alcibiades, Critias, and others seem to have realized Aristophanes' worst fears about the potential effects of the teachings of Socrates and others.[27] Thus Aristophanes' return to many of the themes in *Clouds* is entirely understandable, only here with the ethereal Birds in the place of the ethereal Clouds as the new gods and the hero Peisthetaerus in the place of Socrates as the master sophist who reveals their divinity. But whereas Socrates and the *bômolochos* Strepsiades were ultimately working at cross-purposes, leading to failure for both in *Clouds*, Peisthetaerus is himself the unquestioned protagonist in *Birds*, accompanied by the naive and gullible *bômolochos* Euelpides; what we see is Peisthetaerus experiencing the ultimate triumph of a sophistic will to power of which the miserable Socrates and Strepsiades could only dream.

The identification of Peisthetaerus, "the persuader of aristocratic companions/clubmen,"[28] with the doctrines and techniques of the sophists seems quite clear. He is presented to the birds as a subtle speaker (λεπτὼ λογιστά, 318), an "old man of new ideas" (πρέσβυς καινὸς γνώμην . . . , 255–57) from "wise" (σοφῆς, 409) Greece, and is congratulated with the epithet *sophos* in numerous passages.[29] The birds, previously "unlearned" (ἀμαθής, 471), address Peisthetaerus as their teacher (548) and come to rely upon him for guidance in fulfilling the desire for power he has awakened in them (539–49). Like the sophists, his teaching proceeds by *epideixis* (483), exemplary demonstration.[30] Tereus had taught the birds the rudiments of human language (199–200) and encouraged them to learn more refined arts from the two human visitors; although they belong to an enemy race, enemies can also teach valuable lessons, as in warfare (371–82). As with Protagoras, Prodicus, and other sophists, Peisthetaerus is especially concerned to teach the birds about the origins of civilization, when the cock was first king of the Persians (481–85) and the kite ruled over the Greeks (499–501). Peisthetaerus explains human belief in the gods as a function of *nomos* or "convention," rather than as anything rooted in nature; the ultimate relativity and reversibility of human values is demonstrated by men once having regarded the birds as gods and now seeing them merely as animals and pests (520–38). But this arbitrary belief can just as easily be changed back into reverence for the birds as gods and rejection of the Olympians (561–87). Even as health and sickness are not absolutes but only states of perception in which a man either "fares well" (ἦν εὖ πράττωσ', 604) or "fares ill" (κακῶς πράττων, 605),[31] the gods are whatever men at any historical moment consider to be gods. Peisthetaerus' teaching of the birds covers the full range of sophistic concerns: the theory of culture and religion, nature and convention, language, the relativism of perceptions.

The play introduces religion and the gods as mere tools of political manipulation. Significantly Peisthetaerus and Euelpides announce that they search for their "place uninvolved in affairs" carrying a ritual basket, fire pot, and myrtle wreaths (43), so as to make the proper sacrifice when founding their new city.[32] Peisthetaerus indeed uses these implements in sacrificing to the gods later in the play (848–903); we see the necessity for religion to play a fundamental role in forming and unifying any city. However, it is also significant that the gods to whom sacrifice is made are not by any means the traditional gods of Athenian state religion, but "new gods" (848), not unlike the "new gods" whom Socrates is accused of worshiping (*Clouds* 247–74; Pl. *Apol.* 24B, 26B). *Birds* as a whole dramatizes not only the abandonment of Athenian democracy, but also the overthrow of the city's traditional religion and piety in favor of a new artificially constructed system influenced by the radical subjectivism of sophistic teachings. Presuming to create a new democracy in the interests of the birds (see 1583–85), Peisthetaerus in fact creates a new tyranny (see 1673, 1708) in which he himself holds absolute Basileia ("Sovereignty") and becomes the "highest of the gods" (δαιμόνων ὑπέρτατε, 1765), the final words of the play. As was widely suspected in the case of those responsible for the sacrileges of 415, the undermining of traditional religious institutions is a prelude to subversion of the political order.[33] *Birds* illustrates in comically exaggerated form the ultimate consequences we could expect from the actions of the impious—the overthrow of Zeus and the elevation to divinity of anything the individual thinker desires, including tiny birds and even the thinker himself.[34]

The philosophical/sophistic background to *Birds* is illuminated particularly by the choral portions of the play. The type scenes at the end of the play are punctuated by a series of four responsive odes parodying the techniques of logographic ethnography: we are told of the strange Cleonymus-tree in the land "beyond Cardia" (1470–81), the "region barren of lamps (i.e., Hyperbolus the lampmaker) where men and heroes dine together" (1482–93), the lake where Socrates performs strange necromantic rites "among the Shadowfeet" (1553–64), or the race of "Tongue-Stomach men" like Gorgias and Philip (1694–1705). The last two odes especially illuminate the connection between intellectuals and Athens' current atmosphere of political fratricide and paranoia. The strophe proceeds in a typical Herodotean fashion:

> Among the Shadowfeet there is
> A lake, where unwashed
> Socrates conjures up spirits.
> There even Peisander came,
> Asking to see the spirit which
> Left that man behind, still living.
> Having as sacrificial victim
> A camel-lamb, of which he cut the throat
> Just like Odysseus, he went away.
> And then there came up for him from below
> Toward the bloody neck of the camel
> Chaerephon the bat.
>
> (1553–64)

Peisander, like Cleonymus, was one of the democratic politicians most eager to obtain information about the sacrileges at all costs, even with huge rewards and torture of free citizens.[35] His desire to interrogate the ghost of Cherephon[36] may represent the extremes to which his prosecutorial zeal has taken him. Indeed, Socrates' necromancy constitutes a private mystery ritual[37] not unlike the private rituals at which the Eleusinian mysteries were supposedly parodied.

Socrates himself is an appropriate satirical object here, given the importance of sophistic doctrine in this play and given *Birds*' close relation to the recently revised *Clouds*.[38] Socratic followers such as Critias and Alcibiades played a prominent role in the profanation of the mysteries, and the enthusiasm of such young aristocrats for Socrates' teaching is alluded to in lines 1280–85:

> Before you settled this city,
> All men at the time were mad for Sparta,
> Wore their hair long, were hungry, were dirty, were Socrates-like,
> Carried club-staffs, but now turning around
> They are bird-mad, and with pleasure
> Imitate everything which the birds do.

Socrates' dirty, unwashed appearance (alluded to here in 1554–55; cf. *Clouds* 837) is familiar as are the poverty and hunger of his school (cf. *Clouds* 175, 185–86, 416, 441). Here these habits are assimilated to the traditional customs of the Spartans and are taken to be signs of pro-Spartan sympathy, as was commonly suspected of Athenian aristocrats.[39] In fact this passage may allude to Alcibiades' defection: Plutarch tells us that he adopted Laconian customs of grooming, exercise, and diet after arriving in Sparta.[40] The passage implies that the same kind of people who used to follow Socrates are now "mad for the birds," eager to adopt bird customs; the inference to be drawn is that the characters who soon appear onstage (the parricidal young man, Cinesias, the sycophant) are similar to Socrates' trendy followers,[41] and that Peisthetaerus' revolt against conventional religion and morality is very much the same kind of thing as what Socrates and the other sophists promote. Indeed, Peisthetaerus is twice congratulated with the address ὦ σοφώτατε and other honorific vocatives in 1271–73; the passage in 1274–79, immediately leading up to the reflections on bird madness, makes it clear that his personal magnetism and charisma, like Socrates', have been responsible for these new developments in fashion.

The connection of sophistry, rhetoric, and sycophancy is most sharply articulated by the final antistrophe of the series:

> There is in Phanae near
>> Waterclock a criminal
>> Race of Tongue-Stomach men,
> Who with their tongues
> Reap and sow and harvest
>> And gather figs;
>> They are barbarians by race,
> Gorgiases and Philips,
> And because of those horse-loving
> Tongue-stomach men,
> Everywhere in Attica,
>> The tongue is cut out.

(1694–1705)

This attack on Gorgias and the Englottogasters ("Tongue-Stomach men," men who feed themselves by the art of speaking) is itself quite appropriately made through a string of clever wordplays: Phanae plays on the verb φαίνειν ("to denounce"), Klepsydra refers to the lawcourt's water clock, "gathers figs" (συκάζουσι) puns on the word "sycophant," "horse-loving" (φιλίππων) on the name Philip. Of all the sophists Gorgias was the greatest rhetorician, for whom the persuasive power of *logos* was supreme.[42] We should not forget that Gorgias' original prominence in Athens derived from his leadership of an embassy from Leontini in 427, which convinced Athens to undertake its first direct involvement in Sicilian affairs; indeed, it was ostensibly to settle matters in Leontini and Segesta that Athens was undertaking its much larger expedition contemporary with this play.[43] As in the case of Socrates, however, Gorgias' true danger was not simply his own eloquence so much as his spawning a whole race of imitators, not only Philip but many Gorgiases and Philips

(1701), an entire γένος of "Tongue-Stomach men." Even though many of this race were native Athenians, Aristophanes views the New Rhetoric as something fundamentally un-Athenian and foreign, like Gorgias himself; it is in fact so foreign that the "Tongue-Stomach men," despite their obvious facility in speaking the Greek language, are properly considered a race of *barbaroi* (1700).

The birds' history of their origins in the parabasis fleshes out Peisthetaerus' argument about their antiquity relative to the gods (465–78; cf. 702–3) with an elaborate revisionist cosmogony in the style of the Orphics.[44] Just as human beings imagine the gods in anthropomorphic terms, the birds see their original forebears as winged and aerial creatures, "blackwinged Night" (695), "wind-egg" (695), "Eros, glittering with two golden wings on his back, like windswift eddies" (696–97), "winged Chaos" (698). Of course, the whole genealogy is impossible, since the "wind-egg" from which Eros is born is by definition a sterile, unfertilized egg[45] unable to give birth to anything. The birds themselves are born from the union of Eros and Chaos (= "gap," "yawn," "void") taking place in the depths of Tartarus, the place of death; such an origin explains their lightness and lack of substance, indeed, their unreality. The rest of the universe, however, is born in a more conventional way, "when some things mingled with others" (701–2). The notion of Eros "mingling all things together" (700) is distinctly Empedoclean in nature, even as the picture of "boundless (ἀπείροσι) folds of Darkness" reminds us of Anaximander's *apeirōn*.[46] This whole scheme is itself a skillful fusion of Hesiod's *Theogony*, Orphism, pre-Socratic cosmogony, and sheer nonsense.

One thinker is designated by name in this passage, the sophist Prodicus (692). It has been noted that the repetition of the adverb "correctly" (ὀρθῶς) in lines 690 and 692, where it is the word immediately before Prodicus' name, alludes to Prodicus' doctrine of linguistic "correctness" (ὀρθότης or ὀρθοεπεία).[47] These allusions are more than simply passing references to his supposed "atheism."[48] Aristophanes may have seen something in common between such popular quack religions as Orphism and the "atheistic" teachings of the sophists, for in different ways both had the effect of denying traditional beliefs and undermining the city's established religious institutions.[49] Prodicus' doctrines on the origin of religion are in fact quite relevant to the birds' claim to being the original divinities. Prodicus claimed that men first regarded as gods those things in the perceptible world that benefited and nourished them—the Sun, Moon, rivers, lakes, the four elements, bread, wine—and that these elements later came to be identified as the Olympian gods.[50] Indeed, the birds' chief argument here for their divinity is precisely their usefulness to men, as love gifts (703–7), seasonal indicators (709–15), prophetic signs (716–22), musicians (723–26), general givers of bounty (727–36). This theme has also been adumbrated in Peisthetaerus' discourse to the birds emphasizing their usefulness to men, particularly in agriculture (586–91) and prophecy (592–626). And it is taken up again in the second parabasis, especially 1058–70 on agriculture and 1102–13 on other benefits. Soon after the parabasis we discover the Olympian gods to be themselves identified with different species of birds (863–88), apparently giving further demonstration to Prodicus' doctrine that worship of the Olympians evolved from primeval worship of natural elements and forces.[51] The echo of *Prometheus Bound* at the beginning of the parabasis ("little accomplishing . . . ephemeral . . . dreamlike men," 686–87; cf. *PV* 547–49)[52] has put us into a context of viewing the human race in its helpless infancy, dependent on outside help, whether by gods or by birds; it therefore should not surprise us that the parabasis proceeds to encompass Prodicean anthropology as well as Orphic cosmogony.

In the parabasis epirrhemes the birds offer the audience a world with complete latitude and freedom for self-indulgence of every kind. Whereas the anapests focused on cosmogony and the evolution of religious beliefs, the epirrhemes explore sophistic anthropology further with the opposition between *nomos* and *phusis*, "convention" and "nature."[53] The epirrheme insists upon the distinction between *aischron* ("shameful," 755, 757, 768) and *kalon* ("noble," 756, 758) being purely a matter of *nomos* (755, 757); everything "shameful" among men is "noble" among the birds and hence not restrained or forbidden (755–56). In what appears to be a direct intertextual echo of *Clouds*,[54] the birds tell us that even father beating is noble among them, however dishonorable it may be among men in general. Similarly Athenian anxieties about racial purity and citizenship are shown to be only a matter of convention; the birds welcome to their new city even the lowest Phrygian or Carian slaves like Spintharus or Execestides (762–65).[55] They will open their city up to the *atimoi* (766–68), those recently in exile from Athens for the sacrileges of 415. Peisthetaerus and Euelpides are themselves such *atimoi* fleeing the lawcourts like many Athenian intellectuals of the time. The founding of their new city is itself an act of impiety toward the traditional gods.

In contrast to the epirrheme's emphasis on matters of *nomos* the antepirrheme lists the various ways in which the spectators would be free to satisfy the demands of their *phusis* if they had wings.[56] Our attention shifts from political liberty to personal liberty. Bodily needs for food (786–89), excretion (790–92), and sex (793–96) can be fulfilled at will and without inhibition. The verbal parallelism implies the equivalence of all these bodily processes; even if sex takes the form of adultery, with an important man's wife no less, it is just as natural and acceptable in this context as eating and defecating.[57] By satisfying his need for drink with "winged wicker wine flasks," Dieitrephes is elevated to

the posts of phylarch, hipparch, and "horsecock" (798–800); the ascent to ultimate political power through self-indulgence foreshadows Peisthetaerus' ac-
quisition of power by marrying Basileia. This antepirrheme presents a fantasy
world of total wish fulfillment, not unlike the one imagined by Peisthetaerus
and Euelpides at the beginning of their utopian adventure (127–42), where
friends share only their happy moments and not their times of need, and where
fathers willingly offer their sons as *paidika*. Significantly wings allow men to
leave tragedy behind (787), and with it all care, grief, and social restraint.

The epirrheme's theme of citizenship and the antepirrheme's enumerated
advantages of wings together serve as effective introductions to the play's second half, which exhibits a long series of foreign visitors attempting to profit
from the birds' new city.[58] Peisthetaerus even has loads of feathers brought
onstage to equip the new immigrants with wings (1305–36). Despite the
parabasis's open invitation to new settlers of every sort, however, Peisthetaerus
actually admits no one to his city. We can certainly understand his rejection of
the first group that comes to him; the oracle seller, the urban planner Meton
(perhaps modeled on Hippodamus), the Athenian inspector, and the syco-
phantic decree seller are all characters who try to impose external laws and
restrictions of one sort or another on the new city, thus annihilating its freedom
from restrictions.[59] None of these are really interested in becoming part of
Cloudcuckooland. Even the Pindaric poet, who is treated rather sympathetically by Peisthetaerus, comes as an itinerant seeking monetary profit from his
ready-made encomiastic poetry; only moments after the foundation of Cloudcuckooland (see 917–23) he is already celebrating it in terms identical with
those in which he celebrates every other city. Hence his poetic *nomos* is as
constricting and foreign as the legal, architectural, and religious *nomoi* of the
other parasites.

On the other hand the second group of visitors (the young man, Cinesias,
and the sycophant) are all people who desire to live in Cloudcuckooland
permanently, precisely because of its freedom and lack of conventional Hellenic *nomoi*.[60] But Peisthetaerus rejects them too, sending the young man off to
military service, insulting Cinesias, and beating the sycophant. The rejection of
the young man who wishes to strangle his father and inherit a fortune (1351–
52) strikes us as particularly strange after the parabasis's specific evocation of
father beating as the primary example of what is permitted in bird *nomos* but
not in human *nomos* (757–59), alluded to here by the young man's reference to
the desirability of bird *nomoi* (1345). Peisthetaerus gives the young man some
"fatherly" advice not to beat his father and instead provides him with wings to
undertake a more patriotic and socially useful way of releasing his aggressive
energy—by military service in Thrace (1360–69). In like manner he tries to use

Cinesias in training tribal choruses (1405–7) and with his "noble words" attempts to turn the sycophant toward "lawful work" (ἔργον νόμιμον, 1450).

Some critics interpret this anomaly between the programmatic invitation of the parabasis and Peisthetaerus' actual practice as evidence of the hero's recognition that law is a necessary and integral part of any organized society. Some have even seen Cloudcuckooland in a very positive way as a utopian "just society,"[61] although we are dealing with at least two mutually contradictory versions of utopia here. We should be more suspicious of Peisthetaerus' motives, in view of his subsequent manipulation of the bird state to his own advantage, eating dissident birds and even at the end establishing himself as a "tyrant" (1708) with absolute Sovereignty (Basileia) over them.[62] He may not be defending the claims of morality here so much as using them to consolidate his own social control over Cloudcuckooland. At this point in the play even his old friend Euelpides has disappeared;[63] Peisthetaerus' ideological fervor is no longer undercut by the lightness of his friend's humor, and the new bird city emerges more and more as the private fiefdom of one man. The two named visitors, Meton and Cinesias, were in fact prominent intellectuals of the same class as Peisthetaerus himself; although the kind of people for whom Cloudcuckooland was supposed to be a haven, they represent potential competition for Peisthetaerus' hegemony and must therefore be purged, even if by appeal to conventional antiintellectual prejudices.[64]

The parricide, dithyrambist, and sycophant all introduce disorderly and subversive influences into the ideal state, which, unless channeled into appropriate activities, could threaten the ruler's power even more than the foreign parasites whom he had rejected before. Indeed, Peisthetaerus is himself identified as an "old man" (255, 320, 337) and establishes his position with the birds by using arguments appealing to the patriarchal authority of antiquity and ancestors (472–75; cf. 540–43). It is thus not surprising that he resists the young man's antipatriarchal iconoclasm. Master sophist that he is, Peisthetaerus is able to come up with a counterargument to any contention and can cite another bird *nomos*, that of the stork's obligation to nurture its father (1353–57), to counter the bird *nomos* on which the young man relies.[65] As Peisthetaerus says, "there are many bird laws" (πολλοὶ γὰρ ὀρνίθων νόμοι, 1346); the sophistic concept of legal relativism is most convenient, since it allows him to find support in the body of bird *nomoi* for any position he wishes to take.

The sophistic theory of *nomos* may seem to liberate individuals from any moral obligation to obey absolute *nomoi*; by the same token it also liberates unscrupulous rulers to impose any *nomoi* which they find to be in their self-interest. The dream of absolute personal freedom from *nomos* which the birds offer in the parabasis is dissolved into rule by arbitrary and capricious application of *nomos*, just as the prologue's dream of a τόπον ἀπράγμονα (44) turns into its exact opposite.[66] Even so, our own century has witnessed many hopeful revolutions of social liberation transform themselves into the most oppressive forms of despotism and totalitarianism. The birds' utopian just society is revealed to be a negative dystopia, a classical precursor of Orwell's *Animal Farm*.

A similar process of manipulation and disappointment of the audience's hopes and expectations is at work in Aristophanes' other truly utopian comedy, *Ecclesiazusae*. Produced in 392, this play, along with *Wealth*, has been construed by some critics as a response to deteriorating economic conditions and class polarization in the empire-shorn Athens of the 390s.[67] Some have even regarded Praxagora's utopian program as one with which Aristophanes himself had sympathy, and have therefore seen the play's satire as directed not at the communistic ideas themselves but at the greed and materialism of those who would resist communism.[68] However, there is really very little evidence that the 390s were a decade of radical egalitarianism in Athenian politics: measures such as Agyrrhius' institution of pay for attending the *ekklesia*,[69] obviously alluded to in the title and premise of this play (new people being attracted to assembly meetings), are not really more than an extension of the 420s populism of Cleon. Although the economic depression of the 390s doubtless contributed to the comic interest in economic themes seen in Aristophanes' last two plays, the extreme proposals put forward by Praxagora clearly go beyond anything even seriously considered in the political arena of the time.[70] Again, the source of the utopian ideas is more likely to be found in the intellectual and theoretical realm than in the historical.

The similarities and differences between Praxagora's communism of property and family and the system proposed in Plato's *Republic* have been more than adequately discussed already.[71] Chronology makes it impossible that the *Republic*, even in a preliminary form, could have been a source for Aristophanes' ideas. Nor is it probable that any one treatise was Aristophanes' source here. More likely he was influenced by a long tradition of intellectual speculation and political theory concerning the concept of equality (*isonomia*). This concept was fundamental to pre-Socratic cosmological theory as early as Anaximander,[72] and to the humoral theory of ancient medicine;[73] it may have been applied to political "equality" as early as the reforms of Cleisthenes.[74] The theoretical articulation of a program for sharing wealth as a means of achieving social concord was developed by both Democritus and Archytas.[75] Herodotus informs his readers of several barbarian communities that carry the concepts of shared property and social harmony to the extent of sharing women; as we have noted, this may also have been a topic of sophistic discourse, and seems to have been recognized as such by Euripides (fr. 653 N).[76] Even within the Greek system, social equality and some form of communal family arrangements were a prominent part of what was admired in the Spartan constitution.

One of the most developed theories of property equalization is that of Phaleas of Chalcedon, discussed by Aristotle in *Politics* 2.7 and plausibly dated by modern critics to the end of the fifth century.[77] Aristotle tells us that Phaleas' scheme allowed for equal distribution of property to all in new colonies, but in existing cities tried to achieve this goal through the regulation of marriage agreements. Interestingly, we see property and sexuality linked here, as they are also in *Ecclesiazusae* and, for that matter, in Greek marriage practice generally: as is well known, marriages were arranged among families more for financial purposes than out of any romantic connection. Phaleas' proposal merely extends to the state a certain interest in using the financial calculations for egalitarian purposes. However, Aristotle objects to Phaleas' utopian system on the grounds that mere equalization of property can never be enough to achieve true equality, unless also coupled with equalization of education and honor among all members of the populace. Moreover, he objects that some people will never be satisfied with mere equality, but will aspire for higher honor or more property, and will foment social discord to achieve their desires; as Aristotle points out, criminals are often not motivated by poverty, but by greed. Aristotle's criticisms of Phaleas' fairly moderate egalitarian constitution parallel the flaws which Aristophanes dramatizes in Praxagora's more radical scheme: the problems arising from the fact that all people cannot be equal in terms of beauty and natural gifts, the inevitability of human greed, and the certainty of strife and social discord arising from these problems.

Ecclesiazusae is not as pervaded with explicit allusions to sophists and intellectuals as *Birds* was, but Middle Comedy generally is not quite so oriented to personal satire as Old Comedy. Praxagora, like Peisthetaerus, does seem to be modeled on the sophists. Rothwell has noted the use of intellectually charged terms like ξυνετός, δέξιος, σοφός, and δεινός to characterize her throughout the play and contrasts this semantic cluster with the lack of such terms to characterize the equally dynamic Lysistrata.[78] Her arbitrary intellectual manipulation of arguments becomes especially evident at the beginning of her public proclamation of communism, presented in an agonistic interchange with her husband Blepyrus:[79]

> Chor. Now you must defend your friends, knowing how
> To arouse a shrewd mind and philosophical thought.
> For by common good fortune

> The inventiveness of your tongue is going to delight
> The citizen people
> With countless benefits of life. It is now time to reveal whatever
>   you can.
> Our city needs some clever discovery.
> Only be sure to accomplish
> Things never done nor said before,
> Since they hate it, if they often see old things onstage.
> You must not hesitate, but take hold with high thoughts,
> As being swift wins the most favor among the spectators.

Prax.   And indeed, I trust that I shall teach good things.
> If the spectators wish to start something new and not remain
> In their familiar and ancient customs—this is what I especially fear.

Blep.   Have no fear about starting something new. It is up to us
> To do this in preference to any other rule and to disregard ancient
>   customs.

Prax.   May none of you speak against me or make an uproar
> Until you understand the scheme and have heard out the person
>   explaining it.

(Eccl. 571–89)

Praxagora originally justified her program of rule by women on the grounds of women's traditionalism and preservation of ancestral values: women manage the household and work wool just as their mothers did, and will thus save Athens from its frenzy for experimentation with new and untried methods (*Eccl.* 214–40).[80] But her actual speech to the Assembly justified the proposal on the grounds that this was the one thing never yet tried before (*Eccl.* 455–57). This tension between traditionalism and experimentation becomes the centerpiece of discussion in the present passage: while Praxagora worries about the spectators (i.e., theatrical audience) wanting something new, the chorus praises her precisely for the novelty and subtlety of her ideas, reassuring her (as does Blepyrus) that the audience always wants something new.[81] Just as Peisthetaerus had used the argument that the birds were the original gods and the bird state a reassertion of their primeval dominance, Praxagora cloaks her extremely radical social plan in the rhetoric of a return to traditional family values;[82] presuming to extend the values of the oikos to the whole polis (*Eccl.* 210–12), her plan in fact dissolves the individual oikos and leaves nothing but a polis.

The plot of *Ecclesiazusae* unfolds itself as a progressive demonstration of the unworkability of Praxagora's communistic program. The starting point of her power equalization scheme is the enfranchisement of women, giving them voting rights at the *ekklesia* by dressing them up as men. But the play's prologue demonstrates that they cannot in fact participate in political discussions in a rational way or convincingly imitate their male counterparts, and that all the old stereotypes about women being interested only in sex and wine are true. None of the women other than Praxagora are able to act or speak like men: one tries to card wool at the *ekklesia* meeting (*Eccl.* 88–92), another can speak of nothing but drinking (*Eccl.* 132–46), another can speak only with distinctively feminine mannerisms (*Eccl.* 151–59). Although Praxagora herself does come across as an effective and articulate masculine figure, the comic blunders of the other women demonstrate the absurdity of any attempt at equalization of the sexes, even more of any proposal to give power to women.[83] Aristophanes shows us incorrigible human nature reasserting itself against the confident nostrums of progressive theory.

The most ridiculous extension of Praxagora's program of sexual equality is in the sphere of attempting to equalize sexual attractions, so as to guarantee that all citizens have equal opportunity for sexual activity, whether young or old, beautiful or ugly. It is an inevitable fact of nature that all of us are not equally endowed; the aging process is also an irreversible fact of life. Decreeing that the young and beautiful must first have sex with the old and ugly before pursuing their own inclinations is the ultimate legal intrusion into the concept of personal autonomy. Not only is all private property abolished to become public, but even the privacy of men and women's bodies is abolished to make them available for public appropriation. The result is not social concord, but squabbling among the old to determine who is ugliest and thus most eligible, as well as misery among the young whose personal privacy is violated. The spectacle of Epigenes' rape by three old women is clearly calculated by Aristophanes to be distasteful and unpleasant to the male audience, a vivid symbolic illustration of radical theory spinning out of control, destroying everything the Greek sensibility regarded as beautiful, true, and good.[84]

Systems of redistribution will only work to the extent that people choose to comply with them. While some, like the gullible Chremes, will dutifully contribute every last bowl, flask, pot, and implement in his house (*Eccl.* 728–45), thus making it cease to function as a house, others, like the unidentified neighbor (*Eccl.* 746–832), will hoard their belongings and contribute nothing, even while receiving the common meals along with everyone else.[85] The inevitable result will be even greater inequality, with the selfish keeping everything they had before while obtaining more from the common distribution, and with the public-spirited thus losing out. It is perhaps not insignificant that Praxagora's last appearance in the play was immediately before this scene. Without her personal energy and presence to sustain the system she has put into place, it inevitably degenerates into chaos and falls apart.[86] Even so, we have seen the communist utopias of our own era fall into slow decline and eventual collapse once deprived of the superintendence of charismatic and determined leaders like Stalin or Mao, whose will to power brooked no obstacles. Whereas Peisthetaerus in *Birds* remained ever present, ever in control, Praxagora's departure less than two-thirds of the way through this play reminds us just how tenuous and unstable such visionary systems can become if not enforced with the unflinching and unrepentant despotism of Peisthetaerus' Cloudcuckooland. Utopian attempts to eliminate the autonomy of the individual merely founder if not under the firm leadership of a highly motivated and autonomous individual.

The egalitarian classless society that Praxagora attempts to create is revealed as a mirage, a pretext for a new oligarchy (the women) and ultimately a new tyranny (Praxagora's), since Praxagora is the only one of the women with any real ability to govern and lead. The system depends even more heavily on the utilization of slaves to perform all tasks of manual labor (*Eccl.* 651), and thus voids any pretense of creating a truly egalitarian society.[87] The "ironic" interpretation of this play is surely the correct one;[88] it is possible to view Praxagora's ideas as Aristophanes' only if we dismiss most of the play's scenes as "mere farce" and privilege Praxagora's contradictory and inconsistent speeches as the only part to be taken seriously.

Aristophanic criticism has long been divided by the elusive question of Aristophanes' politics—whether any serious political tendency can be discerned in his work at all, and if so, what tendency.[89] Our discussion of his utopian plays suggests a deep and abiding suspicion of intellectuals and their plans for a better society, with *Birds* (performed in 414) and *Ecclesiazusae* (392) continuing and reinforcing many of the themes already articulated in the early *Banqueters* (427) and *Clouds* (423). What one finds throughout Aristophanes' work is a populist hostility toward elites, whether the political elites dominating Athens from Cleon to Agyrrhius or the intellectual elites who set the tone for the best and brightest among Athens' youth.

At the same time, Aristophanes himself was no boorish reactionary, but was thoroughly conversant with modern intellectual and artistic trends, and in some aspects of his work influenced by them. To the extent that he demonstrates the socially corrosive effects of the sophists and some of their doctrines, his critique is what we might today call "neoconservative." Committed to social justice and sympathetic to the plight of the common man, but suspicious of the intellectual, artistic, and political elitists who presumed to speak for the common man's interests, Aristophanes saw himself engaged in a *Kulturkampf* against those elements of the modernist program that threatened the traditional moral values of the common man. Even so, neoconservative critics of our day (as well as New Left critics in the tradition of Foucault and Deleuze) decry the technocratic "knowledge class" that dominates the media, universities, arts and entertainment industries, foundations, clergy, medical profession, social welfare agencies, judiciary, and regulatory bureaucracies as "coercive utopians" silently bypassing the democratic process to impose upon society a radical agenda in the name of egalitarianism, but in fact designed to perpetuate and enhance the knowledge class's own influence, power, and social control over the masses. The paradox of Athenian politics in Aristophanes' day is that the radicals were in fact the oligarchs, with Athenian democracy being the traditional status quo they wished to overturn, even if in the name of utopian programs that presumed to be more democratic.[90] No state could be more oligarchical than Plato's *Republic* or Praxagora's Women's State, even as no state could be more tyrannical than Cloudcuckooland.

Notes

1. Zimmermann 1983; Konstan 1990 (and above); Dawson 1992. For previous treatments of Aristophanic utopia, working from a similarly inclusive definition, see Schwinge 1977 and Bertelli 1983. For other treatments of the utopian tradition in Greek thought generally, see Salin 1921; Braunert 1969; Finley 1967; Kytzler 1973; and Flashar 1974.

2. Auden 1948, 409. The same dichotomy is also explored in Auden's poem "Vespers," in Auden 1976, 482–84.

3. Auden's Eden/New Jerusalem distinction derives from what Lewis Mumford distinguishes as the "utopias of escape" (golden age mythological utopias) and "utopias of reconstruction" (serious political programs). See Mumford 1922, 16.

4. On this tradition, see the seminal work of Lovejoy and Boas 1935, 23–102. See also Giannini 1967, 101–32; Zimmermann 1983, 59–61; and Dawson 1992, 13–14.

5. See the fragments from these plays collected in Athen. 6.267e–270a. Also see the discussions of Baldry 1953, 49–60; Langerbeck 1963, 192–204; and Heberlein 1980, 11–26.

6. As is well known, Arist. *Poet.* 1449a9, derives comedy's origins from the *phallika* celebrated in the countryside. We obtain an idea of what these fertility rites may have been like from *Ach.* 237–79 as well as from abundant iconographic evidence. See Cornford 1968, 101–14; Herter 1947, 17–31; and, for a more skeptical view, Pickard-Cambridge 1962, 133–47.

7. See Ehrenberg 1951, 73–94.

8. To appropriate Konstan's terminology (see "The Polis and Its Negations" above), all the other utopian forms in Aristophanes—whether anomian, antinomian, or eunomian—eventually gravitate toward the megalonomian and, as such, produce negative outcomes.

9. On Protagoras, see Diog. Laer. 9.55; for Crito and Simon, Diog. Laer. 2.121–22; for Antisthenes, Diog. Laer. 6.16 and Athen. 5.220d; for Hippodamus and Phaleas, Arist. *Pol.* 2.7–8. On this tradition generally, see Henkel 1854, 401–11.

10. In addition to Aristotle, see Strabo 14.2.9; Hesychius, s.v. Ἱπποδάμου νέμησις (1825 Schmidt); ΣAr. *Knights* 327a, c (Koster) and Diod. Sic. 12.10.7. See the studies of Hermann 1841; Erdmann 1884; Bise 1923; Lana 1949; and McCredie 1971.

11. See McCredie 1971, 95–100.

12. For Hippodamus' meteorological interests, see Hesychius, s.v. Ἱπποδάμου νέμησις (1825 Schmidt).

13. Such numerical symmetries in the planning of new colonies clearly went beyond Hippodamus. Hieron's new pan-Dorian colony of Aetna (476/5) was intended for a population of 10,000 Dorians, exactly half from Syracuse and half from the Peloponnese. See Diod. Sic. 11.49.1.

14. Sophistic and pre-Socratic interest in the origins of civilization can be inferred from the accounts in Pl. *Prot.* 320C–323C, Diod. Sic. 1.8.1–7, and the *Sisyphus* fragment often attributed to Critias (= 88B25 D.-K.). See Havelock 1957, 104–24; Reinhardt 1960, 114–32; Cole 1967, 1–147; Guthrie 1961–81, 60–68; and Kerferd 1981, 140–42. For the influence of these theories on *Birds*, see de Carli 1971, 50–54.

15. On this idealizing, utopian tendency in the sophists' use of ethnographic material, see Dümmler 1891, 45–55; and Dawson 1992, 18–21. The community of women is clearly alluded to in fr. 653 N of the sophist-influenced Euripides.

16. For the idealization of Sparta as a topos in late fifth-century oligarchic utopianism, see Dawson 1992, 28–29. Critias' treatises on the Spartan constitution appear to have been the basis for the Xenophontic treatise we possess.

17. For this thesis, see the archeological studies of Hoepfner and Schwandner 1986, 12–20, and Schuller, Hoepfner, and Schwandner 1989. Hippodamus may have been the father of the modern tract development.

18. For a historical survey of what we know about this city's foundation, see Ehrenberg 1948.

19. That Metagenes' play was utopian in nature is suggested by fr. 6 K.-A. and its inclusion in the list of plays discussed in Athen. 6.267e–270a.

20. Cf. Mazon 1904, 110; Croiset 1909, 120–31; Norwood 1931, 241; Gelzer 1960, 259; Händel 1963, 317–20; Murray 1964, 135–36; Whitman 1964, 169; Dover 1972, 145; Maxwell-Stuart 1973, 401–2; Torrance 1978, 53; Koelb 1984, 61–64.

21. This view received its most developed articulation in the seminal work of Süvern 1835. Not all later proponents accept the detailed allegory proposed by Süvern, but some form of allusion to Sicily is maintained by Goossens 1946, 51–60; Turato 1971–72, 115–18; Arrowsmith 1973, 141; Solomos 1974, 178–79; Dalfen 1975, 282; van Looy 1975, 181–82; Katz 1976, 353–81; Newiger 1957, 53–55; and Konstan 1990, 186–88 (and "Polis and Its Negations" above).

22. Nicias is twice alluded to (363, 640). Verses 147 and 1303 mention the messenger ship *Salaminia*, which summoned Alcibiades back from Sicily to stand trial, but this is more an allusion to the trials than to Sicily. Katz 1976, 353–63, argues that the three gods sent to negotiate with Peisthetaerus in 1565–1693 are meant as an allusion to the indecisive troika of generals sent to Sicily in 415; this may be correct, although I am skeptical of his attempt to identify each of the three gods with one of the generals.

23. See Hubbard 1991, 159–61, for a more detailed argument that the play alludes to this historical background. See also Schwinge 1977, 54. The essay of J. Henderson in this volume, "Mass versus Elite," supports my view of Peisthetaerus as an elitist character, but adopts a far more charitable position toward his undertakings.

24. On the connections between sophistic teaching and the profanations, see Guthrie 1961–81, 3.245; Kagan 1981, 205–9; and Ostwald 1986, 324–30.

25. The Clouds' condemnation of Meton's calendar reform (*Clouds* 607–26) suggests that Aristophanes regarded it along with Socrates' speculations as something contrary to Athenian religious tradition. On Cinesias' impiety, see Strattis, fr. 18 K.-A.; Athen. 12.551a (citing Lysias); Pickard-Cambridge 1962, 44–45; Dodds 1951, 188–89; Woodbury 1965, 210; and Turato, 1971–72, 127–31. Andocides 1.35, 1.63, and ΣAv. 766 tell us his father Meletus was one of the violators of both the herms and the Mysteries. The definitive treatment of Diagoras of Melos remains that of Jacoby 1959, who dates his condemnation to 433/32, and accepts his authorship of a pamphlet titled Ἀποπυργίζοντες Λόγοι, denying the existence of the gods. Woodbury 1965,

178–211, challenges Jacoby's conclusions, but is clearly mistaken in his dogmatic assumption (198–99, 206) that a dithyrambic poet could not also write a prose treatise or have unconventional religious ideas. Still less satisfactory is the view of Rosenmeyer 1972, 232–38, that the whole tradition of a decree against Diagoras is a scholiastic fiction; this is disproven by Lysias 6.17–18, as Ostwald 1986, 275 n. 287, notes. Katz 1976, 372–73, raises the interesting possibility that 1576 (ὁ τοὺς θεοὺς ἀποτειχίσας) and the general idea of a fortified city blockading the gods are inspired by the title of Diagoras' work; Jacoby 1959, 30, also sees a possible allusion in *Clouds* 1024 (καλλίπυργον σοφίαν . . . ἐπασκῶν).

26. For interest in the μετέωρα as a leitmotif in *Clouds* symbolizing atheistic naturalism, see *Clouds* 228, 264–66, 333, 360, 404–7, 489–90, 1283–84. On the term and its significance in both plays, see Newiger 1957, 55–56. For the general relation between *Clouds* and *Birds*, see the detailed discussion of Gelzer 1956, 79–82.

27. That Socrates' influence in fact was blamed for the actions of Alcibiades and Critias is recorded by Xen. *Mem.* 1.2.12; Xenophon spends considerable effort in exculpating Socrates from any responsibility for their actions. See also Aeschines' defense of Socrates' condemnation (1.173), which suggests that Critias and his followers are what Socrates' accusers had in mind when charging the philosopher with "corrupting the youth." The essentially antidemocratic character of Socrates' teachings and followers has recently been highlighted by Stone 1988.

28. While there is some scholarly dispute over the exact form of the protagonist's name (Peisthetaerus, Peisetaerus, Peithetaerus, Pisthetaerus—the first is the form of the manuscripts and the one I shall use), it is fairly clear that the prefix has to do with "persuasion" and the root -*hetairos* with the *hetairiai*. See Harman 1920, 87, and on the *peis*- prefix, Dobrov 1988, 98–103. Reckford 1987, 333, thinks the name alludes to Peisistratus, as is appropriate, considering Peisthetaerus' emergence at the end of the play as a "tyrant" (1708) over the birds.

29. See 362–63, 427–31, 1271–75, 1401. On Peisthetaerus' sophistic character, see Süvern 1835, 33–34, and Gelzer 1956, 80. Like any clever rhetorician Peisthetaerus also criticizes his opponents for being "sophists" (1619, 1646). It is significant that *Birds* uses the terms *sophos* and *kainos* more than any other play of Aristophanes except *Clouds*; cf. Moulton 1981, 35.

30. On the sophistic method of *epideixis*, see Guthrie 1961–81, 3.41–44, and Kerferd 1981, 28–29.

31. For Protagoras' doctrine concerning the relative truth of all such quality perceptions, see Kerferd 1981, 83–100. The connection of inner health with external well-being is implied in the concept of πλουθυγιεία (731).

32. This is the interpretation of ΣAv. 43. I do not agree with Hamilton 1985, 235–39, in seeing these implements as sympotic, which is irrelevant to the context, or in believing that verses 47–48 prove that Peisthetaerus and Euelpides expect to join an existing city rather than found a new one: verse 48 in fact expresses doubt of any *apragmōn* city currently existing.

33. See Thuc. 6.27.3, 6.28.2, 6.61.1–4. While most modern historians reject the existence of any plot to overthrow the democracy at this time, the political leanings of the *hetairiai* responsible were certainly oligarchic; see Aurenche 1974, 89–101; Kagan 1981, 205–9; Ostwald 1986, 329–30, 549–50.

34. Peisthetaerus' use of religious beliefs to gain power has much in common with the radical sophistic view that the gods and morality were merely inventions of πυκνός τις καὶ σοφὸς γνώμην ἀνήρ for the purpose of consolidating social and political control: see the fragment from the satyr play *Sisyphus*, probably produced the year before *Birds* and attributed by many to the sophist Critias (= 88B25 D.-K.), one of those involved in the sacrileges of 415. For Aristophanes' familiarity with *Sisyphus*, see de Carli 1971, 52–54, and on its Critian authorship, see Hubbard 1991, 181 n. 69.

35. See Andocides 1.27, 1.36, 1.43.

36. I agree with Cavaignac 1959, 246–47, that the demonstrative ἐκεῖνον in 1558 is more

likely to refer to Socrates than to Peisander, and thus that the ψυχή refers to Chaerephon, who may have died recently. However, the passage may also be meant to have a secondary reference to Peisander's own spirit.

37. Aristophanes also connects Socrates' teaching with the language and procedures of initiation into mysteries in *Clouds* 254–74, 497–508. On the travesty of Socrates' notion of *psuchagogia* in this ode, see Hofmann 1976, 210–11, and Sommerstein 1987, 300–301.

38. For other possible Socratic references in *Birds*, see Stark 1953, 77–89.

39. Peisthetaerus and the Birds have already been associated with Laconizers by Euelpides' proposal to name the new city Sparta (813–14). On Critias' idealization of Spartan society, see n. 16 above.

40. Plut. *Alc.* 23.3–4.

41. Note that the same verb ὀρνιθομανῶ ("I am mad for the birds") is used by the young man in verse 1344.

42. For Gorgias' theory of the irresistible persuasive power of *logos*, see esp. the *Encomium of Helen* (82B11 D.-K.); cf. Segal 1962, 99–155; de Romilly 1973, 155–62; and Kerferd, 1981, 78–82.

43. See Diod. Sic. 12.83.2.

44. For Orphic influence here, especially with respect to the cosmic egg and birth of Eros, see Pollard 1948, 374–75; Hofmann 1976, 184–85; West 1983, 111–12, 201; and Zannini Quirini 1987, 134–45. Of course, the basic starting point of this cosmogony, as of all Greek cosmogonies, is Hesiod.

45. See Whitman 1964, 184; Hofmann 1976, 191–92. In this case it cannot be an egg fertilized by wind, since air has not yet been created; if this is the meaning, then the whole process is still impossible, since there is no wind to fertilize.

46. For Empedocles, see 31B17.7, B20.1–3, B21.8–14, B22.1–5, B26.3–5, B35 D.-K., on the elements coming together to form things through the force of Philotes. For Anaximander's *apeirōn*, see 12B1 D.-K. and the discussions of Guthrie 1961–81, 3.83–87, and Kahn 1960, 231–39.

47. See Hofmann 1976, 181. Nestle 1936, 162, also notes that the repetition of ὥρα (696, 705, 709, 714, 725) and the emphasis on the birds' role as seasonal signs in 709–15 may allude to the title of Prodicus' treatise (῾Ωραι).

48. Henrichs 1976, 21, suggests that Prodicus was not, strictly speaking, seen as an atheist by his contemporaries, because he at least granted some of the gods a past human existence.

49. For the harmful effects of merchandising religion among the public, see Pl. *Rep.* II 364b–365a. Note the contempt with which oracle sellers are treated, both here in 959–91 and in *Peace* 1052–1126 (cf. *Knights* 997–1110).

50. See Prodicus, 84B5 D.-K., and Nestle 1936, 160–63; Untersteiner 1954, 209–11; Guthrie 1961–81, 3.238–42; and Kerferd 1981, 169.

51. The identification of the Olympians with bird species has also been made by Peisthetaerus in verses 514–19.

52. For the allusion, cf. Herington 1963, 237–38; Rau 1967, 176–77; Hofmann 1976, 179–80.

53. For this opposition in Aristophanes, see Hubbard 1991, 124 and the references therein. With regard to *Birds* specifically, see de Carli 1971, 49–53, and Konstan 1990, 189–203.

54. Pheidippides' father beating (*Clouds* 1321–1446) is the climactic turning point of that play, in which Strepsiades sees his whole enterprise turn to his own disadvantage. Significantly Pheidippides also evokes the example of cocks striking their own fathers to demonstrate the relativity of *nomoi* (*Clouds* 1421–29).

55. The citizenship question, particularly with regard to Execestides, appears to be a topical leitmotif in this play; cf. 11, 30–35, 1527.

56. For the concept of *phusis anangkaia* articulated here, cf. *Clouds* 1075–78 (in connection with the Lesser Discourse's justification of adultery), Thuc. 5.105.2 (in connection with the

Melian dialogue), Democritus 68B278 D.-K. (in connection with the sexual drive), and the comments of Heinimann 1945, 167–68; Guthrie 1961–81, 3.99–101; and Turato 1971–72, 123–24. .

57. Concerning the sequence of verbal parallelisms that tend to equate these three acts, see the analysis of Giner and de Hoz 1979, 126–27. On the importance of the erotic element in the play, see Arrowsmith 1973, 130–41, and Paduano 1973, 120–21.

58. See the remarks of Paduano 1973, 125–27. And as Dobrov 1988, 168, notes, the ante-pirrheme, with its final image of Dieitrephes transformed into a "shrill-voiced horsecock," leads directly into Peisthetaerus' and Euelpides' reentry onstage in bird form.

59. See Turato 1971–72, 124–25; and Reckford 1987, 337.

60. Turato 1971–72, 132–33, sees the three newcomers here as violators of each of the three fundamental "unwritten laws" of Greek culture: respectively, (1) honoring parents, (2) worship-ping the gods, and (3) obeying the laws. I would note, however, that although Cinesias' well-known impiety was probably part of the reason for his inclusion here, it is not emphasized in this context so much as his free dithyrambic verse, which violates all poetic *nomoi*; that Aristophanes saw a connection between poetic style and general moral principles is demonstrated by the agon in *Frogs*.

61. For the former view, see Turato 1971–72, 141–43. For the latter, see Gigante 1948, 21–23; Reckford 1987, 334–35; and Zannini Quirini 1987, 86–87. Turato's view is in essence correct, but this should not be seen as a positive enlightenment on Peisthetaerus' part so much as a confirmation of his cynicism in appealing to anomian liberation in the first place.

62. The eating of the birds is done in the name of preserving democracy (1583–85), as the Olympians are overthrown in the name of restoring the birds to supremacy (549–50). Peisthetae-rus' cooking and eating of the birds actualizes the threat made symbolically and theatrically during his first confrontation with the chorus, as he brandishes the cooking pot and spit to defend himself against the birds' attack (356–99). As we have seen, the χύτρα is thematically significant: it is one of the sacrificial implements Peisthetaerus and Euelpides carry onstage at the play's beginning (43), is used to fight off the birds (357, 386, 391), and to sacrifice to the birds (1583–85, 1688–91). Auger 1979, 82–87, examines the inversions of the sacrifice theme in this play and sees it as the vision of a pre-Promethean, presacrificial golden age corrupted into a cannibalis-tic tyranny in which all distinctions between man, god, and animal are erased. See also Romer, "Good Intentions" (in this volume).

63. Strauss 1966, 173–74, has rightly emphasized the importance of Euelpides' disappearance as a turning point in the plot's development.

64. Zimmermann 1993, 267–75, usefully studies the comic techniques used to ridicule Meton and Cinesias here, and sees them as consistent with those employed against intellectuals in the *Clouds*.

65. This patriarchal bird *nomos* has already been adumbrated in verses 472–75. For the general reestablishment of patriarchal authority here, with new gods merely taking the place of the old, see Paduano 1973, 129–31.

66. For an interesting Freudian explanation of the inversion, see Paduano 1973, 141.

67. See esp. Fuks 1984, 19–20, and David 1984, 3–20. For additional references, see Rothwell 1990, 2–5, who offers a corrective revision of this picture.

68. This thesis has been advanced especially by Sommerstein 1984, 314–33. It has been adumbrated in some respects by Barry 1942, 38–50; Konstan and Dillon 1981, 382; Foley 1982, 18–21; and is with modifications also the approach of Rothwell 1990, 9–19. However, Schwinge 1977, 60–65, has seen the opposite development in Aristophanes' work, from a fascination with utopia to a disillusionment with utopian ideas in his last two plays.

69. On this measurè, see the discussion of David 1984, 29–32.

70. Sommerstein 1984, 314–15, bases his argument for a shift in Aristophanes' politics on the

comparatively sympathetic treatment the poor receive and the unsympathetic treatment the rich receive in Aristophanes' last two plays, as opposed to the contrary in the poet's earlier work. But the sympathy for the poor in these plays may simply be a reflection of Aristophanes' audience during a time of economic depression, similar to American popular entertainment of the 1930s, which need not necessarily be interpreted as supporting any particular ideological program. Nor is there validity in the premise that the rich are always treated sympathetically and the poor unsympathetically in the earlier plays: we have no evidence that characters such as Dicaeopolis and Trygaeus are rich, at least in the beginning, and quite certain evidence that the sausage seller is not rich, whereas characters who do seem to be of a somewhat higher status (Strepsiades, Pheidippides, Bdelycleon) are not portrayed in an altogether sympathetic way.

71. For the vast bibliography on the question, see Adam 1963, 345–55, and Ussher 1973, xv–xx. David 1984, 21–23, is probably right in concluding merely that these ideas were "in the air" among philosophers of the time, but not derived from any one text.

72. See the discussion of Vlastos 1947.

73. The word *isonomia* is first attested in Alcmaeon of Croton 24B4 D.-K. For its development as a concept in elemental and humoral theory, see MacKinney 1964.

74. See Frei 1981, 217–18. On the history of the term as a political concept, see the seminal study of Vlastos 1953.

75. Democritus 68B255 D.-K., and Archytas 47B3 D.-K. For discussion of the history of this idea, see Fuks 1984, 172–89.

76. Hdt. 1.216, 4.104, 4.172, 4.176, 4.180; see the discussion of Dawson 1992, 18–21, for the connection of this ethnographic research to sophistic theories of culture. On Euripides' interest in sophistic equality theories, see Dümmler 1891, 8–59.

77. On Phaleas, see von Pöhlmann 1925, 5–8; Lana 1950, 265–76; Dawson 1992, 29–31.

78. Rothwell 1990, 85–91. He sees Praxagora as a dramatic personification of Peitho. See also Heberlein 1980, 59–60.

79. With an ode (*Eccl.* 571–80), katakeleusmos (*Eccl.* 581–82), epirrheme (*Eccl.* 583–688), and pnigos (*Eccl.* 689–709), this passage constitutes the beginning of epirrhematic agon without any responding second half. See Gelzer 1960, 32–34. The point may be that Praxagora's arguments are so forceful and compelling as not to be open to a reply from Blepyrus.

80. Aristophanes' critique of Athens' never-ending desire for political novelty and experimentation with the untried was a major theme of *Frogs*. See Hubbard 1991, 207–16.

81. On the quasi-parabatic interpenetration between the theatrical and political realms, see my remarks in Hubbard 1991, 249–50.

82. On this tension in Praxagora's rhetoric, see Saïd 1979, 35.

83. The prologue of this play seems to be modeled on that of *Lysistrata*, where the protagonist also waits impatiently on the other women to assemble and where the other women also come across as too preoccupied with their feminine interests to be capable of any serious political action.

84. Sommerstein 1984, 320–21, argues that the audience will sympathize with the old women here. See also Konstan and Dillon 1981, 382. But it is not true that the young and beautiful are always treated unsympathetically in Aristophanes (witness the Young Bridegroom in *Acharnians* or the chorus of *Knights*). Nor are the old always sympathetic characters; they too are the object of mockery and fun. See Byl 1977; Henderson 1987; and Hubbard 1989.

85. Sommerstein 1984, 319–20, argues that this character is an unsympathetic rogue. Indeed he is, as are many other type-scene characters in Aristophanes. But such characters do not receive enough sustained attention to be the primary objects of satire in any play. In this case, the point is not that we sympathize or identify with the selfish neighbor, but that human nature is based on a certain selfishness that will thwart schemes like Praxagora's.

86. On the effects of Praxagora's departure and absence, see the remarks of Rothwell, 1990, 73–75.

87. On the problem of slavery as something indispensable to this and all other ancient utopias, see the interesting essay "Slavery and the Rule of Women in Tradition, Myth, and Utopia," in Vidal-Naquet 1986, 205–23.

88. This interpretation of *Ecclesiazusae* has been advanced most notably by Wilamowitz 1927, 203–21; Newiger 1957, 173–76; and Flashar 1967, 154–58. On irony in Aristophanes' late plays generally, see Carrière 1979, 105–10.

89. In favor of finding a serious political tendency, see de Ste. Croix 1972, 355–76; Forrest 1975; and Henderson 1990. Against it, see Gomme 1938; Goldhill 1991, 167–222; and, with qualifications, Heath 1987.

90. On the ultimately oligarchical character of most utopian schemes, see the just remarks of Dawson 1992, 36–37.

Bibliography

Adam, J. 1963. *The Republic of Plato*. 2d ed. London.

Arrowsmith, William. 1973. "Aristophanes' Birds: The Fantasy Politics of Eros." *Arion*, n.s., 1.119–67.

Auden, W. H. 1948. *The Dyer's Hand and Other Essays*. New York.

———. 1976. *Collected Poems*. Edited by E. Mendelson. New York.

Auger, Danielle. 1979. "Le théâtre d'Aristophane: Le mythe, l'utopie et les femmes." In *Aristophane: Les femmes et la cité*, edited by J. Bonnamour and H. Delavault, 71–101. Fontenay-aux-Roses.

Aurenche, O. 1974. *Les groupes d'Alcibiade, de Léogoras et de Teucros*. Paris.

Baldry, H. C. 1953. "The Idler's Paradise in Attic Comedy." *G&R* 22.49–60.

Barry, Eileen. 1942. *The Ecclesiazusae as a Political Satire*. Chicago.

Bertelli, L. 1983. "L'Utopia sulla scena: Aristofane e la parodia della città." *Civiltà Classica e Cristiana* 4.215–61.

Bise, P. 1923. "Hippodamos de Milet." *Archiv für Philosophie* 35.13–42.

Braunert, Horst. 1969. *Utopia: Antworten griechischen Denkens auf die Herausforderung durch soziale Verhältnisse*. Kiel.

Byl, S. 1977. "Le vieillard dans les comédies d'Aristophane." *AC* 46.52–73.

Carrière, J. C. 1979. *Le carnaval et la politique: Une intoduction à la coméde grecque*. Paris.

Carter, L. B. 1986. *The Quiet Athenian*. Oxford.

Cavaignac, E. 1959. "Pythagore et Socrate." *RPh* 33.246–48.

Cole, Thomas. 1967. *Democritus and the Sources of Greek Anthropology*. Cleveland.

Cornford, Francis M. 1968. *The Origin of Attic Comedy*. 2d ed. Gloucester.

Croiset, M. 1909. *Aristophanes and the Political Parties at Athens*. Translated by J. Loeb. London.

Dalfen, Joachim. 1975. "Politik und Utopie in den *Vögeln* des Aristophanes (Zu Ar., *Vögel* 451–638)." *Bolletino dell'Istituto di Filologia Greca* 2.268–87.

David, Ephraim. 1984. *Aristophanes and Athenian Society of the Early Fourth Century BC*. Leiden.

Dawson, Doyne. 1992. *Cities of the Gods: Communist Utopias in Greek Thought*. New York.

de Carli, E. 1971. *Aristofane e la sofistica*. Florence.

de Romilly, Jacqueline. 1973. "Gorgias et le pouvoir de la poésie." *JHS* 93.155–62.

de Ste. Croix, G. E. M. 1972. *The Origins of the Peloponnesian War*. Ithaca.

Dobrov, Gregory. 1988. "Winged Words/Graphic Birds: The Aristophanic Comedy of Language." Ph.D. diss., Cornell University.

Dodds, E. R. 1951. *The Greeks and the Irrational*. Berkeley.

Dover, K. J. 1972. *Aristophanic Comedy*. Berkeley.

Droysen, J. G. 1835, 1836. "Des Aristophanes Vögel und die Hermokopiden." *RhM* 3.161–208, 4.27–62.

Dümmler, F. 1891. *Prolegomena zu Platons Staat*. Basel.

Ehrenberg, Victor. 1948. "The Foundation of Thurii." *AJP* 69.149–70.

——. 1951. *The People of Aristophanes*. 2d ed. Oxford.

Erdmann, M. 1884. "Hippodamos von Milet und die symmetrische Städtebaukunst der Griechen." *Philologus* 42.193–227.

Finley, M. I. 1967. "Utopianism Ancient and Modern." In *The Critical Spirit: Essays in Honor of Herbert Marcuse*, edited by K. Wolff and Barrington Moore Jr., 3–20. Boston.

Flashar, Hellmut. 1967. "Zur Eigenart des aristophanischen Spätwerks." *Poetica* 1.154–75.

——. 1974. *Formen utopischen Denkens bei den Griechen*. Innsbruck.

Foley, Helene P. 1982. "The 'Female Intruder' Reconsidered: Women in Aristophanes' *Lysistrata* and *Ecclesiazusae*." *CP* 77.1–21.

Forrest, W. G. 1975. "Aristophanes and the Athenian Empire." In *The Ancient Historian and His Materials*, edited by B. Levick, 17–29. Farnborough.

Frei, P. 1981. "ISONOMIA: Politik im Spiegel griechischer Wortbildungslehre." *MH* 38.205–19.

Fuks, Alexander. 1984. *Social Conflict in Ancient Greece*. Jerusalem.

Gelzer, Thomas. 1956. "Aristophanes und sein Sokrates." *MH* 13.65–93.

——. 1960. *Der epirrhematische Agon bei Aristophanes*. Munich.

Giannini, A. 1967. "Mito e Utopia nella letteratura Greca prima di Platone." *Rendiconti dell' Istituto Lombardo, Classe di Lettere* 101.101–32.

Gigante, Marcello. 1948. "La città dei giusti in Esiodo e gli 'Uccelli' di Aristofane." *Dioniso* 11.17–25.

Giner, C., and J. de Hoz. 1979. "Aristófanes, Aves 737–800." In *El commentario de textos griegos y latinos*, edited by C. Codoñer, 101–31. Madrid.

Goldhill, Simon. 1991. *The Poet's Voice*. Cambridge.

Gomme, A. W. 1938. "Aristophanes and Politics." *CR* 52.97–109.

Goossens, R. 1946. "Autour de l' expédition de Sicile." *AC* 15.43–60.

Guthrie, W. K. C. 1961–81. *A History of Greek Philosophy*. Vols. 1–6. Cambridge.

Hamilton, Richard. 1985. "The Well-Equipped Traveller: *Birds* 42." *GRBS* 26.235–39.

Händel, Paul. 1963. *Formen und Darstellungsweisen der aristophanischen Komödie*. Heidelberg.

Harman, E. G. 1920. *The Birds of Aristophanes Considered in Relation to Athenian Politics*. London.

Havelock, Eric A. 1957. *The Liberal Temper in Greek Politics*. London.

Heath, Malcolm. 1987. *Political Comedy in Aristophanes*. Göttingen.

Heberlein, F. 1980. *Pluthygieia: Zur Gegenwelt bei Aristophanes*. Frankfurt am Main.

Heinimann, Felix. 1945. *Nomos und Physis: Herkunft und Bedeutung einer Antithese im griechischen Denken des 5. Jahrhundert*. Basel.

Henderson, Jeffrey. 1987. "Older Women in Attic Old Comedy." *TAPA* 117.105–29.

——. 1990. "The Dêmos and the Comic Competition." In *Nothing to Do with Dionysos? Athenian Drama in Its Social Context*, edited by John J. Winkler and Froma I. Zeitlin, 271–313. Princeton.

Henkel, H. 1854. "Studien zu einer geschichte der griechischen Lehre vom Staat." *Philologus* 9.401–11.

Henrichs, Albert. 1976. "The Atheism of Prodicus." *Cronache Ercolanesi* 6.15–21.

Herington, Cecil J. 1963. "A Study in the *Prometheia*, Part II: *Birds* and *Prometheia*." *Phoenix* 17.236–43.

Hermann, F. 1841. *De Hippodamo Milesio ad Aristot. Polit. II,5*. Marburg.

Herter, Hans. 1947. *Vom dionysischen Tanz zum komischen Spiel*. Iserlohn.

Hoepfner, W., and E. L. Schwandner. 1986. *Haus und Stadt im klassischen Griechenland*. Munich.

Hofmann, H. 1976. *Mythos und Komödie: Untersuchungen zu den Vögeln des Aristophanes*. Hildesheim.

Hubbard, Thomas K. 1989. "Old Men in the Youthful Plays of Aristophanes." In *Old Age in Greek and Latin Literature*, edited by Thomas M. Falkner and Judith de Luce, 90–113. Albany.

——. 1991. *The Mask of Comedy: Aristophanes and the Intertextual Parabasis*. Ithaca.

Jacoby, Felix. 1959. *Diagoras* Ὁ Ἄθεος. Berlin.

Kagan, Donald. 1981. *The Peace of Nicias and the Sicilian Expedition.* Ithaca.

Kahn, Charles H. 1960. *Anaximander and the Origins of Greek Cosmogony.* New York.

Kakridis, T. J. 1970. "Phrynicheisches in den Vögeln des Aristophanes." *WS*, n.s., 4.38–51.

Katz, Barry. 1976. "The *Birds* of Aristophanes and Politics." *Athenaeum* 54.353–81.

Kerferd, G. B. 1981. *The Sophistic Movement.* Cambridge.

Koelb, Clayton. 1984. *The Incredulous Reader: Literature and the Function of Disbelief.* Ithaca.

Konstan, David. 1990. "A City in the Air: Aristophanes' *Birds*." *Arethusa* 23.183–207.

Konstan, David, and Matthew Dillon. 1981. "The Ideology of Aristophanes' *Wealth*." *AJP* 102.371–94.

Kytzler, B. 1973. "Utopisches Denken und Handeln in der klassischen Antike." In *Der utopische Roman*, edited by R. Villgradter and F. Krey, 45–68. Darmstadt.

Lana, Italo. 1949. "L' utopia di Ippodamo di Mileto." *Rivista di filosofia* 40.125–51.

———. 1950. "Le teorie egualitarie di Falea di Calcedone." *Rivista critica di storia della filosofia* 5.265–76.

Langerbeck, H. 1963. "Die Vorstellung vom Schlaraffenland in der alten attischen Komödie." *Zeitschrift für Volkskunde* 59.192–204.

Lovejoy, Arthur O., and George Boas. 1935. *Primitivism and Related Ideas in Antiquity.* Baltimore.

McCredie, J. R. 1971. "Hippodamos of Miletos." In *Studies Presented to George M. A. Hanfmann*, edited by David G. Mitten, John G. Pedley, and Jane A. Scott, 95–100. Cambridge, Mass.

MacKinney, Loren. 1964. "The Concept of Isonomia in Greek Medicine." In *Isonomia: Studien zur Gleichheitsvorstellung im griechischen Denken*, edited by Jürgen Mau and Ernst Günther Schmidt, 79–88. Berlin.

Maxwell-Stuart, P. G. 1973. "The Dramatic Poets and the Expedition to Sicily." *Historia* 22.397–404.

Mazon, Paul. 1904. *Essai sur la composition des comédies d'Aristophane.* Paris.

Moulton, Carroll. 1981. *Aristophanic Poetry.* Göttingen.

Mumford, Lewis. 1922. *The Story of Utopias.* London.

Murray, Gilbert. 1964. *Aristophanes: A Study.* 2d ed. New York.

Nestle, Walter. 1936. "Die Horen des Prodikos." *Hermes* 71.151–70.

Newiger, Hans-Joachim. 1957. *Metapher und Allegorie: Studien zu Aristophanes.* Zetemata 16. Munich.

———. 1983. "Gedanken zu Aristophanes' *Vögeln*." In Ἀρετῆς μνήμη· Ἀφιέρωμα εἰς μνήμην τοῦ Κωνσταντίνου I. Βουρβέρη, edited by C. K. Soile, 47–57. Athens.

Norwood, Gilbert. 1931. *Greek Comedy.* London.

Ostwald, Martin. 1986. *From Popular Sovereignty to the Sovereignty of Law.* Berkeley.

Paduano, G. 1973. "La città degli Uccelli e le ambivalenze del nuovo sistema etico-politico." *SCO* 22.115–44.

Pickard-Cambridge, A. W. 1962. *Dithyramb, Tragedy and Comedy.* 2d ed. Oxford.

Pollard, J. R. T. 1948. "The *Birds* of Aristophanes—A Source Book for Old Beliefs." *AJP* 69.353–76.

Rau, Peter. 1967. *Paratragodia: Untersuchungen zu einer komischen Form des Aristophanes.* Zetemata 45. Munich.

Reckford, Kenneth J. 1987. *Aristophanes' Old-and-New Comedy.* Vol. 1: *Six Essays in Perspective.* Chapel Hill.

Reinhardt, Karl. 1960. *Vermächtnis der Antike.* Göttingen.

Rosenmeyer, Thomas G. 1972. "Notes on Aristophanes' *Birds*." *AJP* 93.223–38.

Rothwell, Kenneth S., Jr. 1990. *Politics and Persuasion in Aristophanes' Ecclesiazusae.* Leiden.

Saïd, Suzanne. 1979. "L' assemblée des femmes: Les femmes, l' économie et la politique." In *Aristophane: Les femmes et la cité*, edited by J. Bonnamour and H. Delavault, 33–69. Fontenay aux Roses.

Salin, Edgar. 1921. *Platon und die griechische Utopie*. Munich.

Schuller, W., W. Hoepfner, and E. L. Schwandner. 1989. *Demokratie und Architektur: Der hippodamische Städtebau und die Entstehung der Demokratie*. Munich.

Schwinge, Ernst-Richard. 1977. "Aristophanes und die Utopie." *WJA*, n.s., 3.43–67.

Segal, Charles P. 1962. "Gorgias and the Psychology of the Logos." *HSCP* 66.99–155.

Solomos, Alexis. 1974. *The Living Aristophanes*. Translated by M. Felheim. Ann Arbor.

Sommerstein, Alan H. 1984. "Aristophanes and the Demon Poverty." *CQ* 34.314–33.

———. 1987. *The Comedies of Aristophanes*. Vol. 6: *Birds*. Warminster.

Stark, R. 1953. "Sokratisches in den 'Vögeln' des Aristophanes." *RhM* 96.77–89.

Stone, I. F. 1988. *The Trial of Socrates*. Boston.

Strauss, Leo. 1966. *Socrates and Aristophanes*. Chicago.

Süvern, J. W. 1835. *Essay on "The Birds" of Aristophanes*. Translated by W. R. Hamilton. London.

Torrance, R. M. 1978. *The Comic Hero*. Cambridge, Mass.

Turato, F. 1971–72. "Le leggi non scritte negli 'Uccelli' di Aristofane." *Atti e Memorie dell' Accademia Patavina di Scienze, Lettere, ed Arti* 84.3.113–43.

Untersteiner, M. 1954. *The Sophists*. Translated by K. Freeman. New York.

Ussher, R. G. 1973. *Aristophanes: Ecclesiazusae*. Oxford.

van Looy, H. 1975. "Les 'Oiseaux' d' Aristophane: Essai d' interprétation." In *Le monde grec: Hommages à Claire Préaux*, edited by J. Bingen, G. Cambier, and G. Nachtergael, 177–85. Brussels.

Vidal-Naquet, Pierre. 1986. *The Black Hunter: Forms of Thought and Forms of Society in the Greek World*. Translated by Andrew Szegedy-Maszak. Baltimore.

Villgradter, R., and F. Krey, eds. 1973. *Der utopische Roman*. Darmstadt.

Vlastos, Gregory. 1947. "Equality and Justice in Early Greek Cosmogonies." *CP* 42.156–78.

———. 1953. "Isonomia." *AJP* 64.337–66.

von Pöhlmann, Robert. 1925. *Geschichte der sozialen Frage und des Sozialismus in der antiken Welt*. 3d ed. Munich.

West, Martin L. 1983. *The Orphic Poems*. Oxford.

Whitman, Cedric H. 1964. *Aristophanes and the Comic Hero*. Cambridge, Mass.

Wilamowitz-Moellendorff, Ulrich von. 1927. *Aristophanes: Lysistrate*. Berlin.

Woodbury, Leonard. 1965. "The Date and Atheism of Diagoras of Melos." *Phoenix* 19.178–211.

Zannini Quirini, Bruno. 1987. *Nephelokokkygia: La prospettiva mitica degli Uccelli di Aristofane*. Rome.

Zimmermann, Bernhard. 1983. "Utopisches und Utopie in den Komödien des Aristophanes." *WJA*, n.s., 9.57–77. Reprinted as "Nephelokokkygia." In *Carnevale e utopia nella grecia antica*, edited by W. Rösler and B. Zimmermann, 55–98. Bari, 1991.

———. 1993. "Aristophanes und die Intellektuellen." In *Entretiens sur l' antiquité classique 38: Aristophane*, edited by J. M. Bremer and E. W. Handley, 255–86. Geneva.

F. E. ROMER

Good Intentions and the
ὁδὸς ἡ ἐς κόρακας

I **A**ristophanes constructed Nephelokokkugia in the developing context of pre-utopian myths and proto-utopian literature as they existed in the intellectual life at the end of the fifth century.[1] He pondered the problem of human perfectibility and explored an ideal "no place"—where human nature (albeit in a very Athenian guise) might run its natural course. First, Aristophanes inverted the evolutionary trend of fifth-century anthropology (cf. Anaxagoras and Demokritos),[2] which held that human beings, by virtue of their intellect, had evolved from a primitive state of animality (a θηριώδης βίος as Demokritos apparently put it: 68B5 D.-K.).[3] Second, he had reaffirmed the idea that human life is somehow cyclical, that, however much things change, they return to something very like their original condition, that the new is old. Returning to origins in order to start again provides a key theme in *Birds* and raises suspicions about the play's outcome. I hope in this essay both to provoke and to engender discussion about the implications of this cyclicality for interpreting the play as a whole. Illusion and reality are never what they seem in *Birds*: "a *human being* always is, in fact, by nature a tricky critter in every way" (δολερὸν μὲν ἀεὶ κατὰ πάντα δὴ τρόπον πέφυκεν ἄνθρωπος, 451–52), and humans are also enemies by nature to birds (τὴν φύσιν μὲν ἐχθροί 371; cf. also 334–35).

In this comedy, two disaffected Athenians searching for a happier home and a better world ultimately found a new city among the birds. Peisetairos and Euelpides bring with them the generic paraphernalia with which to conduct a sacrifice (43),[4] but their language does not suggest, strictly speaking, that their initial purpose is to found a new colony. Later, however, Peisetairos does oversee on stage the beginning of a foundation sacrifice for what would become his new colony (848–903, 1033–35) before being driven indoors to complete it, and Nephelokokkugia is referred to in colonial terms (cf. 963–65, 1515). The burden is a double one, for Peisetairos and Euelpides are in the process of either discovering or inventing (cf. ἐξεύροις, 10) a fatherland for themselves, and they also are having trouble in a second dramatic effort— discovering or inventing (ἐξευρεῖν) the ὁδὸς ἡ ἐς κόρακας (28). In ordinary Greek, ἐς κόρακας approximates the English phrase "to hell with you" or "go to hell." Thus, if taken literally, "the road to the crows" (i.e., to the carrion crows) could be heard, approximately, as "the path to hell," and with the help of a resonance from line 1 the phrase echoes even more emphatically from where they are as "the path straight (ὀρθὴν) to hell."[5] At one level, then, for two Athenians to head ἐς κόρακας portends ruin, destruction, death. This phrase establishes a tension between the dramatic action and the audience's expectation. In the process, however, these two adventurers also defy the logic of their own complaints. The pair eventually create a city reminiscent of Athens and no less dependent on law and the political power of vested interests than Athens, but their original language is of discovery and invention, not founding. They seek not anarchy but a world where they are the bosses and where they have the edge.

The relation of any colony to its μητρόπολις ("mother-city") is sometimes paradoxical even in the best cases,[6] and this comic Nephelokokkugia is no exception. The new "foundation" both is and is not an extension of Athens.[7] Peisetairos and Euelpides are tricky Athenians, for whom justice is clearly the working of the laws in favor of those who already hold power, a paradoxically tyrannical but ordinary arrangement. The new world is a mirror image of Athens which inverts, as it were, the haves and the have-nots to Euelpides' and especially to Peisetairos' advantage. To discover or invent this new fatherland, like discovering or inventing the ὁδὸς ἡ ἐς κόρακας, appears at first sight a lot like going to hell in a handbasket. The two adventurers are mauled first and then abandoned by their guide birds, and subsequently they endure a massive air attack from birds who act under the impression that all humans are their natural enemies. It is important at the start of the play to appreciate the basic ambivalence and symmetry of these two processes of discovery or invention, because at the play's end we *expect* to confront the equally basic moral ambivalence that underlies the impending wedding feast for Peisetairos and his bride.[8]

Comedy based on social and political issues depends on moral ambiguities in the stage action and on deep-seated feelings of moral ambivalence in the audience. The political and moral landscape of *Birds* is Athenian, but the play also digs beneath its Athenian veneer to a more primordial level of Greek thinking. The play in general, and the celebratory wedding of the last scene in particular, no doubt did address the demos's contemporary "fantasies of imperial conquest and political unity," as Jeffery Henderson argues in this volume. If, however, *Birds* merely reinforced the community's sense of solidarity only by catering to its fantasies, the meaning of this play would be transparent (as it is not), and critics would have little to discuss. It is clear that comedies could be taken quite literally at Athens—thus Kleon reportedly sued Aristophanes over what the poet said in his *Babylonians*, and Plato's Socrates blamed Aristophanes for whipping up the demos against him in *Clouds*. But however much *Clouds*, for example, may have contributed to the demos's solidarity against Socrates, and to Socrates' condemnation, we do not come away feeling that the poet's purpose was to attack Socrates in a literal vein. The happy ending of comic plays is dictated by the rules of the genre. When Strepsiades burns down the phrontisterion at the end of *Clouds*, it is a satisfying and fantastic (*sic*) conclusion to the play, but it is terrifying as a comment on popular opinion. A successful comedy like *Birds* carries its audience along with the stage action and the laughter it provokes. The wedding feast and Peisetairos' victory over the Olympians are great fun. The audience laughs at what it sees. It is only on reflection, and largely outside the theater, that the moral ambiguities and particularities of a play like *Birds* come home to roost.

In what follows, I argue that the moral ambivalence, from start to finish, of Peisetairos' project underlies what David Konstan earlier called *Birds*' "novel narrative structure," and that, by intersecting all four of his "nomies," this ambivalence both unifies the play and evokes the judgment of its audience in the construction of the play's meaning(s). Konstan has identified key structural elements both in *Birds* and in Nephelokokkugia, thereby describing the mechanism that makes the play work and produce its meaning(s), but in the long run his argument only explains the mechanism of the play without explaining the play itself. *Birds* has a darker side, and its underlying Hesiodic question is not how the possible world of Nephelokokkugia differs structurally from the real one, but whether it does differ and whether it is a *possible* world at all. In this way, instead of being an amorphous bundle of inconsistencies like Konstan's *Birds*, the play's dramatic power actually derives from its audience's engaged response to the tension created between the fantasies it exposes and the underlying psychology and cultural beliefs of its audience. In general, my assumption is that throughout the play, mythic thinking provides a yardstick by which to measure specific details in the dramatic action.[9] *Birds* is a politically engaged play, and the question of what it means to be Athenian is explored more broadly in the Hesiodic terms of what it means to be human. The next section of this essay explores central aspects of Hesiod's *Theogony* as the victory song of Zeus and as a particular version of the cosmic Succession Myth, which Peisetairos' usurpation both extends and parodies. Next the argument turns to an examination of Prometheus' Hesiodic role as civilizer, trickster, and inventor of sacrifice in the context of his presence in *Birds* (section III), while section IV explores the consequences of Promethean sacrifice in view of Peisetairos' intended cannibalism and his roasting of the dissident bird gods. Section V places the deceitful and tricky Peisetairos, *turannos* of the universe, in the Aeschylean and Hesiodic context of his role as new Successor and new Zeus. My argument concludes (section VI) by treating the ambivalent circling back of the final scene and by locating the questions raised in *Birds* (explicitly or implicitly) in the train of Aristophanes' work.

The drama of *Birds* depends heavily on systematic patterns of intertextual allusions. As Sophocles' *Tereus* offered one access to this comic play (in Gregory Dobrov's argument below), so Hesiod's *Theogony* and the cultural values it embodies provide another; both works make explicit foils for the action of the comedy. Rarely is the very act of interpretation so problematized as it is in *Birds*. One of the main unnerving aspects of *Birds* is the way it dramatizes, but does not resolve, both the violence and the trickery in how the universe came to be the way the Athenians and other Greeks experienced it. The interpretation argued here emerges—and can emerge in detail—only outside the immediacy of the theater; it is a product of sustained reflection that, nevertheless, both identifies and addresses important elements in the original audience's response to the play.

II

To return to the opening scene, then, once our two Athenians have proved themselves to the hostile birds and are accepted for what they want to be, they need to provide an ideology for what they now begin to conceive as their new foundation. Their original language about "discovering" or "inventing" a fatherland had suggested at once a process other than starting from scratch. On the other hand, a colony could even rewrite its own history by discovering or inventing a new founder and by reenacting its own foundation, as the Amphipolitans had done in 422 when they ceased to honor Hagnon the Athenian, destroyed his buildings, and replaced them with new monuments to their new founder, Brasidas the Spartan (Thuc. 5.11.1).[10] Rather than start from scratch, our two heroes give the impression of planning a takeover. In Nephelokokkugia they will redo what has already been done. Like the Amphipolitans locally, Peisetairos himself, in the larger picture, cosmically redoes (by reinterpretation) the existing scheme without undertaking any fundamentally new beginning.

Thus, *Birds* ought to be a congenial play for modern critics. Not only does the fantasy deconstruct itself before our eyes,[11] but history is reduced to a set of competing ideologies whose claims cannot be distinguished on the basis of "wie es eigentlich gewesen ist." In his own account Peisetairos reaches back to the beginnings of things, to a time before Kronos and the Titans and Earth (469–70), and he supplants (471–79) Hesiod's account of these beginnings with an otherwise unattested story from Aesop, a fable that proves the temporal priority of the birds over other gods. According to this fable, the primal lark, who existed before Earth, had nowhere to bury her father and so, for want of a better place, she had buried him in her own head. For Peisetairos this simple statement proves that the birds antedate the other gods of more traditional accounts.

This fable not only supersedes Hesiod's narrative of these beginnings but also parodies by inversion key elements in the familiar Hesiodic description of Athena's birth from Zeus' head (*Theog.* 924–26).[12] But although Hesiod's authority is supplanted on this central point of cosmogony, namely the temporal priority of birds over more familiar gods, Hesiod's values and other emphases are not. Nothing is explicitly made, for example, of the fact that the primal lark was a female, only that she was a bird and that her birdness antedated the earliest divinities of the Hesiodic account. In this regard, Peisetairos seems to handle the lark in a way similar to Hesiod's treatment of Gaia, of whom Hesiod had said that she was πάντων ἕδος ἀσφαλὲς αἰεὶ ("ever an unfailing foundation for all," *Theog.* 117). Implicitly, however, the comic fable of the lark assumes the temporal priority of the male over the female (it is, after all, her father she buries),[13] but it also does so in a particular way that *Theogony* does not assume for Gaia. Even so, this fable still reifies and makes natural (in an unnatural way) the same gender hierarchy for which the narrative line of *Theogony* ultimately argues (in equally unnatural ways). Peisetairos both undoes and outdoes Hesiod. Hesiod's *Theogony* therefore remains both a focal text and a challenge for understanding *Birds*,[14] and it does so not least because Hesiod's account of the foundation myth of sacrifice, the story of Prometheus, also provides and explains the machination by which the new bird gods will starve out and overpower the Olympians. This one enterprise alone drives the entire action of *Birds*,[15] the fact that their new physics-defying foundation, Nephelokokkugia, prevents the Olympians from receiving their due share, the savory κνῖσα (i.e., the mixed steam and aroma of roasting meat), which Prometheus had reserved for the gods at the sacrifices made by human beings.

To reinforce his story of the primal lark and this new interpretation of the beginnings of things, Peisetairos offers other proofs that birds once ruled the universe. He uses imagined, present-day survivals of past practices (481–538) to historicize that past and to draw inferences about it: the kingship of the cock in Persia, of the kite over the Greeks, and of the cuckoo in Egypt as well as the eagle's royal power and the history of oaths by birds. It is impossible, of course, to argue the historicity of any description of the beginnings of the universe, but it is nevertheless important for Peisetairos that his description be, as it were, historically credible and compelling to the birds. He therefore uses, in effect, the same method Thucydides relied on when he tried to reconstitute credibly the social conditions in prehistoric Greece (cf. Thuc. 1.5–6). This method assumes a linear connection between past and present in historical time, and in using this method, Peisetairos, of course, goes too far again. He stresses an underlying continuity between the primal mythic past[16] and the historical present, an underlying continuity which the Olympian domination has both obscured and disrupted, but a continuity which in the play's terms is real. He goes still further and assumes that this line of development is patently reversible through action based on exegesis. By restoring the primal order—that is, by overthrowing the Olympian gods and reestablishing the birds as chief deities—Peisetairos becomes a usurper, a type of the anti-Zeus who, in effect, perpetuates the element of crisis in the succession myth of Hesiod's *Theogony*. (And to underscore this point later, when Basileia is transferred from gods to birds, she may even be dressed like Argive Hera in the new *hieros gamos* at the end of this play.)[17]

In Hesiod's *Theogony*, however, the three generations of gods are perversely headed in succession by Ouranos, himself a πατὴρ ἀτασθάλος ("wicked father," *Theog.* 164) who stuffed his children into a recess of the Earth and delighted afterward in his evil deed (*Theog.* 156–59); and next by Kronos who was the most dreadful of Earth's children, hated his father (*Theog.* 137–38), and also devoured his own children (*Theog.* 459–62); and finally by Zeus who acted Kronos-like to prevent his own overthrow by an unknown future son (*Theog.* 886–900). The behaviors of these three gods bespeak a pattern of male violence typified not only by violence against fathers but by violence from fathers against females and children as well. Ouranos, Kronos, and Zeus, like Peisetairos, dominate nature in ways that are themselves most unnatural. Likewise, in *Birds*, the difficult personal history of the human Tereus and Prokne speaks for itself and might have raised, though it did not actually do so, serious questions about how and why Tereus could ever have acquired influence among the birds in the first place: his own tyrannical past underlies his present life among the birds. Suffice it to say, then, that the authority Euelpides and

Peisetairos encountered among the birds when they arrived already reflected gender values implicit in the structure of authority presented in *Theogony*, and nothing either character does in the course of the play actually will subvert that structure.

Likewise, in the process of inverting both the laws of Athens and the laws of physics, Peisetairos also turns the Hesiodic cosmogony upside down in order to restore, so he argues (465–75), their own natural primacy to the birds themselves. Nephelokokkugia—with Peisetairos still in his role of anti-Zeus—eventually becomes a pre-Olympian Khaos (1217–18;[18] cf. also 693). Peisetairos remythologizes the universe, but it is not a fundamentally new beginning, not at all a genuinely new mythologization of the cosmos and its gods. His scheme accepted the abstract principles and metaphysical shape of the Hesiodic cosmos. He merely instituted new holders of divine power for old, but did not cast the mythology of the universe into new and original forms with new and original outcomes.[19] Underneath it all only the masters are changed, and the principles informing the status quo are unchallenged, even though they may be acted on somewhat differently. The claims of the birds to divine power rest merely on their birthright and were ultimately based on the same kinds of claims that were made for Kronos and Zeus in Hesiod's *Theogony*. In other words, the underlying continuity to which Peisetairos appealed in the first place makes the new order mirror the old and precludes the possibility of a radically new mythologization of the universe. The *doubleness* of his course makes its own duplicity and heightens the dramatic tension generated at the outset by the double course of discovering or inventing the ὁδὸς ἡ ἐς κόρακας.

III

These modifications to traditional mythology challenge the priorities of worldly civilization and therefore highlight the figure of Prometheus the great civilizer when he appears on stage. Prometheus' presence in the play raises questions about the structure of the universe, the nature of human civilization, and especially the enterprise of Nephelokokkugia, which, in fact, absorbs the other two sets of questions. These questions occur together because Prometheus invented the form of sacrifice that is being undone here. The commensalism of traditional Greek sacrifice embraces the most basic form of the human community, and the ritual of the sacrificial meal is itself the central feature of traditional religion in the established polis. In *Birds* Prometheus has ceased to act merely "with partiality" (ἑτερωζήλως) as he had in *Theogony* (544). He is no longer the seriocomic trickster Hesiod knew (*Theog.* 510–616; *Erga* 42–89), since he is nervous, frightened, and out both to save his own skin and to overthrow Zeus at all costs. Nor is he the Aeschylean Prometheus with his clear pride in human achievement (PB 442–506). Prometheus' *philanthrôpia* is reduced to simple spite. In *Birds* Prometheus remains the benefactor of humankind, and he still has the secret of Zeus' power, but his eyes are on baser things: his own safety and revenge against Zeus.[20] The paratragic Prometheus is present in *Birds* because he holds the secret of divine power (1534–36), just as he did in *Theogony* and *Prometheus Bound*, but the secret itself has changed. It is no longer the knowledge of a future son who will be greater than his father, but the literal possession of a divine princess who embodies the power Zeus now wields (see note 40). Peisetairos needs to know this secret in order to enforce the new sovereignty of the birds, and because Prometheus is both a "friend to *humans*" (ἀνθρώποις εὔνους, 1545) and a hater of gods (1547–48). Aristophanes' frightened Prometheus, however, turns hopefully to the bird world of the bird men in order to escape, not to meet, the threats of a tyrannical Zeus—a mighty Prometheus who hopes to escape Zeus' violence by passing as a young girl serving in the Panathenaic procession (1550–51)! This new world of birds, rich in the language of political *erôs*,[21] remains a duplicitously human one in several senses, and it is also a heavily gendered world of men, of males, of fatherland and fathers and crimes against fathers—compare especially 1337–71 for the scene of the *patraloias* ("father beater," "patricide") and Poseidon's worry (1605, echoed again at 1643) about Heracles depriving his father of his *turannis*[22] (highlighted here because Heracles' human origin—like Peisetairos'—precedes his metamorphosis to god).

Moreover, females are also routinely disempowered in *Birds*. Prokne is forced to speak only in the birdsong represented by the music of the aulos (223–24, perhaps with the *parepigraphê* after 222; 676–84), not in the language, the *phônê*, Tereus had boasted of teaching (Prometheus-like) the birds to speak (199–200), and she is confronted sexually by Euelpides when she appears on stage later (671–74). Precious little is learned about Basileia despite Peisetairos' direct inquiry of Prometheus—"Who is Basileia?" (1537)—for she remains silent in her cameo appearance at the end of the play (1728–65). And the divine Iris, the only female to speak in words, is pummeled from the sky in a dispute over cosmic territoriality (1205–7), accused by Peisetairos of "dissembling" (εἰρωνεύεται, 1211) when she speaks straight, and threatened by him with rape when she persists in her views (1253–56).[23] No human women appear in the play if we accept Prokne's metamorphosis as complete, or even virtually complete, and consider that she has left her human history behind, although her physical appearance on stage somehow did recall her human form (cf. 670).[24] We have, in effect, returned to the conditions of Mekone and the time when men and gods still banqueted together,[25] a time after Prometheus had stolen fire but before Zeus had punished him, and therefore a time before women had entered the human world.[26]

We recall also that the hoopoe was "manly" (ἀνδρεῖος) for his bravery (91), and the *patraloias* is likewise "manly" for the very actions that define his character (1349). In *Birds*, the audience also routinely understands that all the birds on stage are played by men and that, in mythology, certain prominent birds, here played by men, originally had their own human history to boot. But perhaps most important for my present argument, Prometheus himself enters as a friend to humans (*anthrôpoi*, 1545), *not* to birds as the fiction requires.[27] He is also a hater of "gods," but apparently not a hater of birds, not even of birds as gods. The ultimate self-deception of Peisetairos and Euelpides as bird/men is that, on Prometheus' advice, they wrest the girl Basileia from the gods so that the power she watches over (cf. ταμιεύει at 1538 and 1542)[28] may reside with them. These Athenians have not changed. They want—and ultimately get— power for themselves through a series of inventive deceptions, and that is the danger of their way of life. In Tereus the birds had already been taught to speak by a man-turned-bird, and Peisetairos and Euelpides, who lead the foundation of the new city, are likewise men-turned-bird (virtually before our eyes). Their slick comic πονηρία ("wiliness") threatens their destruction, and Aristophanic mythopoesis again reflects human psychology: their novelty betrays continuity.

In the end, Nephelokokkugia itself emerges as a tyranny, an unsurprising fact that should not be denied.[29] The second herald literally announces Peisetairos as a tyrant (1708),[30] and from an Aristotelian point of view (*Pol.* 1304b7–9), other political orders (πολιτεῖαι) become tyrannies either by force (διὰ βίας) or by deceit (διὰ ἀπάτης). Both force and deceit are at work here. Peisetairos' compelling deceitfulness overrode his promise in the agon to restore to the birds their own sovereignty, which he is seen now to have usurped for himself. And we had already been set up for Peisetairos in his role as tyrant of the birds, for Peisetairos had previously appeared on stage roasting some of his own subjects who had been caught red-handed rebelling against the new avian regime. Peisetairos' deceit and brutality underline the dangers, inconsistencies, and continuities of his new order and recall the universal trickiness of the human species as asserted by the chorus of birds (451–52). Peisetairos' dual role as Promethean trickster and usurper of Zeus' tyranny emerges both from the reinvention of sacrifice in this play and from Hesiod's account of the first sacrifice ever.

IV

It is a critical moment, and probably the most complicated and compelling visual image in the play, when Heracles wants to know what Peisetairos has on his grill.[31] Peisetairos answers in a way that is shocking in context: he is roasting "some birds that have rebelled against the *dêmotikoi* birds" (ἐπανιστάμενοι τοῖς δημοτικοῖσιν ὀρνέοις, 1584). Although the last part of the quotation has been taken to mean "against the bird democracy,"[32] there is no evidence that the birds ever had a democracy. In fact, we do not know what form of government the birds had when Peisetairos and Euelpides arrived, nor even what Tereus' exact authority was. But at the height of his own success Peisetairos is called *turannos*. Thus the enigmatic politics with which Peisetairos describes his barbecue at line 1584 articulates the visual puzzle that the stage action now presents to the audience.

We know from the beginning of the play (at least from 186) that Peisetairos plans to interfere, and later that he does interfere, in the traditional mode of sacrifice that has nourished and supported the gods from time immemorial. Peisetairos' grill further blurs the distinctions in the sacrificial hierarchy established by Prometheus because Peisetairos is a man who is, or claims to be, a bird who in turn is, or claims to be, a god. In Promethean terms Peisetairos is fixing more than a simple barbecue. The meal he is preparing doubles as an act of sacrifice: it is a cooked meal of animal flesh prepared for a god or gods; it is being prepared for a god or gods by a man (as Prometheus implicitly still calls Peisetairos); and it is a meal of cooked meat prepared by a man for a god or gods, but a meal intended to be eaten by the man. This third point does not emerge clearly at first because it appears that the other birds may be expected to share in this grill at Peisetairos' wedding feast (1688–92), but after Prometheus' division of the animate orders as described by Hesiod, eating roasted meat remains a hallmark of human civilization and ties Peisetairos to his human origin.[33] Peisetairos continues to recognize this distinguishing feature when he thanks Prometheus for the power to roast food (1546).[34]

The wedding feast, then, is another mark of how Peisetairos blurs Prometheus' original distinctions and also shows how the new order reconfigures the old. Nevertheless, in Peisetairos' own terms his barbecue is also an undeniable act of intended cannibalism since he considers himself to be a bird god and he is now preparing to eat his own rebellious subjects, whom he will serve also to the bird gods who are his wedding guests. At this point Peisetairos' personal history (bird → cannibal → tyrant) also effectively reverses the direction of Tereus' life (tyrant → cannibal → bird).

Although I have based my arguments on the Hesiodic tradition so far (see note 15), I appeal here, for the moment only, to Orphic doctrine as well. My purpose, however, will not be to pursue the Orphic view for its own sake, but because it offers a counterpoint that helps to contextualize Aristophanes' handling of the Hesiodic material. The Orphics, in particular, developed their

cosmogonies, theogonies, and anthropogonies "in opposition to the official-
ized parlance of Hesiod and Homer, and in total rupture with the value system
found in the Hesiodic account of Prometheus and the first food and blood
sacrifice."[35] According to the Orphic analysis, Promethean sacrifice is, in its
essence, an act of murder (*phonos*). In this view the Promethean community of
human beings is based on a paradigm of murder, the killing of the living by the
living, which is both a crime and an act that effectively makes cannibalism
universal in the polis. The Orphic view deliberately rejects the Promethean
terms that divide living beings into three groups: the rightful beneficiaries of
sacrifice (gods), the rightful sacrificers (humans), and the rightfully sacrificed
(animals). As one consequence of Promethean sacrifice, human civilization is
distinguished by the fact that humans are the only beings that eat cooked meat,
an act that Orphics regard as cannibalistic. The Orphic interpretation of sacrifice offers an instructive counterpoint to Hesiod's account, but it is the traditional Hesiodic account of sacrifice that *Birds* calls into question. Peisetairos
outstripped even the radical Orphic view when, in his self-proclaimed role as
bird god, he not only rejected these Promethean distinctions, but then also
prepared both to eat his divine peers and to feed them to other bird gods.
Nevertheless, Peisetairos' trickiness in reinventing sacrifice to his own advantage echoes the anthropocentric benefits of the Hesiodic first sacrifice.

At that paradigmatic first sacrifice, according to Hesiod, Prometheus had
laid out two disguised portions, and he had asked Zeus to choose between
these servings on condition that his choice was binding ever afterward. One
portion was the meat and innards wrapped in hide, the other consisted of
bones wrapped in the rich fat that cooks so fragrantly. Prometheus' idea, of
course, was to fool Zeus into picking the more visually appealing and aromatic
but less nourishing portion. Hesiod comments succinctly:

φῆ ῥα δολοφρονέων· Ζεὺς δ' ἄφθιτα μήδεα εἰδὼς
γνῶ ῥ' οὐδ' ἠγνοίησε δόλον· κακὰ δ' ὄσσετο θυμῷ
θνητοῖς ἀνθρώποισι, τὰ καὶ τελέεσθαι ἔμελλε.
χερσὶ δ' ὅ γ' ἀμφοτέρῃσιν ἀνείλετο λευκὸν ἄλειφαρ,
χώσατο δὲ φρένας ἀμφί, χόλος δέ μιν ἵκετο θυμόν,
ὡς ἴδεν ὀστέα λευκὰ βοὸς δολίῃ ἐπὶ τέχνῃ.
(*Theog.* 550–55)

He spoke then, planning a trick; but Zeus, knowing indestructible
    counsels,
recognized and did not mistake the trick; evils did he bode in his heart
for mortal humans, [evils] which were even to be fulfilled.
With both hands he took up the white fat,

and he grew angered in his breast, all around, and anger reached him in his
   heart,
when he saw the ox's white bones in the trick's crafty guise.

Sacrifice is a trick, but a trick with moral consequences. To change the hierarchy for sacrifice, just as to create one in the first place, alters both the power
structure and the moral structure of the universe.[36] Zeus saw the trick, *Theogony* says, and did what was wanted anyway. But there was a price: ". . . evils
did [Zeus] bode in his heart for mortal humans, [evils] which were even to be
fulfilled." Paradoxically, Zeus was not fooled, and yet Prometheus' distinctions
work only because of his trick. In other words, Zeus tricked him back and
fooled humans into the bargain. Even to divide the living beings of the universe
neatly into Prometheus' three mutually exclusive categories depends on humans being fooled or fooling themselves. The Promethean world that humans
inhabit descends from a trick or a series of tricks including Prometheus' two
portions, Zeus' complicity, and ultimately human cooperation in perpetuating
the ruse. One of the fundamental stumbling blocks of all Greek rationalizing
theology is that trickery is built into the gods' behavior, and hence into the
structure of the universe, and for that reason trickery is inherent in the relations between *anthrôpoi* and gods. But gods are also made in the image of
humans, as Xenophanes knew (see note 20), and the birds recognized that
trickery is part and parcel of the human condition (451–52).

Peisetairos' behavior, however, exposes these deceitful consequences of Prometheus' original deceit. Peisetairos undoes Prometheus' sacrificial hierarchy,
and in so doing his resegmentation of the roles among gods, men, and animals
again goes back, in effect, to the time of Mekone, that is, to the mythical
moment before women existed.[37] In a comic way Peisetairos has redrawn the
essential lines of civilization's own foundational act. His barbecue reenacts this
paradigmatic dilemma of civilization and offers a radical critique of the polis
both as a community and as a human endeavor—all compounded by the fact
that, as Prometheus indicated, Peisetairos never transcended his human nature.

V

We may go further. Peisetairos was preparing these executed birds by his own
favorite recipe (1579–80, 1637, with 533–38). The recipe, in fact, unmasks
Peisetairos since it demonstrates his essential humanity and links it in an ironic
fusion to his invented role as a bird god. We first learned of this recipe when
he was salivating over the prospect of changing the cosmic power relations
among birds, humans, and Olympians (529–38). In Aristotelian terms (cf. *Pol.*

1279a16–31, 1311a1–5), there could be no clearer, cruder, more tyrannical instance of his subjects existing—or rather, ceasing to exist—for the benefit and pleasure of the ruler alone. Moreover, in this same scene, Peisetairos is negotiating with Poseidon, Heracles, and the unnamed Triballian god to end the war between the birds and the Olympians. For the sake of his stomach (of course!) Heracles is ready to turn over the scepter of Zeus (1603–4),[38] but Poseidon initially balks at depriving Zeus of what Poseidon calls his *turannis* (1605, 1643).

Subsequently, as *turannos* of the birds, Peisetairos comes to possess both the scepter of Zeus and its guardian, the divine princess Basileia, who is, effectively, the incarnation of Zeus' power,[39] and who is promoted from princess among the old gods to queen of the new by her marriage to Peisetairos. Just as Peisetairos serves a dual function as the new Zeus and the new Prometheus, so Basileia has a double role. She is both the new Hera by virtue of her marriage to the new chief divinity and also the new Pandora because she literally bestows on her husband all the bounty of the universe (cf. 971–75), but also functionally because "the transfer of a woman from gods to men marks the change in the nature of the world in both [Hesiod's and Aristophanes'] stories" (Bowie 1993, 163). Commentators generally agree that as used by the oracle monger (971–75), the name Pandora reflects an epithet of Earth as giver of all bounty,[40] but they generally ignore the fact that typically at Athens the attributes of Earth are interchangeable with those of the Hesiodic Pandora, so that in effect the Athenians do not distinguish between the two Pandoras.[41] There is, therefore, absolutely no reason *not* to hear the resonance of Hesiod's Pandora in the oracle monger's self-interested invocation to Pandora, and every reason to do so because of how Hesiod is used in this play, and especially because the Prometheus myth, to which Hesiod's Pandora is attached, plays such a central role in *Birds*' plot. In the play, moreover, Basileia has her own special symmetry with Earth since Earth had been the previous keeper of the bolts and thunder before they were given to Zeus (*Theog.* 503–6).

Peisetairos is, as we have seen, the attacker and usurper of the established Olympian order, a new Prometheus and an anti-Zeus rolled into one. As *turannos* of the birds, however, Peisetairos is prepared also to cannibalize his own subjects, if not literally his own children, and this act of intended cannibalism is symmetrical with, though not perfectly parallel to, similar outrages of Kronos and Zeus as described by Hesiod in *Theogony*.[42] But *Theogony* is also a text that celebrates Zeus' absolute power, his victory, and his consequent legitimacy (cf. *Theog.* 402–3, 506, 613–16, 881–85), just as *Birds* celebrates a similar progress for Peisetairos. It is Aeschylus, however, in *Prometheus Bound* who applies the language of tyranny systematically to Zeus' rule.[43] Just as

Nephelokokkugia both is and is not Athens, so Peisetairos both is and is not a figure of Zeus. On the one hand, he is the anti-Zeus, the attacker and usurper, the figurative son of Zeus "father of gods and men," the son whose secret is the future destruction which the Hesiodic Zeus would have forestalled (*Theog.* 886–900),[44] and the secret of which the Aeschylean Prometheus originally refused to give up to Zeus (cf. *PB* 757–74). On the other hand, as the inheritor of Zeus' *turannis*, Peisetairos also becomes, in effect, the incarnation of Zeus, and, in particular, the paratragic incarnation of the tyrannical Zeus Aeschylus described in *Prometheus Bound*. As Hesiod's victory of Zeus became Zeus' tyranny in Aeschylus' play, so now Peisetairos' victory is shown up explicitly for the tyranny it is, and the foundation of Nephelokokkugia again reflects the order of Hesiod's cosmos. The new beginning brings the action back to the old beginning; the tyrant of the new order reincarnates the tyrant of the old.

Again we have a Peisetairos who undoes the Hesiodic compound only to remake it in symmetrical terms and according to the same principles which the Hesiodic solution embodied in the first place. Thus, while Peisetairos' barbecue enacts on stage a variant of the Orphic dilemma, Aristophanes' presentation remains strictly Hesiodic in structure: Peisetairos again avoids a fundamentally new remythologization of the universe. Just as early in the play the metaphorical *limos Mêlios* (186) had characterized both the strategy and the stratagem of Peisetairos' enterprise, so too the barbecue later in the play instantiates and epitomizes the blurring of Prometheus' distinctions, which Peisetairos has effected through that sacrificial *limos Mêlios*.[45] The distinctions between gods, humans, and animals lay at the heart of Prometheus' first sacrifice and therefore at the center of traditional religion. To reject these distinctions is to unbalance the relations between the natural and the supernatural and to deny the efficacy of the sacrifices that lie at the heart of the human community. Paradoxically, it is Peisetairos' most tyrannical gesture—his barbecue—that challenges Olympian orthodoxy most deeply, but then assures the continuity of Olympian violence into the future.

VI

Only as the wedding feast begins at the end of the play does the audience gain confidence that this ὁδὸς ἡ ἐς κόρακας may not be the road straight to hell. Older critics winced at the ending, and the play was long considered Aristophanes' "most impious" (see note 9). What makes the play seem impious, even if it may not be so, is not that Peisetairos attacks the traditional gods, not that he mocks sacrifice, but that—to all appearances—he succeeds on stage. Peisetairos overthrows the Olympians, deifies himself, and reorders the cosmos! The very words ὁδὸς ἡ ἐς κόρακας to describe Peisetairos and Euelpides' journey, the Melian fast they impose on the gods, the involvement of Prometheus, Peisetairos' intended cannibalism, the tricking of Zeus, and many other things, large and small, in the play all portend a disaster that does not come. The audience has been expecting a massive comic confusion of going to hell, but what it gets is a wedding feast.

The play does not culminate in an apotheosis, as one recent commentator thinks,[46] but in a marriage and a coronation, an enthronement of new ruling powers. Since godhood depends only on birdhood in the new scheme, Peisetairos' divinity was established as soon as he had reentered in feathers right after the parabasis (802). The existence of birds as gods, in and of itself, posed no threat to the Olympians who tolerated—to Peisetairos' bemusement (1525–30)—other divine orders like the Triballian gods. We should note, however, that the new order begins, just as it does in *Theogony*, with the transference of a female from Olympians to men, and with the transference of the female comes marriage. But the psychology of Hesiodic marriage is reversed in this *hieros gamos* in the same way that the Hesiodic etymology of Pandora's name is turned back on itself (see note 13). The actual overpowering of the divine father by his (here figurative) son, though thematically necessary to the motif, is handled allusively and occurs off stage. It is neither centralized in the dramatic action nor dramatized on stage at all—an interesting development, considering the other staged violence in this comedy.

The apparently happy ending of this play—the impending marriage and the expectation of a marvelous feast—is ominous. It *risks* being nothing more than another tricky, man-made illusion and another mark of the power relations between men and women as institutionalized in the structure of the cosmos Hesiod described in his *Theogony*. In the play, neither Peisetairos nor Euelpides fully transcends his status as *anthrôpos* despite the various claims each makes. Basileia, who literally embodies the power of Zeus in her own name (see note 40), remains silent on stage and has been manipulated by various males for their own purposes. As the marriage festivities are begun, the bronteion probably does sound its ominous roar offstage (cf. 1751), and its sound initially raises two haunting questions: Has Peisetairos really pulled off this coup, and how, if at all, does Peisetairos differ from Zeus? With the ominous sounding of the *bronteion* the "trap-for-fools" in this "cloudcuckooville" has been sprung:[47] Discovering or inventing the new colony of Nephelokokkugia and discovering or inventing the ὁδὸς ἡ ἐς κόρακας *are* one and the same. We in the audience are the fools: Peisetairos has won! The larger question for the audience, as it goes away laughing, is less how Peisetairos pulled it off than what the success of this very human tyrant and their admiration for that success says about Athens and the Athenians.

While any comic play reinforces the community's notion of itself, the ideal of ὁμόνοια, absolute like-mindedness that developed in Athens in the fifth century,[48] is itself as nonsensical as it is elusive and illusory. The moment of ὁμόνοια exists in theory only, and in democratic political theory ὁμόνοια is reified by the vote. When a vote is completed, it does not matter whether the individual citizen voted for or against the proposition; it is as if the city has come to an absolute and universally shared understanding, not simply a pragmatic compromise. The fact that there were votes cast on both sides means nothing; the vote is binding on all alike. In like fashion, the celebratory wedding and the victory of Peisetairos provide a moment of universal laughter at the end of *Birds*. It is only afterward that those in the audience discover that they do not all agree. The play is presented to one city assembled in the theater, but the play's interpretation is a tale of no less than two cities (and probably more). The Hesiodic background opens one door to the political discourse of the interpretive community, both the contemporary one and its descendants, and it is in the active and engaged discussion of the political issues raised by the play that *Birds'* meaning resides.

Nephelokokkugia provides a world in which males dominate other males for the sake of a female who turns out to be the embodiment of power in one-man rule. At an intellectual level, Aristophanes has undercut the apparently happy ending so that reflective spectators, and perhaps especially attentive readers, do struggle under the dramatic double burden and necessarily puzzle over the imminent future rather than restrict themselves to the superficial diversion of this marriage celebration. *Birds* is generally disturbing and broadly dystopic in implication and particularly disturbing about the possibility of human perfectibility, because, after all, the happy ending apparently *is*, in the play's own terms, a tricky, man-made illusion and a mark of the power relations between men and women. But Aristophanes has also inverted, and *potentially* even subverted, a literary tradition of violence and distortion stemming from Hesiod in order to expose both the acquisitiveness and the power seeking of ordinary men—of ordinary Athenians. In so doing, Aristophanes also raises the oikos to the level of cosmos, just as he did for the polis, but the inherent questions of oikos in relation to either cosmos or polis are neither articulated in detail nor addressed directly in this play. These questions simply hang in the air.

In 411 when Aristophanes once again turned from the ideal back to the "real," this possessive wresting of Basileia from the gods, this trickiness of male usurpation in power relations, specifically en*gender*ed the questions that issue forth in his next surviving play, *Lysistrate*. As the new Pandora in *Birds*, Basileia is the giver of all things, not the taker and abuser of Hesiodic lore, not the shrew who eats her husband out of house and home (esp. *Theog.* 590–612; *Erga* 702–5). Her role as Pandora figure, like the etymology of the name Pandora in the play, forestalls the evil contributions associated with the Hesiodic Pandora, just as Peisetairos undoes the sacrificial hierarchy established by the Hesiodic Prometheus. Aristophanes suggests, then, the possibility that marriage may be "a metaphor for the triumphal establishment of a new order, one in which the natural blessings of life will not have been perverted,"[49] but he leaves that possibility as a deep and abiding question for his audience. It is this question that makes the play's ending so ambiguous. In *Birds*, the bride is as silent and almost as unobtrusive as the Periclean ideal of womanhood (cf. Thuc. 2.46). Her marriage does introduce a new order, to be sure, but at bottom this new order merely promises to replicate and extend the metaphysical values of the old order—and, in a way, even more advantageous to Peisetairos than he ever stated in the opening scene. The new Pandora figure induces hope and expectation in the audience, but the Hesiodic cycle reinforced in the play does not make this new *elpis* any less evil than the *elpis* once trapped in Pandora's jar.

In *Lysistrate* Aristophanes will go further. He will consider and appreciate in more detail women's roles and contributions to oikos and polis, though in that play (unlike, say, *Ekklesiazousai* much later) he will not also argue for new social and political space for women. After the women's uprising in *Lysistrate*, there will be a return to the status quo in the sexual and institutional dynamics of the city,[50] and, as we have seen in *Birds*, those dynamics replicate the metaphysical dimensions of the universe as described by Hesiod. Nevertheless, one basic connection between *Birds* and *Lysistrate* is clear precisely from the fact that both plays end by supporting the status quo. *Birds*, however, also shows the symmetry between the divine structure of the universe and the structured authority of the polis, which *Lysistrate* does not transcend. The questions raised cosmically about male behaviors and male responsibilities in *Birds* are extended and examined politically in *Lysistrate*. If *Birds* is on the boards, can *Lysistrate* be far behind?

Notes

I cite the Greek from Sommerstein 1987, since the attribution of some lines to speakers is at question, and for the moment he prints an agreeable solution (following Marzullo 1970). I would like to thank Gregory Dobrov who organized the APA seminar (San Francisco, 29 December 1990) at which an early version of this essay first saw light, and Anthony Edwards for his perceptive remarks as discussant on that occasion. A shorter version of this essay also was presented as a paper at the annual meeting of the Israel Society for the Promotion of Classical Studies (University of Haifa, 31 May 1995). My thanks go to Timothy Long, Barbara Pavlock, and David Simpson for pointed comments and hard questions that kept me awake many a night. I also thank Michael Teske for criticizing part of this argument.

1. For utopian aspects, see Konstan 1990, now revised in this volume; Auger 1979; Pozzi 1991, 149–61; and Bowie 1993, 166–77.

2. In general on fifth-century anthropology, see Havelock 1958, 104–54 and 409–14, for a provocative introduction; also Cole 1967.

3. Peisetairos' change from man to bird also inverts the direction of those metamorphoses associated with foundation legends (Bowie 1993, 159–60). On *Birds* and foundation legends, see Bowie 1993, 152–66; on foundation legends in general, McGlew 1993, 17–24, 157–83.

4. Hamilton 1985 argues against the scholia that their paraphernalia were intended to be used at a symposium. Certainly the use of this equipment as a defense against the air attack is coincidental. "It may however be better to regard the items as ambiguous. They could be used at a symposium, but are not so obviously or exclusively sympotic that the possibility of a sacrifice would not have occurred to the audience" (Bowie 1993, 152).

5. Green 1879, 95 on line 28, on the meaning of the Greek phrase; Whitman 1964, 175–76, on the importance of this "dramatized metaphor" and its connection to the play's handling of ambiguities in the fifth-century debate about *nomos* and *phusis*.

6. Practice outdoes theory. Thuc. 1.24–65 reads like a case study in such paradoxes; esp. 1.38.2–3 with McGlew 1993, 176.

7. Sommerstein 1987, 1 n. 3, on general physical and sociopolitical similarities. Cf. Long 1986, 15: "The parabasis may promise a startling new set of *nomoi*, but in the outcome there is a silent assumption of institutions and customs fairly parallel to Athens." Bowie 1993, 160, emphasizes that Nephelokokkugia, "situated in the air, is a world similar to but different in significant ways from the 'real' Athens." Pozzi 1991, 149–52, gives other aspects, esp. pastoral ones, of the "non-Athens" that becomes "a replica of Athens in the sky."

8. Earlier scholars felt the play's moral ambivalence, but perhaps did not appreciate its function *in* the play. See Murray 1933, 155 (on line 1765); and the scholiast on 1753. Zanetto and del Corno 1987, 199 on 186, note that *Birds* was once considered "la più 'empia' delle commedie di Aristofane." Even Katz 1976, 376, paused: "It is not the ending, which has to be 'happy,' but items such as the bitterly ironic political cannibalism (1583–85) as well as the resultant tyranny of Peisetairos which are sufficient signposts of sentiment."

9. See also Auger 1979. My work originated independently of Auger's and was largely completed before hers came to my attention. We have different projects, but with overlapping and mutually reinforcing conclusions. My aim is to provide a reading of *Birds* as it stands; hers is to trace the larger "pensée mythique" that links the utopianizing features in all of Aristophanes' work from *Acharnians* to *Plutus*, with special attention both to *Birds* and to the function of women in the last plays (see note 50). For Auger, *Birds* is a play of deep ambiguity that is a culmination of the themes in the first half of Aristophanes' career (the "young" iron age: rejuvenation of the hero, reaffirmation of sacrifice and marriage, restoration of an age that has disappeared) and anticipates the themes of the second half of his literary corpus (the "old" iron age: degradation of old age to the point of destruction and death). As a result, in her argument, *Birds* is "an ambiguous play that both follows and subverts the pattern of the restoration of the young age" (108, quoted from her English summary).

10. Also Thuc. 6.5.3 on Hippocrates' refounding of Kamarina. See McGlew 1993, 153–54, on the Amphipolitans; 21, on the probability of Syracuse being refounded if Hippocrates had taken it. Elsewhere (18–19) McGlew notes that foundation legends typically involve only a single founder in any one account, even if there may be rival accounts or, as at Amphipolis, a series of accounts. He also suggests (19) that this fact explains why Euelpides disappears in the course of this play.

11. For separate and distinct deconstructions, see Dobrov 1990 and Bowie 1993, 151–77.

12. A similar inversion occurs when the oracle monger calls for a sacrifice to Pandora (971–75). There, the commentators virtually all agree, Aristophanes etymologizes her name as the bountiful "giver of all gifts"—exactly what "Pandora" does not, and cannot, mean in Hesiod since his Pandora receives gifts and bestows evils and grievous sorrows (*kaka* and *kēdea lugra*, *Erga* 42–105), and since Hesiod, *Erga* 81–82, explicitly explains that she was called Pandora because "all [*pantes*] the Olympians gave her a gift [*dōron*]." See notes 41–42 on connections between Hesiod's and Aristophanes' Pandoras.

13. Since his burial place, like that of an *oikistēs*, is memorialized and both literally and narratologically included in the new foundation, the lark's father is being recognized, in essence, as the founder of the new bird order. See McGlew 1993, 14–26, on the inclusion of the founder's burial place and the exclusion of the tyrant's.

14. Kirk, Raven, and Schofield, 1983, 28: "most of Aristophanes' bird-cosmogony is indubitably derived from the Hesiodic *Theogony*, with appropriate modifications. . . . It is a parody of a traditional type of cosmogony; yet the original of a parody must be recognizable, and while the Hesiodic elements are clear enough the egg is non-Hesiodic." One conspicuous element, the non-Hesiodic cosmic egg, usually is considered Orphic, but see Kirk et al. 1983, 26–29, on the problem. In the play the egg appropriately bespeaks the birdness of cosmic origins, but *Birds* likely parodies key features of all previous cosmogonies. Hesiod's *Theogony*, nevertheless, provided the easily recognized model for structuring the parody, just as it later influenced serious cosmogonies like the Orphic *Rhapsodies*.

15. Katz 1976, 370–73, identified how important the title *Apopurgizontes Logoi*, a polemical work by Diagoras the Melian (ὁ ἄθεος), is for the plot of *Birds*. Hubbard 1991, 158–82, returned one focus of criticism to matters of piety and impiety. Romer 1994 links these two developments specifically to the themes of Promethean sacrifice and τὰ πολιτικά. (See also Russo 1990, 147–48, and Romer 1996, 394–98, on other political aspects of *Birds* 1072–75.) It is, in general, amazing how small a role sacrifice has played in criticism of *Birds*, given its centrality to the plot, but then criticism of the play has been nothing short of stupefying for well over a century (a few bright spots excepted). With three major commentaries on *Birds* since 1987, and much else in recent years, there is hope.

16. As opposed to the merely legendary past typified by, say, the Homeric epics and Thucydides' *archaiologia*.

17. Hofmann 1976, 152–60, revives and develops this suggestion about the *hieros gamos* of the finale from Cook 1913. As Peisetairos replaces Zeus, so Basileia replaces Hera, and in the hymenaion (1737–41) Aristophanes compared their wedding with Zeus and Hera's. But the play's language does not reveal Basileia's costume, and other possibilities ought to be considered and have been. (McGlew 1993, 170, notes in passing that this staged marriage accords, mutatis mutandis, with the foundation motif since it shows the *oikistēs* marrying a local woman.)

18. Possibly anticipated at 192 if genuine. Line 192 is deleted rightly by Sommerstein 1987 without explanation (for which see Zanetto and del Corno 1987, 199). Dunbar 1995, 197–98, also gives full discussion and prefers to delete the line.

19. It would be nice to have an analysis of *Birds* in terms of pre-Socratic and fifth-century philosophy. (Rhetorical sophism has received more than its share of attention.) Peisetairos' new cosmos, for example, illustrates, criticizes, and distorts in the extreme the famous principle of cultural relativity identified by Xenophanes (21B14 D.-K.): "And mortals suppose that gods are born of parents and have clothing, speech, and a physical appearance like theirs" (cf. also 21B15–16 D.-K.). For example, the Triballian god speaks Greek about as well as any Triballian, but not as well as the average bird god who is cast linguistically in the mold of those who made birds divine. The plot likewise illustrates and twists the famous idea attributed to Protagoras that human beings are the measure of all things; the play may also twist the anthropological *muthos* Plato assigned to Protagoras (*Prot.* 320C–322D; dramatic date: late 430s), which perhaps deserves critical attention in connection with *Birds* if its association with Protagoras is authentic.

20. Aristophanes in a sense revivifies the stage persona of Prometheus. By 414, Prometheus had become the mythological equivalent of "necessity" or "experience" (cf. Chaeremon, fr. 21 Nauck).

21. As Arrowsmith 1973 demonstrated. Arrowsmith's essay also explored the bird/phallos imagery as a part of the *erōs* theme.

22. Heracles' threat here to Zeus' rule works an interesting change on, and provides a curious proof of, the Hesiodic danger of the chief male deity being overthrown by his stronger son. (See also note 45 on the *patraloias*' similar threat to Peisetairos when he succeeds to Zeus' position.)

23. Henderson 1991, 85, rightly notes the "heroic rejuvenation" of Peisetairos and his hubristic mistreatment of Iris, which reverses the past aggression of Olympian males toward mortal women. (Also Taaffe 1993, 42.) Iris' appearance in the play is less satisfactorily explained by other commentators. Hofmann 1976, 114–15, and Zannini Quirini 1987, 62–65, are interesting for the data they compile, but less engaging as literary criticism of *Birds* itself. Hofmann, for example, offers two uncompelling reasons for Iris' appearance here (her role in the *Iliad* and three slight verbal associations with the structure of *h. Dem.*). Even when he identifies a third reason, her sex, his explanation is mundane: with all the play's male figures, *variatio* is "dramaturgisch erwünscht"; certain double meanings leading up to the threatened rape require a female. For his part, Quirini is more concerned with the theme of Gigantomachy as an entity in its own right than with the play as a whole. For brief, perceptive remarks on both the Titanomachy and the Gigantomachy, see Dunbar 1995, 7–9, who handles them as elements of plot rather than as themes in the play. In any case, both motifs add to the Hesiodic stew, even if "it is impossible to deduce from Aristophanes' use of these two myths how he intended the audience to react to Peisetairos" (Dunbar 8).

24. Romer 1983 discusses the nightingale's possible appearance (*sic*) as an *aulētris*. Based on the evidence of essentially fourth-century South Italian pottery showing scenes from fifth-century comedy, Taplin 1993, 107 n. 6, argues that the idea "can only be salvaged if the nightingale's part were to be metatheatrically played by the official (presumably male) *aulētēs*." I could—and can— accept such casting (Romer 1983, 137 n. 7; *pace* MacDowell 1995, 205 n. 11), but still prefer Webster's costumed mime (1970, 188; see also Dunbar 1995, 421 on 667–74, citing a South Italian kalyx-krater to support her own view). Less convincing is Taplin's reservation about the *parepigraphē* after line 222, which, even though not authorial, certainly reflects a commonsense interpretation of lines 223–24, especially in light of lines 676–84 later. Taplin 1993, 106, argues cleverly and enticingly that the crow-piper described at *Birds* 859–61 also was played by the official *aulētēs*, and that on this occasion he was that same Khairis named in *Peace* 950–55 and *Birds* 857–58. One thing is certain: the piper who played on this occasion had exceptional talent.

25. The chorus's ideology is firm (723–36): the new gods will eschew Olympian remoteness, live among mortals, bring prosperity, and be minutely involved in the intimacies of daily life—a return to the golden age but with a difference.

26. See notes 13, 41–42, on Aristophanes' allusive treatment of Pandora.

27. Hofmann 1976, 120–21, overstates the case. Aristophanes has not changed Prometheus from a friend of humans to a friend of birds. His supposed friendship with the birds is merely incidental and entirely dependent on his friendship with Peisetairos as *anthrōpos*. Aristophanes' twist is that Prometheus remains *philanthropisch* in the most literal sense of Hofmann's word.

28. Contra Zanetto and del Corno 1987, 303 on 1538, who print κεραμεύει ("makes," as one makes pottery), but κεραμεύει produces little, if any, comic (or other) sense here. Dunbar 1995, 704–5 on 1538, discusses the issue.

29. For the suggestion that Nephelokokkugia is to be associated with the theme of Athens *turannis*, see Romer 1994, 360 n. 29. On the theme itself see Hunter 1973–74; Raaflaub 1979; and Connor 1977. But McGlew 1993, 189–90 (cf. also 85–86), puts an important new spin on the theme as a whole: "What I mean to suggest is the city that was labeled by its leaders as a *tyrannis polis*—tyrant city—was home to tyrant citizens. The freedom that was once enjoyed exclusively by tyrants was incorporated into the definition of citizenship." McGlew 1993, 29, had earlier identified this freedom as Aristotle's "vulgar" *eleutheria*: "the ability to do what one wishes"

without restraint of any kind (*Pol.* 1310a32–33). Cf. also Auger 1979, 86: "Les *Oiseaux* montrent comment l'exigence toute démocratique de liberté réalisée par la création d'une cité sans lois, aboutit à la tyrannie du simple citoyen Peithétairos et figurent de manière concrète ce que Platon décrit comme la dégradation du régime démocratique en régime tyrannique."

30. *Turannos* (1708) is sometimes treated as if it simply meant king (as, for example, it *often* may in tragedy). Dunbar 1995, 745, takes it as "king," but does not doubt that Peisetairos is a usurper in the context of the Succession Myth. Sommerstein 1987, 193 and 309 with note ad loc., translates it as "monarch" and observes the emptiness of Peisetairos' promise in the agon to restore the birds to their rightful sovereignty. There can be no doubt, however, that in his own terms (522–38)—and the birds' (cf. 1072–87)—Peisetairos acts tyrannically. Peisetairos' tyrannical violence is alarming—roasting the avian political dissidents, driving out the newcomers, hauling Iris from the sky, and so on. Reading the play, as opposed to watching it, may distract us from noticing how violent the language and stage action are. Auger 1979, 86, is correct: "A la fin de la pièce, le héros qui asseoit son pouvoir sur la force, est présenté par le messager comme un souverain absolu, un tyran (v. 1708). Les ambiguités que le héros concentre en lui finissent par lui faire épouser très exactement les contours de la figure inquiétante et énigmatique du tyran telle qu'on se la représente au Vème et au IVème siècle." See also Pozzi 1991, 157–59, and Katz's remark above, note 9.

31. For the importance of Heracles in this play, see note 39.

32. So Sommerstein 1987, 181, and accepted by Bowie 1993, 171, whose argument it does not fit very well. It is hardly possible to believe with Hubbard 1991, 161, that Peisetairos ὁ τύραννος was "presuming" to benefit the birds by creating a new democracy for them. We have no sense of any alleged "democracy" of the birds, but, if a democracy it was, then it operates very much as Thucydides (2.65.9) described Athens—quite literally as the rule of ὁ πρῶτος ἀνήρ (*sic*). Romer 1994, 360–61, identifies the barbecued birds as rebels against Euelpides and Peisetairos who are the only demesmen (cf. *dēmotikoi*) mentioned in the play; it marks another way in which the two rascals never transcend either their humanity or their Athenian-ness. It should be stated clearly that we are dealing with resonance here: the adjective δημοτικός is not a political word in the same definite sense as the noun δημότης.

33. Tyrell and Brown 1991, 27: "Sacrifice, then, imposes another limitation upon the men at Mekone as well as another definition of civilization: to be civilized is to eat cooked meat." That no fuss is made in the play about what will be served at the wedding feast may suggest that the barbecue also aims metatheatrically at the audience and the actors taking the parts of birds.

34. On line 1546, Green 1879, 161–62; Sommerstein 1987, 299; Zanetto and del Corno 1987, 304; Dunbar 1995, 707, all note that Peisetairos is describing comically the possession of fire. But Peisetairos' remark goes deeper. It responds to Prometheus' claim to be a friend to humans (1545), and he accepts Prometheus' original hierarchy by referring to the Titan as one of the *theoi*. Again Peisetairos blurs both the old and the new distinctions, and he retains this characteristic human feature from Prometheus' hierarchy. Note too that as a bird Tereus still retained human ideas, as Peisetairos realizes ("you think all the things a human does and all that a bird does," 119), and his desires remain consistent too (71–79).

35. Detienne 1989, 7. In this paragraph and the next I am heavily indebted to the argument of Detienne.

36. Tyrell and Brown 1991, 31: "For Hesiod, civilization begins, then, with a breach between men and their gods. Men who sat openly with the gods are now condemned to work and to communicate with the gods through sacrifice." Cf. Vernant 1989, 25: "By eating the edible pieces men, even as they reinvigorate their failing strength, recognize the inferiority of their mortal condition and confirm their complete submission to the Olympians whom the Titan believed he could dupe with impunity when he established the model of the first sacrifice."

37. The barbecue reifies a radical insight into the new order. On the other hand, it is the alteration of the sacrificial hierarchy, even in minute detail, that is shocking because it separates

birds from other animals and raises them above humans. Those humans who do not become bird gods are expected to continue their sacrifices to the old gods but only after they sacrifice to the new ones (561–65). The impact of the new arrangements is otherwise minimal since birds eat— well—like birds.

38. Heracles deserves more attention than I can give him here. First, he is "a prodigious founder of cities" (McGlew 1993, 167 n. 22). Second, "the catastrophic inversion of the sacrificial act would appear to be an essential element in the Herakles myth" (Girard 1977, 41). Third, he is the only Olympian with a human origin, and like Peisetairos the comic Heracles is motivated by the demands of his stomach as here. Finally, in this play Heracles is also a rival claimant to the tyranny of the birds (1673).

39. On Basileia's name, see first Zanetto and del Corno 1987, 303 on 1536; then Bowie, 1993, 164–65 and esp. n. 68, with Taaffe 1993, 161–62 n. 48. (Taaffe points to Pozzi 1991, 159 n. 97, which as it stands, however, mistakes the Greek *de re*.) As guardian of Zeus' bolts, the new queen, Basileia (βασίλεια), stands as the keeper of the instruments of Zeus' power (βασιλεία), and hence her presence here both represents and, in an important sense, *embodies* his power. (MacDowell 1995, 218 n. 33, raises the intriguing possibility that the final alphas on words like these may have been considered variable by Aristophanes and that the words might have been interchangeable for him.) In a familiar Greek way the conveyance of Basileia brings with her the title to Zeus' power. Thus, as so often in mythology, the female embodies the power to bestow power.

40. This etymology reverses Hesiod's explanation of the name (above, note 13). On line 971, Green 1879, 139; Van Leeuwen 1902, 149; Zanetto and del Corno 1987, 257; and Sommerstein 1987, 262, all recognize the association of the name Pandora with Earth (and sometimes with Rheia, as Sommerstein adds), but Dunbar 1995, 546, warns that this Pandora is "a chthonic goddess, sometimes, but perhaps not before late antiquity identified with Γῆ." Green, Van Leeuwen, Zanetto and del Corno, and Dunbar are silent about Hesiod's Pandora here. See following note.

41. Merry 1896, 53 on 970, denies any connection between Aristophanes' and Hesiod's Pandoras. Among the commentators, only Sommerstein 1987, 262 on 971, notes a possible link between the two Pandoras, and he cites West 1978, 164–67 on 81, to show the possible connections between them. West 1978, 165, notes the confusion of the two at Athens, but is reluctant to acknowledge the inherent syncretism. With a slight twist of Hesiod's etymology, the *OCD*[2] 883, s.v. Prometheus, identifies the two and asserts firmly that "the first woman was called Pandora, because she had 'all gifts' from the gods (she probably is in reality an earth-goddess, the All-giver)." See following note. Bowie 1993, 163, connects the two Pandoras (as binary opposites, I suppose) through Basileia in *Birds*.

42. Bowie 1993, 168–69, following Detienne, points out that "no real cannibalism" occurs in *Theogony* because Kronos regurgitates his children and Metis functions inside Zeus. Again Peisetairos remythologizes the process and goes further than Hesiod.

43. Cf. Herington 1963, 236–37, on the characteristically Aeschylean phrase τὴν Διὸς τυραννίδα at *PB* 10 and 357.

44. No wonder Peisetairos drives the father beater away! Among other things, the *patraloias* enacts figuratively those Hesiodic fears about future succession that the new chief deity needs to forestall. It is the endemic paradox of divine sovereignty in Hesiod's *Theogony* that the son both drives out the father and usurps his position. (See note 23.) Repelling the son by force, however, never works in the Succession Myth embedded in Hesiod's *Theogony*, nor did force work in Aeschylus' *Prometheus Bound* to motivate Prometheus to reveal the secret of future succession. Moreover, driving the newly arrived father beater away does not solve the problem since birds actually allow, by law or custom (*nomos*), a young bird to throttle, bite, or beat his father (1344–52; cf. 757–59). Peisetairos succeeds in driving the father beater away by force, but the newcomer is ready to leave, in any case, when he learns that sons are obliged to support their fathers in old age (1358–59, spoken sarcastically).

45. Peisetairos' barbecue enacts in comic form the "sacrificial crisis" which Girard 1977, 39–

67, found widespread in tragedy: "Any change, however slight, in the hierarchical classification of living creatures risks undermining the whole sacrificial structure" (39). According to Girard, the loss of cultural distinctions undermines the order, peace, and fecundity of the human community and motivates that internal or reciprocal violence (49) that it is the sole purpose of religion to prevent (55). Thus, Peisetairos' barbecue exemplifies the reciprocal violence that follows on the breakdown of the established sacrificial hierarchy. (Also note 38.)

46. Pozzi 1991, 149.

47. On the dual etymology of this nonsense word, see Dobrov 1990, 210–11, and 1993, 192.

48. De Romilly 1972 discusses the political history of the term in the fifth century.

49. Pozzi 1991, 160.

50. Cf. Foley 1975, 6–13, on this conclusion and on polis and oikos as mutually defining terms in *Lysistrate*. See also Taaffe 1993, 48–73, on the play. On the other hand, a play like *Lysistrate*, when taken individually, may be interpreted one way, and in quite another way when read in the context of Aristophanes' oeuvre as a whole. Auger 1979, for example, argues that, in the poet's last plays (those after *Birds*), women "serve to reveal the impending catastrophe [for the existing order] and their presence on the stage signifies the disappearance of the civic body and the city" (108, quoted from her English summary).

Bibliography

Arrowsmith, William. 1973. "Aristophanes' *Birds*: The Fantasy Politics of Eros." *Arion*, n.s., 1.119–67.

Auger, Danièle. 1979. "Le théâtre d'Aristophane: Le mythe, l'utopie et les femmes." *Les Cahiers de Fontenay* 17.71–101.

Bowie, Angus. 1993. *Aristophanes: Myth, Ritual and Comedy*. Cambridge.

Cole, Thomas. 1967. *Democritus and the Sources of Greek Anthropology*. American Philological Monographs 25. Cleveland.

Connor, W. R. 1977. "Tyrannis Polis." In *Ancient and Modern: Essays in Honor of Gerald F. Else*, edited by John D'Arms and John Eadie, 95–109. Ann Arbor.

Cook, A. B. 1913. "Nephelokokkugia." In *Studies Presented to William Ridgeway*, edited by E. C. Quiggin, 213–21. Cambridge.

de Romilly, Jaqueline. 1972. "Vocabulaire et propagande, ou les premiers emplois du mot *homonoia*." *Études et Commentaires* 79.199–209.

Detienne, Marcel. "Culinary Practices and the Spirit of Sacrifice." In *Cuisine*, edited by Detienne and Vernant, 1–20.

Detienne, Marcel, and Jean-Pierre Vernant, eds. 1989. *The Cuisine of Sacrifice among the Greeks*. Translated by Paula Wissig. Chicago.

Dobrov, Gregory. 1990. "Aristophanes' *Birds* and the Metaphor of Deferral." *Arethusa* 23.2.209–33.

———. 1993. "The Tragic and Comic Tereus." *AJP* 114.189–234.

Dunbar, Nan. 1995. *Aristophanes' Birds*. Oxford.

Foley, Helene. 1975. "The 'Female Intruder' Reconsidered: Women in Aristophanes' *Lysistrata* and *Ecclesiazusae*." *CP* 77.1–21.

Girard, René. 1977. *Violence and the Sacred*. Translated by Patrick Gregory. Baltimore.

Green, W. C. 1879. *The Birds of Aristophanes*. Cambridge.

Hamilton, Richard. 1985. "The Well-Equipped Traveller: *Birds* 42." *GRBS* 26.235–39.

Havelock, Eric. 1958. *The Liberal Temper in Greek Politics*. New Haven.

Henderson, Jeffrey. 1991. *The Maculate Muse*. 2d ed. New York.

Herington, C. J. 1963. "A Study in the *Prometheia*, Part II: *Birds* and *Prometheia*." *Phoenix* 17.236–43.

Hofmann, Heinz. 1976. *Mythos und Komödie: Untersuchungen zu den Vögeln des Aristophanes.* Spudasmata 33. Hildesheim.

Hubbard, Thomas. 1991. *The Mask of Comedy: Aristophanes and the Intertextual Parabasis.* Ithaca.

Hunter, Virginia. 1973–74. "Athens *Tyrannis*: A New Approach to Thucydides." *CJ* 69.120–26.

Katz, Barry. 1976. "The *Birds* of Aristophanes and Politics." *Athenaeum* 54.353–81.

Kirk, G. S., J. E. Raven, and Malcolm Schofield. 1983. *The Presocratic Philosophers.* 2d ed. Cambridge.

Konstan, David. 1990. "A City in the Air: Aristophanes' *Birds.*" *Arethusa* 23.2.183–207.

Long, Timothy. 1986. *Barbarians in Greek Comedy.* Carbondale, Ill.

MacDowell, Douglas M. 1995. *Aristophanes and Athens: An Introduction to the Plays.* Oxford.

McGlew, James F. 1993. *Tyranny and Political Culture in Ancient Greece.* Ithaca.

Marzullo, B. 1970. "L'interlocuzione negli 'Uccelli' d'Aristofane." *Philologus* 114.181–94.

Merry, W. W. 1896. *Aristophanes: The Birds.* 3d ed. Oxford.

Murray, Gilbert. 1933. *Aristophanes: A Study.* Oxford.

Pozzi, Dora C. 1991. "The Polis in Crisis." In *Myth and the Polis*, edited by Dora C. Pozzi and John Wickersham, 126–63. Ithaca.

Raaflaub, Kurt. 1979. "Polis Tyrannos: Zur Entstehung einer politischen Metapher." In *Arktouros: Hellenic Studies Presented to Bernard M. W. Knox*, edited by G. W. Bowersock, Walter Burkert, and Michael C. J. Putnam, 237–52. Berlin.

Romer, F. E. 1983. "When Is a Bird Not a Bird?" *TAPA* 113.135–42.

———. 1994. "Atheism, Impiety, and the *Limos Mêlios* in Aristophanes' *Birds.*" *AJP* 118.351–65.

———. 1996. "Diagoras the Melian (Diod. Sic. 13.6.7)." *CW* 89.393–401.

Russo, Carlo Fernando. 1994. *Aristophanes: An Author for the Stage.* Translated by Kevin Wren. London.

Sommerstein, Alan. 1987. *The Comedies of Aristophanes.* Vol. 6: *Birds.* Warminster.

Taaffe, Lauren K. 1993. *Aristophanes and Women.* London.

Taplin, Oliver. 1993. *Comic Angels.* Oxford.

Tyrell, William Blake, and Frieda S. Brown. 1991. *Athenian Myths and Institutions: Words in Action.* New York.

van Leeuwen, J. 1902. *Aristophanis Aves.* Leiden.

Vernant, Jean-Pierre. "At Man's Table: Hesiod's Foundation Myth of Sacrifice." In *Cuisine*, edited by Detienne and Vernant, 21–86.

Webster, T. B. L. 1970. *The Greek Chorus.* London.

West, M. L. 1978. *Hesiod: Works and Days.* Oxford.

Whitman, Cedric. 1964. *Aristophanes and the Comic Hero.* Cambridge, Mass.

Zanetto, Giuseppe, and Dario del Corno, eds. 1987. *Aristofane: Gli Uccelli.* Milan.

Zannini Quirini, Bruno. 1987. *Nephelokokkygia: La prospettiva mitica degli Uccelli di Aristofane.* Rome.

NIALL W. SLATER

November 18, 1967:
Artaud is alive at the
walls of the Pentagon.
. . . The Pentagon vibrates
and begins to rise in the
air.—Abbie Hoffman,
Revolution for the Hell of It

Performing the City in *Birds*

One of the most entertaining moments of political theatre during the days of the Vietnam protests occurred when Abbie Hoffman and Co. rallied round to levitate the Pentagon. Though no evidence exists, Hoffman swore that around four in the morning they did succeed in lifting it three or four feet off the ground. The city of Nephelokokkugia in *Birds*, which soars so high in poetic imagination, hovered in actuality about the same distance above the ground, for it was a theatrical city, built to a surprisingly explicit degree on the stage of the Theatre of Dionysos. Though Aristophanes' *Birds* is less obviously metatheatrical than some of his earlier works, the play nonetheless exploits its own performance situation both to increase its comic effects and to literalize the metaphor of the "city in the air." Nephelokokkugia comes into being through a series of enactments, which are sometimes mimetic, sometimes self-consciously nonillusory stage performance. If the critique of spectator politics which Aristophanes launched in the *Acharnians* is more muted in this play, it is nonetheless present. A performance analysis may not resolve the debate between fantastic and allegorical interpretations of the play but should clarify some of the issues.

Birds begins precisely nowhere, a place characterized by its placelessness, an *outopia* as David Konstan points out.[1] Peisetaerus and Euelpides presumably arrive from one of the parodoi into the orchestra but, once there, have no idea how to proceed. The opening lines indicate they are wandering back and forth (and indeed the original production could easily have extended this into a long silent sequence of physical comedy):

Pei. Ὀρθὴν κελεύεις, ᾗ τὸ δένδρον φαίνεται;
Eu.   Διαρραγείης. Ἤδε δ᾿ αὖ κρώζει πάλιν.
Pei. Τί, ὦ πόνηρ᾿, ἄνω κάτω πλανύττομεν;
      Ἀπολούμεθ᾿ ἄλλως τὴν ὁδὸν προφορουμένω.

Their guide birds eventually lead them to some cliffs (κατὰ τῶν πετρῶν, 20), which are represented by the front of the stage.[2] Note too here the expression ἄνω κάτω. This anticipates the direction that the two will eventually locate: up, out of their current dilemma.

Before they find their way out, however, Peisetaerus offers a remarkable direct address to the audience (27–48). The explicit form of his address indicates the audience's participation in the creation of the performance (ὦνδρες οἱ παρόντες ἐν λόγῳ, 30); the passage as a whole signals the political nature of the journey they have undertaken. Unlike the foreigners who are trying to squeeze their way *into* the polis and into Athenian citizenship, these two are trying to escape the city, escape from the oppressive operations of the democracy, especially the lawcourts. Almost as an afterthought, we learn that this journey has, if not a direction, a goal: to find Tereus the hoopoe.

Suddenly we discover that the guide birds *do* know one direction: up.

Eu.   Οὗτος.
Pei.   Τί ἐστιν;
Eu.   Ἡ κορώνη μοι πάλαι
ἄνω τι φράζει.
Pei.   Χὠ κολοιὸς οὑτοσὶ
ἄνω κέχηνεν ὡσπερεὶ δεικνύς μοι,
κοὐκ ἔσθ᾿ ὅπως οὐκ ἔστιν ἐνταῦθ᾿ ὄρνεα.

(49–52)

As Sommerstein notes in his stage directions, Peisetaerus and Euelpides mount the stage at this point: ἄνω is the way one moves in Greek when going on stage, κάτω the direction in which one exits. In other words, they locate themselves, they find a place amid placelessness, by placing themselves on stage, by assuming the proper place for actors in the divided space of the theatre and thereby begin the process of creating Nephelokokkugia.

The appearance of Tereus in response to the knocking of Peisetaerus and Euelpides arguably provides another element of theatrical self-consciousness. The bird who appears is in an advanced state of moulting—and he is specifically Sophocles' *Tereus*.

Ter. Τοιαῦτα μέντοι Σοφοκλέης λυμαίνεται
     ἐν ταῖς τραγῳδίαισιν ἐμέ, τὸν Τηρέα.

(100–101)

This is on its face a quite puzzling passage. To judge from his comments in *Frogs*, Aristophanes admired Sophocles, and the great tragedian nowhere in the fragments of Old Comedy comes in for the severity of criticism that Euripides does. I find very appealing the partial explanation offered by Gregory Dobrov: Sophocles took the risk in his *Tereus* of showing us the title character transformed, though probably only in tableau.[3] This would have been a daring effect and perhaps not fully successful: there was doubtless a considerable danger that some members of the audience would find the transformation not tragic but hilarious,[4] and so Aristophanes may simply be twitting Sophocles with one of his unusual failures. But why is Tereus *shedding* his feathers? He was certainly not represented this way in Sophocles' tragedy. The purported explanation initially puzzles rather than illumines. When asked about his condition, Tereus says:

Pei.   Πότερον ὑπὸ νόσου τινός;
Ter.   Οὔκ, ἀλλὰ τὸν χειμῶνα πάντα τὦρνεα
      πτερορρυεῖ, κᾆτ' αὖθις ἕτερα φύομεν.

(104–6)

This is wrong by 180 degrees. Winter is the least likely time for birds to moult, since they need the protection against cold. So why winter? Perhaps it is a reference to extradramatic time: but *Birds* was a City play, not a Lenaean one, so the season is almost spring rather than fully winter. I am tempted to believe, though I cannot of course prove, that Aristophanes or his producer bought Tereus' costume secondhand from the producer of *Tereus*— and perhaps quite cheaply because after a winter in storage the feathers were already beginning to fall off.[5] The joke makes a virtue of necessity and/or choregic parsimony. It is also, to judge from the Getty birds vase, a joke which was carried through in the costumes of the chorus, once it appears.[6] In any case, comments on the costume as costume remind the audience forcefully that this character is just a shabbily outfitted refugee from the tragic competitions.

Peisetaerus and Euelpides inform Tereus that they are searching for a city— an anticity, in fact, characterized by its difference from the Athens they have left.[7] There *is* such a city, says Tereus, on the Red Sea—but Peisetaerus rejects that because it can be reached by sea from Athens (143– 48). Some Greek cities are mentioned and quickly rejected.

Then comes Peisetaerus' great idea: to found a city among the birds. This alone, he says, will transform the birds from archetypes of helplessness and idiocy[8] into a power to be reckoned with. And what gives this prospective city its potential for power? Its place, its location in the scheme of things, as Peisetaerus proceeds to demonstrate to Tereus:

Pei.   Βλέψον κάτω.
Ter.   Καὶ δὴ βλέπω.
Pei.   Βλέπε νυν ἄνω.
Ter.   Βλέπω.
Pei.   Περίαγε τὸν τράχηλον.
Ter.   Νὴ Δία
ἀπολαύσομαί ⟨τί⟩ γ', εἰ διαστραφήσομαι
Pei.   Εἶδές τι;
Ter.   Τὰς νεφέλας γε καὶ τὸν οὐρανόν.
Pei.   Οὐχ οὗτος οὖω δήπον ῷστὶν ὀρνίθων πόλος;
Ter.   Πόλος; Τίνα τρόπον;
Pei.   ῏Ωσπερ ⟨ἂν⟩ εἴποι τις τόπος.
῝Οτι δὲ πολεῖται τοῦτο καὶ διέρχεται
ἅπαντα διὰ τούτου, καλεῖται νῦν πόλος.
῝Ην δ' οἰκίσητε τοῦτο καὶ φράξηθ' ἄπαξ,
ἐκ τοῦ πόλου τούτου κεκλήσεται πόλις.
῏Ωστ' ἄρξετ' ἀνθρώπων μὲν ὥσπερ παρνόπων,
τοὺς δ' αὖ θεοὺς ἀπολεῖτε λιμῷ Μηλίῳ.
Ter.   Πῶς;
Pei.   Ἐν μέσῳ δήπουθεν ἀήρ ἐστι γῆς.

(175–88)

The pun on πόλος and πόλις in this passage is critical for the establishment of the bird city, as Konstan has seen. He, however, emphasizes it as the establishment of hierarchy: the conversion of the unbounded sky into a bounded and delimited space by the wall that the birds eventually build creates civilization: "It is not just a question of the wall, but of a different way of conceiving space as territorial, a field marked by limits of property."[9] Moreover, the vertical axis of the πόλος sets up a social order, under which the two humans can now dominate the previously unordered, unpoliticized birds.[10]

Yet there is another, less metaphorical way of looking at this critical passage. The terms κάτω and ἄνω have already been established as theatrical terms by the opening. Peisetaerus' elaborate demonstration of where they are establishes that the bird city will be built on stage.[11] It is a theatrical space located midway between god and man, audience (Βλέψον κάτω, 175) and theologeion (Βλέπε νυν ἄνω, 175), inhabited by the gods they plan to starve into submission. And the point of looking around (Περίαγε τὸν τράχηλον, 176)? They will build their city in the presence of the Athenian audience (whom they will eventually invite to join their anticity).

The building of the city begins with teaching the chorus, a process already begun by Tereus, who has taught the birds the Greek language: ἐδίδαξα τὴν φωνήν (202). The teaching role is then assumed by Peisetaerus,[12] a role that is always open to theatrical implication in Aristophanes (cf. Praxagora's "teaching" in *Ecclesiazusae*). Members of the chorus begin to arrive singly, after a simple but perhaps significant joke on Euelpides: he is looking for the birds to arrive from the sky (264), but he has forgotten where they are now located, for the birds arrive from the parodoi.[13] Eventually they are so numerous that they block the theatre entrance—which Euelpides names, reminding us once again that this is a stage city set in a theatre: οὐδ᾽ ἰδεῖν ἔτ᾽ ἔσθ᾽ ὑπ᾽ αὐτῶν πετομένων τὴν εἴσοδον (296).[14]

The chorus, as so often in Aristophanes, initially displays its hostility to the central figure(s). Peisetaerus and Euelpides are humans and therefore the birds' natural enemies. Their gaping beaks indicate at once their hostility and also their ultimate gullibility:

Pei.   Οἴμοι, κεχήνασίν γέ τοι
καὶ βλέπουσιν εἰς σὲ κἀμέ.

(307–8)

The birds, though they may lack the unifying force of a city at this point, nonetheless possess military organization and call upon their taxiarch (Ποῦ 'σθ᾽ ὁ ταξίαρχος; Ἐπαγέτω τὸ δεξιὸν κέρας, 353) to lead the charge against the humans.[15] A pitched battle is about to be joined when Tereus intervenes, once again asserting that the birds have something to learn from humans (διδά-ξοντές, 372; διδάξειάν, 373) precisely because they are enemies: what one learns from enemies is the art of self-defense, more specifically the art of delimiting space by building walls (ἐκπονεῖν θ᾽ ὑψηλὰ τείχη, 379), precisely what the birds will learn from Peisetaerus. The question of how to decide whom to enclose along with the birds inside those walls is conveniently forgotten. Peisetaerus and Euelpides now enact the establishment of just such a defensive perimeter (and proleptically, therefore, of the bird city itself) on the stage, marking the boundary with a pot just used as a helmet (386– 92).[16] Meanwhile the birds, behaving explicitly like hoplite warriors (καὶ τὸν θυμὸν κατάθου κύψας / παρὰ τὴν ὀργὴν ὥσπερ ὁπλίτης, 401–2), suspend hostilities in order to listen to the humans' proposals.[17]

Tereus invites Peisetaerus to "teach" (δίδαξον, 438) the chorus his new λόγοι, a process which describes equally well the *chorodidaskalos*'s task and the process of political persuasion: by becoming *chorodidaskalos* and retraining the chorus, he incorporates it into his version of the new city. The metatheatrical dimensions of the scene are made clear by the terms of the treaty they now swear: if the chorus keeps its oath, it is to win the play competition by a unanimous approval of audience and judges, but if not, by a single-vote margin:[18]

> Pei.   Κατόμοσόν νυν ταῦτά μοι.
> Chor.   Ὄμνυμ' ἐπὶ τούτοις, πᾶσι νικᾶν τοῖς κριταῖς
>   καὶ τοῖς θεαταῖς πᾶσιν—
> Pei.   Ἔσται ταυταγί.
> Chor.   εἰ δὲ παραβαίην, ἐνὶ κριτῇ νικᾶν μόνον.
>
> (444–48)

The terms accepted, Peisetaerus can now disband his "troops"—that is, Euelpides.[19] His preparations for his speech are still not complete: he calls for a garland, and Euelpides asks him whether he is getting ready for a banquet, a particularly meaningful question in light of the fact that at the end of the play Peisetaerus will be dining on birds who rebelled against the new democracy.[20]

Peisetaerus now unfolds his great idea: the birds were once kings of the universe and now have the opportunity to reclaim their realm from the gods. A curious feature of the presentation is that Euelpides is constantly interrupting it. One might regard Euelpides' role as simply the traditional *bōmolochos* figure, designed here simply to get any laughs he can, but we should not dismiss the effect of the presentation so quickly. Euelpides stands aside and apart from Peisetaerus' speech—and consequently the dramatic illusion he creates. Standing outside the dramatic space of persuasion, Euelpides can function as metatheatrical commentator. A key example of this is his comment at 479: Πάνυ τοίνυν χρὴ ῥύγχος βόσκειν σε τὸ λοιπόν. As Sommerstein notes, this must be addressed to the audience in the theatre, not to the birds themselves, since they already possess beaks: in this ironic fashion, Euelpides is inviting the audience to join the bird city which Peisetaerus is proposing—an invitation which will become much more explicit later on. When Peisetaerus tried to use the birds on kings' scepters as part of his proof for their lost kingship, it is Euelpides who plants this firmly in a theatrical context: he has seen this in tragedies (Πρίαμός τις ἔχων ὄρνιν ἐν τοῖσι τραγῳδοῖς, 512). Other ironies or slips in logic go unremarked: a proof of the birds' divinity is that one can still swear by a bird, not a god, but the example is Lampon, who swears *in order to deceive* (Λάμπων δ' ὄμνυσ' ἔτι καὶ νυνὶ τὸν χῆν', ὅταν ἐξαπατᾷ τι, 521). Peisetaerus' speech so overwhelms them that they wish to become his slaves.[21]

Only then does he finally make his concrete suggestion: build a great, walled city. Once again, the languages of the theatre and oratory converge as Peisetaerus teaches the chorus: Καὶ δὴ τοίνυν πρῶτα διδάσκω μίαν ὀρνίθων πόλιν εἶναι, 550. Peisetaerus outlines the operations of the birds' power sharing with the gods in great detail (554ff.). So enraptured with his words are the birds that they swear to join him in a just, forthright, and holy attack on the gods (δίκαιος ἄδολος ὅσιος ἐπὶ θεοὺς ἴῃς, 632)! Only after his persuasion has succeeded does Peisetaerus reveal his own significant name (644).

Much has been written about the motif of Eros in this play, especially about the parabatic anapaests beginning at 685.[22] Whether great poetry or not,[23] in performance it must have been ravishing—and that is the point. It means to entice the viewers just as lovers use gifts of birds to persuade their reluctant beloveds (703ff.).

It is after this passage that the invitation to the spectators to join the new bird city becomes explicit (753ff.). First that city is presented as an antinomia, in Konstan's terms, the place where normal moral categories are inverted. Most of these antinomian characteristics center around the fact that those who cannot be citizens in Athens (slaves, foreigners, and traitors) will be welcomed as citizens here. Then it is presented as the city of excess or megalonomy to use Konstan's term.[24] It is the source of wings that allow one to escape human limitations. In a superb parody of the common tragic choral theme of "I wish I were a bird and could fly away from here," the chorus now describes how wings would allow the *spectators* to fly away from the boring performances of tragedy (πεινῶν τοῖς χοροῖσι τῶν τραγῳδῶν ἤχθετο, 787), either for food or for sex with some woman whose husband is still stuck in the theatre! The performance of tragedy, not the tragic situation itself, becomes the prison and comedy the world of escape.

Peisetaerus and Euelpides return wearing their newly acquired wings to inaugurate the new city. Like any new city (e.g., a colony), it needs a name and a divine patron. Only one name, Sparta, is proposed and rejected (814) before they settle on Nephelokokkugia, and only one goddess, Athena Polias (828), who is rejected (in tragic parody) on the rather feeble grounds that a female deity cannot protect the city well enough. Instead they choose a bird, and Euelpides is immediately dispatched to begin the great wall around the city. In the most economical way possible, then, Aristophanes has assured his audience that his fantasy city is not a Spartan-sympathizer's construct and also (more disingenuously) that the city is not a satire on Athens.

What Nephelokokkugia remains, most obviously, is a city of performance, as Peisetaerus proceeds to demonstrate. He organizes a πομπή (849) and sacrifice in honor of the new avine gods—and includes a metatheatrical joke about the piper (858–61), reminding us or perhaps reassuring us that this is only a representation of a religious ceremony.[25] Even that representation is never completed, since Peisetaerus first interrupts himself, turning on the priest for inviting too many and too rapacious birds to the sacrifice and taking over the ceremony, and then is in turn interrupted by the first of the usual series of *alazones* or impostors, all seeking wings.

Wings in the play function as markers of self-conscious theatricality. While Peisetaerus and Euelpides have acquired their wings through a magic herb, Peisetaerus can now disburse wings to would-be Nephelokokkugians from baskets—that is, as costumes or stage properties. Finally, wings can be bestowed simply by words, whether by Peisetaerus' original persuasion of the chorus to join his performance (λόγων ἀνεπτέρωμαι, 433) or sarcastically, as he drives the informer away (1436ff.).

The first seeker after wings is a poet, continually (mis)quoting Homer and himself a teacher of choruses (912)—and therefore potentially a competitor for Peisetaerus. Perhaps for this reason he comes off reasonably well in the encounter, successfully wheedling some clothes from Peisetaerus.

The next *alazōn* receives much harsher treatment. He is a χρησμολόγος (960), an oracle seller, a type of pest particularly prevalent in Athens as the war dragged on.[26] The most curious feature of his encounter with Peisetaerus is that it turns into a struggle between two textualities, between the oracle seller's *written* collection of prophecies and another book that Peisetaerus suddenly produces. Structurally, the joke works as a running gag: the oracle seller reads an outrageous prophecy, Peisetaerus objects, and the oracle seller replies simply "read the book" (Λαβὲ τὸ βιβλίον, 974ff.). Peisetaerus produces his *own* written authority for hitting the oracle seller and, when questioned, replies Λαβὲ τὸ βιβλίον, hitting him with the book or scroll at the same time. On one level this is Three Stooges–style physical comedy, turning on a simple slippage in the meaning of Λαβὲ between "take (and read)" and "take that!" On another, one wonders what the audience thought when Peisetaerus pulled out his own scroll. Is this Harpo Marx, able to produce a burning blowtorch from his overcoat pocket when he needs one, or might the audience see Peisetaerus' scroll as something more—perhaps even his script?[27]

Meton the surveyor, an unnamed inspector, and a decree seller all receive equally unceremonious treatment. We might pause a moment to consider the choice of Meton. His entrance is welcomed by Peisetaerus in a line now corrupt (994): Τίς ἡπίνοια † τίς ὁ κόθορνος † τῆς ὁδοῦ, "what is the purpose, what the buskin of your journey?" Sommerstein proposes Τίς ἡπίνοια τῆς κοθορνωτῆς

τῆς ὁδοῦ, "what is the purpose of your buskined journey," but notes that the form κοθορνωτῆς is in fact unattested in Greek. In any case, the fact of an allusion to his footgear seems clear, though its purpose is obscure. Sommerstein sees a general allusion to effeminacy, but some allusion to tragedy, where the *kothornos* was standard acting equipment, seems likelier—and yet what would a contemporary character have to do with tragedy?[28] And why, if the power of the birds' city relies precisely in creating boundaries and enclosure where such did not exist before, would a surveyor be chosen as a particular enemy? Perhaps because he would potentially create boundaries and therefore divisions *within* the city. Konstan emphasizes the curious nature of the bird city, which, while marked off from the rest of the universe by its boundary wall, nonetheless retains its "precivic" homogeneity of the populace.[29] Unlike the quarrelsome Athenians, the birds think and will one thing, unanimously. Note the revealing exchange between Meton and Peisetaerus:

Pei.   Ὥσπερ ἐν Λακεδαίμονι
ξενηλατοῦνται καὶ κεκίνηνταί τινες.
Πληγαὶ συχναὶ κατ' ἄστυ.
Me.   Μῶν στασιάζετε;
Pei.   Μὰ τὸν Δί' οὐ δῆτ'.
Me.   Ἀλλὰ πῶς;
Pei.   Ὁμοθυμαδὸν
σποδεῖν ἄπαντας τοὺς ἀλαζόνας δοκεῖ.

(1012–18)

Peisetaerus warns Meton of possible violence against him. Is there a revolution (στασιάζετε) brewing, Meton asks. No, there is a unanimous desire to get rid of frauds and shysters (ἀλαζόνας).[30]

Peisetaerus gives up his attempt to conduct the sacrifice onstage and carries it back into the skene (1057), leaving the chorus to perform the city in another way. The chorus now explicitly incorporates an element of the Dionysiac festival outside the play *within* its own performance and thereby seems to reach out and absorb the festival within itself. The City Dionysia, a major event at which the city displayed itself to the whole Greek world, contained much more than just the performance of the plays and choruses. In addition to the sacrifices, displays of tribute, and parade of orphans (well discussed by Goldhill),[31] there were also public proclamations. What we know of these suggests that decrees of public honors were more common,[32] but on the evidence of the following passage decrees of rewards for the punishment of state enemies were also included:

Τῆδε μέντοι θἠμέρᾳ μάλιστ᾽ ἐπαναγορεύεται·
"'Ην ἀποκτείνῃ τις ὑμῶν Διαγόραν τὸν Μήλιον,
λαμβάνειν τάλαντον, ἤν τε τῶν τυράννων τίς τινα
τῶν τεθνηκότων ἀποκτείνῃ, τάλαντον λαμβάνειν."
Βουλόμεσθ᾽ οὖν νῦν ἀνειπεῖν ταῦτα χἠμεῖς ἐνθάδε·
"'Ην ἀποκτείνῃ τις ὑμῶν Φιλοκράτη τὸν Στρούθιον,
λήψεται τάλαντον, ἢν δὲ ζῶντ᾽ ἀπαγάγῃ, τέτταρα,"

(1072–78)

The birds are in effect hijacking the Dionysia; it is *their* city which, in addition to rewarding tyrant slayers[33] will also offer a bounty for the punishment of a cruel bird seller. The city of Nephelokokkugia, at first a space limited by the very boundaries of the theatre stage, defended by one soldier with a pot for a helmet against the chorus, now has grown so large that it swallows up the mere Athenian festival within itself.

Next the chorus makes an attempt in character to bribe the judges, a piece of business which should be jocular, but one element seems less than light-hearted. In addition to promising the "owls of Laureion" (i.e., drachmas, 1106) and good luck, it promises the judges assistance in political peculation, in plundering from the demos when they happen to be allotted office (1111ff.). This seems less benign, perhaps even reminiscent of the chorus in *Clouds*, tempting the hearers with something they ought not to want. Since the chorus turns immediately to threatening the judges with bird droppings, the point may slip by unnoticed by many, but the chorus has been encouraging the judges to fail in their duty to the demos.

A messenger arrives to recount the astonishing story of the building of the wall, a tour de force of fantasy—which Peisetaerus labels lying (ψεύδεσιν, 1167). Hot on his heels enters another messenger[34] with the news that the walls have already been breached by one of the gods.

Heralded by a sound, which is as likely to be the creaking of the *mechanê* as it is music imitative of rushing wings,[35] Iris swings into view suspended from the crane. Here is an emphatically theatrical (and of course tragic) invasion of the theatre space, showing us once more that the real location of Nephelokokkugia is the stage, the space beneath the theologeion. One wonders if the pun is intended when Iris complains of Peisetaerus' behavior, Ἄτοπόν γε τουτὶ πρᾶγμα (1208). The business seems extraordinary (ἄτοπόν) to Iris, precisely because she fails to recognize that there is a place now, a *topos*, where there was no place, no city before.[36] Nor should we miss the visual comedy of the arrested flight: one imagines that after years of practice the crane operator was capable of quite elegant effects in flying the gods (cf. the Foys in productions of *Peter*

Pan), but once arrested in her flight Iris will dangle there quite obviously an actor on a rope.[37] Peisetaerus charges her with a border violation, not merely for flying through the city but through chaos as well (διὰ τῆς πόλεως τῆς ἀλλοτρίας καὶ τοῦ χάους, 1218), not only reminding us of the great ode on the origin of Love from chaos but also suggesting that the city and chaos, the newly bounded space built in the essence of unboundedness, are one and the same. Threatening this immortal with death and defying the usual divine bluster,[38] Peisetaerus finally sends her back the way she came with a few threats of sexual violence to hasten her on her way.

A herald arrives from earth with the news that the riffraff of humanity (1280ff., those who took Sparta and Socrates as their models before) are now eager to become colonists (ἐποίκοις, 1307, a word suggestive of imperialism)[39] in Nephelokokkugia. The bird chorus is now so besotted with Peisetaerus' vision that it does not detect the irony in its own statement that the city will now become πολυάνορα (1313; cf. καλὸν ἀνδρὶ μετοικεῖν, 1319). The city of the birds is losing its avian identity.

It remains a comic city, however, for while the chorus sings of the graces and wisdom that dwell within it, Peisetaerus is berating and abusing his slave Manes in typical comic fashion for being slow in bringing out the wings he will distribute to the new, would-be colonists. A young man who desires to beat up his father learns from Peisetaerus that he *can* do that here (the antinomian theme) but finds he will still have to support his father and so prefers to fly off to front-line service in Thrace (almost as good a way of getting away from paternal control). The reception accorded Kinesias the dithyrambic poet, in search of ethereal inspiration, is much less cordial, not to say violent, and one wonders why: perhaps because as a κυκλιοδιδάσκαλος (1403) he represents competition for Peisetaerus the *chorodidaskalos*,[40] and so must be sent on his way with a blow or two.

The climax of this particular series is represented by an informer (συκο-φάντης, 1423) seeking after wings, who instead is sent flying like a top with a whipping from Peisetaerus. Just before that, however, in a passage of consider-able significance in this play about words, Peisetaerus says he will give him wings through speaking, Νῦν τοι λέγων πτερῶ σε (1437), a turn of phrase which puzzles the informer. Peisetaerus explains through the analogies of a young man enticed into hoping for a career as a chariot driver through speech and another whose mind is enthralled by tragedy. We are in danger of losing the point here, because the analogies do no justice to the radical conception Peisetaerus has proposed. He claims that his language is "performative" lan-guage,[41] and in doing so he literalizes metaphor in a typically Aristophanic fashion: he has been creating citizens for the bird city by language, and the city is a city of language. The chorus's invitation to the audience to join the city (discussed above, on lines 753ff.) similarly offers to transform father beaters and slaves into birds by renaming them.

After the informer's flagellant dismissal, the chorus once again takes metaphorical flight. The opening lines seem very general:[42]

> Chor.   Πολλὰ δὴ καὶ καινὰ καὶ θαυ-
> μάστ' ἐπεπτόμεσθα καὶ
> δεινὰ πράγματ' εἴδομεν.
>
> (1470–72)

Though he makes no explicit mention of it, Sommerstein's translation of these lines:

> Many and unheard-of and marvelous
> are the places we have overflown, and
> strange the things we have seen.

captures the parody here (first noticed by Moulton)[43] of perhaps the most famous chorus in all of Sophocles, that from *Antigone* which begins:

> Chor.   Πολλὰ τὰ δεινὰ κοὐδὲν ἀν-
> θρώπου δεινότερον πέλει·
>
> (332–33)

The resemblances are few but nonetheless pointed: the same word to begin, and δεινά somewhere further along. The antistrophe in Sophocles does go on to speak of man's dominance over the race of birds (φῦλον ὀρνίθων, 342–43), and perhaps we should count this as a further resemblance. Parody of Sophoclean style it is not—but subversive use of Sophocles' ideas it may be. Has Peisetaerus so ensnared the birds in the noose of words (to steal a phrase from Barbara Goff) that what they present as proof of their power and freedom, an ode on what they have seen flying over the vast world, becomes another demonstration of their subordination to man?

Prometheus now appears, comically muffled up and carrying a parasol. And why? So that the gods will not see him *from above* (ἄνωθεν ὡς ἂν μή μ' ὁρῶσιν οἱ θεοί, 1509).[44] As often in Aristophanes, we are in danger of taking this as natural and obvious when for the Greeks it may have been no such thing. Did the Greeks think the gods could only see them from above? Perhaps children literalized the process in this way, but this is surely a joke for adults.[45] In the theatre, of course, the gods *can* only see from above, since they stand on the theologeion or swing from the crane. The unnecessary emphasis on the spatial dimension here, I suggest, is another reminder that the city is the stage, a platform poised not between heaven and earth but between theologeion and orchestra. Here and only here is Prometheus' parasol a very good defense against snooping gods.

Mythologically Prometheus is a natural ally for subordinates (men or birds) turning on the gods.[46] He not only counsels Peisetaerus to demand Zeus's scepter but also Basileia for his wife, since she is the keeper (ταμιεύει, 1538) of his powers. Prometheus expresses his hatred for the gods and further labels himself a Timon. One wonders if this is a theatrical reference too, for the character was already proverbial in Aristophanes' time (though the scholiasts thought he was historical), and the name turns up as a play title later.[47]

After a very short choral interlude Poseidon appears, accompanied by the dim-witted Heracles and a Triballian god from "up-country," incapable of speaking clear Greek. The scene is broadly comic, turning mostly on the voracious appetite of Heracles and the thick-headedness of the Triballian. The scene has a political agenda nonetheless. First of all, Poseidon laments that democracy has put such gods as the Triballian into office (Ὦ δημοκρατία, ποῖ προβιβᾷς ἡμᾶς ποτε, εἰ τουτονὶ κεχειροτονήκασ' οἱ θεοί; 1570–71). Then we learn that the magnificent feast Peisetaerus is cooking up is (now that he himself has acquired wings, which he continues to wear) a cannibalistic one:

Her.   Τὰ δὲ κρέα τοῦ ταῦτ' ἐστίν;
Pei.   Ὄρνιθές τινες
       ἐπανιστάμενοι τοῖς δημοτικοῖσιν ὀρνέοις
       ἔδοξαν ἀδικεῖν.

(1582–85)

Divine democracy is represented by a glutton and a dolt, while bird democracy devours its own. It is hard to claim we have come very far from Athens after all.

Poseidon does his best to argue the case for the gods, despite his easily distracted companions, but he is hardly the ideal diplomat. He makes a serious faux pas in claiming that the gods will provide "halcyon days" (ἀλκυονίδας ... ἡμέρας, 1594), one thing they are surely capable of providing for themselves.[48] In short order Peisetaerus has reversed the situation, offering the birds' help to the gods (1606ff.) and, true to his name, persuading them to hand over Zeus's scepter.

Peisetaerus' demand for Basileia, however, produced only now when agreement seems at hand, is too much for Poseidon, who then tries to break off negotiations. Heracles, intent mainly on his dinner, is for peace at any price. When Poseidon tries to win him back, claiming that Heracles will be giving up his own expected inheritance from Zeus, the discussion demonstrates that Olympus is just one more version of Athens,[49] for Peisetaerus triumphantly demonstrates that Heracles is a bastard (νόθος, 1650) under Athenian law and therefore not entitled to inherit his father's property.[50] With no property interest in Zeus's continued rule, Heracles is more than willing to hand over sovereignty to the birds. Heracles browbeats the Triballian into agreement, Poseidon is outvoted, and Peisetaerus goes off to receive the scepter of Zeus and Basileia.

The finale, as Peisetaerus returns with his prizes and then dances off to his wedding to Basileia, is so splendid both visually and verbally that it seems almost impossible to question the "happiness" of this ending. Only the faint echo of the thunder machine (the *bronteion*), if indeed it sounds at 1751,[51] seems to mock such an interpretation, coming as it does from the world of tragedy, not that of comedy, and therefore once again reminding us of the status of the performance as performance.

Aristophanes' critique of spectator politics has grown much subtler (perhaps of necessity) in the years since he wrote *Acharnians* as a brash young newcomer to the comic stage. In the war fever that swept Athens with the sailing of the Sicilian expedition, it was not advisable to speak too openly of the democracy's follies. I must confess that I cannot be sure even for myself that the metatheatrical touches of this play mean clearly that Aristophanes saw the new development in the conduct of the war as a dangerous delusion, an *apatē*, as he clearly had seen Cleon and Cleon's policies. If the bird city is indeed monstrous, it is monstrous in ways that Aristophanes knew would not trouble most of his fellow citizens, and there are many pleasures (of language and otherwise) associated with this escape from the confines of besieged, imperial Athens. The bird city, built in a theatre, becomes therefore a model of Aristophanes' own art. As long as he believed in the comedy that he practiced, he could not make his theatrical city a place of misery. Did he then defeat his own purpose?

I hope I will be forgiven a modern analogy in closing. In Preston Sturges's brilliant film comedy, *Sullivan's Travels*, the eponymous hero, a filmmaker famous for his musical comedies during the Depression years, decides he must make socially relevant films instead and goes off to find that social relevance in America's underclass. Having experienced suffering even to the extent of being sentenced to a chain gang, the hero discovers, while watching a cartoon with his fellow prisoners, that comedy and the joy of laughter are gifts too precious ever to discard. The analogy is flawed in many ways: Aristophanes could not have written serious plays about the war, even if he had wanted to, because there was no serious, nonmythological medium in which to work. I think, though, that Aristophanes was a comic artist great enough to know, just as Sturges did, that even when there are serious points to be made, the artist does not abandon comedy's power not only to make us laugh but to console us with a vision of a better life. Neither Peisetaerus nor his play can be reduced to a statement for or against the war, but together they count its costs, both in suffering and to the idea of democracy itself, even as they celebrate the improvisatory powers of the comic hero.

Notes

1. Konstan 1990 (and his essay in this volume).

2. I shall avoid for the moment the question of how high the stage was raised above the orchestra in this period. It need tower like a cliff only in the imagination of performers and audience. Cf. the use of the stage front as a wall under which to hide the male overgarments of the chorus in *Ecclesiazusae* 497, πρὸς τὸ τειχίον. I have argued in Slater 1988 that the *Ecclesiazusae* passage refers to the front edge of the stage and is therefore an indication that the stage of this period was sufficiently raised and cut off from the orchestra to function as a wall.

3. Dobrov 1993, 210. In his published version, Dobrov suggests that the transformation may have been only partly illustrated, by a change in headdress or otherwise, while I would prefer to see a complete costume change.

4. A new play by Frank Manley, *The Evidence*, offers an interesting parallel, though I should emphasize that the idea about Tereus in *Birds* occurred to me before seeing this modern production. Manley's play deals with a man who thinks he has seen a sasquatch. Although a powerful meditation on the dimensions of experience and sanity, the play was weakened by a final tableau in which the back-lit figure of the sasquatch was seen by the audience. The reality did not look otherwise: it simply looked like a man in a gorilla suit.

5. On secondhand trade in costumes, see Slater 1993, 405 and n. 18.

6. Illustrated in Green 1985 (the original publication) and as the frontispiece to Sommerstein's *Birds* edition. Taplin 1987 argued these birds were rather the Logoi from *Clouds*, and Csapo 1993 also doubts they are choristers from *Birds*.

7. They are not jurors (ἡλιασταί), but people characterized by staying away from juries: ἀπηλιαστά, 110, an Aristophanic coinage. Konstan 1990, 190–92 (and in his essay above) defines four kinds of utopias based on their treatment of *nomoi*: here we have the antinomian strain in *Birds*, but it slides easily into the "megalonomian" as well when Peisetaerus and Euelpides begin to describe the fantasy elements of the place they seek: i.e., the "troubles" there are the result of having too many sensual joys (128ff.).

8. The key adjective describing them is κεχηνότες, 165, in which one may hear an echo of Aristophanes' wonderful comic coinage describing the Athenians at the end of *Acharnians*: χαυνοπολίτας (635) or Open-Mouthenians, as Alan Sommerstein 1987 so aptly translates. Peisetaerus will succeed in establishing the bird city precisely because the birds are as gullible as the Athenians. Note also Euelpides' description of his own actions in line 264: Καίτοι κέχηνά γ' εἰς τὸν οὐρανὸν βλέπων.

9. Konstan 1990, 9.

10. Arrowsmith 1973 already saw issues of boundedness versus unboundedness underlying this play. A neglected aspect of his article argues, based on the work of John Fine on boundary stones in Attica, that the alienability of property was a relatively new and revolutionary development in Athenian society of the fifth century. Fine's belief that commerce in (as opposed to inheritability of) property was not possible in Athens until the fifth century has not been widely accepted. Nonetheless, Arrowsmith's discussion of the issue brings out certain important elements. The process of defining boundaries made commerce in land possible. The clash of traditional concepts of land-holding with new, commercial notions is still very much alive in the fifth century and energizes the jokes here in *Birds*. I am reminded of a passage in W. S. Gilbert's

Patience, where the poet Bunthorne remarks: "What's the use of yearning for Elysian Fields when you know you can't get 'em and would only let 'em out on building leases if you had 'em?" Peisetaerus, of course, wants to have his Elysian fields and lease them out, too.

11. Sommerstein 1987, apparently unconsciously, anticipates this reading of the space, for he chooses to translate πόλος as stage (and πόλις as state, for an equivalent pun).

12. See Dobrov 1993, 190, 226, and also Dobrov's essay below.

13. Cf. note 8 above (on gaping). The second bird chorister is greeted with parodies of both a line in Sophocles (175, the *Tyro*, fr. 654) and of a line in Aeschylus' *Edonians* (the beginning of 176 parallels fr. 60 = 75 M, quoted in the scholion). On this play, see Sutton 1971. One would very much like to know if there was a visual as well as verbal parody and whether a revival of *Edonians* figured in the joke, but we simply do not know.

14. This explicit mention is a little puzzling, for it does not seem a very strong joke here. Compare the much funnier moment in *Clouds* 326, where the Cloud chorus is pointed out to Strepsiades:

Strep. τί τὸ χρῆμα;
       ὡς οὐ καθορῶ.
Soc. παρὰ τὴν εἴσοδον.

Incidentally we might note that apparently the birds use only one parodos for their entrance, as did the clouds in their play. One wonders if this was standard procedure.

15. Is there a further dramatic, specifically tragic parody here? On the relation between tragic dancing and military drills, see Winkler 1990, 50–58. Tragic dance was rectangular, as opposed to dithyramb's "circular choruses." A key text that Winkler cites on the the connection between tragic dance and military training is Chamaileon fr. 42 Wehrli [= Athen. 14.268e–f]. On the other hand, the taxiarch was a leader of a *tribal* unit of Athenians troops, and drama's *lack* of a tribal basis (unique among the other Athenian musical competitions) is remarkable. Winkler 1985, 45–46, took this nontribal nature of the tragic chorus to be one of its most significant features (cf. also note 40 below), linking it to Peisistratid reforms of the Panathenaia, a claim he seems to back away from in Winkler 1990. Whatever the origin of this nontribal organization, it remains a significant element.

16. Note that their city already has a public burial ground, and it is the Athenian Kerameikos, an important indication that the anticity is after all Athens itself (395–99).

17. They also wonder about Peisetaerus' motivation: what will *he* get out of it?

Ὁρᾷ τι κέρδος ἐνθάδ' ἄ-
ξιον μονῆς, ὅτῳ πέποιθ'
ἐμοὶ ξυνὼν
κρατεῖν ἂν ἢ τὸν ἐχθρὸν ἢ
φίλοισιν ὠφελεῖν ἔχειν;

For a thorough discussion of this conception of morality and friendship in popular thought, see Blundell 1989, esp. 26–59.

18. The formulation suggests that the vote of the judges (ten picked by lot) occasionally went against the clear demonstration of popular opinion in the theatre. It is tempting to think that there might be a glancing parody of the voting procedure in *Eumenides* here, but we cannot point to a specific Aeschylean revival.

19. It is perhaps pushing a point, but Peisetaerus specifies that new call-up notices will be posted on the πινακίοις, 450, which Sommerstein takes to be the notice boards near the Eponymous Heroes in Athens. But Nephelokokkugia both is and is not Athens: it is the theatrical city as well as the real one, and in this context πινακίοις might well be taken to mean the theatrical backdrop, the changeable scenery in the theatre itself.

20. Sommerstein 1987 notes at 464 that wearing a crown in order to give a speech is otherwise unattested, so Aristophanes' foreshadowing of the feast here may be quite deliberate.

21. At 546–47 the birds say Ἀναθεὶς γὰρ ἐγώ σοι τὰ νεόττια κἀμαυτὸν οἰκετεύσω. To become

part of Peisetaerus' household (οἰκετεύσω) is by no means a power-neutral act: there was no equality in the Greek household. To enroll themselves in his household then is to become his *slaves*—and arguably they do so in the course of the play. One must note that the point here turns on an emendation by Hermann, accepted by Sommerstein, of οἰκετεύσω for the manuscripts' οἰκήσω or οἰκίσω.

22. See esp. Arrowsmith 1973.

23. Silk 1980 is a wide-ranging attack on Aristophanes as a "serious" lyricist. After pillorying Aristophanes for his paucity of "pressure" and "pointedness," as though he and Pindar were writing for the same audience, Silk eventually makes some useful points about the function of the lyrics in context. He buries his disparagement of this particular lyric moment (685ff.) in a footnote *praeteritio* (p. 105 n. 24), quite ignoring Arrowsmith 1973. Perkell 1993 is a vigorous defense of Aristophanes as a lyricist, employing, however, the strategy of separating the Birds and their songs sharply from the characters and events surrounding them.

24. Konstan 1990, 6.

25. Animal sacrifices, just like representations of human violence, do not take place on stage, though in comedy this can be turned into a joke about saving the choregos the expense of a sheep. This is surely not squeamishness so much as some sense of religious reverence, just as, until recently, plays and films in the English-language tradition did not represent God or Christ directly.

26. Smith 1989 has an excellent discussion of the corruption of political discourse Aristophanes saw in the use of oracles at this period.

27. I refer to the scene in the office of the Sylvanian ambassador in *Duck Soup*. On the function of the book in this scene of *Birds*, see further Slater 1996, 101–3.

28. Sommerstein 1987 at 998 notes that Meton seems to have been the donor of a sundial in Kolonos (cf. Philochoros 328 F 122), which explains the otherwise curious joke ὃν οἶδεν Ἑλλὰς χὠ Κολωνός.

29. Konstan 1990, 14.

30. Zimmermann 1993a, esp. 267–75, discusses the scenes with Meton and Kinesias (see below) as examples of Aristophanes' treatment of intellectuals, emphasizing that they are treated more as types than individuals, but also as representatives of those who tend to divide the city.

31. Goldhill 1990. An earlier version appeared in *JHS* 107 (1987) 58– 76.

32. Cf. Pickard-Cambridge 1988, 59, 67.

33. This passage itself is the only evidence for the reading out of such a decree about tyranny at the Dionysia. Sommerstein 1987 accepts it, perhaps too uncritically, as evidence for a practice reaching back to the beginning of the democracy. Given the renewed demagoguery about tyranny in the years preceding this play, which Sommerstein notes (cf. *Wasps* 417, 463– 507; *Lys.* 618– 35), one wonders if the decree was not a more recent innovation within the festival in response to the same demagogic agitation. Another, here decidedly peripheral but nonetheless interesting, issue is raised by the emphatic Τῇδε . . . θἠμέρα. The obvious meaning of this is that the performance of *Birds* takes place on the same day as the proclamation. As honorary decrees were read out on day one of the festival (cf. Pickard-Cambridge 1988, 59, 67), one assumes that such decrees of punishment were read at the same time; certainly there is no other logical point in the festival program for them. Therefore *Birds* was performed on day one of the City Dionysia in 414. This is therefore further evidence in favor of the traditional view that the City Dionysia was shortened to three days of performances (with only three comedies competing) during the war years and against the ingenious argument of Luppe 1972 that there was no restriction, for in its full form, the City Dionysia played all five comedies on *one* day, *after* the three days of tragedies. Luppe discusses (1972, 72–73) the passage at *Birds* 785–96, which is usually taken as proof that comedy was done in the afternoon after tragedy. Luppe says no, that 789, ἐφ' ἡμᾶς, means simply "back to us here in the theatre," not "back to the comedy." Here he relies on the scholion, which reads ἐπὶ τὸ θέατρον—but this is not the point of this phrase, which is rather a notation that the line is metatheatrical, a reference to the actual conditions of performance. Line 1072 is also

incidentally further evidence that the text of plays could be altered up until very shortly before performance, since this statement could not have been made until Aristophanes had been allotted a performance time on that first day.

34. Sommerstein 1987 ad loc. notes the metatheatricality of the verb for his appearance, εἰσθεῖ πρὸς ἡμᾶς δεῦρο, 1169, which means "enter" in the sense of "come on stage." He takes πυρρίχην in the same line in its primary sense of "war dance," interpreting it in light of the coming confrontation with the gods. We might also note, though, that the πυρρίχη (see Winkler 1990, 55–57) is closely associated with tragic dance as well: coupled with the verb εἰσθεῖ, it suggests that this messenger, not unlike the one before him, is a refugee from the tragic stage.

35. Line 1196 is a dimeter instead of the expected trimeter. Sommerstein 1987 ad loc. suggests connecting it with the music effect for the sound of her wings, but φθόγγος, 1198, can equally well be a discordant sound.

36. I would dearly love for Peisetaerus' comment on her at 1211, εἰρωνεύεται, to be equally self-conscious, but there is no evidence that the fifth century thought of this as a technical term, "to play the *eiron*."

37. See Mastronarde 1990, esp. 287.

38. There is a significant parody here, too. Peisetaerus asks Iris to whom she thinks she is speaking, πότερα Λυδὸν ἢ Φρύγα (1244), reminding us of the beginning of Pheres' speech to his son in *Alcestis*, ὦ παῖ, τίν' αὐχεῖς, πότερα Λυδὸν ἢ Φρύγα (675). It must have been quite a famous speech to be worth parodying nearly a quarter century after *Alcestis* first played in Athens (438 B.C.). Even more interesting is the implication: "do you think you're talking to a *barbarian*? No, you're speaking to a Greek." Peisetaerus does not now speak for birds who are fundamentally different from humanity, but for birds who, thanks to Tereus' teaching (Ἐγὼ γὰρ αὐτοὺς βαρβάρους ὄντας πρὸ τοῦ / ἐδίδαξα τὴν φωνήν, 199–200), have become speakers of Greek and therefore, as antiquity measured it, Greeks.

39. LSJ give as the second meaning for the verb ἐποικέω "to be settled with hostile views against" and cite Thuc. 6.86. These are carpetbaggers, not philosophical enthusiasts.

40. There is a possible relation to Konstan's theme of the unity of the birds. The dithyrambic competition, for which Kinesias' services are fought over (ὃς ταῖσι φυλαῖς περιμάχητός εἰμ' ἀεί, 1404), was tribal: it *fostered* rivalry among divisions of the citizen body, whereas comedy (before the fourth century: Arist. *Ath. Pol.* 56.3) and tragedy were the only nontribal *agones* at the festivals. Cf. note 15 above and Winkler 1985, 45: "[T]ragedy seems never to have been organized as a competition by tribe or by naucrary or by any other subgrouping of the polis. It was from the first a celebration of the polis as a whole (here we slide over into interpretation) and not of its constituent parts." Certainly there is also criticism of contemporary dithyramb, too: see Zimmermann 1993b.

41. The concept of performative language was introduced by Austin and Searle (see in particular Searle 1969 and Austin 1962) in contradistinction to constative, or simply descriptive, language. Performative language creates reality (typical examples are a judge's sentence upon an offender, a ritual curse, ordination, or a marriage ceremony). For a valuable discussion of these topics in relation to the example of *Coriolanus*, see Fish 1980, 197–245. Philosophically the distinction collapses rather quickly, because *all* language is ultimately performative, informing observed reality with structures generated by the human mind ("man," "woman," and "child" are all imposed constructs, not pure descriptions, for example). The term still has some use, since what Austin and Searle began by defining as performative utterances usually call attention to their performance or are produced within strongly marked frames. Peisetaerus here calls attention explicitly to the performative power of his own language, and we need to ask why.

42. Silk 1980, 125, predictably hears only "topical satire" here. For a much more sensitive appreciation of the poetry of the passage, see Moulton 1981, 28–46, especially for the wonderful image of the Cleonymus-tree. Rau 1967 makes no mention of possible parody.

43. Moulton 1981, 34, who also compares *Birds* 451–52.

44. The word ἄνωθεν is later repeated in contexts where it appears to mean "from up-country," as Sommerstein translates it (e.g., 1522, 1526), but nothing activates this meaning at 1509, and it clearly once again means from above vertically at 1551, when Prometheus once again worries about Zeus seeing him. The word also occurs at 844, in relation to the birds' relation to man.

45. Cf. Ko-Ko and Pooh-Bah discussing the financing of the former's wedding in Gilbert and Sullivan's *The Mikado*:

Ko.   But you said just now "Don't stint yourself, do it well."
Pooh.   As Private Secretary.
Ko.   And now you say that due economy must be observed.
Pooh.   As Chancellor of the Exchequer.
Ko.   I see. Come over here, where the Chancellor can't hear us.

46. On his role in *Birds*, see esp. Rau 1967, 175–77.

47. Antiphanes fr. 204 K.-A.; cf. Plato com. fr. 237 K.-A. See Sommerstein 1987 at 1549. Phrynichus was in fact competing against Aristophanes at this very festival with his play *The Hermit*, whose title character was very similar, as his fr. 19 K.-A. shows: ὄνομα δὲ μοῦστι Μονότροπος / ζῶ δὲ Τίμωνος βίον. . . . We cannot speculate what made Timon so topical in 414.

48. See Sommerstein 1987 ad loc. on the halcyon.

49. In light of the use of the theme of *apatē* elsewhere in Aristophanes (see esp. Slater 1993), the two competitors' terms for each others' activities are of interest here. Poseidon warns Heracles against Peisetaerus' deceptive speech (ἐξαπατώμενος, 1641), while Peisetaerus, the consummate demagogic politician, accuses his opponent Poseidon of sophistry (περισοφίζεται, 1646). The echo of sophistic debates about the origin of the Trojan War and Helen's responsibility or innocence in line 1639 (Ἡμεῖς περὶ γυναικὸς μιᾶς πολεμήσομεν;) encourages us to read this in the light of contemporary sophism.

50. Patterson 1990 is the best and most recent treatment of the νόθος in Athenian law and society. She does take Peisetaerus' citation of Solon in lines 1661–66 as generally accurate (51), although given what we know of Peisetaerus' methods of argument, there is ample room for doubt.

51. See Sommerstein 1987 ad loc. on the force of νῦν in this line. Its use is not definitely proven for the fifth-century theatre, although Sommerstein cites *Clouds* 292 (ἤσθου φωνῆς ἄμα καὶ βροντῆς) and Sophocles *OC* 1456ff. as parallels.

Bibliography

Arrowsmith, William. 1973. "Aristophanes' *Birds*: The Fantasy Politics of Eros." *Arion*, n.s., 1.1.119–67.

Austin, J. L. 1962. *How to Do Things with Words*. Oxford.

Blundell, Mary Whitlock. 1989. *Helping Friends and Harming Enemies*. Cambridge.

Csapo, Eric. 1993. "Deep Ambivalence: Notes on a Greek Cockfight." *Phoenix* 47.1–28, pls. 1–4; 115–24.

Dobrov, Gregory. 1993. "The Tragic and the Comic Tereus." *AJP* 114.2.189–234.

Fish, Stanley. 1980. *Is There a Text in This Class?* Cambridge, Mass.

Goldhill, Simon. 1990. "The Great Dionysia and Civic Ideology." In *Nothing to Do with Dionysos? Athenian Drama in Its Social Context*, edited by John J. Winkler and Froma I. Zeitlin, 97–129. Princeton.

Green, J. R. 1985. "A Representation of the *Birds* of Aristophanes." *Greek Vases in the J. Paul Getty Museum*, 2.95–118. Malibu.

Konstan, David. 1990. "A City in the Air: Aristophanes' *Birds*." *Arethusa* 23.183–207.

Luppe, W. 1972. "Die Zahl der Konkurrenten an den komischen Agonen zur Zeit des peloponnesischen Krieges." *Philologus* 116.53–75.

Mastronarde, D. J. 1990. "Actors on High: The Skene Roof, the Crane, and the Gods in Attic Drama." *CA* 9.247–94.

Moulton, Carroll. 1981. *Aristophanic Poetry*. Hypomnemata 68. Göttingen.

Patterson, Cynthia B. 1990. "Those Athenian Bastards." *CA* 9.40–73.

Perkell, Christine. 1993. "On the Two Voices of the Birds in *Birds*." *Ramus* 22.1–18.

Pickard-Cambridge, A. W. 1988. *The Dramatic Festivals of Athens*. 2d ed. Revised by J. Gould and D. M. Lewis, reissued with supplement and corrections. Oxford.

Rau, Peter. 1967. *Paratragodia: Untersuchung einer komischen Form des Aristophanes*. Zetemata 45. Munich.

Searle, John. 1969. *Speech Acts*. Cambridge.

Silk, Michael. 1980. "Aristophanes as a Lyric Poet." In *Aristophanes: Essays in Interpretation*, edited by Jeffrey Henderson. Yale Classical Studies 26. Cambridge.

Slater, Niall W. 1986. "The Lenaean Theatre." *ZPE* 66.255–64.

——. 1988. "The τειχίον of *Ecclesiazusae* 497." *Liverpool Classical Monthly* 13.105.

——. 1993. "Space, Character, and ΑΠΑΤΗ: Transformation and Transvaluation in the *Acharnians*." In *Tragedy, Comedy, and the Polis*, edited by Alan Sommerstein, Stephen Halliwell, Jeffrey Henderson, and Bernhard Zimmermann, 397–415. Papers from the Greek Drama Conference, Nottingham, 18–20 July 1990. Bari.

——. 1996. "Literacy and Old Comedy." In *Voice into Text: Orality and Literacy in Ancient Greece*, edited by Ian Worthington, 99–112. *Mnemosyne* Suppl. 157. Leiden.

Smith, Nicholas D. 1989. "Diviners and Divination in Aristophanic Comedy." *CA* 8.140–58.

Sommerstein, Alan. 1987. *The Comedies of Aristophanes*. Vol. 6: *Birds*. Warminster.

Sutton, Dana F. 1971. "Aeschylus' *Edonians*." In *Fons Perennis*, 387–411. Turin.

Taplin, Oliver. 1987. "Phallology, *Phlyakes*, Iconography and Aristophanes." *PCPS* 213, n.s., 33.92–104.

Winkler, John J. 1985. "The Ephebes' Song: *Tragōidia* and *Polis*." *Representations* 11:26–62.

——. 1990. "The Ephebes' Song: *Tragōidia* and *Polis*." In *Nothing to Do with Dionysos? Athenian Drama in Its Social Context*, edited by John J. Winkler and Froma I. Zeitlin, 20–62. Princeton.

Zimmermann, Bernhard. 1993a. "Aristophanes und die Intellectuellen." In *Aristophane*, edited by J. M. Bremer and E. W. Handley, 256–86. Geneva.

——. 1993b. "Comedy's Criticism of Music." *Drama* 2: *Intertextualität in der griechisch-römischen Komödie*. 1–13.

GREGORY W. DOBROV

ἐκ τοῦ "πόλου" τούτου
κεκλήσεται "πόλις"
—Aristophanes,
Birds 184

Language, Fiction, and Utopia

I   **U**topia, by definition, is a conundrum expressed vividly in the punning names of those most famous examples, Aristophanes' Cloudcuckooland and Samuel Butler's Erewhon. Popularly used of an idealized place or visionary scheme since its coinage by Thomas More nearly five hundred years ago, "utopia" (οὐ + τόπος) remains a token of hope undercut by futility.[1] The ancient comic polis in the air and More's fantastic island, after all, are "nowhere" and the designation of something as utopia(n) implies a degree of irreality or impossibility. The first two essays in this collection refine the vocabulary of utopian discourse by making important distinctions (e.g., Arcadian vs. utopian) and building on Eco's terms for parameters other than "place"—especially "nomos"—with operators beyond simple negation such as "eu-" and "anti-."[2] Indeed, for the purposes of appreciating the Other dimensions of fantastic literature, Greek comedy in particular, we are better served by considering the ways in which space, time, and society are represented as *different*: better, worse, or in the process of change. In this essay I focus on the linguistic and theatrical aspects of political invention in *Birds*—the discovery and foundation of Cloudcuckooland—that is precipitated by the abandonment of the polis in quest for a solution of its real and imagined ills. This metatopia, "transformation of place," is articulated to the spectators in the prologue by being projected into fantastic transformations of language, form, and genre. The prologue's bold enactment of linguistic process, I shall argue, colludes with a large-scale transformation of a model drawn from a "rival" festival genre (Sophocles' *Tereus*). Thus salvation from the polis is imagined as an experiment in dramatic (meta)language and (meta)fiction that operates simultaneously as an autonomous narrative and, on a deeper level, as a comment by one discourse on various other discourses of the polis. The catalyst for this experiment is the deconstruction of metaphor and traditional dramatic forms in a display whereby comedy makes a political comment on the poetics of its sister genre: whereas tragedy *studies* political crisis in veiled terms of a limiting mythos, comedy presents a solution (μηχανὴ σωτηρίας) in a *contemporary* scenario improvised freely from the linguistic, theatrical, and social materials to hand. Aristophanes flaunts his mastery over language and tragedy (and comic rivals as well) in a competitive display of his genre's preeminence as a mode of entertainment and persuasion. The outrageously successful metatopia of *Birds*, in other words, is erected on a scaffolding of metaphor and metafiction as the bird *polos* (sphere, stage) becomes a polis.

Metaphor and the Comedy of Language

Birds is unlike any other extant play of Aristophanes. We are struck immediately by the opening action whose bewildering indeterminacy is studied well by Niall Slater in his essay above. The pattern throughout the 420s had been to start with a concrete situation within Attica—for example, the Pnyx, Strepsiades' house in (the deme) Kikunna—from which a central problem was traced throughout the play. In the very first sequence of *Birds*, however, the adventures of Peisetaerus and Euelpides are already underway in an unspecified space outside the polis and entail the invention of a rather unfamiliar future. *Birds* is unique in the Aristophanic menagerie for the obstinacy with which it has resisted attempts to capture its general theme. Is the play that was produced for an Athenian audience at the City Dionysia of 414 B.C. an allegory of political and military events, a parable concerning human nature, a criticism of modernity and sophistic technique, sheer fantasy, or some blend of these and other motives? From its origins in Hellenistic scholarship, the controversy over the meaning of *Birds* developed by the end of the nineteenth century to the point where a bibliography could classify work on the play under six categories, each representing a distinct band in the interpretive spectrum.[3] The implicit and explicit debates between critics—those who emphasize political tendency and those inclined toward escapist fantasy—persist as the byways of the various approaches continue to be explored.[4] I submit, however, that this scholarly dialectic is not a cacophony of conflicting opinion, but rather a predictable reaction to a unique play whose prologue (and much else besides) is profoundly aporetic, that is, taunting our desire for sense and closure.

Instead of seeking to identify a single unifying content or theme, I shall study *Birds* as a bold dramatic experiment, a "comedy of language," whose polysemy is rooted in its exploitation of the originary transference (meta-

phoricity) and deferral (différance) of the signifying process.[5] It is the extent
and depth of this exploitation that marks *Birds* as unique and allows the play
to float, as it were, relatively free of focused satire ad hominem and topical
themes. The first part of *Birds* distorts the well-established prologue pattern of
problem-solution-agon to innovate a comic series of pointed deferrals and
repressions that suspend us for a moment between sense and nonsense: Aristophanes first establishes a semantic vacuum colored by the general language
of desire[6] (despite the promise of lines 30–54) and then fills the void in a grand
act of metaphor formation, which playfully represses and defers both the acute
political anxiety of the moment and the grim dystopia of the play's tragic
model, *Tereus*.

Aristophanes destabilizes his main metaphor to interact with its inversion:
"man as bird" colludes throughout with "bird as man" informing the microstructure of jokes, puns, and allusions. When we are introduced to Peisetaerus'
comic invention "bird as god," the metaphors interact to produce the final
absurdity "man as god." At the same time language—as a system, structure, and
creative force—is projected outward to govern the dramatic design of *Birds* in
an essential way. We confront first the eros, or open-ended search of Peisetaerus and Euelpides for a father(land) elsewhere, which, in its otherness, has
them speaking in terms of a possible future that must be invented; the inter-
view with Tereus that follows is catalytic in the development of the plot by
allowing Peisetaerus to read in it the metaphor of his destiny as a bird and,
finally, a god, the supreme *daimōn* of the exodus. From a suspension of sense
we reach the turning point at which the cloudy "meaning" of Nephelokokkugia
emerges to be poured retroactively into the initial semantic void: the play with
language reveals a metafictional program in which the themes and characters of
Sophocles' *Tereus* are transformed to become the new polis in the air. The very
name of this city, Nephelokokkugia, is pregnant with meaning: on one level it
identifies the topographic and ethnic coordinates of a city of bird folk situated
in an unspecified sector of the air (νεφέλη, as "cloud(y)" physically and intellectually);[7] on another level, the name reveals Peisetaerus' sophistic snare of
language (νεφέλη, or gauze net) in which fools (κόκκυγες as flighty folk, light-
weights) become hopelessly entwined.

A suitable point of departure in a study of *Birds* is Hypothesis II[8] as the
earliest extant critical attempt to set forth the play's general meaning. This text
appears to "report a controversy between philologists in antiquity (without our
being able to distinguish the participants) over the methods of Aristophanic
plot-construction."[9] A salient feature of this brief commentary is an awareness
of *Birds* as significantly different from other Aristophanic plays: (1) in the
elusiveness of its main idea or intention, which, nevertheless, appears to be

"something grand"; (2) in its departure from sustained series of jokes ad hominem toward a more oblique and general satire; (3) in its display of a "transformation in form and nature" that links hypothetical changes in society and politics with the manipulation of language and genre. The hypothesis concludes
with a discussion of chronology that quotes lines 145–48 as a weak allusion to
Alcibiades recalling an earlier allusion to some restriction on κωμικὴ ἄδεια,
"comic indemnity."[10]

Why does *Birds* appear so different from the earlier plays? Recent scholarship has attempted to find a partial answer to this question in the scholion on
line 1297[11] concerning legislation restricting ὀνομαστὶ κωμῳδεῖν, "lampoon-
ing by name"—an impossibly general notion, which Droysen proposed to limit
by applying exclusively to the hermokopid *atimoi*.[12] Clearly the "decree of
Syracosius"—if in fact historical—will help explain why Alcibiades, for example, and others disenfranchised in wake of the scandal of 415 are not named in
the play.[13] We cannot be certain, however, that such legislation existed in 414
and must always be on our guard against imaginative scholiasts "[eager] to re-
create the assumed factual background of Aristophanic jokes."[14] In any event,
there is little explanatory power at stake, and Hubbard's compromise is a
judicious statement of the limit: "Syracosius' decree had the effect of merely
encouraging the comic poets to seek more creative and indirect ways of criticizing the forbidden targets."[15]

Süvern's essay (discussed by Konstan above) attempted to ground the elusive text in historical fact by constructing an intricate and explicit allegory,[16] an
ambitious interpretation that has not, however, won general acceptance.[17]
"Some critics," notes Hubbard in an oblique response to Süvern, "have observed that this is fundamentally a play about the power of language."[18] This
looks toward the other end of the spectrum where *Birds* is regarded as an
escapist fantasy involving a more general criticism of the "Athenian character"
or human nature.[19] An extreme example of this approach is seen in the work of
Cedric Whitman, who goes beyond simple utopianism to define the comic
protagonist as an *alazôn*, "the Great Impostor, Nature's exile, the absurdity of a
self against a selfless Absurd," who is master of trickery (πονηρία), especially
"the ability to turn metaphors into facts."[20] *Birds*, he claims, is a fantastic
representation of absurdity or "nothingness" since "the nothing that people
talk is the reality which they possess."[21] Identifying metaphor as an important
force—indeed a main "idea"—informing the nonsensical aspects of the play,
Whitman made an important contribution by placing language and textuality
in the focus of his discussion.

Naturally, much work falls between the poles of history and escapist fantasy.
This middle ground is occupied largely by attempts to modify or integrate the

two extremes.[22] Thus, William Arrowsmith sought to reconnect *Birds* with politics by reading the play as a comic warning and satire of Athenian greed (πλεονεξία): "The real subject of the play," he notes, is indeed politics "as fantasy, a disease of the human spirit, a spirit represented, incarnated, in the Athenian imperial city."[23] The readings of Newiger, Alink, and Pozzi articulate milder "Mittelstellungen" to use Behaghel's term.[24] "A clear presentation of the sort of thing that happens whenever Athenians deal with politics," *Birds*, in Alink's view, reveals Aristophanes playing gentle tricks on his audience by luring it away from the Earth and subjecting it to a performance in which, by praising "birds," he praises himself.[25] Newiger clarifies why, for all their figurality and personification, the early Aristophanic plays (including *Birds*) cannot be allegories.[26]

More recently Taaffe and Bowie have reviewed the familiar issues in the interpretation of *Birds* from the perspectives of feminist criticism and ritual, respectively.[27] Most discussions of *Birds* from Süvern to Dunbar[28] have entered the fray with some ritual metacriticism in which the problem is delineated, allegiances declared, and opponents confronted. The historicist/escapist dialectic will doubtless engage many more students of the play as it continues to demonstrate an uncanny ability to generate writing by polarizing its scholarly audience.[29] I shall attempt, however, to escape the venerable holding-pattern to investigate the properties responsible for the text's elusiveness: how does an apparent anomaly in the Aristophanic oeuvre that is "regarded as the poet's masterpiece"[30] continue to oscillate in critical opinion between playful nonsense and urgent, structured meaning? To seek an answer we need to step outside the closed circle outlined above and take a bird's-eye view of Aristophanes' *Birds*.

Metaphor, Deferral, and the Comic Truth

I argue elsewhere[31] that the plot or λόγος of comedy differs from its tragic counterpart in being a sort of *hapax drōmenon*. Thus, whereas the "myth" of Orestes mutates variously throughout a number of tragedies, Trygaeus' flight on a dung beetle or the infiltration of the Thesmophoria by Euripides' Kinsman are unique to their respective texts. Although we do, of course, distinguish the interpretation of myth from the interpretation of a tragic script, "both may evolve in a hermeneutic circle" in the words of Walter Burkert,[32] "and remain mutually dependent on each other." The comic "myth," however, is coextensive with its form and, despite connections with epic and tragic articulations of legend, is much more immediately a unique text and performance. Old Comedy exhibits an acute awareness of itself as such and, by involvement with its own textuality, sets itself apart from the other festival genres. Foregrounding this reflexivity, Aristophanes' bird "myth" derives its problem-and-solution (νόσος-μηχανὴ σωτηρίας) from a linguistic moment: the man-as-bird meta-phor, which is deconstructively conflated with its inversion (bird-as-man). Reversing the Homeric ἔπεα πτερόεντα, "winged words," Aristophanes hatches a world of preposterous constructed birds (cf. the χὴν γεγραμμένος, "sketched goose," of line 805) from the fertile nest of writing.

"Birds," notes Sommerstein, "differs from all other fifth-century plays of Aristophanes that survive in having no strong and obvious connection with a topical question of public interest."[33] Appearing to brush such topics into the periphery, Aristophanes derives a great deal of his design from the central metaphor suggested by the transformed Tereus, the specifics of which I take up in the second half of this essay. Informed on many levels by playful contradic-tions and innovations, this comedy suspends us for a time between sense and nonsense without offering the comfort of resolution. In distinction from the comedies of the 420s in which linguistic play may figure as a seasoning, so to speak, the prologue and Great Idea of Birds are essentially displays of the creative power of language. Language and its properties are foregrounded here in a way that does not have obvious parallels in Greek drama of the classical period. Throughout the prologue—a dramatic form conventionally devoted to the establishment of a concrete situation and story—Aristophanes presents a rather abstract journey "to Tereus" (or is it ἐς κόρακας?) that culminates in an equally abstract "Great Idea" and agon. We must wait until after the parabasis to catch the thread of something akin to a familiar place (Cloudcuckooland as an antitype of Athens) and situation (the comic hero vs. the intruders). It is quite natural that this striking deferral of the expected engagement with so-ciopolitical themes continues to encourage readers to seek extraordinary so-cial, personal, or psychological explanations.

Central to the display of language and its creative powers in Birds is a series of metaphorical strategies extending from abstract to concrete: (1) the poten-tial, at the heart of language, of one sign to replace or suppress another[34] in what we call "word coinage," "metaphor," "metonymy," and the like; (2) the lyric and tragic visualization of metaphor as physical transformation in the topos "I wish I were a bird";[35] (3) the concretization this lyric-tragic linguistic topos in the figure of Tereus (lines 92–675); (4) the multiple resulting confla-tions of the human and avian. At first glance, as an extended example of the concretization of metaphor (an Aristophanic favorite),[36] this series, in fact, transcends simple "literalization" to upset the workings of metaphor to allow fully reciprocal interpenetration of "tenor" and "vehicle" in a single figure. The customary collusion of poetry and figural language is thus turned on its head before the spectators in a dramatic deconstruction of metaphor. Are men birds, and birds men? We can never be certain. The plot is sure to thicken, moreover, when Peisetaerus revises the game so that birds become gods, indeed *superior* to the gods. At least we can now guess what this con man is up to: his colonization of the bird community is merely a prelude to riding their tail feathers to a position above Olympus.

Aristophanes' complex bird myth, therefore, operates on a number of levels:

1. As a rather abstract μεταφορά or *translatio* of two men, motivated only by an unspecified eros ("desire" or "lack"), from a familiar Athenian past into an apparently "other" future that is to be improvised from the resources of language and tragic myth. I return below to the link between metaphor and translation that informs the linguistic dimension of *Birds*. The language of the birds—the chorus's native tongue—fuses at times with human speech as the natural flock of Tereus seeks to "translate" its avian concerns into Greek; Athens is "translated" into the fantastic terms of Peisetaerus' vision. The point here is to notice how much is actually lost or changed in the process!

2. As the comic subversion of a lyric topos: Tereus, the Thracian lingual castrator, acts as the disseminator of language in *Birds* and enables men and birds to communicate. "They were mere barbarians before," he says of the chorus in lines 199–200, "but I've taught them language, having spent a long time here." Simultaneously embodying the desiderative metaphor and mocking it, Tereus is a vivid example of violence deferred and suppressed, indeed the living blueprint for Peisetaerus' Great Idea and megalomaniacal scheme. The Thracian ruler raped Philomela and cut out her tongue only to be overcome by the Athenian woman's *textum* revealing his crime. He was transformed into a bird at the moment of crisis: having unwittingly eaten the flesh of his son Itys, he was chasing Procne and her sister in order to kill them when Zeus decided to suspend the entire tragedy in metamorphosis. This violently polysemous narrative mutates in *Birds* to form a new set of associations.[37] In a remarkable strategy of repression (foreclosure), Tereus becomes, in his Aristophanic context, a benign father, teacher of language, and an endearing, comic intermediary between two worlds. Peisetaerus, for his part, appropriates the glossectomy of the "Tongue-Stomach men" in his capacity as sophist (cf. 1705, with Hubbard's commentary, above). "In modes of symbolic transformation," notes Charles Segal, "we operate within a chain of signifiers which convey the repressed contents of the unconscious through metaphorical and metonymic substitutions. *Repression is itself a species of metaphor formulation* [emphasis added]. The repressed contents of the unconscious, which for Lacan had the structure of language, become visible through the translucent barrier of language," that is, linguistic substitution and figuration.[38] Tereus, then, to whom the men's eros leads them, embodies and catalyzes the grand metaphor which, as a large-scale and playful exercise in comic repression, serves marvelously to

repress, in turn, the extreme anxiety and tension surrounding recent events, especially the ambitious military undertaking and attendant scandal.

3. As the exploitation by Aristophanes of a scenic ambiguity: the men, essentially unchanged in birdhood, cheerfully flaunt the fine distinction between "costume," "disguise," and "metamorphosis." In a comedy so concerned with transformation and the manifold dichotomies between form and content, such theatrical play with costume is especially effective.

4. As a vehicle for paradoxical characters (Tereus, the bird chorus) that are at once the object of a transformation (men seek to become birds) and its subject (birds assimilate to the general human sphere of language and politics while claiming to be gods).

These and many other moments, charged by an essential equivocation, will necessarily continue to suggest widely divergent readings. Although it may be futile to demand a traditional "theme" from the play of signs that is *Birds*, Aristophanes' choice to foreground textuality in the play is certainly meaningful, a point I will take up after a brief review of the metaphorical complex outlined above.

"Metaphor," writes Lacan, "occurs at the precise point at which sense emerges from nonsense, that is, at the frontier which, as Freud discovered, when crossed the other way produces . . . the signifier *esprit* ['wit,' 'sense']; it is at this frontier that we realize that man defies his very destiny when he derides the signifier."[39] This aphoristic insight hints at the way language—into which man is born and which "speaks man"—is a systemic prison from which jokes and metaphors can offer only the illusion of escape. Any attempt to shake the bonds of language, to paraphrase Lacan, is doomed to failure; the best we can do is to challenge the limits of our being—as constructed by language—through metaphor, jokes, and other modes of "deriding the signifier." Metaphors, in the words of K. Harries, are "weapons directed against reality, instruments to break the referentiality of language, to deliver language from its ontological function,"[40] while in their resolution jokes can offer a pleasurable relief on intellectual and emotional levels.

Comedy, especially the Aristophanic variety, thrives on rattling its fetters in a perpetual show of escape from the linguistic prison through humor and transference. This will to freedom cannot fully respect an artificial dichotomy between the "literal" and the "figural" since comic discourse depends on all language (not simply metaphors and jokes) being, at some level, "nonsense" in critical need of construal and interpretation. "The picturesque saying that 'language is a book of faded metaphors' is the reverse of the truth," notes L. Bloomfield, "for poetry is rather a blazoned book of language."[41] What we misleadingly call "metaphor," then, is not an anomalous substitution of transference for reference but rather a strategy foregrounding the transferential and differential essence of how language produces meaning, be it the collective acceptance of a new coinage or a poetic flash of brilliance.[42]

Already important (if implicit) in Saussure's diacritical notion of language, the transference and deferral inherent in the signification process have been variously articulated in the wide variety of postmodern discourses. Language, both in its paradigmatic lexical network as well as in the syntagmatic chain of signifiers, is essentially constituted by multiple, complex exchanges of signs for other signs. In a classic essay Paul de Man challenged the priority of "transparent" (direct, primary) over "figurative" language—that is, the priority of a higher signified ("idea," "sense") revealed in "definition" over the simple sign, which, in the "epistemological vacuum" (or "disease") of translation and metaphor, is merely exchanged for another sign.[43] Deconstructing this hierarchy, de Man reveals the substitutional common denominator of all these processes structured by the chain of signification.[44] What we call "metaphorical language," then, is marked only in that it forces us to confront what we usually forget or choose to ignore. "The creative spark of metaphor," according to Lacan, "flashes between two signifiers one of which has taken the place of the other in the signifying chain, the occulted signifier remaining present through its (metonymic) connection with the rest of the chain."[45] If a metaphor is used with such frequency as to become cliché, it ceases to be felt as unusual, the suppressed signifier is erased, and the image "fades" or becomes "ossified" (to use an example). Although a continuum thus extends from the most brilliant poetic metaphors to opaque etymologies, "literal" language (as an antidote to figuration) is an illusion that must always be maintained by certain discourses with specific intellectual, political, or ideological agendas.

D. Davidson has argued that the debate about the cognitive content and function of metaphor[46] is largely misguided: "To suppose that [metaphor] can be effective only by conveying a coded message" he notes, "is like thinking a joke or a dream makes some statement which a clever interpreter can restate in plain prose. Joke, or dream or metaphor can, like a picture or a bump on the head, make us appreciate some fact—but not by standing for, or expressing, the fact . . . there is no limit to what a metaphor calls to our attention, and much of what we are caused to notice is not propositional in character."[47] The great collision of man and bird is just such a "bump on the head" with which Aristophanes surprises us into laughter. Delighting in the root metaphoricity of signification, *Birds* offers little indeed for propositional restatement by "clever interpreters."[48] Though far from expressing anything approaching an explicit theory of the comic, Aristophanes demonstrates an uncanny practical grasp of much that has been articulated on a theoretical level in modern scholarship. The exuberant and often highly innovative wordplay in his comedies, especially the extensive interaction between "human" and "avian" registers in *Birds*, is indeed a practical demonstration of this "radical superfluousness" in the sense of taunting and challenging the stranglehold of language, jabbing at the very mechanisms of meaning, which, profoundly arbitrary as they are, hardly seem worthy of the tyrannical rule they enjoy. The following are a few of many general imagistic strategies employed by the poet of *Birds* in this "demonstration" of comedy's rebellious textuality and its parasitic relation to other discourses:

1. Images that deconstruct metaphor: In addition to upsetting the supplementarity of the categories "literal" and "figural," the highly reflexive discourse of comedy—characterized by one critic as an "anti-discourse"[49]—deconstructs the conventional supplementarity of "vehicle" and "tenor" in metaphor.[50] Any intellectual or ideological impulse to control figurality must keep potential nonsense at bay by regarding the "vehicle" as a semantic supplement in the imaginary periphery (e.g., "That devil in the Vatican" may not "seriously" imply that *Satan* is a Catholic). In a move that includes, but is not limited to, so-called literalization, Aristophanes likes to force two terms to recognize each other in a reciprocal transference: for example, the comic names κατωφαγᾶς (288–89), ὑποδειδιώς (65), ἐπικεχοδώς (68), which fuse the morphology of bird names with stock comic themes of gluttony and cowardice. By rejecting supplementarities enforced in other discourses and by openly admitting its awareness of their "rules" and textual strategies, the script of a comic performance draws attention to (its own) textuality as temperamentally parasitic and omnivorous. This rejection, moreover, deconstructs any future attempt, however useful, to place it in a supplementary relation to another, "serious" discourse (i.e., to relegate it to the "unserious" and "marked" periphery). It is a remarkable paradox that, for all its intense involvement with its sociopolitical milieu, Aristophanic comedy manifests a uniquely reflexive awareness of its textuality and imposes the least ideological restrictions on its language.

2. Images "translated" from other discourses: the lyric yearning to be a bird expressed by the parricide (1337–39), the distortion of Pindaric metaphor (lines 924–30, 941–45, 950–51), and the manipulation of proverbs involve images structured by their source texts and amusing as comic grafts (whether altered or not). As multiple translations (cf. μεταφορεῖν), they are allegories of their own potentially endless recontextualization and rereading. The most prominent and pervasive "borrowed image" is the metaphor expressed in lyric poetry and tragedy as an unfulfillable yearning, which becomes, in *Birds*, a fully realized, governing paradigm of human ambition (see note 22).

3. Images set up as vehicles for phonetically or semantically disruptive substitutions παρὰ προσδοκίαν: for example, the cicada-Athenians who are

said to "sit on *lawsuits*, singing their whole life long" (40–41), and men who in their bird mania "alight on books, and feed on decrees" (1288–89). "I wish I were . . ." becomes, "I hereby pronounce myself (a bird)."

4. Images amusing simply in their content that participate in what could be described as the "linguistics of the grotesque," that is, language mirroring the confusion of species and natural spheres associated with grotesque imagery.[51] Thus the "Cleonymus tree" of lines 1473–77 splices together a botanical image with a stock comic theme (cowardice) with one of its standard representatives in Old Comedy, Cleonymus. Aristophanes then pursues his hybrid to the absurd point where the tree sprouts "denunciations" (συκοφαντεῖ) in the spring and casts off its "shields" in winter.

Another dimension of *Birds* in which dramatic design reflects the deeper structures of language is the enactment of the deferral outlined above. The profound rift between human language and the world of phenomena (referents)[52]—a manifestation of what Derrida termed différance (difference-differing-deferral)[53]—is put on display both in the initial deferral of comic meaning as well as in the later reversal whereby previously nonexistent entities (Cloudcuckooland and the Hellenized birds) are allowed to appear by virtue of linguistic accident and mere invocation. Within language, of course, the chain of signification is characterized by deferral:[54] one word leads to—"is defined by"—another while the referent recedes, forever outside the realm of language in a way that reveals lack or desire as essential to the process of signification.[55]

The opening of *Birds* is marked by a critical différance, or suspension of meaning structured by Aristophanes as the open-ended search by two men for an absent πατρίς or Father(land), a search for the primal father, in the Lacanian sense, "not as a living, real father but in language and as an absence, the Symbolical father, whose signifier is the Name of the Father, *the locus of the Law and of the demands of the social and moral order* [emphasis added]."[56] The "paradox that the very act of naming the Symbolical Father represses that for which the name stands" sheds an interesting light on the curious hesitancy on the part of Peisetaerus and Euelpides to name their own fatherland. The remapping of Athenian features in Nephelokokkugia, however, comically reveals the ethereal city as a return to the Father(land).

The underdetermination of the central "problem" in *Birds* poses a major obstacle to commonsense exegesis: why, after a glancing reference to their countrymen's litigiousness, do Peisetaerus and Euelpides fail to name Athens again and continue their journey in the absence of any motivation whatever?[57] A productive approach is suggested by Arrowsmith, who identifies their motive as "want—the want that in Greek thought always underlies desire, the mortal imperfection, the human craving that can only be fulfilled briefly and is always renewed."[58] Aristophanes, I submit, pours his meaning, that is, the fabulous, autonomous metaphor, into the gap, the fundamental lack (ἔρως)[59] that yawns at the opening of the play and is felt as a contextual vacuum that starkly highlights anything suspended in it. Oppressed by the absent (deferred) signifier promised and yet withheld by the text of his (dis)course—"I left Athens because . . . I am searching for . . ."—Peisetaerus is made to fasten arbitrarily upon one transference ("bird" for "man"), which structures an invented future into which he inscribes the past. This move then opens up a series of metaphorical substitutions that progress along the chain of signification: man becomes bird becomes a god who is comically supplementary to man! Lacan illustrates the "oppressiveness" or "tyranny" of the signifier with a series of such sentences interrupted before the significant term and notes that "[they] are not without meaning, a meaning all the more oppressive in that it is content to make us wait for it."[60] The fluid triple metaphor-metamorphosis of *Birds* (man-bird-god) that retroactively fills the initial lack with meaning is indeed a spectacle in which the comic hero "defies his own destiny by deriding the signifier" in a shameless apotheosis.

Nephelokokkugia, the winged construct that rises from the ashes of faltering discourse, is thus revealed as a supplement,[61] a comic fulfillment of an originary lack. As a delightful fiction, however, the grand Aristophanic supplement will tell us neither its name nor what it completes, what it compensates for. It has tempted many to regard it as an outlandish substitute for Athens with the comic implication that human politics is merely a subspecies of "flighty [i.e., 'bird'] behavior" with all the attendant arbitrariness and instability. Alternatively, we can regard it as supplementary to the human condition, in which case our life is revealed as only an allomorph of a more general "birdhood"! In the broadest possible terms, we can read *Birds* as setting forth the supplementarity of the terms in the Greek comic polarity: νόσος "disease," "problem" and μηχανὴ σωτηρίας "solution," "cure" (cf. σῶς = salvus): the νόσος, a structure of ailment and crisis, pushes man outward in search of a "cure," which, when achieved, turns out to contain a new crisis. Thus, although the νόσος of Athenian life (line 31) is apparently cured by the final metamorphoses, the brave new birds infected with metaphor succumb to a different strain of the original political virus (cf. Hubbard's essay above).

The metaphorical sparks catch and *Birds* is soon ablaze with writing as Peisetaerus composes the script of Cloudcuckooland in the agon (more precisely, lines 162–205 and 461–672). The protagonist emerges as an active "sophist-teacher" and "city planner" who invokes a new world through language in the first and most important step toward "deriding his own destiny" as a mere mortal (i.e., his final ascent to godhood). Appointing him protagonist in an ether where, in Whitman's phrase, "the word is all," Aristophanes retraces in Peisetaerus' rhetorical creativity his own function as writer of comedy: Peisetaerus trains the chorus for the spectacular parabatic performance by "writing" the text for its sham "divinity," a play he populates with a series of verbal constructs, that is, the graphic bird exempla (τεκμήρια) of the agon. Deriving the attendant politics from a simple pun (πόλος / πόλις, lines 182–84), he proceeds to vie with a number of other "writers" (the interloping poets, oracle monger, decree seller,[62] et al.) for command of this new text which he has named Nephelokokkugia, a comic formation that neatly captures the connection, noted by critics such as MacMathúna, Alink, and Hubbard between the δόλοι, "ruses," of characters within comedy and the governing, textual tricks of the comic poet himself.[63] In his superficially clever coinage that means "ethereal (νεφέλαι as 'clouds') city of the *Birds* (κόκκυγες 'cuckoos')," Peisetaerus expresses his role as writer of comedy who captures idiots in the net of his discourse, that is, Nephelokokkugia as a booby (κόκκυξ "fool") trap (νεφέλη "subtle snare"). Revealing through the protagonist his own deep involvement with language and textuality, Aristophanes also demonstrates a mastery of its scenic correlate: just as the signifiers of a text call attention to themselves, so the playwright makes the physical (con)text call attention to itself in metatheatrical strategies, which are the subject of the next section of this essay.[64]

What is the "meaning" of Aristophanes' deconstructive enactment of metaphor? Why does he defer the customary topicality and amplify the forces and tensions inherent in language to release a comic play of signs in a pointed act of repression and metaphor-formation? Why does he, while deconstructing the conventional supplementarity implicit in the notion of "figuration," ironically expose the trace of originary lack (in language) to fill it with his own comic supplement? "The irony of the comic hero," suggests Whitman, "from one point of view, is merely a means to a greater and more inclusive *alazoneia*, impostorship; so that one might say that there is no real *eiron*, but only a variety of *alazones*, and the biggest fraud wins, on the theory that if the fraud be carried far enough, into the limitless, it becomes a template of a higher truth."[65] Aristophanic textual *alazoneia* is certainly as limitless as the chain of signification and, inasmuch as every metaphor *qua* nonsense is a fraud, Aristophanes is the poetic *alazōn* who (to distort Shakespeare) weaves a complex, "mingled yarn" of tricks and frauds into a "web of life" that is his higher comic truth. "Truths are illusions about which one has forgotten that this is what they are," observed Nietzsche, "metaphors which are worn out and without sensuous power; coins which have lost their pictures and now matter only as metal, no longer as coins."[66] Herein, I submit, is the "serious" comic motive that, as a cultural menace, has been strategically overlooked by a sullen positivism: to startle us into remembering through laughter. Through the sensuality of its metaphor and other textual strategies, comedy stages an *anagnōrisis* in which, laughing, we recognize the illusion, of all (constructed) truth. In a splendid act of comic repression involving a grotesquely fluid triple metaphor, Aristophanes defers a comforting and habitual "meaning" in explicit involvement with his immediate sociopolitical context to expose the prison of language itself. This is one of his main "topics" or "themes" in the exploration of which he implicitly exposes truth-in-language as a concealer that denies its concealing (cf. ἀλήθεια as "unconcealedness"). *Birds* is a powerful comic jolt, a "bump on the head," which inspires us to pretend a celebratory return to our selves-as-bodies, to our language, to our earth thrown free of the bitter gravity of the Transcendent. It is only natural that the exodus of *Birds* should celebrate the apotheosis of the comic hero who, "defying his destiny by deriding the signifier," is established as his own comic truth.

II

Metafictions of the Polis

On a rather abstract level, Aristophanes' "comedy of language" is constructed along the lines of substitution and transformation inherent in metaphor. More concretely, as we have seen in the essay of Frank Romer above, the comic bird city is systematically erected on a scaffolding of other narratives. I would like to complement Romer's exploration of the connection between Hesiod and Aristophanes to foreground another important text, Sophocles' *Tereus*, which *Birds* appropriates aesthetically and ideologically. Mastery over other discourses is an accomplice (and close relative) to the more general mastery of language. My analysis moves, then, from the linguistic transformation of metaphor to metafictional transformations of one narrative by another. The thoroughgoing exploitation and deconstruction of figural language in *Birds* is directly connected with the play's ability to borrow eclectically from Hesiod to Sophocles and to fabricate a bold new myth of the comic polis in the air.

Aristophanes' transformation of "reality" in *Birds* has already brought the reflexivity of comic discourse to our attention. An important ingredient of this comedy is the way the playwright transforms the comic topos of "abandoning the city" (in the prologue) and the barbarian-metamorphic thematics of Sophocles' *Tereus* (through the parabasis and beyond). This metafictional moment has neither been fully appreciated nor explored as the study of Aristophanic metatheater is far from mature, and has much to learn from work in other fields (e.g., film and Shakespeare studies). Even in terms of descriptive groundwork,

Christian Metz's most recent work, for example, is impressively comprehensive[67] in a way that finds no counterpart in classics.[68] I shall begin by outlining a preliminary framework within which I can situate the varieties of metafiction exhibited in *Birds*. Comic metadrama features a number of phenomenal modes of which I shall single out "surface play," "*mise en abyme*," and "contrafact." These modes are simple to articulate but their realization is complex and varied. To imagine an inventory à la Metz, each of my categories would turn out to subsume scores of individual techniques and related substrategies with different distributions in tragedy and comedy.[69] A comprehensive review of this subject is beyond the scope of this essay. *Birds* offers a fine point of departure for this inquiry, however, as it is an unusually rich and complex specimen.

1. *Surface Play*: I designate as "surface play" moments in which an element of the performance *briefly*—and this is important—admits and exploits its duplicity, moving horizontally from inside the play and theatrical space to the sphere outside the dramatic fiction or between the script of the given performance and a text external to it. This mode is the stock-in-trade of comedy, which commonly foregrounds a basic duality in this connection: actor/role, theatron/dramatis locus, object/prop, face/mask, one's own speech/"borrowed" speech. Surface play is usually brought to our attention, moreover, by certain clues or even explicit marking in the script, that is, by being verbally (sometimes gesturally) signposted.[70] A list of strategies belonging to the category of surface metatheater would include so-called ruptures of dramatic illusion: audience address, commentary on the circumstances of production, explicit mention and manipulation of dramatic convention, reference to extradramatic phenomena, brief parody, quotation. A particularly subtle type of surface play might be seen in the pointed use of ambiguous terms (e.g., *agôn*, *theasthai*) that look both inward to the fiction and outward to the festival and political context. The spectator is ever reminded of the fiction-making process itself by an unsettling tension inherent in the multivalent signifier whose semantic range may extend from Homer to the contemporary fields of rhetoric, law, and the theater itself. Surface play enriches the dramatic fable at a given point by delimiting the boundaries of the fiction as a construct and, simultaneously, linking this construct in a self-conscious way to phenomena external to it.

2. *Mise en Abyme*: Play with the "deep structure" of the theatrical event, on the other hand, engages the mechanics of a dramatic situation within the larger, "framing" fiction. As a species of the *mise en abyme*,[71] the "internal plays" of Greek tragedy and comedy differ from Renaissance examples such as "The Murder of Gonzago" (*Hamlet*) by being seamlessly incorporated into the dramatic fiction with more subtle verbal marking, if any. This metarepresentational strategy embeds a miniature theatrical *situation*—one involving the

mimetic dynamics of director-actor-audience—within a larger, similarly structured dramatic framework. The spectator is invited to contemplate the very
process in which he or she is involved at a given moment from a newly
constructed distance, which paradoxically mixes irony with self-recognition.
Nowhere in Greek drama is the spectator jarred into acknowledging that an
internal sequence is a *formal dramatic production*, a play-within-a-play (though
the merchant scene in *Philoctetes* comes close). Herein is the seductive power of
the *mise en abyme*: it beckons to the spectator without admitting to its purpose.
The ironic potential of this strategy, moreover, makes it particularly effective in
tragedy as Helene Foley, Charles Segal, and others have shown in the case of
Euripides' *Bacchae*. Although these first two metatheatrical modes cannot be
separated strictly along generic lines, we must maintain full awareness of the
asymmetry of their distribution: in shifting from the world of the play to the
world "framing" the performance in surface play, for example, tragedy falls far
short of the explicitness and the frequency which we find in Aristophanes.
Setting aside the questions of quantity and intensity that have engaged Taplin
and others, however, I think it valuable first to make a qualitative distinction between the ways in which a dramatist might incorporate theatrical self-
awareness into the design of his plays.[72]

3. *Contrafact*: This is a term I have taken from music theory to designate a
composition of which a *sustained portion* (and sometimes the whole) is based in
a significant and systematic way on another composition. Effectively coined for
the field of jazz studies in 1975 by musicologist James Patrick in a study of the
harmonic sources of early modern jazz, "contrafact" or "melodic contrafact"
has entered the mainstream theoretical vocabulary to describe the "general
procedure of the borrowed-harmony technique" whereby "an original piece is
selected; the original harmony is retained and the original melody is discarded;
a new melody is then fitted to the borrowed chord structure, yielding a new
composition."[73] The field (kind, species, genre) of the contrafact and that of its
model are necessarily at some remove from each other in time, form, or style.
The model of the contrafact, by definition, should be accessible and, at some
level, discernible. An important aspect of the contrafact is the interplay between "old" and "new" material—elements of the model retained and those
replaced or altered. The "old" material remains to establish connection with the
model, while the "new" material is the contrafact's creative focus. This term,
modified appropriately, suggests a poetics of transformation governing the
refashioning of a model into a new "original" and offers the Aristophanic critic
a refreshing alternative to "parody" and "travesty," which necessarily imply
mockery and distortion in the service of humor. I follow here the lead of Pietro
Pucci who reserved the terms "tragicomedy" and "paratragedy" for much the

same purpose.[74] Besides being potentially misleading, however, these terms lack a certain breadth. A dramatic contrafact, like its musical analog, will often involve various types of parody (and much else besides) but the latter term does not suffice to capture the full phenomenon.[75] Regarded in light of the musical metaphor, for example, the first half of Virgil's *Aeneid* and Joyce's *Ulysses* might be contrasted as contrafacts of the *Odyssey*, each with its own poetics of transformation and literary agenda. What these works have in common is the systematic reworking of Homer, not any particular humorous purpose (though *Ulysses* does involve a fair amount of parody and travesty in the strict sense). Similarly, Euripides' various transformations of the *Oresteia* and Aristophanes' extended reworkings of Euripides are both contrafacts of tragedy, but constructed from very different perspectives.

Important ingredients of *Birds* (and a number of other plays) are the contrafacts in which significant elements—language, character, spectacle, theme, or situation—of one performance (the dramatic model) are creatively engaged and transformed into a utopian (metatopian) scenario by the comic protagonist. Dramatic contrafacts share another important feature with their musical kin: they thrive on, indeed *require*, a display of explicit or implicit improvisation on the underlying material in a way best exemplified perhaps by the way Dicaeopolis hijacks the script, plot, and costume of a tragic hero (Telephus) to serve his private agenda. For all their superficial differences, most Aristophanic contrafacts arise from the common process of creative manipulation of tragic elements (although comic and dithyrambic models also occur, as we shall see). More precisely, Aristophanes has his characters, as they go along, appear to be improvising their own scenarios from other "literary" material that is to hand. In most of the fifth-century utopian comedies, the lead role is closely bound up with, indeed *defined* by means of, a tragic model. In this case we appear to be dealing not only with an Athenian style of metafiction but with a specifically Aristophanic trademark.

Peisetaerus chorodidaskalos: *Protagonist as* Metteur en Abyme

Metatheater on the level of the "deep structure" of drama differs from surface play in that it does not depend simply on exposing the duplicity of isolated theatrical elements to bridge the inner and outer worlds of a play. Instead, the playwright amplifies the theatricality of a whole scene by structuring it *internally* like a dramatic performance, that is, with internal "director," "player(s)," and "audience," all of whom participate in the fiction underway. This process of studying the theatrical process itself is more comprehensively metafictional—a display of the theater in its three-dimensional totality as a leading site of cultural production. In the mock trial at *Wasps* 835–43, 891–1108, for example, we are struck by the equation between the legal and dramatic agons as the two kinds of spectacle presented for the entertainment and enjoyment of the audience.[76] Indeed, the comic picture of the poet as behind-the-scenes master of language and representation suggests a great deal about drama as a means of persuasion and influence. "The power of Comedy," notes Hubbard in this connection, "is the power to manipulate public imagination into new modes of perception and, it is hoped, new modes of judgment."[77]

For all its sophistication, as I have noted, the fifth-century *comédie mise en abyme* never quite attains to Lionel Abel's Shakespearean "antiform" of a play-within-the-play. The most obvious explanation for this, in the case of tragedy, is the absence of the theater from its source culture (i.e., the heroic past of the tragic mythos). Importing a theater into the court of Agamemnon, for example, would strain the genre's well-known tolerance for anachronism to the breaking point.[78] There is, moreover, the risk of banality in pushing metatheater to the limit of making a formal theatrical performance a rank-and-file dramatic event within the fiction—literally incorporating the performance of a play into the plot, witness countless films-within-films that have little, if any, metafictional point.[79] Shakespeare's ability to exploit this device owes far less to the technique per se than to the poet who was able to make splendid drama from even the humblest of materials. Aristophanes' approximation to this technique in *Thesmophoriazusae*, discussed by Elizabeth Bobrick below, is well known and represents the nearest we have to explicit play(s)-within-the-play on the classical stage.[80]

An extensive but neglected comic *mise en abyme* is centered about the parabasis in *Birds*, a passage often admired for its splendor and uniqueness.[81] For the first time in the extant comedies (414 B.C.—thirteen years into Aristophanes' career), the poet's voice is heard neither in the anapaests nor in the following epirrhematic syzygy. Attempts to interpret the apparent anomaly[82] have failed to take into account the wider context of the parabasis, which involves the shaping of a disorganized "natural" community of "birds" into a well-rehearsed chorus of citizens of Cloudcuckooland. The transformation of the chorus accompanies an equally significant transformation on the part of the protagonist, Peisetaerus, from an elitist *apragmôn* to active sophist and city planner to tyrant-god. The metatheatrics of *Birds* fuses drama and politics in a novel manner: Nephelokokkugia, as I argue above, is a manifestly linguistic construct involving the enactment of polis "nowhere"—suspended in mid-air whose name appropriately connotes a booby trap set for the gullible followers of Peisetaerus' teaching. In his essay above Niall Slater sets forth in performative terms how this διδασκαλία—"teaching," "choreography"—leads to the invention and enactment of an outlandish colony, a city based on a pun whose justification and "foreign policy" rest on a tangle of specious arguments and farcical episodes. It is striking that Peisetaerus' bizarre scenario within the play is given an explicit political form—*it is supposed to be a polis*. The erstwhile quiet Athenian becomes a busybody who combines the functions of demagogue and poet-director (χοροδιδάσκαλος) as he hijacks the action for his own purposes. Nephelokokkugia unfolds as a performance composed and directed by Peisetaerus who supervises the entrances and exits of characters from his polis-as-comedy. It is the transformation of the chorus, however, that foregrounds most vividly the way in which a metafictional strategy can prompt innovation in generic form.

The first encounter of the Athenian refugees and the bird chorus is a disaster in which the two sides array against each other in the ephirrhematic agon (327–99). A "military" confrontation is avoided, however, owing to Tereus' diplomacy, whereby he facilitates a temporary pact (445) between men and birds on the condition that the birds (as chorus and play) win the dramatic competition. Peisetaerus, characterized as a sophist in familiar comic terms (427–30 and 372–73; see Hubbard's essay above), is invited to *teach* the birds. The several forms of διδάσκω ("teach") used in this context (438, 548, 550; cf. also 375–80, 912) economically express his dual role as sophistic teacher and poet-director: he will convert the hostile array of birds into a chorus by teaching his revisionist theology and new political mythos in the form of an epidictic speech, which is simultaneously an act of training and choreography. The double διδασκαλία of the main agon is a great success and may be regarded as illustrating the complementary distribution of military and choral disciplines in a comic corollary of J. J. Winkler's famous "ephebic" hypothesis:[83] the array of bird "hoplites" in military formation (cf. the explicit language at lines 353, 400–402, and 408) is brilliantly transformed into a stately chorus of Nephelokokkugians, compliant citizens (κόκκυγες = young fools) of Peisetaerus' tricky scheme. Perhaps further play with the theatrical process, tragedy in particular, is intended in the fact that the foundation of Nephelokokkugia involves the sacrifice of a billy-goat (902, 959, 1056–57). Comedy as τρυγῳδία inaugurates its fictional polis with the one genuine instance of τραγῳδία on the fifth-century stage, an etymological jab, perhaps, at the sacrificial thematics of tragedy!

The fact that in the parabasis of *Birds* Aristophanes forgoes the customary direct appeal has a metafictional explanation: the "stepping forth" is reserved for the first entrance of this new chorus, the chorus of Nephelokokkugia, Peisetaerus' new city-as-comedy. A point-by-point analysis of the "sophist's" teaching (465–626)[84] reveals that the birds assimilate the choreography well and accurately reproduce their lesson in an amplified poetic form. It is significant also that in the main agon (451–626) the contest of earlier comedies yields to Peisetaerus' directorial monologue.[85] Aristophanes now replaces his erstwhile dialectic (of the agon) and polyphony (of the parabasis) with performances in which we hear only the protagonist in one and the "new" chorus in the other. *Birds* thus stands out as an experiment in the manipulation of established forms. The "rules" of the agon are not inviolable and the parabasis has already undergone changes toward the end of the 420s. Whether or not the latter was the earliest ritual kernel of the Old Comic form and substitute for the parodos (and this is doubtful),[86] the anapaestic tetrameter is ideally suited for comic allusion to the conventional presentation of the chorus in tragedy. Again, dramatic convention is important: Aristophanes has sublimated the moment of direct address in the famous cosmogonic contrafact:[87]

Ἄγε δή, φύσιν ἄνδρες ἀμαυρόβιοι, φύλλων γενεᾷ προσόμοιοι,
ὀλιγοδρανέες, πλάσματα πηλοῦ, σκιοειδέα φῦλ' ἀμενηνά,
ἀπτῆνες ἐφημέριοι, ταλαοὶ βροτοί, ἀνέρες εἰκελόνειροι,
προσέχετε τὸν νοῦν τοῖς ἀθανάτοις ἡμῖν, τοῖς αἰὲν ἐοῦσιν,
τοῖς αἰθερίοις, τοῖσιν ἀγήρῳς, τοῖς ἄφθιτα μηδομένοισιν,
ἵν' ἀκούσαντες πάντα παρ' ἡμῶν ὀρθῶς περὶ τῶν μετεώρων,
φύσιν οἰωνῶν γένεσίν τε θεῶν ποταμῶν τ' Ἐρέβους τε Χάους τε
εἰδότες ὀρθῶς, Προδίκῳ παρ' ἐμοῦ κλάειν εἴπητε τὸ λοιπόν.
Χάος ἦν καὶ Νὺξ Ἔρεβός τε μέλαν πρῶτον καὶ Τάρταρος εὐρύς·
γῆ δ' οὐδ' ἀὴρ οὐδ' οὐρανὸς ἦν.

(685–94)

Come now, you men whom nature gives but feeble life, like to the race of leaves, weaklings modeled from clay, shadowy strengthless tribes, flightless creatures of a day, suffering mortals, men like the figures of dreams—pay attention to us, the immortal, the everlasting, the celestial, the ageless, whose counsels are imperishable, so that you may hear correctly from us all about the things on high, and with accurate knowledge of the birth of birds and of the origin of gods and rivers and Erebus and Chaos may tell Prodicus from me that in the future he can get lost! In the beginning there was Chaos and Night and black Erebus and broad Tartarus, and there was no earth or air or heaven.

It would be inappropriate for Aristophanes' voice to be heard here as it would interfere with this presentation. His "representative," Peisetaerus, is also significantly silent throughout the parabasis, which is thus played as the parodos of a new chorus: the stately formation reveals a new persona, which has assumed the authoritative verbal mask of cosmogonic poetry. The Nephelokokkugians step forward, identify themselves, deliver the impressive ornithogony, and invite all spectators to join their play and their polis. As "gods" and "muses," they need not admit to an antecedent discourse. Consequently, their authoritative text conceals its source, that is, the ideas and training of the sophist-poet Peisetaerus. The birds' dismissal of Prodicus (692), moreover, harmonizes well with their promotion of the new avian order in an effort to secure the first prize for their choreographer. Peisetaerus' status as "director" and the birds' self-awareness as the chorus-as-demos of a new performance (Nephelokokkugia) are emphasized in a sequence of fairly standard parabatic surface play in the syzygy (e.g., lines 753–68). Thus the preliminary exercises of agon and parabasis establish a framework *en abyme* within which the comic polis, as it unfolds in the second half of *Birds*, is presented as a "theatrical" production within the play.

Reinventing the Barbarian: Contrafacts of Pherecrates and Sophocles

Old Comedy, as Hubbard points out above, "is the most immanently 'political' of all literary genres." In play after play, the polis, in whole or in part, figures variously as the dramatis locus, the source of the action, a character, the chorus, and, in the case of *Birds*, a spectacle coextensive with several constituent elements of the comedy. The foundation and business of Nephelokokkugia, in fact, occupy most of *Birds* from the first syzygy to the exodus (801–1719) making it the most autonomous and sustained representation of a polis in Old Comedy. As we have seen, owing to its complex and innovative design, *Birds* is quite capable, ironically, of appearing to have "no strong and obvious connection with a topical question of public interest, whether political, literary-theatrical, or intellectual-educational."[88] On the level of its transformation of other narratives, however, *Birds* exhibits important connections indeed with its literary and political context. In this respect the contrafact emerges as an important mechanism whereby Aristophanes reverses the initial suspension of "meaning" in the prologue to invent his anti-Athens in the air.

Peisetaerus leaves his polis in an uncertain quest for the quiet life (ἀπρα-γμοσύνη) and, for the time being, the spectators must be content with his stated purpose of literally seeking the way ἐς κόρακας (28). Paradoxically, he speaks of a homeland both in terms of flight (ἀνεπτόμεσθα, 35) and discovery (ἐξευρεῖν, 10, 29). The opening scene with its pointed involvement with Pherecrates' *Savages* is only superficially a spectacle of aimless wandering and sheds light on what Peisetaerus means by "going to birdition." *Savages* (produced 420 B.C.), which was critical of the naive Cockaigne theme (cf. Athen. 6.267e ff.), depicted two refugees from Athens setting out to search for a simpler life in some sort of "natural" community (fr. 10 K.-A.). To their horror, they discover that this "Eldorado" is a miserable place: the savages "live on chervil, weeds, and wild olives; but when really hungry they gnaw their own toes at night like octopuses" (fr. 14 K.-A.), words Peisetaerus appears to echo when he complains that he has "ground down his toenails at the bidding of a jackdaw" (*Birds* 7–8). We must remember that Peisetaerus speaks of himself and his sidekick as "having the full status of tribe and clan membership, citizens among citizens" (lines 33–34). Whatever they find in their flight from the polis, it must be better than the rustic struggle of a "natural" life ἐν ἀγρῷ, in the radical sense. In Protagoras' Great Speech (*Prot.* 327 d), Plato has the sophist cite *Savages* in support of his view that the vilest Athenian is still superior to, and incompatible with, his anomian counterpart. The subsequent action of *Birds* agrees with this reading of Pherecrates' play, a point supported by Alink's study of νόμος:[89] "logos/polis/nomos are human concepts which together form the only way to civilization. . . . Aristophanes maps this way to civilization and tells us the story of the birth of society . . . in the realm of the birds." The birds, of course, acquire language, build a polis, and greatly expand the semantic field of what νόμος signifies for them.

Pherecrates drove a wedge between the anomian and the eunomian topoi: life in a natural community unstructured by human laws is far worse than life in the Athenian polis; it is, in fact, intolerable. Knowing this, the spectators are suspended in disbelief: can Peisetaerus and Euelpides indeed be repeating the error of Pherecrates' protagonists? Certainly not! Aristophanes builds upon Pherecrates' criticism of a comic theme to create the following sequence: having left Athens, Peisetaerus and Euelpides certainly desire eutopia: a good place, a *better* place. Their motives, however, cannot include a nostalgia for a golden age with an edible landscape in the spirit of Telecleides' *Amphictyones* (fr. 1 K.-A.), nor are they in the least bit capable of a "natural" life amid beasts or bushmen. As creatures of the polis, they must seek a political alternative: that is, they must find a great polis, or found one. It is for this reason that the quasi-Orphic/Pythagorean challenge that *Birds* poses to the boundaries between men and beasts, men and gods, is devious and, at best, a comic illusion enhanced by Aristophanes' destabilization of metaphor outlined above.

Peisetaerus speaks of Athens as great and prosperous (37) and admits to Tereus that he cannot hope to find a greater polis but yearns for one that is somehow "more suitable, more profitable" (24). The precise sense of the advantage is still not specified, however. The subsequent exchange between Tereus and the Athenians (125–61) involves only a series of weak puns and reveals that Peisetaerus really has no clear idea of what he is seeking. For the moment, "topical questions of public interest" are deferred as the poet fills the void with the language of eros.[90] Current discussions of *Birds* emphasize that Nephelo-kokkugia, as an impossible alternative to Athens, is an elaborate hybrid—for

Hofmann a fusion of the past (paradise) and future (utopia), for Konstan a fusion of anomia, antinomia, eunomia, and megalonomia.[91] A hybrid cannot be found in nature but must be invented, and the process of invention will be heuristic: it is the character and physical presence of Tereus—himself a complex hybrid of man and bird, Athenian and Thracian, tragedy and comedy—that allows the protagonist to invent the fantastic contrafactual polis quite literally "nowhere" between the gods and earth (186). At this point the economy of a pun comes in handy as the Sophocles character catalyzes the utopian foundation of Nephelokokkugia, a polis that is indeed contrary-to-fact.

Following the brief revision of Pherecrates, then, Aristophanes develops the action around a famous tragic model: Tereus is first sought by the Athenian "suppliants" (120) as a source of information about alternatives, as a guide to something Other. The bird man is quickly stripped of his role as guru, however, to become Peisetaerus' living blueprint for the future.[92] The comic Tereus (*Birds* 92–675) is a brilliant and unusual contrafact that serves, catalytically, to transform the very performance in which he participates. He enters the action, facilitates a powerful reaction, and disappears leaving as a trace only the profound consequences of his presence: Nephelokokkugia arises as a metafictional affirmation of the fact that nowhere (literally) is there a place or polis greater than Athens!

Peisetaerus' most concrete statement of purpose involves Tereus: "Our journey now is to see Tereus the hoopoe, wanting to find out from him if he's seen a city of that kind (τόπος ἀπράγμων) anywhere he's flown over" (46–48). Although Tereus will only later identify himself as a refugee from the Sophoclean stage (100–101), his status as a tragic model is unmistakable.[93] Having set out to learn from tragedy, however, Peisetaerus quickly evolves from spectator and "suppliant" to comprise the active roles of sophist, demagogue, and *chorodidaskalos*. Aristophanes appears eager to demonstrate creative control of his tragic model and to engage the spectators in a fantasy of a polis evoked by the powers of a comic playwright. The resulting contrafact involves translating the pathetic Sophoclean final solution (metamorphosis as metaphor for death) into a governing metaphor for his comedy. Flight to birdhood furnishes a marvelous rescue strategy (μηχανὴ σωτηρίας) and starting point for the political myth to follow. An important feature of this translation, as I have argued above, is the comic destabilization of the desiderative lyric-tragic metaphor "I wish I were a bird": the signifiers ἄνθρωπος and ὄρνις are conflated in mutual intersubstitution.

To backtrack somewhat: in a recent study of the lost tragedy *Tereus* and its relation to *Birds*,[94] I argue (1) that it was Sophocles who imparted the definitive form to the legend made famous by Ovid (*Met.* 6.422–676); (2) that these dramatic innovations were extensive and made a profound impression on the

Athenian audience; and (3) that the transformation of *Tereus* as a tragic model in *Birds* is essential to the basic design of the latter, its governing metaphor, and the (partial) identification of Aristophanes with Peisetaerus in particular. It is remarkable, moreover, that Aristophanes, in reacting to Sophocles' *Tereus*, concentrates on features innovated by the tragedian. The most salient of these are:

Dramatis Locus: Sophocles emphasizes Tereus' barbarian status by innovatively removing the king of Daulis from his natural homeland in Phocis (cf. his alliance with Pandion) to Thrace. Thereafter, the name of Tereus was synonymous with Thrace, barbarism, and misogyny.[95]

Myth: Instead of the traditional hawk (cf. Aesch. *Supp*. 62), Sophocles has his Thracian fittingly transformed into the exotic hoopoe, a crested bird which, in comedy, is symbolic of what is "other" or unfamiliar to the Athenians (cf. the response to the peacock at *Acharnians* 63). "Tereus the Hoopoe" is a Sophoclean trademark as a later joke in *Birds* makes clear (280–86).[96] Though Sophocles did not invent the *redende Name*, there can be little doubt that his tragedy established it over the other variants (Zethus, Polytechnus). Thucydides' defense of Teres, the Athenians' Thracian ally,[97] against the infamy of Tereus is most likely a reaction specifically to Sophocles' play.

Plot: Sophocles has Tereus both incarcerate Philomela *and* cut out her tongue in order to set up the recognition by means of the "voice of the shuttle" (*Poet*. 16.1454b 30–37). Occurring nowhere else in Greek legend as a means of preventing communication, this "lingual castration" is highly marked and serves to emphasize Tereus' savagery.[98] Aristophanes foregrounds this motif in the antistrophe (1694–1705) that characterizes sophists as Tongue-Stomach men whose monopoly of the logos yields the result that "throughout Attica, tongues are cut out." The revelation of Tereus' crime by means of writing is a device designed for the tragic stage by Sophocles, as Aristotle makes clear. The immediate result is the victory of literate cunning of the Athenian women over their oppressive and crude Thracian environment.

Ritual and Theater: Sophocles has Procne and Philomela use the occasion of the Dionysiac Trieterica to carry out their revenge.[99] The ritual context provides the costume and setting for the Athenian sisters' own *mise en abyme* in anticipation of *Bacchae*. Their "theater of revenge"—the maenad disguise, the sacred meal, the gift of a special robe, the bloodshed, and the sacrifice—is motivated, dramatically and thematically, by the Dionysiac context.[100]

Transformation: In addition to the innovative plot features noted above, the conclusion of *Tereus* exhibits an innovation in dramatic technique: Sophocles enacted the lyric topos "I wish I were a bird" as a visual metaphor for death on the *ekkuklêma*. The metamorphosis of Tereus into a crested hoopoe was thus both thematically and visually motivated: the *akrokomos* Thracian becomes a crested bird.[101] Hofmann shows that Sophocles transformed a punishment into a solution.[102] Aristophanes, in turn, fashions a contrafact by transforming this final solution into his basic idea and point of departure. This is but one example of how a comic contrafact transforms tragic crisis into something productive, a new plan or strategy of rescue.

The common denominator of these innovations to the tradition is Sophocles' success, drawing on contemporary ill feeling toward the Thracians, in establishing a stark Atheno-Thracian antithesis. The purpose of this antithesis is complex and finally results in the ironic undermining of Athenian superiority in the spectacle of Pandion's daughters willfully outdoing their host and ill-chosen ally in savagery.[103] The Aristophanic reversal is spectacular: Tereus speaks a colloquial (as well as mock-tragic) Attic Greek, has a servant, and eats Athenian delicacies using a bowl, pot, and stirring-spoon. His name occurs naturally to Philocrates, the Athenian vendor who recommended him to Peisetaerus and Euelpides. Tereus' Thracian past and ethnic character are lost in moulting, so to speak, and he wears a hilarious hybrid costume that challenges our distinctions between "metamorphosis," "costume," and "disguise." Far from being ignorant, threatening, or savage, he is a widely traveled bird man and pacifist who inspires laughter and sympathy. Sophocles had Tereus' suppression of language trigger the Athenian sisters' Dionysiac theater of revenge. A Thracian "full of scorn for writing," in Detienne's phrase,[104] seeking "to destroy in fury everything which concerned the intellectual sphere," the tragic Tereus was himself destroyed by writing and the superior intellectual abilities of the Athenians. Aristophanes, on the other hand, makes him a benevolent teacher and disseminator of language, and not any language at that, but Greek! This Aristophanic counterinvention provides Peisetaerus with a linguistic context for his city-planning activities and triggers, in turn, a metatheatrical response. The fact that this Thracian has taught Greek to the "barbarians" (as he condescendingly calls the birds) unleashes a new wave of rhetorical and poetic creativity, which surfaces as a comedy-within-a-comedy. It is now the "barbarian" sophists who cut out the Athenians' tongues (1705). Aristophanes thus promotes Tereus to the forefront as an intermediary and banishes Sophocles' eloquent female protagonist: Procne has no speaking part in the comedy, and does not even appear onstage as a bird. Finally, Peisetaerus and Euelpides find their tragic "Watcher" (cf. τηρεῖν) asleep and the tragic wordplay is extended so as to adapt Tereus to his new role as guide and catalyst.

In designing his thematic synthesis, Aristophanes fastened on the Sophoclean opposition between Athens and the barbarian Other expressed in a dramatic intersection of language and spectacle: the poetic flight from an intolerable situation and the "human condition" becomes a comic flight from the

Athenian condition, with the potential flight of Athenians in droves from their city to Nephelokokkugia. The question posed by the Pherecratean prologue— "where to discover a more profitable native polis?"—finds its concrete answer in the countercharacter, Tereus. This stands in stimulating contrast to other Aristophanic contrafacts that emphasize narrative and situation (e.g., *Telephus* in *Acharnians*). Aristophanes' and Peisetaerus' collaborative mastery of their tragic model is programmatic: they translate the Sophoclean scenic metaphor onto the comic stage where this metaphor is destabilized and reconcretized in the role of the hoopoe. Sophocles had enacted the lyric-tragic topos "I wish I were a bird" in a final tableau that, for all its poignancy, only suspended the crisis and enforced the stark opposition between man and bird, life and death, Athens and Thrace, "tenor" and "vehicle." *Birds* systematically dismantles these oppositions, first in the person of Tereus and, subsequently, in Nephelokokkugia. On the most abstract level, Aristophanes reveals his comic deconstruction of metaphor through his transformation of a tragic model: whereas in tragic discourse "bird" represented escape, death, and the "Other," in comedy men assimilate to birds, and birds to men in a cheerful intersubstitution. Escape into the unknown thus becomes a return to the familiar. As long-standing generic and sociopolitical oppositions collapse, we realize that Nephelokokkugia will be comic anti-Athens with a hybrid charter.

The instant Peisetaerus realizes the significance of what the "new" Tereus embodies, he is illuminated with comic invention: "Yow! I see in the race of birds what could be a grand design [μέγα βούλευμα] and a mighty power, were you to be *persuaded* by me" (163–64). This passage with its triple repetition of the latter verb (πιθέσθαι) signals a new turn in the play. The protagonist fulfills the omen of his name and assumes a new role a "persuader," a role in which he is clearly identified, at least in part, with Aristophanes. Peisetaerus' city-planning activities will soon take the form of composition and choreography (χοροδιδασκαλία) discussed above and his polis-as-comedy will be inaugurated in what I have described as the parodos of a new chorus (Nephelokokkugians!). In the double training of the birds, Aristophanes once again "exposes the dangerous effects of high-style rhetoric on a gullible and volatile audience (pun intended)" to quote Helene Foley.[105] Peisetaerus' Great Idea is sparked by a mere pun and his city-planning activities *in vacuo* are possible only in the realm of language and the theater. A fascinating aspect of these activities is the fusion of rhetorical and poetic prowess in a fantasy of poet as founder of a city and leader-god of the demos. In Nephelokokkugia, like the author of a script and choreographer, Peisetaerus' authority is supreme as he manages the entrances and exits of the many visitors, rival poets among them, in his polis-as-comedy.[106] The deployment of dramatic models is another aspect of this authority and illuminates Aristophanes' complex design. The catalytic role of Tereus, in which linguistic and ethnic oppositions collapse, is especially important: he is a guide to us as spectators and readers in revealing how the Athenians' fantasy of change and translation into something Other in Nephelokokkugia is necessarily undermined by their own "political" nature, that is, their traditions, language, customs, laws, and values.

Utopia is almost invariably a metatopia, "change of place," and I have attempted to complement the discussions of Konstan and Hubbard above by studying the transformational modalities involved in the construction of Aristophanes' grandest comic utopia. Abstractly, the medium of language, and more concretely, scripts of other plays, are ostentatiously transformed on the comic stage in a display of the genre's mastery and persuasive power. A scenic representative of the poet himself, Peisetaerus exhibits limitless persuasion (*nomen est omen*) and creative energy. He begins "nowhere" with little idea of his future and ends by colonizing a natural community, founding a city-state for them, and taking charge of its outrageous "foreign policy." Having successfully defied his destiny as a mere mortal, Peisetaerus illustrates the fabulous rewards of gaining mastery over language and dramatic representation as he celebrates his marriage to Basileia and leaves the stage to the hyperbolic acclaim of the chorus. The final invocation—and the play's last words—leave no doubt as to the totality of his achievement:

ὦ δαιμόνων ὑπέρτατος,

O, most exalted of the gods!

Notes

The first section of this essay is modified from Dobrov 1990.

1. For More and the coinage of "utopia" see Konstan's essay above.

2. See Konstan's essay above.

3. Coulon 1925, 73–98, proposes solutions to several textual problems in the second hypothesis to the play. Boissonade's emendation σκοπός for στίχος, in particular (Dunbar prints στόχος), yields good sense that points to an ancient scholarly controversy. For the bibliography, see Behaghel 1878–79. Throughout, I use the text of Sommerstein 1987, unless noted otherwise. For a review of the important issue of speaker assignments, see Nesselrath 1996 (who, however, defends the traditional distribution).

4. The political approach is well reviewed in Katz 1976 and Newiger 1983. On the utopian side are studies such as Schwinge 1977 and Zimmermann, "Nephelokkygia," in Rösler and Zimmermann 1991, 55–98. More exploratory are the classic essays of Whitman "The Anatomy of Nothingness" (1964, 167–99) and Arrowsmith 1973. Recent work of note includes Pozzi 1991; Hubbard 1991, 157–82; and Bowie 1993, 151–77.

5. "Transference" lies at the heart of word coinage as any sampling will reveal: we "grasp" concepts, for example, "digest" ideas, and "swallow" truths. Any new discourse necessarily plun-

ders the existing lexicon for terms to appropriate by transferring, by engaging "metaphor" (e.g., the new *epidemic* of electronic *viruses*). This process is sometimes misleadingly expressed by the cliché that "language is a book of faded metaphors." Deferral characterizes the way in which the "true" meaning and presence of an external referent or signified can never be finally captured, summoned, or made identical with a given sign. We are able only to offer one sign(s) in exchange for another. The dream of fusing a sign and the "real" presence of the external referent is ever deferred.

6. The erotic language of *Birds* has attracted much attention (see esp. Arrowsmith 1973) and stands in stark contrast to the play's failure to explain Peisetaerus' and Euelpides' enigmatic quest. For ἔρως in various nominal and verbal forms see lines 135, 136, 143, 324, 412, 574, 593, 696, 699, 703, 704, 707, 1279, 1316, 1343, 1634, 1659, 1737.

7. Hubbard 1991 (and above) comments on the metaphorical thematics of "clouds" in Aristophanes' play of that name. "Like the Clouds themselves," he notes on 111–12, "poets are mutable creatures without fixed allegiances or programs who use the powers of mimetic illusion to engage and mirror men's fantasies and follies."

8. "In *Birds* also something rather grand is intended, . . . As his city-state is afflicted with an incurable illness. . . . [Aristophanes] intimates another city. . . . He suggests, moreover, a complete metamorphosis in form and nature, if necessary, in order to secure a life of peace. This is his intention. The blasphemy against the gods is skillfully handled. . . . The general aim, however, is as follows: to openly expose the Athenians to general reproach for their foolish attitudes rather than randomly criticize citizens individually. . . . Some say that, whereas in other comedies the poet had ridiculed the tales of marvels in tragedy, in the given play he reveals the theme of gigantomachic conflict as trite by having the birds challenge the gods' (supreme) authority." I am following Coulon's text of the hypotheses (the translations are mine) which differs from Dunbar's in certain important respects. L. Radermacher and others have discerned in Hypothesis II the influence of a rather astute critical biography of Aristophanes (see Coulon 1925, 73). On the subject of the hypotheses to Aristophanes, see Gröbl 1889–90.

9. Hofmann 1976, 79. ἐν δὲ τοῖς Ὄρνισι καὶ μέγα τι διανενόηται. ὡς γὰρ ἀδιόρθωτον ἤδη νόσον τῆς πολιτείας νοσούσης . . ., ἄλλην τινὰ πολιτείαν αἰνίττεται. . . . οὐ μόνον δὲ τοῦτο, ἀλλὰ καὶ τὸ σχῆμα ὅλον καὶ τὴν φύσιν, εἰ δέοι, συμβουλεύει μετατίθεσθαι πρὸς τὸ ἠρεμαίως βιοῦν. καὶ ἡ μὲν ἀπότασις αὕτη. τὰ δὲ κατὰ θεῶν βλάσφημα ἐπιτηδείως ᾠκονόμηται. . . . ἀλλ' ὁ μὲν καθόλου σκοπὸς τοιοῦτος. ἕκαστον δὲ τῶν κατὰ μέρος οὐκ εἰκῇ, ἀλλ' ἄντικρυς Ἀθηναίων . . . ἐλέγχει τὴν φαύλην διάθεσιν. . . .

. . . τινὲς δέ φασι τὸν ποιητὴν τὰς ἐν ταῖς τραγῳδίαις τερατολογίας ἐν μὲν ἄλλοις διελέγχειν, ἐν δὲ τοῖς νῦν τὴν τῆς γιγαντομαχίας συμπλοκὴν ἑώλων ἀποφαίνων ὄρνισιν ἔδωκε διαφέρεσθαι πρὸς θεοὺς περὶ τῆς ἀρχῆς.

10. καὶ ἐν μὲν ἄλλοις δράμασι διὰ τῆς κωμικῆς ἀδείας ἤλεγχεν Ἀριστοφάνης τοὺς κακῶς πολιτευομένους ⟨φανερῶς⟩. ἐν δὲ τοῖς Ὄρνισι καὶ μέγα τι διανενόηται, φανερῶς μὲν οὐδαμῶς,— οὐ γὰρ ἔτι τούτου ἦν ἐξουσία,—ληθότως δέ, ὅσον ἀνῆκεν ἀπὸ κωμῳδίας προσκρούειν. So Coulon 1925 and *Aristophane* ad loc., improving upon the rather confused manuscripts.

11. I cite the text of White 1914, 234: οὗτος γὰρ τῶν περὶ τὸ βῆμα, καὶ Εὔπολις ὡς λάλον ἐν Πόλεσι διασύρει· 'Συρακόσιος δ' ἔοικεν, ἡνίκ' ἂν λέγῃ, / τοῖς κυνιδίοισι τοῖσιν ἐπὶ τῶν τειχίων· / ἀναβὰς γὰρ ἐπὶ τὸ βῆμ' ὑλακτεῖ περιτρέχων." δοκεῖ δὲ καὶ ψήφισμα τεθηκέναι μὴ κωμῳδεῖσθαι ὀνομαστί τινα, ὡς Φρύνιχος ἐν Μονοτρόπῳ φησί. "Ψῶζ' ἔχοι Συρακόσιον. / ἐπιφανὲς γὰρ αὐτῷ καὶ μέγα τύχοι. / ἀφείλετο γὰρ κωμῳδεῖν οὓς ἐπεθύμουν." διὸ πικρότερον αὐτῷ προσφέρονται, ὡς λάλῳ δὲ τὴν 'κίτταν' παρέθηκεν.

12. See, e.g., Sommerstein 1986 who revives the thesis of Droysen 1836; Halliwell 1984; and Hubbard 1991, 159–60.

13. Despite its manifold depatures from Aristophanes' style of the 420s, *Birds* does mention thirty-one contemporary Athenians by name, including the putative legislator, Syracosius, him-

self. We have also six oblique references: three patronymics and three nicknames (see lines 17, 31, 126, 712 [and 1491], 766, 1292). See Sommerstein 1986, 102.

14. "If I am right about the general tendency of ancient interpreters to draw unjustified inferences from comic texts, then an agnostic attitude to Syracosios' decree would be wise. If this decree was an invention, the motivation may well have come from the knowledge of the one decree of this kind which . . . may reasonably be regarded as genuine—the one attested in Σ RE Ach. 67."

15. Hubbard 1991, 160.

16. Refuting the views of A. W. Schlegel who held that *Birds* is "the most innocent buffoonery or farce, touching upon all subjects . . . without entering deeply into any, like a fanciful fairy-tale," Süvern presents his learned and detailed reading by means of curiously circular reasoning: the failure of scholars to detect it is itself proof of the allegory's "fine construction and masterly perfection" (Süvern 1830). Attempting to refine the simplistic analysis of the "byzantine schoolmaster" (Hypothesis II), he detects an "intricate confusion" that has "thrown a veil over the fundamental idea of the poem, and has led to the opinion, that the author had merely in view a general satire, on the notions and relations of man, though with a special reference to the Athenian people" (Süvern 1830, 12). This "confusion" turns out to be simply the resistance of *Birds* to Süvern's allegorical trap.

17. While the gods represent the Spartans and the hoopoe is Lamachus, the Athenians are represented sometimes by birds and sometimes by "real" men. Peisetaerus seems to be a composite portrait of Alcibiades and Gorgias whereas Euelpides comprises the gullible Athenians and Gorgias' pupil Polus. For a recent synthesis of historical approaches, see Hubbard 1991, 157–82, which emphasizes Aristophanes' ongoing project of self-presentation in the parabases.

18. Ibid., 181.

19. This approach can be traced from A. W. Schlegel's well-known views through much scholarship in the nineteenth (Vögelin 1858; Curtius 1874, 629–31; Droysen 1836; Schroeder 1927, introd.; Behaghel 1878–79, 20) and twentieth centuries (van Leeuwen 1908; Cataudella 1934; Gigante 1948; and Blaiklock 1954).

20. Whitman 1964, 79.

21. Ibid., 172. "The word is all, it creates consciousness, and its enormous vitality stubbornly resists fact. A word becomes image or metaphor, and the image or metaphor lives in the mind, independent of reason and far more compelling. . . . Images and metaphors are dream substance and make dream worlds, and every world is an absurdity, a verbal nothing. All this is beyond satire, as handled in the *Birds*; it is a poetic weft comically adumbrating the world in which we live, the world where there can be no tragic reversal or recognition, the world of *poneria* and the self, where the persuasive and manipulable word is king."

22. For nineteenth-century bibliography see Behaghel 1978–79, 18–21, who lists a number of works occupying a middle position between a "Speciell-politische Tendenz" and "Tendenzlosigkeit."

23. Arrowsmith 1973, 146.

24. Newiger 1983; Alink 1983; and Pozzi 1991, 149–61.

25. Alink 1983, 324.

26. Newiger 1957, 102. "Es darf abschließend festgestellt werden, daß auch die Chorpersonifikationen sich uns nicht als allegorische Figuren dargestellt haben. Ihre Rolle in den einzelnen Komödien ist verschieden, auch die angewandte Technik der Darstellung, wie wir sahen; aber das Wesentliche ist Wolken, Wespen und Vögeln gemeinsam: sie bedeuten nicht durchgänig etwas anderes, als sie sind, sondern nur gelegentlich. Sie werden durch Wortspiel, Metapher, Vergleich zu einem anderen in Beziehung gesetzt, aber nicht a priori geglichen, es wird auf sie nicht Zug um Zug des Gemeinten übertragen, sondern die Übertragungen gehen hin und her. Wir sind nur zeitweise 'im Bilde.' Ein im ganzen einheitliches Bild hatten wir nur in den 'Vögeln,' aber da war wieder kein deutlich und ständig Gemeintes feststellbar."

27. See Taaffe 1987, 54–63; and Bowie 1993, 151–77.

28. Nan Dunbar has been helpful in sharing her knowledge and views with me (per litt.) reflecting the long experience of writing this fullest of Oxford commentaries, and I must here acknowledge my debt to her.

29. Studies that explore other aspects of *Birds* are Hofmann 1976 and Pozzi 1991, which contrast with the more strictly historical approaches of Gomme 1938, Katz 1976, and Stark 1982. Zannini Quirini 1987 sees *Birds* (especially the latter half of the play) as an ominous return to a pre-Olympian religion that is as horrific as it is comical.

30. Whitman 1964, 168.

31. Dobrov 1988b, 26–29.

32. Burkert 1979, 56.

33. Sommerstein 1987, 1.

34. "*One word for another*: that is the formula for the metaphor," asserts Lacan 1966, 157, "and if you are a poet you will produce for your own delight a continuous stream, a dazzling tissue of metaphors." He goes on to speak of comedy's perfectly convincing "demonstration of the radical superfluousness of all signification."

35. The yearning to become a bird is a common lyric topos, Alcman fr. 26 being perhaps the most famous example: "Ah, how I wish I were a sea-bird who with the halcyons would skim the crests of the waves! etc." More or less contemporary tragic examples include Euripides *Hipp.* 732–51, *Hel.* 1478–94, *Andro.* 861–62; Soph. *OC* 1080–84, fr. 476 (*Oenomaus*) etc. This desiderative metaphor often expresses an implicit death wish. See Euripides *Ion* 1238–45, *Heracl.* 1157–62, *Hec.* 1096–94. The song from Sophocles' *Oenomaus* is transplanted into a comic context when quoted by the young man in the second sequence of intruders, *Birds* 1337–39.

36. A. W. Schlegel in Newiger 1957, 181.

37. For a discussion of Sophocles' tragedy and its metafictional transformation, see section II.

38. Segal 1986, 19.

39. Lacan 1966, 158.

40. Harries 1978, 80.

41. Bloomfield 1933, 443.

42. A. Wilden (Lacan and Wilden 1968, 220), citing F. Bresson's comment that "languages are *simultaneously* doubly articulated and devoid of symbolic value," suggests that "metaphor as usually conceived (dependent on resemblance) is not something developed out of an originally digital language, but rather that language itself, as Vico, Condillac, Rousseau, and others believed, is originally metaphorical."

43. De Man 1978, 13, explores philosophy's attempt to "control figuration by keeping it, so to speak, in its place, by delimiting the boundaries of its influence and thus restricting the epistemological damage that it may cause."

44. Concerning Locke's dismissal as "mere translation" of a well-known "definition"—"motion is the passage from one place to another"—de Man notes (1978, 17) that "Locke's own 'passage' is bound to continue this perpetual motion that never moves beyond tautology: motion is passage and passage is a translation; translation, once again, means motion, piles motion upon motion. It is no mere play of words that 'translate' is translated in German as 'übersetzen' which itself translates the Greek 'meta phorein' or metaphor. Metaphor gives itself the totality which it then claims to define, but it is in fact the tautology of its own position. The discourse of simple ideas is figural discourse or translation and, as such, creates the fallacious illusion of definition."

45. Lacan 1966, 157.

46. The two rival theories implying a "cognitive content" in metaphor appeal, respectively, to (1) "collusion" (similarity): although the vehicle is predicated of, or suppresses, the tenor, "meaningful" metaphor is possible insofar as the two terms share certain aspects. The semantic sphere of the vehicle is thereby extended to make metaphor intelligible; or (2) the "collision" of two (preferably dissimilar) terms: meaning arises in the resulting tension. Davidson's quasi-performative

view of metaphor (1978), on the other hand, denies to it any intrinsic cognitive content. Standard guides to research in this field are the annotated bibliographies of Shibles (1971) and van Noppen (1985).

47. Davidson 1978, 76.

48. Let alone allegorical restatement, cf. Newiger's point 1957, 102, that the birds of the Aristophanic play succeed in "meaning" something other than they are only incidentally.

49. Roland Barthes 1970, 174 n. 1, who describes comedy as the parasitic "black" rhetoric that "traces with severity and precision the transgressive place where the taboos of language and sex are lifted."

50. The "tenor" is the signifier suppressed or replaced, i.e., the metaphorical "subject." The vehicle or "object" (often referred to simply as the "metaphor") is the term predicated of, or replacing, the tenor.

51. On the grotesque see Bakhtin 1984, 30–32, and Steiger 1934, 161–84, 275–85, 416–32.

52. In contrast to the "anaglog" world of phenomena, human language is "digital" and "doubly articulated." It is "Digital" in the sense that its work of representation and signification is performed by means of discrete bits: phonemes, words, etc. It is also "Doubly articulated": on one level, language consists of material bits forming a nonsemantic code (digits, letters, phonemes) whose relationship to what they represent is constitutively arbitrary; on a second level, it consits of syntagms (words, sentences), which combine into further syntagms thereby generating meaning. Analog: there is a direct rational or quantitative relationship between the scale and what it represents (e.g., mercury in a thermometer, a cry of pain) that precludes negation, and the true/false distinction.

53. "The *a* of *différance* indicates [an] indecision as concerns activity and passivity, that which cannot be governed by or distributed between the terms of [the] opposition [presence/absence]." Derrida 1972a, 27.

54. Decentering the system of language by depriving it of a transcendental signified, Derrida (1972a, 26) argues that every sign marks a place of difference: "The play of differences supposes, in effect, syntheses and referrals which forbid at any moment, or in any sense, that a simple element is present in and of itself, referring only to itself. Whether in the order of spoken or written discourse, no element can function as a sign without referring to another element which itself is not simply present. This interweaving results in each 'element'—phoneme or grapheme— being constituted on the basis of the trace within it of the other elements of the chain or system. This interweaving, this textile, is the text produced only in the transformation of another text. Nothing, neither among the elements nor within the system, is anywhere ever simply present or absent. There are only, everywhere, differences and traces of traces."

55. "It is [the] implied circularity and autonomy of language," writes A. Wilden in Lacan and Wilden 1968, 217, "that lead Lacan into postulating a sort of fault in the system, a hole, a fundamental lack into which, one might say, meaning is poured. It is this fundamental *manque* which allows substitutions, the movement of language essential to signification, to take place."

56. Segal 1986, 16–17.

57. In lines 30–54 Aristophanes seems to promise a conventional comic problem that will structure the subsequent events. This promise is notoriously violated as the parabasis reveals an entirely unfamiliar world that springs spontaneously from the interacting metaphors represented by Tereus and the intense political life of Cloudcuckooland (replete with laws and "culture").

58. Arrowsmith 1973, 131.

59. The centrality of the concept of desire has been most recently and forcefully presented by Arrowsmith 1973, 130: "No other play of Aristophanes, not even *Lysistrata*, is so pervaded, so saturated by the language of desire."

60. Lacan 1966, 153.

61. I invoke the Derridean notion expressed most fully in the reading of Rousseau in *Of*

Grammatology. Essentially, it comprehends the irreconcilable notions "an inessential extra added to something already complete" and "something essential added to fulfill a lack in something that was supposed to be complete."

62. On such textual charlatans, see Smith 1989.

63. On the way Aristophanes' protagonists reflect the playwright's creative energy, see Hubbard 1991, 45–47, 136–38.

64. The so-called rupture of dramatic illusion in the parabasis, e.g., has the birds summon the spectators directly to join them and to leave the theater (Athens by synecdoche) whose physical constraints are equated with abstract limitations of the human condition (lines 785–800).

65. Whitman 1964, 27.

66. Nietzsche 1873, 46–47.

67. E.g., Metz 1991.

68. To be sure, the works of David Bain on the one hand and those of Peter Rau and Pietro Pucci on the other (treating tragedy and comedy, respectively) are of comparable value and precision, and are a fine start: Bain 1977; Rau 1967; and Pucci 1961.

69. While I would certainly not presume to collapse generic distinctions when it comes to dramatic reflexivity, tragedy and comedy share significant common ground (more than is traditionally acknowledged, e.g., Taplin 1986). This is especially interesting in the case of sustained sequences *mise en abyme* outlined below. For a fuller discussion of these categories and their application to a wide range of tragic and comic drama, see *Figures of Play* (forthcoming).

70. Such "signposting" often consists in a clue such as a sudden change in meter or register of speech. See the introductory discussions in Schlesinger 1936 and Chapman 1983.

71. This term, coined in 1893 by André Gide, is a metaphor from heraldry in which a coat of arms may have a plate at its center that duplicates, in miniature, the outlines of the main escutcheon. I use *mise en abyme* here specifically to represent the way in which the poetics of a given "text" in the most general sense is self-consciously foregrounded or retraced within the narrative itself. For a history of the term, see Ron 1987.

72. See Taplin 1986. For a different view of the relationship between tragedy and comedy on this level, see Seidensticker 1982; and Zeitlin 1980.

73. Patrick 1975, 3: "Thus, George Gershwin's 'I Got Rhythm' (1930) may be transformed into Sidney Bechet's 'Shag' (1932) or into Charlie Parker's 'Dexterity' (1947). Similarly, new blues compositions may be created by fitting a newly-composed melodic line to a basic I-IV-I-V-I harmonic scheme. By analogy to text substitution in medieval music, I call this general technique the 'melodic contrafact' (*contrafactum*)." The genre of modern jazz ("bebop") does much more than parody or "respond" to its model. It uses a significant aspect of its structure to produce a entirely new composition. For theatrical improvisation, see Greenblatt 1980.

74. For a careful philological review of the terms "parody" and "travesty," see Rau 1967, 7–18, and Hutcheon 1991, 30, 49. For paratragedy as distinct from parody, see Pucci 1961, 277–78. I have not followed Niall Slater's recent suggestion (1992, 403) of "recycling" to capture the true spirit of the Aristophanic contrafact (cf. the term's vivid and perhaps pejorative connotations in contemporary debates about waste management).

75. The notions of "parody" and "travesty" when applied to Aristophanic comedy misleadingly limit the dramatic range and importance of this phenomenon. Far from challenging the admirable work of scholars such as P. Rau and W. Horn, however, I would submit "contrafact" as a more general term that transcends the specific functions of parody (i.e., achieving humorous effect through mythical travesty, incongruity, exaggeration, and mockery of the original).

76. Hubbard 1991, 132.

77. Ibid., 132–33.

78. The Roman poet, by contrast, does not seem to have been bothered by such anachronism as we can appreciate from the details of theater construction prominent in the description of Carthage at *Aeneid* 1.426–28.

79. A few delightful exceptions in the category of films-within-films include *Lilly in Love*, *Farewell My Concubine*, and Robert Altman's *The Player*.

80. Cf. Taplin 1986, 171: "There is no surviving example even in comedy of a fully fledged play within a play; but the use of *Telephus* in *Acharnians*, or of *Helen* and *Andromeda* in *Thesm.*, is half way there. The nearest that tragedy approaches to this is in certain uses of contrived disguise such as the 'merchant' in *Philoctetes* and the escape scene in *Helen*. Such scenes seem to occur in the 'outer periods' of fifth-century tragedy."

81. The status of *Birds* (with the parabasis as a highlight) as a masterpiece is *communis opinio*; Henderson 1991, 82, refers to it as "the culmination of Aristophanes' earlier technique." For studies of important problems unique to *Birds*, see Hofmann 1976 and Hubbard 1991, 158–60. The unique position of the play in the Aristophanic corpus is well analyzed in Newiger 1975, 266–82.

82. The recent historicizing trend such as the revival of Droysen's hypothesis concerning the law of Syracosius is discussed above.

83. That is to say, choral and military service were mutually exclusive for young men of ephebic age. See Winkler 1990, 20–62. For the connection between sophistry and comic poesis in *Clouds*, see "Misunderstood Intellectuals and Poets," in Hubbard 1991, chap. 5, 88–112 (n. 22, p. 95, in particular).

84. See Dobrov 1988a, 111–65. It is important that Peisetaerus reaffirms his status as choreographer and director in the later episodes. Note, for example, his clement dismissal of the poet with whom he apparently sympathizes as with a poetic competitor (cf. 947) who is a rival choral *didaskalos* (912).

85. See Gelzer 1960, 22, 130, 135; Händel 1963, 317; and Gelzer 1976, 9.

86. See Sifakis 1971, 62, who is arguing against the work of scholars such as Francis Cornford who held the parabasis to be a cultic remnant of sorts that first replaced the parodos and to which dramatic scenes were added. Although certainly not identical to the so-called marching anapaests of tragedy, the anapaestic tetrameter in combination with a new persona (bird-god citizens of Nephelokokkugia) cannot have failed to allude to the convention of a first choral entrance. On this question see Harsh 1934.

87. Text and translation from Sommerstein 1987.

88. Sommerstein 1987, 1.

89. Alink 1983, 323.

90. See Arrowsmith 1973.

91. See Hofmann 1976, Henderson 1991, and Konstan 1990.

92. The famous black-figure oinochoe depicting bird choristers as well as references to the bird choruses of Magnes (cf. *Knights* 522) and, perhaps, Crates suggest that Aristophanes had a precedent to draw upon as a choral context for his comic polis.

93. In a memorable performance (ca. 430) the Thracian king underwent metamorphosis into a hoopoe, a feature innovated by Sophocles. For a reconstruction and discussion of this play, see Dobrov 1993, 197–214.

94. Ibid.

95. For a detailed discussion of this question, see Mayer 1892, 489–94, and Halliday 1933, 104–6, who argues that Tereus was originally a Megarian hero. Other important secondary literature on this myth includes Hiller von Gärtringen 1986; Robert 1920, 154–62; Chandler 1935; Cazzaniga 1950; Mihailov 1955; Fontenrose 1948; Schroeder 1926; Zaganiaris 1973; and Segal 1990.

96. See Pearson 1917, 224, and Dobrov 1993, 218–20.

97. Thuc. 2.63: "Men like these [*apragmones*] would soon ruin a state, either here, if they should persuade others, or if they should settle in some other land founding an independent state all to themselves; for retiring and unambitious men are not secure unless flanked by men of action" (trans. Rex Warner).

98. Aeschylean drama attests a simpler pre-Sophoclean tradition: as in the case of the passage in *Suppliants* (line 62, hawk instead of hoopoe), *Ag.* 1050–51 reflects an earlier version of the legend which makes no mention of shearing Philomela's tongue. Clytaemnestra says she will "persuade Cassandra (in Greek)" provided that she is not a monolingual barbarian who can only chatter like a swallow. This is the familiar association of swallow song and foreign languages, which, if anything, foreshadows Cassandra's mantic loquacity, *not* her inability to speak.

99. The crux at *Birds* 16, ἐκ τῶν ὀρνέων, no doubt conceals a phrase that anticipates Peisetaerus' explanation (46–48) of his interest in Tereus. A compelling solution is offered by Koenen 1959, 83–87, who emends to ἐκ τῶν ὀργίων, restoring an allusion to the Dionysian cult context of Tereus' metamorphosis. We should then translate "Tereus, the hoopoe, who became a bird from the rites (of Dionysus)." In this case ἐκ + genitive would denote both a causal and a temporal connection between the Dionysian Trieterica and Tereus' metamorphosis. Dunbar 1995 ad loc., on the other hand, considers it an interpolation, a gloss on the preceding line.

100. Cf. Ovid *Met.* 6.594–96: Concita per silvas truba comitante suarum / Terribilis Procne furiisque agitata doloris, / Bacche, tuas *simulat*; "Surrounded by her (female) attendants Prokne rushes through the forest frightful in her frenzied rage of pain, *feigning* your fury, Bacchus."

101. It is conceivable that the moment of metamorphosis was illustrated by the display of Tereus, Procne, and Philomela on the ἐκκύκλημα in a superimposition of the death tableau of the *Choephori* exodus and the familiar Euripidean deus ex machina. The rapid succession of events would seem to preclude a full costume change. I suggest that we imagine this moment marking the conclusion of the tragedy as an arrangement of three characters (Tereus in pursuit?) in which their metamorphosis is marked symbolically by certain prominent signs—a token change of clothing or headdress, perhaps. The death wish implicit in the desiderative metaphor of lyric and tragic poetry "Would that I were a bird" (i.e., the desire to flee from life and the human condition) is well known and would make quite natural the association of this desperate tableau of metamorphosis-in-crisis with the scenes of death that had already been presented on the *ekkuklēma*. Thus Sophocles would achieve a counterpoint of sorts between this final image of the unfortunate "birds" and his audience's expectation of a death scene.

102. Hofmann 1976, 74.

103. Anticipating Hall's *Inventing the Barbarian* (1989), Kiso (1984) emphasizes how much our understanding of the Sophoclean corpus is distorted by the (nonrandom) process responsible for preserving the seven extant scripts. Much of the lost material appears to resemble late Euripides (much more so than do the extant seven)!

104. Detienne 1987, 2–3.

105. Foley 1985, 46.

106. For a discussion of the performative aspects of Peisetaerus' role, see the essay by Slater above.

Bibliography

Alink, M. 1983. *De Vogels van Aristophanes: een structuuranalyse en interpretatie*. Amsterdam.

Arnott, Geoffrey. 1973. "Euripides and the Unexpected." *G&R* 20.49–64.

Arrowsmith, William. 1973. "Aristophanes' *Birds*: The Fantasy Politics of Eros." *Arion*, n.s., 1.119–67.

Bain, David. 1975. "Audience Address in Greek Tragedy." *CQ* 25.13–25.

———. 1977. *Actors and Audience*. Oxford.

Bakhtin, Mikhail. 1984. *Rabelais and His World*. Translated by H. Iswolsky. Bloomington.

Barchiesi, M. 1970. "Plauto e il 'metateatro' antico." *Il Verri* 31.113–30.

Barthes, Roland. 1970. "L'ancienne rhetorique." *Communications* 16.170–97.

Behaghel, W. 1878–79. *Geschichte der Auffassung der Aristophanischen Vögel*. Parts 1–2. Heidelberg.

Bertelli, L. 1983. "L'utopia sulla scena di Aristofane e la parodia della città." *Civiltà classica e cristiana* 9.215–61.

Blaiklock, E. 1954. "Walking Away from the News: An Autobiographical Interpretation of Aristophanes's *Birds*." *G&R* 2.1.98–111.

Bloomfield, Leonard. 1933. *Language*. Chicago.

Bonanno, M. G. 1987. "Παρατραγῳδία in Aristofane." *Dioniso* 61.135–67.

Bowie, A. M. 1993. *Aristophanes: Myth, Ritual and Comedy*. Cambridge.

Burkert, W. 1979. *Structure and History in Greek Mythology and Ritual*. Sather Lectures 47. Berkeley.

Calderwood, James L. 1971. *Shakespearean Metadrama*. Minneapolis.

——. 1979. *Metadrama in Shakespeare's Henriad: Richard II to Henry V*. Berkeley.

——. 1983. *To Be and Not to Be: Negation and Metadrama in "Hamlet."* New York.

Carpenter, T., and C. A. Faraone, eds. 1993. *Masks of Dionysus*. Ithaca.

Cataudella, Q. 1934. *La poesia di Aristofane*. Bari.

Cazzaniga, Ignazio. 1950. *La saga di Itis nella tradizione letteraria e mitografica greco-romana, I: Da Omero a Nonno Panopolitano*. Verona.

Chandler, A. 1935. "The Nightingale in Greek and Latin Poetry." *CJ* 30.78–84.

Chapman, G. A. H. 1983. "Some Notes on Dramatic Illusion in Aristophanes." *AJP* 104.1–23.

Coulon, Victor. 1925. "Observations critiques et éxegétiques sur l'argument II des *Oiseaux* et sur le texte d'Aristophane." *Revue des Études Greques* 38.73–98.

——, ed. 1928. *Aristophane*. Vol. 3. Translated by H. Van Daele. Paris.

Curtius, E. 1874. *Griechische Geschichte*. Vol. 2. 4th ed. Berlin.

Davidson, D. 1978. "What Metaphors Mean." *Critical Inquiry* 5.1.31–48.

de Man, Paul. 1978. "The Epistemology of Metaphor." *Critical Inquiry* 5.1.13–30.

Derrida, Jacques. 1967. *Of Grammatology*. Translated by G. Spivak, 1976. Baltimore.

——. 1972a. *Positions*. Translated by A. Bass, 1981. Chicago.

——. 1972b. "White Mythology." In *Margins of Philosophy*, 207–71. Translated by A. Bass, 1982. Chicago.

Detienne, Marcel. 1987. "The Voice and the Book of Orpheus." Translated by Richard Klein. Townsend Lecture no. 4, Cornell University, 10 March 1987.

——. 1989. *L'ecriture d'Orphée*. Paris.

Dobrov, G. W. 1988a. "Winged Words/Graphic *Birds*: The Aristophanic Comedy of Language." Ph.D. diss., Cornell University.

——. 1988b. "The Dawn of Farce: Aristophanes." *Themes in Drama* 10.15–31.

——. 1990. "Aristophanes' *Birds* and the Metaphor of Deferral." *Arethusa* 23.2.209–33.

——. 1993. "The Tragic and the Comic Tereus." *AJP* 14.2.189–234.

——. Forthcoming. *Figures of Play: Greek Drama and Metafictional Poetics*. Oxford.

——, ed. 1995. *Beyond Aristophanes: Transition and Diversity in Greek Comedy*. Atlanta.

Dover, K. J. 1993. *Aristophanes' Frogs*. Oxford.

Droysen, J. 1836. "Des Aristophanes *Vögel* und die Hermokopiden." *Rheinisches Museum* 4.27–62.

Dunbar, Nan. 1995. *Aristophanes' Birds*. Oxford.

Foley, Helene. 1985. "Tragedy and Politics in Aristophanes' *Acharnians*." *JHS* 108.33–47.

Fontenrose, J. E. 1948. "The Sorrows of Ino and Procne." *TAPA* 79.125–67.

Forbes-Irving, P. M. C. 1990. *Metamorphosis in Greek Myths*. Oxford.

Gelzer, Thomas. 1960. *Der epirrhematische Agon bei Aristophanes. Untersuchungen zur Struktur der attischen Alten Komödie*. Munich.

——. 1976. "Some Aspects of Aristophanes' Dramatic Art in the *Birds*." *BICS* 23.1–14.

Gigante, M. 1948. "La città dei giusti in Esiodo e gli Uccelli di Aristofane." *Dioniso* 2.17–25.

Goldhill, Simon. 1986. *Reading Greek Tragedy*. Cambridge.

———. 1990. *The Poet's Voice: Essays on Poetics and Greek Literature*. Cambridge.

Gomme, A. W. 1938. "Aristophanes and Politics." *CR* 52.97–109.

Green, J. Richard. 1991. "On Seeing and Depicting the Theatre in Classical Athens." *GRBS* 32.15–50.

Greenblatt, Stephen. 1980. *Renaissance Self-Fashioning: From More to Shakespeare*. Chicago.

Gröbl, J. N. 1889–90. *Die ältesten Hypotheseis zu Aristophanes*. Dillingen.

Gruber, William E. 1981. "The Wild Men of Comedy: Transformation in the Comic Hero from Aristophanes to Pirandello." *Genre* 14.207–27.

———. 1983. "Systematized Delirium: The Craft, Form, and Meaning of Aristophanic Comedy." *Helios* 10.97–110.

Hall, Edith. 1989. *Inventing the Barbarian: Greek Self-Definition through Tragedy*. Oxford.

Halliday, W. R. 1933. *Indo-European Folk-Tales and Greek Legend*. Cambridge.

Halliwell, Stephen. 1984. "Ancient Interpretations of ὀνομαστὶ κωμῳδεῖν in Aristophanes." *CQ* 34.83–88.

Händel, Paul. 1963. *Formen und Darstellungsweisen in der Aristophanischen Komödie*. Heidelberg.

Harries, K. 1978. "The Many Uses of Metaphor." *Critical Inquiry* 5.1.73–90.

Harsh, P. W. 1934. "The Position of the Parabasis in the Plays of Aristophanes." *TAPA* 65.178–97.

Henderson, Jeffrey. 1991. *The Maculate Muse: Obscene Language in Attic Comedy*. 2d ed. New York.

Hiller von Gärtringen, Friedrich F. 1986. *De Graecorum fabulis ad Thraces pertinentibus quaestiones criticae*. Berlin.

Hofmann, Heinz. 1976. *Mythos und Komödie: Untersuchungen zu den Vögeln des Aristophanes*. Spudasmata 33. New York.

Horn, W. 1970. *Gebet und Gebetsparodie in den Komödien des Aristophanes*. Nürnberg.

Hornby, Richard. 1986. *Drama, Metadrama, and Perception*. Lewisburg.

Hubbard, Thomas. 1991. *The Mask of Comedy: Aristophanes and the Intertextual Parabasis*. Ithaca.

Hubert, Judd D. 1991. *Metatheater: The Example of Shakespeare*. London.

Hutcheon, L. 1991. *A Theory of Parody: The Teachings of Contemporary Art Forms*. New York.

Katz, B. 1976. "The *Birds* of Aristophanes and Politics." *Athenaeum* 54.353–81.

Kiso, Akiko. 1984. *The Lost Sophocles*. New York.

Kock, T. 1927–. *Ausgewählte Komödien des Aristophanes erklärt von Theodor Kock*. Berlin.

Koenen, Ludwig. 1959. "Tereus in den *Vögeln* des Aristophanes." In *Studien zu Textgeschichte und Textkritik*, edited by Hellfried Dahlmann and Reinhold Merkelbach, 83–87. Cologne.

Kölb, C. 1984. *The Incredulous Reader: Literature and the Function of Disbelief*. Ithaca.

Konstan, David. 1990. "A City in the Air: Aristophanes' *Birds*." *Arethusa* 23.2.183–207.

Kowzan, T. 1983. "Les cómedies d'Aristophane, véhicule de la critique dramatique." *Dioniso* 54.83–100.

Lacan, Jacques. 1966. *Écrits, a Selection*. Translated by A. Sheridan. New York.

Lacan, Jacques, and Anthony Wilden. 1968. *Speech and Language in Psychoanalysis*. Baltimore.

MacDowell, D. M. 1995. *Aristophanes and Athens: An Introduction to the Plays*. Oxford.

MacMathúna, S. 1971. "Trickery in Aristophanes." Ph.D. diss., Cornell University.

Mayer, M. 1892. "Mythistorica 3: Tereus." *Hermes* 27.489–99.

Meinecke, A. 1839–57. *Fragmenta Comicorum Graecorum*. Berlin.

Metz, Christian. 1974. *Film Language: A Semiotics of the Cinema*. New York.

———. 1991. *L'enonciation impersonelle, ou le site du film*. Paris.

Mihailov, Georgi. 1955. "La lègende de Terée." *Annuaire de l'Université de Sophia, Faculté des Lettres* 50.2.77–199.

Muecke, F. 1977. "Playing with the Play: Theatrical Self-Consciousness in Aristophanes." *Antichthon* 11.52–67.

Nesselrath, Heinz-Günther. 1996. "Die Tücken der Sprecherverteilung: Euelpides, Peisetairos und ihre Rollen in der Eingangspartie der aristophanischen *Vögel*." *Museum Helveticum* 53.91–99.

Newiger, H.-J. 1957. *Metapher und Allegorie: Studien zu Aristophanes*. Zetemata 16. Munich.

———, ed. 1975. "Die *Vögel* und ihre Stellung im Gesamtwerk des Aristophanes." In *Aristophanes und die alte Komödie*, 266–82. Darmstadt.

———. 1983. "Gedanken zu Aristophanes' *Vögeln*." In Ἀρετῆς μνήμη · Ἀφιέρωμα εἰς μνήμην τοῦ Κωνσταντίνου Ι. Βουρβέρη, edited by C. K. Soile, 47–57. Athens.

Nietzsche, F. 1873. "On Truth and Lie in an Extra-Moral Sense." In *The Portable Nietzsche*, 42–47. Translated by W. Kaufmann, 1954. London.

Patrick, James. 1975. "Charlie Parker and Harmonic Sources of Bebop Composition: Thoughts on the Repertory of New Jazz in the 1940's." *Journal of Jazz Studies* 2.2.3–23.

Pearson, A. C. 1917. *The Fragments of Sophocles*. Cambridge.

Pozzi, Dora. 1986. "The Pastoral Ideal in the *Birds* of Aristophanes." *Classical Journal* 81.119–29.

———. 1991. "The Polis in Crisis." In *Myth and the Polis*, edited by D. Pozzi and J. Wickersham, 126–63. Ithaca.

Pozzi, Dora, and John Wickersham. 1991. *Myth and the Polis*. Ithaca.

Pucci, Pietro. 1961. *Aristofane ed Euripide. ricerche metriche e stilistiche*. Atti dell' Academia Nazionale dei Lincei 358, Memorie, Cl. di Scienze mor., stor. e filol., Ser. 8, vol. 10, fasc. 5. Rome.

Rau, Peter. 1967. *Paratragodia: Untersuchungen einer kömischen Form des Aristophanes*. Zetemata 45. Munich.

Robert, Carl. 1920. *Griechische Heldensage*. Berlin. Vol. 2 [in 3 "books"] of Preller's *Griechische Mythologie*, 4th ed.

Romer, Frank. 1983. "When Is a Bird Not a Bird?" *TAPA* 113.135–42.

Ron, Moshe. 1987. "The Restricted Abyss: Nine Problems in the Theory of *Mise en Abyme*." *Poetics Today* 8.2.417–38.

Rösler, Wolfgang, and Bernhard Zimmermann. 1991. *Carnevale e utopia nella grecia antica*. Bari.

Schlegel, A. W. 1809. *Vorlesungen über dramtische Kunst und Litteratur*. Vol. 1. Heidelberg. Translated by John Black as *A Course of Lectures on Dramatic Art and Literature*. London, 1846.

Schlesinger, Alfred E. 1936. "Identifications of Parody in Aristophanes." *TAPA* 67.296–314.

Schroeder, Otto. 1926. "ΠΡΟΚΝΗ." *Hermes* 61.423–36.

———. 1927. *Ausgewählte Komödien des Aristophanes. Erklärt von Th. Kock*. Vol. 4: *Die Vögel* (4 Aufl., neue Bearbeitung von O. Schroeder). Berlin.

Schwinge, E. 1977. "Aristophanes und die Utopie." *Würzburger Jarbücher für die Altertumswissenschaft* 3.43–67.

Segal, Charles P. 1986. *Language and Desire in Seneca's Phaedra*. Princeton.

———. 1990. "Philomela's Web and the Pleasures of the Text: Ovid's Myth of Tereus in the *Metamorphoses*." Lecture version. University of California at Berkeley, March.

Seidensticker, Bernd. 1978. "Comic Elements in Euripides' *Bacchae*." *AJP* 99.303–20.

———. 1982. *Palintonos Harmonia. Studien su komischen Elementen in der griechischen Tragödie*. Hypomnemata 72. Göttingen.

Shibles, W. 1971. *Metaphor: An Annotated Bibliography and History*. Whitewater, Wis.

Sifakis, G. M. 1971. *Parabasis and Animal Choruses*. London.

Slater, Niall. 1985. *Plautus in Performance: The Theatre of the Mind*. Princeton.

———. 1992. "Space, Character, and ΑΠΑΤΗ: Transformation and Transvaluation in the *Acharnians*." In *Tragedy, Comedy and the Polis*, edited by Sommerstein et al., 397–415.

Smith, N. 1989. "Diviners and Divination in Aristophanic Comedy." *Classical Antiquity* 8.1.140–58.

Sommerstein, Alan. 1986. "The Decree of Syrakosios." *CQ* 36.1.101–8.

———. 1987. *Aristophanes' Birds*. Warminster.

Sommerstein, Alan, Stephen Halliwell, Jeffrey Henderson, and Bernhard Zimmermann, eds. 1993. *Tragedy, Comedy and the Polis*. Papers from the Greek Drama Conference, Nottingham, 18–20 July 1990. Bari.

Stark, I. 1982. "Die Aristophanische Komödienfigur als Suject der Geschichte." *Klio* 64.67–74.

Steiger, H. 1934. "Die Groteske und die Burleske bei Aristophanes." *Philologus* 89.2.161–84, 89.3.275–85, 89.4.416–32.

Süvern, J. 1830. *Essay on "The Birds" of Aristophanes*. Translated by W. Hamilton, 1835. London.

Taaffe, Lauren. 1987. "Gender, Deception, and Metatheatre in Aristophanes' *Ecclesiazusae*." Ph.D. diss., Cornell University.

——. 1993. *Aristophanes and Women*. London.

Taplin, Oliver. 1986. "Greek Tragedy and Comedy: A *Synkrisis*." *JHS* 106.163–74.

van Leeuwen, J. 1908. *Prolegomena ad Aristophanem*. Leiden.

van Noppen, J. 1985. *Metaphor: A Bibliography of Post-1970 Publications*. Amsterdam.

Vögelin, A. 1858. *Ein Blatt an Herrn Prof. Köchly zum Feste des fünf-und-zwanzigjärigen Bestandes der zürcherischen Hochschule*. Zurich.

White, John. 1914. *The Scholia on the Aves of Aristophanes*. Boston.

Whitman, Cedric. 1964. *Aristophanes and the Comic Hero*. Cambridge, Mass.

Winkler, J. J. 1990. "The Ephebes' Song: *Tragoidia* and *Polis*." In *Dionysos*, edited by Winkler and Zeitlin, 20–62.

Winkler, J. J., and F. I. Zeitlin, eds. 1990. *Nothing to Do with Dionysos? Athenian Drama in Its Social Context*. Princeton.

Zaganiaris, Nicholas J. 1973. "Le mythe de Térée dans la litterature greque et latine." *Platon* 25.208–32.

Zannini Quirini, Bruno. 1987. *Nephelokokkygia: La prospettiva mitica degli Uccelli di Aristofane*. Rome.

Zeitlin, Froma. 1980. "The Closet of Masks: Role-Playing and Myth-Making in the *Orestes* of Euripides." *Ramus* 9.51–77.

——. 1981. "Travesties of Gender and Genre in Aristophanes' *Thesmophoriazusae*." In *Reflections of Women in Antiquity*, edited by H. P. Foley, 169–217. New York.

PART TWO

Playing along the Fault Lines

JEFFREY HENDERSON

Mass versus Elite and the
Comic Heroism of Peisetairos

Peisetairos, the hero of *Birds*, in some important respects differs typologically from Aristophanes' other five hero(in)es.[1] This essay assesses these differences and their possible significance for the interpretation of the play as a whole. In studying how the comic hero is institutionally and socially determined I respond to the utopian analyses in the first section—especially those of Romer and Hubbard—while placing emphasis on a new feature of the genre, namely how comedy exploits fissures in the social fabric to generate its meaning.

Evaluation of Peisetairos' heroism is complicated by the play's remote setting far from Athens and far from anywhere, and by its hero's detachment from topical concerns. Every play of Aristophanes subordinates topical reality to comic fantasy to some extent, so that any interpretation of its satirical thrust involves determining the extent of that subordination, mainly by applying external controls. The interpretation of *Birds* has been unusually difficult because of the unusual autonomy of its fantasy.[2] Unlike the other extant plays, *Birds* contains no debate on any current question of public interest; recommends no reform of current political habits; and advocates no particular policy decisions. The poet forgoes his customary appearance in the parabatic anapaests, and the hero takes great pains to make his bird polis as distant and as distinct from Athens or any other actual polis as can be. Its name will not be Sparta but the fantastic Nephelokokkugia (814–20); its citadel god will not be Athena but a fighting cock (826–36); its prayers will not include the Khians

(880); it rejects membership in the Athenian Empire (1021ff.); it denies entry to anyone who would import Athenian laws, customs, or institutions; it holds to be lawful whatever is unlawful in Athens (753ff.). Peisetairos himself is hard to identify with in the usual ways. To unify and become the almighty king of the birds is an odd sort of ambition for an Athenian, not to mention its elision of the distinctions between human and beast, mortal and divine. Peisetairos ends up being both man and bird, ruler and god. All very fine, but what to do with Athens?

Some regard *Birds* as a detached escapist fantasy, a flight from the harsh realities of the actual polis to some sort of poetic fantasy world.[3] But that cannot be right. Neither in the play nor in any external source is there the slightest suggestion that in spring 414 the Athenians generally were in an escapist mood; on the contrary, Thucydides portrays their mood as buoyant to the point of hubris (6.24–31). Nor in beholding Nephelokokkugia do we seem to have "escaped" from Athens: Athens and the Athenians are constantly in view, and the hero, in spite of his metamorphosis, remains very much an Athenian. In the most fundamental ways, Nephelokokkugia is a utopia defined by its lack of what Athenians found annoying and its possession of what Athenians desired. The resemblance of the plot to the sensational events of the preceding year, though not explicit, is close enough that no spectator could fail to see it, and this resemblance clearly suggests that among the play's agenda was satire of the lofty imperial ambitions engendered in the Athenians by contemporary rhetors, just as the name of the hero suggests satire of their persuasive rhetoric. For the spectators, then, Nephelokokkugia was not a distraction from Athens but a beguiling new way to contemplate it.

At the same time, the resemblance of the plot to contemporary reality is not exact enough to reward an allegorical interpretation of the kind invited by *Knights* or *Wasps*. All attempts to identify characters, actions, or situations in the play with particular topical counterparts fail from lack of consistency and from insufficient clues in the text.[4] The utopian fantasy of *Birds* was indeed generated by contemporary realities, but it is too large, distant, and autonomous to be limited by them; it subsumes rather than merely reflects the actual world, and Peisetairos in particular corresponds to no simple character type or category. What is more, *Birds* reflects not so much the actual world inhabited by the Athenians, which the hero rejects, but the fantasy world of their corporate imagination: fantasies of national solidarity and imperial conquest on which Aristophanes puts his particular spin.

In these circumstances the meaning of the satire—the way it comments on reality—is bound to be ambiguous and complex, and its mode suggestive or "interrogative"[5] rather than allegorical or didactic. Like the Assembly debaters of 415, *Birds* was designed to evoke responses to a grandiose vision of Athens that were at once contradictory and equally compelling. The interpreter's task is thus not to find one "correct" meaning but rather to determine a range of meanings whose coexistence is topically significant. Whether Peisetairos' triumphant realization of his characteristically Athenian fantasy was intended to be encouraging or ironic—expressing Aristophanic disapproval and warning of the disappointment that was in fact to come—is a related question that we will have to face.

In the straightforward terms of his heroic trajectory and success, Peisetairos is typical, to judge by his fellow Aristophanic hero(in)es. In typical profile, the Aristophanic hero(ine) is an ordinary, marginal, or even unenfranchised Athenian citizen, fed up with the burdens and annoyances of contemporary Athens, who hits on a plan either to evade or eliminate them and ends up restoring or establishing a utopian polis.[6] This (re)new(ed) polis is portrayed in terms of festivity, prosperity, and personal autonomy—a hog heaven of food, wine, sex, and carefree living. The hero(ine)'s success amounts to vicarious wish fulfillment for most of the spectators, who were themselves ordinary Athenians weary of the same burdens and annoyances and whose own idea of utopia was much like the hero(ine)'s. Standing between the hero(ine) and success are the powers that be: current and would-be leaders and celebrities, those ambitious members of the elite whom ordinary Athenians both respected and distrusted, envied and resented.[7] The hero(ine) denounces these authorities as inept or maleficent, blames them for the play's motive troubles, and exposes them as being *alazones*: people who falsely claim to possess the sort of wisdom or expertise that entitles them to authority.[8] In discrediting the authorities and expelling them from the (re)new(ed) polis, the hero(ine) shows that it is (s)*he* who actually possesses superior wisdom and expertise; the elite are at best an unnecessary bother. This triumph of the ordinary citizen seems to reflect democratic faith in the basic goodness of the ordinary Athenian, and in the justice and ultimate wisdom of popular sovereignty.[9]

In spite of his typical heroic actions, however, Peisetairos has some strikingly atypical features as a character. He is complex to the point of being self-contradictory: first a dropout, an expatriate, and a would-be hermit, then a demagogue, an imperialist, and an absolute ruler, not to mention a bird man. He entirely lacks a righteous cause and (at least initially) a grand vision. And far from exemplifying the ordinary citizen who discredits or overthrows elite authorities, Peisetairos himself embodies some of their stereotypical comic traits: rhetorical glibness, intellectual sophistry, disdain for the gods, hubristic ambition, readiness to use others for his own advancement. In portraying Peisetairos as a successful comic hero, was Aristophanes being ironic? If so, what was the point? Or was Aristophanes' notion of comic heroism different in 414 than it had been in the 420s and would be again in 411 (*Lysistrata*)?

A question about Peisetairos not prompted by other Aristophanic hero(in)es is, what kind of Athenian was he supposed to be? Initially the seeker of a τόπος ἀπράγμων (44), exhausted by life in Athens with its debts, litigation, and civic involvement; the sort of man sympathetically described in *Knights* as "naive, well-to-do, not wicked, afraid of πράγματα," who lives in some quiet refuge until a Kleon targets him for fleecing in court (258–65). Realizing that not even the far corners of the earth are safe from Athenian πράγματα, Peisetairos leaves the earth entirely and finds refuge with Tereus, whose wife was Athenian (368). Seeing that Tereus is the ineffectual leader of a weak but potentially strong race, Peisetairos becomes his expert advisor, showing him how the birds, if they could be persuaded to follow a bold plan, might win an empire and so become masters of the universe. Since men are the great oppressors of birds, the birds are initially hostile to Peisetairos. However, in a series of speeches Peisetairos lives up to his name by persuading the birds to adopt his plan. The birds then naturalize him and invite him to lead them in carrying out the plan. It is a complete success: the birds become a master race, supplanting even the gods, and Peisetairos becomes their sovereign.

These elements hardly add up to any conventional type. True, Aristophanic heroes are always to a degree fictitious composites,[10] but they are based in conventional character types. These heroes represent actual social categories: independent farmers like Dikaiopolis and Trygaios; a cultivated gentleman who hates Kleon, like Bdelykleon; a man of the markets, like the sausage seller; a housewife like Lysistrata. Peisetairos comes before us virtually without a past, and then we are at a loss to recognize in him a generic category that could contain both an ἀπράγμων and a persuader of the masses, a quietist and an imperialist, an alien expert and a ruler. Peisetairos' only typical characteristic seems to be his outsider status vis-à-vis Athenian πράγματα—the minimal requirement for comic heroism.

Peisetairos is clearly a complex composite, then, not based on a recognizable character type. His constituent elements do fit a recognizable social stratum, however one not previously represented by a comic hero: the intellectual and social elite, that small minority of well-to-do and cultivated Athenians who, being born and raised to rule, were positioned to seek power by cultivating the goodwill of the sovereign masses through benefactions and persuasion. Some of them nevertheless decided not be be ambitious for public distinction—in short, to become ἀπράγμονες.[11] In Peisetairos we see a man who opts for the life of an ἀπράγμων but then changes his mind when he spots a chance to rule on his own terms. That Aristophanes chose in 414 to explore the relationship of such a man to the polis (actual and ideal) is unsurprising when we take into account the role actually played by the elite in the events of 415 and the fantasies that their vision for Athens aroused in the populace.

In that year, ambitious members of the Athenian elite under the leadership of Alcibiades had persuaded the demos to undertake the Sicilian expedition: a bold plan to incorporate Sicily into the empire, then blockade the Peloponnesians and thus become masters of a world empire. In the same way, Peisetairos and his companion persuade the birds to incorporate humanity into the bird empire, blockade the gods, and become masters of the universe. Like Peisetairos and Euelpides, Alcibiades and his friends were making their first bid for leadership. Since the death of Pericles in 429 leadership had been in the hands of men who were, or who could represent themselves as being, nonelite: the "demagogues" who styled themselves champions of the demos and its defenders against elite tyranny.[12] During that period the younger generation of the "true" elite, not yet old enough for leadership, were building careers as sophistically trained prosecutors, while many members of the older generation had become ἀπράγμονες, avoiding court and Assembly, even avoiding Athens itself.[13]

Like many ἀπράγμονες Peisetairos avoids participation in democratic life and leaves Athens in search of a quiet refuge. Like Alcibiades, who faced initial hostility from a demos ever wary of elite tyranny, Peisetairos must face initial hostility from the birds, the traditional victims of human tyranny who, in the play, bear a distinct resemblance to the demos.[14] And like Alcibiades, who in 415 challenged Nicias, architect of the peace of 421 and current leader of a quiet Athens, Peisetairos challenges the quietist Tereus. On their side, the Athenians, who had not added to their empire during the war and who had been quiescent since 421, are reminded, like the birds, of their former imperial glory and recalled to activism. In the end, the Athenians accepted Alcibiades' plan and his leadership, just as the birds accept Peisetairos and his plan.

Not only are these events reflected in the play but also the arguments underlying them. Nicias had warned the Athenians that by accepting the plan they would be "going off to found a city among alien tribesmen [ἀλλοφύλοις] and enemies," but after hearing Alcibiades the Athenians were all the more εὐέλπιδες (Thuc. 6.23.2, 24.3). Alcibiades had promised a dream of power that could be realized only if the Athenians were willing to put aside their factionalism to create a new unity of mass and elite, of young and old, of poor and rich. Peisetairos does the same, pleading for a new unity of man and bird as the recipe for power.[15] Moreover, Alcibiades had argued that this unity would depend on the demos' willingness once again to accept leadership by those, like himself, who were naturally fit to lead. As Peisetairos puts it to the birds, adapting Gorgias' phrase, I will be your brains (γνώμη), you will be my brawn (ῥώμη) (636–37), and together we will all have what we truly want: power and happiness.

But Peisetairos is much more than an echo of Alcibiades the politician and commander. He also displays that "sophistic" intellectualism, relativism, internationalism, atheism, and rhetorical agility that so appealed to ambitious members of the elite. Essential to Peisetairos' success is his ability as a sophist, a teacher of statecraft and persuasion whose pupils are the elite leaders or would-be leaders of the native demos. In this role he is for Tereus what Anaxagoras was for Pericles, what Socrates was for Alcibiades, and what Plato would someday be for Dion of Syracuse. For the birds he is what Protagoras was to the colonists of Thourioi and Gorgias was to the Athenians: the expert, the master of persuasion, the magician who can make reality out of dreams.

For Peisetairos' arguments are thoroughly sophistic. He argues the superiority of φύσις to νόμος; upholds the natural right of the strong to rule the weak; rejects patriotism in favor of cosmopolitanism, welcoming into his polis anyone who brings no νόμοι; appeals to myth, poetry, history, ethnography, and natural science to correct false majority beliefs; argues from words and names; expresses cheerful scorn for all laws and limits; and inaugurates a truly rational polis by overthrowing the gods. And his pupils, the birds, are apt. They follow suit by delivering, in the parabasis, a learned and sophistic theocosmogony in which they trace their origin to a pair of qualities that would aptly describe the Athenian demos of 414: chaos and eros. And finally, Peisetairos realizes the dream of every sophist and his elite pupils since the days of Pericles: he actually persuades the demos to acknowledge his superiority and grant him power.

And here is where *Birds* and reality part company. In reality, Alcibiades and his fellow activists had convinced the demos to enact their plan, but they had not sold the idea of unity under their own leadership. On the eve of the expedition the demagogues persuaded the demos to indict Alcibiades and some 300 other members of his class on charges of impiety and antidemocratic agitation, that is, for scorning the gods and aiming for tyranny. Alcibiades fled to Sparta and leadership of the expedition reverted to Nicias, the old-fashioned democrat who had been least enthusiastic for it and whose grandest accomplishment until then had been the peace treaty that now bears his name.

The plot of *Birds* thus differs from actuality principally by ignoring the democratic attack on the elite and the fall of Alcibiades. Aristophanes even takes pains to distinguish Alcibiades from the self-exile Peisetairos, who tells us that he has left Athens not out of hatred or ill will or because anyone had "shooed" him away, and that he refuses to flee to an aristocratic state or anywhere the Salaminia might find him. In the play, the birds grant Peisetairos' dream of personal rulership and thus realize their own dream of imperial rulership; in actuality, the demos pursued its own dream while smashing that of Alcibiades and rejecting the elite culture that had produced him. It is hard to avoid the conclusion that in *Birds* Aristophanes presented a fantasy of what might have happened had the demos in fact united behind Alcibiades, if it had in fact accepted not merely his plan but his culture as well. And what Aristophanes shows us is a fantasy of success and happiness for all, a dream that all Athenians could share but have not yet realized.

In this dream the birds benefit by reclaiming an imperial sovereignty that they deserve by birth and natural right: Athenians may substitute autochthony and inherent superiority. They replace the gods as enforcers and benefactors, and this is portrayed as just. The birds will truly bless those who accept their beneficent sovereignty, while the gods' rule is a true tyranny: they have not kept their promises, do nothing to earn their sacrifices, and travel to Earth only to seduce mortal women—rather like the comic caricature of demagogue-tyrants like Kleon. The gods' rule is in fact very like the present Athenian Empire under the radical democratic regime: Greek, with barbarian allies. Where Poseidon swears by democracy, Herakles is subject to Athenian inheritance law, and Iris parallels the Athenian imperial officers that come to bother Peisetairos. The gods, like the present Hellenic power structure, are merely an obstacle to freedom and happiness, and their removal both restores an old paradise and inaugurates a new utopia. In this fantastic scenario, Peisetairos has his revenge on the Athenians who had made an exile of him: his empire is superior by being at once universally dominant and loved by its subjects.

On the personal side, Peisetairos benefits by finding an outlet for his natural capacities, turning from frustrated ἀπράγμων to σωτήρ (545), ἄρχων (1123), τύραννος (1708), and finally δαιμόνων ὑπέρτατος (1765), receiving a gold crown from humans and winning scepter, thunderbolt, and sovereignty from Zeus, while enjoying the sensual rewards of the typical comic hero in the process. Like the birds (the new gods), Peisetairos is a beneficent master, sharing the benefits of his plan in common (458–59) and deriving power from the consent of the birds (629ff.). In bringing about a utopia for himself and for all, Peisetairos resembles all other Aristophanic heroes except Dikaiopolis: but he had been victimized by the whole polis and justifiably refuses to share the blessings of his private peace. In *Birds* all are happy because each member of the new polis does what nature best suits him for (the Platonic ideal!). As a result, Nephelokokkugia has none of the annoyances that plague the Athenians, and none are allowed in. No philosopher king would quarrel with this arrangement, nor indeed would Pericles, whom Thucydides describes in his famous postmortem as the ideal democratic leader, who ruled by persuasion (2.65).

On any straightforward reading or viewing of the play, then, Peisetairos is portrayed as a typical sympathetic hero, updated to suit the Athens of 414, whose plan is a success and who brings utopia (back) to the world for all to enjoy except current authority figures (human and divine) and other unsavory types. Nevertheless, most scholars who deal at all with the topical aspects of *Birds* seem to think that its utopia must have been intended ironically, either because it is self-evidently impossible or because it is self-evidently sinister.[16] But utopias are by definition impossible, and before we declare anything sinister we must first try to imagine whether contemporary Athenians would have seen it the same way. Only if there are good reasons to think they would should we resort to an interpretative category like irony, which as a wholesale device seems so alien to Old Comedy.[17] In my view, there is no reason to doubt that most spectators would have regarded the fantasy of *Birds* as enjoyable, and few would have seen anything sinister or ominous in Peisetairos' success. Precisely because Nephelokokkugia had so much in common with the Athens that most Athenians in 414 hoped for, I doubt that Aristophanes would have wanted to evoke ominous responses. After all, a comic poet's job was to win a prize by creating reassuring laughter, not gloomy foreboding.

First, there is no reason to think that the imperialistic dream of conquest that had spurred the Sicilian expedition was self-evidently sinister,[18] that is, that at the time of *Birds* the Athenians had dropped their enthusiasm for the initiative in Sicily, were troubled about the immoderate passion that had spurred them to launch it, or did not expect that it would turn out as well as the birds' initiative does in the play. We should not be misled by Thucydides, since in 414 he had not yet published his famous portrayal of the expedition as doomed hubris and in any case had not set foot in Athens for ten years. In *Trojan Women* of 415, Euripides did remind the spectators in a general way about the horrors of war and the evils of unprincipled aggression, and somewhat more pointedly about the power of the West Greek poleis (220–29) over whom advocates of the expedition had predicted an easy victory, but he stops far short of anything that could be construed as disapproval.

In the comic world of *Birds* there is no trace even of such general qualms. Quite the opposite: there is no expression of any desire for peace in this play and quite a lot of enthusiasm for aggression. Neither Peisetairos nor the birds make any apology about their ambition for power, Peisetairos cheerfully adopts the successful Athenian tactic of starving out the Melians (186),[19] and he reforms a father beater by sending him to fight at the Thracian front (1360–71), while the birds happily execute their duties and missions. Nicias is praised for his successful strategems at Syracuse (362–63) and chided for his subsequent failure to follow up that victory (639), while the only contemporaries ridiculed in the play are demagogues and those who had opposed the expedition: Nicias (639), Meton (992ff.), and Socrates (1553ff.). If anything, *Birds* suggests that the Athenians were showing not too much imperial ambition but too little, just as Alcibiades had argued against the cautious Nicias (Thuc. 6.18). If all this was meant to be taken as ironic, then Aristophanes might have given us some slight clue.

The hypothesis that desire for empire must self-evidently have disturbed the Athenians finds precious little support in comedy. Aristophanes may have criticized the demagogues' management of the imperial cities in his lost play *Babylonians* (426: cf. *Ach.* 641–45), but nowhere does he express the slightest doubt that possession of an empire was a very good thing for the Athenians.[20] Even in the view of private critics like Thucydides and the Old Oligarch, whose main gripe against the empire was that it buttressed the regime of full popular sovereignty, Athens' problem was not that its rule was immoral but that it was resented and resisted by its subjects. By contrast, Aristophanes' bird empire is welcomed by everyone, except of course the undeserving rulers (the gods) whom it replaces.

The idea of overthrowing the gods was no more self-evidently sinister than the lust for imperial power. The Athenians were notoriously skeptical about the gods.[21] Thucydides represents their envoys as recently arguing to the Melians that they should not hope for divine assistance against Athenian strength, since even the gods are subject to *phusis* and its dictate that the strong shall master the weak, a dictate, incidentally, that the Athenians had used from the beginning of the war to justify imperial ambition (e.g., Thuc. 1.76; 2.36, 41, 62–64). It is no great comic stretch to imagine that the gods, too, should bow to superior strength, if such could be brought to bear on them. This idea was certainly not alien to the Attic stage. In *Peace* and *Wealth* men similarly call the gods to account for misgoverning the universe and for unjust interference in human affairs. So too Aischylos in the *Oresteia*, the author of *Prometheus Bound* (who is close thematically, perhaps also chronologically, to *Birds*), and Euripides routinely. Dunbar notes that Peisetairos "is assisted in his defeat of the Olympians by Prometheus, a god particularly popular in Athens, who personified the ingenuity on which Athenians prided themselves" and also that Peisetairos' and the (other) birds' triumph over the Olympians reveals "interesting limits."[22]

To be sure, a flippant attitude toward the gods is characteristically sophistic, but that does not make it self-evidently sinister,[23] since fondness for sophistic thinking was characteristic of the Athenians themselves, as Aristophanes' *Clouds* and many passages of Thucydides demonstrate.[24] This was never more true than in 415, when Alcibiades held the floor. To say that Aristophanes at any rate must have been hostile to sophism because he had ridiculed certain sophists in the 420s is incogent, for here sophism is differently portrayed. We are not now dealing with Socrates and his school or with amoral young prosecutors, but with the sort of arguments that had recently been embraced and acted upon by elite and demotic Athenians alike, and which promised to bring the war to a resolution more glorious than even Pericles had imagined. The question of Peisetairos' hubris—mortal aspiration to godlike immunity—is in any case mooted by his apotheosis.

But what about the one aspect of the play that clearly departs from reality, that truly was fantastic in 414: the return of elite rule? Here matters are more ambiguous. Peisetairos has much in common with other intellectual portraits of the elite created in response to the class warfare that began in 415: those in Euripides' *Ion* and *Antiope*, in Sophokles' *Philoktetes*, in Thucydides' history, in Plato's dialogues. All asked what place there might be for the elite minority, by nature born to rule, in a world of ordinary people who refused to see that their nature was to be ruled? Aristophanes' answer in *Birds* seems to be: only in their dreams, only in Nephelokokkugia. The Athenians had recently returned a similar verdict when they disenfranchised Alcibiades and so many others of his class. But then the Athenians had felt threatened, assuming that elite rule would mean tyranny, as the "demagogues" constantly warned. *Birds* seems to allay this fear of elite rule by portraying Peisetairos' hegemony over polis and empire as beneficial, almost in such a way as to imply that the Athenians' fears had been wrong.[25]

The only hint in the play to the contrary, if it is one, is Peisetairos' remark that he is roasting and eating birds who "are guilty of attempting a rebellion against the demos of the birds" (*dēmotikoisin orneois*, 1583–85). Why the birds in question had wanted to rebel, and how they had been found guilty, Aristophanes does not reveal, but no spectator could miss the allusion to the sort of oligarchic or "tyrannical" conspiracies that were so much in the air in the aftermath of the scandals of 415. Do we see here, as some have, a warning that Peisetairos' rule is not as benign as it otherwise seems to be?[26] That if people like Peisetairos were really in power they would roast and eat us without a fair trial? I doubt it: the absence of any other references to faction in Nephelokok-kugia suggest that this is merely an incidental joke about the Athenians' para-noia.[27] But not a joke that would evoke popular revulsion: Peisetairos is not acting much differently than the Athenian demos itself in 415, when it had condemned so many elite "rebels" to death and/or confiscated their property. We may also recall a passage in *Knights* where the knights had approved of Mr. Demos' tactic of fattening up and then eating thieving politicians (1131–40). Thus the joke about condemned rebel birds may suggest either tyrannical or demotic savagery, but in either case a rebellion against the demos is not some-thing that most Athenians in 414 would have been any more prepared to be lenient about than they had been in 415. If anything, Peisetairos has adopted a tactic that most members of the audience would be hypocritical to condemn. The significant feature of the passage is that it is the elite tyrant Peisetairos, not the "demos of birds," who punishes those who threaten the new regime; again the utopian fantasy emphasizes civic solidarity across class lines.

It seems to me that *Birds* is at once critical and hopeful, with the emphasis on hopeful.[28] An ironical or satirical utopia typically removes some known prob-lems only to exaggerate others. But *Birds*, where no undesirable consequences of the new regime are visible, does not seem to fit that model. Once we jettison the unwarranted assumption of wholesale irony—which derives from our own prejudices, seasoned by Thucydides, rather than from the play itself—Nephe-lokokkugia appears to be a superior alternative to Athens that implicitly crit-icizes the real Athens. As a superior version of Athens it is hopeful, an encour-aging ideal. In imperial terms, the enterprise of the birds differs from that of the Athenians primarily in being more successful. In ideological terms there are the usual complaints about the factional and litigious habits of the Athenians that make them their own worst enemies. There is also implied disappointment at the failure of the demos to accept Alcibiades' leadership, and there is a vision of what a new unity of mass and elite might be like. The real-life difficulties that such a vision would encounter in practice Aristophanes elides by including very few details about Nephelokokkugia as a polity.[29]

On this reading, *Birds* would certainly chide the spectators about their short-comings, including their errors of 415, while still anticipating victory in the West, much as *Peace* had scolded them about the war while anticipating the treaty of 421. And along with victory might there not also be an achievement of political unity, and a better polis, under the leadership of "the best"? In the event, Aristophanes was wrong about the expedition and wrong about the prospects for, and the benefits of, a return to elite rule in Athens. But on that account we should not deny his hero of 414 the full fruits of his fantastic accomplishment.

Notes

1. Dikaiopolis in *Acharnians*, the sausage seller in *Knights*, Trygaios in *Peace*, Lysistrata in *Lysistrata*, and Praxagora in *Ekklesiazousai*.

2. For a concise survey of current interpretative approaches, see MacDowell 1995, 221–28; for the nineteenth century, see Behaghel 1878–79.

3. So, e.g., Murray 1933, 135–63, and Whitman 1964, 167–99.

4. Representative examples of allegorical readings are Süvern 1830, Katz 1976, and Vickers 1989; for the workings of true allegory in Aristophanes, see esp. Newiger 1957.

5. So Konstan above.

6. For the comic utopia, see esp. Zimmermann 1983, and Konstan above.

7. "Ambitious" is an important qualification, since Aristophanes entirely spares from ridicule "quiet" and nonambitious members of the elite (for whom see Carter 1986).

8. For *alazoneia*, see MacDowell 1990.

9. For the "Old Oligarch" (writing in the mid 420s), Old Comedy's ridicule of the ambitious elite even helped to *enforce* democratic rule ([Xen.] *Ath.* 2.18); Plato was later to express a similar view of drama's institutional role in catering to and reinforcing democratic polity. In general see Henderson 1990, 1993.

10. As opposed to Aristophanic villains, who typically represent particular individuals or groups.

11. For the politically ambitious class as a small citizen elite, see in general Carter 1986; Rhodes 1986; Sinclair 1988, 33–34, 136–61; Ober 1989.

12. For this phenomenon, denounced particularly in Aristophanes' *Knights*, see Connor 1971; Rhodes 1981, 345.

13. Like Kleon's typical victim, the rich man who tries to live a quiet life in the Chersonnese (*Knights* 261–65).

14. The matrons of the three women's plays play a similar role.

15. Peisetairos' vision, but also his vocabulary, is distinctly elitist, even oligarchic: 1539–40; cf. Zimmermann 1988, 351.

16. Zannini Quirini 1987 claims both, reading Nephelokokkugia as an anti-Athens whose absurdity and sinister politics make the actual Athens look good; for critiques see Sommerstein 1989 and Zimmermann 1989.

17. See the remarks of Reinhardt 1975, 62, for whom irony is a tragic and Socratic mode.

18. As, e.g., Arrowsmith 1973, Newiger 1983.

19. In our time we are used to the idea that Thucydides expected readers to sympathize with the Melians, but actually there is nothing in the text to refute the claim of Perry 1937, 427, that "in the Melian Dialogue . . . the folly of the Melians rather than the cruelty of the Athenians is the chief subject of contemplation," nor is there any more reason to take Peisetairos' reference as sinister humor than there is to frown at the starving Megarian jokes in *Acharnians*.

20. See Meiggs 1972, 392–96.

21. See Nilsson 1948, 77–78.

22. Dunbar 1995, 12–15. The idea (already ancient: Hofmann 1976, 79–90) that *Birds* is a parody particularly of the myth of the Gigantomachy, with the birds equaling the impious Giants (e.g. Zannini Quirini 1987, 47–87), is too narrow a straitjacket for the play; in addition, the birds resemble the Titans more than the Giants, and the myth's major motif—the battle itself—has no analogue in the play, where the gods are diplomatically outmaneuvered. For a balanced review of the mythical sources, see Dunbar 1995, 7–9.

23. As for example Hubbard 1991, 158–92, and above.

24. Athenian irreligiosity versus Peloponnesian piety is one of the major contrasts in Thucydides.

25. It is this positive portrayal of Peisetairos' "tyranny" in terms of traditional comic heroism that makes the presence of minatory irony (e.g., Bowie 1993, 168–72) implausible.

26. See Sommerstein 1987, 303.

27. So Dunbar 1995, 720, who compares the references to Peisandros in 1074–75 and 1556–58, with Thuc. 6.60.1.

28. For "striving after a perhaps unattainable ideal society" as characteristic both of Old Comedy and of Athens, see Sommerstein 1989, 384.

29. MacDowell 1995, 226–27, makes the point that it is precisely this vagueness that allows scholars, by filling in the picture with their own ideas, to construct contradictory political readings.

Bibliography

Arrowsmith, W. A. 1973. "Aristophanes' *Birds*: The Fantasy Politics of Eros." *Arion* 1.119–67.

Behaghel, W. 1878–79. *Geschichte der Auffassung der aristophanischen Vögel.* Parts 1–2. Heidelberg.

Bowie, A. M. 1993. *Aristophanes: Myth, Ritual and Comedy.* Cambridge.

Carter, L. B. 1986. *The Quiet Athenian.* Oxford.

Connor, R. W. 1971. *The New Politicians of Fifth-Century Athens.* Princeton.

Dover, K. J. 1993. *Aristophanes' Frogs.* Oxford.

Dunbar, N. V. 1995. *Aristophanes' Birds.* Oxford.

Henderson, J. 1990. "The Demos and the Comic Competition." In *Nothing to Do with Dionysos?*, edited by Winkler and Zeitlin, 271–313.

———. 1993. "Comic Hero versus Political Elite." In *Tragedy, Comedy and the Polis*, edited by Sommerstein et al., 307–19.

Hofmann, H. 1976. *Mythos und Komödie, Untersuchungen zu den Vögeln des Aristophanes.* Spudasmata 33. Hildesheim.

Hubbard, T. 1991. *The Mask of Comedy: Aristophanes and the Intertextual Parabasis.* Ithaca.

Katz, B. 1976. "The *Birds* of Aristophanes and Politics." *Athenaeum* 54.353–81.

MacDowell, D. M. 1990. "The Meaning of ἀλαζών." In *Owls to Athens: Essays on Classical Subjects Presented to Sir Kenneth Dover*, edited by E. M. Craik, 287–92. Oxford.

———. 1995. *Aristophanes and Athens.* Oxford.

Meiggs, R. 1972. *The Athenian Empire.* Oxford.

Murray, G. 1933. *Aristophanes: A Study.* Oxford.

Newiger, H.-J. 1957. *Metapher und Allegorie. Studien zu Aristophanes.* Zetemata 16. Munich.

———, ed. 1975. *Aristophanes und die alte Komödie.* WdF 265. Stuttgart.

———. 1983. "Gedanken zu Aristophanes' *Vögeln*." In Ἀρετῆς μνήμη · Ἀφιέρωμα εἰς μνήμην τοῦ Κωνσταντίνου Ι. Βουρβέρη, edited by C. K. Soile, 47–57. Athens.

Nilsson, M. P. 1948. *Greek Piety.* Oxford.

Ober, J. 1989. *Mass and Elite in Democratic Athens: Rhetoric, Ideology, and the Power of the People.* Princeton.

Perry, B. E. 1937. "The Early Greek Capacity for Viewing Things Separately." *TAPA* 68.403–27.

Reinhardt, K. 1975. "Aristophanes und Athen." In *Aristophanes*, edited by Newiger, 55–74.

Rhodes, P. J. 1981. *A Commentary on the Aristotelian Athenaion Politeia.* Oxford.

———. 1986. "Political Activity in Classical Athens." *JHS* 106.132–44.

Sinclair, R. K. 1988. *Democracy and Participation in Athens.* Cambridge.

Sommerstein, A. H. 1987. *The Comedies of Aristophanes.* Vol. 6: *Birds.* Warminster.

———. 1989. Review of Zannini Quirini, *Nephelokokkygia. CR* 39.383–84.

Sommerstein, A. H., S. Halliwell, J. Henderson, and B. Zimmermann, eds. 1993. *Tragedy, Comedy, and the Polis.* Papers from the Greek Drama Conference, Nottingham, 18–20 July 1990. Bari.

Süvern, J. 1830. *Essay on the Birds of Aristophanes*. Translated by W. Hamilton, 1835. London.

Vickers, B. 1989. "Alcibiades on Stage: Aristophanes' *Birds*." *Historia* 38.3.267–99.

Whitman, C. 1964. *Aristophanes and the Comic Hero*. Cambridge, Mass.

Winkler, J., and F. Zeitlin, eds. 1990. *Nothing to Do with Dionysos? Athenian Drama in Its Social Context*. Princeton.

Zannini Quirini, B. 1987. *Nephelokokkygia: La prospettiva mitica degli Ucelli di Aristofane*. Rome.

Zimmermann, B. 1983. "Utopisches und Utopie in den Komödien des Aristophanes." *Würzburger Jahrbücher für die Altertumswissenschaft* 9.57–77.

——. 1988. Review of Zannini Quirini, *Nephelokokkygia*. *Gnomon* 61.350–51.

RALPH M. ROSEN

The Gendered Polis in Eupolis' *Cities*

Ever since Antiphanes brought on the stage a character, perhaps Comedy herself, complaining that comedy was more difficult to compose than tragedy (fr. 189.17–23 K.-A.), it has become something of a truism to say that the poets of Old Comedy had at their disposal much richer and less generically restricted literary possibilities than their colleagues working in tragedy. In the area of the chorus this is certainly the case: whereas a tragedian was limited in his choice of a chorus by the demands of the particular myth he was dramatizing, the comic poet's great freedom in plot construction led to enormous variations in the composition and deployment of his choruses. The extant plays of Aristophanes give us a fair sampling of the range of choruses available to the comic poet, from the animal choruses of *Birds* and *Frogs*, through the quasi-divine meteorological chorus of *Clouds*, to the choruses representing various human constituencies involved in the plot (e.g., knights, demesmen, women). But it so happens that the extant Aristophanic plays offer no examples of another important type of comic chorus, known to us from the fragmentary authors, in which the chorus members represented allegorically inanimate abstractions or institutions.

Although, as so often happens with the fragmentary material, we can capture only a fleeting glimpse of how this conceit might have been employed in the plays, some cases are particularly tantalizing for what they seem to reveal about how the Athenians conceptualized the abstractions represented by these choruses. Theatrical allegory, after all, compels the playwright to conceive of abstractions in ways that go beyond ordinary discourse, since he must ascribe flesh and blood to a lifeless intellectual construct. A "law," a "demos," an "island" must suddenly wear a costume and a mask, sing, dance, and gesticulate in front of an audience intended to recognize at some level what the allegory means. The playwright must make practical decisions not only about what sort of human accoutrements will best convey his conception of the abstraction at hand, but, even more importantly, about how to give appropriate voice and character to a normally mute and incorporeal "thing." The poet, then, must conceive of the abstraction behind his chorus in an entirely new mode, and it is precisely this necessity to articulate its nature in unfamiliar ways that leads him to invent new metaphors and representational devices for it. In the end, the very novelty and unconventionality of the way in which these choruses are portrayed often reveal particular cultural modes of conceptualizing that might otherwise be concealed by the terms of discourse more normally used to describe them.

Choruses such as these are fairly common in explicitly political comedies, where they were used to personify a social or political abstraction or institution that helped define the central issues of the play. Perhaps the most famous example occurs in Eupolis' *Demoi*[1] in which the men of the chorus represented the Athenian demes, who in the course of the play sought political counsel from famous generals of the past brought up from the underworld. Even though attempts to reconstruct their role in the play have been largely unsuccessful,[2] the very fact that Athenians could conceive of the deme as a corporate entity with identifiable, idiosyncratic characteristics capable of being transformed into intelligible human analogues is not inconsequential, especially in view of the relatively recent contrivance of the deme system in Attica.[3] Moreover, we may legitimately suppose that the interrogation of Athenian politicians by the demes that we find in the papyrus fragments of *Demoi* reflects at some level a mechanism of democratic control over political leadership in Athens that adds to our understanding of the relationship between deme and polis in the fifth century.

Just how the chorus of demes was presented, what its costumes and masks were like, what physical or verbal idiosyncrasies were used to associate individual choreutai with actual demes, we cannot tell. Some scholars have imagined that there were in fact two choruses of demes, one in the underworld representing "old demes," the other demes of contemporary Athens.[4] But how and to what end such choruses might have been distinguished from each other remains inaccessible to us. One fact that we can be sure of, however, one easily overlooked—perhaps because it seems too obvious to merit comment—is that the chorus was composed of male members of various demes. Few would dispute the assumption that the poet envisioned a chorus that looked like Attic males and acted accordingly, combining, however unconsciously, the rhetoric, physiognomy, and body language appropriate to the gendered aspects of their roles. But we must not forget that this kind of a chorus represents a social institution, and while the decision to render the demes as a collection of "males" may seem "natural," insofar as political business such as that transacted in *Demoi* was by and large a male affair, just *how* these metaphorical demes looked and behaved on the stage as living and breathing males must have been in keeping with current ways of conceptualizing them.

In the absence of more fragments, of course, little more can be said about the significance of gender in the chorus of *Demoi*, especially since an audience would notice nothing very peculiar in itself about a group of males representing demes. The "maleness" of such a chorus, in other words, is perhaps best considered an "unmarked," default aspect of its characterization, and would probably not have encouraged any particular ruminations about gender in the minds of the audience.[5] But if we turn to another of Eupolis' political plays, *Poleis* (*Cities*), which featured a chorus of *women* representing allied Athenian states, the conspicuously marked gender of this chorus (a fact highlighted by the play itself) offers, as we shall see, an unusual and subtle perspective on the ways Athenians conceived of their polity and the corporate psychology that gave rise to such a choral self-presentation.[6]

While *Demoi* clearly took up internal political issues such as domestic leadership and civic and judicial administration, *Poleis* was evidently concerned with the international political arena—how, in particular, Athens treated its subject states. The demes in the chorus of the former play, in other words, were (from the vantage point of the Athenian audience) local sociopolitical units, while the cities of the latter chorus represented foreign entities. Would this distinction help explain why the former chorus was male and the latter female? Was there something about the Athenian conception of a "deme" that demanded it be represented as "male," while a "polis" was conceived of as "female"? In addressing questions such as these in this essay, I will argue that even the apparently unremarkable gender categories found in the composition of a comic chorus can be shown to reflect subtle, but significant, aspects of Athenian self-conception.

One obvious objection to imputing so much significance to the gender of the choruses of *Demoi* and *Poleis* is that the poet would have been compelled to compose a chorus in accordance with the linguistic gender of the noun he intended to represent with actors. Δῆμος, in other words, was linguistically a masculine noun, and πόλις feminine. A poet who decided to stage a chorus of demes, one might argue, would have little choice but to personify them as men, and, along the same lines, we would expect a chorus of "cities" to be women.[7] Even if we grant, however, that the poet would automatically base the gender of a nonhuman chorus on the natural gender of the noun it represented,[8] he alone must make the many decisions about how to transform the abstraction into a recognizable human being along the road to actual production.[9] In the process of this transformation, of assigning a humanized gender to a "thing," the poet enters into a new imaginative realm, in which he is at liberty to explore on the stage all the ramifications of his novel creation, including all the associations that a particular gender will call forth in the minds of his audience. Many of these associations no doubt operated at an unconscious level, as we might expect in the case of an unobtrusively gendered chorus, such as the male demes of *Demoi*. But a chorus of "marked" gender, such as we find in *Poleis*, compels the audience (and the poet) to confront an explicitly feminized polis on the stage, and to consider whether portraying cities as women, incarnating them with stereotypically feminine attributes, accurately reflected contemporary aspects of conceptualizing the polis.

Just how the Athenians "conceptualized the polis," however, is hardly a simple or singular problem, since different contexts called for different descriptive and analytical approaches, and, as is the case for most complex societies, true consensus about national self-definition is virtually impossible to find at any given time in classical Athens. Moreover, Athens was but one Greek polis among many, and Athenians were characteristically fond of viewing themselves in relation to other cities. Their sense of a corporate self was therefore deeply implicated in their conception of outsiders, and this dynamic in turn inspired a variety of ways to delineate both their own political institutions and ideologies, and those of others.

Recent scholarship has done much to illuminate Athenian discourse at the intersection of national and international politics, and we have acquired a good sense, at least, of how Athenians expressed their views on their power and their role in the larger international arena. The politically oriented allegorical choruses of Old Comedy are particularly interesting in this regard in that they can dramatize tangibly what would ordinarily remain mere metaphors within current political discourse. For example, in the broadest and most general sense, Athenians perceived their hegemony at the height of the empire as the morally legitimate rule of a "superior" over less worthy subordinates—states that were, from the Athenian point of view anyway, felt to be actually in need of Athens' leadership. A variety of metaphors were current that conveyed Athens' conception of its hegemonic relationship with other states, expressed in terms of such relational pairs as masters and slaves, parents and children, humans and animals—all of them, obviously, emphasizing the authority of the one and the subjection of the other.[10] When Eupolis in his *Poleis*, or Aristophanes in his *Nêsoi*, chose to represent subject cities as women, in keeping with the linguistic gender of the noun *polis* or *nêsos*, they are exploiting yet another metaphoric strand of the same political attitude. These choruses of foreign subject states depicted as females interacting with Athenian (male) citizens, in other words, affirm the close connection between gender and politics in dominant Athenian culture that recent scholars have been stressing.[11] We find in these instances, then, rather unusual examples of how the political relations between states are articulated with a kind of discourse that derives from the realm of domestic gender relationships within Athenian society in general, and within the oikos in particular.

It is not enough, however, to say that the choruses of these plays obviously portray women because their customary status in the fifth century was one of subjection and subordination. Such a formulation, while true enough in a general sense, ignores the cultural subtleties that the metaphor of a female allegorical chorus invites us to contemplate. Allied cities were not "women" in reality, after all; these choruses represented serious and very real political entities whose relationship with Athens was essential for the success of its empire. Figuring this relationship in terms of the domestic interaction between male and female no doubt provided a good deal of comic novelty, but beyond that, it also raises a number of further questions, including questions about how Athenians themselves conceived of their own city. In the Athens as represented on the comic stage, we find male Athenians engaged in one sort of gendered relationship with the female chorus, rooted in traditionally conceived roles. But since Athens itself was, after all, a *polis*, we might suppose that it too was conceptualized in these comedies in the same way as foreign cities were by virtue of the feminine gender of that noun. What, then, is the interplay between the gendered discourse about Athens within Athens itself and the gendered conceptualization of foreign Greek cities that we find in comic choruses? To begin to suggest some answers to such questions we may turn to the most conspicuous allegorical chorus of this sort in Eupolis' *Poleis*.

Even the relatively few fragments that survive from this play have led scholars to suppose that its main theatrical focus was an elaborately conceived and adorned chorus. Norwood has imagined with characteristic enthusiasm that it was a "beautiful, stirring and brilliant comedy," largely based on the assumption that the chorus of allied states offered a colorful spectacle concerned with weighty matters of contemporary politics. Elsewhere he calls it "probably one of the most charming and vigorous comedies ever produced in Athens."[12] Although it is difficult to judge exactly how much theatrical emphasis was placed on the chorus, the fragments do indeed suggest that at least some of the individual chorus members in *Poleis* were singled out for commentary by the actors, such as we find in the parodos of Aristophanes' *Birds* (260–304), where the hoopoe identifies for Peisthetaerus and Euelpides individual birds of the chorus as they make their entrance.[13]

Several fragments in *Poleis* are traditionally adduced to support a scene of this sort, and although quite brief, they are especially revealing when we keep in mind the interplay between sexual and political discourse in Athenian society. Fragment 246 K.-A., which derives from a scholium on Aristophanes' *Birds*, leaves little doubt that one character announces and comments upon the identity and appearance of chorus members as they make their entrance:

αὕτη Χίος, καλὴ πόλις ⟨ ⟩
πέμπει γὰρ ὑμῖν ναῦς μακρὰς ἄνδρας θ' ὅταν δεήσῃ,
καὶ τἄλλα πειθαρχεῖ καλῶς, ἄπληκτος ὥσπερ ἵππος

and here's Khios—and a fine city ⟨she is⟩!—
since she sends you long ships[14] and men whenever there's a need,
and she takes orders wonderfully, just like an obedient horse

These lines clearly indicate the stage business at hand: the demonstrative αὕτη indicates the ceremonious entrance of Khios, and the aesthetic comment (καλὴ πόλις) implies that she is accoutred according to her status as a valuable ally and rich city.[15] But on the stage this abstraction of a city is also a woman, and this situation allows for the male actors to interact with them and comment upon them as explicitly human and female. The language immediately becomes susceptible to the standard double entendre of Old Comedy, and reveals at the same time how an Athenian[16] can easily speak about the relationship between Athens and its allies as he would the relationship between male and female. Khios is praised, in other words, as a city who actively aids the Athenian war effort with ships and men, yet the speaker seems as pleased with the notion of Khios' *obedience* to a superior authority (πειθαρχεῖ καλῶς, ἄπληκτος ὥσπερ ἵππος) as he is with its material aid. In this fragment, then, we find the discourse of political power coalescing with that of sexual relations, where the relationship between the ideal ally and its putative leader (Athens) is portrayed much as the relationship between the ideal wife and her husband is supposed to be. The animal metaphor of the horse, in particular, may work easily enough in its own right to describe a well-behaved city, but with a female character marching across the stage, the reference to her as an "obedient horse who doesn't need goading" introduces, no doubt with intentional comic effect, female stereotypes that extend in the extant tradition at least from Hesiod and Semonides to Aristotle and beyond.

Aristotle is particularly revealing on this point, in that he conceives of the relationship between male and female within a household in a way that can be seen as analogous to the relationship between Athens and other Greek cities. For Aristotle, that is, the "female" is allied with the "slave" by virtue of the fact that they both are deficient in the composition of their souls. Specifically, slaves lack the deliberative capacity (τὸ βουλευτικόν) entirely, while women possess it, though it remains inoperative (ἄκυρον; cf. 1260a10–12). It is natural, and therefore just, according to Aristotle, that both women and slaves be ruled by a male element with full psychic capacities. But Aristotle was also aware that the social status of Athenian women, at any rate, within the oikos and the polis was different from that of slaves, though he never explicitly lays out a distinction between rule over women and rule over slaves.[17] Roger Just attempts to resolve the problem: "if the rational faculty of women's *psyche* was *akyron*, 'inoperative,' 'without command,' then the obvious solution to the problem of their very necessary accommodation within the organization of the civilized community was to place them under a *kyrios*, a male, who could supply for them that rational command which they lacked."[18] Just is not clear about exactly how this would differ from Athenian rule over slaves, who also require a ruling element, but he rightly stresses the difference in the actual contemporary discourse about the two categories: a woman whose deliberative function is ἄκυρον, but who then acquires a κύριος to make up somehow for this lack, would have been perceived and treated differently from a slave whose deliberative capacity was simply nonexistent. A natural slave, in other words, will always lack τὸ βουλευτικόν and so will always exist at a lower social status than a woman, who at least in theory has a capacity for deliberation.[19]

According to Aristotle, then, the relationship between a man and woman, though capable of being characterized philosophically as "slavish," was in reality a good deal more subtle than might first appear. The famous scene in Xenophon's *Oeconomicus* (7–10) where a rather unctuous Ischomachus describes his attempts to domesticate his young wife, illustrates well Aristotle's fundamental attitude in which women are simultaneously viewed as chronically in need of male intellectual guidance, yet also worthy of some sort of respect.[20] Aristotle holds to his more rigid formulation of "slavishness" in the case of barbarians, male and female alike, whose souls are by nature constructed differently from those of Greeks.[21]

To return to the fragment from *Poleis* under discussion, I would suggest that the idea of having women embody allied states in the play would have worked particularly well in Athens precisely because it conflated so well the sexual attitudes we have noted in Aristotle with analogous contemporary attitudes towards the allied states. Just as women represented for Aristotle an element within society that needed by nature a form of rule, so were non-Athenian Greek states regarded as best served when they had Athens ruling over them.[22] Moreover, just as a woman's social status was not as low as the true slave's, so were Athenian subject states differentiated from non-Greek (i.e., barbarian) states. Athenian men (in the case of domestic relations) and the corporate Athenian polis (in the case of international relations) would surely subscribe to Aristotle's observation that "ruling and being ruled not only belongs to the category of things necessary, but also to that of things expedient" (1252a21– 22, trans. Barker). Such an attitude certainly governs the rhetoric of the Athenians in the "Melian dialogue" in Thucydides 5.85–111, as a few examples illustrate:

. . . ὡς δὲ ἐπ᾽ ὠφελίᾳ τε πάρεσμεν τῆς ἡμετέρας ἀρχῆς καὶ ἐπὶ σωτηρίᾳ νῦν τοὺς λόγους ἐροῦμεν τῆς ἡμετέρας πόλεως, ταῦτα δηλώσομεν, βουλόμενοι ἀπόνως μὲν ὑμῶν ἄρξαι, χρησίμως δ᾽ ὑμᾶς ἀμφοτέροις σωθῆναι. (91.2.1)

We will now proceed to show you that we are come here in the *interest of our empire*, and that we shall say what we are now going to say, for the *preservation of your country*, as we would fain exercise that empire over you without trouble, and see you preserved *for the good of us both*. (trans Crawley)

ἡγούμεθα γὰρ τό τε θεῖον δόξῃ τὸ ἀνθρώπειόν τε σαφῶς διὰ παντὸς ὑπὸ φύσεως ἀναγκαίας, οὗ ἂν κρατῇ, ἄρχειν. (105.2)

Of the gods we believe, and of men we know, that by a *necessary* law of their *nature* they *rule* wherever they can. (trans. Crawley)

"Expediency," "mutual benefit," "necessary rule," "natural rule"—such are the concepts that undergird the ideology of Athenian hegemony during the later fifth century, and which provided the rationale for the way the Athenians dealt with their allies.[23]

The little parable about the origins of gender roles which Ischomachus relates to his wife in Xenophon's *Oeconomicus* offers a strikingly parallel set of concepts to justify his injunctions to her:

ἐμοὶ γάρ τοι, ἔφη φάναι, καὶ οἱ θεοί, ὦ γύναι, δοκοῦσι πολὺ διεσκεμμένως μάλιστα τὸ ζεῦγος τοῦτο συντεθεικέναι ὃ καλεῖται θῆλυ καὶ ἄρρεν, ὅπως ὅτι ὠφελιμώτατον ᾖ αὐτῷ εἰς τὴν κοινωνίαν. (7.18)

For it seems to me, woman . . . that the gods have used great consideration in joining together the pair called male and female so that it may be of the *greatest benefit to itself and the community*.

διὰ δὲ τὸ τὴν φύσιν μὴ πρὸς πάντα ταὐτὰ ἀμφοτέρων εὖ πεφυκέναι, διὰ
τοῦτο καὶ δέονται μᾶλλον ἀλλήλων καὶ τὸ ζεῦγος ὠφελιμώτερον ἑαυτῷ
γεγενῆται. . . . (7.28)

Since, then, the *nature* of each has not been brought forth to be *naturally* apt
for all the same things, each has need of the other, and their pairing is *more
beneficial* to each. . . .

Ischomachus' attitude to his wife is probably much more generous than was
the norm,[24] though it illustrates well how Athenian men could conceive of
their marriages as partnerships while at the same time asserting their natural
right to ultimate authority within the oikos as a whole.[25] Such passages from
Thucydides and Xenophon do not, of course, necessarily lead to the conclusion that Athenians consciously and publicly thought of their allies as "feminine" in any general sense. But there is no question that Eupolis is able to
"feminize" Khios and the other states in *Poleis* precisely because the allies were
expected to assume a specifically defined subordinate role in a power relationship remarkably similar to that between husband and wife.

The strong likelihood of sexual double entendre in fragment 246, moreover,
reinforces the conflation of the sexual and political spheres. Khios is praised for
sending "long ships and men whenever there's a need," and for acting like an
obedient "horse." The first phrase, mentioning ships and men, of course, was
practically formulaic in contexts involving allies and, by itself, need raise no
eyebrows. But the metaphor of the "horse" is so charged with sexual overtones
in Attic comedy that it is difficult not to assume a lewd coloration for it here,
and we are probably justified in reading the previous line in this manner as
well.[26] The horse metaphor appears in a variety of contexts in comedy, though
one of the most common involves the mode of copulation in which the woman
is "on top," as if riding a horse. The horse metaphor in comedy is actually used
without great precision; that is, in descriptions of this form of copulation, the
man technically becomes the horse, and the woman the rider.[27] Yet, as Aristophanes' *Lysistrata* 677 indicates, the metaphor of the horse can be transferred
to the "riding" woman as well: "a woman is a very horsey creature and knows
well how to mount."[28] At *Ecclesiazusae* 846–47, furthermore, a man named
Smoios is said to put on his "horseman's garb" in order to prepare himself to
"wipe clean the women's cups" (. . . ἱππικὴν στολὴν ἔχων / τὰ γυναικῶν
διακαθαίρει τρύβλια), a passage that clearly conjures up the image of a human
male in control of a female sexual partner conceived of as a horse.

Implicit in the metaphor of Khios as an obedient horse, moreover, is the
notion that both as a female choreut and as an allied city, she represents an

element that requires domestication by a controlling and civilizing force. The idea that for Athenian men women were fundamentally creatures of the wild, of nature, lacked self-control and rationality, and ultimately presented an impediment to the progress of civilization, is evident at every turn in their myths, rituals, and cultural representations. Much recent scholarship within classics has emphasized this fact, and feminist scholars outside the discipline have shown just how pervasive, if not universal, this attitude seems to be.[29] The conflation of women and allies in Eupolis fragment 246 within the metaphor of a tamed, serviceable beast, therefore, is a direct reflection of this mode of thought, and illuminates an aspect of Athenian self-perception that only Attic comedy is capable of articulating in just such a way. Non-Athenian Greek states could have all the allure of women as aesthetic, sexual objects (as the accoutrement of the chorus no doubt emphasized); they could assist in Athens' aggrandizement just as a woman assisted in the prosperity of the oikos within the polis. But ultimately the Athenians conceptualized their allies as "wild," as they did women, or at least as less thoroughly civilized than an Athenian citizen, and thereby could bolster their claims to political leadership and superiority.[30]

The nature of the relationship between Athens and her allies can be further specified in Eupolis' *Poleis* from fragment 223 K.-A., in which gender and politics once again merge:

ὁ Φιλῖνος οὗτος, τί ἄρα πρὸς ταύτην βλέπεις;
οὐκ ἀπολιβάξεις εἰς ἀποικίαν τινά;

Hey Philinos! Why're you gawking at her?
Make yourself disappear, would you? Off to the colonies with you!

Ever since Raspe,[31] it has commonly been supposed that the ταύτην of the first line refers to one of the cities of the chorus on display, and this seems reasonable, not only in view of the fact that fragments 245 and 246, as we discussed above, strongly suggest such a scene but also because the humor of the second line ("off to a colony with you") depends on a context that has something to do with foreign cities.

Kock offered several parallels from Aristophanes to suggest that Philinos was a spectator rather than a character in the play.[32] Such a comic conceit, in which the poet disrupts the dramatic illusion in order to register the reaction of the audience, supports the likelihood that this scene offers considerable spectacle of some sort, and it allows the poet to call attention to his own dramaturgy. If we are right, then, to suppose that Philinos is here lewdly ogling one of the cities of the chorus, the details complement our discussion of fragment 246 by offering an even more nuanced commentary on how the Athenians perceived their relationship to their allies. To begin with, the name Philinos almost certainly was chosen for its erotic connotations, where the root φιλ- would suggest the usual associations of "love" and "kisses" (φιλήματα).[33] If the name refers to a generic member of the audience eyeing a female character with erotic intention, the humor of the scene is all the more assured by making it appropriate to his actions. The protective attitude of the speaker toward the woman, however, is noteworthy, and seems to imply that these women, in any event, ought to receive more respect than one might afford, say, a woman of lesser status, such as a prostitute, slave, or barbarian.

It would be helpful, of course, to know exactly who spoke the lines of this fragment. Although it is possible that they belong to a male character adopting the posture of a husband, indignant at an affront to his wife's honor, I think it is more likely that one of the female chorus members themselves, offended at the locker-room attitude displayed by the characters as they comment on the parade of female cities, is here chastising the general male populace at Athens. In this case the sexual dynamics of the scene are subtle: the fragment strongly implies that the woman referred to (ταύτην) is costumed in a suggestive manner, hence the stock male response of ogling. As such, she appears on the stage more as a typical slave or prostitute than a respectable Athenian housewife.[34] Yet the speaker seems to be objecting to such an assumption, and appeals for an attitude of greater respect toward the female choreut. This sort of small-scale female rebellion against male attitudes is, of course, well known to us from several Aristophanic plays, but it is particularly interesting here for what it says about the chorus's identity as allied cities. As women, in other words, they insist on maintaining their respectable status even if they choose to make themselves sexually attractive; as allies, they ask for analogous treatment, namely, to be taken seriously as political partners, even while asserting a certain degree of autonomy as the subordinate partner of a ruler-ruled relationship.

Indeed, the second line of fragment 223 (οὐκ ἀπολιβάξεις εἰς ἀποικίαν τινά;) calls attention to the female chorus as political entities, if only by turning the joke in on themselves. The verb ἀπολιβάζω appears for us only in comic diction,[35] and occasions the gloss that supplies this fragment. Its literal meaning of "causing to drop away" has developed into an idiom meaning little more than "get the hell outta here!" In this fragment, then, the speaker consigns the offending spectator to a colony for his bad behavior. Whether spoken in mock earnestness by a male Athenian or with self-irony by a female chorus member, the import is clear: sending an Athenian citizen off to a colony represents a demotion in status, implying as it does physical removal from Athens and presumably relinquishment of Athenian citizenship.[36] Once again, Athenian attitudes toward its allies are quietly reinforced: being sent to a "colony" is not, perhaps, as terrifying as being sent to a barbarian country, but neverthe-less non-Athenian Greek cities are by definition inferior to Athens and occupy the same sort of intermediate position in politics (Athenian—non-Athenian Greek—barbarian) as women did in gender relations (male citizen—female birthright Athenian—female slave/prostitute).[37]

Norwood himself sensed that fragments of *Poleis* such as 223 K.-A. and 246 K.-A. indicate that the comedy played up the sexual tensions between a female chorus and male principals.[38] His suggestion that the cities' "appeal for clem-ency—naturally successful in the poet's hands—resulted in a marriage or pairing-off of 'cities' and Athenians"[39] cannot be substantiated with the avail-able evidence, but fragment 243 K.-A., "for I've got just the right man for her" (ἔχω γὰρ ἐπιτήδειον ἄνδρ' αὐτῇ πάνυ), does suggest that marriage is at least addressed in the play, if it does not play a substantial role in the action.[40] However this theme was played out, we may be fairly certain that this fragment does highlight a particular attitude of the male Athenian actor(s) toward the female chorus, and supports my argument that the Athenians were viewing their allies here in much the same way as they would view their own wives. Their desire for a "marriage" with individual allies, therefore, was analogous to the desire for a "real" marriage with a woman: in each case the relationship ideally was intended to foster the higher goal of managing, maintaining, and enriching an oikos, whether it be the actual one of the Athenian household, or the metaphorical one of the international hegemony which Athens claimed for itself. This would surely explain why in fragment 223 we saw that a man was castigated for lecherous intentions toward one of the cities. Sexual gratification seems not to have been a necessary, defining component of an Athenian mar-riage, and even though, as many have rightly emphasized, we must treat the incomplete and often conflicting evidence we have with extreme care, it is safe to say that marriage was not seen in any way, for males anyway, as a necessary sanction for sexual activity.[41] Extramarital sex of all sorts was available and tolerated, and only excessive sexual activity in general seems to have been subject to moralizing. In circumspect, male-centered discourse, wives were not generally viewed as sexual creatures, and indeed to do so could be construed as a slight against their character.[42] Hence, when Philinos ogles one of the cities in fragment 223, viewing them as sexual objects rather than functional elements of a social institution, he repudiates (and thereby calls attention to) their implicit claim to a higher political/domestic status.

Nowhere is this male "double-standard" more evident in the fragments of *Poleis* than in fragment 247, where the formal entrance of the choreut portray-ing Kyzikos reminds a character of a great debauch he once experienced there as a guard.

ἡ δ᾽ ὑστάτη ποῦ ᾽σθ᾽; ἥδε Κύζικος πλέα στατήρων.
ἐν τῇδε τοίνυν τῇ πόλει φρουρῶν ⟨ἐγώ⟩ ποτ᾽ αὐτὸς
γυναῖκ᾽ ἐκίνουν κολλύβου καὶ παῖδα καὶ γέροντα,
κἀξῆν ὅλην τὴν ἡμέραν τὸν κύσθον ἐκκορίζειν

But where's the last one? There's Kyzikos, full of staters.
Yes, that reminds me of the time when I was on guard duty in that city
and I got to screw a woman, a boy, and an old man for only a penny,
and I could spend the whole day rooting out pussy

It did not take much, of course, to inspire boastful characters in comedy to reminisce fondly about their peccadillos while on military service ("fortia memorabiliaque facinora patrare callent Atheniensium praesidia," Kassel and Austin wryly note),[43] but this example is especially noteworthy for the way in which the speaker's sexual escapades resonate within the context of the scene. There is virtual consensus that this fragment probably comes from the same scene as fragments 246 and 247 (discussed above), that is, as a part of the formal paradelike entrance of the chorus of cities. Like the other cities, Kyzikos was evidently distinguished by her costuming or accoutrements, as the end of the first verse suggests (Κύζικος πλέα στατήρων).[44] Kyzikos was famous at this time for its opulence and its contributions of gold staters[45] to the league, and as such, the allegorical depiction of the city as a woman calls to mind the same nexus of associations that we have seen in the case of Khios. Like the feminized Khios, that is, Kyzikos is a subordinate, but respected player in an international relationship analogous to that between a husband and a wife within a household. In this particular case, the explicit emphasis on Kyzikos as a financial asset is especially significant in that, as Henderson has recently argued, women (especially older women) seem to have been thought of as excellent money managers at Athens, and were evidently allotted considerable financial responsibility both within the oikos and in certain public offices, such as priesthoods.[46] The speaker of fragment 247, however, like Philinos in fragment 223, can only react to the allegorized city as a sexual object. He does not, of course, treat Kyzikos herself specifically as an opportunity for sexual gratification, as Philinos apparently views the unnamed city of fragment 223, but it is clear that Kyzikos functions as nothing more than a mnemonic springboard for his own sexual bravado. In fact, the last thing on his mind is the kind of male-female relationship that one associates with an ideally functioning oikos. Indeed, what he reveals here, as is the case in all such passages in which characters recount rakish escapades on military service, is precisely a sense of sexual freedom that derives from the fact that he is *away* from Athens, away from the constraints of decorum, not to mention law, that would inhibit the pursuit of his most bestial

desires at home. The speaker's energies while in Kyzikos are focused on undifferentiated heterosexual and homosexual activity of all varieties (γυναῖκ᾽
ἐκίνουν κολλύβου καὶ παῖδα καὶ γέροντα, / κἀξῆν ὅλην τὴν ἡμέραν τὸν
κύσθον ἐκκορίζειν), and the implicit contrast between Kyzikos as a place
where such libertine behavior is tolerated (if not encouraged) and Athens,
where it is not, ultimately reflects a deep conflict in the conceptualizing of
Athenian and non-Athenian national characters. The speaker revels, in other
words, in the opportunity for unbridled sexuality in Kyzikos, yet the thrill of
his experience there seems contingent on the fact that it occurs in a place that is
not Athens. For the speaker, Athens remains morally superior even as he seeks
to transgress the principles upon which this superiority is felt to be grounded.

We see in this fragment, therefore, a tension between two divergent attitudes. On the one hand, the poet has created an instantiation of Kyzikos,
reinforced by costume and gesture, that would signal its stature as a respected
player in international politics. This portrait derives from the realm of "official"
discourse about how Athens publicly acknowledged its allies. The city is valuable to Athens as a source of wealth (πλέα στατήρων), and deserves the respect
that all the other cities on parade deserve (cf. above on fr. 223). But Kyzikos,
like the others, is still subject to Athens and must always acquiesce to Athenian
hegemony. Allegorized as a woman on the stage, then, the city plays the role of
the respected and valued, yet ultimately subordinate, housewife.

On the other hand, however, the fragment in the end undermines this rather
polite portrayal of Kyzikos, as the speaker launches into the litany of sexual
escapades that the city allegedly afforded him. It is difficult not to see in this
fragment, then, the sort of ambivalence and anxiety toward women on the part
of Athenian men that Loraux and others have emphasized.[47] In this case, it is as
if the speaker's self-indulgent sexual anecdote is an attempt to counter a perceived threat to the proper hierarchies of power and value that the polis/
woman Kyzikos poses for him. Indeed, the sexual partners of line 3 (a woman,
a boy, an old man) share the common feature of being physically or politically
weak (or both), and the fact that on Kyzikos the speaker could gratify his lusts
for only "a penny" (especially in contrast to Kyzikos' repute as a wealthy city, as
noted in line 1), further emphasizes the deliberate devaluation of these individuals, and their status as mere commodities of appetitive desire.

Indeed, the scholiast on Aristophanes Peace 1176, who cites this fragment
from Eupolis, affirms this sort of attitude toward Kyzikos. The lemma from
Aristophanes that he glosses is the phrase "he has been dipped in Kyzicene
dye" (βέβαπται βάμμα Κυζικηνικόν), which he takes to refer to someone who
cannot control his bowels because of excessive homosexual anal sex:

. . . εἰς κιναιδίαν διαβάλλεται, ὥστε μηδὲ τῶν ἀναγκαίων διὰ τὴν εὐ-
ρύτητα κρατεῖν δύνασθαι, ὡς καὶ Εὔπολις ἐν Πόλεσιν [Eupolis fr. 247]·
ἄλλως· τουτέστι κατασχημονεῖ. οἱ γὰρ Κυζικηνοὶ ἐπὶ δειλίᾳ καὶ θηλύτητι
ἐκωμῳδοῦντο

. . . the person is ridiculed for homosexual activity, implying that he is unable
to control his bowels because they have been stretched out so much, as
Eupolis too [has] in *Poleis* [Eupolis fr. 247]; used differently here; in other
words [the speaker] acts indecently, for the Kyzicenians were ridiculed in
comedy for their cowardice and femininity

It is difficult to judge from the wording whether the scholiast also sees a
specific connection between the explicit homosexual innuendo of the Aristophanes passage and the reference to Kyzikos in Eupolis 247, but the nexus of
associations is clear enough. Even if the scholiast would not push for such a
connection, he sees that Kyzikos was an appropriate venue for the sort of
activity and attitude displayed by the speaker of the Eupolis fragment, precisely because the city was characterized by emblems of subjection and cultural
inferiority, namely cinaedic homosexuality and femininity.[48] The speaker of the
fragment, therefore, manages to ridicule this portrait of the Athenian ally by
literally wielding his own phallus in a conspicuous show of virility intended to
cover all the bases, as it were. Once again, the discourse of politics and gender
intertwine, freely exchanging metaphors of power and status that reflect the
complex public posturing of the Athenian male persona.

Fragment 247 seems to have occurred near or at the end of the parade of
female city-choreuts (ἡ δ᾽ ὑστάτη ποῦ ᾽σθ᾽; ἥδε Κύζικος . . . , "but where's the
last one? There's Kyzikos . . ."), and its position here, even as a passing comic
remark, summarizes what was probably a basic ambivalence toward the chorus
on the part of the male characters in the play. On the one hand, the chorus's
apparent criticism of Athenian policies toward the allies amounts to the sort of
political self-criticism we associate with Old Comedy. In keeping with this
agenda, the chorus presumably strove to enlist the sympathies of the audience
(and judges), lodging complaints against an imperialistic Athens and warning,
perhaps, of the dangers of political arrogance in international affairs. On the
other hand, attitudes such as those voiced by the speaker of fragment 247
suggest that Eupolis was not particularly interested in repudiating the fundamental structure of the Athenian Empire, and that, despite any reasonable
pleas by the allies for a better relationship with Athens, Athens' interests were
ultimately best served by ensuring that the allies remained, at least metaphorically, perennially servile.

In practice, of course, Athenians made a clear distinction between a slave and a Greek ally, as they did between an Athenian woman and a household slave. But, as we noted earlier, all of such categories share the fundamental trait of being socially and politically subordinate to Athenian males. It is not surprising, therefore, to find the discourse of "servility" in all contexts that involve relationships between superiors and subordinates, even when slavery per se is not literally at issue. We find just this sort of discourse, in fact, in fragment 229 of *Poleis*, where a member of the chorus,[49] in lamenting his current status, alludes to a law that allowed slaves to change their masters:

> κακὰ τοιάδε
> πάσχουσιν οὐδὲ πρᾶσιν αἰτῶ

> they suffer such ills,
> and I don't even ask to be sold

The fragment is quoted by Pollux (7.13) alongside a similar usage of πρᾶσιν in Aristophanes (fr. 577 K.-A.), and a passage in Plutarch (*Superst.* 166d) clarifies the idiom: "even for slaves who have given up the hope of freedom, there is a law that allows them to ask to be put up for sale and to switch to a better master" (ἔστι καὶ δούλοις νόμος ἐλευθερίαν ἀπογνοῦσι πρᾶσιν αἰτεῖσθαι καὶ δεσπότην μεταβάλλειν ἐπιεικέστερον). The speaker is evidently outraged at the suffering of her fellow cities and characterizes the relationship they have with some superior force, presumably Athens, as that between master and slave. Here, the speaker expresses additional indignation that she, at any rate, has been willing to endure a good deal of ill treatment without rebelling— without, that is, asking to be "put up for sale" to a better master (οὐδὲ πρᾶσιν αἰτῶ). Her attitude, in other words, is one of basic compliance with the general social order, and the point she seems to be trying to make in this fragment is that her outrage at Athens is all the more valid precisely because she accepts her status as a subordinate of Athens. The Athenian citizenry must have heard a good deal of criticism in this play about its foreign policy, but this fragment, along with the others we have examined, certainly suggests that the traditional stereotypes remained intact: the fundamental assumption that Athens was naturally suited to rule over the Greek world does not seem here to be called into question, nor is the assumption that non-Athenians were naturally inferior. By allegorizing the cities of the chorus as women, moreover, Eupolis conflates in one stroke several sociopolitical categories—the political ally, the female, the slave—and thus emphatically dramatizes how monolithic and polarized a segment of the Greek world the masculine Athenian citizen body conceived itself to be.

Eupolis' allegory in the chorus of *Poleis*, as we have seen, relies upon the dominant Athenian conception of women and non-Athenian Greek cities as intrinsically subordinate and in need of a ruling power. My argument has assumed that Eupolis was exploiting the feminine gender of the noun "polis" in his allegory of the chorus to highlight this conception. But how did the Athenian citizen conceptualize his own polis, Athens itself? The relationship between the allied cities and Athens in *Poleis* was, after all, a relationship between two conceptualizations of a polis; but only one of these seems to have been portrayed on the stage as an allegorical character. The audience, rather, witnessed the interaction between the allegorized allies and Athenian *men*, who, though representing at some level the polis of Athens, did not *embody* it the same way the chorus did its own. The question remains, then, whether the allies were feminized only by virtue of the fact that their political status demanded as much (they were inferior to Athens, and so were like women), or whether the abstract notion of a polis itself, of whatever kind, was "feminine" at some level in the Athenian mind. If the latter, how would a feminized conception of the *Athenian* polis differ from that of the allies in *Poleis*?

Nicole Loraux's analysis of the Periclean funeral oration in Thucydides discusses in some detail fifth-century conceptualizations of the polis, and touches on a number of the concerns I have voiced about the representation of the polis in Old Comedy. Loraux notes that in the funeral oration in particular, and in the orators in general, there is a distinct tendency to efface the diversity and multiplicity of the actual polis in favor of a unified abstraction.[50] She contrasts this unified portrayal of the polis in oratory with its various concrete representations in everyday life (e.g., public iconography, representations on the stage), where multiplicity seems to be celebrated, and concludes that "[n]o face . . . must come between the orators and the men whom it is their duty to celebrate." In other words, the polis, when conceived of as an entity "is abstract through and through, and, being addressed to an imaginary without image, it exists in opposition to figured abstractions, which are based on a certain type of representation."[51]

As for the representations of the polis that we find in dramatic allegories of the fifth century—one of Loraux's "figured abstractions"—Loraux seems to imply, without quite articulating it as such, that they are less ideological, or, perhaps, less productive of ideology, than the "ideality" of the polis that emerges from the epitaphios. When a comic chorus or a sculpture puts a face on an abstraction, such allegoresis can represent concretely only a partial ideological framework. As Loraux says of the figure of Demos in Athens: "When the sculptors represent Demos as a bearded old man, they are borrowing from comedy a figure that was already fully formed: because Demos is embodied in

Knights, we can forget that demos, in Athenian political practice, is first defined as a number." Allegory, in other words, cannot hope to encompass the full range of ideological associations inherent in an abstraction.[52]

Our analysis of Eupolis' allegory of the polis in *Poleis* helps to demonstrate the extent to which "figured abstractions" could in fact reflect important aspects of the Athenian imaginary landscape. Loraux might argue that Eupolis' allegory is particularized to refer to non-Athenian cities, and illuminates more specifically the issue of how Athenians perceived *other* poleis, rather than their own. But the construction of the polis as essentially "female" need not be dismissed as a convenient device simply to put down all cities that were not Athenian. The allegory can only work to the fullest extent, it seems, if we assume that the abstract entity itself—the figure of a polis—can be articulated most meaningfully to an Athenian audience with the metaphor of the female. To illustrate this, we might try to imagine what Eupolis would have done if he had wanted to represent the city of Athens among the other choreuts of *Poleis*. Would he, in other words, have felt compelled to represent Athens as a male figure, in contrast to the non-Athenian cities, in order to highlight the political inequities that obtained between the two categories? This is, of course, a purely hypothetical question, but not, I think, an idle one, for there is plenty of evidence indicating that Athens itself was figured as a female in the various material representations of the later fifth and fourth centuries,[53] and a male choreut representing Athens in a comedy would surely seem completely inappropriate to a contemporary audience. Indeed, one of the remarkable features of the representations of the Athenian polis in literary sources, at any rate, is that it seems to transcend gender categories, while visual representations of Athens tend to be figured as distinctly female.[54]

It is clear, therefore, that an allegory of any polis in fifth-century Athens, whether of Athens itself or of a non-Athenian polis, whether verbally or visually, would have appeared as a female figure. In discussing the particular allegory in Eupolis' *Poleis*, we were able to suggest how contemporary conceptions of the "female" intersected with conceptions of non-Athenian Greek states. But did such discourse reflect a more general and abstract way of thinking about the polis that could include Athens as well? Certainly Athenians did not portray their own polis with metaphors or allegories that would impute to themselves the subordinate and weak status generally associated with Athenian women or, worse yet, slaves. Insofar as Athenian males regarded their own city as superior in force and moral legitimacy to foreign, subject cities, it would obviously be inappropriate for them to apply to Athens the metaphors of subordination and servility that they associated with their subject states. In conceiving of a feminized Athens, rather, Athenians had to draw on the strictly positive stereotypes of "the female" while obscuring the more negative ones which seem to have predominated in most other areas of Athenian cultural discourse.

It is especially interesting in this regard that the most conspicuous metaphor used to describe Athens specifically as the caretaker of an empire is that of the "metropolis," the "mother city." This metaphor, though, could only operate when the Athenians viewed their empire as a relationship specifically between *an abstract polis* (their own) and *other subordinate ones* (their allies), in which case the relationship could be figured as that between a mother and child. In other contexts, when Athens was conceived of as a *collection of Athenian males*, such as was evidently the case in Eupolis' *Poleis*, the city-ally relationship was more explicitly figured as one between male and female. Athens could, in short, be allegorized as a female, just as the allies had been, but Athenians would have certainly invested such a figure with an entirely different set of female attributes than those used for the allegorized allied states, since they would hardly have imagined their own city in anything but a positive light.

In the metaphor of the metropolis, then, we find just such a feminized image that manages also to incorporate an essentially masculine agenda (power, control, hegemony) within a "feminine" framework of motherhood, birth, nurture, and domestic economics. It is, of course, difficult to ascertain how vividly the maternal image inherent in the term would have been in the minds of a fifth-century Athenian, especially since the word has lost so much of its imagistic force in modern Western culture. Still, we must remember that a μητρόπολις in fifth-century Greek had a rather limited and specified meaning, referring mostly to a city that managed its own "progeny," usually in the form of colonies.[55]

Just how "technical" the term μητρόπολις must have been at this time becomes clear when one contrasts it to the very common term πατρίς, "fatherland," referring to Athens as the place of a citizen's birth and belonging. Indeed, this term reflected a tendency to conceptualize one's genealogical ties to Attica as essentially patrilineal.[56] Such an emphasis on a male conceptualization of citizenship and politics contrasts vividly with the metaphor of the polis in its capacity specifically *as the parent of her colonies and/or allies*. When it was a matter of their own identity, Athenian citizens tended to gender their polis as male—fatherly, masculine, warlike, ordered by a πάτριος πολιτεία—and their relationship with the polis paralleled that between a father and a son. But when the polis was conceived as an international "parent," we find a shift in the metaphor from paternity to maternity, giving rise to an Athens visualized as a μητρόπολις.

A curious fragment from the fourth-century comic poet Antiphanes illustrates well how actively gendered the metaphor of the μητρόπολις could be at this time. Only one fragment survives from a play entitled Φιλομήτωρ, quoted by Athenaeus in a playful discussion of the delicacy known as the μήτρα:

ἔμμητρον ἂν ᾖ τὸ ξύλον, βλάστην ἔχει·
μητρόπολίς ἐστιν, οὐχὶ πατρόπολις ⟨πόλις⟩·
μήτραν τινὲς πωλοῦσιν ἥδιστον κρέας·
Μητρᾶς ὁ Χῖός ἐστι τῷ δήμῳ φίλος

(Antiphanes fr. 219)

If wood is full of pith, it can sprout;
⟨a city⟩ is a "mother-city" (*metropolis*), not a "father-city" (*patropolis*)
Some sell the pig's uterus (*metra*) as the greatest delicacy;
Metras the Chian is a friend to the people.

In the Athenaean passage Ulpian adduces the fragment as part of his disquisition on the term μήτρα, but offers no commentary on it. The context of the fragment within Antiphanes, therefore, remains uncertain, although clearly its main purpose was to introduce the extended pun on μήτρα/μήτηρ. The joke here merges with actual etymology, since μήτρα refers to the "uterus" as the defining locus of maternity, and thus is derived linguistically from μήτηρ. Kock suggested that the lines were spoken by someone who was trying to show that a mother deserved more respect than a father,[57] and such a scenario does not seem unlikely.[58] The lack of a context makes it difficult to decide whether these lines offer merely a random list of humorous puns on μήτηρ, or whether there is some sequence of thought in them. The striking lack of any particles or conjunctions that might establish a logical flow between the lines does encourage us to treat each line as independent of the others. Still, the first two lines especially seem connected by a single thought: motherhood means growth and fecundity. By using the word ἔμμητρον of wood in the first line, the speaker implies that it can grow precisely because it has a "maternal element" inherent in it. The mention of the βλάστη, the result of this growth, segues meaningfully into the following line, which can be read as an attempt to corroborate the point of the first line: to paraphrase the thought, then: "If wood is 'motherized' [full of pith], it can sprout; I mean, we call a city a '*mother* city,' after all, not a '*father* city,' and that's because the city, like pithy wood, can produce progeny of a sort." The implication of this paraphrase, of course, is that the metaphor of paternity would not only be contrary to current linguistic convention, but inappropriate to the ways Athenians conceptualized the role of their city, at least in its capacity as an international power. Part of the humor of the passage may arise from the assumption that most people in the original audience would not routinely think through the literal ramifications of calling a city a "metropolis," but even so, the joke does suggest that Athenians were capable of quite a remarkable degree of self-consciousness about a metaphor that we might otherwise assume to be "dead" or insignificant.

It seems, therefore, that in spite of the various metaphors available to Athenians in talking about their own city, when it came to thinking *allegorically* about Athens, actually instantiating the abstraction of the polis, the result was an idiosyncratic version of the more general tendency to construct poleis as feminized entities, as we have seen in the case of Eupolis' *Poleis*. The conceptual shift from non-Athenian cities to Athens itself accompanies a shift in the conception of the female as a negative and subordinate construct to one that was positive and commanding. But the interplay of gender models implicit in these shifts is subtle. Athens, on the one hand, played out the role of a "mother" city in the international arena by viewing the world metaphorically as an oikos. Since, in the real Athenian oikos the mother seems typically to have been the financial manager and general administrator of domestic affairs, including parenting,[59] Athens was easily and appropriately "maternalized" in the Athenian imagination. Within the context of the oikos, then, the figure of the mother in fact represented a degree of control and power, and in the metaphorical, worldwide oikos of international relations, foreign cities could be figured as children—incomplete humans in need of a controlling rationality and educational guidance. It is easy to see, therefore, how the various metaphors for cities align themselves according to who is actually conceptualizing them. The following chart may help to illustrate the situation:

	"*Athens*" *as leader*	"*Athenians*" *as leaders*
Athens	mother	husbands
Foreign cities	children	wives

Here the headings at the top indicate who is doing the conceptualizing, and the left-hand items indicate what is being conceptualized. The chart clearly shows how an allegorized Athens becomes feminized, while a *group of males self-identifying corporately as Athenians* adduce their maleness in constructing a role for themselves in international relations. It is significant, in any event, that the polis per se, when construed abstractly, is never viewed as a distinctly marked male entity. The maternalized Athens is surely felt to be a positive and powerful force, but it is feminine nevertheless.

I have spent some time speculating about how Athenians might have allegorized their own city on a comic stage as a way of exploring the implications of the chorus of allied cities in Eupolis' *Poleis*. For the presence of an allegorical chorus on the Athenian stage demands that the audience (ancient and modern) tries to ascribe meaning to the allegory, and in this particular case, if a woman can make sense as a city, then we will want to know whether it makes sense only because the cities are *foreign* cities, or because all cities were somehow feminized in the Athenian imagination. Our discussion suggests, I believe, that in fact the latter holds and that at some fundamental level the chorus of cities in *Poleis* made sense as women precisely because the abstraction itself of a city was invested with stereotypically "feminine" attributes by contemporary male culture. But as in our own culture, the notion of the "feminine" in fifth-century Athens is neither monolithic nor consistent, and we have seen its conceptual fluidity in the Athenian mind. Two parallel notions of the "feminine" emerge here. In the case of the allied states, the female is seen as a subordinate player in a relationship with males based on the exercise of power. Hence we find the female cities of Eupolis' *Poleis* portrayed "negatively," for example, as erotic objects, prostitutes, or slaves. But when it comes to Athens, more "positive" images of the female arise, such as those of maternal nurturer and household manager. Beneath this apparent ambivalence, however, there remains an inherent otherness about the female in the Athenian male imagination.[60] Athenian men may indeed have felt reasonably well disposed toward women, at least insofar as they could be mothers and oeconomists worthy of respect, but it is the citizen body of *males* who ran the empire, fought the wars, and brought glory to their polis. Any allegorized Athenian polis must remain the abstraction that it is, and hence, like the women to whom it could be likened, functionally static and ultimately ornamental.

Notes

I owe thanks to Ian Storey, Keith Sidwell, and A. J. Graham for their comments on an earlier draft of this essay.

1. For other examples cf. Cratinus' *Nomoi*, Aristophanes' *Nēsoi*, or Plato Comicus' *Nikai*.

2. Cf. Whitehead 1986, 329 n. 17; Whitehead's anxiety (329–30) about extrapolating too much about the nature of fragmentary comedies from their titles is prudent, though I hope to show that, even if we cannot establish anything of the plot of these plays from their choruses, the few apparent facts about certain choruses that we can extract from the fragments is often incidentally revealing of significant cultural attitudes.

3. Cf. Ober 1989, 30–33; Whitehead 1986.

4. On the issue of the "two choruses," cf. Schmid and Stählin 1946, 127–28; Plepelits 1970, 69–76; Page 1970, 203–4.

5. See Loraux 1993, 118–19, on the cases in Aristophanes where women appropriate the term δῆμος in describing their own "subversive" assemblies (e.g., in *Lysistrata* and *Thesmophoriazusae*). Loraux argues that when the women refer to themselves as a δῆμος, they cannot divest the term from its masculine connotations; they cannot, she maintains, refer to themselves as the "people of female Athenians" or the like, but must call themselves a *"people of women*, as if every intrusion of women into the political universe had to be offset by a reminder about their connection to a particular sex."

6. Loraux 1993, 117, on Attic comedy as a reflection of Athenian conceptions of gender relations: "[S]ince the woman is an effective source of laughter, especially when she dares to stray out of her normal role, the comic stage is a precious reserve of glimpses into the Athenian imagination about the division between the sexes."

7. In fact, the chorus of Aristophanes' *Peace* clearly shows that a poet did have some alternatives in how he represented his abstractions. Although there remains a controversy over the precise composition of the chorus of *Peace*—are they men from Attica or from other Greek states? Are they farmers, or members of other professions?—they refer to themselves in their first lines (302) as Πανέλληνες, and when they haul up Peace, they can single out Boeotians (466), Argives (475), Laconians (478), and Megarians (480) in their number. Whatever the ultimate configuration of the chorus (some have suggested two half-choruses, others that the chorus's identity actually changes within the play; cf. Platnauer 1964, xiv–xv), it is clear that Aristophanes wanted to represent a number of Greek cities in some capacity. He chose to do this by having as choreuts *not* allegorical representatives of those cities, but actual "flesh-and-blood" representatives of them. In this case, it is unremarkable that the chorus members are male insofar as they function as little more than "ambassadors" or "emissaries" of these cities. Eupolis in *Poleis* could likewise have avoided the "problem" of portraying cities as women, since he could have had male choreuts act as real-life representatives of their respective homelands. Presumably in *Peace* the chorus needed to be men in order to help with the "masculine" task of hauling up Peace. I suspect that Eupolis' decision to employ a female allegorical chorus in *Poleis* was also deliberate, as I argue below.

8. Enough evidence survives from the fifth century to suggest, at any rate, that incongruities between gender and meaning did not go unnoticed. Cf. Guthrie 1971, 221, who discusses Protagoras' interest in the gender of nouns; cf. also Guthrie 205–6 on the notion of "correctness of names" in sophistic thought. Certainly the passage in Aristophanes' *Clouds*, which Guthrie discusses, shows that people were attuned to the apparent dissonances created when certain words have a particular gender attached to them, hence the injunction at *Clouds* 680–81: "It is necessary for you to learn which words are masculine, and which are feminine."

9. It is probably true that once Eupolis decided to write a play about cities, and to have the chorus represent the cities, he could not very realistically have had them appear as men. But we may still wonder whether the chorus of cities was cast as female *only* because the noun was feminine or whether the poet himself was actually interested in the ways in which Athenians conceptualized them as feminine. Without venturing too far down the cul-de-sac of "intentionality," I would suggest simply that the answer probably lies somewhere in between: once Eupolis decided to compose a comedy about Greek cities, the choice of a female chorus would have seemed inescapable. Still, whether fully aware of it or not, his need to flesh out a role for this otherwise inanimate chorus carried with it a commitment to exploring and exploiting its gendering.

10. Tompkins 1994, 20–21.

11. For example, Halperin 1990, 96–104.

12. Norwood 1931, 197, 192. On the dating of the play, cf. Geissler 1925, 39, who places it at the City Dionysia of 422. Most scholars place it more tentatively somewhere between 422 and 413. Geissler's arguments are essentially in line with nineteenth-century attempts at dating the play (Brandes 1886, 6; Meineke 1839–57, 1.140), which rely on several termini furnished by the fragments: fr. 246 K.-A. mentions Khios as an ally, which places production before its revolt from Athens in 412; fr. 225 K.-A. mentions the seer Stilbides, who died in 413. The reference to Amynias in fr. 222 K.-A., general in 423/2, however, clinches 422 for Geissler. The evidence is discussed in detail in Storey 1990, 18–20, who also opts for 422. Contra, cf. Luppe 1972, 75 n. 91, and Sidwell 1994, 99–101.

13. Cf. Meineke 1839–57, 2.508, and Raspe 1832, 84–85. Norwood 1931, 187, speculates that the choreuts of *Demes* may also have been given some "particularity." Scholarly evaluation of the evidence is revealing, however: Norwood's attraction to the perceived theatricality of *Poleis*

allows him to rank it as among Eupolis' best work. Raspe, on the other hand, finds that it pales in comparison to *Demoi*: ". . . videri nostram fabulam multo minus nobilem illustremque fuisse, quam Δήμους, ut non iniuria eam Lenaeis assignare possis [!]: quae sententia hac etiam re confirmatur [!], quod inspectantibus sociis vix Atheniensium iniquitas atque occultae insidiae, quas sociis struebant, aperiri potuerunt" (. . . our play evidently was far less noble and distinguished than *Demes*, so that one might comfortably assign it to the Lenaean Festival: this suggestion is confirmed by the fact that the unfair treatment and hidden agenda of the Athenians against their allies could hardly have been portrayed on the stage if the allies were present in the theater). Cf. also Storey 1994, 109–11, on the chorus of *Poleis*. Storey's article came to my attention after this essay was written. He too sensed the essential dichotomies of male/female, master/slave, human/animal, Athens/allies in *Poleis*, which I examine in detail below, but he was not concerned to explore them in his piece.

14. The pronoun ὑμῖν implies that the speaker is addressing an interlocutor, possibly a non-Athenian one; Meineke, however, emended to ἡμῖν, thereby making the speaker Athenian. Khios had been a reliable source of ships for Athens until 413, as Thucydides attests (1.116.2, 1.117.2, 4.129.2, 6.43, 7.57.4).

15. "Probably the Chian chorister was decked with naval gear," suggests Norwood (1931, 193), on the basis of fr. 245 K.-A. (on which see below).

16. See note 15. More relevant than whether the speaker is Athenian or not is, in this case, the fact that he is almost certainly a male, addressing a predominantly male audience.

17. Cf. *Politics* 1252a34–69, where Aristotle contrasts non-Greek communities that fail to distinguish between female and slave because they lack a natural ruling element completely (and so they are all slaves) to communities (such as Athens presumably) in which there is an element naturally fit to rule. Just 1989, 190–91.

18. Just 1989, 191.

19. Cf. *Politics* 1254b20–23, where Aristotle is more explicit about the slave: "a man is thus by nature a slave if he is capable of becoming (and this is the reason why he actually becomes) the property of another, and if he participates in reason to the extent of apprehending it in another, though destitute of it himself" (trans. Barker).

20. Cf. Murnaghan 1988 and Just 1989, 114–18. Pomeroy 1994, 66–67, takes the *Oeconomicus* rather more at face value, and in fact concludes, somewhat surprisingly, it seems to me, that "in the *Oeconomicus*, there is no natural hierarchy among human beings according to gender, race or class" (66).

21. It is not entirely clear whether Aristotle regards *all* non-Greeks as naturally "slavish." *Politics* 1327b16–1328a21 discusses the character of several non-Greek people in a way that suggests that Aristotle is open to the notion that some non-Greeks are more or less "slavish" than others. On the equation of slaves and barbarians in Greek tragedy, see Hall 1989, 196–97.

22. Note that in *Poleis* fr. 250 K.-A., someone addresses another as "master" (*despotes*): ὦ δέσποτα, καὶ τάδε νῦν ἄκουσον ἃν λέγω σοι. Storey 1994, 111, notes that the Archilochean meter used in this line is associated with the chorus elsewhere in Old Comedy; obviously, it would be in keeping with the role of the *Poleis* chorus as "servile" allies to use this term of an Athenian "master," but the fragment remains without a context.

23. Despite such a general ideology, not all Athenians were comfortable with Pericles' own imperialistic rhetoric. Many, particularly those of aristocratic background, suspected him of aiming at a sole tyranny. See Ostwald 1986, 185–88.

24. No doubt the situation between Kritoboulos and his wife described in *Oeconomicus* 3.12–14 was more typical. Here Kritoboulos reveals that he barely speaks to his wife in spite of her significant duties within the house. Cf. Just 1989, 135–36.

25. Ischomachus illustrates more clearly what was implicit in Aristotle, namely the peculiar status of a woman as a natural subordinate, but somehow different from a servile subordinate.

26. On the use of nautical imagery in sexual contexts, cf. Henderson 1975, 162–63.

27. Cf. Henderson 1975, 164–65, on the related obscenities surrounding the *kēles*.

28. ἵππος also appears in comedy referring to the phallus (cf. Ar. *Lys.* 191, *Eccl.* 146); on the comic name Ἱπποβῖνος at *Frogs* 433, cf. Henderson 1975, 165 n. 66.

29. Just 1989, 217–79; Ortner 1974.

30. Halperin's remarks about the "democratizing" effect of Athenian prostitution are apposite here. He argues that cheap and readily available sex (male and female) in Athens allowed even the poorer citizens to avoid being "effeminized" by poverty, and that the effect was "to promote a new collective image of the citizen body as masculine and assertive . . . and as perpetually on the superordinate side of a series of hierarchical and roughly congruent distinctions in status: master versus slave, free versus unfree, dominant versus submissive, active versus passive, insertive versus receptive, customer versus prostitute, citizen versus non-citizen, man versus woman" (1990, 102). The last two categories here are particularly appropriate, as they highlight the conflation of "female" and "non-Athenian Greek" that we find in Eupolis' chorus. Cf. also Winkler 1990a, 45–70.

31. Raspe 1832, 91.

32. Kock ad loc.; he cites *Wasps* 74, 78, 81; *Peace* 81.

33. Cf. Henderson 1975, 181–82, and Aristophanes' use of names such as Φίλιννα at *Clouds* 684 (said by the scholiast to refer to a prostitute, though also apparently a common enough name for an Athenian woman; cf. Dover 1968, ad loc. pp. 184–85), and Φιλίστη at *Thesm.* 568 (of a servant).

34. Ischomachus' attitude at Xen. *Oec.* 10.12–13 is probably typical. Here he takes his wife to task for indulging in cosmetics, judging them unseemly for a respectable woman: "a wife's looks, *when in contrast to a waiting maid she is purer and more suitably dressed*, become attractive . . ." (12); "On the other hand, women who always sit about in pretentious solemnity lend themselves to comparison with *those who use adornments and deceit*" (13).

35. Cf. Aristophanes *Birds* 1467, Pherecydes fr. 42 K.

36. Graham 1983, 166–92, discusses in detail the differences between Athenian colonies proper (*apoikiai*) and cleruchies, the latter being "a settlement of Athenians living abroad" (167) as opposed to an autonomous city-state. Technically speaking, cleruchies were inhabited by Athenian citizens and were regarded as extensions of the state, but it is often extremely difficult, as Graham makes clear, to distinguish between the two in our evidence, since the terminology was not always used with great precision (Thucydides, e.g., apparently uses the term *apoikia* for *klērukhia*; cf. Graham 1983, 170–84). We cannot tell for sure, therefore, whether the *apoikia* of the Eupolis fragment refers to a bona fide colony, though the negative tone of the line implies that going to such a place would be a form of punishment for poor behavior. It seems likely that a "colony," where an Athenian would no longer retain citizen privileges, is, in fact, meant here. On the issue of mutual citizenship between mother-city and colony, cf. Graham, chaps. 5 and 6. Cyzicus and Miletus, for example, colony and mother-city respectively, seem to have shared citizen rights (Graham 1983, 108), but Athens evidently did not routinely grant isopolity to its colonies. The issue is far from settled, however. Figueira 1991, 72, for example, concludes that "fifth-century Athenian colonists as well as cleruchs retained their Athenian citizenship. *Apoikoi* possessed a status which might truly be called sympolity, since ἀποικίαι were *poleis* with a form of local citizenship."

37. Hall 1989, 201–5, discusses how in Greek tragedy women, both Greek and non-Greek, who transgress Athenian (patriarchal) norms are frequently associated with "barbarian" behavior. See her discussion of the "carpet scene" in Aesch. *Ag.* 205–8, in which, she argues, "the antipathy between Greek and barbarian [is] an analogue to that between male and female."

38. "That the sexual possibilities of a 'female' chorus would not be overlooked is certain" (Norwood 1931, 196).

39. Ibid.; Norwood further speculates "that there was a marriage—procession of these pairs to rites in the *opisthodomos* or rear-chamber of the Acropolis," which he infers from the exhibition at

the festival of treasure brought by each of the cities (cf. fr. 254 K.-A., on which see below). Cf. Dougherty 1993, 61–80, on the prevalence of marriage metaphors in the discourse of Greek colonialization. She notes (68) that "the rhetoric of marriage articulates the representation of archaic colonization. First, the view of marriage as a harmonious union of opposites (male and female) becomes symbolic of another kind of union as well—that of Greek and indigenous populations." In this sense, "Greece" as civilizing male/husband/superior colonizes other lands characterized as female/subordinate, in need of acculturation and civilizing. Dougherty is speaking specifically of colonies, but this sort of rhetoric is easily extended, as it evidently was in Eupolis' play, to include all states with which Athens had some sort of hegemonic relationship.

40. On fr. 243 cf. also Kaibel's unpublished remark, cited by K.-A., ad loc.: "videtur maritus quaeri uni ex Civitatibus"; Schmid 1946, 1.4.118 n. 7.

41. Cf. Just 1989, 135–41, drawing on earlier work by Dover and Pomeroy.

42. Cf. Pomeroy 1994, 35–36. Note also the prurient tone of Ar. *Lys.* 151 where Lysistrata mentions pubic depilation as a sexual attraction for husbands; as Henderson notes (1987, 130): "a practice especially associated with hetaerae and other female sex-objects."

43. Cf. *Wasps* 236, 1201.

44. We can only guess about how she would have been dressed, though it would not be unthinkable that she was dressed in extravagant gold garments, reflecting the famed gold coinage of the city, as well as the color of the famous dye known as "Kyzicene" (on which see below).

45. References to the wealth of Kyzikos are collected ad loc. in K.-A.

46. Cf. Henderson 1987b.

47. Loraux 1993; Rabinowitz 1993.

48. On "cinaedism" cf. Winkler 1990a, 45–70.

49. It is not entirely clear who speaks these lines, since it is impossible to be certain whom the third person of πάσχουσιν and the first person of αἰτῶ refer to. Raspe 1832 understands πάσχουσ(α), with this explanation: "loquitur rursus Πόλις quaedam, quae quum admodum dure tractata esset a demagogis, se cum servis comparat, qui herum mutare poterant apud Graecos . . ." (90) (again a City speaks, who, as as result of past ill treatment at the hands of demagogues, compares herself to slaves who were able to change masters in Greece at that time). Kassel and Austin (1983–) are prudently conservative, though imagining the scene on their reading becomes less clear. Possibly one of the chorus members speaks about her colleagues, and then implicates herself in their plight. In any event, the first-person form of αἰτῶ indicates that the speaker envisions herself to be of servile status.

50. Loraux 1986, 279–80: "*He polis* absorbs plurality in an abstract singularity. . . . As the product of an official oration, the entity of the polis is nevertheless only one of the possible forms of an imaginary relationship between the Athenian community and itself."

51. Ibid., 282.

52. Ibid., 283. Loraux is certainly right to contrast the deeply abstract nature of the "polis" as it emerges from the epitaphios with its particular representations throughout Athenian culture as a whole. I would modify her focus, however, by stressing that even the "figured abstractions" of the polis in such areas as drama often appear to reflect a coherent "imaginary," even if more obliquely and less consistently than the polis imaginary she articulates for the epitaphios. To use her own example, it is true that a comic "demos-as-old-man" does not strive for a unified or unprejudicial representation of the Athenian citizenry, but it does suggest that the characteristics that the audience would commonly associate with such a real-life figure—irascibility, forgetfulness, physical weakness, for example—depict negative aspects of an implied ideal.

53. On associations in the visual arts between Athens and Athena, and between Athens and Demokratia, cf. Kleinknecht 1975, 149; Picard 1935, 3.98; Loraux 1986, 282–83.

54. Loraux 1986, 283–84. "Both classical and Hellenistic iconography present the cities as women, goddesses in the classical period and personified abstractions in the Hellenistic" (ibid.,

450 n. 111). Thus, the comic poets who portrayed cities as allegorical women evidently antici-pated later trends in the visual arts.

55. Even small deviations from this technical meaning, such as when it appears as a synonym for "homeland" (e.g., Pind. *Nem*. 5.8, Soph. *OC* 707, *Ant*. 1122) or for "capital city" of a country (Xen. *An*. 5.2.3) imply a "maternal" relationship between the city so designated and the individual or group whose "mother-city" it is said to be. For cities in antiquity called "Metropolis," cf. *RE* sv. See also Radt 1958, 33–39.

56. Loraux (1993) has argued that the evolution of Athenian self-identification as citizens in the classical period involved a persistent effort to repress a mythological narrative about Athenian autochthony with originally "feminine" associations. On the primacy of the father metaphor in the discourse about the Athenian polis as a "metaphorical family," see also Loraux 1993, 65–66.

57. Kock 208 ad fr. 220.2. Kock made this suggestion in response to Meineke (3.129), who reads "Metropolis" and "Patropolis" as proper names of cities: "at non opus est nomine proprio: siquidem is qui loquitur matri plus quam patri verecundiae deberi comice exemplis demonstrat. sic μητρόπολιν urbem dici ex qua coloniae deducantur, non πατρόπολιν."

58. I suspect that the punning on μήτρα/μήτηρ in this fragment operates simultaneously on a coarser level as well. Μήτρα is not readily attested as an obscene metonym for female genitalia, though it is not difficult to imagine that it might be, especially in the light of its use in this particular passage: κρέας is a well attested comic term for the female sexual organs (Henderson 1975, 144, which also offers a list of various food delicacies with obscene connotations), and someone selling Μήτρα as the "sweetest meat" (line 3) might easily be intended to refer to a pimp of some sort. This might help to explain line 4, which refers to one Metras who is a "friend to the demos." In other words, the mention in line 3 of purveyors of Μήτρα (taken obscenely) might remind the speaker of a well-known example of such a person. Meineke's speculation, in any event, that Metras was actually the fourth-century philosopher Metrodorus of Khios, seems far-fetched.

59. Cf. Henderson 1987b.

60. See Elizabeth Bobrick's essay in this collection for a discussion of male-female stereotypes as they are played out in *Thesmophoriazusae*.

Bibliography

Brandes, E. 1886. "Observationes criticae de comoediarum aliquot Atticarum temporibus." Diss. Rostock.

Dougherty, Carol. 1993. *The Poetics of Colonization*. Oxford.

Dover, K. J. 1968. *Aristophanes' Clouds*. Oxford.

Ehrenberg, V. 1962. *The People of Aristophanes: A Sociology of Old Attic Comedy*. New York.

Figueira, Thomas J. 1991. *Athens and Aegina in the Age of Imperial Colonization*. Baltimore.

Geissler, P. 1925. *Chronologie der altattischen Komödie*. Berlin.

Graham, A. J. 1983 [1964]. *Colony and Mother City in Ancient Greece*. 2d ed. New York.

Guthrie, W. K. C. 1971. *The Sophists*. Cambridge. Originally published in *A History of Greek Philosophy* I.3. Cambridge, 1969.

Hall, Edith. 1989. *Inventing the Barbarian: Greek Self-Definition through Tragedy*. Oxford.

Halperin, David M. 1990. *One Hundred Years of Homosexuality and Other Essays on Greek Love*. New York.

Henderson, Jeffrey. 1975. *The Maculate Muse: Obscene Language in Attic Old Comedy*. New Haven.

———. 1987a. *Aristophanes' Lysistrata*. Oxford.

———. 1987b. "Older Women in Attic Old Comedy." *TAPA* 117.105–29.

Just, Roger. 1989. *Women in Athenian Law and Life*. New York.

Kassel, R., and C. Austin. 1983–. *Poetae Comici Graeci*. Berlin.

Kleinknecht, H. 1975. "Die Epiphanie des Demos in Aristophanes' *Rittern*." In *Aristophanes und die alte Komödie*, edited by H. J. Newiger, 144–54. Darmstadt. Originally published in *Hermes* 77 (1939): 58–65.

Kock, T., ed. 1880–88. *Comicorum Atticorum Fragmenta*. 3 vols. Leipzig.

Loraux, Nicole. 1986. *The Invention of Athens: The Funeral Oration in the Classical City*. Cambridge, Mass.

———. 1993. *The Children of Athena: Athenian Attitudes about Citizenship and the Division between the Sexes*. Princeton.

Luppe, Wolfgang. 1972. "Die Zahl der Konkurrenten an den komischen Agonen zur Zeit des Peloponnesischen Krieges." *Philologus* 116.53–75.

Meineke, A. 1839–57. *Fragmenta Comicorum Graecorum*. Berlin.

Murnaghan, Sheila. 1988. "How a Woman Can Be More Like a Man: The Dialogue between Ischomachus and His Wife in Xenophon's *Oeconomicus*." *Helios* 15.9–22.

Norwood, Gilbert. 1931. *Greek Comedy*. London.

Ober, J. 1989. *Mass and Elite in Democratic Athens: Rhetoric, Ideology, and the Power of the People*. Princeton.

Ortner, Sherry B. 1974. "Is Female to Male as Nature Is to Culture?" In *Woman, Culture and Society*, edited by M. Zimbalist Rosaldo and L. Lamphere, 67–87. Stanford.

Ostwald, Martin. 1986. *From Popular Sovereignty to the Sovereignty of Law: Law, Society and Politics in Fifth-Century Athens*. Berkeley.

Page, Denys. 1970. *Select Papyri*. Vol. 3: *Literary Papyri: Poetry*. Cambridge, Mass.

Picard, Charles. 1935. *Manuel d'archéologie grecque*. Vol. 3: *La sculpture*. Paris.

Platnauer, Maurice. 1964. *Aristophanes' Peace*. Oxford.

Plepelits, K. 1970. *Die Fragmente der Demen des Eupolis*. Vienna.

Pomeroy, Sarah B. 1975. *Goddesses, Whores, Wives and Slaves: Women in Classical Antiquity*. New York.

———. 1994. *Xenophon, Oeconomicus: A Social and Historical Commentary*. Oxford.

Rabinowitz, Nancy Sorkin. 1993. *Anxiety Veiled: Euripides and the Traffic in Women*. New York.

Radt, S. L. 1958. *Pindars zweiter und sechster Paian*. Amsterdam.

Raspe, G. C. H. 1832. *De Eupolidis Δήμοις αψ Πόλεσιν*. Leipzig.

Schmid, W., and O. Stählin. 1946. *Geschichte der griechische Literatur* 1.4. Munich.

Sidwell, Keith. 1994. "Aristophanes' *Acharnians* and Eupolis." *Classica et Mediaevalia* 45.71–115.

Storey, Ian C. 1990. "Dating and Re-dating Eupolis." *Phoenix* 44.1–30.

———. 1994. "The Politics of 'Angry Eupolis.'" *Ancient History Bulletin* 8.4.107–20.

Taaffe, Lauren. 1994. *Aristophanes and Women*. London.

Tompkins, Daniel P. 1994. "'What Has This to Do with the Praetor's Edict?': Classical Studies and Contemporary Society." *Arethusa* 27.1.11–39.

Whitehead, David. 1986. *The Demes of Attica, 508/7–ca. 250 BC*. Princeton.

Winkler, John J. 1990a. *The Constraints of Desire: The Anthropology of Sex and Gender in Ancient Greece*. New York.

———. 1990b. "*Phallos Politikos*: Representing the Body Politic in Athens." *Differences: A Journal of Feminist Cultural Studies* 2.1.29–45.

ELIZABETH BOBRICK

Husband and wife may exchange roles but never escape the tyranny of roles themselves. . . . Theatrical narratives appear to promote the very ideology of difference they expose as arbitrary.

—Barbara Freedman, "Frame-Up"

The Tyranny of Roles

Playacting and Privilege in Aristophanes' *Thesmophoriazusae*

Thesmophoriazusae contains many of the features we expect from Old Comedy: an upside-down world in which traditional social roles are reversed or abandoned altogether,[1] a bawdy celebration of the pleasures of the body, a pair of bumbling heroes who foment the chaos yet ultimately triumph. At the same time, the play stands out in the Aristophanic corpus for the extent of its parody and the complexity and coherence of its plot. *Thesmophoriazusae* is a Euripidean play of intrigue rewritten by Aristophanes, a vehicle he uses not only to play with plays but to represent the control playwrights have, or fail to have, over the members of their audience. Behind the mask of tried-and-true comic formula is a self-referential representation of theatrical narratives and their power to establish civic ideology.

Thesmophoriazusae appears to share little ground with Aristophanes' overtly political plays. No civic crisis is ever stated, as in, say, the beginning of *Acharnians*, where Dicaeopolis waits outside the Pnyx, hoping to force talk of peace in the Assembly, or *Knights*, where two slaves fret that their master Demos has fallen under the influence of the evil Paphlagon. The chorus of women here does not step out of character in order to speak in Aristophanes' theatrical persona as *didaskalos* of the city. The trouble in *Thesmophoriazusae* appears to be solely Euripides' own: how is he going to keep the women from killing him?

Nonetheless, this is a deeply political play concerned with the definition of social roles in the context of the theater as a public space.

The play's framework is this: the Athens of *Thesmophoriazusae* is one in which a single tragedian has successfully dictated the terms of relations between married men and women. Euripides' plays have taught the men to treat their wives as potential Medeas and Phaedras. From the women's point of view, Euripides' grip on the public imagination is so strong that only his death can break it. At their festival of the Thesmophoria, in which the women had rare license to be together, away from their homes, they issue a formal indictment for Euripides' death.

Euripides gets wind of the plot and comes back with one of his own, one that pits his theatrical narratives against the women's attempted resistance to them. The fey tragedian Agathon refuses Euripides' request to plead his case with the women, but agrees to act as costumer for the invasion. He enables Euripides' unnamed Kinsman (here called "Mnesilochus," following tradition) to go in drag to the festival.

Once inside the festival, Mnesilochus tries to convince the women that Euripides is no real threat. He is almost immediately detected for the fraud that he is. He and Euripides (in the role of rescuer) adapt the strategems employed by the heroes and heroines of Euripidean escape plays in hopes of getting home in one piece. They perform parodic scenes from the tragic stage to a variety of unreceptive audiences, entering into and stepping out of identities before the spectators' eyes. Through the miracle of transvestism, men become women, and every woman is really a man. Thesmophoria is quickly transformed into Dionysia. The women speak in their own defense, in their imitation of a male ecclesia and in the parabasis, but for the most part the stage belongs to the two men. For the finale, Euripides stars in a comedy of his own devising, in which he tricks the Scythian archer-policeman into letting Mnesilochus escape.

As *Thesmophoriazusae* unfolds, social roles dictated by gender become unsettlingly arbitrary. In the theater, a man can be a woman if he chooses to, and for Euripides the world is a theater. Aristophanes initially appears to eradicate boundaries of gender and status by allowing his characters to change personae and class within the action of the play. With its abundance of parody and role playing within the role (e.g., actor as Mnesilochus as matron as Telephus), *Thesmophoriazusae* raises questions of theatrical and social genuineness, *mimesis*, and authorship. It appears to question the rigidity of social roles, yet even as it does so, it delimits the extent to which members of three political categories—citizen male, female, and barbarian—may participate in the civic spectacle that was theater and hence influence the public imagination.

I shall argue that *Thesmophoriazusae* ultimately leaves social boundaries largely intact. The power to represent the underrepresented is, after all, securely in the hands of free adult male playwrights. By the play's end the apparent instability of categories within the theater has been used to promote and secure an ideology of difference outside the theater, in the city. The women return to their homes unavenged, but with a concession from Euripides. They are still enemies, but enemies who have agreed to a peace treaty. When the women agree to let Euripides get Mnesilochus away from the Scythian policeman if he can, the opposition between male and female is realigned to one between Greek and barbarian. Aristophanes' mock exposure of both tragedians' and Thesmophorians' trade secrets eventually puts the city to rights again by depicting effeminate male and masculine female as subcategories of the dominant class, citizen male. As such, these subcategories are not so much to be defeated as enlisted in the aid of another citizen male and his prerogatives. The "tyranny of roles," to use Freedman's phrase, is not overthrown. It is vigorously shaken, with festival license, but essentially unchanged.[2]

In what follows, I shall examine the roles taken by Agathon, the women, and the Scythian in the escape plays concocted by Mnesilochus and Euripides. I argue that, as alliances within the play are redrawn for the finale, the preexisting roles of political life are reestablished, but not without comic reconsideration of their correctness—and not without raising the question of what oblique commentary Aristophanes offers on his own theatrical art, which I will address in the conclusion of this essay.

Clothes Make the Woman

At the play's beginning, the audience is given a hint of what promises to be an irregular state of affairs. In the opening lines, prior to their meeting with Agathon, Euripides tells his kinsman that he will soon hear what is not seen, and see what cannot be heard (5–6). This cryptic remark leads to some predictably comic confusion on the part of Mnesilochus. Euripides' response to his kinsman (13–18), in which a mock-sophistic cosmology is invoked to explain the difference between hearing and seeing, leaves the audience with the expectation that it is about to take part in a Gorgian fantasy in which that which is not, is, and in which appearance becomes reality.[3]

The confusion of appearance with reality is made manifest when the poet Agathon appears. His interchange with Euripides and Mnesilochus is relatively brief but significant. It serves as a sort of *mise en abyme*, an internal mirror in miniature of the play's constant prodding at the boundaries of gender categories.[4] This scene is the first example of how theatricality—the use of clothes to fashion a persona and a script to create appearance—allows its practitioners to remake identity.[5] Not only is Agathon a transvestite, but he is the first character who openly takes on another persona, or, as he says, makes use of μίμησις ("imitation," 156).[6] He gives us a peek at the poet in rehearsal, and his performance is the first of many to be rejected by a hostile inner audience—in this case, Mnesilochus, who later has the tables turned on him by the women.

Agathon is brought out by his servant, reclining on a platform used to represent interior scenes on the tragic stage, the ἐκκύκλημα (96).[7] He is in the process of composing a choral ode for mixed male and female voices. Dressed in women's clothes, he sings both the men's and women's parts. Scandalized but aroused, Mnesilochus threatens Agathon sexually and condemns Agathon's appearance as a τάραξις τοῦ βίου (137), "a confounding of life-styles." Agathon tries to explain to the unsympathetic old man that his creative process, his μίμησις (156), is more than superficial imitation:

ἐγὼ δὲ τὴν ἐσθῆθ' ἅμα τῇ γνώμῃ φορῶ.
χρὴ γὰρ ποιητὴν ἄνδρα πρὸς τὰ δράματα
ἃ δεῖ ποιεῖν, πρὸς ταῦτα τοὺς τρόπους ἔχειν.
αὐτίκα γυναικεῖ' ἢν ποιῇ τις δράματα,
μετουσίαν δεῖ τῶν τρόπων τὸ σῶμ' ἔχειν.

(148–52)[8]

I wear the clothes that suit my state of mind.
The man who is a poet must match his manner
to the roles he's creating. So when the poet is
writing women's roles, you see, his body mustn't
clash with the way women look and act.

The playwright, he says, must identify on a physical level with the roles he creates, and "if one is writing a play about women, his body must have something of their manner."[9] As he explains to the increasingly agitated Mnesilochus, "one must create things that are like unto one's nature" (τῇ φύσει, 167). Agathon, at least in his own mind, is no fake. He identifies himself with the feminine.

The success of Agathon's transvestism is unsettling: things are not what they seem, for not every man is a real man. Agathon is able to masquerade sexually as well as theatrically, so convincingly, he claims, that the women are jealous of him (204–5). Little wonder that the young playwright so fills Mnesilochus with dread. His anxiety gives the comedy its edge. If a man can so easily become a woman, can a woman easily become a man? Can women control men, which is to say, ruin them, in the way that all women in tragedy who get control over men ruin them?

Of course, Agathon has not really become a woman. This exposure of the playwright at work does not show that he has transformed himself biologically. To the contrary, it makes clear that he is very much a man. His gender combined with his social class makes him a member of a political category whose privileges, both sexual and theatrical, extend to pretending to be a woman when he wishes to.

Agathon's transvestism at once represents a convention of ancient theatrical performance and a transgression of ancient cultural norms. All actors were men; all playwrights were men; but drag queens received no cultural benediction. Still, Agathon is no Cleisthenes, who later champions the women. He comes down on the men's side. Despite his questionable behavior, Agathon shows that his heart is in the right place in his male body when he joins Mnesilochus and Euripides in their cause.[10] He helps Euripides even though he is sympathetic to the women's complaints. For all Agathon's dubious allegiances, he is unquestionably a playwright. His ability to represent women so faithfully may be due, as he says, to his nature, but his ability to do so in public venues is due to his profession, one open to men only. Even though the clothes make the man a woman, Agathon's body shows where the permeability of gender category ends. His freedom to transgress as well as create stands in stark contrast to the women's emerging but ultimately limited voice as censors of public art. His gender bending makes both his authorial power and his womanly delicacy completely natural in his own eyes.

Agathon chooses to assist Euripides in his subterfuge, not by entering the festival himself and pleading the elder tragedian's case, as Euripides has asked, but by transforming Mnesilochus into the compleat matron. Agathon gives him the dress off his back as well as one of his very own razors to shave off his beard. This scene is particularly significant, as it demonstrates the amazingly simple process for engendering theatrical characters: take off the whiskers, put on a wig, get something new to wear. More importantly, it shows how easy it is for men to play at being women: just shave, and pull a few things out of the lingerie chest.[11] By contrast, women need a great deal more from men in order even to play secretly at being men. They need permission and financial support for the rare opportunity to gather in numbers without male supervision.[12]

Agathon disappears from center stage by choice. He declines to play along with Euripides, and is wheeled back inside on his ἐκκύκλημα. Unlike the women, he does not have to struggle against the producers of culture for control of the stage. However effeminate Agathon may be, his masculinity is not in question when he presents his tragedies for consideration in the Dionysia. The μίμησις that works for him is not open to the women. In short, dramatic personae may be male or female, but authors must be male.

Agathon gives entrance into a hidden world of women that is about to be exposed. He sets the stage for the two intruders, both literally and figuratively. Agathon, the transvestite catamite male, draws the the audience's laughter early on as playwright and actor, a man who thinks he can really be a woman just by dressing up. He is soon followed by Mnesilochus and Euripides, who think that they can make other women believe they are women, just by dressing up.

Immediately after Agathon's exit, Aristophanes' satire of stage conventions is implicitly turned on itself. The stage is filled with the "female" celebrants of the festival, every one a man dressed as a woman.

Thesmophoria and Dionysia

Thesmophoriazusae comically enacts a civic festival that in real life was never seen by its male citizens but which was celebrated in a secret, three-day gathering by their wives. As such, the play is as much a burlesque of the imagined Thesmophoria as it is a travesty of the Dionysia. Like the Dionysia, the real Thesmophoria held an important place in Athenian civic life; and like the Dionysia, *mimesis* and ritual were at its core. Not only did the women ritually represent the story of Demeter and Kore (Persephone), but they did so in civic spaces that were normally open solely to men. The Athenian matrons have a voice inside the space of their festival, but because the real Thesmophoria was a secret space, that voice could not be heard by men. As A. M. Bowie observes, the lawcourts and the ecclesia did not sit during the Thesmophoria, so that "when the women gathered at the Thesmophorion on the Pnyx, they were symbolically replacing the men at the political centre of the city."[13] In *Thesmophoriazusae*, however, Mnesilochus and Euripides gradually supplant the women.

As soon as Mnesilochus enters the Pnyx in drag, the "real" world as presented by the play appears to be organized on the same principles as the theater. When the polis becomes a stage, what part do women get to play? The trespassing males attempt to recast the women of the festival. Euripides and Mnesilochus treat the celebrants of the Thesmophoria as if they were merely supporting characters in a newly improvised play, *Escape from the Thesmophoria*. First, they change the women from principal actors in their own ritual drama to reactors in supporting roles.

Our first view of the women at the festival, in their *ecclesia*, shows them angry and defiant (295ff.). Although they devote considerable time to prayer in this mock Thesmophoria, an important goal of their gathering is to indict Euripides for crimes against the women and the state. By *mimesis* of men, specifically of a male ecclesia and the issuance of an assembly decree against

Euripides, they hope to get rid of their enemy. The women imitate the ecclesia earnestly, more to confer legitimacy on their gathering than to lampoon the innate silliness of the proceedings (unlike the ecclesia scene in *Acharnians*, which we see through the cynical eyes of Dikaiopolis).

Thanks to Euripides, say the women, the men live in suspicion of their wives, putting more complicated locks on the door, accusing them of love affairs, watching them always for signs of pilfering from the household stocks (384–432). As if that weren't enough, Euripides has made the men atheists (450–51). For their part, the women reject the authenticity of Euripides' destructive female characters (e.g., Medea, Phaedra) and the credibility of those characters as models for real women. They refuse to be the gullible audiences for Euripidean tragedy that their husbands have proved to be.

Euripides' authorial crimes against women are not in themselves the cause of the women's wrath. Rather, it is the male spectators' enthusiastic reception of the tragedian's representations of the female that propels the women's anger. If their husbands had ignored his Medeas and Phaedras, the women would not be seeking Euripides' death. Even the charge of atheism against him has its foundation in economics rather than moral philosophy: it comes from a garland-seller, the sole support of her family, who says that her business has fallen off sharply since Euripides got men to stop believing in the gods (442–58). Eliminating Euripides, the enemy of the δῆμος τῶν γυναικῶν ("the people [body politic] of the women," 306–7, 335–36), is a measure for correcting men's behavior, not for keeping Athenian morals on track or maintaining proper aesthetic standards.[14]

The assembly is interrupted by a strange woman who would have them excuse Euripides on the grounds that he either doesn't know or doesn't talk about the worst of women's routine transgressions, adultery with a variety of partners and presenting husbands with illegitimate children.[15] The strange woman is, of course, Mnesilochus. His speech detailing the secrets of female behavior that Euripides hasn't yet presented on stage is so outrageous that he attracts the women's suspicion and is found out.

Mnesilochus' infiltration of the festival is ostensibly a defensive tactic. He must persuade the women that Euripides is really not so bad. Once inside, however, the old man cannot help himself from switching to a more offensive stance, the reordering of what he sees as the women's all-too-free sexuality. It seems that the celebrants need more than persuading; they need correcting. As soon as Euripides joins his kinsman inside the festival, he implicitly agrees with Mnesilochus' tactic of moving the focus away from his own perceived transgressions onto the women's behavior. Paradoxically, therefore, the permeability and instability of male sexual categories in a theatrical context is used to confirm the traditionally set boundaries of female sexuality. Men can play at being women in order to get women back under control.

Mnesilochus demonstrates a touching faith that Euripides' schemes, which got him into this scrape, will get him out. *Telephus* is the first of four Euripidean dramas of escape to be parodied here (659–758). It is followed by a brief parody of *Palamedes* (765–84), and by longer adaptions of *Helen* (855–925) and *Andromeda* (1008–1126), for which the Scythian alone is the audience and unwitting participant, the women having by this time left the stage.[16] In these adaptations, Mnesilochus and later Euripides try to transform the women from protagonists enacting their own festival to subordinate actors. They recast these women, as it were, to move them away from center stage, where they are actors in their own ritual drama, to the fringe roles of those who only react. The women resist these efforts to make them into cooperative extras, but cannot hold out against the two men.

Mnesilochus' first speech in the female assembly (466–520) centers on men's fears about their wives supplanting "false" babies for "real" ones. This fear is immediately borne out by the appearance of a wineskin dressed in baby bunting (590ff.) which Mnesilochus holds hostage and ultimately sacrifices in his parody of *Telephus*.[17]

After the *Telephus* parody the women regain the upper hand, but only partially and temporarily. Mnesilochus must be officially arrested by a real citizen, that is, a man. The prytanis must be summoned (763–64). The women lose a considerable degree of their authority by having to turn to the men, even at a time when they are celebrating their own power in the city.

The chorus retreats, its indictment of Euripides subverted. The invaders then enact adaptations of Euripidean plays in which the female is represented as increasingly powerless and dependent on salvation by the male. The plays they choose are Euripides' *Helen* and *Andromeda*. Their heroines are damsels in distress: helpless, alluring objects of desire rather than the active and dangerous Medea and Phaedra about whom the women originally complained.

For the *Helen* parody, only one woman, Critylla, is left on stage. Her duty is to watch Mnesilochus until the prytanis arrives, and the two men try to draw her in as a participant. Sommerstein declares her to be the priestess of the Thesmophoria and a principal speaker in the assembly.[18] If he is correct, Mnesilochus and Euripides have degraded her role from the most important woman on the stage to the least. In her exchanges with the two men as they pretend to be Helen and Menelaus (852–923), she is shown to be very dense indeed. Just as the transvestite Agathon is a forerunner to Mnesilochus in drag, so Critylla's refusal to be a receptive audience for this adaptation of Euripidean theater presages the Scythian archer's lack of appreciation for the fictive imperatives of *Andromeda*.

The parodies of *Helen* and *Andromeda* have been the subjects of such thorough commentary that there is little purpose in repeating what little would fit here.[19] As has been amply demonstrated, they mock tragedy in general and the idiosyncrasies of Euripidean tragedy in particular and they challenge the women's self-representation at the Thesmophoria. What I would like to emphasize here is that these parodies momentarily reverse the women's relationship to their sacred space from actors to audience, so that even the city's legitimized forms of female separateness and initiative are rewritten and hence controlled. Actors in ritual drama (Thesmophorians) have their script changed; a story of female rescue of female (Persephone and Demeter) is transformed to male rescue of female.[20] The importance of the mother-daughter blood relationship is transferred to the marriage bond between man and woman (Menelaus-Helen, Perseus-Andromeda).[21]

After the first third of the play, the ecclesia scene and the *Telephus* parody, the women's most sustained appearance on stage is in the parabasis. Here they attempt to defend themselves against Mnesilochus' and Euripides' explicit and implicit charges by demonstrating their loyalty as citizen wives. The women's efforts to turn away suspicions from what has been represented as their disordered sexuality and toward their useful function as mothers is as much a support of the patriarchal order as a self-protective device. We see this in their most articulate resistance, the speech of self-defense they give in the parabasis. Here, ironically, the women are at their most "masculine": they imitate male forms of political self-justification.[22]

The women begin their defense by listing the evils for which "everyone," presumably every man (πᾶς τις, 786), holds them responsible: ἔριδες, νείκη, στάσις ἀργαλέα, λύπη, πόλεμος ("wranglings, quarrels, grievous civil strife, sorrow, war," 788). Women, they say, are accused of causing trouble not just at home but in the city and between cities—hardly a novel charge in a culture steeped in Homeric epic.

The women's next point concerns what in modern academic terminology is called the male gaze,[23] the desire of men to watch and objectify women (789–94): if we are truly an evil to men, the women ask, why do you men marry us and then make such a fuss over safeguarding this evil? Why do you always want to look at us, and why do you take such pains to make sure no other man looks at us?

The women then turn to their first argument, a βάσανος of their superiority "to you," that is, the male spectators.[24] Ironically, the women's proof is not initially based on bodies but on names, and not just any names, but names that make women into symbols of traditionally masculine virtues in male spheres of activity (802–9). The chorus "proves" the superiority of women to men etymologically.[25] For example:

οὕτως ἡμεῖς ἐπιδήλως
ὑμῶν ἐσμεν πολὺ βελτίους, βάσανός τε πάρεστιν ἰδέσθαι.
βάσανον δῶμεν, πότεροι χείρους. ἡμεῖς μὲν γάρ φαμεν ὑμᾶς,
ὑμεῖς δ᾽ ἡμᾶς. σκεψώμεθα δὴ κἀντιτιθῶμεν πρὸς ἕκαστον,
παραβάλλουσαι τῆς τε γυναικὸς καὶ τἀνδρὸς τοὔνομ᾽ ἑκάστου.
Ναυσιμάχης μέν γ᾽ ἥττων ἐστὶν Χαρμῖνος—δῆλα δὲ τἄργα—
καὶ μὲν δὴ καὶ Κλεοφῶν χείρων πάντως δήπου Σαλαβακχοῦς.

(799–805)

There's clear proof that we are better by far than you.
We'll put to the test which of us is worse—of course, you say it's us, and we say it's you. Let us scrutinize and compare on a case-by-case basis, comparing a woman's name to a man's. Now, Charminos is inferior to Nausimache; it's obvious. And Cleophon is so much worse than Salabaccho.

The hypothetical Nausimache ("victory at sea"), they say, must prima facie be a better general than the real Charminos. Any girl named Salabaccho ("trumpet") would make a better leader in battle than Cleophon. The chorus continues in this vein: Aristomache ("best at battle") and Stratonike ("victorious army") are both better than any general. Euboule ("good at giving counsel") is wiser than any real member of the assembly.

In short, women's names are testimony to their superiority over men even in the male spheres of politics and war. This βάσανος is one of the play's most vivid illustrations of its own construction of the female: what is praiseworthy about the feminine is an echo of the male; or, as Luce Irigaray wrote in another context, "the feminine finds itself defined as lack, deficiency, or as imitation and negative image of the [male] subject."[26]

Finally, the chorus's etymological proof of its superiority is an attempt to manipulate signs as men do. By the same token, however, sign = self in this "proof," and a sign can be manipulated by men as readily as a body.[27] Through their proof, the women have consigned themselves to being symbols. As Loraux notes, the women do not really act; they symbolize action.[28] According to their own proof, they participate in public life in name only.

The women conclude their self-defense with a speech about their usefulness to men rather than their superiority. Here, their utility comes not from their significant names but from their bodies. A man must have a citizen mother in order to have citizen status himself.[29] Likewise, in the play as a whole, as in the real city, the civic identity of male and female are drawn in large part from the production of children.

The final argument in the parabasis responds to Mnesilochus' earlier charges before his detection as a fraud in the assembly. The women protest his slurs on their own genuineness, even though they have already admitted to them (339–40). They insist on being honored for their contribution to the state as mothers (836–47).

Not only do the women declare their value as bearers of cultural symbols, but with their wordplay at 845 on τόκος/τέκος ("interest" or "income producing"/"progeny") make a punning link between the respective spheres of men and women. The mother of Hyperbolus the politician, they say, should be chastised for appearing in public next to the mother of the hero Lamachus. Hyperbolus' mother, who lends money, should be told:

ἀξία γοῦν εἶ τόκου τεκοῦσα τοιοῦτον τόκον

(845)

You're a fine one to be making interest-bearing loans,
after bearing a son like the one you bore.[30]

The joke establishes a parallel between the male business of property owning and moneymaking, and the female business of childbearing. Each is a means of contributing to the health and continuity of the city. Further, the pun suggests that women purchase their legitimate participation in public life through the production of children. For them, children are tokens with which they can purchase affiliation, if not membership, in the exclusive club of citizenship.

In the action following the parabasis, the women are largely absent as players who interact with Euripides and Mnesilochus. Instead, as an undifferentiated chorus, they offer two prayers (947–1000 and 1136–59). The first, which begins as a prayer to Demeter and Persephone, also summons the aid of other gods—but never Aphrodite, despite their alleged and admitted sexual licentiousness—and ultimately turns into a paean in honor of Dionysus. The second entreats Pallas Athene for protection of the city, and ends with a prayer to the goddesses of the Thesmophoria. In the first, the goddesses of one festival give way to the god of another, just as the women's festival has been reworked by the male intruders from Thesmophoria to Dionysia. The second echoes the general tenor of the parabasis: all the women really care about is the good of the city.

The women's emerging voice and its subsequent silencing follows a pattern we see in this play's contemporary, *Lysistrata*, and in the later *Ecclesiazusae* as well: ordinarily voiceless women claim a public voice only to reorder wayward men. Once that reordering has taken place, the women retreat from the public arena and are heard from no more. They surrender their place on center stage by agreeing to let the two imposters escape in return for Euripides' promise to cease slandering them in future. This is female power, but it is corrective rather than creative.[31]

Unlike Agathon, who is a successful creator, however, the women are merely unsuccessful imitators. Here we see the power of those who produce culture as opposed to those who merely consume it by imitating its forms. Agathon's presence as an effeminate male playwright seems at first to be simply another opportunity for Aristophanes to show that denizens of the theater are extravagantly out of touch with reality. The flamboyant tragedian's role as an exemplar of male privilege becomes clear only when we see what happens when the women take center stage. His freedom to create and self-invent stands in opposition to the women who try to assume male privilege and control the production of culture by censoring Euripides. The women are much more limited in the variety of their self-presentation. Their response to Euripides' calumny is not to put on a play about the virtues of women; that, apparently, would have strained the credulity of any audience. All they can do is plot to kill him and, failing that, to bargain with him for a cease-fire.

Although by play's end the invading males have attempted to transform Thesmophoria into Dionysia, they are only partially successful. *Thesmophoriazusae* itself has the myth of Demeter and Persephone as its own paradigm. Like the myth of Demeter's loss of Persephone, the play's story is one of initial female resistance and rage (Demeter's creation of eternal winter in revenge for the rape of her daughter) followed by compromise and submission (Zeus' intervention to allow Persephone's partial return to her mother). The women's response to Euripides follows this pattern. Ultimately they acquiesce in Euripides' attempts to silence them, but not without first attempting to establish their important cultural role as mothers of citizens.[32]

Just as the women's actions have a double allegiance to the paradigm of the Demeter/Persephone myth and to Aristophanes' script, so do Euripides' and Mnesilochus' actions have a double allegiance. The first is to the Aristophanic script, following its typical pattern of reversal of the status quo for the purpose of ultimate reaffirmation of the same, with slight reordering. The second is to the Euripidean script of rescue and intrigue, for Aristophanes' plot depends on typically Euripidean features of δόλος, ἀπάτη, μηχανή, and σωτηρία (subterfuge, deceit, device, salvation). Aristophanes adapts Euripides' scripts handily to his own. In the first two parodies (of *Telephus* and *Palamedes*), Mnesilochus plays the Euripidean hero who has found himself helpless. Outside his own territory, cut off from friends and resources, he must rely on his wits rather than on an epic deed of bravery to save himself. In the second two parodies (of *Helen* and *Andromeda*), Mnesilochus' damsels in distress are in settings that contrast Greek to barbarian values. Greeks versus barbarians becomes the theme of the final scene of the play.

The Fall of Tragedy Crushes the Barbarian

With the women rendered harmless, Euripides' work of subjection is focused on the Scythian policeman rather than the women, and with him he is successful. As the parodied play changes from *Helen* to *Andromeda*, the onstage audience changes as well, from Critylla to the Scythian. Critylla resisted Euripides' and Mnesilochus' efforts to cast her as Theomene, and was angered and bewildered by their playing at Helen and Menelaus. In contrast, the Scythian, although momentarily confused and angered by the character Echo from the *Andromeda* parody (1056–96), is for the most part in control of the situation. He responds to Mnesilochus and Euripides with what might be called good-natured cruelty, tightening Mnesilochus' bonds when asked to loosen them, and making an obscene suggestion to Euripides as to how he (as Perseus) might get closer to his fair Andromeda (1118–20, 1123–24). His control comes from his lack of understanding; he does not share the Athenians' cultural context.

When the archer does not take on his assigned role as expected, Euripides comes to the realization that the Scythian doesn't understand theater. The barbarian is too unsophisticated to participate as an audience should. He does not fall under the playwright's spell as the Athenian husbands already have. A desperate Euripides declaims a soliloquy, in the manner of one of his own tragic heroes:

αἰαῖ τί δράσω; πρὸς τίνας στρεφθῶ λόγους;
ἀλλ' οὐκ ἂν ἐνδέξαιτο βάρβαρος φύσις.
σκαιοῖσι γάρ τοι καινὰ προσφέρων σοφὰ
μάτην ἀναλίσκοις ἄν. ἀλλ' ἄλλην τινὰ
τούτῳ πρέπουσαν μηχανὴν προσοιστέον.

(1128–32)

Oh no! What shall I do? What speeches shall I turn to now?
But his uncouth nature wouldn't take them in. You'd be
wasting your time to use the latest subtleties
on idiots. No, some other device must be put to work,
one more suitable for him.

So Euripides must trick himself out as an old female pimp, one "Artemisia," who offers to watch the Scythian's prisoner while he buys some offstage time with the dancing-girl Elaphion ("Fawn," 1172). As I have discussed elsewhere, this too is a theatrical subterfuge, a parody of the escape mechanism of Euripides' own *Iphigeneia at Aulis*.[33] Even in appearing to give up on his theater as an effective weapon against the Scythian, Euripides cannot stop drawing on it as a source.

At this point the spectators' sympathies are subtly redirected: instead of laughing at Mnesilochus' and Euripides' attempts to make the women play along, we are asked to root for their success in duping the Scythian. Euripides again relies on female sexuality to act as the ruin of men, but here it is a sexuality that is known, expected, and socially ordered: a dancing-girl is supposed to be licentious. Her use of her body as a means of manipulating men does not threaten the legitimacy of male citizens' heirs and, hence, civic identity.

Thus a hierarchy of domination is established, or reestablished, after a brief threat to its stability. Male citizens control their women, and male and female Greeks work together to disempower the foreigner. Difference based on gender is masked, and the opposition of men versus women is realigned into one of Greek versus barbarian.[34] In this way, the play ultimately reinforces the legitimate male citizens' superiority over all, a feeling of superiority that appears in every genre of Greek literature.

The comedy illustrates what Paul Cartledge has called "the characteristically 'Greek' way of defining the citizen . . . precisely by negative opposition to a whole series of 'others'—the unfree, minors, females, and non-Greeks." The true Other in this play is the Scythian, a publicly owned slave and a barbarian. The women and their enemy Euripides, the effeminate Agathon and the stoutly masculine Mnesilochus, have more in common with each other than they do with this alien.[35]

But even here the hall of mirrors that is *Thesmophoriazusae* holds up yet another unflattering reflection to its audience. The Scythian, a crude, credulous, irresponsible idiot, has more than a little in common with the Athenian husbands who were so terrified by Euripides' Phaedra and Medea. Like them, he has been taken in by the playwright. Barbarian and citizen may be at opposite ends of the spectrum in terms of sophistication, but they are on the same spectrum nonetheless.

Euripides must stoop even lower than Mnesilochus did to conquer his enemy; for although Mnesilochus had to play at being female heroines of royal blood, Euripides has to impersonate a female pimp. Tragedy must bow to comedy in order to save its hide, but comedy does not escape uninjured. For as Aristophanes aims the comic weapon of exposure against Euripides and Agathon, men who put on shows, he does so, ironically and indirectly, against himself.

Aristophanes *didaskalos*?

By play's end, the tyranny of roles that governs the theater has been clearly defined. Agathon, Euripides, and Mnesilochus are creators and producers. The repressive husbands are credulous spectators who appear to have lost their hold on reality. The women of the chorus are at first primary actors, then marginalized reactors, then unwilling spectators. The Scythian archer is so uncouth that he cannot recognize theater at all.

Yet *Thesmophoriazusae* should not be understood simply as a standard-bearer for the ruling patriarchy. It would be simplistic to maintain that the major objects of this play are to show the superiority of comedy to tragedy and to shore up established social conventions.[36] The anarchy central to Aristophanes' particular style does not permit any message or statement to stand absolutely pat. In *Thesmophoriazusae*, Aristophanes tears down at least as much as he establishes. He dismantles the theatrical constructs that create what used to be called dramatic illusion. The added dimension of theatrical self-consciousness in *Thesmophoriazusae* confuses not just social but theatrical roles. A play that has as its inspiration other plays, whose plot is the comic adaptation of those plays, is in essence metatheatrical; and metatheater, if nothing else, mixes up the usual roles assigned to audience, actors, and author.[37] The audience is given what appears to be an authorial privilege: a behind-the-scenes look at composition, costuming, and the art of acting. The characters "become" actors within the play, discarding their roles and taking on new ones. The play exposes as sham the cross-dressing and stage props on which theater, and the play itself, rely for its effect.

Much like the Cretan liar of the famous paradox who declared that everything he said was false, Aristophanes constantly encourages his audience to view theatrical constructs as a sham reality. The premise on which the play is built—that Athenian husbands have been so swayed by a playwright that their wives revolt—is itself founded on an assumption about the importance of theater in the spectators' lives. While appearing to attack the tyranny of roles, Aristophanes presents a comically subversive portrait of the tyranny of theater over the hearts and minds of Athenian citizens.

Mnesilochus and Euripides present theater, particularly the tragic theater, within a frame of fakery. That is, they declare that they are acting in order to manipulate their intended audience, the women. They pretend to expose the players behind the mask.[38] Mnesilochus is discovered and exposed on stage by those he has shown to be false and is punished for his falsity by them. The creation of this pervasive sense of fraudulence creates pleasure for the spectators in two ways. Their sense of their own genuineness is confirmed, and they are titillated by the exposure of what is usually kept hidden. They are induced to believe that they are "seeing the backstage of something."[39] Here, backstage = backside.

Tragedians are fools, actors are fakes, spectators are the biggest dupes of all. As a self-declared teacher of the city, what is Aristophanes teaching by creating this widespread sense of fraudulence? That theater, for all its power, is a fake? Or that its power resides in its very falsity?

Kenneth Reckford has made a strong case for Aristophanes as a *didaskalos* whose comedies have restorative and constructive powers to diagnose and heal an ailing city.[40] While agreeing with much of his argument, I prefer to emphasize here a darker side to Aristophanic comedy, indeed to all serious comedy, and that is the destruction, even the self-destruction, that must occur prior to restoration.

In Aristophanes' comedy, the destroyer is hero. To be sure, he or she is never a general or any other state-appointed, publicly sanctioned destroyer, but a destroyer nonetheless. One has only to flip through the extant works to see the destroyer of the army (Lysistrata); the destroyer of the Phrontisterion (Strepsiades), himself a dupe of the vengeful and destructive Clouds; the destroyer of pretense, both dramatic and civic (Dikaiopolis); or the destroyer of the harmony in which birds, gods and humans once lived (Peisetaerus).

The destroyer is seldom able to come up with a successful solution, even when he or she tries. Lysistrata ultimately offers a symbolic woman's body to be carved up by the warring parties, so that the men end up in possession of the only weapon found effective against them.[41] Dionysus leads Aeschylus back to the light so that the Athenians can get remedial instruction in statecraft and manly virtue, but it is clear that his nostalgia is just that, and not a solution to contemporary Athens' problems: the very men who grew up under Aeschylus' tutelage, after all, were responsible to no small degree for the city's ills, brought on by the Peloponnesian War. The mirror that the comic playwright holds up to his audience is an excellent diagnostic tool but poor medicine. It can do nothing for the patients beyond restoring them to consciousness of their errors.

Destruction is not limited to the confines of the plot; as mentioned, Aristophanes cheerfully dismantles his own theatrical constructs into the bargain. What was for years referred to as comedy's "rupture of dramatic illusion"[42] can now with the wider acceptance of deconstructive reading be more accurately seen as the comic playwright's design of leaving nothing whole. Every sacred cow must be milked for comic effect, including and most especially tragedy's requirement for near-seamless illusion, the better to engage the audience's emotions. In Attic tragedy, the audience is encouraged to give itself over to the dramatist's control. By contrast, Aristophanes' comedy gives the audience the illusion of control, of being able to see through travesty, of joining the author backstage in full knowledge that this is just a play. Just a play, in which they have been encouraged to view every claim to principle and genuineness as sham.

Destruction is not alien to the worship of Dionysus, the god who is at once healer and destroyer. Aristophanes' penchant for chaos shows his genuine affinity for Euripides, who holds a place of honor as his favorite target. Euripides too understood that the theater is a place for tearing things apart, for punishing those convinced of the importance of their own principles. Obviously, Euripides' *Bacchae* bears more than a surface resemblance to *Thesmophoriazusae*, and not just in plot.[43] In both plays, a man dresses up as a woman in order to infiltrate rites closed to him. More importantly, both plays imply that once humans give themselves over to the allure of spectatorship, of looking and listening, they have put their hearts and minds at the disposal of the showman. When the spectacle is over, they are on their own. The sight of the howling Scythian at *Thesmophoriazusae*'s finale does not compare with that of Agave coming to her senses over the severed head of her son, to be sure; but both are victims of the rites of Dionysus and his followers.

Thesmophoriazusae is a theater of exposure but hardly an exposé. In appearing to lay bare all the tricks of theatricality, Aristophanes paradoxically celebrates them and hence his own power. By staging Euripides' ultimate theatrical triumph over the forces of law and order in the play's finale, he includes the tragedian in the select company of those who can put one over on the spectator. (Of course, the tragedian must first bow to comedy before he is allowed to prevail.)

Who are the winners of the struggle for power and freedom of expression set up in *Thesmophoriazusae*? Neither the suspicious husbands of Euripides' audience, nor the indignant women, but the playwrights, both real and imagined; and not even the winners enjoy a total victory.

Notes

The author wishes to express her appreciation to Gregory Dobrov for his efforts in bringing this essay to print, to the UNC Press's anonymous reader for his/her valuable criticism, and to Andrew Szegedy-Maszak and David Konstan for their helpful suggestions.

1. For full discussion of the play's role-reversals, see Muecke 1977 and Zeitlin 1996.

2. For a discussion of the ways in which civic festivals allow for the strengthening of the social order by temporarily violating its codes, see Goldhill 1991, 176–88.

3. See Porter 1993. I am grateful to Gregory Dobrov for the reference.

4. *Mise en abyme* is in this way the inverse of a frame story. For a discussion of the term with its history, see Ron 1987 and Dobrov's essay in this volume.

5. Burn 1973 provides a valuable survey and discussion of this and other social uses of stage conventions.

6. See Muecke 1982 for a detailed discussion of this speech and the Agathon scene in general.

7. For a summary of the arguments about the use of the *ekkuklēma* here, see Hansen 1976, 170–73. He and Arnott 1962, 78–90, agree that Agathon is here brought out on an actual *ekkuklēma* rather than a wheeled couch. See also Dearden 1976 for the use of this and other stage machinery in Aristophanes.

8. The Greek text follows that of Sommerstein 1994; translations are my own unless otherwise noted.

9. Silk 1990, 164, points out that this speech prefigures "the wonderful repeated joke in the second half of *Thesmophoriazusae*, that by appearing to be Menelaus, Euripides can rescue Mnesilochus, if Mnesilochus appears to be Helen; and by appearing to be Perseus, Euripides can rescue Mnesilochus, if Mnesilochus appears to be Andromeda."

10. Cf. by contrast the cameo appearance of Cleisthenes (582ff.), who alerts the women of a male intruder. This most ubiquitous of Aristophanes' laughingstocks (he appears eleven times in the extant comedies) is accepted or at least tolerated by the celebrants as an honorary woman, and calls himself their *proxenos* (576).

11. As Ferris 1989, 28, has it, "The prop phallus promoting the real penis is a major source of Aristophanic comedy. There is no parallel joke for female characters. Unlike that of the phallus, the theatrical code for woman derives from her social clothing: costume apes costume, in this case, and not some real *part* of the woman. . . . Aristophanes' comedy tells us how easy it is to be a woman, a metonymic piece of skirt."

12. The festival was, of course, financed by men as well: see Bowie 1993, 205 n. 2.

13. Ibid., 206–7.

14. *Pace* Hubbard 1991, 182, who says, "The women of the *Lysistrata* conspire with political motives in view, while those of the *Thesmophoriazusae* are more concerned with addressing a literary and artistic issue." The women of *Thesmophoriazusae* are in their own eyes very much concerned with political motives: they want to defeat the enemy of their people. They care less about the literary and artistic issues of Euripidean tragedy than they do the entirely mundane but oppressive results of his stage portraits of women.

15. Note that the women admit to much in their assembly that they later deny when they realize that they have an audience. Their crimes center chiefly on excessive drinking, adultery, and trying to pass off children they have bought from other women as their own (331–51).

16. Rau 1967 thoroughly discusses the individual parodies of Euripidean plays and the paratragic style of these scenes. Sommerstein 1994, 212, 223, gives very useful "Tables of Quotations and Adaptations" for the parodies of *Helen* and *Andromeda*.

17. For a full discussion of male anxiety about illegitimacy and women's sexuality in this play and other comedies, see Gardner 1989.

18. Sommerstein 1994, 176, n. to 295. He assigns her the lines the scholiast gives to "woman imitating a herald" and to the unnamed woman who helps Cleisthenes search Mnesilochus' body.

19. See Zeitlin 1996, esp. 392–405.

20. When we speak of "actors" and "roles" in ritual, of course, the meaning is not identical to that of the same words used in reference to a text-based play. Rather, they are, as Turner has said, "roles which carry with them, if not precisely recorded scripts, deeply engraved tendencies to act and speak in suprapersonal or 'representative' ways appropriate to the role taken, and to prepare the way for a certain climax given in a certain central myth of the death or victory of a hero or heroes in which they have been deeply indoctrinated or 'socialized' or 'enculturated' "; see Turner 1974, 123.

21. In this it is oddly reminiscent of the central theme of Aeschylus' *Oresteia*, the primacy of the husband-wife bond over the mother-child bond.

22. For use of rhetorical themes by women in dramatic speeches that follow standard male forms of political self-justification, see Ober and Strauss 1990, 264.

23. In the last decade or so, the objectification of the female by the male spectator has taken center stage in feminist performance criticism. "The male gaze" has become common shorthand to describe the process; this was the term used by Mulvey 1988, writing about modern cinema. She described "the gaze" as "taking other people as objects, subjecting them to a controlling and curious gaze." The gaze is that of the male director and his predominantly male audience, who have an interest in seeing women conform to the ideological paradigms of a patriarchy. Other scholars have since applied Mulvey's work to texts, and some have produced new readings of authors who predate the movies by many years, notably Shakespeare; see, e.g., Freedman 1991 and Dolan 1988.

As Taafe 1994 has shown, this approach is particularly useful for Aristophanes, whose representations of the feminine in *Lysistrata*, *Thesmophoriazusae*, and *Ecclesiazusae* are constructed according to male models. In *Thesmophoriazusae*, the male gaze is not directed at women only. It is directed at anyone who puts himself or herself up for display.

24. For the complicated history of the semantic shift of βάσανος from "proof" to "torture," i.e., from *logos* to *soma*, and its literary usage in tragedy and in *Frogs*, see du Bois 1991, 20–34.

25. It is possible that these etymologies were also meant to be understood as further parodies of Euripidean style, given his fondness for etymological wordplay, in regard to which see Woodhead 1928; Wilson 1968; and van Looy 1978. Van Looy cites as examples of Euripidean etymologizing one fragment each from *Telephus* and *Andromeda* (351 and 352, respectively), and lines 1674–75 from *Helen* (356). Others have pointed out the puns involved in these etymologies: see Taafe 1994, 77–78; Moulton 1981, 131; and Zeitlin 1996, 391.

26. Irigaray 1985, 78.

27. Ferris 1989, 29–30: "The more symbolic and mediatory 'woman' becomes, the less she herself is and can be culturally creative. . . . The notion of women as symbolic objects, existing purely and passively as signs, in contrast to men who use signs, has a particularly striking relation to a theatre where for centuries only men took the stage."

28. Loraux 1980–81, 145 n. 137.

29. See Plut. *Per.* 37.2–5 on the citizenship legislation of 451/0; see also Patterson 1988; and cf. *Eccl.* 233–34 and 635–49 on women's roles as producers of male children.

30. Sommerstein's translation, 1994, 99.

31. What Zeitlin has said about women in Greek tragedy applies equally to the female characters in this comedy: "Women as individuals or chorus may give their names as titles to plays. . . . But functionally women are never an end in themselves, and nothing changes for them once they have lived out their drama onstage. Rather, they play the roles of catalysts, agents, instruments, blockers, spoilers, destroyers, and sometimes helpers or saviors for the male characters." See 1996, 347.

32. Bowie 1993, 212–17, sees an even closer parallel between the Demeter-Persephone story and the plot of this play, arguing that Euripides' rescue of Mnesilochus is a perverted retelling of Demeter's rescue of her daughter. For the relationship between the worship of Dionysus and Demeter in other plays, see Zeitlin 1982, 129–58; Padilla 1992; and Taafe 1994, 99.

33. Bobrick 1991.

34. Hall 1989 suggests that Aristophanes' unflattering portrait of the Scythian is due to the archers' allegiance to the oligarch Aristarchus and their "infamous defection to Oenoe" (54).

35. Cartledge 1993, 4. Cartledge (54–55) mentions Thucydides' "emphatic cross-cultural judgement of Scythian inferiority" as an example of the Greek mode of self-definition by denigration of others.

36. Winkler 1990 argues convincingly that the reader can always find some aspect of resistance to patriarchy from within cultural products.

37. See Dobrov's essay in this collection for a thorough and original analysis of the varieties of theatrical self-consciousness and reflexivity in both tragedy and comedy; for a more traditional vocabulary of criticism, see Taplin 1986.

38. Bassi 1989 discusses a similar exposure in Euripides' seriocomic tragedy: the playwright exposes the presence of the male actor behind the female mask.

39. Goffman 1974, 474–75.

40. Reckford 1987.

41. On this see Konstan 1993.

42. See, e.g., Chapman 1983.

43. For discussion of their similarity, see Foley 1980.

Bibliography

Arnott, Peter. 1962. *Greek Scenic Conventions in the Fifth Century BC*. Oxford.

Bassi, Karen. 1989. "The Actor as Actress in Euripides' *Alcestis*." In *Themes in Drama 11: Women in Theatre*, edited by J. Redmond, 19–30. Cambridge.

Bobrick, Elizabeth. 1991. "Iphigeneia Revisited: *Thesmophoriazusae*. 1160–1225." *Arethusa* 24.1.67–76.

Bowie, A. M. 1993. *Aristophanes: Myth, Ritual and Comedy*. Cambridge.

Burn, Elizabeth. 1973. *Theatricality: A Study of Convention in the Theatre and Social Life*. New York.

Cartledge, Paul. 1993. *The Greeks*. London.

Case, Sue-Ellen, ed. 1990. *Performing Feminisms: Feminist Critical Theory and Theatre*. Baltimore.

Chapman, G. A. H. 1983. "Some Notes on Dramatic Illusion in Aristophanes." *AJP* 104.1–23.

Dearden, C. W. 1976. *The Stage of Aristophanes*. London.

Dolan, Jill. 1988. *The Feminist Spectator as Critic*. Ann Arbor.

du Bois, Page. 1991. *Torture and Truth*. New York.

Ferris, Lesley. 1989. *Acting Women: Images of Women in Theatre*. New York.

Foley, Helena. 1980. "The Masque of Dionysus." *TAPA* 110.107–33.

Freedman, Barbara. 1991. *Staging the Gaze: Postmodernism, Psychoanalysis, and Shakespearean Drama*. Ithaca.

Gardner, J. F. 1989. "Aristophanes and Male Anxiety: The Defence of the *Oikos*." *G&R* 36.51–62.

Geldart, W. M., and F. W. Hall, eds. 1978. *Aristophanis Comoediae*. New York.

Goffman, Erving. 1974. *Frame Analysis*. Cambridge, Mass.

Goldhill, Simon. 1991. *The Poet's Voice: Essays on Poetics and Greek Literature*. London.

Green, J. Richard. 1991. "On Seeing and Depicting the Theatre in Classical Athens." *GRBS* 32.15–50.

Hall, E. M. 1989. "The Archer Scene in Aristophanes' *Thesmophoriazusae*." *Philologus* 133.38–54.

Hansen, Hardy. 1976. "Aristophanes' *Thesmophoriazusae*: Theme, Structure, Production." *Philologus* 120.165–85.

Horn, W. 1970. *Gebet und Gebetsparodie in den Komödien des Aristophanes*. Nürnberg.

Hubbard, Thomas. 1991. *The Mask of Comedy: Aristophanes and the Intertextual Parabasis*. Ithaca.

Irigaray, Luce. 1985. "The Power of Discourse and the Subordination of the Feminine." In *This Sex Which Is Not One*, 68–55. Translated by Catherine Porter. Ithaca.

Konstan, David. 1990. "A City in the Air: Aristophanes' *Birds*." *Arethusa* 23.2.183–208.

———. 1993. "Aristophanes' *Lysistrata*: Women and the Body Politic." In *Tragedy, Comedy and the Polis*, Papers from the Greek Drama Conference, Nottingham, 18–20 July 1990, edited by A. H. Sommerstein, S. Halliwell, J. Henderson, and B. Zimmermann, 431–44. Bari.

Loraux, Nicole. 1980–81. "L'acropole comique." *Ancient Society* 11–12.119–50.

Moulton, C. 1981. *Aristophanic Poetry*. Hypomnemata 68. Göttingen.

Muecke, Frances. 1977. "Playing with the Play: Theatrical Self-Consciousness in Aristophanes." *Antichthon* 11.52–67.

———. 1982. "Portrait of the Artist as a Young Woman." *CQ* 32.41–55.

Mulvey, Laura. 1988. "Visual Pleasure and Narrative Cinema." In *Feminism and Film Theory*, edited by C. Penley, 199.57–68. New York.

Ober, J., and B. Strauss. 1990. "Drama, Rhetoric, Discourse." In *Dionysus*, edited by Winkler and Zeitlin, 237–70.

Padilla, Mark. 1992. "Theatrical and Social Renewal in Aristophanes' *Frogs*." *Arethusa* 25.3.359–84.

Patterson, Cynthia. 1988. *Pericles' Citizenship Law of 451–50 BC*. Salem, N.H.

Porter, James. 1993. "The Seductions of Gorgias." *CA* 12.2.267–99.

Rau, Peter. 1967. *Paratragodia: Untersuchungen einer komischen Form des Aristophanes*. Zetemata 45. Munich.

Reckford, Kenneth. 1987. *Aristophanes' Old-and-New Comedy*. Vol. 1. Chapel Hill.

Ron, Moshe. 1987. "The Restricted Abyss: Nine Problems in the Theory of *Mise en Abyme*." *Poetics Today* 8.2.415–38.

Silk, Michael. 1990. "The People of Aristophanes." In *Characterization and Individuality in Greek Literature*, edited by C. Pelling, 150–73. London.

Sommerstein, Alan. 1994. *Thesmophoriazusae*. Warminster.

Taafe, Lauren. 1994. *Aristophanes and Women*. New York.

Taplin, Oliver. 1986. "Fifth-Century Tragedy and Comedy: A Synkrisis." *JHS* 106.163–74.

Turner, Victor. 1974. *Dramas, Fields, and Metaphors: Symbolic Action in Human Society*. Ithaca.

van Looy, H. 1978. "παρετυμολογεῖ ὁ Εὐρίπδης." In *Zetesis: album amicorum*, edited by E. de Strycker, 345–66. Antwerpen.

Wilson, J. R. 1968. "The Etymology in Euripides' *Trojan Women* 13–14." *AJP* 89.66–71.

Winkler, J. J. 1990. *The Constraints of Desire*. New York.

Winkler, J. J., and Froma Zeitlin, eds. 1990. *Nothing to Do with Dionysos? Athenian Drama in Its Social Context*. Princeton.

Woodhead, H. D. 1928. *Etymologizing in Greek Literature*. Ph.D. diss., University of Chicago.

Zeitlin, Froma. 1982. "Cultic Models of the Female: Rites of Dionysus and Demeter." *Arethusa* 15.1–2.129–58.

———. 1996. *Playing the Other: Gender and Society in Classical Greek Literature*. Chicago.

GREGORY CRANE

Oikos and Agora

Mapping the Polis in Aristophanes' *Wasps*

Wasps articulates a struggle between the individual oikos ("household") and the polis that threatens to subsume it. This tension is the direct product of material conditions that emerged in the classical period, the appearance of a monetary economy, and, in Athens, the growth of an empire, whose revenues gave money an aberrant power. Aristophanic discourse textualizes this conflict according to its own internal logic.

The first section, "Transgression and Material Reference in Aristophanic Discourse," locates Aristophanic poetry within the larger framework of Greek poetry as a whole. The poetics of transgression in Aristophanes' *Wasps* goes far beyond scatalogical and sexual language, and includes the detailed references to material culture and to the peculiar aspects of the Athenian polis, which mature Panhellenic poetry would not tolerate in such densely concentrated form. The following section, "From the Archaic to the Classical Agora: Filling the Empty Center," contrasts the archaic agora with the civic center of centralized, redistributive societies such as that best known to, and most feared by, Greeks of the classical period, the Persian Empire. It argues that the archaic polis required an "empty" civic center that no individual or family could appropriate (hence, the unpopularity of tyranny, which threatened to do just that). The third section, "Money, the Athenian Agora, and the *Wasps*," discusses the way in which the classical Athenian agora differed from this archaic model: it was the site for both monetary exchange and an increasingly centralized and powerful governmental machine (of which the lawcourts are a part). This section traces the connections between money and power, and their implications for Bdelycleon and the oikos. The fourth section, "Mapping the Oikos: Territory and Integrity," outlines the way in which Greek authors textualized the ideal forms of civic and domestic space, and then contrasts this practice as it appears in Aristotle, Xenophon, and Solon with Aristophanic discourse. The final section, "Conclusion: Dialectical Space and Synthesis (?)," explores the various degrees to which Aristophanes offers and denies a resolution to the tension between oikos and polis.

Transgression and Material Reference in Aristophanic Discourse

No author occupies a more unsettling position in the canon of Greek literature than does Aristophanes. In modern literary criticism he seems less to resemble his representation in Plato's *Symposium* than Alcibiades, entering late and unexpected, a bit too drunk but more charming still, a gate crasher in the sedate symposiastic space constructed by Plato, and yet fascinating. With one foot in the canon and one foot—where?—Aristophanes' work is a contradiction, and in contradictions critics have sought unity for his sprawling plays.[1] Young versus old, rich versus poor, aristocrats versus common people, nature versus convention, nature versus education, social criticism versus humor—critics have traced how each of these oppositions helps shape the *Wasps* of Aristophanes, the play on which this essay will focus.

Yet not all such oppositions are equally helpful, for as we map the scripts of Aristophanes' plays into our own sensibilities, we can only approximate and suggest. If nothing else, postmodernism has allowed us to rethink the opposition between serious criticism and apolitical humor. Certainly, Aristophanes felt keenly that he was balancing intellectual aims with gross humor: "Our little subject is not wanting in sense," remarks Xanthias at the opening of *Wasps* (64–66). "It is well within your capacity and at the same time cleverer than many vulgar comedies."[2] This essay will touch upon the sacrosanct sphere of aesthetic experience, separate from politics or vulgar concerns. However, the particular "sacred space" of a literary text as it employed by modern critics is itself—and must in some measure be, given the nature of our own production in history—a reaction against the Industrial Revolution and the power of the monetary exchange in developed capitalist society.[3] Humor is a powerful force that shapes and coerces, as Socrates and Cleon both learned. Jeffrey Henderson has recently argued against "the carnivalists" who "separate festivals and the state: the poets' seriousness was somehow detached from the 'real' world of the spectators as being 'mere' entertainment." The comic poets were "the constituent intellectuals of the demos during the period of full popular sovereignty that began with the reforms of Ephialtes in 462/1, and in their institutionalized competitions they influenced the formulation of its ideology and the public standing of its individuals."[4]

Of all the inconcinnities in Aristophanes' plays, their obscenity, the shift between the sexual/scatological and *to prepon*, "that which is fitting," has attracted the most intense and (often suppressed) attention of critics. After the landmark decision on James Joyce's *Ulysses* by the U.S. Supreme Court allowed more faithful renderings of Aristophanes to be published, Random House printed them—but the author chose to remain anonymous rather than affix his name to these moderately scandalous translations.[5] Our understanding of the sexual and scatological matters in Aristophanes has increased dramatically in the past two decades,[6] and we can much more fully—and freely—appreciate this dimension of Aristophanes' plays. And yet Aristophanic "obscenity" strikes so raw a nerve in the bourgeois sensibilities that took shape primarily in the nineteenth century[7] that it has assumed an exaggerated role in our view of Aristophanic comedy. For Aristophanes transgressed against many norms, not all of which translate into the dichotomy of "high" and "low." Greek—or, more properly, Attic—tragedy, for example, had a different internal economy of what was and was not *to prepon*, and this economy excluded not only matters "below the belt" but other areas of experience as well.

Aristophanic comedy is at once radical and regressive, and it stands further along in an intellectual vector which separates Panhellenic lyric from Attic tragedy.[8] Simonides, Pindar, and Bacchylides composed poems for patrons from a particular polis who had won a particular athletic event. These poems were composed for performance, but at same time they had limited value for their patrons unless they caught the imagination of Greeks in cities scattered throughout the Mediterranean and Black Seas. Hieron, strongman of Syracuse, may have been the richest and most powerful man of his time, but he had no direct power over a Greek citizen of Tegea on the Greek mainland, Halikarnassos on the coast of Turkey, or Olbia in South Russia. The epinician poet needed to construct a persona for his patrons that would freely engage the willing attention and admiration of a contentious Greek world. And yet, the language of epinician, and especially of Pindar, is elitist and exclusive.[9]

Tragedy, on the other hand, is not Greek, in the sense that it is not primarily aimed at a Panhellenic audience. It is Attic tragedy, composed normally (though not always) by an Athenian poet[10] for an Athenian audience at an Athenian festival to be judged by Athenian judges. The Great Dionysia, the festival of Dionysus at which tragedy was performed, was an elaborate, ceremonial event that celebrated the Athenian polis as a grand, unified entity. Later in the fifth century, representatives of the Athenian allies would be present at the Dionysia, but not to pass judgment: they arrived to deliver their tribute and they stayed to observe the Athenians celebrate the power and majesty of their city—as Isocrates observed, the Athenians of the fifth century excelled at getting themselves hated.[11] The theater and the popular assembly are largely homologous, in that each organizes the citizen body for a shared, performative experience.[12] If tragedy did not appeal to both mass and elite, then it would fail and the playwright would stand less of a chance to receive a chorus the following year. The Attic playwright, however, needed first and foremost to charm the Athenian public, the admiration of Therans, Thessalians, or Thebans would not win places in future competitions at Athens. Attic tragedy had to cut deeply across class lines, for the elite could not wholly dominate the masses when time came for judgment.[13] The playwrights could only push their audiences so far— to paraphrase Barthes, they needed to balance the "readerly" and the "writerly" if they were to survive as poets. Euripides and Aristophanes never quite established a comfortable relationship with their audiences,[14] but even Sophocles, the most successful playwright of the fifth century, suffered occasional setbacks.[15] The Athenian public found Aeschylus hard to understand, but, if *Frogs* presents a recognizable picture, Aeschylean complexity made the Athenians feel grand rather than small, enhancing their sense of worth more than emphasizing their intellectual inadequacy. Tragedy abounds in events gone awry, but most of these take place safely over the border in Thebes, the conservative, land-based power with whom Athens clashed repeatedly.[16]

But where the Attic dimension to tragedy is often implicit and effaced from the surface, comedy, even when it criticizes Athens in the most biting terms, celebrates its local, Athenian nature more concretely and pervasively than the most patriotic surviving tragedies, such as *Persians* of Aeschylus or *Suppliants* of Euripides. Whatever its specific, historical origins, comedy is the local genre that almost by accident inscribed itself into the textual canon of "Greek" literature. Comedy belongs to the small face-to-face society of the Attic country villages,[17] and comedy only became an official part of the City Dionysia in 486, after more than forty years of tragic competitions. As part of a festival celebrating the centralized Athenian polis, comedy is itself a transgression. The body, as producer of excrement and object of sexual pleasure, scandalizes the decorum of formal epic, choral lyric, and tragedy, but sex and scatology are only parts of a more general transgression, one that rests on gritty materialism and physicality of reference. Panhellenic poetry filters out the local and the particular, its achievement was to create a common mythological and poetic space that

Hellenes who hated one another could nonetheless share. The in-jokes about Cleonymos, Theoros, Amynias, Nikostratos, and the like transgress against a decorum of reference, for only the labors of scholiasts and prosopographers can render these allusions comprehensible, and none can fully resuscitate their initial punch. And yet, like paleontologists with a fossil, we can create models that portray the manner in which emotional flesh covered these bonelike allusions.

Aristophanic and Pindaric poetry are in some measure calculated opposites and thus mirror images of each other. Each poet consciously aims to fashion an audience by selective inclusion and exclusion. Both authors are full of personal names and challenge the modern reader, but Aristophanes' prosopography is generally more elliptical than that of Pindar. Pindar is consciously framing the people to whom he refers in a monumental poetic form. He is reading these names into the literary record, so that they may be preserved. Aristophanes, however, makes jokes about these characters, and leaves it to us to understand the point. He is as uncompromising to his audience as Pindar, for he sets the burden of understanding firmly on the shoulders of his audience. The Athenian demos had challenged the international *agathoi* of Hellas as the dominant elite in the Greek-speaking world. We might more properly say that Aristophanes' audience is not so much the opposite, but the transformation, of Pindar's elite. The relentless stream of obscure nouns and topical references of the Greek text renders Aristophanes almost as inaccessible to the intermediate reader of Greek as Pindar. But whereas Pindar challenges his audience to follow his meaning and thus to place itself within the select group of the *sophoi*, Aristophanes challenges those in his audience to be Athenian, completely immersed in the concerns of their city, its ambitions and its fears.

Of course, Pindar and Aristophanes are very different. We would be in sorry shape if we depended upon Pindar's Olympian odes for our knowledge of Olympic topography. Aristophanes is no Pausanias or even Herodotus. But if he does not set out to present a comprehensible picture of space, Aristophanes inscribes his plays in the physical, detailed space of the polis. For Aristophanes, the polis is what we might call an idealized object: we can abstract from the plays general intellectual themes, but Aristophanes is not a philosopher and his polis is not some Hegelian abstraction. The polis is a *somatic*, sensible entity, shaped by intellectual forces, yet present in its parts and its grainy particularity.

This essay will focus on the constituent elements of the polis and on the way in which they interact in the *Wasps*. This play revolves less around individual men or classes of men than around the tension between institutions such as the oikos and the polis. Much earlier scholarship focused on the contrast between the first part of the play, which focuses on the lawcourt, and the concluding sections, which revolve around the symposium and its aftermath.[18] While this essay does not primarily set out to pursue the formalist project of extracting a normative unity from the play, it does argue that the two parts are intimately connected, for the play articulates the tension between the oikos and the polis, as mediated by the space of the agora. Much recent work has focused on the way in which sanctuaries at the center or periphery define a polis,[19] or on the role of the great panhellenic sanctuaries in defining poleis from the outside.[20] This essay focuses squarely on the agora, for if the sanctuary was constitutive of "la cité culturelle" (de Polignac's phrase) in the archaic period, the agora began to assume a competing role in the classical period. Recent work has focused on the countryside and the constants of agrarian Greek life,[21] but social conditions did change and especially in Athens. Within a decade following the reforms of Ephialtes in 461/0, the Delian League had effectively completed its transformation into the Athenian Empire. Enormously expanded prestige and wealth reinforced popular sovereignty, but the power which the Athenian polis now possessed could be applied in many ways. *Wasps* reflects the tension as the oikos, the individual household, wrestles with a polis that threatens to subsume it. The two parts of the play thus address primary loci, the lawcourts, which are generally in the agora, and the symposium, which takes place within the oikos.

From the Archaic to the Classical Agora: Filling the Empty Center

A strictly hierarchical society has, by definition, a top, and when this society finds itself expressed in spatial form, the top becomes a center. The palace economies of the Bronze Age revolved around centers that accumulated and redistributed wealth.[22] The great courtyard at Knossos, for example, was the center of a massive palace complex, filled with storage facilities and many rooms. The entrances into this palace led any visitor through a series of narrow hallways, which separated and framed the open courtyard at the center. At palaces such as Pylos, the dynast and his family stood at the center of their society. The Persian Empire was, to the Greek way of thinking, both vast and precisely defined: exactly ninety days journey separates Susa from Sardis, ninety-three from the coast (Hdt. 5.52–53). When Aristagoras attempts to woo the Spartan Kleomenes into a campaign against Persia, Susa is the target, and the various lands under Persian domination all point inward to this rich and inviting prize. Displaced potentates from Greece find themselves in Susa as the center of power, either looking for the means to reverse their fortunes (e.g., Demaratos at

Hdt. 7.3.1, the Peisistridai at Hdt. 7.8.3) or called in for preventive custody (e.g., Histiaios at Hdt. 5.24.4). The center itself had a center: Histiaios is not only Darius' councilor (5.24.4: *sumboulos*) but his companion at meals as well (*sussitos*). Susa is not, properly speaking, the oikos of the Persian Emperor, for the Persian Emperor is the *despotês*, the master and owner of all things: the empire itself is his oikos. Later, Xerxes becomes enraged at Pythios, one of the richest men in the empire, reminding him that he was nothing but Xerxes' slave (*doulos*) and that his own oikos (*panoikia*) stood at the disposal of the great king. The Persian Empire is a kind of super-oikos, in which all members have their allotted rank and in which all alike are slaves, *douloi*, of the king.[23]

Herodotus shows a keen sensitivity to the relationship between civic space and social structure. When Deiokes became the first king of the Medes, he not only acquired a dwelling place "worthy of royal power" (*oikia axia tês basileias*, 1.98.2) and a personal bodyguard (to the Greeks, a sign of the tyrant), but surrounded his palace and treasuries with seven walls. The outermost wall was as long as the city walls of Athens, and the whole complex thus rivaled Athens in size. Large as this complex may have been, its form was designed to gesture emphatically inwards. The palace sat atop a hill and each of these seven walls grew higher as they approached the center (1.98.4). Different colors marked each of the first five walls (98.5); silver coated the sixth, and the seventh, inmost, wall was covered with gold (98.6).

The palace complex did not just dramatize, but also helped generate, the king's dignity. The great walls separated him from the world. No one was allowed to come into his presence, and all communication took place through messengers (1.99.1). "He put on these haughty airs for this reason, so that those who were of the same age as he, who had grown up with him, who came from equally illustrious *oikiai*, and who were his equals in moral qualities . . . might, because they could not see him, think of him as a kind of different being."[24] Herodotus concedes that the king's power is absolute, but he emphasizes that it rests on concealment and deception. The shaping of civic (or perhaps imperial) space and the construction of the royal authority are, in this scheme, intimately linked. Deiokes' position, at the center of his palace, wrapped within its walls and perched atop its hill, both signifies and produces his power.

If we turn back a bit and consider the polis (or proto-polis) in the *Odyssey*, we find that this social formation has as its center the agora. The Homeric agora does not seem to be the economic center of the early polis—indeed, it is not even clear that the polis of the Homeric epics really has an economic center, since the term "economic center" presupposes that this early polis is a centralized economic unit. Clearly, the polis, as it appears in our epics, is dominated by "household production," as the economic anthropologists call it: each oikos produces most of its own goods and turns only when necessary to exchange and external sources.

In the *Odyssey*, the agora is not primarily a market or place of exchange, but still fulfills its etymological role: the noun agora comes from the verb *ageirô*, "to gather, assemble," and thus denotes, most simply, a "gathering" or "assembly." In the *Odyssey*, an agora can still be an action rather than a place. The Atreids summon a poorly timed and ill-fated agora (3.137–40), and Odysseus simply "establishes an agora" when he wants to address his men (9.171 = 10.188 = 12.319). Nevertheless, the agora can occupy a defined space and function. When Odysseus and his men find the wife of the Laistrygonian king in her house (*dômata*), she calls her husband out of the agora (10.112–14)—already, the narrative expects to locate women in the household and men in the agora. The agora has a natural place in the acropolis (8.502–4). The Phaiacians have many agorai (7.43–45), but at least one built around a handsome shrine of Poseidon and surrounded by a wall of quarried stones,[25] and one phrase[26] suggests that an agora would have regular places in which to sit.

The agora is the center of the state, and its presence is a clear sign of civilization, for if people do not assemble to make decisions as a group and to follow shared customs, then, to the archaic and classical Greek, no society can be said to exist. The Cyclopes, for example, have neither agorai in which decisions are made (*agorai boulêphoroi*, 9.112) nor customary laws (*themistes*). They live on mountaintops in caves (113–14). The Cyclopes each separately determine their own private *themistes* for their wives and children, and they pay no heed to one another (114–15). In opening an agora, one can call upon Zeus and upon Themis, the divine personification of law, for she is the one who breaks up and sets in motion the agorai of men (2.69).

Above all, the agora is free space, not the preserve of any one family, but the place where decisions are made that dominate the polis as a whole. Thus, Telemachos naturally brings the stranger Theoclymenos from the agora to his home (17.52) and the suitor Eurymachos rudely threatens to expel him from the house and back into the agora (20.362). Later, when each oikos has collected and buried its suitor, killed by Odysseus, they gather together as a group into the agora (24.420ff.). The families of the suitors do not need to meet like conspirators in some unusual place. They openly assemble in the agora and debate among themselves whether they should rush off to kill Odysseus. In Phaiacia, Alcinous has no qualms about handing his daughter off to Odysseus (7.311–14) and he is the acknowledged leader of the Phaiacians (7.12), but his personal support is only a starting point for Odysseus. Odysseus must present himself before the other Phaiacians at the agora and win their favor. When Telemachos calls his fellow citizens to an agora, the aged Aigyptios remarks it is the first such assembly in the twenty years since Odysseus left for Troy, but he clearly assumes that an agora can properly be called with or without Odysseus (2.25–34).

Penelope frets that Telemachos is not a grown man "well experienced in both toils [ponoi] and in assemblies [agorai]" (4.818), and the collocation is not casual. The agora is a free space, in which men compete and win (or lose) prestige, and nothing is guaranteed once the discussion begins. Nestor's affection for Odysseus rests in part on the fact that they supported one another in agorai (3.126–29). When the Atreids quarrel after Troy's fall, they use the agora as a kind of theater to determine which of the two will prevail (3.148–50). While blood ultimately resolves the contest between Telemachos and the suitors, Athena visits Ithaca to urge Telemachos to begin this dispute properly, by calling the Achaeans into an agora and there denouncing the suitors (1.88–91). The agora is the space in which "big men," to use the anthropological term, such as Odysseus establish and constantly reestablish their authority. The world of Odysseus lacks the mechanisms for the creation of "symbolic capital." "Relations of domination can be set up and maintained only at the cost of strategies which must be endlessly renewed."[27] Those who wish to exert control in such societies "have to work directly, daily, personally, to produce and reproduce conditions of domination which are even then never entirely trustworthy."[28] The agora is one arena within which leaders acquire and maintain prestige within the society as a whole.

Viewed from another perspective, that of the demos, the Homeric agora is an instrument of resistance and of autonomy. The agora remains, in a sense, "empty," or "neutral" space, which reproduces within the confines of the polis the organizational influence which the great Panhellenic sanctuaries exert in inter-polis affairs. The Panhellenic sanctuaries exerted authority only insofar as they were not dominated by any one major power. Suborning the priestess at Delphi was thus an especially disturbing crime, in that it eroded the image of autonomy and thus attacked a source of the oracle's authority.[29] Just as jealously independent poleis came to dominate "Greek" affairs, the polis itself was built around individual oikoi that retained a high degree of autonomy. The oikos of Odysseus does not subsume the individual oikoi of Ithaca and the surrounding islands. Odysseus, like Alcinous, must leave his own domestic space behind and visit the agora when he chooses to influence the polis as a whole. Neither man can summon his fellows to wait upon him in his own home, the way a Dareios or a Xerxes could summon or attract needy Greeks to his palace. The relative autonomy of the oikos stands at the moral center of the polis. The agora, which forms the functional, empty center of the polis, both signifies and produces this autonomy.

Money, the Athenian Agora, and the Wasps

The physical topography of the Athenian agora allows us to trace the way in which the Athenians had constructed for themselves in material form an empty center to their polis. If Philocleon and his cohorts approached the Athenian agora from the north, they would have passed between two stoas. These were buildings, open at one side, with a roof and colonnade that offered shelter from rain or sun and a space in which Athenians would congregate. Peculiarly Greek structures, the stoas optimally suited the needs of the agora, for they allowed visitors to the agora to seek protection from the elements without concealing themselves in a wholly enclosed space.[30] A passerby could easily see who was inside and stop to chat: thus, in Xenophon's *Oikonomikos*, Socrates begins his extended conversation with Ischomachos when he sees him sitting at his leisure in the stoa of Zeus Eleutherios, which Philocleon would have seen to his right as he entered the agora (7.1). There were many such spots, and we hear from a fourth-century speech that most Athenians had some particular place in or near the agora that they would frequent: the perfume sellers, the barbershop, the leather workers (Lys. 24.20).

The stoa immediately to Philocleon's right (between him and the Stoa of Zeus Eleutherios) would have been the Royal Stoa, the place from which the "royal archon," *archon basileus*, the official primarily responsible for religious affairs, exercised his duties (Paus. 1.3.1). The term *basileus*, in fact, means "king," and the office is called the "kingship" (*basileia*), but a different Athenian citizen each year filled the position of "king archon."[31] Even as Athens maintained the archaic office of kingship, no one citizen was allowed to appropriate it to himself or his family. A few meters down the Panathenaic Way, which cuts diagonally across the agora, Philocleon would have passed on his right the Altar of the Twelve Gods, a sixth-century shrine from which distances were measured and which functioned quite literally as the central point of the Athenian polis.[32] These two structures, the Royal Stoa and the Altar of the Twelve Gods, both date from the archaic period, and together they mark the Athenian agora with characteristics similar to those of the agora in the *Odyssey*. The agora is the functional center of the state, it is the intellectual heart of the state which no one person or family can dominate, and it is a place in which citizens conveniently gather and mix with one another.

But if Philocleon and his friends were bound for the old sixth-century court on the southwest corner of the agora, they would, however, have passed by a very different space than the *Odyssey* suggests. Small wooden booths and stalls filled the center of the agora. One could buy anything there: wine, oil, pots, garlic, onions, fine clothes, and meat, or one could hire the butchers who would carve up an animal (Pollux 9.47–48). Excavations have revealed the workshops of bronze workers, marble workers, shoemakers, and other tradesmen clustered around the agora.[33] The young boys who guide the aged chorus in *Wasps* ask for figs (297), but the old men, scandalized at this extravagance, reply that they must buy grain, firewood, and other necessities.

The Athenian agora, like its counterparts in the *Odyssey*, remains a gathering place, but it has also become the locus within which commercial exchanges take place. In the agora at Athens, social intercourse, shops for every commodity, and lawcourts were all intermingled. The crusty Dicaiopolis detests life in the city because in the city everything—charcoal, wine, oil—costs money. Back in his village, he supposedly didn't even know the meaning of the word "buy": in his own home, Dicaiopolis claims that he could live entirely outside the money economy (*Ach.* 33–37). The Athenian agora is a place to buy, sell, bargain, and extract profit from one's opponent in an exchange. When in Herodotus the Spartans sent a delegation to tell the Persian king Cyrus to keep clear of the Ionian Greeks, the king disdainfully responds: "I have never yet feared men of this kind, who have a place designated in the middle of their polis, in which they gather to cheat each other under oath" (Hdt. 1.153.1). As in the *Odyssey*, the agora is the center of the polis and a mechanism that in part shapes the polis. Now, however, the agora is not just the empty center of the state: it is the center where money changes hands and where Greeks show themselves at their worst.[34]

Money is the medium for exchange in the agora, and money is the central force that shapes much of what goes on both there and in *Wasps*. In the play, money operates at two distinct and parallel levels. On the one hand, money is the mechanism whereby Cleon supports the old jurors and is the foundation of his power. Aside from Philocleon, the jurors in *Wasps* literally depend upon the three-obol "little payment" (*mistharion*, 300). On the opposite extreme stand the enormous sums calculated in talents. (A single talent, consisting of 6,000 drachmas would support a single juror for forty years, or a skilled workman for fifty years.) Philocleon and the jurors are obsessed with the massive peculations of public officials (*Wasps* 102, 240–41) and they begin to turn upon their demagogue supporters when they suspect them of accepting fifty-talent bribes. Vast sums bring power with them, and the old men feel that such wealth threatens those of moderate means (*hoi penêtes*, 463) with tyranny. Certainly, this idea was deeply ingrained in Greek thought: when in Herodotus Deiokes invents the imperial palace, he encloses in the innermost sanctuary not only himself and his palace, but his treasuries (*thêsauroi*, Hdt. 1.98.5). For Athens in particular, money was the foundation of its power over its allies and its greatest strategic asset over its enemies in the Peloponnesian War.[35] The Athenian agora, unlike its Homeric counterpart, is thus intimately associated with money, because it is the center for both petty commercial exchange and for the supervision of enormous government expenditures.

The attitude toward jury payment, however, sharply distinguishes the jurors from Bdelycleon. The jurors look beyond the payment: they call Cleon their *kêdemôn* (242), a loaded word, for it describes a "guardian" or "patron" who is not a relative.[36] Thus, at *Wasps* 731 the chorus wishes it had either a *kêdemôn* or *suggenês* ("kinsman") such as Bdelycleon to advise it. In tragedy, the term *kêdemôn* can absorb a powerful emotional charge. In Aeschylus, the suppliant women, bitterly opposed to their proper *philoi*, that is, their cousins and thus members of their family (*Supp.* 74), scramble on shore in Argos in search of others who will serve as *kêdemôn*, patrons who will protect them against their immediate family. In Sophocles, Ismene asks plaintively what life will be dear (*philos*) for her when her sister Antigone is gone, but Antigone rejects her concern and taunts her: "Ask Kreon! He's the one of whom you are the *kêdemôn* (*Ant.* 548–49)." In Euripides, the chorus chastises Jason for abandoning his proper wife Medea and seeking the tyrant Kreon's daughter: "You wretch, miserably wedded patron (*kêdemôn*) of tyrants! (*Med.* 991)."[37] The *kêdemôn* is not just a patron or supporter, but one who intervenes, for better or worse, in the natural order of the family.

Philocleon makes this point graphically clear. Cleon is not simply a source for revenue, but treats the aged Philocleon with a tender concern that Philocleon's son reportedly cannot match: "We are the only ones whom Cleon, the great bawler, does not badger. On the contrary, he protects and caresses us; he keeps off the flies, which is what you have never done for your father" (596–98). As Bourdieu remarks of such patron-client relationships, domination "cannot take place overtly and must be disguised under the veil of enchanted relationships, the official model of which is presented by relations between kinsmen; in order to be socially recognized it must get itself misrecognized."[38] Cleon does not dominate Philocleon and the other jurors, but cares for them lovingly. They do not submit to his will, but enjoy his affection.

A bit earlier in the play, Philocleon provides another example of power relations embedded within the affective. In a comic travesty of such relationships, Philocleon expresses outrage that Xanthias and Sosias would oppose him with force (438–47). "Even now those two are manhandling their old master, having no thought of the leather coats (*diphtherai*) and the tunics (*exōmides*) [445] and the caps (*kunai*) he bought for them; in winter he watched that their feet should not get frozen. And only see them now; there is no gentleness in their look nor any recollection of the shoes (*embades*) of other days" (443–47). Each of these garments was a cheap and rough piece of work,[39] and this passage is one of our best testimonia for the wardrobe of a slave. Philocleon assumes that the slaves should be grateful for these small presents. These lines seem to be relatively "straight," for they set up the comic reversal of Philocleon's next remarks. At 451, he claims that he made his slave "an object of envy" (*zēlōtos*) and the slave was *acharistos*, that is, did not return the appropriate affectionate gratitude (*charis*). Philocleon's great gift was a harsh flogging which he administered in a fine "manly" fashion (450). Comic discourse freely deconstructs this relationship, bringing to the fore the physical violence that underlies the relationship between master and slave.

In *Wasps* money is a more important comic target than violence. Before he begins the debate with his father, the chorus's repeated accusations of conspiracy and tyranny (409–11, 417–19, 463–70, 471–76, 482–90) wholly exasperate Bdelycleon. At 488–99 he explodes:

Everything is now tyranny with us, no matter what is concerned, whether it be large or small. Tyranny! I have not heard the word mentioned once in fifty years, and now it is cheaper [*axiōtera*] than salt-fish so that the word tyranny is passed back and forth in the agora. If you are buying [*ōnētai*] one kind of fish and don't want another, the huckster [*ho pōlōn*] next door, who is selling the latter, at once exclaims, "That is a man who is stocking his kitchen with a view to being a tyrant!" If you ask for onions to season your fish, the woman selling vegetables [*hē lachanapōlis*] winks one eye and asks, "Ha! you ask for onions! are you seeking to to be a tyrant, or do you think that Athens must pay you your seasonings as a tribute?"

Even before he addresses Cleon personally, we can see how his mind revolves around the agora, around commercial exchange and money. When he expresses his frustrations about the goading suspicions of the old jurors, he thinks immediately of small retailers from the agora. The term "tyranny" is now a commodity with a price, cheaply available in the marketplace. The petty hucksters working their small booths jealously look to guard their share of trade, and associate anyone who might not add to their business with tyranny. When Bdelycleon imagines the cause for the suspicion and disorder of the polis, his mind is drawn to the market and to those so poor and low on the social scale that their women must stand in the public space of the agora and sell vegetables. Money and desire for petty profit are the source of these charges of tyranny and conspiracy.

Thus, Bdelycleon sees the relationship between Philocleon and Cleon very differently than does his father. Where Philocleon resolutely chooses to view the economic benefits (the three-obol payment) as part of a more complex, affective relationship, Bdelycleon focuses on the money. He ultimately deconstructs the affectionate superstructure Cleon has carefully erected over these small payments, shifting from the "obol and drachma" level of the agora to the talents stolen by greedy politicians such as Cleon. Bdelycleon has Philocleon calculate that the state receives roughly 2,000 talents of income but pays its jurors a maximum of 150 talents per year (655–63). "Not even the tenth part of the income," laments the increasingly dejected Philocleon (665) "comes to us as payment!"

More than one critic has remarked that Bdelycleon "does not expose the faults or inadequacies of the court system in order to recommend remedies, some of which, given the arguments he employs, might well run counter to views that may be plausibly attributed to Aristophanes himself, as in the matter of pay for jurors."[40] "Logically . . . the chorus might have responded to Bdelycleon's argument by demanding an increase in the juror's daily fee."[41] But such an analysis is excessively logical and perceptive in that it assumes a consistency of analysis, which the old jurors deliberately eschew. Whether or not the jurors actually need their pay, they ultimately base their loyalty to Cleon on the affection and respect they seem to derive from him. The money is not entirely an instrument for a particular material goal. The money is a signifier that points to a larger, more complex relationship. When Bdelycleon prods Philocleon into his rough calculations, he does not open the possibility for higher pay. He shatters the "false consciousness" which Philocleon and his fellows have developed and reveals the misrecognized truth about their relationship to Cleon.

The intellectual terrain of *Wasps* is extremely complex, for its characters interweave money, kinship, emotions, and raw power. The "three-obol" wage is a starting point for the jurors, but, where the other jurors imply that they would starve without this wage, Philocleon praises his life as a juror because of the power it conveys and the respect which this power allows him to extract from others. In the nervously sacred space of comic discourse, this old man can bring to light the uncomfortable relationships between power and affection.

But I am forgetting the most pleasing thing of all. When I return home with my pay [*misthos*], everyone runs to greet me because of my money [*argurion*]. First my daughter bathes me, anoints my feet, stoops to kiss me and, while she is calling me "her dearest father," fishes out my three obols [*triôbolon*] with her tongue; then my little wife comes to wheedle me and brings a nice light cake; she sits beside me and entreats me in a thousand ways, "Do take this now; do have some more." All this delights me hugely, and I have no need to turn toward you or the steward to know when it shall please him to serve my dinner, all the while cursing and grumbling. But if he does not quickly knead my cake, I have something which is my defense, my shield against all ills. If you do not pour me out drink, I have brought this long-eared jar full of wine. How it brays, when I bend back and bury its neck in my mouth! It farts like a whole army, and how I laugh at your wine-skins. (605–18)

The *misthos* gives Philocleon a variety of privileges. His daughter treats him with unaccustomed affection (and somewhat scandalously: Dover points out that "french kisses" are generally erotic).[42] His wife pushes dainties upon him—thus he is not dependent on receiving food from the surly steward of the oikos. Finally, he has been able to purchase his own jug of wine and can drink as much as he pleases. Philocleon thus claims to have increased his status within the oikos. Money, whether the obols of the juror or the talents of the demagogue, exerts power that transcends and undermines more static ties such as kinship, and money can support new affective relationships (such as that of Cleon, the *kēdemōn* of the jurors).

Raw power also attracts Philocleon: he loves his job because his power as a juror locates him above wealth. After Philocleon has described the pathetic spectacle that defendants present, he triumphantly declares: "Is not this great power [*archē*] indeed, which allows even wealth to be disdained [*ploutou katachēnē*]?" (575). His son, who has writing tablet in hand, picks up on this as a key point: "A second point to note, the disdain of wealth" (576). A bit later Philocleon sums up his defense of the jurors' life: "If I let loose the lightning, the richest [*hoi ploutountes*] and most pretentious are half dead with terror and crap for fright" (625–27). The little three-obol wage of the juror "dis-embeds" the economic power normally embedded within the oikos. The three-obol wage also, by supporting the jurors, allows them to compel the wealthy men who come before them to embed their wealth in a larger structure based on pity and submission—affective ties which appeal to the jurors' emotions.

When Bdelycleon deconstructs the persona Cleon has fashioned for himself, he takes money as his starting point, but quickly moves on to nonmonetary issues. First, he argues that the demagogues buy the old men off with a few obols, while pocketing fifty-talent bribes (666–71). But the bulk of Bdelycleon's accusation focuses on acts of subordination and prestige. The jurors have been tricked into giving him their affections (*agapō*, 672). Bdelycleon rattles off a long list of elaborate presents that come to the demagogues: "they [the allies] count you for nothing, for not more than the vote of Connos; it is on those wretches that they lavish everything, dishes of salt fish, wine, tapestries, cheese, honey, sesame-fruit, cushions, flagons, rich clothing, chaplets, necklets, drinking-cups, all that yields pleasure and health. And you, their master, to you as a reward for all your toil both on land and sea, nothing is given, not even a clove of garlic to eat with your little fish" (675–79). The presents that the allies lavish upon the demagogues are not simply utilitarian objects to be consumed or converted into cash. Gifts of this kind are, in fact, an end in themselves, for the giving acknowledges and celebrates the power of the recipient. The allies seek favor and protection, thus placing themselves in a subordinate position and locating the recipient of these gifts above them.[43] The demagogues have not simply appropriated wealth, but the prestige and authority to which wealth is only a means. When Bdelycleon presents his view of a more fitting relationship between jurors and state (706–11), he does not suggest a monetary wage. Rather, each city in the Athenian Empire should directly support twenty citizens "with all kinds of hare, crowns, cream, and cream-cheese" (709–10).[44] Likewise, the Persian king establishes his friends by providing them with cities rather than with money.[45]

To summarize, money and market exchanges occupy an ambiguous role. Money is enormously powerful, but its significance is hard to assess, for characters such as Philocleon and demagogues such as Cleon employ money as the means to an end. The means, the beginning, and the end are, however, intermixed. Philocleon and Cleon use money to weaken the individual oikos and fashion, as do Deiokes and other eastern potentates, the polis into a kind of super-oikos. This project is by no means new: the Greeks both consciously and unconsciously modeled the polis after the most viable social entity with which they were familiar, the oikos.[46] Each of the ten Athenian tribes took a turn presiding over the state, and its fifty representatives spent their time at the Tholos, a round structure which Philocleon would have passed on his way from the Royal Stoa to the lawcourt. The prytaneis, as these officers were called, took their meals here,[47] and a third of them spent the night in this building.[48] The prytaneion was a separate building which seems to have been situated between the agora and the acropolis.[49] This was the common hearth of the state, and the location at which the polis entertained delegations of friendly powers, individual representatives of Athens abroad,[50] and particular benefactors of the state. The privilege of eating along with the prytaneis at public expense was one of the highest honors that the polis could confer, for this privilege provided not merely access to food (which was simple and not elaborate), but prestige.[51] The polis was thus, in part, an objectified oikos, common to all the citizens.

Even after the Athenians had driven their own tyrants out, they exploited the same symbolic mechanisms. Access to the hospitality of the polis supplanted access to the personal table and company of the Peisistratids as a mark of favor.[52] The latter part of *Wasps* is one of our best testimonia for the symposium, the ritualized drinking party, as a central practice that helped define the space and sphere of the oikos. As with the king, however, this privilege became objectified: no single individual oikos or group could appropriate it. The transference may have been almost heavy-handed: the excavators at the agora have located below the Tholos another structure, labeled simply "Building F." Its form is that of a private house, though a very large one, and two cooking trenches were found associated with it. Pottery found on the site indicates that the building was erected in circa 550–525, and it has been suggested that this building was the actual home of the Peisistratids. The Athenian democracy may have built the Tholos directly on top of the old Peisistratid household.[53]

The polis could in the sixth and early fifth centuries readily model itself on the oikos, without threatening to overwhelm it, because the polis lacked the means to challenge the integrity of the oikos. The effective shift from alliance to empire, however, typified by the transfer of the league treasury from Delos to Athens in around 454, changed the relationship of polis and oikos. The Athenian state accumulated within its own treasuries so much liquid wealth that this wealth could upset the balance between the empty center and the thousands of oikoi within the state. A new structure, labeled "South Stoa 1," seems to have been constructed in the agora around 430–420, the same period in which *Wasps* was produced. The large number of coins found in this structure suggests that it was a commercial establishment, but many of its rooms have the off-center doorway peculiar to dining rooms: this design was necessary in order to fit couches into the room, since the Greeks reclined while dining—see, for example, the parody of elegant reclining at *Wasps* 1208ff. Some of the finds suggest that these rooms were the official space in which officials who oversaw exchange in the agora held office and, like the prytaneis, took their meals.

Whether or not this building had already been erected before the Lenaia of 422, the conditions necessary for it were in place: the agora had grown in power and wealth, and could support a new physical structure that attracted both monetary exchange and dining.[54] Similarly, it is not only possible for Philocleon to challenge his role as retired *despotês*, but for the impoverished chorus members to eke out a living entirely based on their jury pay. Philocleon could, in theory anyway, thus break entirely loose from the redistributive center of the oikos. The empire had "filled" the empty center of the polis, charging it with a power that it had previously lacked and setting loose forces that threatened to destabilize the social formations of the time. The agora had become not only a "gathering place," but the center of commercial exchange and of centralized, objectified governmental power. These two new functions equally threaten Bdelycleon, who conflates them in his language and attacks both at once.

Mapping the Oikos: Territory and Integrity

Our sources reflect considerable sensitivity to the organization, real, supposed, or desired, of the agora. At Xenophon, *Oikonomikos* 8.21–23, Ischomachos portrays the agora as the classic example of organized space. His wife has expressed dismay at the thought of organizing the oikos, but Ischomachos consoles her with the problems of the polis. "We know that our polis contains tens of thousands of things [*murioplasia hapanta*]. All the same, whichever one of the servants you dispatch to buy you something in the agora, none of them has any trouble, but each one will show that he knows where he has to go to get everything. The reason for this, I assert, is none other than the fact that these things have been placed in an organized space [*en tetagmenêi xôrâi*]" (8.22). Thompson and Wycherly write that "surely Xenophon's Ischomachos, who is reading his young wife a lecture on the virtue of domestic tidiness, gives an exaggerated impression. There must have been a certain amount of intermingling and distribution. The excavations show that the major trades of Athens, such as metal-work, marble cutting, and especially pottery, were scattered over a fairly wide area."[55] The gap between the perception of Xenophon and the evidence of the excavations is revealing, for it reflects the kind of order which Xenophon felt an agora should have and to which he believed he could safely point in the Athenian agora.

However regularly the fish stalls and book sellers all clustered together in well-known areas, Xenophon does not attribute another kind of organization to the agora. Lawcourts, government buildings, and small booths filled with commodities of every kind seem to have been distributed throughout the Athenian agora. Aristotle in the *Politics* (1331a30–1331b4) argues that a proper polis should have not one but two agorai. He cites that Thessalians as an example of proper behavior. They have a "free" (*eleuthera*) agora. This is kept "pure" (*katharê*) of all things that are bought and sold (*ta ônia panta*)—a strong expression, with very negative implications for *ta ônia*. No craftsman (*banausos*), farmer (*geôrgos*), or any other such person may approach this space unless called by one of those in charge (*hoi archontes*). This "free" agora should be an attractive spot (*eucharis topos*) so that the gymnasia for grown men may be placed there. It should be further divided into sections for the young and the old: a few magistrates (*archontes*) should spend time among the younger men, while the older men should spend their time among the *archontes*. Aristotle makes explicit the point for this subdivision of the agora: the presence of the *archontes* instills a "true sense of shame" (*alêthinê aidôs*) and "that awe which characterizes a free man" (*ho tôn eleutherôn phobos*). "It is necessary to have another agora for things bought and sold [*ta ônia*] which is different, and physically separate, from this." Of the commercial agora, Aristotle says simply that it should be a convenient place for collecting (*eusunagôgos*) those things which are imported by sea and all those goods which come from the countryside.

Aristotle's ideal agora is extremely revealing. It champions a negative attitude toward the money economy, and attributes great importance to the location of activities, stressing both absence and presence. Just as Aristotle would banish all those who support themselves by their own labor from his "free" agora, he ordains that magistrates be present among the young, because they will exert a positive influence. Nor is Aristotle the only author to portray such a division. In his *Cyropaedia* (1.2.3), Xenophon claims that the Persians have an agora that is termed "free" (*eleuthera agora kaloumenê*). In this space, the royal (*ta basileia*) and the other governmental offices (*ta alla archeia*) have all been built. Not only do the Persians banish "things that are bought and sold" (*ta ônia*) and "the kind of people who frequent the agora" (*hoi agoraioi*) who are relegated to a separate area, but also banish the very sound of their voices (*hai toutôn phônai*) and vulgarities (*apeirokaliai*). The latter term is a plural form of a noun that literally means "inexperience with what is *kalos*," *kalos* being the term that designates at once what is beautiful and "upper class." The confusion (*turbê*) of these venal souls should not be intermingled with "the good order of those who are properly educated" (*hê tôn pepaideumenôn eukosmia*).

Aristotle and Xenophon thus frame in words the revulsion which Bdelycleon implies at *Wasps* 488–99. An agora in which money changes hands lowers the moral climate of the polis and is no place for people of proper breeding. Doubtless, Bdelycleon would have been glad to see a separate commercial agora constructed in some part of Athens where it would not offend him and where it would not affect the character of government. Bdelycleon, however, has his own concerns and cannot turn to the idealized solutions of other Greek cities or of foreigners, but he remains acutely sensitive to the importance of space and to the implied homology between location and behavior.

It is almost a truism of Aristophanic scholarship to see in Bdelycleon and similar cultivated figures an example of the well-bred Athenians withdrawing from active political life in the latter part of the fifth century. "Thucydides (2.65), the Comic Poets and Aristotle (*Ath. Pol.* 28.1) tell us that Pericles was the last fifth-century leader who was both rich and well-born."[56] In one early fourth-century speech attributed to Lysias (19.55), the speaker defends himself on the grounds that, although he lives geographically near the agora, he had never before been seen by anyone near either a lawcourt (*dikastêrion*) or the council house (*bouleutêrion*)—note that the preposition is *pros* ("near") rather than *en* ("in"), as if proximity to these buildings were alone a sign of bad character. At the age of thirty he has never spoken in opposition to his father nor has any fellow citizen dragged him into court. This speaker keeps to himself, his family and his friends, and takes pride in having nothing to do with the center of the polis.[57] Location and behavior reflect one another, and the farther one stays from the political power in the agora (no mention is made of commercial activity), the better.

But if the old families of Athens retreated from the competition with demagogues such as Cleon and Hyperbolos, we should not stress this almost proleptic interpretation of Bdelycleon. A major irony in this play (as elsewhere) is the perceived difference in wealth not just between classes but between generations. Bdelycleon is simply better off than his own father was when he grew up. The chorus identifies itself with the whole generation that fought the Persians (*Wasps* 1071–90), and implies a general contrast between its modest, but hard won positions and the more comfortable situation of those who enjoyed what their elders had earned (1114–21).

And yet, Bdelycleon sees his prosperity as a means to participate in the cultivated, sheltered and, above all, cosmopolitan life-style of the old elite which evolved in the archaic period. His cloak comes from Persia (1137), his shoes are Laconian (1158), and familiarity with the Lydian city of Sardis, three days into the more than ninety-day trip from the coast to Susa, is for Bdelycleon a minimum requirement for sophistication (1139). Bdelycleon and his friends value tokens of prestige from among non-Athenians: a *theôria* (1187), participation in an official embassy to one of the great cultural missions; consultation of an oracle or representing the Athenian polis at one of the international games; personal knowledge of the great athletes from other states in Greece such as Ephoudion from Arkadia[58] or Phayllos from Croton (1206); presence at a symposium that includes not only prominent Athenians but at least one foreigner as well (1221), and knowledge of "Sybaritic tales," associated in some way with Sybaris, the proverbially wealthy Greek city in southern Italy. If Bdelycleon typifies a class of young men who have become wealthier than their fathers, and if Bdelycleon's pretensions are familiar to the audience, his behavior is ironic: Bdelycleon's generation derives its increased wealth from the Athenian Empire and the domination of non-Athenians, but he clearly bases his own self-image on the prestige which he and his fellows derive from those outside of Athens. The ideal of *apragmosunê*, detachment from business and other people's affairs, is a classic conservative trait.[59] Bdelycleon may foreshadow the detached elite of the fourth century, but his models would surely have been men of the old style, such as Cimon, who named one of his sons Lacedaimonius, "the Spartan."

Faced with the chaos (and, more pertinently, the competition) of the agora, Bdelycleon retreats and turns inward. His reflex is hardly new. Six generations before, in the *Eunomia* (fr. 1 West), Solon had criticized those who felt that they could retreat from the polis. "Thus, the troubles which afflict the demos [*dēmosion kakon*, fr. 1.26] penetrate the oikos of each person [*ērchetai oikad' hekastôi*].[60] The outer doors which separate the courtyard from the street [*auleioi thurai*, 27] no longer hold this evil outside. It leaps above the high protective wall [*hupsêlon herkos*, 28] and it finds you, even if you flee into the innermost recess of the house [*feugôn en muxôi . . . thalamou*, 29]." The *despotês* of a household feels that his dwelling is a fortress, and that its barriers, the gate and wall, seal it off from what goes on outside. The oikos is a physical as well as a social unit, and its integrity (or lack of it) as a separate and separable entity is a contested issue. Solon graphically portrays the frailty of this barrier, as the *dēmosion kakon*, like a beast, leaps over the high walls, and pursues its prey into the innermost sanctuary of the house.

Wasps likewise explores the integrity of the household, presenting us with a neat transformation of Solon's putative individual hiding with his home. Both Solon (fr. 1 West) and *Wasps* treat the oikos as a fortress. Each of these works focuses on the barriers which articulate the inside of the oikos from the outside and on the struggle to make this barrier absolute. In Solon, the oikos seeks in vain to keep the troubles that threaten it outside. In Aristophanes, however, the polarity is reversed: Bdelycleon finds his household threatened, but he discovers that he must keep his old father from getting out. The *dēmosion kakon* that threatens to burst inward in Solon becomes the old man pictured as a "monster" or "wild beast" (*knôdalon*, 4) threatening to burst *outward* at the very beginning of *Wasps*. The trouble is located as always outside the oikos, but it works through the person of Philocleon, exerting a malevolent attraction upon him. The servants who are on stage at the opening of the play, Sosias and Xanthias, immediately tell us that they are on guard duty (*phulakê nukterinê*, *Wasps* 2, 69), and Philocleon describes them as hoplites under arms (359–60). The besiegers act as if besieged, barricading the door of the house, but from the outside (198–202).

But where Solon speaks briefly, if graphically, of the "gates to the courtyard," the "high wall," and the "innermost recess," Aristophanes develops the physical reality of the oikos with the obsessive intensity open to comic discourse. The play constitutes perhaps our best textual map of a classical Greek house.[61] Philocleon tries to squeeze out through the gutters (*hudroroai*, 126) and chinks in the wall (*opai*, 127), so the servants stuff rags into these tiny openings (128). Philocleon then drives pegs into the wall (*toichos*, 130), up which he can climb like a tame bird hopping up a ladder (129). The servants respond by spreading nets all the way around the courtyard (*aulê*, 131). Philocleon rushes into the kitchen (*ipnos*, 139) so that he can slip through the drain in the bathroom (*kata tês puelou to trêma*, 141).[62] He temporarily outsmarts his guards and noisily emerges from the chimney (*hê kapnê*, 143). When Philocleon asserts that he is smoke (144), Bdelycleon asks what kind of wood is the source for this smoke (145). Bdelycleon then secures this escape route by weighing down a chimney cover (*têlia*, 147) with a heavy piece of wood. When Philocleon attempts to burst out of the door (*thura*, 152), Bdelycleon secures the lock (*katakleis*, 154) with a bolt (*mochlos*), but frets that Philocleon might gnaw through the pin that holds the bolt in place (*balanos*, 155). A small clod of dirt (*bôlion*, 203) spills out from the roof, and Philocleon threatens to burst out from under the tiles (*hupo tôn keramidôn*, 206) of the roof (*orophia*). When the chorus arrives, it asks if Philocleon cannot dig his way through the wall (*dioruxai*, 350) or lower himself by a rope (*kalôidion*, 379) from the window (*hê thuris*). When Philocleon does presume to lower himself out a window, Xanthias takes up a "harvest wreath" (*eiresiônê*, 399), an olive or laurel branch, "adorned with wool, figs, and other fruits, small loaves or cakes and small jars of olive oil, wine, and honey,"[63] mounted on the outside of the house during a festival in October and left there until the next year's festival. The play moves from top to bottom, inside and outside, probing the physical oikos. The detail with which Aristophanes draws this description is typical of his style, but the relentless string of mundane referents, taken as a whole, would be as inappropriate in Pindar or Aeschylus as Aristophanes' individual scatalogical or sexual references.

Philocleon and Bdelycleon contest space and its articulation in the material world as much as they contest ideas. Philocleon renders his obsession a "total social fact" run wild, for it touches upon and refashions all aspects of his life. Philocleon is fascinated with the physical tokens of his beloved lawcourt. The physical landmarks of the lawcourt attract him like the erotic charms of a lover's body. He groans if he is not seated on the front-most bench in the court (89–90). He does not sleep a wink, because at night his mind hovers about the water clock that times the trials (92–93). His fascination marks his own body, for he rises with three fingers clenched permanently together because of his habit of clutching his voting pebble (94–96), and it drives him to mark what he sees to serve as signs of his condition: when he sees that someone has marked erotic graffiti on a door, he feels compelled to scratch a similar remark in praise of the voting urn (97–99).[64] The lawcourts draw his body physically to them, and he attaches himself to the pillar in front of the court like a limpet.[65] Philocleon's obsession not only fixates his imagination, but compels him to reshape the world around him in its image. He compulsively structures his entire environment as a signifier pointing to his beloved role as a juror.

Where the chorus of wasps initially view its *kēdemōn* Cleon as a replacement for inadequate kin, Philocleon and the chorus convert the *dikastērion* into his oikos. Access to space and physical location constitute identity, and Philocleon draws upon the homology of position and identity. As Philocleon prepares for his final escape attempt, he tells the wasps in the chorus that, should anything happen to him, they should do two things. They should first take up his body and mourn him (*anelontes kai kataklausantes*, 386), and then bury him under the railings of the lawcourt (*theinai hupo druphaktois*). Participation in a private funeral was not a casual act, but signified a close attachment to the deceased and often a claim on the estate.[66] When Philocleon asks his fellow jurors to conduct his funeral, he shows the extent to which he has cut himself off from his natural family.

Second, the physical burial place was one of the primary elements that constituted the identity of an Athenian. When the Athenian state formally reviewed a particular individual, he would be asked, among other things, "whether he possessed family tombs [*ēria*], and where these were" (*Ath. Pol.* 55.3). Elsewhere in Greece, desperate exiles from Epidamnos had recently won aid from Corcyra (their mother colony) by physically pointing to the tombs of their ancestors and thus proving their consanguinity (*tafous te apodeiknuntes kai xuggeneian*, Thuc. 1.26.3).[67] When Philocleon asks to be buried in the lawcourt, he is not simply making a comic gesture, but is touching sensitive and deeply placed nerves.

Third, the chorus urges Philocleon to pray to his "ancestral gods" (*toisi patrōioisi theoisin*, 388)—a strong plea, for each *genos* had its own cults peculiar to itself and thus its own special relationship to supernatural forces. At *Athenaion Politeia* 55.3, we also hear that representatives of the Athenian state reviewing someone would specifically inquire as to where his particular family cults were (*pou tauta ta hiera estin*). Philocleon follows this recommendation by crying "O master Lykos! hero who dwells near to me!" (*ō Luke despota, geitōn hērōs*, 389). Lykos was a hero whose cult resided in the agora near a lawcourt, and this turn toward Lykos is another sign powerfully indicating where Philocleon's psychic center has located itself. As far as Philocleon is concerned, the lawcourt in the agora is his personal oikos.[68]

In the end, Bdelycleon must not only defeat Philocleon by argument (which he does) but must accept, and refashion, the identification of lawcourt and oikos. Philocleon accepts the logic of Bdelycleon's argument—but he cannot bear to give up serving on juries (760–63). In response, Bdelycleon offers to set up a private court at home so that his dejected father may continue passing judgment. "Remaining here," Bdelycleon suggests at 766, "pass judgment over the household slaves [*oiketai*]." Where the agora had modeled itself on the oikos, and had pushed this identification so far that it threatened the integrity of the household, in this scene the oikos strikes back, appropriating to itself the symbols and practices of the lawcourts. When Bdelycleon recites a catalog of comforts for the oikos juror (770–85, 805–18), he reembeds the practice of the juror within the framework and affective ties of the household. Every physical house (*oikia*) in Athens will one day, Philocleon has heard (800–804), have its own mini-lawcourt (*dikastêridion*, 803), as common as the small shrines to Hekate that stand before the front door. Where Philocleon had before transcoded the oikos into the lawcourts and agora, he now begins to reverse this process, remapping the attributes of the oikos to convert it into a lawcourt. He asks for the hero shrine of Lykos to be placed within his home (818–23).

The shrine is not the only spatial token which Philocleon demands. A few lines later, a scandalized Philocleon stops his son from beginning a trial: "Hold on there, you! You almost ruined us! You were just about to call the court into session without a railing [*druphaktos*, 830], which is the first of our sacred objects" (829–31). "Damn it, that's not here," the exasperated Bdelycleon replies. When Philocleon volunteers to run off and fetch one, Bdelycleon grumbles about the old man's *philokhôria*, his meticulous attention to the details of space. Yet the court railing is critical to Philocleon, because it is a both a barrier and a sign: it separates the inside from the out, the juror from the nonjuror. Just as Bdelycleon had anxiously scanned the chinks, drains, and gutters that threatened the outer shell of the oikos, Philocleon clings to the *druphaktos* as token of his status as juror. Subsequently, Philocleon transcodes ladles (*arustichoi*, 855) into voting urns (*kadiskoi*, 853–54) and a chamber pot (*amis*) into a water clock (*klepsudra*, 857–59). The chorus ends this set of preparations by calling the blessings of Pythian Apollo down upon Bdelycleon, for contriving this business "right in front of the household gates" (871) so that all in the chorus can ultimately rest from their wanderings (872–73).

Conclusion: Dialectical Space and Synthesis (?)

In the end, Bdelycleon does manage to wean his father away from the lawcourts and the agora. The shock of an accidental acquittal finally breaks the grip that judging had upon the old man, and Bdelycleon is free to refashion his father according to his own ideas. Earlier scholarship on the play found problematic the contrast between the first part of *Wasps*, which focuses upon the lawcourts, and the latter part, where Philocleon explores high society. The latter portion of the play is a logical counterpart to the opening sections. Having rescued (as he sees it) his father from the agora and the lawcourt, Bdelycleon now attempts to settle his father properly in the sphere of the oikos. Bdelycleon seeks, however, only to establish an antithesis to the control of polis and agora, and his attempts are not surprisingly doomed.[69] Synthesis does not come, if at all, until the final scene of the play (1474–1537).

Bdelycleon dresses his father in luxurious clothes, adorning him with marks of wealth and elite status (1121–73). He attempts, unsuccessfully, to train his father for polite company, prompting him with hints as to witty stories (1174–1207), urges him to move in an elegant and fitting manner (1208–15), and rehearses the drinking songs that will be sung (1216–50). All of this prepares them, Bdelycleon remarks, to get good and drunk (1251–52).

The discussion of drink reveals much about Bdelycleon's model of social behavior. His querulous old father is horrified at the idea of a drinking party: "Drinking is a terrible thing! From wine comes breaking open doors and fistfights and throwing things, and then afterward the paying of fines on top of a hangover!" (1253–55). Bdelycleon demurs from this interpretation: those with his urbane background construct society according to their own designs. If you consult with those in the elite (andres kaloi kagathoi, 1256), they talk the one who has been injured out of his anger (1257), or they tell some clever story that they learned at the symposium, thus breaking the tension and converting a serious affair into something lighthearted (1258–61). By their refined and charming comportment, they create their own space within which they can move gracefully and, by a kind of urbane sympathetic magic, convert their environment into something equally smooth and unthreatening for those initiated into it. Bdelycleon seeks to be independent of physical location: whether in the symposium or on the street, his dress, the movement of his body and, above all, his use of refined language set him apart and create a protective aura that travels with him.

Bdelycleon soon learns, however, that there is nothing smooth, graceful, or charming about his father, who offends everyone at the symposium and ends up carrying off the flute girl. Three typical Aristophanic walk-ons enter to complain about their treatment: a man representing a group attacked by Philocleon in the street (1332–40);[70] a female bread seller into whose booth Philocleon careened (1388–1416); a man assaulted by Philocleon (1417–41). None of these figures, however, comes from the symposium. They are all people whom Philocleon has encountered in the street, the neutral space that neither belongs to the oikos nor is even especially constitutive of the polis (those guilty of sacrilege may remain, like Andocides, in the polis but be barred from agora and from the sacred places or rituals).[71] However offensive he may have been in the symposium, Philocleon gets into real trouble when he ventures outside the oikos into which he had been invited, and runs wild in the street, the no-man's land, where the bonds of oikos and polis are weakest. Dutifully following his son's instructions, he tells stories of famous athletes at Olympia (1381–87) and of famous poets (1409–11), Sybaritic tales (1427–32, 1435–40), and a story about Aisop (1446–49). But his "wasplike" nature transgresses wildly against the easygoing urbanity that Bdelycleon attributes to such verbal tools, and the old man simply aggravates his existing troubles. In the end, Bdelycleon physically hoists his father up and drags him away indoors (1442–49), and he is left in the same position that he occupied at the opening of the play, as his father's jailer, desperately holding Philocleon within the limits of the oikos. Bdelycleon may object to the jury duty, but he has no more effective formula that will integrate his cantankerous father into the community.

But Bdelycleon does not appear at the play's conclusion, Philocleon does ultimately escape from his oikos (1482ff.), and he does, in the final analysis, find a role for himself in the polis, in the Theater of Dionysus, a space that belongs neither to the oikos nor to the agora. He does not find his resolution in tranquillity or in urbane behavior, but in a wild dance (1484–86).[72] The comic hero calls upon the sons of the tragic poet Carcinus to join him in his dance (1496–1515). Comedy and tragedy as genres vie with one another, as Philocleon does not turn to cooperation so much as the controlled competition of the theater. Within the framework of the polis, strife moves from the periphery to the theater at its center, where it is contained and drives the wild dance with which the play concludes (1518–37).

And yet, the manner of this resolution literally dramatizes its limits: comedy and tragedy eschew their natural medium—the spoken or sung word—and plunge into the nonverbal sphere of motion. Language—on which Aristophanes and Bdelycleon depend—plays a role secondary to the physical spectacle of the leaping, whirling bodies that bring the play to its frenetic close. This is the final (and ultimate) transgression against literary form, for if the complex allusions to realia and minutiae defy the standards of normal literature, Aristophanes here undermines literary form altogether. The words that end the play point outward, away from themselves and into the nonverbal realm. To the extent that Aristophanes offers a resolution to the tension between oikos and polis, that resolution exists outside of, and ironizes, the sphere of comedy as text.[73] But if the textuality of comic discourse mocks itself, it mocks the reader as well, for the ending of the play forever excludes us from the joyful and wild resolution in which the original audience partook. Where the literary texts of Greece strove to reproduce themselves so that they could live forever within the Panhellenic canon, Aristophanes concludes *Wasps* with the ultimate transgression, effacing the medium and rejecting the reading public at the climactic moment of the play.

Notes

1. Note the manner in which Strauss 1966, 135, summarizes his view of *Wasps*: "The Aristophanean comedy achieves the right mean, not by avoiding vulgarity on the one hand and transcendent wisdom on the other, but by integrating vulgarity and transcendent wisdom into a whole that can, among other things, convey the moderate political message. The Aristophanean comedy circles around the mean between vulgarity and transcendent wisdom, i.e., it avoids it while points toward it." Strauss thus summarizes the play in terms of high and low, but his analysis subtly privileges the "mean," averaging out, as it were, the rough edges and extremes of the play to sanitize it and lend it a less troubling position in the canon.

2. *Wasps* 64–66: ἀλλ' ἔστιν ἡμῖν λογίδιον γνώμην ἔχον, / ὑμῶν μὲν αὐτῶν οὐχὶ δεξιώτερον, / κωμῳδίας δὲ φορτικῆς σοφώτερον.

3. Succinctly put, e.g., by J.-C. Agnew 1986, 6–7; for the development of this idea in England, see Williams 1958, 130–58; for the role of aestheticism in Germanic thought, see now Terry Eagleton 1990.

4. Henderson 1990b, 272; contrast Redfield 1990, 334: Aristophanes "may have wanted to do more with his art, to make it a vehicle of genuine teaching and of public education. In so doing, he stretched his genre to and beyond its limit, for Old Comedy cannot, ultimately, be used to correct the world; it can only enjoy it."

5. See Oates and O'Neill 1938, which ascribes "Translator Anonymous" to ten of Aristophanes' plays.

6. On Aristophanes in particular, see Henderson 1990b; see also Dover 1978.

7. On this, see Stallybrass and White 1986.

8. For an extended, if different, analysis of Panhellenic poetry, see Nagy 1990, 82–115.

9. Pindar's poetic utterances are arrows that "speak to the wise, while the mass of mankind needs interpreters" (*Ol.* 2.85–86). Praise counts, but only from the intelligent (*Pyth.* 5.107). Pindar coyly asks whether his patron (and, through him, the audience) knows how to understand "the true essence of words" (*Pyth.* 3.80–81). "You are wise" (*essi gar ôn sophos, Isth.* 2.12), the poem asserts and challenges at once. "Wise" (*sophos*) and "wisdom" are favorite words for Pindar, appearing thirty and twelve times respectively in his epinician poetry. The poet must entice the attention of his audience and must spread his net wide, but not so very deep—the Pindaric ode is aimed at an elite which it seductively defines. Only the elite of the Greek world can appreciate his poems, and this exclusivity of discourse is both a challenge and an offer.

10. E.g., Aristarchus of Tegea (*TrGF* 1.14), Ion of Chios (*TrGF* 1.19), Achaios of Eretria (*TrGF* 1.20), Spintharos of Herakleia (*TrGF* 1.40).

11. See Goldhill 1987, 97–129; for Isocrates' judgment, see *De Pace* 82: οὕτω γὰρ ἀκριβῶς εὕρισκον ἐξ ὧν ἄνθρωποι μάλιστ' ἂν μισηθεῖεν.

12. See Kolb 1981; note also Longo 1990, 16: "the community of the plays' *spectators*, arranged in the auditorium according to battle order (no different from what happened on the field of battle or in the burial of the war dead), was not distinct from the community of citizens."

13. See Ober and Strauss 1990, 237–70.

14. Individual playwrights were, of course, to some extent subordinate to the normative values of the polis, but a Marxist analysis which views poets as "products" of the normative values in the polis is too reductive; see, e.g., Longo 1990, 14: "In the total machine of the '*polis* theater,' the author is but one of many mechanisms of dramatic production, located between two acts of selection: the preliminary selection . . . administered to his text outline, . . . and the subsequent

selection made by the public." Aristophanes and the surviving fragments of the other comic playwrights vividly portray the importance which the Athenian public attributed to the quirks and peculiarities of its individual playwrights: thus, see Aeschylus in *Frogs*, Agathon at the opening of *Thesmophoriazousai* and Euripides throughout.

15. Bdelycleon remarks at *Wasps* 462 that the chorus would have been much harsher had it eaten the verses of Philocles, and other passages in comedy comment on the bitter quality of Philocles' work, but this poet, now all but forgotten, defeated Sophocles' *Oedipus Rex*. The Tragedians had to work with the tastes of their audience. On Philocles victory, see Soph. *OT* Hypoth. 2; on Philocles (*TrGF* 1.24), see *Birds* 281 (with scholia), *Thesm.* 168 (with scholia), Cratinas 292, Telecleides 14.

16. See Zeitlin 1982, and 1990, 130–67.

17. Aristotle (*Poet.* 3.1448a36) notes the Doric tradition that *kōmazein* was derived from the word for "village" (*kōmē*): the Greek verb *kōmazein*, according to this tradition, inscribes the fact that those who performed comedy had been driven from the city and forced to wander about the countryside; on comedy (in this case Megarian) as the source for a "counterideology," see Figueira, in Figueira and Nagy 1985, 132–43.

18. On discussions of the contrast between the first and second portions of the play, see Vaio 1971, who himself argues various thematic links binding the two sections; see also Konstan 1985, 42–43.

19. See de Polignac 1984, 41–92; Osborne 1985, esp. his discussion of Brauron at 154–82.

20. Morgan 1990, 1–25.

21. See Osborne 1985 and 1987, de Polignac 1984, and Van Andel and Runnels 1987.

22. For a brief summary of Mycenean society as it emerges from the linear B texts, see, still, Ventris and Chadwick 1973, 119–25; for more extended discussion, see Chadwick 1976.

23. See Hdt. 7.38–39; it was a basic tenet of the Persian Empire (at least in Greek eyes) that all the king's subjects were his personal slaves, see also Artemisia's advice to Xerxes at Hdt. 8.102.2–3, where she distinguishes between Xerxes' personal oikos with the rest of his subjects. The great Persian nobleman Mardonios, who will command the force that remains in Greece, is only Xerxes' *doulos*.

24. Hdt. 1.99.2: ταῦτα δὲ περὶ ἑωυτὸν ἐσέμνυνε τῶνδε εἵνεκεν, ὅκως ἂν μὴ ὁρῶντες οἱ ὁμήλικες, ἐόντες σύντροφοί τε ἐκείνῳ καὶ οἰκίης οὐ φλαυροτέρης οὐδὲ ἐς ἀνδραγαθίην λειπόμενοι, λυπεοίατο καὶ ἐπιβουλεύοιεν, ἀλλ᾽ ἑτεροῖός σφι δοκέοι εἶναι μὴ ὁρῶσι.

25. Homer, *Od.* 7. 266–67: ἔνθα δέ τέ σφ᾽ ἀγορὴ καλὸν Ποσιδήιον ἀμφίς, / ῥυτοῖσιν λάεσσι κατωρυχέεσσ᾽ ἀραρυῖα.

26. *Od.* 8.16: ἀγοραί τε καὶ ἕδραι.

27. Bourdieu 1977, 183.

28. Ibid., 190.

29. On the interplay of neutral space and international sanctuary, see Morgan 1990, 16–25; on the interdynamics of competing "peer" states, see Cherry and Renfrew 1986.

30. On the form and function of the Greek stoa, see Coulton 1976.

31. See Thompson and Wycherly 1972, 83–90; Camp 1986, 53–57.

32. See Wycherly 1978, 64–66; Camp 1986, 40–42; on the altar as the center of Athens, see Hdt. 2.7 who defines the length between Athens and Olympia as the length between the Altar of the Twelve Gods and the Temple of Zeus at Olympia; a milestone from ca. 400 B.C. (IG 2² 2640) defines the distance between the harbor and the Altar of the Twelve Gods.

33. See Thompson and Wycherly 1972, 170–3; Wycherly 1978, 91–103; Camp 1986, 135–47.

34. On the effects of market exchange on society, see Polanyi 1944; on Polanyi, see Humphreys 1978, 31–75; for a recent application of Polanyi's ideas to classics, see Kurke 1991, and in particular her discussion of Pindar *Isth.* 2 at 240–56, where she outlines the manner in which Pindaric poetry deals with monetary exchange.

35. Thus, e.g., the Corinthians and Pericles articulate very different strategic perspectives, but both attribute great importance to money (*chrēmata*) for projecting power during war (Thuc. 1.121 and 142).

36. For general examples of the term, see Homer, *Il.* 23.163, 23.674; Theognis 360, 645–46; Soph. *Phil.* 195; Xen. *Mem.* 2.7.12, *Anab.* 3.1.17, *Cyrop.* 3.3.22; Pl. *Rep.* 412c, 463d.

37. Note, however, that Page 1938, commenting ad loc., assumes that *kēdemōn*, here alone in classical Greek, is equivalent to *kēdestēs* ("connection by marriage").

38. Bourdieu 1977, 191.

39. On the *diphthera*, *exōmis*, and *kunē*, see MacDowell 1971 on 444 and 445; on the *embades* as basic but not luxurious footwear, see Bdelycleon and Philocleon at *Wasps* 1157ff.

40. Konstan 1985, 31.

41. Konstan 1985, 38, who cites Lenz 1980, 25: "Logisch läge es viel näher, dass die Choreuten-Heliasten auf Erhöhung ihres Tagegeldes drängten."

42. Dover 1972, 127.

43. The symbolic value of gift exchange and its role in defining social hierarchies has been intensively studied by anthropologists: see, e.g., Malinowski 1922; Mauss 1990, with the new introduction by Mary Douglas; on the importance of gift exchange in the classical period, see Herman 1987.

44. Rendering of this line is tricky: the "hare" (*en pasi lagōiois*) and crowns (*stephanoi*) are simple enough, but *puos* is "colostrum," the first milk produced after birth, and *puatē* is colostrum that has been curdled "by heating over embers" (LSJ). The translation "cream and cream-cheese" is suggested by MacDowell ad loc.

45. See, e.g., Themistocles at Thuc. 1.138.5; he receives from the great king Magnesia for his bread, Lampsakos for his wine, and Myous for the rest of his provisions (*opson*); at Hdt. 5.11.2, Darius offers to Histiaios Myrkinos in the land of the Edonioi and to Koes of Mytilene the possession of his own polis; on grants of landed estates, see Herman 1987, 106–15.

46. The similarity between polis and oikos seems to have been a well-known idea in antiquity, since Aristotle singles it out for criticism in the opening sentence of the *Politics*.

47. Thompson and Wycherly 1972, 41–46; Paus. 1.5.1: "Near to the Council Chamber of the Five Hundred is what is called the Tholos; here the prytaneis sacrifice, and there are a few small statues made of silver"; *Ath. Pol.* 43.3: "the prytaneis dine together [*sussitousin*] in the Tholos"; Camp 1986, 94–97; a kitchen was a standard feature of this building throughout its various incarnations, Thompson and Wycherly 1972, 43–44.

48. Arist. *Ath. Pol.* 44.1; Andocides 1.45 (which seems to imply that in an emergency all the prytaneis might spend the night in the Tholos).

49. Thompson and Wycherly 1972, 46–47; Paus. 1.18.3–4.

50. See Meiggs and Lewis 1989, no. 37.14–15 (d. ca. 458–457), e.g., where representatives of Egesta are to be summoned to the official building of the *prytaneis* (*es prutaneion*) to receive formal hospitality (*epi xenia*), and thus become the *xenoi* of the Athenian state; a logical place for them to have received this hospitality would have been at the Tholos. See the same formula applied to the people of Selymbria in the Propontis: Meiggs and Lewis, no. 87.45–46, to the Carthaginians (?) (92.17–18: where the formula is almost entirely restored) and to the individual Oiniades, an official representative of the Athenian people at Skiathos (no. 90.24–25). The *proxenos* was the official guest friend (*xenos*) of the Athenian state as a whole, and this institution perfectly captures the manner in which the polis could constitute itself out of institutions which developed for the individual oikos; on this, see Herman 1987, 130–42.

51. For this custom, see Pl. *Apol.* 36d–e, where Socrates argues that a man such as himself, who makes his fellow citizens truly fortunate (*eudaimōn*) deserves to take his meals in the official building of the prytaneis (*en prutaneiōi siteisthai*) far more than a person who triumphed in one of the horse races at Olympia. In particular, Socrates points out that such a man has no need of the subsistence offered (*kai ho men trofēs ouden deitai*), but he himself does. This is certainly true, for

anyone who could afford the enormous expenses involved in international horse racing maintained a large household himself. The honor had far more to do with prestige than with material comforts. For studies of the *sitêsis*, see Thompson and Wycherly 1972, 47 n. 132.

52. On the importance of shared hospitality in archaic and classical Greece, see Herman 1987; Kurke 1991, 135–59.

53. See Camp 1986, 44–45.

54. See Thompson and Wycherly 1972, 74–78, who describe the remains beneath these as "dignified quarters" for magistrates, located behind a "fine colonnade" and "with a fine view over the whole area"; Camp 1986, 122–26. In 1967, an inscription regarding the *metronomoi*, dated to 222/1 B.C., was discovered and seems to have come from the South Stoa 1. The *metronomoi* were officials who, according to *Ath. Pol.* 51.2, were responsible for all weights and measures. The outraged "bread seller" in the *Wasps* threatens to report Philocleon to the *agoranomoi*, officials charged with regulating trade in the agora (see *Ath. Pol.* 51.1).

55. Thompson and Wycherly 1972, 171.

56. Henderson 1990b, 279–80; on evidence for this shift in the comic poets, he cites *Knights* 180–222, *Frogs* 732–33, Eupolis, fr. 219, 384.

57. Lysias 19.55, cited by Konstan 1985, 39, who in turn refers to Lateiner 1982b. Konstan follows Lateiner in characterizing this separation from politics as typical of the upper classes in post-Periclean Athens; Lateiner (11) cites "The democratization of Athens, the relaxation of traditional social and political maneuvering in the courts" and concludes that "as the men of traditional status were deprived of their monopoly of political power, they came to devalue political participation." See also Connor 1971, 175–94; Lateiner 1982a, 151–52, 158; on the proleptic aspect of this attitude, see also Whitman 1964, 152: "The elegant world of dinner parties and small talk into which he tries to bring his father anticipates, in a way, the retired conceptions of the good life which characterizes the fourth century or the Hellenistic philosophies."

58. See Ehrenberg 1947, 46–67; Demont 1990; on *apragmosunê* in Athens in particular, see also Carter 1986.

59. MacDowell, on *Wasps* 1191.

60. So also Schwinge 1975, 35–47, esp. 42ff.

61. See, e.g., its use by Robinson and Graham 1938, 176 (where *Wasps* 1215 is adduced as literary evidence for the elaborate nature which roofs could take), 189 (where 139–48 is "the best known and most detailed passage" relating to the kitchen flue), 199 n. 72 and 200 n. 73 (the drain, *puelos*, at 141).

62. On the identification of the *puelos* with the bathroom—as well as kitchen—drain, see Robinson and Graham 1938, 199 n. 72, who point out that bathrooms excavated at Olynthus typically open off into the kitchen.

63. MacDowell 1971, on *Wasps* 398.

64. *Wasps* 97–99, καὶ νὴ Δί᾽ ἢν ἴδῃ γέ που γεγραμμένον / υἱὸν Πυριλάμπους ἐν θύρᾳ Δῆμον καλόν, / ἰὼν παρέγραψε πλησίον "κημὸς καλός." The formula "So and So is *kalos*," was a standard amatory remark, and occurs as a common feature on Greek vases; see also *Ach.* 144, where the Thracian king Sitalkes is supposedly so taken with Athens that he scrawls "the Athenians are *kalos*" on walls.

65. *Wasps* 104–5: κἄπειτ᾽ ἐκεῖσ᾽ ἐλθὼν προκαθεύδει πρῲ πάνυ, / ὥσπερ λεπὰς προσεχόμενος τῷ κίονι.

66. Osborne 1985, 139: "Participation in the funerary rites of a man constituted an important way of both showing and claiming kinship, and hence a stake in the inheritance; helping non-kin with the expenses of burial, which could be considerable, is a demonstration of *philia*"; as examples of competition for the right to conduct a burial, he cites Isaeus 8.21–22, 3.8–9; Dem. 43.65, 54.32; Lys. fr. 64.

67. The importance attached to the location of a grave is particularly prominent in hero cult: the physical remains of a dead *heros* are the source of his power, and thus possession of a grave

brings with it the support and protection of its occupant. The classic examples of this are the grave of Orestes at Hdt. 1.67, where the Spartans steal the bones of Orestes from Tegea and thus gain military superiority over the Tegeans; see also the significance of Oedipus' grave in the *OC* 1518–23. On the hero as a local figure, see Rohde 1898, 184–89; Burkert 1985, 206.

68. On the manner in which a hero near a particular house might be "domesticated" and "receive regular greetings and offerings from his mortal neighbors," see Rusten 1989, 289–97.

69. Bdelycleon, of course, sees this as a resolution; see Konstan 1985, 40: "The genteel class could cloak its withdrawal from public life and encounters at law in an idealized memory of a time before the law, representing their class attitude as a gesture of pristine social harmony."

70. On the identification of this character, see MacDowell 1971 on 1332.

71. The term *hiera* can describe sacred objects, a sacred space, or the actions involved in religious ritual. On the importance of agora and *hiera*, see, e.g., Lys. 6.9, 24, where we hear that Andocides has been banned from these parts of the polis; note also Lys. 12.96, where the Thirty Tyrants were so outrageous that they plucked their victims from the agora and the *hiera*.

72. On the importance of the dance, see Whitman 1964, 160–61: "The whole scene, far from being inorganic, is of great importance for the structure of the play. The futility of education and the incorrigibility of nature is the principal theme, and the finale completes it. . . . Far from cured, Philocleon has merely a new disease, worse than the first, but with equally contentious, agonistic purport; according to Xanthias and Bdelycleon he is outright mad. The threads are now all pulled together and the final dance begins, a whirling dance which seems to convey symbolically the underlying idea of the vicious circle where all things return upon themselves. . . . It is the dance of the world's madness, the dizzying, infectious course of self-assertive, irrepressible nature, the great divine *Dinos*, Vortex, who has deposed Zeus and rules in his stead." Vaio 1971, 344, points out that the dance consists of more than just circular motions, and gives a fuller appreciation of its physical dimension.

73. See Whitman 1964, 166, who praises the "irresolution of the end" of the play and praises it as "a token of dramatic honesty far superior to the weak moralizing of the finale" of the *Clouds*.

Bibliography

Agnew, J.-C. 1986. *Worlds Apart: The Market and the Theater in Anglo-American Thought. 1550–1750.* Cambridge.

Bourdieu, Pierre. 1977. *Outline of a Theory of Practice.* Cambridge.

Burkert, Walter. 1985. *Greek Religion.* Cambridge, Mass.

Camp, John. 1986. *The Athenian Agora: Excavations at the Heart of Athens.* London.

Carter, L. B. 1986. *The Quiet Athenian.* Oxford.

Chadwick, John. 1976. *The Mycenaean World.* Cambridge.

Cherry, C., and Colin Renfrew. 1986. *Peer Polity Interaction and Socio-political Change.* Cambridge.

Connor, W. Robert 1971. *The New Politicians of Fifth-Century Athens.* Princeton.

Coulton, J. J. 1976. *The Architectural Development of the Greek Stoa.* Oxford.

Demont, Paul. 1990. *La cité grecque archaïque et classique et l'idéal de tranquillité.* Paris.

de Polignac, François. 1984. *La Naissance de la Cité Grecque.* Paris.

Dover, K. J. 1972. *Aristophanic Comedy.* Berkeley.

———. 1978. *Greek Homosexuality.* Cambridge, Mass.

Eagleton, Terry. 1990. *Ideology.* Cambridge.

Ehrenberg, Victor. 1947. "*Polypagramosyne*: A Study in Greek Politics." *JHS* 67.46–67.

Figueira, T. J., and G. Nagy, eds. 1985. *Theognis of Megara: Poetry and the Polis.* Baltimore.

Goldhill, Simon. 1990. "The Great Dionysia and Civic Ideology." In *Dionysus*, edited by Winkler and Zeitlin, 97–129.

Henderson, Jeffrey. 1990a. *The Maculate Muse.* 2d ed. New York.

——. 1990b. "The Demos and the Comic Competition." In *Dionysus*, edited by Winkler and Zeitlin, 271–313.

Herman, Gabriel. 1987. *Ritualized Friendship and the Greek City*. Cambridge.

Humphreys, S. C. 1978. *Anthropology and the Greeks*. London.

Kolb, Frank. 1981. *Agora und Theater: Volks- und Festversammlung*. Berlin.

Konstan, David. 1985. "The Politics of Aristophanes' *Wasps*." *TAPA* 115.27–46.

Kurke, Leslie. 1991. *The Traffic in Praise: Pindar and the Poetics of Social Economy*. Ithaca.

Lateiner, Donald. 1982a. "An Analysis of Lysias' Political Defense Speeches." *RSA* 11.151–58.

——. 1982b. " 'The Man Who Does Not Meddle in Politics': A Topos in Lysias." *CW* 76.1–12.

Longo, Oddone. 1990. "The Theater of the *Polis*." In *Dionysus*, edited by Winkler and Zeitlin, 12–19.

MacDowell, Douglas M. 1971. *Aristophanes' Wasps*. Oxford.

Malinowski, Bronislaw. 1922. *Argonauts of the Western Pacific*. London.

Mauss, Marcel. 1990. *The Gift: The Form and Reason for Exchange in Archaic Societies*. London.

Meiggs, Russell, and David Lewis. 1989. *Greek Historical Inscriptions*. Oxford.

Morgan, Catherine. 1990. *Athletes and Oracles: The Transformation of Olympia and Delphi in the Eighth Century BC*. Cambridge.

Nagy, Gregory. 1990. *Pindar's Homer: The Lyric Possession of an Epic Past*. Baltimore.

Oates, Whitney J., and Eugene O'Neill Jr., eds. 1938. *The Complete Greek Drama*. New York.

Ober, J., and B. Strauss. 1990. "Drama, Political Rhetoric, and the Discourse of Athenian Democracy." In *Dionysus*, edited by Winkler and Zeitlin, 237–70.

Osborne, Robin. 1985. *Demos: The Discovery of Classical Attika*. Cambridge.

——. 1987. *Classical Landscape with Figures: The Ancient Greek City and Its Countryside*. London.

Page, Denys. 1938. *Medea*. Oxford.

Polanyi, Karl. 1944. *The Great Transformation*. New York.

Redfield, James. 1990. "Drama and Community: Aristophanes and Some of His Rivals." In *Dionysus*, edited by Winkler and Zeitlin, 314–35.

Robinson, David M., and Walter J. Graham. 1938. *Excavations at Olynthus*. Part 8: *The Hellenic House*. Baltimore.

Rohde, E. 1898. *Psyche: Seelencult und Unsterblichkeitsglaube der Griechen*. Freiburg.

Rusten, J. S. 1983. "Γείτων Ἥρως: Pindar's Prayer to Heracles (N.7.86–101) and Greek Popular Religion." *HSCP* 87.289–97.

Schwinge, E.-R. 1975. "Kritik und Komik. Gedanken zu Aristophanes' Wespen." In *Dialogos: Festschrift Harald Patzer*, edited by J. Cobet, R. Leimbach, and A. Neschke-Hentschke, 35–47. Wiesbaden.

Stallybrass, Peter, and Allon White. 1986. *The Politics and Poetics of Transgression*. London.

Strauss, Leo. 1966. *Socrates and Aristophanes*, 112–35. Chicago.

Thompson, Homer A., and R. E. Wycherly. 1972. *The Agora of Athens*. Princeton.

Vaio, John. 1971. "Aristophanes' Wasps: The Relevance of the Final Scenes." *GRBS* 12.335–51.

Van Andel, T. H., and Curtis Runnels. 1987. *Beyond the Acropolis: A Rural Greek Past*. Stanford.

Ventris, Michael, and John Chadwick. 1973. *Documents in Mycenaean Greek*. 2d ed. Cambridge.

Whitman, Cedric H. 1964. *Aristophanes and the Comic Hero*, 143–66. Cambridge, Mass.

Williams, Raymond. 1958. *Culture and Society: 1780–1950*. New York.

Winkler John J., and Froma I. Zeitlin, eds. 1990. *Nothing to Do with Dionysus? Athenian Drama in Its Social Context*. Princeton.

Wycherly, R. E. 1978. *The Stones of Athens*. Princeton.

Zeitlin, Froma I. 1982. *Under the Sign of the Shield: Semiotics and Aeschylus' Seven against Thebes*. Rome.

——. 1990. "Thebes: Theater of Self and Society in Athenian Drama." In *Dionysus*, edited by Winkler and Zeitlin, 130–67.

MALCOLM HEATH

Aristophanes and the
Discourse of Politics

Aristophanic comedy contains echoes and representations of contemporary political discourse. If we are to identify these allusions and interpret them, we must know something of the political discourse that is being echoed and represented—or (as it may be) misrepresented. But how much do we really know about the discourse of late fifth-century Athenian politics, and what are the sources of our knowledge?

To a limited extent we enjoy direct access. For example, when we read pseudo-Xenophon's essay on the Athenian constitution we are reading a late fifth-century political text; but within the whole domain of contemporary Athenian politics this text is manifestly eccentric. Comedy played to, and was appreciated by, a mass audience; our primary concern, therefore, must be its relation to the political discourse in which the majority of the citizens participated. But our access to this mass political discourse is much more problematic; we do not, for example, have any speeches addressed to the fifth-century assembly.

We do have some fifth-century representations of speeches to the assembly. In particular, Thucydides offers a compelling representation of political debate in Athens, and one that has been extremely influential. How far should we trust it? Doubts arise when one tries to correlate what we read in Thucydides with the implications of other indirect evidence. Consider for example how the topic of justice features in Athenian attitudes to foreign policy—or fails to feature: in

Thucydides Athenian speakers are broadly consistent and wholly isolated in openly dismissing justice as irrelevant to questions of international policy. This is utterly unlike the observable practice of political speakers in fourth-century Athens, and I have argued elsewhere[1] that there are sufficiently strong pointers toward a broad continuity of rhetorical theory and practice from the late fifth to the fourth century to make Thucydides' portrayal of Athenian speakers look less than plausible. This is not to say that late fifth-century Athenians never argued in the way that Thucydides portrays; but it is hard to believe that they typically argued in the way that Thucydides typically portrays them as arguing. The overall impression which Thucydides gives may therefore be profoundly misleading, and his evidence must be used with caution.

The claim that justice is likely to have been an important rhetorical topos for Athenians in the late fifth century, as in the fourth, finds some support in Aristophanes himself. In the *Birds* Iris is intercepted flying through avian territory and Peisetaerus tells her that it would be intolerable if, when the birds rule everyone else, the gods remain insubordinate; the gods must learn to obey "the stronger" (*Birds* 1225–28). Taken in isolation these lines might be thought to confirm Thucydides' picture of Athenian attitudes, in which the key concept is power; but the broader context does not bear this interpretation out. Peisetaerus is careful to ground the birds' foreign policy on claims of justice. From the outset he argues that the birds have a prior title to rule, and that the gods are usurpers and aggressors. In lines 467 and 477–78 he explains to the birds that they preexisted the gods, and therefore have a right to kingship; thereafter the birds consistently refer to *their* kingship (549), *their* scepter (634–35). During the negotiations with the gods Peisetaerus claims that they initiated hostilities, and that peace is still possible if they will act justly, that is, restore the birds' scepter to its proper owners (1596–1601);[2] in due course Heracles formally recognizes the justice of the birds' claim (1674). Hence Peisetaerus' insistence that the gods must obey the stronger cannot be separated from his insistence that this obedience is something to which the birds have a just claim. It would be shameful for a city with the power to enforce its rights to allow them to be flouted; but it will wish to be seen to possess the rights it enforces.

There is other evidence in Aristophanes for the continuity of political rhetoric from the late fifth century to the fourth. In *Frogs* Euripides is asked how the city can be saved and says (first in a clever epigram, then in a paraphrase labored enough for even Dionysus to comprehend) that Athens should abandon its present leaders and adopt new ones: "if *now* we're doing badly in *these* circumstances, naturally if we do the opposite we shall be saved" (1449–50).[3] Compare with this argument the beginning of the *First Philippic*. Demosthenes offers the encouraging reflection that the Athenians have got themselves into difficulties by doing everything wrong. If they had got into difficulties by doing the right things the situation would be hopeless; as it is, there is the possibility that the situation can be retrieved by adopting a new policy. Of course, adopting a new policy implies adopting a new adviser on policy; the speech opens with a pointed contrast between "the usual people," whose advice has got the Athenians into trouble, and Demosthenes, whose advice will presumably get them out of it. Demosthenes, like the comic Euripides, invites a fallacious inference from the failure of current policy to the efficacy of the proposed alternative.[4] We need not assume that Demosthenes borrowed his line of thought from Aristophanes; it is more probable that he was using, and Aristophanes was imitating, a pattern of argument current among Athenian politicians both in the late fifth century and in the fourth century. The same inference suggests itself when we compare the defensive tone of Demosthenes' reference to "the usual people" (he would have preferred to keep quiet, but circumstances compel him to speak) with the similar gesture of apology for putting oneself forward at the beginning of the second woman's speech in *Ecclesiazusae* 151.[5]

Another obvious area of continuity in political rhetoric is invective.[6] In *Knights* a number of unpleasant characteristics are attributed to Cleon: he engages in deception (48, 809), flattery (48, 215–16), slander (7, 45, 64, 262, 288), sycophancy (62–70, 437), and financial corruption (66, 79, 296, 802); he exploits fears of conspiracy for his own political ends (236, 257, 452, 461–79, 628, 862) while conspiring with foreign powers (465–69) and undermining democracy himself (847–59, 1044); he embroils Athens in wars to suit his own ends (801–4); he is of foreign and servile origin (hence "Paphlagon");[7] he is sexually depraved (78); he is shameless (277, 324, 409, 1206); and he has a deplorably vulgar rhetorical style (256, 275–76, 286).

What a difference there was between this vile demagogue and the great fourth-century statesman and patriot Demosthenes! Or was there? According to Aeschines, Demosthenes engaged in deception (2.124, 3.99), flattery (2.113, 3.76), slander (2.109, 3.216), sycophancy (2.99, 145), financial corruption (3.58, 91, 94, 103–5, etc.); he exploited fears of conspiracy for his own political ends (2.10, 3.225), while conspiring with foreign powers (2.123–28, 141, 143) and undermining democracy himself (2.177; 3.23, 145, 220); he embroiled Athens in wars to suit his own ends (2.13, 79, 161); he was of foreign and servile origin (2.22–23, 78, 180; 3.171–72); he was sexually depraved (2.23, 88, 99, 149; 3.162); he was shameless (2.150; 3.16, 99); and he had a deplorably vulgar rhetorical style (3.166–67, 218).

And what of Demosthenes' opponents? Strangely enough, they too (so Demosthenes assures us) engaged in deception (16.3, 18.282), flattery (8.34), slander (9.54; 18.11, 122ff., 126), sycophancy (8.71, 19.2), financial corruption (9.34; 15.32; 18.52, 131; 19.101); they conspired with foreign powers (2.4; 6.32–34; 8.66; 9.53; 14.18; 18.41, 149, 158–59, 284; 19.27–28, 69, 110, etc.) and undermined democracy (2.30; 15.33; 19.2, 294–97, 300, 314; 21.207–9; 22.32; 24.75–76, 90, 153–54);[8] they embroiled Athens in wars to suit their own ends (18.143, 19.88); they were of foreign and servile origin (18.129–31, 257–66, 284; 19.237); they were sexually depraved (18.130; 19.287, 309; 22.21–24, 73); they were shameless (18.285; 19.16, 72, 175, 199–200, 206; 21.194); and they had a deplorably vulgar rhetorical style (18.82, 122, 126–28, 132, 308; 19.209).

It is clear, therefore, that conventions of political invective similar to those observable in the fourth century underlie Aristophanes' portrayal of Cleon.

The assembly debate in *Knights* provides further evidence for the continuity of rhetorical practice. The question at issue in this debate is which of the two rivals has greater goodwill toward the people (748). This is something to which fourth-century political speakers too laid competing claim in their struggle for political influence; Demosthenes opens *On the Crown* with a prayer that his goodwill toward the people will be reciprocated by the jury in the present case (Dem. 18.1, 8), and commentators have often noted the close parallel between this prayer and the Paphlagonian's opening move (763–68). The latter's contributions to this scene can be read as a speech interrupted (and increasingly disrupted) by hostile interjections.[9] A brief synopsis may help to make clear the many topoi it shares with later political speeches:[10]

[A] I have deserved well of the people (764–65); [B] I alone fight for the people (767); [C] I am the greatest lover of the people (773); this is proved by the fact that [D] I have conferred benefits on you (773–76). By contrast, my opponent's claim to goodwill rests on [E] flattery (788). Hence [B] I am your greatest defender (790) and [C] lover (791). [F] My policy will secure Athens' power and prosperity (797–800). [G] I am being slandered (810–11), although [H] I have done the city more good than Themistocles (811–12). This is because [C] I am a lover of the people (820–21).

But it is not only in overt parodies of political debate that we can observe such parallels: Aristophanes presents himself to his audience in a way that mimics the devices of political oratory.[11] In the parabasis of *Acharnians*, for example, we find a similar cluster of rhetorical topoi:

[I] I am reluctant to put myself forward (628–29); but [G] I am being slandered (630–31), and [J] the Athenians are liable to jump to rash conclusions (630, 632). [D] I have conferred benefits on you (633–42), in opposition to [K] deception (634, 636) and [E] flattery (635, 639). [L] I have taken a risk in speaking frankly (643–45); but [F] my advice will bring you victory (645–54) and prosperity (656), and I will not [E] flatter or [K] deceive you (657–57).

Behind this passage lies Cleon's prosecution of the poet in the preceding year: Aristophanes responds to this attack with a parody of the way in which a politician would seek to justify himself in the face of an attack by a political opponent.

There are, then, pervasive parallels with later political oratory in Aristophanes. These parallels suggest that he was influenced by a contemporary practice of political rhetoric standing in substantial continuity with that of the fourth century. It follows that the fourth-century orators will be crucial in reconstructing the discourse of late fifth-century politics, and thus in establishing the relation between Aristophanic comedy and extratheatrical political discourse. Of course the orators do not constitute direct contemporary evidence for the late fifth century; times and circumstances had changed. We must use them critically, therefore—but we must use them.

One weakness of recent work on Aristophanes has been its neglect of fourth-century oratory. I do not except myself from this charge: my monograph on *Political Comedy in Aristophanes* makes no more than a single casual reference to the exchange of invective between Demosthenes and Aeschines. Jeffrey Henderson's essays "The *Dêmos* and the Comic Competition" and "Mass versus Elite" add perhaps half a dozen other references to those two orators (mostly for matters of law and the like); his primary points of reference are pseudo-Xenophon and Thucydides. Lowell Edmunds' book *Cleon, Knights and Aristophanes' Politics* makes no reference to Demosthenes or Aeschines in its attempt to map out the ideological background of *Knights*, although chapters are devoted to Pindar and Theognis.

How damaging is this omission? Let us take as a test case the contrast between quiet (ἡσυχία) and disturbance (ταραχή), which is central to Edmunds' interpretation of *Knights*. Edmunds correlates quiet with disengagement from public affairs (ἀπραγμοσύνη) in opposition to disturbance and civil strife (στάσις), and he clearly sees this opposition as ideological in the sense of embodying the values of one political tendency rather than another; thus he talks of "the ideology opposed to 'disturbance,'" refers to "the Athenian *apragmones*," and concludes that "the Athenian *apragmones* . . . had to face . . . a political order founded on principles different from and even opposed to ἡσυχία."[12]

The theme of ἡσυχία is one we have already met: Demosthenes in the *First*

Philippic and the woman in *Ecclesiazusae* begin their speeches by saying that they would have preferred to keep quiet. This apologetic opening implies an ideology in which keeping quiet is approved, and putting oneself forward may be resented. Now consider in this light the following passages from the orators:[13]

1. Aeschines 3.82: Demosthenes was supported by "those who make war on the city's quiet," and he provided them with "the beginnings of war and disturbance."
2. Demosthenes 18.307–8: There is such a thing as "quiet that is just and in the city's best interest," but that is not Aeschines' way; often he keeps quiet, but when something disagreeable befalls the city "suddenly out of his quiet, there he is—a politician."
3. Demosthenes 19.88: Aeschines will sing the praises of peace, but in doing so will condemn himself: "for if what is a source of blessings for others has become a source of so much trouble and disturbance for us," then this surely proves that their bribery has corrupted the peace.

What can we infer from these passages? First, that quiet has good connotations and disturbance bad; this is hardly surprising. Second, both speakers wish to charge the other with causing disturbance. Naturally, it is easier for a speaker who advocates peace to bring this charge; but the other party is able to represent his opponent's apparent quietness as fraudulent and productive in reality of disturbance. So the assertion of either side of the opposition is always reversible. The opposition does not embody the values of one political tendency rather than another but expresses an ideological common ground, the possession of which is contested by all sides.

Can this conclusion be projected back into the late fifth century? The parabasis of *Acharnians*, which begins with the customary apology for putting oneself forward, suggests that it can. On the other hand, if Thucydides is to be trusted, it was then possible for a politician to reject ἡσυχία and ἀπραγμοσύνη as the bases for Athenian policy; Alcibiades does so in the Sicilian debate (6.18). But we should be cautious: Alcibiades was an unusually flamboyant politician; in the same speech he takes up a charge of madness and ironically makes a virtue of it (6.17.1). Moreover, even in this context Alcibiades speaks of "the ἀπραγμοσύνη of Nicias' words, and his sowing dissension (διάστασις) between young and old" (6.18.6); that is, he seeks to discredit Nicias' claim to the positive connotations of ἀπραγμοσύνη by implying, first, that it is merely a pose ("of his *words*") and, second, that the reality behind it is an attempt to stir up internal disharmony. These polemical tactics are exactly comparable with those we have seen Demosthenes using against Aeschines' claim to the virtues

of quiet. Furthermore the accusation of fomenting discord and causing disturbance must have been familiar in late fifth-century political debate, since the
notion that the internal conflicts generated by political rivalries were a main
source of Athenian weakness (a topos well-attested in fourth-century oratory)
seems already to have been a commonplace in the fifth century.[14] Further
evidence that the opposition was, in the fifth century as in the fourth, common
ground to which conflicting claims might be laid can be found in the well-
known passage of Thucydides in which Pericles characterizes the politically
inactive citizen as "not ἀπράγμων but worthless" (2.40.2); there is little point
in contesting an opponent's self-description unless the values to which it lays
claim are commonly recognized ones.

So in the fifth century, as in the fourth, quiet has positive connotations and
disturbance negative ones; any politician will try to rob his opponents of the
former and to tar them with the latter. One may doubt, therefore, whether the
charge of causing disturbance was ideologically distinctive within democratic
political discourse at the time of *Knights*. It is more likely to have been a topos of
political invective that any politician could in principle use against any other.[15]
If so, then Aristophanes' association of Cleon with ταραχή is not dissimilar
from his accusations of financial or sexual corruption; it tells us little more than
that his representation of Cleon is a hostile one—which we already knew.

We have seen that the representation of political discourse in Aristophanes
corresponds at many points with the likely realities of contemporary political
oratory, both in its echoes of rhetorical techniques and (most extensively) in its
use of the topics of invective.

These correspondences are in part a consequence of the way in which Aristophanes' characters speak to and about each other; the political discourse of
contemporary Athens is echoed and exaggerated in the political discourse of
the comic world. We cannot assume that what comic characters say is true
within the comedy itself, for comic characters are prone to engage in deception.[16] Nevertheless, it is clear that many of the scurrilous lies that politicians
tell about each other in the real world are true in comedy; the sausage seller
lives in a world in which politicians really are thieves, prostitutes, and so forth.
So comedy constructs not only the political discourse of its fictive world, but
also the fictive world itself, on a pattern provided by real political discourse.

But it is not just the fictive comic world that Aristophanes constructs according to this pattern. Although there is much in the comic world that is not true
of the real world, and not meant to be true (e.g., the possibility of establishing a
polis of birds), there is also much that is true and is meant to be recognized as

true (e.g., the existence of a polis called Athens). No precise line of demarcation can be drawn between these two extremes; we cannot, for example, state definitively which features the Athenian polis in comedy is to be seen as sharing with its real archetype. So when he explicitly constructs a fictive comic world on the pattern provided by political invective Aristophanes may also, to an indeterminate degree, be doing the same by implication to the real world. Moreover, Aristophanic comedy includes direct statements about the primary world—that is, statements that break out (or appear to break out) of the fictive framework of the plot.[17] These statements about the primary world exploit elements of the same political discourse, as we saw in the parabasis of *Acharnians*; so Aristophanes seems explicitly as well as implicitly to construct the primary world on the pattern of political discourse.

Aristophanic comedy therefore echoes contemporary political discourse on a number of different levels: in the speech of comic characters; in the design of the comic world; in the account of the primary world which that comic world implies; in its explicit commentary on the primary world; and in its presentation of Aristophanes himself as a commentator on the primary world. The question therefore arises: in view of these pervasive parallels, should we not see Aristophanic comedy as a form of political discourse, sharing its ends?

This has brought us to a central contention of Henderson's "Comic Competition." In his view the parallelism between comic and political discourse constitutes a problem for those skeptical of political intent in comedy:[18]

> The skeptics have not explained away the fact that the comic poets . . . argue vehemently and purposefully about the most important and divisive issues of the day. The positions they advance or denounce represent those of actual groups, and their techniques of persuasion and abuse are practically identical with those used in political and forensic disputes.

This point is backed up by an analysis of the festival context in which comedy was produced, which—Henderson argues—is also significantly parallel to that of political debate:[19]

> Comic festivals, as occasions for competitive display . . . , show not only as much institutional structure as the deliberative occasions with which the Old Oligarch aligns them, but also much the same structure. And, like all festivals organized by the demos, they had social and political as well as religious significance: no decisions were made about the city or its individual citizens, but the city and its citizens were the festival's theme and focus.

In sum, "comedy portrays political debate and deliberation, and is itself a competition [as are political debate and deliberation]"[20] and these points of convergence imply that comic poets are (in their own way) doing something similar to the politicians; so, for example, "if we deny to comic ridicule any persuasive intention, we must deny it also to the orators."[21]

There are weaknesses in this argument. Nothing follows from the festival context with its competitive structure as such. A race at the Panathenaea was a competitive event in an institutional context of great civic significance, but this does not make it (in any relevant sense) political. The festival context cannot coerce us into a political reading of any event occurring in that context independently of our assessment of the event's intrinsic political content and function. Second, there are differences as well as parallels between the political and comic contests, and consequent differences also in their use of shared techniques of persuasion and abuse. Politicians and comic poets both sought to gain the approval of an audience by means of political invective. But the politician's invective was directed against other politicians, with whom he was in direct rivalry. The comic poet was not in direct rivalry with the politicians against whom he directed his invective;[22] rather, he was striving to outdo other comic poets in the abuse of the politicians as a third party. This prima facie asymmetry suggests the possibility of an underlying asymmetry of intent. Henderson is right to say that we must attribute persuasive intent to comic poets as well as to orators, and in a very broad sense the persuasive intent is the same: both wished to persuade their audience to accord them victory in a competition. But for the comic poet, unlike the orator, winning the competition did not entail establishing direct competitive ascendancy over the victim of the abuse, since the comic poet was not in direct competition with the victim. Henderson's statement that the comic poets "argue . . . purposefully" is not in dispute, therefore; the question is, What was that purpose?

One approach to this question might be to look at what Aristophanes is willing to count as success. In *Clouds* he says that he attacked Cleon when he was at the peak of his power and refrained from attacking him when he was down. The implication of lines 549–50, in which the chorus refers first to Aristophanes' blow to Cleon's stomach and then to the restraint he showed in not jumping on him when he was down, must be that it was Aristophanes' blow which put him down. Likewise in the parabasis of *Wasps*, when Aristophanes assimilates himself to Heracles the monster slayer (1030, 1043) the implication is that the monsters against which Aristophanes had been fighting were actually slain; he could not otherwise claim to have won a triumph and to have performed a public service. These claims notoriously do not correspond to any actual reverse in Cleon's political career. The point, often made, that *Knights* won first prize shortly before Cleon's election to the generalship can thus be given a sharper formulation: that sequence of events was consistent with Aristophanes claiming that he had slain the monster and floored his opponent. This may suggest that the success that Aristophanes sought did not lie in the sphere of extratheatrical politics but was internal to comedy, or else that it was a pretense.[23] Such a pretense would be consistent with Aristophanes' habit of making blatantly untrue statements about himself, and with his tendency to claim credit for putting an end to abuses that he treats elsewhere as continuing.[24]

Against this one might urge that the many passages in which Aristophanes claims to be the people's adviser point to a genuine design on extratheatrical politics; thus Henderson writes that "the poets consistently said that their advice and admonishments to the spectators were true and just."[25] Of course, no one says "let me give you some bad advice"; but there are ways and ways of offering "good" advice. The skeptical reader's caution in taking the comic poet's adoption of the adviser's role seriously is not arbitrary; it is a response to genuine complexities in Aristophanes' self-presentation, such as those we have just observed.[26] Indeed, Aristophanes' appropriation of the terms of political discourse is itself fraught with ambiguity, given his relentless mockery of that discourse. The audience is surely not meant to accept uncritically Aristophanes' application to himself of topoi that he satirizes in the discourse of politicians; and as soon as self-subverting irony is admitted into Aristophanes' appropriation of political discourse, the parallelism on which Henderson's case rests is compromised. Perhaps, then, Henderson's position can be reversed: the more closely Aristophanes imitates the political discourse he satirizes, the less likely it is to be politically (as distinct from comically) persuasive.

The parallels we have observed so far have been primarily with that part of political rhetoric designed to manage the audience's perception of the speaker and his opponents. For a political speaker this is not an end in itself, but provides a framework for bids to win the audience's support for particular policies. Does comedy provide a parallel for this aspect of political discourse as well?

The war is an obvious and much-discussed test case. On one side are those who argue that Aristophanes makes clear his hope of persuading the audience to "abandon its aggressive war-policy" in *Acharnians* "by unmistakably identifying himself with his hero,"[27] on the other, those who wonder whether (for example) it is prudent to ignore the fact that the hero in question is a self-professed liar.[28] Here we may return to the play's parabasis. In a context in which (as we have seen) Aristophanes portrays himself as an adviser in a way that mimics the politician's self-presentation, he tells his audience not to surrender Aegina (*Ach.* 652–55);[29] this is the one piece of specific advice (as distinct from self-advertisement) that can be construed from that context. Should we therefore infer that Aristophanes is advocating a hard line on the status of Aegina? If so, how is this related to the advocacy of peace that some detect in the play as a whole? *Acharnians* is not usually seen as advocating peace *provided that* the Spartans back down from certain specified demands; but why not? The anodyne proposition that peace is nicer than war may generate good drama, but it lacks political substance; the real question the Athenians faced in 425 was, What would be acceptable peace conditions? If we are to say that Aristophanes positively advocated a particular position (as distinct from a conventional platitude) on this issue, this is the kind of question we must make him answer. It would not have been absurd in 425 to argue that a compromise was desirable on the Megarian decrees, but not on Aegina; but I doubt whether many will come forward to argue that *Acharnians* aims to persuade its audience to accept that nuanced position.

The need to identify a stance on particular policies and issues is noted by MacDowell in his review of Edmunds' book on *Knights*. On "the catalogue of Demos' plans for the future" at the end of *Knights*, MacDowell comments, "presumably Kleon was associated with the ills which Demos wants to suppress."[30] Note that "presumably": how well does the presumption survive an assessment of the whole context as a piece of political analysis? The first criticism of Demos' past behavior in this scene relates to his susceptibility to flattery in the assembly (1340–44); this reproduces a topos of political debate which we have already met, and has no specific policy content. The second criticism, of Demos' preference for public pay over shipbuilding (1350–55), is more specific; but it would be rash to assume that the alleged preference has strong roots in reality. A trireme's active life has been estimated at twenty years;[31] if that is right, then Athens must have replaced at least half its fleet in the course of the Archidamian War (and probably more, since the conditions of active service are likely to have shortened a ship's life) if it wished to maintain its fleet at a constant strength. There is no documentary proof that Athens did so;[32] but there is no evidence of any shortage of ships, and it would have been curious if the Athenians had chosen to save money for public pay by running down their navy at the same time as voting for the continuation of a vastly expensive war in which they depended on that navy.[33] It will not do to say that the war was continued because military service was a source of public pay, and that shipbuilding was skimped to finance that pay; another of the faults of the old regime according to *Knights* was a failure to pay the rowers in full (1366–68), implying (if we were to accept this passage as reliable political commentary) that the war was not an efficient way of ensuring that public pay reached the poor. Indeed, if public pay was all that the Athenians wanted, they could have avoided the trouble of serving in what must (if we believe the sausage seller) have been an ever smaller and less seaworthy fleet by adopting a suggestion which Bdelycleon makes in *Wasps* (706–12). His idea is that the Athenians should simply divide the tribute out among themselves. This is the culmination of a speech in which a sensible character who shares Aristophanes' animus against Cleon and claims to be trying to cure a disease in the city (650–51) convinces his opponents; so if we are looking for policies in Aristophanes, why not this one too?[34]

If it is hard to pin Aristophanes down to policies, what of politicians? After all, in the one passage that even most skeptics acknowledge as offering serious advice, the parabasis of *Frogs*, the point is that the Athenians should adopt a particular set of leaders.[35] It is true that certain leaders, such as Nicias, although not exempt from satirical attack,[36] are not systematically assaulted in the way that Cleon is; this unequal distribution of invective may reflect Aristophanes' political sympathies. But a symptom of political sympathy is not in itself evidence of an intent to exercise political influence. Moreover, as Henderson observes, "praise is actively avoided."[37] There is a prima facie sympathetic reference to Thucydides, son of Melesias, at *Acharnians* 703–18. But this does not offer support to an active politician; at most it expresses retrospective sympathy for a retired (perhaps, by 425, dead) one, and the portrayal of him as a bewildered old dodderer might be thought barbed (the phrasing of *Wasps* 947–48 also suggests that Aristophanes was turning the incident into mockery). Otherwise, those who look for a positive treatment of politically active individuals have not done better than Laches; but Laches himself might not have agreed that it was flattering to be portrayed as a malfeasant and ill-educated dog.[38] The failure to cross the boundary between the absence of criticism and the presence of commendation is another fundamental difference between comic and extratheatrical politics.

Or is this difference the point? Part of the function of political comedy, according to Henderson, was to get the Athenians "to think about their lives and civic duties in ways not encouraged on other occasions."[39] More specifically, "comic poets particularly wanted the *dêmos* to look through the lies, compromises, self-interest, and general arrogance of their leaders and to remember who was ultimately in charge." But were the Athenians ever in danger of forgetting that they, not their leaders, were in charge? The structure of Athenian democracy made that difficult to forget; the frequency with which the Athenians deposed, fined, and even executed their leaders[40] proves that it was not in fact forgotten. If this is what Aristophanes wanted to tell those in his audience, then he was telling them what they already knew very well, and what they no doubt liked to be told. I am far from wanting to deny that this is what

Aristophanes was doing; indeed, it is part of what I am asserting when I claim that Aristophanic comedy was in one sense political, and in another not.[41]

I said earlier that no precise line of demarcation can be drawn between features of the comic world that are and are not to be seen as shared with the primary world. Strictly speaking this is not true; such a line *can* be drawn, in many different places. One could say that all statements about the comic world are meant to apply to the real world, although many of them are highly metaphorical; or that none of them apply, even statements that happen to be true of the primary world being referred solely to a self-contained fantasy;[42] or one could draw a line at any point between these two extremes; or one could say (more cautiously) that a sharp line of demarcation was intended, but that we lack the evidence to locate it. I do not myself believe that any of these claims would be correct, but in rejecting them one is not uttering a *necessary* truth; one is making a normative judgment about the most appropriate way to read Aristophanic comedy. In other words, the denial of a precise line of demarcation between the comic and the primary world is an interpretative hypothesis. This does not mean that the hypothesis is arbitrary (there is a broad middle ground between being necessary and being arbitrary); but it is irreducibly *contingent*.

This contingency compels us to reject all approaches to Aristophanes that limit the range of possible readings a priori, including those politically skeptical readings to which Henderson refers, which rely on the assumption "that humour . . . is not a moral or political determinant: what makes people laugh cannot affect their choice of action when they are not laughing."[43] I am not convinced that anyone does argue from that assumption;[44] but if they do, Henderson's retort ("in the case of fifth-century Athens . . . this assumption has insufficient explanatory power") is too tame: the assumption is simply *wrong*. There is no limit in principle to the possible uses of humor, or of literary and dramatic art in general; the problem that confronts us is therefore always the concrete, historical problem of making sense of a particular text, or group of texts, in a particular context.

We must be cautious, however, about the notion of interpreting a text in context. The point made earlier, that the festival context of comedy does not in itself coerce our interpretation, can be generalized. Context as such never controls interpretation, but always and only as it is mediated by interpretation; *what* context is relevant and *how* it is relevant always depend on particular interpretative practices. What this point implies in practice will depend on our aims. If we are content simply to produce "a reading" of comedy, we need give it no further thought; that the context we deem relevant is determined by our own practice of interpretation is self-evident. But if (and to the extent that) we aim to understand Aristophanic comedy as a fifth-century discourse, then it will follow that our interpretation needs to embrace questions about Aristophanes' fifth-century audience as well. That audience, with its presuppositions about and strategies for making sense of comedy, is an ineliminable part of our problem, since context is, in the first instance, mediated through those presuppositions and strategies.[45]

This position is flatly opposed to that taken by Simon Goldhill in an influential contribution to the current discussion of the festival context of drama. According to Goldhill "we cannot expect to know how an Athenian audience would react to any tragedy."[46] So he applies himself to an interpretative project in which that question can be bypassed: "What I hope to describe is a tension between the festival of drama as a civic institution and a reading of the texts of that institution. How different Athenians reconciled or conceived that tension is simply not known."

But this is not as easy as it seems. One pole of the tension that Goldhill hopes to describe is "a reading"; the tension is therefore not a prior datum, but the product of a particular way of reading the text. So we cannot know whether the tension existed for an Athenian audience to reconcile or conceive without knowing whether it read the text that way—which, on Goldhill's premise, we cannot know. But the status of the reading which generates the tension now becomes an urgent question. *Ex hypothesi* we do not know whether this reading was or could have been appropriated in fifth-century Athens; but then it needs to be explained with some care how and why it is thought to throw light on tragedy as a fifth-century Athenian discourse. The mere fact that there is *some possible* reading that generates a tension of the kind Goldhill describes is meaningless: there will always be *some possible* way of reading a text that places it in tension with a given context. But Goldhill does not address this issue; instead he sidesteps the problem by at once redefining the tension with which he is concerned as one "between the texts of tragedy and the ideology of the city." The remarkable sleight-of-hand which substitutes "the text" for "a reading" as one pole of the tension distracts from the reading's contingency, and evades the question about the status and significance of that reading.

In more recent work on comedy Goldhill has affirmed the centrality of reception: "this determination of relevance or significance depends on the active involvement of an audience."[47] Moreover, when he observes of fifth-century Athenian drama's "willingness . . . publicly to question the values of a culture" that "such an institution could exist only in a democracy and in Athens in particular,"[48] he is clearly now willing to commit himself to a definite (and contestable) view on how drama was read in the fifth century. For if we were to say (what I suspect is true) that fifth-century audiences typically read tragedy as confirming rather than as questioning their culture's values, there would be no need to invoke Athenian democracy as an explanatory factor. Any institution *can* be read by external observers as standing in tension with, and so questioning, the values of its own culture; it is only when an institution *is* so read by internal observers, and is nevertheless officially sponsored, that the society's structure and values have something to explain.

Goldhill argues that "what is to be taken from Aristophanes inevitably remains a question replayed with every audience member's or reader's engagement with the comic."[49] This conclusion is, in one sense, uncontroversial; the only way to take anything from any text is to hear or read it, and what is taken depends (of course) on how one hears or reads it. This is simply another way of formulating the centrality of "the active involvement of an audience," and tells us nothing about Aristophanes in particular. But we should be wary of any implication that there is some one question that is inevitably replayed with every audience member's or reader's engagement, such as "the question of how seriously, how comically, how literally to take (the) play."[50] Since nothing that depends on the contingencies of a given audience's mode of reception can be "inevitable," this view would risk a retreat into antihistorical abstraction. Whether the question of seriousness is posed for a given audience, and if so in what form it is posed, will depend on its presuppositions about comedy and its strategies for making sense of comedy. It is possible for a member of an audience or for a reader to approach comedy with presuppositions that preempt the question of seriousness, or which allow it to be raised in one way but not another, or which allow it to be raised but tend to prejudge it. To rule out this diversity of possible modes of reception by the claim that some particular question is "inevitable" would be to impose another, if more subtle, a priori.

This point prompts a reflection on the concept of "negotiation," which Goldhill makes crucial to his discussion of comedy.[51] The parties to a negotiation always start from some prior position, and these initial positions determine both the range of outcomes accessible through the negotiation, and the relative accessibility of those outcomes. The only way, therefore, in which we can give concrete, historical content to the notion of Old Comedy as "a constant renegotiation of licence"[52] is to investigate the positions from which this negotiation proceeded, and the consequent range of accessible outcomes. In other words, we are driven back to the problem of reconstructing the presuppositions and strategies of reception that Aristophanes' audiences brought to comedy, and to which Aristophanes addressed himself. The concept of comedy as negotiation should not therefore be placed (as Goldhill places it) in opposition to the wish "to find some external control, evidence independent of our reading of the plays that would help us calibrate our estimation of their tone and mood."[53] Without evidence about the political and literary assumptions and behavior of the parties to comic negotiation in late fifth-century Athens, informed conjecture about the scope of such negotiation is manifestly impossible.

To ask for such a control is not to rule out in advance any conclusion about the range of possible outcomes accessible by negotiation in Old Comedy; it does not imply, for example, that the range must be narrowly constricted or static. My view of the parabasis of *Frogs*, in which Aristophanes seems to have tried actively to appropriate a role that tradition in theory made available to him, but which was in practice generally disarmed, obviously commits me to a recognition that the limits of comic license were renegotiable.[54] The point is rather that the range of outcomes accessible in a given transaction can be established (if at all) only through historical enquiry. Since the notion of a wholly indeterminate process of negotiation is vacuous, the alternative is not to approach the interpretation of fifth-century comedy without controls; it is to acquiesce in the control of our interpretation by presuppositions and procedures which have not been brought into a critically considered relationship with our (inevitably limited and negotiable) understanding of the ways in which comedy may have functioned as a form of late fifth-century Athenian discourse.

Notes

1. For the argument of this paragraph see Heath 1990b.
2. Sommerstein 1987 ad loc. refers to lines 554–56 to show that it was in fact Peisetaerus who declared war; but Peisetaerus' contention is surely that the gods' usurpation of power constitutes aggression, to which the declaration of war is a legitimate and necessary response.
3. A notoriously problematic context; I agree with Sommerstein's analysis of the textual problem (1993, 469–73). In Dover's reconstruction (1993 ad loc.) the advice is assigned to Aeschylus, and (following MacDowell) these two lines are given separately to Dionysus.
4. Compare the well-known Politician's Syllogism: "Something must be done. This is something. Therefore this must be done."
5. Cf. Isoc. 6.2; Fränkel 1962, 138–40.
6. The references in the following paragraphs are illustrative rather than comprehensive. Cf. Dover 1974, 30–33; Halliwell 1991, 293–94. Harding 1994 argues for the influence of the comic stage on the orators: I would contend that the influence was reciprocal.
7. MacDowell 1995, 86 n. 9, denies that this choice of name implies a joke about Cleon's origin. I am not convinced, and note that the discussion in MacDowell 1993 takes no account of parallels in oratory.
8. Demosthenes apparently does not accuse his opponents of exploiting fears of conspiracy.
9. On interrupted speeches in Aristophanes, see Murphy 1938, 80–81 (where, however, this example is overlooked); also useful for the general question of Aristophanes and oratory is Burckhardt 1924.
10. Again my references are illustrative only:

[A] for the phrase βέλτιστος περὶ τὸν δῆμον see (e.g.) Lys. 13.2 (ἄνδρας ... ἀγαθοὺς περὶ τὸ πλῆθος); in *Knights* 873 it is paired with "goodwill" (εὔνοια), for which see Aeschin. 1.159, 2.181, 3.248; Dem. 18.173, 320, 322, 25.64–68; *Rhet. ad Alex.* 1376b22–23; Brock 1991, 165 n. 25. Goodwill as grounds for an honorific award: Aesch. 2.46, 3.246; goodwill linked to democratic sentiments: Aesch. 3.248, Dem. 18.6.

[B] *Wasps* 593, 666–67; cf. Cleon as "watch-dog" (references are collected in Brock 1991, 161 n. 3); Dem. 18.107 (βοηθῆσαι τοῖς πένησιν ὑμῶν); Aeschin. 2.8 mocks a claim to be sole κηδεμών; for the claim to uniqueness cf. Dem. 25.64.

[C] cf. *Knights* 1341 with Brock 1991, 161 n. 4.

[D] Dem. 5.4–10, 8.70–73, 18.88–89, 102–9, 229–30; *Rhet. ad Alex.* 1436b23–24. On the Council's financial responsibility see Rhodes 1972, 88–113; the smear about corrupt ways of raising revenue is paralleled at Lysias 30.22.

[E] opponents flatter: Aeschin. 2.177; Dem. 3.13, 8.34; Dein. 1.103; Isoc. 12.140; assembly susceptible to flattery: Aeschin. 3.234, Dem. 3.21–24, 8.34, 9.4; I am not a flatterer: Dem. 3.3, 6.31, 8.24, 9.3–4.

[F] military and financial resources as themes of deliberative oratory: *Rhet. ad Alex.* 1422a12–14; Ar. *Rhet.* 1358b20–25, 59a30–60a11; cf. (e.g.) Dem. 8.71–72, 14.41, 18.322.

[G] victim of slander: e.g., Aeschin. 2.81, 181; opponents slander: Aeschin. 1.3, 2.145, 3.215; Dem. 18.10, 34, 126, 180, 242, 19.210, 251, 25.41; *Rhet. ad Alex.* 1436b36–37a323. Assembly enjoys slander: Dem. 8.23, 30, 9.54, 18.138; cf. Halliwell 1991, 293.

[H] unprecedented service: Dem. 18.94; Themistocles as standard of comparison: Aeschin. 1.25, 2.9, 3.181, 259; Dem. 19.303, 23.196–98; Themistocles surpassed: Dem. 20.71–74; cf. Anderson 1989.

[I]: *Thesm.* 383–84; Dem. 4.1; *Rhet. ad Alex.* 1437a32–b17.

[J] Dem. 5.2, 19.135–36, 26.18; Isoc. 8.52, 15.19; Dover 1974, 24f.

[K] opponents deceive: Aeschin. 2.124, 153; Dem. 16.3, 18.276, 282, 19.43–44, 23.188; Dein. 1.91, 99, 110–11; assembly susceptible to deception: Aeschin. 1.178; Dem. 18.159, 23.145, 185.

[L] risk in speaking freely: Dem. 1.16, 3.11–13, 32, 4.51, 8.69, 9.3–4, 18.219–20, 22.59.

11. Halliwell 1984, 17.

12. Edmunds 1987, 17, 31.

13. Also relevant: Aeschin. 2.106, 207–8, 3.216; Dem. 4.1, 8.67, 18.111 (ἄνω καὶ κάτω διακυκῶν), 198, 19.187, 25.42, 50, 52; Thrasymachus 85 B1 D.-K.

14. Heath 1990c.

15. See further Allison 1979; Harding 1981.

16. Heath 1990a.

17. I distinguish here between fiction (which is not a statement about the primary world, although it may be used *inter alia* to make a statement about the primary world obliquely) and falsehood (which is a statement about the primary world, although its function is not necessarily to win credence: e.g., some of the falsehoods which orators uttered about each other were probably designed to humiliate the opponent rather than to convince the audience of the truth of the claims made).

18. Henderson 1990, 273.

19. Ibid., 286.

20. Ibid., 311.

21. Ibid., 300.

22. I say "direct" rivalry, because on Henderson's reading the politicians were indirectly the comic poet's rival; but that is the conclusion of Henderson's argument, not a premise.

23. Halliwell 1984, 18–19.

24. Heath 1987, 22–23. This does not apply only in the political sphere; in *Peace* 739ff. he says

that he has stopped his rivals using various kinds of low-grade comic material; really? Cf. Murray 1987.

25. Henderson 1990, 271.

26. Heath 1987, 18–24; Heath 1990a, 237.

27. Henderson 1990, 306.

28. Heath 1990a, 233–37.

29. Heath 1987, 18–19.

30. MacDowell 1988, 216.

31. Casson 1971, 96.

32. Andoc. 3.8 and Aeschin. 2.175 do not inspire much confidence. Evidence for the funding of shipbuilding is discussed in Rhodes 1972, 115–17; Gabrielsen 1994.

33. Cf. Hansen 1991, 315–16, on the relative cost of public pay and warfare in the fourth century.

34. A foolish policy, to be sure, but this way of dealing with a surplus was one that a Greek state could seriously entertain (Hdt. 3.57.2, 7.144.1); and in view of the *Frogs* parabasis (see below) we cannot take the soundness of Aristophanes' political judgment for granted (Arnott 1991; cf. Sommerstein 1993, 476). Murphy 1938, 105–6, briefly analyses Bdelycleon's speech; its portrayal of relations between people and politicians offers further parallels with fourth-century oratory (cf. Dem. 3.29–32, 23.209–10). I have doubts about Bdelycleon's, as about Dicaeopolis', integrity: Heath 1990a, 234–35. MacDowell 1995, 166 n. 25, is right to question my description of Bdelycleon's speech in defense of Labes as "utterly mendacious"; it is, nevertheless, a deliberate and systematic attempt to mislead.

35. MacDowell 1988, 217, and 1995, 5, suggests that I undermine the whole case of my *Political Comedy* by admitting this exception. But the question is not whether comic choruses "give good advice" regularly, but whether the posture of "giving good advice" is regularly taken seriously (note that the claim to be giving good advice in lines 686–87 is not the sole reason for accepting the seriousness of this parabasis: the passage is significantly lacking in the kinds of textual cue that make it plausible to discount the claim elsewhere). There is no inconsistency in holding that Aristophanes attempted on this occasion to appropriate seriously a role that tradition made available to poets in theory, but which he was in general content to treat with lighthearted irony (cf. Heath 1987, 42).

36. Heath 1987, 34 n. 73.

37. Henderson 1990, 308 n. 133.

38. Heath 1987, 32.

39. Henderson 1987, 312.

40. Hansen 1991, 216–18.

41. Heath 1987, 42–43.

42. The advocate of such a position would point out that the boundary between primary and comic worlds is debatable in two directions: is the comic "I" the comic poet talking about his own world (which would still leave open the question of whether his aim is to win credence), or a comic persona talking about a fictional world—as much a character as the characters?

43. Henderson 1990, 273.

44. Gomme 1938 has an a priori tendency, but its premises are concerned with drama and art, not humor.

45. This not to say that the interpretation of comedy should (or could) be *limited* to a reconstruction of how it was understood in the fifth century; but I would contend that (quite apart from its intrinsic interest) such a reconstruction is indispensable in answering certain other questions we may want to ask. Note also the conditional clause in the text. To say that we must make sense of a text in a particular context is not to say in *which* particular context the text is to be made sense of; it is self-evidently not *necessary* to relate a text to its context of utterance, and self-evidently

impossible to relate a text to its context of utterance *alone* (for the modern interpreter is also a context).

46. Goldhill 1990, 115. Some of the statements that Goldhill makes in this paragraph suggest that he means to deny only that we can know how *all* members, or any *individual* member, of an audience responded; but who pretends otherwise? At fault here may be the assumption that talking about an audience's reaction implies "that an audience for a drama has only a uniform, homogeneous collective identity or response . . ."—"an intolerably naive idea," as Goldhill says. It would be equally naive to suppose that the Athenians had only a uniform, homogeneous collective ideology, but it does not follow that we can dismiss Goldhill's references to Athenian ideology, which only a caricaturist would interpret as implying such homogeneity.

47. Goldhill 1991, 201.

48. Ibid., 174.

49. Ibid., 201.

50. Ibid.

51. Ibid., 188.

52. Ibid.

53. Goldhill 1991, 201, quoting Heath 1987, 8. I should perhaps have stated explicitly (what I take as axiomatic on hermeneutic grounds: it is one manifestation of the hermeneutic circle) that "external" and "independent" are relative terms: our reading of the context of comedy is open to influence from, even though it is not wholly dependent on, our reading of comedy itself.

54. Cf. note 18 above; and see further Carey 1994, 80–83.

Bibliography

Allison, J. W. 1979. "Thucydides and πολυπραγμοσύνη." *AJAH* 4.10–22, 157–58.

Anderson, Carl A. 1989. "Themistocles and Cleon in Aristophanes' *Knights*, 763ff." *AJP* 10.10–15.

Arnott, W. G. 1991. "A Lesson from the *Frogs*." *G&R* 38.18–23.

Brock, R. W. 1991. "The Emergence of Democratic Ideology." *Historia* 40.160–69.

Burckhardt, A. 1924. "Spuren der athenischen Volksrede in der alten Komödie." Ph.D. diss., Basel.

Carey, C. 1994. "Comic Ridicule and Democracy." In *Ritual, Finance, Politics*, edited by Osborne and Hornblower, 68–83.

Casson, L. 1971. *Ships and Seamanship in the Ancient World*. Princeton.

Dover, K. J. 1974. *Greek Popular Morality*. Oxford.

———. 1993. *Aristophanes' Frogs*. Oxford.

Edmunds, L. 1987. *Cleon, Knights and Aristophanes' Politics*. Lanham, Md.

Fraenkel, E. 1962. *Beobachtungen zu Aristophanes*. Rome.

Gabrielsen, V. 1994. *Financing the Athenian Fleet*. Baltimore.

Goldhill, S. 1990. "The Great Dionysia and Civic Ideology." In *Dionysus*, edited by Winkler and Zeitlin, 97–129.

———. 1991. *The Poet's Voice*. Cambridge.

Gomme, A. W. 1938. "Aristophanes and Politics." *CR* 52.97–109.

Halliwell, S. 1984. "Aristophanic Satire." *Yearbook of English Studies* 14.6–20.

———. 1991. "The Uses of Laughter in Greek Culture." *CQ* 41.279–96.

Hansen, M. H. 1991. *The Athenian Democracy in the Age of Demosthenes*. Cambridge.

Harding, P. 1981. "In Search of a Polypragmatist." In *Classical Contributions: Studies in Honour of Malcolm Francis McGregor*, edited by G. S. Shrimpton and D. J. McCargar, 41–50. Locust Valley, N.Y.

——. 1994. "Comedy and Rhetoric." In *Persuasion: Greek Rhetoric in Action*, edited by I. Worthington, 196–221. London.

Heath, M. 1987. *Political Comedy in Aristophanes*. Hypomnemata 87. Göttingen.

——. 1990a. "Some Deceptions in Aristophanes." *PLLS* 6.229–40.

——. 1990b. "Justice in Thucydides' Athenian Speeches." *Historia* 39.385–400.

——. 1990c. "Thucydides' Political Judgement." *LCM* 15.158–60.

Henderson, J. 1990. "The *Dēmos* and the Comic Competition." In *Dionysus*, edited by Winkler and Zeitlin, 271–313.

MacDowell, D. M. 1988. "Aristophanes and Politics." *CR* 38.215–17.

——. 1993. "Foreign Birth and Athenian Citizenship in Aristophanes." In *Tragedy, Comedy and the Polis*, edited by Sommerstein et al., 359–71.

——. 1995. *Aristophanes and Athens*. Oxford.

Murphy, C. T. 1938. "Aristophanes and the Art of Rhetoric." *HSCP* 49.69–113.

Murray, R. J. 1987. "Aristophanic Protest." *Hermes* 115.146–54.

Osborne R., and S. Hornblower, eds. *Ritual, Finance, Politics: Athenian Democratic Accounts Presented to David Lewis*. Oxford.

Rhodes, P. 1972. *The Athenian Boule*. Oxford.

Sommerstein, A. H. 1987. *Aristophanes' Birds*. Warminster.

——. 1993. "Kleophon and the Restaging of *Frogs*." In *Tragedy, Comedy and the Polis*, edited by Sommerstein et al., 461–76.

Sommerstein, A. H., S. Halliwell, J. Henderson, and B. Zimmermann, eds. 1993. *Tragedy, Comedy and the Polis*. Papers from the Greek Drama Conference, Nottingham, 18–20 July 1990. Bari.

Winkler, J., and F. Zeitlin, eds. 1990. *Nothing to Do with Dionysus? Athenian Drama in Its Social Context*. Princeton.

JOHN WILKINS

Comic Cuisine

Food and Eating in the Comic Polis

I

The production and consumption of food is of major importance for the comic polis. This is partly because the comic polis reflects the agricultural production, import of commodities, and consumption of foods that sustained the polis of Athens. At the same time, in many of the surviving plays of Aristophanes the good order that is achieved at the end of the play is celebrated with the consumption of foods in a context of social or religious ritual. Consideration of the place of food in Greek comedy is timely: recent work on food in other cultures offers valuable approaches. Douglas and Powers and Powers have shown the overwhelming importance of symbolic significances in foods in both native and immigrant communities in the United States, especially in the context of social and religious ritual.[1] Powers and Powers discuss the cultural incomprehension between the native American for whom the hunting of the buffalo over the plains was an act that embraced the physical and metaphysical worlds—gods, ancestors, and landscape all gave meaning to the hunt—and the federal government, which supposed that the animals formerly hunted by native Americans could be replaced by meat on the hoof, delivered to a corral at the head of the railroad. For the native American, corralled cattle standing in their own excrement were not an equivalent of the buffalo of the plains. Complexities within a single cultural system are suggested for China by Chang who notes "the Chinese are probably among the peoples of the world most preoccupied with eating. . . . There has been an attempt to see Chinese poverty as a culinary virtue . . . but poverty and the consequent exhaustive search for reasons provide only a favorable environment for culinary inventiveness and cannot be said to be its cause. If so, there would be as many culinary giants as there are poor peoples. Besides, the Chinese may be poor, but . . . by and large they have been well fed. The Chinese have shown inventiveness in this area perhaps for the simple reason that food and eating are among things central to the Chinese way of life and part of the Chinese ethos."[2]

Approaches to the significance of foods specific to Greek culture have been developed in several sources.[3] With this background to food in Greek culture, we may approach more confidently the representation of food in Greek comedy, and specifically food in the fragments of Greek comedy. A high proportion of the comic fragments refer in some way to food and eating, partly because large numbers have been preserved by Athenaeus of Naucratis in his vast testament to ancient eating, the *Deipnosophistae*, written in the late second or early third century A.D. For reasons of space, this essay confines its study to Old Comedy and suggests ways of looking at representative categories of fragments within the framework of trade and agriculture modified by social and religious ritual, as outlined above.[4] (Some pertinent observations on appetite and the consumption of fish in Middle Comedy, eight hundred of whose plays Athenaeus claims to have read [8.336d], will be found below in the essay by Nesselrath.) Surviving plays are also considered in order to establish the ways in which foods are approached through a whole work.

Food in Comedy: A "Low" Form of Culture in a "Low" Form of Drama

Food is at the heart of the polis, in many of its dealings and negotiations and in the center of its social organization. Food is not mere fuel and nutrition, any more than the buffalo is mere meat on the hoof: it is an important part of trade and agriculture; it is a vital component of exchanges between humans and gods (in sacrifice and festival), between cities (in hospitality to ambassadors and other delegations), and between individuals (in hospitality and commensality among citizens, kinsmen, and religious groups); its symbolic significance expresses within a culture multiple meanings that will normally differ from meanings within another culture. Choice of food product, the means of preparation and the means of consumption will normally reinforce the identity of the polis or group within the polis and distinguish that group from others with different rituals of eating. The comparable use in the modern world of foods and patterns of eating to identify a group (African Americans or Italian Americans) within a larger culture (the United States) is the subject of Douglas.[5] The self-image of Athens is investigated in section III of this essay.

From another point of view, food is all too substantial, the tangible and olfactory[6] reality to which abstractions may be reduced in the comic polis, as for example in the scene in *Wasps* in which the dog is tried for stealing a cheese (760–1018). There is more to justice than dogs, cheeses, and cheese graters. In an essential way the humor here derives from banality, from what Gregory Crane terms "material reference," but humor is also generated from the combination of the judicial (which is organized by the polis or the community of oikoi) with the domestic (the oikos running its own affairs). In addition, the cheese conventionally represents Sicily and the dog political rapacity: we thus see a version of the political world expressed in material form.

Banality is a strong element earlier in *Wasps*, in the remarks of the market-stall holders who discuss politics in the context of vegetables and fish (488–99: cf. Crane above). At the same time, the location of the political opinions of the day in the lively discourse of the market is entirely fitting, for the agora embraces goods for sale, buildings housing institutions of the democracy, and that class of citizen most feared by oligarchs, the *agoraios*. (On the complex nature of the agora, see Crane above and section II of this essay). Elsewhere in *Wasps* there is reference to imperial revenues (648–724) and to proper deportment at the symposium (1122–1537). In the case of revenues, food products are appropriate for consideration as commodities imported into the city, but the matter is approached in a personal way, in terms of items to be enjoyed at the dinner and symposium; the polis has once again been reduced to the level of the pleasures of the individual citizen. (For a different perspective see Crane above.) It is an approach regularly adopted in comedy, to which foodstuffs may contribute. So too in the scene training the old man for the rituals of the symposium, the trainee approaches his task at a buffoonish level. In all of these cases, foodstuffs and the context of their consumption have an extensive symbolic significance in the social, religious, and political organization of the city-state. Food is culture-specific and polysemous within that culture. A better term than banality would be humility, something closer to the φαυλότερα (more humble things or persons) which Aristotle declares proper to comedy (*Poet.* 1449a32–34). Foods and comedy each represent a humble level which on the one hand stresses their apparent lack of status but on the other carries great significance within the cultural system.

Some of those signs may be highlighted by unexpected juxtapositions, and such incongruity is a major interest of Old Comedy. A well-known case is the Euripides of *Acharnians* and his vegetable-selling mother, the products of whose stall invade lines from the tragedies (396–489: see esp. 480, 885– 94). Here, comedy assimilates tragedy to itself and comments on the "domesticity" of Euripides as demonstrated later in the culinary and medical details of *Frogs* (936–91). Euripides, after all, is the poet whose Electra provides meat, wine, and cheese to the new arrivals in the recognition scene (*El.* 493–500). The incongruity achieved by such juxtapositions produces new perspectives of wonderful imagination. Archippus in his *Fishes* has the fish address their assembly as "gentlemen, fish" (fr. 30), and various humans—probably fishmongers—are denounced for their cruelty to fish (fr. 23). This idea resembles comment on the selling and roasting of birds in Aristophanes' *Birds*, and the eating of animals in the *Beasts* of Krates (fr. 19):

A: You must boil cabbages, and roast fish and saltfish, and keep your hands off us.

B: Are we then going to be eating no more meat whatsoever? Is that what you are saying? No meat from the agora? And no making of rissoles or black puddings?

Food is closely associated with the products of the natural world, animals, fish, and plants. In the comic polis, access to that world may be gained through the animal chorus: in comedy the food talks back. The chorus of beasts in Krates' play appears to have been removed from the menu: *Beasts* is one of a series of plays quoted by Athenaeus for their provision of automatic foods which serve themselves at table. In *Beasts* (fr. 16) the food other than meat cooks and serves itself, and the fish is even asked to turn itself over on the grill to cook on the other side: automated cooking and serving is discussed below in section III.

A notable juxtaposition may be achieved by the combination of a food of low status with a religious ritual. The comic polis presents many simple and apparently humble foodstuffs, such as the porridge (πόλτος) of Epicharmus (fr. 23), the small grilled fish (ἐπανθρακίδες) of the parabasis of *Acharnians* (670), or the lentil soup (φακῆ) of *Wasps* (811). These simple foodstuffs may sometimes have a symbolic value within the home or at the center of cult, as, for example, the beans and pulses consumed at the Pyanopsia and Anthesteria.[7] Similarly, when comedy refers to foods ritually consumed at a festival, the food selected is often of low status; so, at *Acharnians* 146, the Apaturia is represented by a sausage or black pudding, and at *Clouds* 386 the Panathenaia is represented by a soup of meat broth. A possible example in comedy of a humble food that carries great significance is the spit-loaf, ὀβελίας, mentioned by Aristophanes in *Farmers* (fr. 105). There are many references to Athenian loaves in Athenian comedy: they, together with barley cakes (*maza*), constitute a basic part of the diet, and Athens' greater access to imported wheat allowed it special breads unknown to many of its neighbors. Thus, mention of breads may be merely of a staple or may imply a celebration of Athenian excellence (Thearion, one of the few known commercial bakers in Greece, is named in Aristophanes' *Aiolosikon* [fr. 1] and *Gerutades* [fr. 177]). The *Breadsellers* of Hermippus appears to have had an extra dimension in introducing the mother of Hyperbolus—an analogy perhaps for the vegetable-vending mother of Euripides. That play may have exploited bread-making terms applicable to the political arena, as *Knights* exploits meat-producing terms (see below). Now spit-bearers (ὀβελιαφόροι) appear on two vases (though there is a slight possibility that the foodstuff carried could be roast meat and not bread).[8] The spit-bearers may be the cult members of Dionysus or of another god who carried the bread on their shoulders in procession.[9] We may suppose that some, all, or quite different aspects of spit-bread were drawn on by Ephippus in his *Spit-bearers*, written in the fourth century. Cratinus creates a similar effect in fragment 300: "I swear by Solon and by Draco on whose tablets they now roast barley."

The point appears to be that the tablets (κύρβεις) of the laws of the ancestral lawgivers are no longer respected. Bergk attributed the fragment to *Laws*, probably one of those plays contrasting the present unfavorably with the past. But the tablets, as Plutarch explains (*Solon* 25) with the help of this fragment, were held in the prytaneion, near the city's hearth, where the city's cooking was done—the production of meals for the executive of the council and honored guests of the state (see below on *Knights*). The form of disrespect, the toasting of barley, is then drawn from another of the uses of the building—the cooking is a central part of the life of the polis. Is it in fact an insult at all? It is a powerful juxtaposition. A final striking example is provided by a well-known fragment of Hermippus from his *Basketbearers* (63):

> Tell me now Muses who dwell in the houses of Olympus
> How many blessings for humans Dionysus has brought here in his black
>   ship
> Since he captained his ship over the wine-dark sea.
> From Cyrene silphium stalk and ox hides,
> From the Hellespont mackerel and all kinds of salt fish,
> From Thessaly rough-ground wheat and ox ribs,
> From Sitalces a mange for the Spartans
> And from Perdiccas lies for a good many ships.
> Syracuse sends hogs and cheeses . . .

The list continues. The primary importance of this passage is its celebration of the Athenian polis as a trading center that draws in goods from around the Mediterranean. This is a comic reflection of one of the primary sources of wealth in the polis, the others being agricultural production and mining. Agriculture is frequently celebrated in comedy as a source of blessings—ἀγαθά (see section III). In addition to the recognition of economic reality—which in comedy is comparable with the imports listed in the *Merchant Ships* of Aristophanes, and elsewhere to luxury goods noted at Thucydides 2.38, Xenophon, *Ways and Means* iii, [Xenophon], *Athenaion Politeia* 2.7–10—Hermippus' fragment 63 parodies hexameter poetry, locates particular goods in particular places (this is Athenaeus' reason for quoting this and similar passages at 1.27d–28d), throws in political jokes against enemies, and, most important, has Dionysus preside over this trade by sea. It is likely that the importation of food is thereby incorporated into Dionysus' own journey by sea to Athens and his arrival at the city at the beginning of the sailing season for his Anthesteria festival at which the god's journey was probably represented by the ship cart (unless this took place at the City Dionysia).[10] In this way Hermippus combines cultural features from different categories into a powerful whole in a way characteristic of the comic polis. Just as Dionysus presides over the symposium, his festivals, and drama itself, so in the comic polis his influence is extended to trade by sea. The presiding by Dionysus over the wealth-creation of the polis may be compared with Aristophanes' *Acharnians* in which four of the god's festivals—Rural Dionysia, Lenaia, City Dionysia, and Anthesteria—are combined with other Dionysiac elements: a celebration of wine in a symbolic and material form (186–200: libations sealing a peace treaty) and the triumph of the god's vine over the enemy of comedy (1178), all in the context of the "automatic" provision of good things (977) at the agricultural market of Dicaeopolis. The play concludes with festive eating (1000–1234) at the Anthesteria in addition to the the ritual drinking of the new wine: comedy alone in Greek literature concerns itself with what was eaten at this festival.

A food may have a positive cultural value as a simple food: it may speak of the people, the poor and unpretentious who do not share in the luxuries and extravagance of the rich. It may speak for Athens in contrast with other cities that are considered more self-indulgent. It may have a flavor or texture particularly associated with a place or occasion. Alternatively its significance may be derided, as at *Peace* 923–24 where the standard vegetable offering for the restoration of a statue is thought insufficient for Peace, and an animal is used. Two important aspects of comedy's discourse are the list and the detailing of parts. Lists, apparently prosaic in themselves, give an impression of joyful plenty, as in Hermippus' fragment 63 and *Acharnians* 1098–1112: they may provide a comment on each item, as the list of wines in Hermippus' fragment 77; they may simply run through a series of similar products, as the goat chorus on edible shrubs in Eupolis *Goats* (fr. 13) or the chorus on the fruits of peace at *Peace* 570–81. That play also offers a fine example of the detailing of parts, in the sacrifice of the sheep. There are the preliminary operations (956–74), followed by the dismemberment of the animal after death: the thigh bones, vital organs, and grain mixed with honey and wine (1039–40) are

roasted, and then the loin, the tail, the tongue and the lungs are taken separately. Such detailed description of the sacrifice is rare in fifth-century literature. Now if the parts of animals are referred to rather than the best meats, then
a humbler level of consumption is implied. The ears, trotters, head meat,
womb, and entrails are commonly cited in comedy, as Athenaeus demonstrates
in quoting liberally from comedy in his section on "meats boiled in water" at
3.94c–101e. For example Aristophanes' *Tagenistae* (fr. 520):

> That's enough sprats for me.
> I'm torturing myself eating all this oily food.
> [corrupt text] . . . a little liver, the neck of a young boar.
> If not that, then bring here rib or tongue or
> spleen or gut or the stomach of a young pig in autumn
> with hot rolls.

But that is not to say that the humbler level is dishonored in the culture. The
tongue of the sheep is one of the parts reserved for the priest, and in secular
eating, the consumption of the head meat of a fish or animal was sought after
for flavor and texture by those who had the power to choose.[11] Once again
comedy presents the humble as culturally significant.

Because of their symbolic values of this kind, foods often appear in a wide
range of literary texts, those of high status, such as Homer's *Odyssey*, as well as
those which may draw on the humbler levels of society, such as elegy and
invective. In the fifth century, comedy was the standard-bearer of food texts, as
is demonstrated by the extent to which Athenaeus draws on comedy for his
examples. For this late author, comedy has much to say about food, and is
organized under such headings as sea bass, radish, cabbage, trotters. Comedy
also concerns itself with the ritual accompaniments of the *deipnon* (meal) and
sumposion (drinking party), the garlands, the party girls, the drinking songs,
and the games. Athenaeus often approaches food on a material level; hence his
lists of vegetables and fruits may pick out comic fragments for the mere mention of radish or cabbage, while in fact the fragment may have a greater depth,
as in the case of Hermippus' fragment 63. Sometimes Athenaeus will consider a
social or ethnographical aspect of eating, as for example in his discussion of the
parasite or of styles of dining in Greek and other cities.

Much of what we know of foods in Athens itself comes from comedy
through Athenaeus, names of various breads, fish consumed, fruits, and so on.
In this respect Athenaeus resembles Pollux whose *Onomastikon* lists fish, chefs,
breads and other items, some of which he supports with quotation from comedy. In many respects we know more of food in the comic polis than we do in
Athens itself. There is no space here to explore the relationship between them

in their foods, but our understanding of that relationship depends on the approach adopted. At a statistical level, Gallant finds comedy useless for the analysis of fish consumption in Athens;[12] at the level of material culture, Sparkes finds a good correlation between comedy and the cooking equipment found in the agora;[13] at an ideological level, Davidson finds the comic polis analogous to Athens in its association of fish with luxurious eating.[14] For his part, Athenaeus' most common qualification of comic poets is not of censure for inaccuracy but of praise for their wit (χάρις) and their witness to an ancient reality.

Foods are frequently represented in comedy through the medium of social organization: in Old Comedy the food is often (but not always—see below) presented in the context of festival or religious ritual at the triumphant conclusion of the play; in later comedy, the symposium and entertainments associated with drinking became more important. That is not to say that sympotic themes are not to be found in Old Comedy or sacrifice and festival in Middle, but there has been a significant change in emphasis. The change may be illustrated by comparing the scene of feasting at the end of *Acharnians*, in which the protagonist's delight in his splendid feast at the Anthesteria is incorporated into his contest with the hungry warrior Lamachus, with a typical speech by a chef of Middle Comedy, in which the nature of the food and the chef's skills of preparation are the focus of attention. Athenaeus gives examples of such speeches at 7.290b–293e and 8.403d–405f.

The importance of the social and religious codes of dining is reflected in comedy by the representation of the ritual outsider, the figure who does not partake in the ritual system, and whose differentness highlights the sense of participation of the group. Such figures in comedy include the *bômolochos* (one who, though not a member of the group of sacrificers, steals meat from the altar), the parasite (one who is not invited but shares the meal), and to a lesser extent the cook who makes extravagant claims for his skill, which others consider mundane or utilitarian. The *bômolochos* is rare in comedy: Aristophanes denies a place in his comedy for behavior metaphorically associated with the *bômolochos* (*Clouds* 969, *Peace* 748, *Frogs* 358, 1085, 1521),[15] but the importance of this character is more structural than apparent on the stage. There is some trace in Old Comedy of the chef and parasite, but they are important later, in Middle and New Comedy as Nesselrath has illustrated.[16] Dohm was hard-pressed to identify the sausage seller of *Knights* as a full comic chef (μάγειρος), despite his skills in the preparation, cooking, and vending of meat,[17] and Arnott has argued that the comic parasite as such is rightly assigned to Alexis (Middle Comedy) even though the social phenomenon was reflected in comedy much earlier, in the *Hope or Wealth* of Epicharmus, the *Flatterers* of Eupolis and perhaps in the *Chiron* of Pherecrates.[18] Athenaeus discusses Eupolis in his treatment of the parasite (6.236e–237a): Eupolis' flatterers were the hangers-on of rich men on their way to banquets, one of the rich men being Callias, son of Hipponicus (Eupolis test. ii K.-A.). Many of the fragments lead us to expect that expenditure was on luxurious foods, contrasting with the frugality or meanness in buying foods of Hipponicus, father of Callias (fr. 156). The presence of the parasite or flatterer implies both ritualized eating among a peer group to which he does not belong and eating at a level which makes gate-crashing worthwhile. The chef and the parasite live by their words and their wit as much as by their culinary and social skills, and in later comedy take on a literary and dramatic life of their own, to such an extent that in the *Pseudolus* of Plautus the chef adopts a metatheatrical aspect as poet.[19]

II

Gregory Crane demonstrates in his essay the material world into which comedy casts the affairs of the Athenian state. That material world is rich in association with many aspects of religious, social, and cultural life, as I have shown above. This section demonstrates how Aristophanes' *Knights*, the play that above all others reduces Athenian politicians to screaming market hawkers and creatures of appetite and animality, at the same time maintains a strict adherence to the sacrificial code of the city. While on one level the exuberant hawkers challenge the power structure of the city in forms of Bakhtinian festivity, on another level order is maintained in the ritualized treatment of animals.

Aristophanes' Knights

Knights concerns the Athenian demos and the operation of the political system under the domination of Cleon, which is represented in terms deriving from the processing of animals, the tanning of hides, and the preparation, cooking, and eating of foods. In addition to the processing of animals, the play is structured around systems of eating. Cleon has been honored by the polis, apparently for his success as general at Pylos,[20] and is given food in the prytaneion at the city's hearth.[21] As the play proceeds, his feasting at the prytaneion comes to be viewed from a different perspective, as the fattening-up of the *pharmakos* at the Thargelia festival prior to expulsion from the city. The play concludes with the expulsion of Cleon from the prytaneion: no longer the honored citizen, he is now the φαρμακός (1405). Cleon's place at the hearth is taken by the black-pudding seller, the seller of the lesser sacrificial meats. Demos meanwhile, the gullible old fool who has been spoon-fed like a baby, regains his wits, reveals that contrary to appearances he has in fact controlled the consumption of food for his own benefit, and is rejuvenated to his full powers by boiling in the cauldron of the black-pudding seller.

The play reduces leading politicians to slaves, and matters of state and military policy to the level of the material, the physical, and the bestial. The focus is on the agora, largely to the exclusion of the Acropolis and Pnyx, and within this space two areas of activity dominate: eating at the hearth of the polis in the prytaneion, and preparing animal carcasses for sale. (Though we do not know the precise site of the prytaneion on the southern edge of the agora, it is to be considered, if not as part of the agora, at least in close association with it.)[22] The protagonists, the Paphlagonian slave and the black-pudding seller, each struggle for inclusion in the agora and at the sacred hearth of the prytaneion, and seek to exclude the other from these spaces. In presenting two spaces, the prytaneion as a place of honorific eating and the agora as civic space, Aristophanes has created a special agora for his protagonists who fear exclusion from it and expulsion beyond the city gates: in Athens itself, the sale of goods was conducted both within the agora and beyond the gates. Tanning was almost certainly conducted outside.

Trade in Animal Products Both the black-pudding seller and Paphlagon are sellers of animal products. The commercial activity in the agora is not often attacked in other plays (see, e.g., *Peace* 999), but here it is linked with the selling of political favors (cf. Crane above on *Wasps*). In addition, the commerce in this case offends the nose (tanning) and is a terrible trade (black-pudding selling). Terms deriving from food processes abound in the play, and are frequently applied as metaphors with a political significance to the contest between the black-pudding seller and Paphlagon (there are many tanning terms, which I do not cite here): lines 55–57 (making barley cakes), 213–16 (sausage making), 364, 372, 374, 375–81 (meat processing), and 769–72 (food preparation).

Now the antagonists are at the same time processors of meat products (the one treats the outside of the beast, the other the inside) and terrible monsters who tear each other apart tooth and claw and greedily fill their bellies just as Paphlagon cuts up strips of animal hide for his shoes and the black-pudding seller stuffs forcemeat into animal guts. They are dealers in animals, who are themselves presented as various kinds of animal, human and otherwise. In an oracle they are represented as eagle and serpent (197–98); Paphlagon is hit in the guts by the bestial chorus (ὑφ' οἵων θηρίων γαστρίζομαι, line 273), and again at lines 453–56; at lines 284–304 the contest is characterized by a screaming voice; they threaten each other with various processes (369–80), including the treatment of Paphlagon as a pig; at lines 708–9 they threaten to claw each other apart; at lines 1121–40 politicians fed at state expense are seen as sacrificial victims. Animality is important in this comedy (just as in *Peace* the focus is on cereals and plants, represented in human form by the vegetative protagonist Trygaeus [Vintage Man] and his bride Opora [Autumn Fruits]). The combatants take on the bad qualities of animals (swinishness); their physicality and their ferocious aggression are stressed; they become potential sacrificial victims. These terms allow the poet to dwell on the physical aspects of meat eating and on the ways in which parts of animals resemble parts of humans,[23] and human aggression can be reduced to bestiality. Within this debate, however, there is a notable division between the black-pudding seller—who in his trade and in his rhetoric operates within the sacrificial system, as it were as a *mageiros*, a sacrificer and seller of meat—and Paphlagon, who draws on foods outside the sacrificial system (e.g., Milesian sea bass), is represented as the pig who suffers the violence of the *mageiros*, and at the end of the play is forced to take over the trade of the black-pudding seller, but outside the gates and outside the sacrificial system, since he will sell donkey and dog meat.[24]

The Stealing of Foods At 457–58, the black-pudding seller is greeted by the chorus: ὦ γεννικώτατον κρέας ψυχήν τ' ἄριστε πάντων / καὶ τῇ πόλει σωτὴρ φανεὶς ἡμῖν τε τοῖς πολίταις ("O most noble meat and best of all in spirit, and savior manifest for our city and us citizens"). What is signified in the chorus's warm approval for this "noble meat" and "manifest savior for the city"? He is an ironic savior, loathsome at the outset and desired only as the vanquisher of Paphlagon (143–49), but by the end of the play he has transformed the city. The *bōmolochos*, the thief of meat, literally, in this case, from the butcher's stalls in the market (411–28), has become savior of the city.

Paphlagon too is a thief of food (52, 56, 205), of the Spartan barley cake which comically represents the victory at Pylos, a victory that, it is implied, belonged to Demosthenes. The greedy snatching of food and the greedy consumption of food have negative and positive charges: corruption and political rapacity is suggested, but at the same time there is a triumphing in rascality, and it is through stealing Paphlagon's hare that the black-pudding seller wins the contest. Theft from the prytaneion is not acceptable. Much of the plot concerns the removal of the unworthy Cleon/Paphlagon from his honorific eating at state expense with those who are deserving, the tyrannicides, Olympic victors, and benefactors. Cleon is the earliest Athenian general so honored,[25] according to Osborne (1981). Instead of the frugal eating appropriate to the sacred hearth and exemplified by generals of an earlier generation (575–78),

Paphlagon feasts to his heart's content: he "eats up the public assets" (258); he licks the cakes (103–4); he goes in with an empty stomach, comes out with a full, and brings out bread, meat, and saltfish (280–83); and he does nothing in return for this honorific feasting (765–66). The prytaneion is humorously presented as a possible location for other pleasures to two others, Cratinus, who is said on account of his comedies to deserve drink rather than food in the prytaneion (535),[26] and the black-pudding seller who is offered oral sex instead of feasting at lines 167–68 (as if he were going to a rowdy private symposium). Both the black-pudding seller and Paphlagon in their verbal contests are, in addition to thieves, consumers with large appetites. Paphlagon, for example, wolfs down tuna and wine and Milesian sea bass (353–61), while the black-pudding seller consumes entrails, meat soup, and beef ribs (356–62). At lines 691–709 the "animals" express their verbal aggression in threats to eat each other. Appetite is both to be deprecated in a metaphorical system in which it represents political corruption, and to be admired in the contest for control in the city. Both antagonists, furthermore, vie to offer food to Demos, to control him by controlling his diet, as if he were a child. At lines 716ff., food is not consumed, but is masticated for Demos, that is, presented to him in a controlled way, regulating the quantity and perhaps quality of what he eats.

Sacrifice Control, however, is not quite what it seems. As the play proceeds, the violence becomes rather different in focus, and moves from the animality and secular processing to the ritual violence of the Thargelia,[27] the driving out of the *pharmakos*, and the animal sacrifice.[28] Demos is no longer the idiotic childlike dotard but the controller of sacrificial violence; at the same time, the black-pudding seller realizes his promise sought earlier in the play—that he would save the city. Demos aims to kill the politicians as *dêmosia*, a term explained by the scholiast on line 1136 as "the so-called scapegoats who purify the cities with their own blood, or the creatures fed at public expense by the city." He claims that far from being fed as if a child by politicians while they, exploiting his naiveté, stole the people's foods, he was in fact fattening them for slaughter. Cleon, prepared earlier with feeding in the prytaneion, is now ready in all his swinishness and animality for sacrifice. However, he is not sacrificed. He suffers the alternative ritual violence of being driven out, and the black-pudding seller uses his skills as *mageiros* to boil Demos as he would the entrails and lesser meats. Boiling restores both his youth and the integrity of politics in Athens. It seems to be important that this is a ritualized action properly performed: this is not some metaphorical or literary effect such as that found in *Pseudolus* and in the rejuvenation of Philemon's fragment 82. There we find extravagant boasts made by a commercial cook, here a symbolic action. I have shown elsewhere that the imagery in this play is remarkably tightly controlled, and also that the apportionment of foods to Paphlagon and the black-pudding seller is coherent and controlled with care.[29]

I have discussed *Knights* from an alimentary perspective in order to highlight the complex ways in which Aristophanes has adapted associations of foods into the play. There are many related considerations, the most important of which—mythical and festive elements, gigantomachy and the triumph of the outsider—have been discussed by Bowie.[30] It is clear, however, that the themes related to food are particularly prominent in the play, and do not merely provide a ridiculous background against which the political debate may be played out. *Knights* is, as we have seen, replete with the popular-festive elements of the marketplace, aggressive animality, and the grotesque. As the play proceeds, there appear the further elements of sacrifice and festival of purification for which the aggressive "animals" have been prepared.

III

Simplicity and Abundance in Attica

The hostility to the marketing of foods is unusually pronounced in *Knights*, but is found elsewhere. The foods associated with Paphlagon, the fish and cakes, may not necessarily imply luxury and corruption, as they do in this play, though fish will often do so, as Davidson has demonstrated.[31] The loathsome nature of the trade of the dealer in forcemeats and identifiable parts of the animal is not stressed when these products are cited elsewhere,[32] though those are the parts of the animal that are particularly prominent in comedy. Demos' preference for the countryside and the rustic diet possible in peacetime (805–6: χῖδρα, "rough wheat"; στέμφυλος, "pressed olives") is familiar elsewhere in comedy, but is not a universal preference. The country is preferred in Aristophanes' *Farmers* (fr. 111) and *Islands* (fr. 402), and there is a clear preference for the benefits of peace and the countryside in plays such as *Acharnians* and *Peace*. This may be because of wartime privation but it is also because the countryside is a center for food production, and a location for the ideas of plenty and the traditional, which comedy espouses. Food comes from the countryside and in comedy is powerfully associated with the comic gods Demeter and Dionysus. Thus in the all-Greek countryside of *Peace*, plays of Sophocles and Euripides and festivals Dionysiac and otherwise return in peacetime as well as the possibilities of vine production. (Drama *was* produced at the Dionysiac festivals in wartime, but comedy claims it was not.) With fertility of the soil will come fertility of humans, weddings, and drinking, which brings fertility of invention in the poetic mind. Blessings (ἀγαθά) of this kind are central to comedy. The Dionysiac takes over. I have shown the ways in which foods in a wide cultural context are important in some plays of Aristophanes. *Plutus* or *Ecclesiazousae* could as easily have been chosen as plays from the period of the Peloponnesian War. What is clear in the surviving plays of Aristophanes is prima facie to be hypothesized elsewhere, not necessarily in terms of whole plays, but in individual passages at least.

Toward the end of *Knights*, Athena is presented as both the bather of Demos (1090–91) and as the manufacturer of bread scoops (1168–69), a soup stirrer (1172), and provider of other foods. The bathing is of a special kind, for the goddess is ladling health and wealth over Demos, but the tasks are in general humble tasks for a goddess. Gods often occur in such contexts in comedy. In *The Basketbearers* of Hermippus, Dionysus takes over the importation of foods in the spring. In the *Phaon* of Plato Comicus—a mythological love story presumably—the fragments which survive demonstrate comedy's adaptation of the themes of food and sex in a context of festival, and fragment 188 is a speech by Courotrophus giving lewd instructions for festive offerings.

Comic gods are prominent in the *Marriage of Hebe* of Epicharmus. Here is a comic tradition earlier than Attic, and based in another polis. The thirty-five surviving fragments record lists of fish, birds, and breads; these are foods for a feast (eating is clear in frr. 42, 56, 63; there are eating vessels in fr. 70). Three fragments imply that gods are eating these fish (frr. 42, 54, 71). That gods should show any concern for low-grade molluscs (fr. 42.11), the excrement of the parrotfish (fr. 54), or the salting of the *elops* is a feature of the comic polis in which human and divine come closer. Humans in the real polis may share foods with gods at *theoxeniai*, but in comedy the gods can feast as if they were humans. We do not know enough of this play or of Syracuse to make any large claims, whether for instance this magnificent banquet of fish—presumably the wedding feast of Heracles and Hebe—in any way reflected dining at the court of Hiero. What we can say is that nothing comparable is known for Attica until the fourth century.

There are lists of foods in Old Comedy, as we have seen, including fish; there are banqueting scenes, but nothing on this scale. Does this reflect local conditions of dining and their representation? This is likely, though hazardous to assert in view of our Athenocentric perception of the ancient world, and the dependence of that perception on the comic polis. Certainly Attic comedy constructs a contrasting picture of lavish dining elsewhere (Athenaeus in book 4 cites plentiful material, much of it comedy from the fourth century, for the extravagance of such peoples as the Thessalians and Persians, and such cities as Thebes and Syracuse) and of the Athenians' comparative simplicity. Thus the bad son in Aristophanes' *Banqueters* is said to have learned "how to drink, to sing badly, about Syracusan dining and the feasts of Sybaris" (fr. 225). Attica, it is asserted, is not a location of rich dining. This comic presentation may be a considerable distortion of eating in the city, but it is an important element in the identity of the comic polis.

Attica identifies itself as a place of modest consumption in both Old and Middle Comedy, to be contrasted with its greedy and unrestrained neighbors. Food in Old Comedy, when not contrasted with Persians or others, appears to be based on the comic polis in festive mode or in rustic bliss. There may be some exceptions in fragmentary plays which show lists of foods consumed without their context, but the majority testify to some form of festivity such as that found in Aristophanes *Tagenistae* and *Thesmophoriazousae* B. There is in addition a remarkable series of fragments based on dining of a special kind, in other places and with unlimited and effortless production based on the era before slavery, the "ancient life" or "golden age." Athenaeus, through the voice of the character Democritus (6.267e–270a), presents the fragments in chronological order from *Wealths* of Cratinus, *Beasts* of Crates, *Amphictyons* of Telekleides, *Miners* and *Persians* of Pherecrates, *Tagenistae* of Aristophanes, *Sirens* of Nicophon, and *Thurio-Persians* of Metagenes. In these passages, the food provided is plentiful and in most cases automatic: by no use of slaves Athenaeus clearly means that they were not needed for food production or preparation (slaves are present as servers and as players of games). These passages complement the passages about Attica in which a return to agricultural production is earnestly sought (*Acharnians*, *Peace*, *Farmers*), and an abundant supply is granted by the agricultural gods (there is "automatic" food at *Ach*. 969 and *Peace* 1313–15). They are idealized and, most importantly, located in other times and places, in the Age of Cronus (the Ploutoi or Wealths of Cratinus are Titans under their lord Cronus), in the underworld (*Miners* and *Tagenistae*), to the East (*Persians*) and to the West (*Thurio-Persians*). From the point of view of presentation, parody of other texts is clearly present, and the passages also have something in common with the Cockaigne scenes in later European literature.[33] They also show the way in which contemporaries worked very closely in parallel (this is expressed as plagiarism in Aristophanes' *Clouds* and Cratinus' *Wine Flask*). There is more to these fragments than parody and the life of ease, however, for some of them hint at anodoi of gods and the provision of good things by the earth or the divine forces under the earth. I cite only the *Miners* of Pherecrates (fr. 113):

They were all blended with wealth,
Worked in all good things in every way.
Rivers full of porridge and black soup
Flowed murmuring through the narrows
Together with the bread scoops. There were bits of cheese cake too.
All this made it easy for a rich oily mouthful automatically
To slip down the throats of the dead.
There were blood puddings and boiling slices of black pudding
Sizzling on the riverbanks, scattered like shells.
There were roast steaks nicely presented in various sauces
And eel steaks wrapped in beet leaves . . .

A woman describes her visit to the underworld, but the rivers of fear and forgetfulness and wailing have been replaced by streams of porridge and cooked meats that feast the dead. The earth is the provider of good things and here provides the dead (the blessed) with all the goods for which the living have to labor endlessly. (The blessed are presented as the truly happy ones in Aristophanes' *Tagenistae* fr. 504.) The dead are present at a kind of symposium, combined with the geography of the underworld. This vision of the dead feasting perhaps resembles the gods feasting in *The Marriage of Hebe*: in comedy human eating patterns and human foods may be enjoyed by other categories of being that in the everyday polis were accessible only by strictly defined ritual foods. For the comic polis, this is a description of others (humans, gods, or the dead) feasting in a way better than was possible for the typical citizen of the comic polis of Athens.

In some plays, the gods who protect Athens do not feast extensively either. In Chionides' *Beggars* (fr. 7), which describes a simple meal given by the Athenians to the Dioscuri, the gods receive, in a form of *theoxenia*, cheese, barley cake, olives, and leeks in the prytaneion "in memory," according to Athenaeus (4.137e), "of the old way of life." Here there are combined simplicity, antiquity, and that central hearth of the polis. The ideal form of eating in Athens, or at least in comic Athens, is exemplified in the food of its gods at its civic hearth. Its self-image is contained in ritual and tradition. For the comic polis these two sanctions are as important as economic and agricultural strength, if not more so. Other humble eating by the gods verges on the burlesque: Heracles in Attic comedy, as far as we know, consumes pea soup in the fifth century. Heracles the mighty carnivore, established early in comedy by Epicharmus (fr. 21), does not appear in the Attic comic polis until the fourth century—Hermes is the god hungry for meat.[34] In Old Comedy, the gods are as likely to be starved as feasted, and in that way reflect an important feature of

Athens' self-image. For the comic polis, such gods maintain the important combination of the humble with the powerfully symbolic.

Notes

1. Douglas 1984 and Powers and Powers 1984.

2. Chang 1977, 1–22 n. 4.

3. Approaches to the significance of foods specific to Greek culture have been developed in, e.g., Longo and Scarpi 1989, Detienne and Vernant 1989 on sacrificial ritual, Detienne 1977 on structural approaches to religious ritual, Schmitt-Pantel 1992 on eating in the context of the polis, and Murray 1990 on the significance of the symposium in the polis. To these may be added Garnsey 1988 on trade and famine and Forbes and Foxhall 1982 on comparative ethnography. Gowers 1993 has examined the representation of foods in Latin poetry, and is one of a number of studies that draw on the festive model of Bakhtin 1968, which has been so influential in studies of comedy. Some of the fragments discussed in this essay are treated in Fauth 1973.

4. The comic fragments are cited from R. Kassel and C. Austin, *Poetae Comici Graeci* (Berlin, 1984–), except for Epicharmus who is cited from G. Kaibel, *Comicorum Graecorum Fragmenta I* (Leipzig, 1899).

5. Douglas 1984.

6. See Thiercy 1993.

7. On these festivals see Burkert 1985, 101, 240.

8. An Attic oenochoe from the Athenian Agora, P23907, and an Apulian bell-krater, St. Petersburg, Hermitage Museum inv. 2074, both of the fourth century.

9. Athenaeus 3.111b; Pickard-Cambridge 1968, 61–62, 213.

10. Burkert 1983, 200–201; Pickard-Cambridge 1968, 12–13.

11. Wilkins and Hill 1994.

12. Gallant 1985.

13. Sparkes 1962.

14. Davidson 1993.

15. In these passages the language of the *bōmolochos* is at issue as much as his behavior: cf. Ar. *Gerutades* fr. 171 χαριεντίζμ καὶ καταπαίζεις ἡμῶν καὶ βωμολοχεύηι· ("you are witty and mocking at our expense and are a *bōmolochos*").

16. Nesselrath 1990.

17. Dohm 1964.

18. Arnott 1968.

19. Gowers 1993, 93–107.

20. Osborne 1981, 162.

21. For the importance of the prytaneion as the hearth of the polis, for categories of persons feasted there, for the role of the prytaneis and the relationship between prytaneion and Tholos, see Miller 1978 and Osborne 1981.

22. Cf. Crane above and Schmitt-Pantel 1992, esp. 145–77.

23. Bakhtin 1968, 303–67, and Gowers 1993, 74–76.

24. See further Wilkins 1994.

25. Osborne 1981. It does not affect the argument here if this honor for Cleon is a construction only of the comic polis, though the question is a concern for the relationship between polis and comic polis.

26. The drinking of Cratinus may have been a trademark, his special Dionysiac activity: it certainly featured in his *Wine Flask* of 423.

27. The scholiast on εἰρεσιώνη (729) links the sacred branch with the festivals of the Thargelia

and Pyanopsia: see Burkert 1985, 101. Sommerstein (ad loc.) prefers the latter, but the driving out of the scapegoat (1405) is a feature of the Thargelia, not the Pyanopsia.

28. For the relationship between the expulsion of the scapegoat and the controlled violence of animal sacrifice, see Bremmer 1983, 299–320, esp. 315–18.

29. Wilkins 1994.

30. Bowie 1993.

31. Davidson 1993.

32. Wilkins and Hill 1994.

33. Baldry 1953.

34. A possible exception to this is *Birds* 1583ff. where Heracles is certainly interested in the birds being roasted.

Bibliography

Arnott, W. G. 1968. "Studies in Comedy, I: Alexis and the Parasite's Name." *GRBS* 9.161–68.

Bakhtin, M. 1968. *Rabelais and His World*. Boston.

Baldry, H. 1953. "The Idlers' Paradise in Attic Comedy." *G&R* 22.49–60.

Bowie, A. M. 1993. *Aristophanes: Myth, Ritual and Society*. Cambridge.

Bremmer, J. 1983. "Scapegoat Rituals in Ancient Greece." *HSCP* 87.299–320.

Burkert W. 1983. *Homo Necans*. Berkeley.

———. 1985. *Greek Religion*. Translated by J. Raffan. Oxford.

Chang, K. 1977. *Food in Chinese Culture*. New Haven.

Davidson, J. 1993. "Fish, Sex and Revolution." *Classical Quarterly* 43.53–66.

Detienne, M. 1977. *The Gardens of Adonis*. Atlantic Highlands, N.J.

Detienne, M., and J.-P. Vernant. 1989. *The Cuisine of Sacrifice among the Greeks*. Chicago.

Dohm, H. 1964. *Mageiros*. Munich.

Douglas, M. 1984. *Food in the Social Order: Studies of Food and Festivities in Three American Communities*. New York.

Fauth, W. 1973. "Kulinarisches und Utopisches in der griechischen Komödie." *Wiener Studien* 7.39–62.

Forbes, H., and L. Foxhall. 1982. "*Sitometreia*: The Role of Grain as a Staple Food in Classical Antiquity." *Chiron* 12.41–90.

Gallant, T. 1985. *A Fisherman's Tale*. Ghent.

Garnsey, P. D. A. 1988. *Famine and Food Supply in the Graeco-Roman World*. Cambridge.

Gowers, E. 1993. *The Loaded Table*. Oxford.

Longo, O., and P. Scarpi. 1989. *Homo Edens*. Verona.

Miller, S. G. 1978. *The Prytaneion: Its Function and Architectural Form*. Berkeley.

Murray, O. 1990. *Sympotica*. Oxford.

Nesselrath, H.-G. 1990. *Die attische Mittlere Komödie: Ihre Stellung in der antiken Literaturkritik und Literaturgeschichte*. Berlin.

Osborne, M. J. 1981. "Entertainment in the Prytaneion at Athens." *ZPE* 41.153–70.

Pickard-Cambridge, A. W. 1968. *The Dramatic Festivals of Athens*. Oxford.

Powers, W. K., and M. M. N. Powers. 1984. "Metaphysical Aspects of the Oglala Food System." In *Food in the Social Order*, edited by Douglas, 40–96.

Schmitt-Pantel, P. 1992. *La cité au banquet: Histoire des repas publics dans les cités grecques*. Rome.

Sparkes, B. A. 1962. "The Greek Kitchen." *JHS* 82.121–37.

Thiercy, P. 1993. "Les odeurs de la Polis ou le 'nez' d' Aristophane." In *Tragedy, Comedy and the Polis*, edited by A. H. Sommerstein, S. Halliwell, J. Henderson, and B. Zimmermann, 505–26. Papers from the Greek Drama Conference, Nottingham, 18–20 July 1990. Bari.

Wilkins, J. M. 1993. "The Significance of Food and Eating in Greek Comedy." *Liverpool Classical Monthly* 18.66–74.

——. 1994. "The Regulation of Meat in the *Knights* of Aristophanes." In *Tria Lustra*, edited by H. D. Jocelyn and H. Hurt, 119–26. Liverpool.

Wilkins, J. M., and S. Hill. 1994. "Fishheads of Ancient Greece." In *Proceedings of the Oxford Food Symposium* (1993), edited by H. Walker, 241–44. London.

PART THREE

The New Comic Polis

HEINZ-GÜNTHER NESSELRATH

The Polis of Athens
in Middle Comedy

Greek comedy has always been one of the most valuable sources for investigating and reconstructing the life of that Greek polis where most of the plays about which we still know something were written and performed: Athens. Within the roughly 250 years of development that Athenian comedy went through, the depiction of Athenian life changed considerably. In the so-called Old Comedy we get a really broad, all-encompassing view of Athens and its inhabitants, of their public and private life, of the functioning of their political institutions, and of their numerous involvements with the outside world. In New Comedy many of these aspects have either vanished completely or have been reduced to a minimum: what we now usually see is a quiet street in some residential quarter of Athens, with a few people pursuing their private lives and having to cope with some temporary disturbances that befall them. Of politics we hear almost nothing, and the only contact with the big outside world—in most cases—may be a pompous mercenary soldier who blunders into this little bourgeois world and usually plays a prominent part in its temporary disruption.

Between Old and New Comedy, there lie six to eight decades of what is usually called Middle Comedy. What does Athens look like in the comic plays of this period? Answering this question is much more difficult than for either Old or New Comedy, because instead of complete plays (as in Old Comedy) or nearly complete plays (as in New) we have to make do with a mass of mostly unconnected and unconnectable fragments, which in very many cases look like pathetic little pieces left over from vast puzzles. Still, some fragments are not as hopeless as others; and in this essay I shall try to gather and discuss some of those that may even today give us an insight into what aspects of Athenian polis life were presented—and seem to have been most prominent and characteristic—on the comic stage between approximately 380 and 320 B.C.

First of all, what about politics? In the fragments of the Middle Comic poets, one encounters the names of more than twenty Athenians who were more or less prominently involved in the politics of their time; many of them are still identifiable from other sources, but some appear only in those fragments (which makes the task of placing them more accurately within the political history of Athens in those times almost hopeless). Still, the very number of these people mentioned in Middle Comedy indicates that political awareness and reflections of political life in these plays are on a level still comparable with those of Old Comedy. In what we might call the "first generation" of Middle Comic poets, a very prominent position is held by Eubulus who seems to have started producing plays around 375 B.C.[1] and, in the course of several decades, wrote more than one hundred of them. We still have some scathing comments by Eubulus on prominent Athenian politicians of the 360s and 350s that might readily be assigned to a poet of Old Comedy. Just like them, he acidly ridicules the very influential Callistratus of Aphidna for being a passive homosexual ('Αντιόπη, fr. 10 K.-A.); in one fragment, Callistratus is even downright identified with the broad πρωκτός that he needs for this activity (Eubulus, Σφιγγοκαρίων fr. 106.5 K.-A.).

Eubulus' jokes do not stop at the borders of Attica. There is a considerable number (six in all, more than any other comic poet has to offer) of fragments in which he makes fun of the boorish Boeotians who do nothing but eat all day. With these attacks, Eubulus probably reflects the palpable tensions that had arisen between Athens and Thebes in the years after the startling Theban victory over the Spartans at Leuctra in 372. In those years Thebes looked like it was becoming the foremost hegemonial power in Greece, a prospect that was very little to the taste of the old imperial power, Athens. On the other side, Eubulus was not stinting with satiric forays against the inner-Athenian political system, either. In a fragment from his play Γλαῦκος, someone relates how he once was able to persuade the Athenians to take up their weapons and go on an expedition against, of all things, gold-digging ants and their treasuries that some rumor had detected in Mount Hymettus (fr. 19 K.-A.)! This is surely a dig against the lighthearted credulity of the Athenian body politic,[2] and the speaker could be one of those politicians who apparently were able to convince their followers of anything. Even more cynical is a fragment from the play Ὀλβία,[3] 74 K.-A., in which two people rival with each other in enumerating all the good things that can be had for money in Athens: Speaker A happily—and naively—thinks of the wondrous varieties of foodstuffs, while his sardonic interlocutor B bitingly adds, how everything in the legislating assemblies and the lawcourts can be bought for money, too.

Another comic poet quite contemporary with Eubulus, Anaxandrides,[4] did not spare the Athenian politicians of those times, either. In his Πρωτεσίλαος, a play that probably still belonged to the 380s, he not only castigated the dubious behavior of the opportunistic politician Melanopos (fr. 41 K.-A.), he also commemorated—in a very exuberant passage— the lavish nuptials of the Athenian general Iphicrates with a Thracian princess (fr. 42 K.-A.). Even the obviously mythical theme of this play (the hero Protesilaus was the first Greek hero to get killed in the Trojan war)[5] did not prevent the poet from bringing in contemporary politics. Like Eubulus, Anaxandrides' stage comments on the contemporary world did not remain within Athenian boundaries. In a play called Πόλεις, a speaker waxes very eloquent about why he can't imagine being an ally of Egyptians (fr. 40 K.-A.). In the late 360s there arose indeed a situation when Egyptians, rebelling against their Persian overlords, sought assistance from various Greek powers, Athens among them. Even more significant than this fragment may be the title of the play to which it once belonged. A rather famous play[6] called Πόλεις had already been produced by Eupolis; in it, the title apparently indicated the various Greek allies—or, to put it more realistically, subjects—of the sea-ruling Athenians, and these Πόλεις seemingly formed the (allegorical) chorus of the play. Could there have been something similar in Anaxandrides' play? It might at least have been produced in a similar political landscape: In 377/6 the second Athenian maritime alliance had come into existence, and for the next two decades at least there was once more a sizable number of Greek cities around the Aegean following Athens' lead.

Something like the political allegory that we may assume in Old Comedy plays with titles like Πόλεις, Νῆσοι, Δῆμοι was still possible about half a century later in Middle Comedy, as can be shown from a long fragment of Ephippus, yet another poet of those decades between 375 and 340.[7] In fragment 5 K.-A. (from his play Γηρυόνης) a speaker describes how a giant fish (bigger, in fact, than Crete) is being prepared for the dinner table of the even more gigantic king Geryones; within the course of the description there appear the names of various peoples (and city populations), so that in the end one gets the impression that the whole Aegean forms the vast cauldron in which the giant fish is being broiled, with the adjacent peoples providing various assisting services. What— obviously vast—political enterprise, encompassing the whole Aegean and maybe even more, is being alluded to in this description? Could it have been a bold design planned by an even bolder Athenian leader wanting to restore his native city to its former greatness? It has been proposed that the Athenian general Timotheos might lurk behind the totally oversized Geryones;[8] but if we try to get much more specific about the other details of the situation here hinted at, we very soon run into serious difficulties.[9] In any case, the Athenian audience surely knew what Ephippus' speaker was talking about, and it certainly enjoyed his ingenious depiction of the Aegean situation.

Perhaps the most interesting allegorizing fragment that apparently comments on the contemporary Greek political situation is to be found in Heniochus, a Middle Comic poet of whom there is not much left. If we didn't have the explicit statement of the Suda Lexicon that Heniochus belonged to Middle Comedy (test. 1 K.-A.), we would be hard put to assign this very little known poet (of whom only five fragments and the titles of eight plays have been preserved) to any definite period of Attic comedy at all.[10] For all the obscurity surrounding Heniochus, however, the last of his five fragments (and we do not even know to which of his plays it once belonged) may be called a real gem. It is a passage of eighteen iambic lines, which probably once formed part of a prologue; the speaker of these lines introduces us to an assembly of (as he makes clear already in line 2) the Greek poleis themselves who have come together in Olympia, a place of Panhellenic implication, as is well known, to celebrate a sacrificial feast because of their newly won freedom. After this celebration, however, they have all sunk into a debilitating torpor: "Since that feast indecision has brought them low, being their host from day to day and holding them under her sway for a long time already. Moreover, two women are always with them and throw them into disarray: one is named Demokratia, the other Aristokratia; on behalf of them, they've already often lost their minds . . ." (12–18). The antagonism of democratic and oligarchic governments was a constant feature of inner-Greek political strife at least since the times of the Peloponnesian War; it was especially virulent in the first half of the fourth century, until the rise of Philip II forced the Greek city-states to assign first priority to the Macedonian threat.[11] But what is the situation alluded to in line 11, "when they [the poleis] more or less got free from the φόροι"? Wilamowitz[12] connected this allusion with the time, when the Second Athenian League was founded (377/6), Breitenbach[13] with the aftermath of the battle of Chaeronea (338).[14] One might, however, consider also a period in the middle of the 350s, after the Athenians had lost the Social War (which effectively meant the end of the Second League) and a sizable number of poleis really got free once more from Athenian overlordship.[15] The remarks about the debilitating constraints of ἀβουλία also might remind us of the words with which Xenophon described the effects of the battle at Mantinea in 363 and concluded his *Hellenica*: ἀκρισία δὲ καὶ ταραχὴ ἔτι πλείων μετὰ τὴν μάχην ἐγένετο ἢ πρόσθεν ἐν τῇ Ἑλλάδι ("After the battle, confusion and disturbance got even bigger in Greece than they had been before").

So far, we have considered several comic poets and their comments on the Athenian and Greek political situation, which probably belong to the decades between 380 and 350. After reviewing these comments, can we really say that they are only a weak echo of the bold political statements of Old Comedy? Quite the contrary, for they seem to tell of a sustained interest of those poets in Athenian and general Greek political developments. Moreover, even after 350 one cannot lightly talk about a decline of statements on politics in comedy: as far as a chronological sequence can at all be established, there is between 380 and 320 no real sign that mentionings of politics and politicians in the fragments are decreasing. If anything, one might even observe a sort of increase of "political" fragments right up to the end of the life and times of Demosthenes. One of the most political poets of those later decades[16] of the Middle Comic period was Timocles, who was active from about the middle of the 340s onward and whose fragments yield a wealth of political allusion and invective that easily rivals the corresponding material of most Old Comic poets. One must remember that those decades were, after all, one of the most decisive periods in the political history of Athens. In the course of those years Athens, the one-time leader of much of the Greek world, entered into the final struggle with Philip II and, because of the battle of Chaeronea and its aftermath, at last succumbed to the rise of Macedonian power. Until the end of the 320s it was still able to preserve some sort of maneuvering room as an independent polis, but after the death of Demosthenes and with the beginning of the great struggles of Alexander's successors, all independence and freedom were lost.[17] It is probably more than coincidental that by then we have the fully developed type of New Comedy in which almost no allusions to actual political developments of the contemporary world can be found.

Many fragments of Timocles still reflect the heady political atmosphere of the two decades before the hiatus of 322 (marked by the end of the Lamian War and the death of Demosthenes), but he was not the only comic poet who commented on the political developments in his plays, as one especially significant example may show. In 342/1 a memorable incident happened in the already long-standing struggle between Athens and Philip II. The Macedonian king grandly declared that he wanted to give the island of Halonnesos to the Athenians, but Demosthenes angrily reacted by saying that this island could not be given, but only be given *back* to Athens, since it already belonged to the city by right and tradition.[18] A whole cluster of comic plays took up this famous retort (which played on the meaning of the verbs δίδωμι and ἀποδίδωμι) and made fun of it. The deipnological polymath Athenaeus, one of our most important sources for Middle Comic fragments, cites five passages from five different plays of those times, where the words of Philip's offer and Demosthenes' rejection are reused in comic quarrels, and even a sixth instance of a similar wordplay—which was doubtlessly recognized by alert Athenian spectators—may probably be added.[19] Two of these fragments belong to plays of the already mentioned Timocles (Ἥρωες and Καύνιοι), two others to one of the most prolific writers of Middle Comedy, Alexis (Ἀδελφοί and Στρατιώτης), and numbers 5 and 6 were provided by Antiphanes and Anaxilas respectively. Presumably not all of these six plays were performed in one and the same year; the two plays each by Timocles and Alexis may well have been brought on stage in succeeding years (e.g., 341 and 340), but, in any case, not too long after the incident itself, for the joke might have become too stale after a certain time.

In other instances, too, Demosthenes—without doubt the most prominent Athenian politician of his time—proved a welcome target for comic jibes. At least two plays (maybe there once were more) ridiculed his penchant for extravagant and pathetic oath formulas;[20] the already mentioned fragment from Timocles' Ἥρωες describes him as a weapon-eating war hero.[21] Some years later he is castigated in yet another of Timocles' plays (Δῆλος) for his involvement in the corruption scandal centering on Harpalus (the minister of finance for Alexander the Great, who after embezzling huge sums fled to Athens in 324, was arrested there, but set free again after buying a number of politicians, Demosthenes apparently among them).

As prominent as he is, however, Demosthenes is *not* the Athenian politician most often mentioned in the comic fragments of his time; that perhaps dubious distinction belongs to a person who today is—and rightly so—considered as only a minor player in the political games around Athens' dying political independence. This is Callimedon, called the "Crayfish," because he was an avid gobbler of that kind of seafood, and this reason for his nickname already tells us a lot about those aspects of his person that were most considered worthy of comic comment in those days. Callimedon probably began his career sometime in the 340s as a politician of pro-Macedonian sentiment and, as such, an opponent of the politics of Demosthenes;[22] he had his heyday after 322 when the formerly strong anti-Macedonian faction in Athens had been crushed and when the city had been reduced to a mere shadow of its former independent self. It was very probably before those dark days that Callimedon had become a stock figure in comic plays. He appears in no fewer than fourteen fragments (from thirteen different plays), but—and this is very interesting—he is almost nowhere ridiculed for being a politician;[23] he is much more frequently taken to task because of the squint in his eyes[24] and most of all because of his gluttony and his prowess in eating tremendous quantities of fish and other edible stuff.[25] Callimedon, moreover, is not the only politician to be thus ridiculed in a rather unpolitical way. The well-known Hypereides is not only mentioned because of his complicity in the Harpalus scandal,[26] but also, in the same fragment and in another one,[27] because he too is a great lover (and eater) of fish. There are still other people (some of whom may have been politically active as well), who are included in comic verse for their love of food and drink; moreover, within the remains of Middle Comedy there still exist several rather impressive catalogs of such ὀψοφάγοι[28] who apparently were of no little interest to spectators.

I have mentioned the cases of Callimedon and Hypereides because with them we are already transgressing the boundaries of politics proper and passing into what might be called the wider realm of social life. Something similar can, of course, already be found in Aristophanes and other poets of Old Comedy, who provided their audiences with news and gossip of the kind that nowadays can mostly be found in the pages of the boulevard press: more or less substantial rumors and grapevine about the penchants and vices of more or less prominent people of Athenian society. As long as comedy does not turn itself totally away from the world by which it is surrounded, this yellow-press matter forms a permanent part of the comic repertoire. Still, one might get the impression that comments on certain kinds of social behavior are much more prominent in Middle Comedy than in Old and even more than in New Comedy, and that surely tells something about the ways in which contemporary life is reflected on the stage. We have already encountered a certain species of glutton-politicians who are frequently a target of Middle Comic poets; politicians, however, were not the only gluttons, and so there appear many other people, too, in the fragments because of their liking of large quantities of food and drink. Our richest source for Middle Comic fragments, Athenaeus, has carefully collected a number of sometimes rather extensive catalogs of ὀψοφάγοι and τρεχέδειπνοι. With this wealth of material, one could go far in compiling a "Who is who in food gobbling and wine swilling" in fourth-century Athens. It has often been claimed that Athenaeus' almost pathological penchant for everything about food and drink is very much to blame for a distorted picture we get about those comedies he cites from; the fact is, however, that no other period of Attic comedy provided him with more material on big eaters and drinkers in Athens than Middle Comedy;[29] this can be no mere coincidence with Athenaeus' interests.

Now gluttons need a steady supply to satisfy their vice, and the people who provide this supply constitute a steady source for comic comment and jokes on the Middle Comic stage. With meat being something of a rarity in the everyday Athenian cuisine, fish was the most sought-after replacement for it, and the fishmongers who sell this delight—at much less delightful prices—on the market are the butt of many a joke and sarcastic comment on the stage. There are fourteen fragments from thirteen different plays of Middle Comic poets in which the fishmongers are ridiculed or reviled, while there is little about them in New Comedy and well-nigh nothing in Old.[30] No other professional group as such is so prominent in comedy except for one of even more dubious distinction: hetairai.

Hetairai do play a role already in Old Comedy, but, it seems, only a minor one. They are not really prominent in the plays of the "political" poets,[31] but rather in that sideline of Old Comedy which was represented by Crates and Pherecrates and in some poets that were active only toward the end of this period. In New Comedy, on the other hand, hetairai are quite often an important part of cast and plot, but—and this is a major difference if we look back to Old and especially to Middle Comedy—they are all fictitious, invented by the poets themselves, like all the other characters in their plays. In Middle Comedy, the hetairai mentioned and sometimes described in no little detail are very often figures from real contemporary life about whom theatergoers could hear often when they gossiped in the streets and whose services they might even be able to enjoy (if they had enough money to pay for them). Some of them even seem to have become title figures of comedies, which would have made them important characters within those plays.[32] From the famous Lais of the early decades of the fourth century down to the no less famous Pythionice who became the mistress of the later infamous Harpalus and died in Babylon, there are all in all thirty-seven names of hetairai mentioned in Middle Comic poets, all of whom probably are historical (even if we don't hear of them outside of comic fragments). Some of them are so prominent that Giuseppe Schiassi was able to draw up a chronological table in 1951 of those plays in the fragments of which these hetairai appear. He did this by carefully putting together the various fragments in which they are mentioned. This tentative chronology is still very helpful in giving us at least an idea of how things developed on the comic stage between 380 and 320; moreover, this kind of evidence is so peculiar to Middle Comedy, that in no other period of Athenian comedy could a similar study ever be undertaken. This tells us something about the ubiquitousness that this group of female "professionals" enjoys in these plays.

The areas of Athenian life which have been discussed so far may seem to be rather prominent in the remains of Middle Comedy, more prominent, in fact, than in the remains of the other periods. These areas are, of course, in the plays themselves not kept as separate from each other as my discussion up to now may have suggested; rather they are quite often intertwined and thus form intriguing pictures of Athenian life as the comic poets wanted it to appear before their spectators. To see how these pictures are built up, one has to look at some longer fragments which have still been preserved by the grace of fate (and, again, by the deipnological whim of Athenaeus) and which may show how the various areas of public and semipublic life mentioned so far—the world of politics, the world of gluttons and their providers, and the world of hetairai and their customers—do indeed form a peculiar whole in these fragments. For example, we get quite an interesting view of this comic Athens which surely is a distorted, but still somehow "real" picture of the contemporary city, in twenty-four lines preserved from Antiphanes' Ἁλιευομένη (fr. 27 K.-A.):

τὰς σηπίας δὸς πρῶτον. Ἡράκλεις ἄναξ,
ἅπαντα τεθολώκασιν. οὐ βαλεῖς πάλιν
εἰς τὴν θάλατταν καὶ πλυνεῖς; μὴ φῶσί σε
†Δωριάς, ἀλλ᾿ ὀυε† σηπίας εἰληφέναι.
5   τὸν *κάραβον* δὲ τόνδε πρὸς τὰς *μαινίδας*
ἀπόδος· παχύς γε νὴ Δί᾿. ὦ Ζεῦ, τίς ποτε,
ὦ *Καλλιμέδων*, σὲ κατέδετ᾿ ἄρτι τῶν φίλων;
οὐδεὶς ὃς ἂν μὴ κατατιθῇ τὰς συμβολάς.
ὑμᾶς δ᾿ ἔταξα δεῦρο πρὸς τὰ δεξιά,
10 *τρίγλας*, ἔδεσμα τοῦ καλοῦ *Καλλισθένους*·
κατεσθίει γοῦν ἐπὶ μιᾷ τὴν οὐσίαν.
καὶ τὸν Σινώπης *γόγγρον* ἤδη παχυτέρας
ἔχοντ᾿ ἀκάνθας τουτονὶ τίς λήψεται
πρῶτος προσελθών; *Μισγόλας* γὰρ οὐ πάνυ
15 τούτων ἐδεστής. ἀλλὰ *κίθαρος* οὑτοσί,
ὃν ἂν ἴδῃ τὰς χεῖρας οὐκ ἀφέξεται.
καὶ μὴν ἀληθῶς τοῖς κιθαρῳδοῖς ὡς σφόδρα
ἅπασιν οὗτος ἐπιπεφυκὼς λανθάνει.
ἀνδρῶν δ᾿ ἄριστον *Κωβιὸν* πηδῶντ᾿ ἔτι
20 πρὸς *Πυθιονίκην* τὴν καλὴν πέμψαι με δεῖ·
ἁδρὸς γάρ ἐστιν. ἀλλ᾿ ὅμως οὐ γεύσεται·
ἐπὶ τὸ *τάριχός* ἐστιν ὡρμηκυῖα γάρ.
ἀφύας δὲ λεπτὰς τάσδε καὶ τὴν *τρυγόνα*
χωρὶς *Θεανοῖ* δεῦρ᾿ ἔθηκ᾿ ἀντιρρόπους.

Give me first the cuttle-fishes. Lord Heracles! They've squirted and messed everything. Throw them back into the sea, won't you, and clean up! Never let them say that you've got . . . no cuttle-fishes.[33]—(5) Now set aside this crayfish where the sprats are. It's a fat one, by Zeus. My goodness, Callimedon, who among your friends will presently eat you up? Well, nobody who doesn't put up the price.—As for you, blonde mullets, I put you here on the right; (10) you're the dish of the beautiful Callisthenes—he is in fact gobbling up his estate for the sake of one of them.—Now, who will be the first to come forward and buy this conger-eel with spikes thicker than Sinope's?[34] For Misgolas isn't exactly (15) an eater of these! But now this turbot[35] here: if Misgolas sees *him*, he won't keep his hands off: this chap really—on my word—clandestinely manages to get into hotly close contact with all cithara players.—As for Kobios, the best of men, still jumping about, I must send him (20) to the beautiful Pythionice; for he is a lusty one. But no, she won't taste him; for she has by now devoted all her keenness on Old Salted Fish.—These tiny small fry and this spiketail I've set aside here for Theano; they're just her weight.[36]

Athenaeus presents this passage as another catalog of well-known Athenians who love to eat fish;[37] on closer inspection, however, Antiphanes seems to do something much more ingenious. The play from which these lines once were excerpted is titled Ἀλιευομένη, *The Fisherwoman*, and the person speaking is ordering another one—probably a servant—to hand her various kinds of fish so that she may properly display them for sale. Thus it is without doubt the title figure herself who speaks this passage; but what kind of fish is this fisher-woman *really* displaying? Antiphanes' Athenian spectators probably knew from the start that these were no ordinary fish; we get the first inkling that something is wrong in lines 5–7, when suddenly among all these fish the fat "crayfish" Callimedon turns up. Soon afterward another contemporary figure is named: Callisthenes is probably the same person who gets stung by Timocles somewhat later (fr. 4 K.-A.) for being implicated in the Harpalus scandal. Here he is not, like Callimedon, presented as a fish but as a fish eater. But are the mullets on one of which he is apparently spending his whole estate really only expensive fish? With Misgolas in lines 14–18 we are finally getting near the whole scandalous truth: Misgolas can't keep his hands off the fish κίθαρος and off nice κιθαρῳδοί—his penchant for young boys is amply demonstrated in other fragments too.[38] Our source, Athenaeus himself, sets out the relevant material (which ultimately derives from a Hellenistic commentary) soon after to explain the Antiphanes passage, and he comments on the next fish person as well: Kobios (who is probably identical with the glutton we meet in two fragments of Alexis[39]) once was the lover of the hetaira Pythionice, who capped her career by becoming the mistress of first famous and then infamous Harpalus. At the time of our Antiphanes passage, Pythionice had not yet reached this stage, but had already diverted her favors from Kobios to the sons of a rich merchant in salted fish, Chaerephilus. That's why Antiphanes' fisherwoman says that Pythionice does not touch anymore the sort of fish named κώβιος, but has by now developed a craze for salted fish. Our passage concludes with another hetaira, Theano, who is rather unkindly mentioned by another comic poet, too.[40] Theano, however, compared with Pythionice, has to make do with small fry indeed.[41]

If we now look back to the beginning of the fragment, we may well suspect that the σηπίαι of line 1 and the μαινίδες of line 5 and the τρίγλαι of line 10 were no simple fish, but nicknames of hetairai with whom men like Callimedon and Callisthenes consorted. A woman named Σηπία ἡ Θύρσου can already be found in the Ἰχθύες of Archippus,[42] and already Schweighäuser (in his massive commentary on Athenaeus, which he produced at the beginning of the nineteenth century) thought that μαινίδες and τρίγλαι concealed the names and identities of courtesans. What, finally, about the speaking fisherwoman herself? Maybe she fishes not only or perhaps not at all for ordinary seafish, but men for her "institution" (which may have been more like a brothel than a stand for vending fish). Or does she act as a procuress or go-between for high-fashioned call girls and wealthy clients, providing even Misgolas with the boys he craves? So our Ἁλιευομένη might more appropriately be called a female pornoboskos or—if she were in a Roman comedy—a *lena*.[43] Fragment 27 K.-A. may have belonged to what possibly was her grand introductory monologue, showing her in full command of her trade and exactly knowing whom to bring into lucrative contact with whom, and at the same time providing her delighted spectators with an intriguing and ingenious tableau of quite a range of Athenian VIPs and their fish- and prostitute-loving ways. One would indeed, I think, be hard put to find another instance in Greek Comedy where a comparable double-entendre between fish-eating habits and sexual entanglements of the rich and famous in society is kept up so well and so consistently in such a long versified passage.

The Antiphanes fragment just discussed is not the only one to show us how the comedy of the 340s and 330s depicted contemporary Athenian society life on the stage. Another fragment of the same poet very vividly describes how something like a minor political crisis develops because of an insufficient supply of fish (Antiphanes, Πλούσιοι fr. 188 K.-A.):

> Εὔθυνος δ' ἔχων
> σανδάλια καὶ σφραγῖδα καὶ μεμυρισμένος
> ἐλογίζετο † τῶν πραγμάτων οὐκ οἶδ' ὅ τι·
> Φοινικίδης δὲ Ταυρέας θ' ὁ φίλτατος,
> 5 ἄνδρες † πάλαι ὀψοφάγοι τοιοῦτοί † τινες
> οἷοι καταβροχθίζειν ἐν ἀγορᾷ τὰ τεμάχη,
> ὁρῶντες ἐξέθνησκον ἐπὶ τῷ πράγματι

ἔφερόν τε δεινῶς τὴν ἀνοψίαν πάνυ.
κύκλους δὲ συναγείροντες ἔλεγον † τάδε,
10 ὡς οὐ βιωτόν ἐστιν οὐδ' ἀνασχετὸν
τῆς μὲν θαλάττης ἀντιποιεῖσθαί τινας
ὑμῶν ἀναλίσκειν τε πολλὰ χρήματα,
ὄψου δὲ μηδὲ – ∪ εἰσπλεῖν μηδὲ γρῦ.
τί οὖν ὄφελος τῶν νησιάρχων; ἔστι δὴ
15 νόμῳ κατακλεῖσαι τοῦτο, παραπομπὴν ποιεῖν
τῶν ἰχθύων. νυνδὶ *Μάτων* συνήρπακεν
τοὺς ἁλιέας, καὶ ⟨δὴ⟩ *Διογείτων* νὴ Δία
ἅπαντας ἀναπέπεικεν ὡς αὐτὸν φέρειν,
κοὐ δημοτικόν γε τοῦτο δρᾷ τοσαῦτα φλῶν.
20 γάμοι δ' ἐκεῖνοι καὶ πότοι νεανικοὶ
ἦσαν . . .

Euthynus, wearing sandals and signet ring and drenched in perfume, was reckoning about matters I don't know what;[44] while Phoenicides and dearest Taureas, (5) gentlemen of long standing in gourmandry[45] and of the kind that greedily gulp down the best cuts in the market, were about to expire when they saw this happening; they were furious at the scarcity of fish. Gathering circles around them, they said (10) that life was not worth living and that one could not tolerate that certain men among you should claim ownership of the sea and spend so much money, while not even the slightest bit of fish was coming in. What, then, is the use of having island prefects? Surely it's possible (15) to order by law the establishment of a special convoy for fish! But now Maton has monopolized all the fishermen, and what is more, Diogeiton—by Zeus!—has persuaded them all to bring their catch to him. It's not democratic what he's doing, greedily grabbing so much! (20) Those were wedding parties and extravagant drinking bouts . . .[46]

Most of the characters mentioned in these lines are well known from other fragments. The first to be named, Euthynus, is a wealthy saltfish merchant just like Chaerephilus (whose sons could afford one of the most expensive hetairai in Athens). Here this Euthynus seems to cause not a little anguish to two fish-loving gourmands, Phoenicides and Taureas, who on another occasion are shown fighting lustily between themselves because of an eel (Antiphanes, Αὐλητρὶς ἢ Δίδυμαι fr. 50 K.-A.),[47] but who in this instance had to join forces because they saw themselves excluded from their most beloved source of nourishment by the machinations of greedy rivals like Maton and Diogeiton. Of those two, at least Maton is mentioned in other places too as a greedy fish eater;[48] to stop them, Phoenicides and Taureas even envision legal action so that fish can "safely" arrive on the Athenian market for all who want to buy them. This is not the only fragment where the fish supply is considered a matter of politics. In Alexis, Λέβης fragments 130 and 131 K.-A., the politician Aristonicus is highly applauded for curbing the mean practices of the fishmongers; in Alexis, Δορκὶς ἢ Ποππύζουσα fragment 57 K.-A., on the other hand, the fishmongers themselves have decided to set up an honorary statue for Callimedon, for this fish-eating politician has proved to be their only savior. We know, in fact, of real-life instances in fourth-century Athens, where fish supply was a matter of politics: the already mentioned saltfish merchant Chaerephilus got Athenian citizenship after he had considerably lessened a real shortage of food by generously donating a large amount of saltfish to the city.[49]

Back to Antiphanes fragment 188 K.-A.: it is not clear by whom it once was spoken; in its first half, it sounds very much like a messenger speech (like, for instance, that in the *Sicyonians*[50] of Menander, which itself imitated the famous messenger-speech in Euripides' *Orestes*),[51] so these words might come from a slave who had just gone to market[52] and observed what happened there. In the second half of the passage, however, the speaker doesn't any more seem just to relate what he saw and heard, but rather to express his own sentiments, which are very much in agreement with the indignation exhibited by Phoenicides and Taureas. Like them, he doesn't seem very much to like the scarcity of fish brought about by those other greedy fish lovers, so he might either be one of the Πλούσιοι, who are the title figures of this play, or—and this seems even more probable—a rather poor chap who is somewhat annoyed that the rich people deprive the less wealthy of even the little bit of seafood they would like to enjoy themselves.

These examples may suffice here to illustrate in what ways Athenian public and semipublic life was represented on the comic stage in the time of the Middle Comic poets. Athenian politics as a topic of allusion remains prominent, almost as prominent as in the times of Old Comedy, though the way—not the frequency—in which politicians are ridiculed seems to change somewhat, particularly in the later decades of this period. Many politicians now are taken to task more for their private vices (eating and sex) than for their public actions. These vices by themselves fill up a very considerable part of the fragments we still have left over from Middle Comedy; and this, as I already said, cannot—at least not exclusively—be explained by the curious interests of our most important source, Athenaeus, but must correspond to a real interest in these things among the Athenian theatergoing public of those decades. Obviously the poets would not have included these things in their plays if they hadn't counted on getting the spectators' favor by displaying them. In no other period of Athenian dramatic history do real-life hetairai and real-life gluttons (or gluttonous politicians) loom so large on the stage, and this even in plays the titles of which suggest the treatment of a mythical story that had nothing at all to do with the phenomena of contemporary Athenian society.

Many plays of those times must have contained a curious mélange: on the one hand, a fictional story line (mythical or nonmythical) that was more or less invented by the poet; on the other, repeated references (sometimes longer, sometimes shorter; sometimes quite explicit, at other times more enigmatic) to Athenian life and to those figures and events in it that were at the moment most gossiped about. Thus Athens as a living and exciting polis, with all its amusing and sometimes scandalous happenings, constantly intruded into Middle Comedy, whose poets never lost track of the reality surrounding them. A short glance at two areas which have not yet been mentioned in this essay may additionally confirm this. It is well known that in the course of the fourth century, Athens (apart from her varied and finally sagging political fortunes) was on its way to becoming the philosophical capital of the Greek world, most of all due to the rise of Plato's Academy. It is certainly no coincidence that Plato's name (and more than once he himself, as a living character) appears in at least fifteen fragments of fifteen different Middle Comic plays. The most interesting of them is Epicrates fragment 10 K.-A., with its superb description of the Academy being eagerly at work exploring new dihaereses. It is well known, too, that in the history of the Athenian theater the fourth century is the period when single actors attain an ever increasing prominence, beginning to direct the staging of plays themselves (mainly the restaging of old plays) and, in this process, quite often becoming more important than the playwrights. So, again, it is no coincidence that among the Middle Comic fragments referring to artists of various professions (tragic and comic poets, musicians etc.) we find at least six instances[53] where dramatic actors are evoked. The poets of Middle Comedy seem to have captured all aspects of contemporary public life—political, social, and cultural—of Athens. They combined the various elements of polis life into a sometimes curious mixture, which certainly distorted the picture of this polis, but was nevertheless recognizable by its theatergoing inhabitants and highlighted the more peculiar sides of it for them.

All this seems to change considerably once we get past the year 322 and into New Comedy in its fully developed stage: here or there a philosopher's or a contemporary parasite's name may still crop up, but as for real-life hetairai or politicians or other prominent members of society, we mostly look for them in vain.[54] What happened? The final downfall of the democratic constitution after the short-lived rebellion against Macedonian supremacy in 323/2, the establishment of a new government, which mostly took its orders from Macedonian overlords (who made their menacing presence felt by placing a garrison in the harbor fortress Munychia and who did not leave until 307), and the abolition of the choregic system by Demetrius of Phalerum in 317 or soon after (which resulted in the state assuming a much bigger role in organizing Athenian theater than before) may all have played an important part in it. The end of the Peloponnesian War has always been recognized as a very important date within the development not only of Athenian political history but of its cultural history, too, for it coincided with the end of classical tragedy and of Old Comedy. The evidence gathered in this essay seems to suggest that with the death of Alexander the Great and its bloody aftermath the history of Athenian comic theater reached a watershed of similar importance. From then on (and for the first time in theater history), Athens as a polis was present in comedy only in a very much dehistoricized and deactualized form, a fictionalized shadow of its former self.

Notes

1. See Nesselrath 1990, 195–96. Fragments are cited from Kassel and Austin 1983 (K.-A.).

2. Regarding this credulity, already Herodotus (5.97.1–2) has a significant story to tell.

3. As for the title, Graf 1885, 69, suggested that Ὀλβία signifies Athens herself, which would make the whole play a highly political one.

4. He seems to have put plays on the stage from the mid-380s until at least the early 340s, and with the recorded number of sixty-five plays he was only slightly less productive than Eubulus; see Nesselrath 1990, 194–95.

5. On the treatment of this myth in Anaxandrides' play, see Nesselrath 1990, 212–15.

6. More than forty fragments are still to be found under its heading: Eupolis fr. 218–58 K.-A.

7. On his dating see Nesselrath 1990, 196–97.

8. See Dušanič (1985) 10–29.

9. See Nesselrath 1990, 219–20 with notes 119–20.

10. This is probably the best argument that the *Suda*'s ascription must derive from an ancient source; there was simply no reason to invent it. See Nesselrath 1990, 61.

11. Of course, internal strife within the Greek poleis did not automatically cease when the Macedonians appeared on the political stage, as is well known from Athens itself (see now Habicht 1995, 19–46); it even reappeared in force, when the constant conflicts between the successor states of Alexander's empire precipitated major turnarounds in the balance of power (see below note 54).

12. Wilamowitz 1925, 145 n. 1.

13. Breitenbach 1908, 40.

14. Kock even wanted to go down into the third century B.C., to the end of the Chremonidean War (261 B.C.); but "hoc sane absonum a 'mediae comoediae' poeta, vid. test. 1" (K.-A. ad loc.).

15. According to Aeschines (2.70), Athens lost seventy-five allies at the end of the Social War; see now Radicke 1995, 24.

16. One might, perhaps, talk more appropriately of the "intermediate time" between "real" Middle and "real" New Comedy, as I have done in Nesselrath 1990, 334–38.

17. See now Habicht 1995, 47–75.

18. See Aeschin. 3.83; Plut. *Dem.* 9.6; Wankel 1976, 410, on Dem. 18.69.

19. Timocles, Καύνιοι fr. 20 K.-A., with the editors' comment on lines 4ff.

20. Antiphanes fr. 288 K.-A. and Timocles fr. 41 K.-A. (μὰ γῆν, μὰ κρήνας . . .).

21. It would be uncautious to interpret this as a particularly unpleasant way of reminding the audience that this militant war preacher once quite ingloriously ran away from a battlefield (Plut. *Dem.* 20.2), because that supposedly happened at Chaeronea in 338, and Ἥρωες might have been put on stage a few years earlier.

22. See Swoboda 1919.

23. He is called ψυχρός in Theophilus, Ἰατρός fr. 4 K.-A. Does that refer to his shortcomings as an orator? In Alexis, Δορκὶς ἢ Ποππύζουσα fr. 57 K.-A. he is to be honored on behalf of the fish vendors, which may suggest that he took political action to support them, but may, on the other hand, again be only a joke making fun of his love of seafood.

24. Cp. Alexis, Κρατεία ἢ Φαρμακοπώλης fr. 117 K.-A. and Timocles, Πολυπράγμων fr. 29 K.-A.

25. Alexis, Μανδραγοριζομένη fr. 149 K.-A.; Alexis, Ποντικός fr. 198 K.-A.; Alexis, Φαίδων ἢ Φαιδρίας fr. 249 K.-A.; Antiphanes, Γόργυθος fr. 77 K.-A.; Eubulus, Ἀνασῳζόμενοι fr. 8 K.-A.

26. Timocles, Δῆλος fr. 4 K.-A.

27. Timocles, Ἰκάριοι Σάτυροι fr. 17 K.-A.

28. Antiphanes, Ἁλιευομένη fr. 27 K.-A.; Antiphanes, Πλούσιοι fr. 188 K.-A.; Euphanes, Μοῦσαι fr. 1 K.-A.

29. Wilkins in his essay above demonstrates the importance of food in Old Comedy; Middle Comic poets not only seem to keep up this interest in things gastronomical, but add a new focus on notorious eaters and drinkers.

30. For New Comedy, see Diphilus fr. 32 K.-A. (Ἔμπορος) and 67 K.-A. (Πολυπράγμων); the earliest mention of a fishmonger with high prices may be in Aristophanes' Νῆσοι fr. 402.9–10 K.-A.; cp. Archippus' Ἰχθύες, fr. 23 K.-A.

31. See Nesselrath 1990, 318–19.

32. Antiphanes, Ἄντεια (?); Epigenes, Βακχίς (?); Antiphanes, Λαμπάς (?); Antiphanes, Ὀμφάλη (?); Ephippus, Φιλύρα (?); Eubulus, Νάννιον.

33. The first words of this line are corrupt. The most appealing solution may be Kaibel's, who reads Δωριάδας, ἀλλ' οὐ σηπίας εἰληφέναι: "don't let them say, that you've only got fish [or girls?] like Doris and not like Sepia!" See K.-A.'s textual comment on this line.

34. Or is it "this conger-eel of Sinope's"?

35. κίθαρος is echoed by κιθαρῳδοῖς in the line after the next one; this wordplay is well-nigh impossible to imitate in English (or in another modern language).

36. The translation is based on that by Gulick 1930, 37–39, with some modifications, not least because the text is somewhat different in K.-A.

37. Compare his introductory words: Ἀντιφάνης δ' ἐν Ἁλιευομένῃ φιληδοῦντάς τινας καταλέγων ἰχθύσιν φησί . . .

38. See Alexis, Ἀγωνὶς ἢ Ἱππίσκος fr. 3 K.-A.; Antiphanes, Ἁλιευομένη fr. 27 K.-A.; Timocles, Σαπφώ fr. 32 K.-A.

39. Alexis, Ἰσοστάσιον fr. 102 K.-A.; Alexis, Παγκρατιαστής fr. 173 K.-A. This Kobios of the second half of the fourth century B.C. is probably not identical with the one named in Archippus fr. 27 K.-A. There seem to be no other instances of this name (see Osborne and Byrne 1994, 277), which, in fact, signifies a certain kind of fish (see Thompson 1947). In both cases, then, we probably only have a nickname and do not know what the real names of their owners were.

40. Anaxilas, Νεοττίς fr. 22.20 K.-A.

41. The ἀφυαί and the τρυγών mentioned in line 23 are usually taken as further nicknames for hetairai (see K.-A. ad loc.); within their context, however, they would make better sense alluding to the species of common and unimportant "customers" that Theano has to "feed" on, just as in the lines before Kobios at one time was the really "big" morsel that Pythionice could gorge herself upon. Perhaps the γόγγρος mentioned in line 12 similarly means an aged lover, who provided food for Sinope.

42. Fr. 27.2 K.-A.; see K.-A. ad loc.

43. There was a certain number of plays in which male πορνοβοσκοί played the central or title part: see Nesselrath 1990, 324.

44. The translation tries to take into account the textual doubtfulness of this line.

45. Another problematic line, which Dobree 1832, 318, and Richards 1909, 76–77, even considered deleting.

46. The translation is again based on Gulick's 1930, 53–55, modified in some places because of the somewhat different text in K.-A.

47. In yet another fragment (Euphanes, Μοῦσαι fr. 1 K.-A.) Phoenicides is depicted like a Homeric hero, provoking all around to rival him in emptying a still-boiling-hot plate of seafood.

48. See Anaxilas, Μονότροπος fr. 20 K.-A., and Antiphanes, Κιθαρῳδός fr. 117 K.-A.

49. See Kirchner 1899; Davies 1971, 566sq.

50. This title is probably to be preferred to *Sicyonius*; see now Belardinelli 1994, 56–59.

51. Men. Sic. 176–271; Eur. Or. 866–956; see Hofmeister's essay below.

52. This is a duty slaves very often have to fulfill in the fragments of Middle Comedy; see Nesselrath 1990, 285–95.

53. See Alexis, Γυναικοκρατία fr. 43 K.-A. (Hippocles); Eubulus fr. 134 K.-A. (Nicostratus); Timocles, Ἥρωες fr. 14 K.-A. (Satyrus); Alexis, Λίνος fr. 140.12–16 K.-A. (Simus); Ephippus, Ὅμοιοι ἢ Ὀβελιαφόροι fr. 16 K.-A. (Theodorus); Antiphanes, Λύκων (?).

54. Exceptions are few and apparently concentrated within a couple of years after the upheaval of 307, when the Macedonian garrison in Munychia and Demetrius of Phalerum (who reigned in Athens by the grace of King Cassander) were thrown out by Demetrius Poliorcetes, who subsequently became the new overlord of the reestablished democracy (see now Habicht 1995, 74–87, 107): in a fragment of the comic poet Alexis (who by now had been active on the Athenian stage for about half a century), a speaker effusively welcomes a political measure proposed by the politician Sophocles and favored by Demosthenes' nephew Demochares and apparently by Demetrius Poliorcetes himself that aimed at bringing the philosophical schools under the control of the Athenian demos (Alexis fr. 99 K.-A.). In a lost play of the comic poet Archedicus, a severe invective seems to have been vented against the just-mentioned Demochares (Archedicus fr. 4 K.-A.); and a similarly severe invective was brought forth against the politician Stratocles (the foremost henchman of Demetrius Poliorcetes in Athens) by the comic poet Philippides (fr. 25 K.-A.), who himself was politically active in those decades (see test. 3 K.-A.) and had enduring connections with another important diadoch, Lysimachus. All these instances of politics once more surfacing in comedy significantly occur between 307 and about 300 B.C.; those years may therefore have been the last phase in Athenian history when comedy raised something like a political voice, which, however, looks only like a rather feeble echo of the headier years before 322. From none of the "big three" of New Comedy (Menander, Diphilus, Philemon) is any expression of overtly political significance extant within the remains of their comedies. Menander may have endorsed the institutions of his native polis, as Hofmeister's essay below shows, but he remains studiously vague (the assembly at Eleusis treated at length in *Sicyonians* was surely possible even under the conditions of restricted franchise in the years immediately after 322 and under Demetrius of Phalerum). Menander himself briefly got into political trouble in 307 because he seemed to have been too closely connected with the now banished Demetrius (test. 8 Koerte); but this was probably not because of any explicit statements in support of Demetrius' politics in his comedies.

Bibliography

Belardinelli, Anna Maria. 1994. *Menandro, Sicioni. Introduzione, testo e commento*. Bari.

Breitenbach, H. 1908. *De genere quodam titulorum comoediae Atticae*. Basel.

Davies, J. K. 1971. *Athenian Propertied Families*. Oxford.

Dobree, P. P. 1832. *Adversaria II*. Edited by J. Scholefield. Cambridge.

Dušanič, S. 1980–81. "Athens, Crete and the Aegean after 366/5 BC." *Talanta* 12–13 (pr. 1985). 7–29.

Graf, H. E. 1885. *Ad aureae aetatis fabulam symbola*. Ph.D. diss., Leipzig.

Gulick, C. B. 1930. *Athenaeus: The Deipnosophists*. Vol. 4. London.

Habicht, Chr. 1995. *Athen. Die Geschichte der Stadt in hellenistischer Zeit*. Munich.

Kassel, R., and C. Austin, eds. 1983–. *Poetae Comici Graeci*. Vols. II (Agathenor—Aristonymus); III 2 (Aristophanes, testimonia et fragmenta); IV (Aristophon—Crobylus); V (Damoxenus—Magnes); VII (Menecrates—Xenophon). Berlin.

Kirchner, J. 1899. "Chairephilos." *RE* III 2.2027–28.

Kock, T. 1880–88. *Comicorum Atticorum Fragmenta*. Leipzig.

Nesselrath, H.-G. 1990. *Die attische Mittlere Komödie. Ihre Stellung in der antiken Literaturkritik und Literaturgeschichte*. Berlin.

Osborne, M. J., and S. G. Byrne. 1994. *A Lexicon of Greek Personal Names*. Vol. 2: *Attica*. Oxford.

Radicke, J. 1995. *Die Rede des Demosthenes für die Freiheit der Rhodier*. Stuttgart.

Richards, H. 1909. *Aristophanes and Others*. London.

Schiassi, G. 1951. "De temporum quaestionibus ad Atticas IV saeculi meretrices et eiusdem comicas fabulas pertinentibus." *RFIC* 79.217–45.

Schweighäuser, J. 1801–7. *Athenaei . . . Deipnosophistarum Libri XV . . . emend. ac suppl. nova Lat. vers. et animadv. cum Js. Casauboni aliorumque tum suis illustravit. . . .* 14 vols. Biponti.

Swoboda, H. 1919. "Kallimedon." *RE* X 2.1647–48.

Thompson, D'Arcy W. 1947. *A Glossary of Greek Fishes*. London.

Wankel, H. 1976. *Demosthenes, Rede für Ktesiphon über den Kranz, erläutert und mit einer Einleitung versehen*. Heidelberg.

Wilamowitz-Moellendorff, U. von. 1925. *Menander, Das Schiedsgericht erklärt*. Berlin.

αἰ πᾶσαι πόλεις

Polis and *Oikoumenê* in Menander

Where then is the polis in Menander? For some time it has been assumed that in Menander the polis is not present. After Athens had mostly ceased to project its power, or even in some instances to rule itself without outside interference, Menander turned away, it is said, from the depressing political failure of the city-state. The stage of New Comedy no longer reflected the enterprise of a dynamic, hegemonistic Athens; its world entailed instead a widely spread network of Greeks, which was forged in the expedition of Alexander and shaped by his successors.[1]

New Comedy reveals this changed background most by confining itself within a sharply restricted foreground. The setting of its plays represents a stereotypical locale found anywhere, purportedly, in the cities of an increasingly homogeneous Hellenistic world. The plots elaborate a variety of universal concerns about marriages, property, citizen rights, and relations within families and between neighbors, while characters enact common traits of personality (impetuosity, avarice, naiveté) and basic biological and social roles (father, neighbor, master). Comedy has exchanged the parochial for the ecumenical. Consider the first plays (of those extant) of Aristophanes and Menander, *Acharnians* and *Dyskolos*, for example. In the former, Dikaiopolis, the sooty Acharnians whom he defies, and the Boeotians and starving Megarians whom he welcomes into his entrepôt all have identities that are geographically and historically particular; in *Dyskolos*, by contrast, two pairs of fathers and (step)sons, Kallipedes and Sostratos, Knemon and Gorgias, individually represent certain generic traits (e.g., Knemon's ἀπανθρωπία, "unsociability"), and collectively a set of abstract social relations (e.g., wealthy vs. less wealthy).

Niall Slater expressed the view of New Comedy outlined here in a lucid essay published in the *Themes in Drama* series:[2]

> The world of New Comedy is purely domestic, most often a quiet residential street in Athens where private comedies of marriage or reconciliation are played out with no effect on anyone beyond the participants. . . . The subject matter of comedy becomes domestic and thereby broadens its appeal greatly. The political comedy of Aristophanes had no appeal outside Athens; we have no records of any performances after his lifetime outside the city. Menander's young lovers, though, appealed to Greek-speaking audiences from Athens to Alexandria to Syracuse. Wherever conquest and trade carried the Hellenistic Greeks, the touring Artists of Dionysos followed.

Surely the assumption that Menander's art is more universal than Aristophanes' is reasonable, if it is not pressed. Its acceptance explains why for at least two generations scholarship on Menander has largely ignored "politics," in the sense of Menander's treatment or representation of the polis. Scholars have focused instead on questions of artistic form or intellectual milieu: Menander's innovation in conventions of plot and characterization; his imitation or transformation of scenes and motifs from tragedy, especially Euripides; the dramatization of philosophical doctrine, with an emphasis on ethics, particularly of the Peripatos. This work has aided an understanding of Menander, and was both prudent and necessary, given his textual history. Yet this approach to Menander also fostered the notion that the polis was lacking in his drama;[3] it is the purpose of this essay to challenge that notion.

I would like to discuss two important points, however, before attempting to identify the polis in Menander and describe its significance within his drama. The first point involves one way in which the city becomes apprehensible in Menander. The second has to do with the nature of this city of Menander.

To begin to discuss the ways in which Menander dramatizes the polis, I borrow a term from Hanna Scolnicov: "the theatrical space without." Scolnicov defines this "space without" as "extrapolations of the concrete visible space on stage," and explains its significance thus:[4]

> The theatrical space without adds an extra dimension to the performance. For, whereas the visible theatrical space is wholly within the given theatre space, the theatrical space without extends as far as the playwright wills it to, thus demanding an imaginative response on the part of the spectators. . . . far from being accidental or arbitrary, the articulation of the theatrical space is,

at its best, an expression of the playwright's philosophical stance. As such, it becomes of thematic and structural importance to the play. An analysis of the spatial conception of a play, especially of the theatrical space without, can thus lead us directly to a consideration of its innermost problems.

In this "extra dimension" Scolnicov offers a means for revising the cliché of Menander's theater as highly constricted, especially in comparison with Aristophanes. Even if his stereotyped settings are far less varied than those of Aristophanes, and less fantastic,[5] nevertheless Menander was able to supplement a monotonous stage set[6] with the sort of allusive extensions of space that Scolnicov describes.[7] This technique is fundamental to Menander's creation of the polis within his plays. The examples I will discuss are drawn from several texts: *Samia*, *Sicyonios*, and *Epitrepontes*. In each case I will attempt to show how the city, or parts of the city, are called forth in speech and thus realized within the "imaginative space" of the play; I will also discuss how the city functions in the drama, once or whenever it is invoked in this manner.

A second point on which I must touch briefly concerns the kind of city one is likely to see, once one has isolated it within a given play. Menander's polis will naturally take on the colors of Menander's plays themselves. Insofar as these typically deal with the intersection of the public and private, with people's lives as they are affected by basic social institutions and practices such as marriage, citizenship, and ownership of property, the features of his city relate to these concerns. The topography of his city, likewise, is marked by structures which connote other activities than those of war or high politics. Menander's polis is not imperial and has no dynamic or aggressive foreign policy.

The polis in Menander differs from the polis in Aristophanes chiefly in this respect, that Menander's city is not the hegemonic city of Aristophanes. One will find nothing in Menander, at least as he has been preserved for us at present, to match such a sequence concerning the polis as the following from *Lysistrata*.

> I hear it's the same old thing again—the unbridled nature of the female sex coming out. All their banging of drums in honour of that Sabazius god, and singing to Adonis on the roofs of houses, and all that nonsense. I remember once in the Assembly—Demostratus, may he come to no good end, was saying we ought to send the expedition to Sicily, and this woman, who was dancing on the roof, she cried, "O woe for Adonis!," and then he went on and said we should include some heavy infantry from Zacynthus, and the woman on the roof—she'd had a bit to drink, I fancy—she shouted, "Mourn for Adonis, all ye people!" But the damnable scoundrel from Angeriae just blustered on and on. (*Lys.* 391–97, trans. Sommerstein)

In this passage the proboulos invokes the "theatrical space without": he juxtaposes two locations, one the locus of the fundamental political activity of the city, the ekklesia, and the other a private space, the roof of a nearby house on which a woman celebrates the Adoneia.[8] The audience of this play ought to have expected the proboulos to privilege the public space and to diminish the private one, even more so in this instance because the scene on the rooftop is meant to illustrate the irrationality of women. Surely the proboulos does not intend not to privilege the public space.[9] But, oddly enough, the way he makes his point does just that. In his narrative the disconcerting performance of the adorateuse is intertwined with that of the assembly meeting at which a certain Demostratus spoke.[10] What Demostratus had to say—that is, his advocacy of the disastrous mission to Sicily—turns out to be more harmful by far than the rooftop lamentations. Unconsciously, it would seem, the proboulos' complaint against the unbridled nature of women in fact transforms itself into an angry outburst against the unbridled discourse of the Athenian assembly.[11]

At the same time, the proboulos' implied comparison of Demostratus and the Adonis singer suggests the same role reversal between the genders that the proboulos resists throughout the play. He unintentionally makes the very case that is Lysistrata's, for example, in her speech in 555–58: "Let's put a stop first of all to men going into the marketplace in full armor and acting as though they were mad . . . they go around the vegetable and pottery stalls in all their equipment just like Corybants!" Ironically, then, the proboulos corroborates Lysistrata's claim that the men are quite mad, and so incapable of running the city.[12]

Aristophanes sharpens this point by referring so boldly to public policy in the proboulos' opening speech, in particular to a failed policy whose consequences must have devastated many households of the polis. Indeed, he makes this reference to the Sicilian debacle less than two years after news of the calamity had come back to the city.[13] To judge from this example, Aristophanes does not just allude to the city in order to create additional ways to broach his dramatic themes; when he does so, there is such an overlay of intense "political" experience, actions of the most profound consequence for the whole community, and not segments of it only, that Aristophanes' adversions to the city therefore resonate deeply and produce automatically, as it were, a sense of pathos.

Given the meager references to politics in the surviving fragments of New Comedy, whether due to the harsher realities of Macedonian overlordship or simply to the accidents of textual transmission, one hardly expects Menander to advert to the city in a similar way, or engage in topical allusion with such a raw edge.[14] But this difference between the two poets does not mean that the polis is lacking in Menander's comedy, or that Aristophanes' manner of referring to it is the only one possible, that *his* polis is the only comic polis.[15]

On the contrary, the polis of Menander resembles that one which Oswyn Murray has described in this fashion:[16]

> The developed Greek city was a network of associations: as Aristotle saw, it was such associations which created the sense of community, of belonging, which was an essential feature of the polis: the ties of kinship by blood were matched with multiple forms of political and religious and social groupings, and of companionship for a purpose, whether it be voyaging or drinking or burial.

Menander's polis is no less a polis because his drama does not resonate so often with allusions to activities in the external world, that is, the armed competition with other Greek states that occurred outside the city. Instead Menander seems to focus on matters internal to the city, represented in that "network of associations" which made for civilized life, or life in a community such as the ancient Greek polis was claimed to be, not least by Aristotle, as Murray reminds us.[17]

In addition to opening the important issue of the existence of the polis in Menander, I will argue at the end of this essay for a reconsideration of Menander's point of view regarding the fate of the polis in his own time as well as its prospects. It is often claimed that an enlightened humanism underlies Menander's drama, and likewise a tolerance of the new Macedonian-led version of the *oikoumenê gê*. Scholars have grounded this view in two approaches. One involves hints of a cosmopolitan and humane attitude in certain of Menander's context-less fragments; more on this later. Another depends on an historicizing argument according to which, the world having changed so rapidly around Menander, he is caught up willy-nilly in the antichauvinist trends of his age. An expansion of the Greek world had dissolved the narrow boundaries of the individual poleis and with that their blinkered parochialism, the argument goes; Menander, in line with the kind of thinking that becomes familiar from Zeno, for instance, found the new interconnectedness of poleis and peoples congenial. Sophisticated as he was, Menander must also have been an eager and convinced cosmopolite. Yet such notions as these are false and misleading.

If Menander perceived imminent changes in his world (and I believe he did), far from filling him with wonder, the incipient Hellenistic age, with its colossal (and contentious) political structures and concomitant erosion of the autonomous polis, probably filled him with anxiety and unease, perhaps also regret. It is important then to uncover Menander's polis, for this reason, to help judge the claim that Menander remained loyal to an ideal of the autonomous city-state. Alternatives to the polis did not interest him in life, just as the anecdote has it in which Menander refuses Ptolemy's invitation to the royal court at Alexandria. I will argue that in his art as well Menander not only defended the integrity of the polis (just as Aristophanes did in his own way); Menander also debunked and ultimately rejected the evolving *oikoumenē*, or world community, as any adequate substitute for the life inside one's native polis.

Menander on "Friendship" and the Polis

Menander's theatrical space is not monotonous or incapable of symbolic meaning. The setting of a majority of the extant plays seems stereotyped, hence restricted (though a play like *Dyskolos* is set outside the town), and yet the two *parodoi* of the theater nevertheless *imply* the world beyond the theater. It has been maintained that these two wings represented the way to the country in one direction and to the city in the opposite direction, a configuration that would encompass the polis in its two essential aspects—*astu* and *chora*.[18] Thus, inasmuch as the theater entrances extend the physical theater toward city, field, or harbor—that is, into the civic space—in that sense the city is immanent in Menander's drama. With this in mind, it seems less odd to claim that the poet should invoke a part of the polis (or beyond) at the verbal level of the play and thereby extend the reach of the physical set in this way too. The poet may direct the audience to imagine any of the city's constituent elements, then, in order to put in play the associations that reside in these elements.

To illustrate this technique I turn first to a scene in *Samia* involving the two neighbors, Demeas and Nikeratos, who are, along with Demeas' son Moschion, the main figures of the play. At this point in the drama, in act 4 (439ff.), all three men are on stage together. Demeas has just succumbed to the mistaken impression that Moschion has fathered a child on Demeas' mistress, Chrysis. Demeas at first attempts to keep the matter from Nikeratos; but Moschion's interventions on Chrysis' behalf not to have her thrown from the house—Moschion does not perceive Demeas' error—anger Demeas so much that he allows Nikeratos (Moschion's prospective father-in-law) to guess the "truth." Nikeratos' reaction soon outsizes Demeas' own indignation, however, for Nikeratos in fact takes advantage of the situation to construct a self-aggrandizing fantasy:

> ἀνδράποδ[ον εἶ, Δημέα.
> εἰ γὰρ ἐμὸν ἤι[σχυνε λέ]κτρον, οὐκ ἄν εἰς ἄλλον ποτὲ
> ὕβρισ' οὐδ' ἡ συγ[κλ]ιθεῖσα· παλλακὴν δ' ἄν αὔριον
> πρῶτος ἀνθρώπων ἐπώλουν, συναποκηρύττων ἅμα
> υἱόν, ὥστε μηθὲν εἶναι μήτε κουρεῖον κενόν,
> μὴ στοάν, καθημένους δὲ πάντας ἐξ ἑωθινοῦ
> περὶ ἐμοῦ λαλεῖν λέγοντας ὡς ἀνὴρ Νικήρατος
> γέγον' ἐπεξελθὼν δικαίως τῶι φόνωι.

(Sam. 506–13)

You're a slave, Demeas. If he were shaming *my* bed, he would never again commit such an outrage against anyone else—nor would the one he's sleeping with. That whore I would sell off tomorrow, before anyone else sold anything, and at the same time I would publicly disinherit your son. No barbershop or stoa would be empty, but everyone would sit there from early in the morning and chatter away about me, and they would be saying what a man Nikeratos was, to deal with this vicious murder so righteously!

Here, as elsewhere in the play, Nikeratos' reaction places him in clear contrast to Demeas.[19] While Nikeratos is impulsive and bloody-minded, as he shows throughout this scene, Demeas, though not wholly above passion, is slower to anger.[20] Once Demeas explodes, moreover, he recovers quickly, and in fact comprehends the true situation within a scant sixteen lines of his outburst. Nikeratos meanwhile hunts for Chrysis offstage, to expel her from his own house.

Nikeratos' "barbershop speech" provides the opportunity to draw additional distinctions between himself and Demeas. Nikeratos makes clear by the middle of his speech what revenge he would take, were he the victim of a vicious "Helen" and reprobate son. At that point Nikeratos divagates on the reputation that would stem from his bold actions. Nowhere in the city, not in barbershop or stoa, would anyone sit and not talk about him. In this way Nikeratos emphasizes the publicity of his revenge. Such publicity, however, would be anathema to Demeas. Repeatedly in the play Demeas reveals how crucial it is that his difficulty be resolved in a way that involves no one outside his household. Although Demeas does mention a concern to protect his son's reputation, it seems that Demeas is habituated to this discretion by long practice and that an instinct for privacy is central to his disposition.[21]

Nikeratos' invocation of the barbershop and the pedestrian stoa exposes the gulf between the two men, despite their attempts to bridge it, in another way. These are "low places"; men loiter about them from early on, with little better to do than retail the latest gossip: καθημένους δὲ πάντας ἐξ ἑωθινοῦ / περὶ ἐμοῦ λαλεῖν (511–12).[22] Even without Demeas' obsession with privacy, the barbershop and the street are the last places he would want his name bandied about. Yet here Nikeratos feels at home. He naturally associates such demotic locations with the most auspicious venue of his κλέος ("fame"). Nikeratos' phrasing in 510–11, it has been noted, turns "tragic" (μηθὲν . . . μήτε . . . μὴ: cf. Sandbach ad loc.) and grandiloquent, as though he were referring sweepingly to the entire city by a kind of metonymy. To Nikeratos, in other words, this *is* the polis.

Furthermore, although Nikeratos may feel horror at Moschion's supposed betrayal out of a natural revulsion, or even out of a feeling of solidarity with

Demeas (despite their underlying differences), the "poor" neighbor also feels a delight in debasing his richer, more successful "partner": ἀνδράποδ[ον εἶ, Δημέα (506). Nikeratos imagines himself specifically as acting in a manly way (see 512: ὡς ἀνὴρ Νικήρατος γέγον'), and this implies that Demeas is less of a man than he should be, or certainly less of one than his social inferior, Nikeratos. Though he seems to ally with Demeas, at the same time Nikeratos makes this a capital occasion for redressing the imbalance in their relationship, which arises from their differences in status and wealth.[23]

Menander expresses the sizable difference between Nikeratos' and Demeas' sense of status, as well as personal honor, via Nikeratos' sense of the polis, which comes into play by means of the allusive technique that we identified above. The natural question at this juncture is whether Demeas also invokes the polis at some point in the play, as Nikeratos does. If so, what is the nature of the space to which Demeas alludes? Given his overriding concern with preserving privacy amid the ostensible disaster in his household, it makes sense that Demeas *does not* allude to the public sphere after the onset of the crisis. In his entrance at the beginning of act 4, the last restful moment until Nikeratos leaves the stage with Demeas at the end of the act, Demeas looks no farther abroad than to offer a prayer to the image of Apollo Agyieus that stands before his house.

In his prayer to Apollo (444–49), Demeas indicates a resolve to carry through with the wedding despite his upset. That Demeas addresses Apollo also has symbolic significance. The god's image stands on the border of house and street, and serves, in Demeas' perspective, as a buffer between the household and the public sphere. When little else has proved stable, the god must seem to protect the privacy to which Demeas clings, as Demeas' imperative to Apollo—τήρει— confirms: while the verb figuratively suggests that Apollo should watch over Demeas lest he make a slip at the wedding and display his annoyance to anyone, it also has the literal sense of "stand guard," "keep secure."

Demeas' concern transcends a simple wish not to be "obvious" ('πίδηλος) about his recent frustrations. This concern becomes more plain just twenty-five lines later. Because Moschion, as Demeas sees it, appears evasive, Demeas addresses Apollo in a different tone:

> ταῦτ' οὐ γνώριμα,
> οὐ σαφῆ; μαρτύρομαί σε, Λοξία, συνόμνυται
> τοῖς ἐμοῖς ἐχθροῖς τις. οἴμοι· καὶ διαρραγήσομαι.
>
> (Sam. 473–75)

Isn't it obvious, and plain to see? I call you to witness, Loxias, someone is in league with my enemies. Confound it! I will surely burst.

Now, when Demeas does acknowledge the public sphere, he is combative. He speaks as if he were giving evidence before Apollo: μαρτύρομαί σε, Λοξία. Demeas immediately suspects that his enemies conspire against him, to exploit Moschion's embarrassment—or Moschion (τις) is even collaborating with them.[24] It is difficult to know who Demeas means by the phrase τοῖς ἐμοῖς ἐχθροῖς. One gathers that Demeas has been active enough in the polis to incur enmity among certain rivals; or he simply anticipates a natural hostility among the envious.[25] If Demeas knows who he means by τοῖς ἐμοῖς ἐχθροῖς, the object of his anxiety is concrete, so that the insistence on privacy seems calculated rather than paranoid. Consequently Demeas' allusions to space, both in speech and action, tend to outline the oikos; he not only draws no comfort from those outside it, quite contrary to Nikeratos, but views suspiciously the world that begins at the street.[26]

To return to the prayer in 444–49 from this subsequent outcry to Apollo, it is curious that there Demeas directs an aside to the audience—μέλλω γὰρ ποεῖν / τοὺς γάμους, ἄνδρες, καταπιὼν τὴν χωλήν ("For I intend to celebrate the wedding, gentlemen, and swallow my anger")—which is sandwiched inside the two sentences of the prayer to Apollo (= 446–47). This is odd first of all because Demeas is fairly busy at this time; as Blume notes, the addressee of Demeas' monologue changes three times within a brief space.[27] Besides, as I just demonstrated, Demeas is both upset and fearful. He exhorts Apollo to guarantee his discretion and self-control at the wedding, but also to watch over him more generally. If Demeas fears exposing his distress in front of other people, or himself to his enemies' mirth, it is strange that he should suddenly open up to over ten thousand witnesses!

Walther Kraus explained Demeas' earlier address to the audience in act 3 (verse 269) by saying that the relationship stood outside the "world of the play": ". . . seinen Nachbarn etwa oder Vorübergehenden auf der Straße würde Demeas sein vermeintliches Mißgeschick gewiß nicht so brühwarm erzählen." Or Menander here purposefully ignores these boundaries. The intimacy Demeas develops with the audience results from Menander's manipulation of the convention of audience address. In the candor and frequency with which Demeas comments to the audience on his own behavior, he privileges it, an openness remarkable precisely because Demeas reveals such intense concern with "enemies" (ἐχθροί), as shown above. In fact, whereas one might expect the connection between Demeas and the audience of the play to be ephemeral, it is not.[28]

That Demeas' relationship with the audience has thematic significance is suggested early in the play, when Demeas and Nikeratos first enter. This entrance scene borrows on yet another comic convention, what Gaiser in his study of *Fragmentum Didotianum* b called the "praise of Athens."[29] In this fragment an anonymous character describes his feeling of wonder at the sight of Athens, after he has apparently undergone a transformative experience of some sort. In *Samia*, likewise, Demeas praises the sight of Athens with an enthusiasm fostered by his absence in the Pontus. In both cases, the familiar emotion of greeting one's native land is heightened by the added feeling of a temporary alienation.[30] If the playwright executes the convention with skillful enough variation to make the praise seem genuine, or at least cleverly done, then the topos ought (if only momentarily) to produce a sense of solidarity within the community-in-microcosm that the actors and spectators together represent.[31]

The rebirth into a new world of sight is reiterated throughout the fragment.[32] Owing to this emphasis, perhaps, the experience of the theater itself becomes an object of praise, because the theater combines the notions of physical vision with perception and understanding (διάνοια); hence the theater is magnified as an integral part of the overall civic experience of an Athenian.

> νῦν θ' οἷον εὕρημ' ἄνδρες· ἐν τῇ σήμερον
> ὑμᾶς ὁρῶ νῦν αἰθρίᾳ, τὸν ἀέρα,
> τὴν ἀκρόπολιν, τὸ θέατρον.
>
> (frag. *Didot.* b 13–15)

What a discovery this is, gentlemen: in the clear light of today I now see you all, this brilliant atmosphere, the acropolis, the theater.

It is tempting to see the same sort of reference in Demeas' comparison of the light of Athens and of Byzantium in *Samia* 110–11. Assumedly, Demeas' far-fetched comparison of the gloom over Byzantium to the brilliant light around Athens is all part of a joke on Nikeratos' gullibility. Otherwise, since the clear atmosphere of the city is a routine element of its praise,[33] Demeas' remarks may be attributed simply to Menander's need to vary the motif. It is also possible, however, that Demeas means the comic spectacle when he claims of Byzantium: ἀλλὰ σεμνὸν οὐδὲν ἐθεᾶτ' αὐτόθι ("But there was nothing worth seeing there," 110); that is, Demeas is actually saying that what is worth looking at here, in Athens, as opposed to Byzantium, is comedy, that is, edifying drama. Appropriately, Nikeratos' asseverative oath: νὴ τὸν Διόνυσον, εὖ λέγεις, indeed names the god of the theater.[34] Just as the speaker in the fragment unites light, acropolis, and theater as the constituents of Athenian self-consciousness, Demeas praises the theater as much as the city, and thus flatters the spectators in a double sense, both as citizens of the polis and as the audience of that day's comedy.

From all this Nikeratos is excluded. If Sandbach is correct that Nikeratos is the speaker of lines 98–101, then Nikeratos' speech is not party to any praise of the city. His final apothegm "undiluted good for the poor" reverses the expectation of praise that was raised by his complaints against the Pontus. Instead of rounding off the sarcasm of "Byzantion/apsinthion" with something like "But here it is much better," Nikeratos instead shoots a bolt of sarcasm at his native polis. The complaint suits Nikeratos, however, insofar as he makes an issue of his poverty at several points in the play.[35] Yet Nikeratos' sarcasm only serves as a springboard for Demeas' praise, which is launched without Nikeratos' having finished out the line. If this assignment of lines is correct, then Demeas' μακαριώτατοι constitutes a deliberate counterpoint to Nikeratos' πενήτων. We must return to these lines (102–4), in fact, at the end of the section. The relevant point here is simply that at the very outset of the drama Menander dramatizes the potential for division between these two "friends," and roots that potential in their unequal socioeconomic positions.

Thus the audience aside within Demeas' prayer to Apollo is another hint that the relationship with Nikeratos is flawed. At that instant it seems as if Demeas, feeling embattled (εἰσανάγκασόν με σύ, 449), falls in with the Aristotelian teaching on the value of friends in a time of misfortune: "Pain is alleviated when friends share the sorrow" (1171a29). In this spirit, then, he establishes his intimate rapport with the audience by means of the asides. But this reflects badly on his relationship with Nikeratos, since the friendship on that side, also judged by Aristotelian criteria, falls far short of the ideal form of friendship. In fact, the relationship between Demeas and Nikeratos seems most like the third, or least desirable, of those discussed in the typology of friendships in book 8 of the *Nicomachean Ethics*: the type based on τὸ χρήσιμον (see 1156a6–23). This is so, at least, judging from Nikeratos' motivation. What Nikeratos derives from Demeas is usefulness, particularly in the economic sense. His "poverty," as I just said, is alluded to at several points in the play; yet Demeas for his part has decided to marry his son to Nikeratos' daughter without the dowry. Indeed, as the misunderstanding in act 4 begins to mount, Nikeratos blurts out that he would prefer to be father-in-law to Diomnestos, whose story apparently (as Dedoussi has shown)[36] signified the sudden loss of a fortune. Nikeratos' outburst reveals how he sees Moschion, namely, as a very rich prospective son-in-law, and likewise that Nikeratos' relation with Demeas stands largely for profit.

From a final vantage point, Moschion's remark at 458–59, τί τ]οὺς φίλους / προσδοκαῖς ἐρεῖν πυθομένους; ("What do you expect your friends to say when they learn about this?") refers to an essential function of friends, to take a concern in one's affairs and to give advice. Demeas' primary group of friends is never present in the drama, except in this reference. Yet Moschion's passing remark briefly lends them a presence. They must be of roughly the same class and financial standing as Demeas; what is important in the present context is that this group of Demeas' friends indicated by Moschion need not, and probably does not, include Nikeratos.[37] It is true that Demeas' comment in 518 reveals his expectation of Nikeratos to act the "proper" friend: συναδικοῦ γνησίως ὡς ἂν φίλος ("Suffer along with me, nobly, as a friend would").[38] But Demeas says this at a moment of supreme agitation, and also when Demeas is in the midst of error. When Demeas comes to his senses, the distance between himself and Nikeratos is reestablished. Within only fifty lines the two nearly come to blows; to avoid a serious row Demeas has to becalm Nikeratos with the same guileful species of conversation (587–614) that marked the apparent teasing of lines 106–12 in their entrance scene.

The same differences made plain by Nikeratos' and Demeas' constructions of "space"—Nikeratos' evocation of the barbershops and idlers' haunts, Demeas' emphasis on the protective privacy of his own oikos—originate in the intrinsic nature of their relationship. Menander has dramatized between the two men a relationship whose fault lines run along the coordinates of class and wealth. The friendship would not on Aristotle's prediction tend to be harmonious, or to last. (Granted, the friendship of unequals is described in *Nicomachean Ethics* 1163b1–16; yet it is doubtful that Nikeratos, except occasionally, gives Demeas honor in the proportion Aristotle suggests is appropriate as a return for the "better" man, who stands to offer more in the way of material benefit.) But the relationship functions very well as a symbol of the type of relations within a community as differentiated as Athens was in terms of social and economic status.[39] Because the tensions that Aristotle predicts in an unequal friendship correspond to tensions among the classes of the polis itself, they are of prime concern to the φιλόπολις, Menander.

Such tensions are reflected in Demeas' prayer to Athens:

> ᾿Αθῆναι φίλταται,
> πῶς ἂν γένοιθ᾿ ὑμῖν ὅσων ἔστ᾿ ἄξιαι,
> ἵν᾿ ὦμεν ἡμεῖς πάντα μακαριώτατοι
> οἱ τὴν πόλιν φιλοῦντες.

(Sam. 101–4)

Dearest Athens, how I wish you might have all you are worthy of, so that we who love our city may be blessed in all ways!

Though this sort of remark is again familiar from the dramatic convention to which it belongs, nevertheless the lines, particularly in connection with this point about μακαρία, also have special relevance within the immediate context. Demeas is responding to Nikeratos' facetious remarks (if Nikeratos is facetious), either sympathetically, or in an attempt to ride hard over Nikeratos' criticism of the polis. In either case, Demeas seeks to correct his partner; it is only a question of the sharpness of Demeas' reply. If Demeas' meaning is something like "*We* are well enough off—may we only remain so—you should not blame the city for *your* problems," then the tone is arch, even oligarchical. More likely, Demeas feels less impatience than embarrassment at Nikeratos' comments: in such a case, Demeas' "we" *includes* Nikeratos, and addresses him, though indirectly, as φιλόπολις, and also as one who has been disadvantaged—unjustly—by a decline in the city's fortunes.

"The prayer that Athens may have what she deserves may have had some topical allusion to a danger or misfortune in which she was involved."[40] Were we able to date the *Samia* precisely, we might know better if Menander had a particular misfortune in mind. Webster dated the play very early: 320–318 B.C. This would provide a suggestive background: the disruptions that followed the Lamian War, especially those due to the interference of Macedonians in the internal politics of Athens.[41] In 322, when the city fell under Antipater's control, he revised the citizenship drastically so that at a stroke thousands of citizens were disqualified by a higher property qualification. Such an action should have intensified the tension between rich and poor, insofar as it converted inequality of wealth from an underlying issue to an overtly political one.[42] However, Antipater's proxy rule did not last, and the exclusionary higher qualification, though not eliminated, was at least modified in 317, when Demetrius of Phaleron, supported by Cassander, instituted his *epimeleia* of Athens.

If the play was produced before 317 B.C., then the resonance of Demeas' words might be deeper, for his wish would touch on the restitution of the fortunes (both literally and figuratively) of former citizens. If the play came after 317, then the wish would not refer to suffering as acute as in the immediate aftermath of Antipater's policy.[43] The invidious distinctions inherent in Antipater's order would have been mitigated, to some extent, though even in Demetrius' more liberal citizenship criteria, these distinctions remained. In this scenario Demeas' wish embodies a conciliatory spirit, which, though disparities in wealth still have political consequences, nevertheless seeks to deny it.

It has been argued that the audience of Menander's comedy was upper class—especially if payments out of the theoric fund were finished—and therefore financially comfortable.[44] If one chooses to read such passages as Demeas' prayer for prosperity as "conciliatory," then the question arises, what possible relevance might have attached to the idea of "conciliation" for this audience, since it was quite possibly a homogeneous gathering, and therefore, both as audience and social group, not subject within itself to the tensions generated by the competition of unequal economic classes?

The sense in which Menander adopts a "conciliatory" tone with his audience, first of all, has nothing to do with his own relation to that audience, of course; instead, he addresses the idea of conciliation, or social tact, as it relates to the lives of that audience outside the theater and within the web of relations which, as stated at the start of this essay, constitute the polis. The way in which Menander serves that audience by dramatizing the relation of rich and poor, governed by a spirit of conciliation, falls under two headings: admonition and consolation.

The issue of rich and poor surfaces frequently in Menander's early drama, not only in *Samia*, but also, for example, in *Dyskolos*.[45] Menander there makes the point several times that a poor man may be very sensitive in dealings with a rich one, and that the rich must be careful to avoid even an appearance of taking advantage of the poor man: Gorgias puts the issue clearly at the end of his first speech to Sostratos (*Dyskolos* 295–98). But Demeas and Nikeratos successfully avoid at least open conflict on those grounds. It is instructive for the audience to witness this disparity in fortunes negotiated so satisfactorily for both men. Both receive from the relationship what they need, so that, at least at first sight, there seems to obtain something like the proportionality that Aristotle spoke of in connection with friendships of inequality. After all, Nikeratos obtains his son-in-law free of expense (see 727–28), and Demeas obtains from the match what is most important to him, that Moschion upon marriage becomes the gentleman Demeas desires of him: πύκαζε σὺ κράτα καὶ κόσμει σεαυτόν ("Put the crown on your head, and compose yourself," 732–33).[46]

The price of this relationship will be high for Demeas, however, not simply in terms of the financial outlay required to service his friend. The true cost for Demeas accrues more to his spiritual account. One suspects at the end of the play that these two men, with their different financial means, alien tastes, and unequal standings, may find their relation trying at times, and even somewhat turbulent. Beside the material reviewed above, there is in addition the last image that Menander leaves in the minds of the audience: that of Demeas standing in between Nikeratos and his son, Moschion, who has just drawn his sword on his father's friend! Demeas seemed to have sorted the situation out by the end of act 4; yet he no sooner assuages Moschion than Nikeratos appears and at once introduces confusion back into the bargain, and the potential disruption of all their plans. The strenuous negotiations Demeas will face (for the foreseeable future) are on display in this final scene.[47]

The play provides a lesson in tolerance among classes and statuses, yet at the same time subtly reinforces the social hierarchy. Menander orients *Samia* around Demeas, perhaps for a mostly upper-class audience, therefore a man very much like them. In dramatizing Demeas' accommodation to a man who does not share his fortune or his views, the play offers consolation as well as a gentle warning to the "better sort," who similarly have to accommodate themselves, in their lives outside the theater, to the likes of Nikeratos. The polis that Menander addresses in the *Samia*, then, is one in which the upper class, though secure in its property, its other advantages, and its sense of superiority, must nevertheless adjust itself to the participation of others of lower status in many aspects of the life of the polis, which all inhabit in common.

Mass and Elite in Menander's Polis

By the technique of allusion to the "theatrical space without," Menander evokes the physical reality of the polis and uses the details of its topography to suggest different aspects of the polis as a social and political construct. For another example of Menander's enactment of the polis in this way, I turn to a scene from the *Sicyonian*, in which the Eleusinian demos deliberates on the citizenship and custody of young Philumena.

The relevant topographical detail in this instance is the great Propylaea, in the north wall of the sanctuary at Eleusis:

ἐξ] ἄστεως δ' ἥκων—ἵν' ἐντύχοιμί τωι
τῶν δημοτῶν μέλλοντι λεπτὸν βοΐδιον
νέμειν ἀκούειν θ' ὅσα προσέστ' αὐτῶι κακὰ
ὑπὸ τῶν λαβόντων μερίδα—τούτων δ' αὐτὸς ἦν·
τοῦ τῆς θεοῦ δήμου γάρ εἰμ' ἐπώνυμος,
Βλέπης Ἐλευσίνιος—ἐπέστην ὄχλον ἰδὼν
πρὸς τοῖς προπυλαίοις, καὶ "πάρες μ'" εἰπὼν ὁρῶ
καθημένην παῖδ' εἰς τε τούτων τῶν κύκλωι
γενόμενος. εὐθὺς δῆμος ἦν καὶ κύριον
   τ]ῆς καθημένης κόρης

(183–92)

I was leaving the town to meet up with one of my own demesmen, who was about to share out a pretty pathetic little ox, and to hear plenty of complaints from those who were getting a portion—I myself was going to be one of these; for I am a bona fide member of the goddess' own deme, Blepes the Eleusinian—when I saw a crowd at the gates of the city, and I stood up next to it, saying "excuse me," and could see a young girl sitting there, so I myself became one of those who were in a circle. All at once it was like a meeting of the *demos*.

Here Blepes (who narrates the entire scene, for this is an example of an ἐξαγγελία, or messenger scene) describes how he happened on a meeting of the demos. The purpose of this meeting apparently is to discover the rightful guardian of Philumena, who sits in supplication before the assembled deme. (Such is the sense if one accepts something like Sandbach's supplement of 192: εὑρεῖν ἐπεθύμει.)

At stake for Philumena is citizenship (social, not political) and thus identity, for both depend on the discovery of her proper *kurios*. Without a citizen father, she forfeits her own claim to freeborn status and remains in Stratophanes' control. At stake for the community is a principle whose importance is shown by the frequent appearance of the theme of citizenship in Menander. By Pericles' citizenship-law of 451 B.C. only offspring of two Athenian parents were entitled to Athenian citizenship.[48] This restriction of the franchise obviously strengthened the connection between citizenship and marriage. Doubts over the status of a marriageable young woman therefore are a concern for the social group as well as for the individual, for any ambiguity in this regard threatens the set of definitions that protects the citizen body from tampering and maintains citizenship itself as undiluted, that is, highly restricted.

In this sense, then, a drama of the polis is present in the drama of Philumena. But the scene also relates to the polis in another sense. For as much as the scene exposes a threat to citizens and the citizen body posed by cases of mistaken or lost identity, it comments additionally on the very process of the political assembly. In the narration of the assembly the process of democratic government stands on prominent display. Menander is therefore airing a view of democracy itself—perhaps a view of Athenian democracy, moreover, dressed up in the guise of a local deme meeting.

The scene has an additional significance that confirms this interpretation; as has been widely observed, Menander's scene resembles the messenger scene in Euripides' *Orestes*.[49] In the scene from *Orestes* a messenger reports the Argive assembly's debate on whether to condemn Orestes. Certainly this play engages the core of the Greek mythical tradition, like so many other Euripidean plays; but *Orestes*, especially within the scene in question, also seems to address various problems of Athenian-style democracy, for example, in the relation of the discourse of popular assemblies to leadership and decision making.[50] If the Euripidean scene dealt with politics and political discourse, then it seems natural to assume that Menander would place that scene in the background of his own scene primarily in order to open a dialogue on politics. While some have discussed Menander's borrowing, or transformation of the Euripidean episode, no one has described the relationship of the two dramatic passages as a dialogue in which Menander echoes the Euripidean passage in his own messenger scene in order to comment on political behavior in the democratic city.[51] This approach may provide at least one way of describing the effect of Menander's composition of this scene, by seeing its adversion to the place of assembly within the polis as leading to a dialogue on politics with Euripides' scene in the *Orestes*.

Menander is careful to signal the relation of his own scene to the Euripidean original. Menander's messenger, who names himself in 187–88—Blepes of Eleusis—opens his account of the assembly meeting with the words

ἐτύγχανον μὲν οὐ[κ ἀγρόθε πυλῶν ἔσω
βαίνων, μὰ τὸν Δι', οὔτε τ[

(Sic. 176–77)

I happened to be on my way, not from the countryside, but inside the gates, by Zeus . . .

which resemble those of the messenger in Euripides' play (at some risk of circularity, since the lines above are restored on the basis of the Euripidean text below):

ἐτύγχανον μὲν ἀγρόθεν πυλῶν ἔσω
βαίνων, πύθεσθαι δεόμενος τὰ τ' ἀμφὶ σοῦ
τὰ τ' ἀμφ' Ὀρέστου·

(Or. 866–68)

I happened to be on my way from the countryside, inside the gates, as I wanted to learn how things stood with you, and with Orestes . . .

On the other hand, Blepes' description of himself—δημο] τικός, οἵ καὶ μόνοι σῶιζουσι γῆν ("a democrat, the sort who alone preserves our land")—resembles the description of the last speaker at the Argive assembly, before Orestes himself: αὐτουργός, οἵ καὶ μόνοι σῶιζουσι γῆν ("a man who works the land himself, the sort who alone preserves our land"). Therefore, even though Menander makes certain connections explicit between his and the Euripidean ἐξαγγελία, there is obviously not a complete correspondence between the two scenes, nor does Blepes, most importantly of all, have a straightforward analog. To sort out the ways in which Menander has linked these two passages, then, we need to move cautiously. It will be helpful first to outline the Euripidean scene, by describing its three key players: the farmer (αὐτουργός) who advocates the cause of Orestes and Electra, the messenger himself, and the demagogue who speaks (on Tyndareus' behalf) for a condemnation and the death sentence; then to examine the character of Blepes, as Menander constructs it, as well as Blepes' narrative of the meeting of the Eleusinians.

The farmer is an important figure in the Euripidean messenger scene. He alone speaks for Orestes without equivocation. This farmer is also presented in a flattering light because he seems to embody the values of the narrator himself. For the narrator reveals his own sympathies by referring to his gratitude to the royal family of Argos (see *Or.* 866–70). At the least, we can describe the αὐτουργός as a conservative, though the approval of the narrator is insufficient to prove that the farmer is, like this messenger himself, a royalist.

As much as he speaks for the monarchy, or even for the son, Orestes, the farmer speaks for the injured father. He condemns Clytemnestra in general terms, that is, in reference to the norms of religion and morality (κακὴν γυναῖκα κἄθεον—"wicked, godless woman," 925), but worst of all, the farmer insinuates, is the harm she has done the state, specifically the war-making ability of the state and its capacity to defend its interests. This is made clear in lines 926–29, in which the farmer warns that no man will march on campaign if his wife and property are threatened by nonservers (like Aegisthus) and by Clytemnestra's precedent. The narrator foreshadowed this disposition within his introduction of the farmer into the debate: ξυνετὸς δὲ χωρεῖν ὁμόσε τοῖς λόγοις θέλων ("shrewd, and willing to come to close quarters in debate," 921), for χωρεῖν ὁμόσε lends the line a military connotation—to be precise, a connotation of the close-in fighting characteristic of hoplite warfare. On this evidence the farmer represents the sort of moderate conservative who might equate service in arms with the right to share in the duties and privileges of citizens.[52]

There is a hint that the farmer is apolitical—ὀλιγάκις ἄστυ κἀγορᾶς χραίνων κύκλον ("rarely in the town or the marketplace," 919). But to the narrator this amounts to nothing more than a praiseworthy self-restraint. The messenger at the same time insists that this farmer is an effective speaker (921). Indeed, in this debate his speech persuades, though only within a smaller audience—καὶ τοῖς γε χρηστοῖς εὖ λέγειν ἐφαίνετο ("and he seemed to the good sort at least to speak well," 930); the farmer fails to move the democratic mass: νικᾷ δ᾽ ἐκεῖνος ὁ κακὸς ἐν πλήθει λέγων ("but that scoundrel won over the mob with what he said," 944).

Here the αὐτουργός loses out to the demagogue, whom the narrator presents as unfavorably as he describes the farmer flatteringly:

ἀνὴρ τις ἀθυρόγλωσσος, ἰσχύων θράσει,
Ἀργεῖος οὐκ Ἀργεῖος, ἠναγκασμένος,
θορύβῳ τε πίσυνος κἀμαθεῖ παρρησίᾳ,
πιθανὸς ἔτ᾽ αὐτοὺς περιβαλεῖν κακῷ τινι.

(*Or.* 903–6)

A certain man who does not mind his tongue, who feeds on his own audacity, an Argive in name only, always someone's creature, who himself depends on a commotion and on thoughtless, wild speech, and who can be depended on to get people into trouble.

The demagogue, according to the narrator, lacks decency, is bold without real courage, obstreperous, ignorant, and dangerous to the state, insofar as he readily serves a bad cause. Possessing no abiding loyalty (Ἀργεῖος οὐκ Ἀργεῖος), the demagogue serves nothing outside of what accords with his self-interest: in this connection the narrator claims that the demagogue in this assembly functioned as the tool of Tyndareus (915–16). Likewise, the assembly in which the demagogue triumphs takes on his characteristics, and represents the democratic process in a brutal and biased form.

With this in mind, let us move to the scene in the *Sicyonian* and the characterization of Blepes. In terms of the verbal and structural parallels between Menander's scene (at its start) and the Euripidean scene, Blepes ought to correspond to the farmer and the narrator. As a vigorous democrat, however, he is the opposite of the conservative αὐτουργός, not to mention the "royalist" messenger. Blepes is by his own claim δημο]τικός, or ἐργα]τικός: it is difficult to choose the correct supplement. The former suits Blepes as he himself describes his tendency: ὄχλος ὤν (161).[53] If the phrase φοβερὸς εἰς τριώβολον (180) is in fact a reference to his fancy for the jury court, this phrase would likewise indicate Blepes' democratic leanings. Blepes further characterizes himself in the following lines:

] καὶ τὰ τῶν ἄλλων κακὰ
ἐξ] ἄστεως δ᾽ ἥκων ἵν᾽ ἐντύχοιμί τωι
τῶν δημοτῶν μέλλοντι λεπτὸν βοΐδιον
νέμειν ἀκούειν θ᾽ ὅσα πρόσεστ᾽ αὐτῶι κακὰ
ὑπὸ τῶν λαβόντων μερίδα—τούτων δ᾽ αὐτὸς ἦν·

(Sic. 183–86)

. . . and other people's troubles . . . I was leaving the city to meet up with one of my own demesmen, who was about to share out a pretty pathetic little ox, and to hear plenty of complaints from those who were getting a portion—I myself was going to be one of these . . .

The first line above is difficult to interpret since the context is abbreviated by damage to the text; but some level of interest in others' troubles is indicated. The rest similarly betrays a mild malice—Blepes expects the ox sharer to be abused or mocked by the feasters; the last half of line 186 suggests both "I was going to be there" and "I would be adding to his troubles too."

Blepes' attitude appears aggressive, echoing the stereotypical manner of a "democratic" personality;[54] his language elsewhere gives a similar impression, e.g.: μισῶ σε καὶ τοὺς ὀφρῦς ἐπη[ρκότας/ἅπαντας ("I hate you, and all your sort who raise their eyebrows," 160). Not only is μισῶ harsh, but ἅπαντας seems indiscriminate. This manner of speaking again conveys the impression of a popular-leaning democrat, yet one might argue to the contrary that in this last instance Blepes is simply giving it back fairly to Smikrines, if in fact that is his dialogue partner in lines 150–55.[55] In any event, despite these hints of a pugnacious nature, Blepes seems to back down from Smikrines at line 167— perhaps Blepes is less dangerous than simply voluble. It may be safer to say that, while Blepes is the democratic man, to be sure, even so any judgment on his seeming excesses ought to be withheld until the conclusion of his narration.

A detail that associates Blepes with the democratic element but is less compromising, for example, comes in the phrase with which he describes himself entering the meeting on Philumena's case: εἷς τε τούτων τῶν κύκλωι γενόμενος ("joining in as one of these in the circle"). This phrase portrays democratic behavior in concrete terms, and very nicely enmeshes the key terms, "one" and "those in the circle," in order to represent the unity of individual and body of citizens in a democratic society. The line appears to contrast with Euripides' messenger's comment on the αὐτουργός: ὀλιγάκις ἄστυ κἀγορᾶς χραίνων κύκλον ("rarely in the town or the marketplace," 919). In the account of Euripides' messenger, ἀγορᾶς κύκλον (the "circle of the agora") is an archaic phrase[56] well suited to the assembly place of Argos in the heroic age. In Blepes' narrative, on the other hand, the phrase τούτων τῶν κύκλωι refers to a different sort of event, a local democratic proceeding, and to its quality of immediacy and the intimacy of its participants.

We may now turn to that assembly as Blepes narrates it. True to the care with which Menander characterizes Blepes (though in a brief space), the assembly takes its color less from the actual event itself than from Blepes' perception of it. By Blepes' account it is full of sudden alarms and just as rapid decrescendos and silences. At several points Blepes punctuates his speech with verbs of loud vocal noise to render the outcries of the crowd at key moments in the presentations of Dromon, Moschion, and Stratophanes. According to Blepes the crowd is intent on the actors before it and is highly susceptible to the impressions that each succeeding speaker produces.

This treatment returns us to *Orestes*, for it resembles a description of the behavior of the democratic mass offered in that play: namely, Menelaus', to Orestes just before Orestes' "trial." Though the controlling metaphor in Menelaus' account is fire, nevertheless, as Blepes does (though unconsciously), Menelaus characterizes the demos as a volatile element:

ὅταν γὰρ ἡβᾷ δῆμος, εἰς ὀργὴν πεσών,
ὅμοιον ὥστε πῦρ κατασβέσαι λάβρον·
εἰ δ' ἡσύχως τις αὐτὸς ἐντείνοντι μὲν
χαλῶν ὑπείκοι, καιρὸν εὐλαβούμενος,
ἴσως ἂν ἐκπνεύσει· ὅταν δ' ἀνῇ πνοάς,
τύχοις ἂν αὐτοῦ ῥᾳδίως ὅσον θέλεις.
ἔνεστι δ' οἶκτος, ἔνι δὲ καὶ θυμός μέγας,
καραδοκοῦντι κτῆμα τιμιώτατον.

(*Or.* 696–702)

Whenever the people in a body are at full pitch, having succumbed to passion, just like when one tries to extinguish a ferocious fire, if one does not fan it, when it is most intense, but watches carefully for the right moment, it may well exhaust itself. Once it remits its fiercest blasts, you might have better luck with it, surprisingly so. There is pity in the people assembled, and also considerable compassion—a very valuable possession for the man who knows what to look for.

Menelaus' calculating approach at this point in the play does not of itself disqualify his testimony.[57] Indeed, it is difficult to say whether the assembly meeting that turns out so disastrously for Orestes proves Menelaus wrong or right. Menelaus does not condemn the demos in an unqualified way, but places an onus on the leader, or speaker, in a democratic proceeding. The speaker must act with considerable poise (εἰ δ' ἡσύχως τις αὐτὸς ἐντείνοντι μὲν χαλῶν ὑπείκοι) and prove himself not just an astute but an agile judge of the public mood (καιρὸν εὐλαβούμενος, ἴσως ἂν ἐκπνεύσει). It may be laid at Orestes' door that Orestes himself fails to live up to these requirements; he is unpersuasive with the demos, as he was before with Tyndareus. On the other hand, several options were available to the demos, for example, Diomedes', not to mention the proposal of the αὐτουργός.[58] These cannot have been so far undermined by Orestes, even if he is as displeasing to the people as this line of argument suggests, unless the proceeding is indeed unfair.

The assembly trial that condemns Orestes and Electra is a harsh proceeding, determined not by quality of argument but by partial interests, which are mostly at work, moreover, outside the proper arena of the discourse. Whatever the merit of Tyndareus' position, the proceeding in the assembly is a sham; Tyndareus has his way behind a thin covering of legal procedure. The success of this manipulation, and the pivotal role played by the demagogue, seem not only to accentuate Menelaus' implicit critique of the fickle mob, but simultaneously to engender a sharper critique of democracy by negating his sanguine assertions of the potential for constructive leadership.

Both Menander's interest in the failure of Orestes in this mythic politics, and his keenness on his audience's remembering the bitter outcome of the political process in the *Orestes*, suggest the likely relation of Menander's transformed scene and the Euripidean original. In respect to the latter, the parallel of the *Orestes* scene is meant to be felt as an omen of disaster. Menander's Blepes is intended at first to raise doubts over the happy, or just, outcome of the "trial," which may well settle the fate of Philumena and also of Stratophanes. As a matter of fact, the more one recalls the Euripidean play, the greater the apprehension over the scene to be described by this Blepes character, for the "demotic" in that play of Euripides seems to stand for unjust and intemperate policy. On the other hand, in connection with the former, Orestes' inability is contrasted, as we will see, by Stratophanes' success with the Eleusinians. Interestingly enough, Menelaus' view on the role of the speaker in a democracy will fare much better in Menander's assembly scene than in Euripides'.

To deal first with the negative expectations raised by reminiscences of the assembly in *Orestes*, it is disturbing that at one moment Blepes is contemplating a portion of his fellow demesman's ox roast, then abruptly at the next is taking his share in the public business. The easy shift from one sort of banquet to another is an eerie reminder of the gluttonous agon of Agoracritus and the Paphlagonian in *Knights*. The disquieting proximity of feasting to politics suggests that one sort of appetite is just like another, and that for many within the great mass of the demos state business falls under the heading of pleasure, not dutiful service. What is more, the "noise" of the proceedings that Blepes describes suggests the worst side of democratic politics, and prompts another unwholesome recollection of *Orestes*, namely, in the description of the demagogue as ἀθυρόγλωσσος and θορύβῳ τε πίσυνος.[59]

Yet one must recall how Philumena's affair / Blepes' meeting turns out. Contrary to the depression of expectations produced by Menander's evocation of the Euripidean parallel, Stratophanes wins in the assembly, despite Moschion's attempts to shake his credibility. Indeed the crowd of Eleusinians only suspects Moschion; their reaction is impeccable. Despite all outward appearances, its noise and bluster, mutability of affect, and of course Blepes' class coloration in the background, the demos reveals a basic sense of decency on account of which it responds instinctively to Stratophanes, then to the merits of his case once he presents them in order.

The crowd resists a natural but parochial instinct to distrust Stratophanes, because he is not only ξένος but στρατιώτης as well (cf. fr. 439 K). In fact it strikes up an affinity with Stratophanes before he even speaks: ὄ]ψει τις ἀν-δρικὸς πάνυ ("looking like a *real man*," 215). In line with the *Orestes* parallel, Stratophanes now resembles the αὐτουργός of the debate scene there—μορφῇ μὲν οὐκ εὐωπός, ἀνδρεῖος δ' ἀνὴρ ("not much to look at, yet every inch a man," *Or.* 918)—not in respect to the first phrase, but the second. Menander does not need the audience's marking the precise verbal parallel. Once he has placed the audience within the framework of the *Orestes* play, it naturally responds to the thematic cue "ἀνδρικὸς" by associating this character with its similar type in the parallel play.[60] Menander assimilates Stratophanes to the farmer (who is "manly," that is to say, "decent" or "honorable") by means of the key word ἀνδρικὸς, which arises out of the perception of the assembly crowd.

Stratophanes' positive reception is in contrast, of course, to Moschion's, whose less robust appearance makes him appear shifty. The crowd sees in Moschion something unsavory—μοιχώδης δὲ μᾶλλον κατεφάνη ("he appeared to be a creep, really," *Sic.* 210). This reaction again defies the expectations raised by the Euripides parallel, and prepares for that moment in Blepes' narration (215–16) when the crowd responds to the noble character who in the original acted for the losing cause.[61]

In fact, Menander has amended the scene of his original in order to produce a more wholesome outcome. To put it another way, Menelaus' advice has been vindicated in a different environment. The higher instincts of the demos are engaged first of all because a fellow citizen is at risk: "πολῖτίς ἐστιν ἡ παῖς" ("the girl is a citizen!") is the first uproar, which follows immediately on Blepes' report of what Dromon said, most of which is lost to a lacuna in the text, unfortunately. And it is to this sensitivity that Stratophanes pitches his appeal. Stratophanes mentions his expense in Philumena's upbringing only to repudiate it along with his claim over her, sensible especially as this claim has no legal standing any more. And if Dromon had said anything unfavorable of him (in 194?), Stratophanes deflects this when he gives up the slave, too, with the girl. At line 238, finally, he emphasizes the issue of citizenship: the girl must find her family in order to be reintegrated as soon as possible into her rightful community, which in turn guarantees her appropriate status and standing. Stratophanes asserts only self-restraint: οὐκ ἀντιτάττομ' οὐθέν ("I am not going to offer opposition").

In a masterstroke, Stratophanes recommends that those in the assembly itself take responsibility for their fellow citizen, and stand as κύριος for the girl, until her father and family retrieve her from their guardianship and the custody of the priestess in Demeter's precinct. After hearing the applause that follows this gambit, Stratophanes reveals his own recent self-discoveries, and his hopes regarding Philumena as well, which after all are fairly straightforward.

Stratophanes' presentation to the Eleusinians embodies two related principles: that an individual's identity within the community is guaranteed in that person's identity within the basic unit of the community, the oikos; and that the community has an interest in safeguarding the oikoi of which it is composed, for the sake of its own stability and good order. It is by now common to point out the constant attention paid in New Comedy to a deep concern over citizen status (and the complementary dependence of the polis upon its citizens). The dread of losing a place within one's polis, and, one supposes, the utter dependence of the individual upon it, prompted the comic poets of this period to reproduce again and again this drama of status and security lost and regained.

In exposing the essential fabric of the polis, the scene rehearses this collective fetish of fourth-century Athenians. But the amount of anxiety normally involved with this motif is in fact increased by Menander's skillful handling of this scene over against its "original" in the *Orestes*. Through the juxtaposition of Blepes' speech and the messenger scene in *Orestes*, the audience is unsettled momentarily by suggestions of the sharp divisions within Athenian society and the instability of the democratic temperament in general. The outcome of the assembly settles this anxiety, however; the polis holds to its essential ways faithfully and the assurance of sympathy between community and individual, polis and πολίτης, is not revoked, but reaffirmed. The comrades of Blepes do the proper thing; they respond to the principles to which Stratophanes refers, and by these principles he is able to elicit the "correct" behavior from them.

I would like to broaden this interpretation by applying some of J. Ober's conclusions regarding Athenian democratic ideology (in his book *Mass and Elite*) to Menander's scene. Indeed Stratophanes' performance among the Eleusinians strikingly resembles the performances of elite speakers before the mass audiences of Athens' various political contexts, which Ober analyzes throughout his book. In general, Ober argues that, because of the difficulties inherent in constitutional change, "tensions generated by simultaneously maintaining social inequality and political equality . . . had to be resolved on the ideological plane. The sociopolitical order operated smoothly as long as the social power of the elites was balanced by the political power of the masses."[62]

His observations on the performance of the elite litigant before a mass audience of jurors demonstrate this problem in its acute form:

> The need for mediation was particularly acute in the law courts, where the people sat in collective judgement on the individual citizen. As an individual confronting the group, the litigant was in a high-risk position. . . . The elite litigant . . . was in a particularly delicate spot. Communication with the jurymen was his only way out of the dangerous individual-versus-community and elite-versus-mass situation. The elite litigant who could persuade the jurors that, despite his elite privileges, his interests and theirs were identical, would win their sympathy and so save himself.[63]

This description is particularly applicable to Stratophanes. Not surprisingly, Stratophanes' rhetorical performance illustrates many of the techniques identified by Ober as necessary for success before the mass audience: the elite litigant must (1) "make clear to the jury his generalized adherence to egalitarian principles, his acceptance of the correctness of mass rule and mass judgement"; (2) "[show] himself to be a good citizen, a demotikos, the sort who would be likely to use his elite attributes for the good of the demos"; (3) "By lowering himself and elevating the members of the jury in status, . . . put himself on the same social footing as his audience."[64]

By observing these requirements, the elite orator may arouse the sense of a "community of interest," which assures him a good hearing. It should be clear from the above summary of Stratophanes' speech that he indeed puts these very ideas into practice. His tears and tearing of hair produce an impression of powerlessness (219–21); he suggests his loyalty to the demos by addressing Tyche in its behalf (224–25), and more emphatically by referring to the institution of κυρία, in a way, moreover, which establishes the demos as the singular locus of authority within the polis (ὄντες αὐτοὶ κύριοι, 240); and, finally, he forgoes his "elite" advantages: wealth (226 and 237, 235–36) and stratiotic skill (239). Stratophanes is successful because he puts himself on a level with the Eleusinian demos. The perfection of this strategy comes at the climax of his speech, when he offers himself as a fellow citizen (246–51), and—to emphasize his humility vis-à-vis the mass—a brand new one: Σικυώνιος τὸ πρότερον (246). All in all, then, Stratophanes' performance belies the anxiety that attaches to the relation of the individual (most acutely the elite individual) and the social mass. Ober fairly describes the process in the *Sicyonian* when he concludes:

> For their part, the jurors—and, on a society-wide level, the demos as a whole—were persuaded that there was no need to bring their collective political power to bear against the elite. The individual who played his role correctly was no longer perceived as a threat, and hence there was no need to act preemptively against him. In short, having shown himself to be at the mercy of the masses, the individual had reason to expect merciful treatment from them.[65]

Stratophanes very much "plays his role correctly." For that reason he wins a relation with Blepes and his colleagues in which an ethical discourse plays the dominant part. The way they together sort out the difficulty surrounding Philumena is a model of humane consideration and tact. How this comes about is best laid bare with the help of Ober's analysis of the large body of fourth-century evidence on the mass-elite relationship.[66]

Ironically, Moschion himself unveils the nature of Stratophanes' role in the assembly in an unintended way when he casts aspersions on Stratophanes' sudden discovery of a citizen's pedigree: ἐξαίφνης πολίτης [ἀνεφάνης· / γεν-ναῖον ("suddenly it turned out you are a citizen—magnificent!," 274–75). But Moschion only reinforces the thematic parallel of Stratophanes' character and performance to the messenger and farmer in *Orestes*. As the messenger in the *Orestes* says of himself: χρῆσθαι δὲ γενναῖον φίλοις ("but noble when it comes to aiding friends," 870); and indeed he and the αὐτουργός represent the noble spirit in that play, but in its corrupt atmosphere remain frustrated and ineffectual. Moschion's sarcasm misses, but he reveals the way Stratophanes has redeemed the notion of γενναῖον ("noble"), particularly in relation to the passage from *Orestes*. Menander has brought the Euripidean text full circle, by circumvention of the despairing belief that the individual, especially a decent one, is liable to be a victim of the community, given the corruption of (democratic) governments. In his comic play Menander, in order to redeem (democratic) government, unites the banausic and the heroic, the democratic and the noble, Blepes with Orestes' advocate and Stratophanes.

In the sense that the polis itself entails the unity of banausic and heroic, democratic and noble, then the polis is the virtual subject of the scene in the *Sicyonian*. The city is first physically manifested by scant reference to the Propylaea (if one assumes that in some sense Eleusis stands in for the city proper at Athens). This landmark itself helps to locate the assembly, which is both space and civic function at the same time. The scene then evolves into a consideration of the polis in more abstract terms, in the way it dramatizes the operation of political discourse within the assembly of citizens. The object of that discourse, moreover, consists less in specific concerns, like an individual's guarantee of citizen status, than in the more general question of how the debate transpires when important issues are decided: will the process of public discussion operate in a humane and civilized manner, that is, can it operate properly at all?

This question must concern a community which is apprehensive about its equilibrium. Within such a community an unequal distribution of status, money, and power produces different groups who tend to pursue different interests. As he did in *Samia*, however, Menander implies here that social and/or economic inequality need not always lead to unworkable relationships among individuals; common goals are not impossible, though the level of comfort even in fairly sound relationships may not be as high as one might wish. The same concern over the coordination of interests within a society is present in Aristotle, of course. We may employ Aristotle at this juncture as a nearly contemporary source for Menander to complement the modern perspective just derived from Ober's work.

Aristotle reveals at several points in the *Politics* a desire to reconcile the two broad constituencies which compete in the polis, that is, the "better sort" and those who are their social inferiors (or, simply, rich and "poor").[67] In fact, in a passage that treats democracy favorably, Aristotle entertains the possibility that the many, though not highly capable as individuals, are wise in the aggregate and in that way may govern well. (See *Pol.* 1282a7, 1295b6, 1318b1.) This suggestion is particularly apt to the scene in the *Sicyonian*: it helps explain how Blepes by himself might seem untrustworthy yet together with his peers perform admirably.

Another passage that discusses cooperation between different classes, from the *Ethics*, also applies to the scene in act 4 of the *Sicyonian*.

> For concord does not consist in two persons having identical thoughts of any kind at all, but in having them in relation to the same person, e.g., when both the common people [ὁ δῆμος] and the better classes [οἱ ἐπιεικεῖς] wish that the best men should rule [τοὺς ἀρίστους ἄρχειν]. For in this way only does everyone attain his goal. We see, consequently, that concord is friendship among fellow citizens. . . . Now this kind of concord exists among good men [ἐν τοῖς ἐπιεικέσιν]. They are of the same mind each with himself and all with one another, since—to use the expression—they never shift their position: the wishes of people like this remain constant and do not flow this way and that, as the Euripus does. They wish for what is just and what is in the common interest, and these are their common goals. (*NE* 1167a33–1167b9, trans. M. Ostwald)

There follows in Aristotle's discussion an explanation of what occurs when "bad men" (οἱ φαῦλοι) attempt to live according to *homonoia*. They cannot in fact sustain the attempt, since they are too keen on their own advantage, do not exert themselves for the common good, and are jealous of their neighbors: "So faction comes to be rife among them, when they force one another to do what is just, though they are themselves unwilling to do it" (1167b14–16). The pessimistic note on which the chapter ends can be construed as Aristotle's effort to maintain consistency, namely, with his own position that there is no real friendship among bad men.[68] This should not obscure the fundamental point of the argument, however, that concord consists not in "having identical thoughts" but in "having them in relation to the same person," a principle that makes mixed government possible, nor the corollary of this crucial point, which constitutes the underlying thrust of the chapter, that the union of the common people and the "better classes" will encompass the best interest of all so long as the driving force within the arrangement is the "better people."

This proposition of Aristotle's is reflected in *Sicyonian* in the way the assembly is managed successfully by Stratophanes, himself representing the kind of "best men" Aristotle refers to, whom the people will elect if harmony exists in the polis. Likewise, Aristotle's image of the Euripus recalls the image of raging fire which Menelaus in *Orestes* applied to the democratic mass; but also the raucous crowd of Eleusinians, in the *Sicyonian's* assembly scene, before it feels the effect of Stratophanes' speech. Just as Aristotle uses the image to illustrate what a well-mannered community will *not* resemble, so in Menander's assembly the noise dies away (or is successfully directed) under the influence of Stratophanes' oratory.

Menander dramatizes a community in which harmony arises among the disparate orders of society under the guidance of a "right-thinking" individual. This good order results when everyone seems not "unwilling" to do "what is just." Indeed the Eleusinians do not have to be "forced" to do "what is just," as the only "force" required—the persuasion of Stratophanes—is scarcely force at all. Therefore the polis that Menander enacts in *Sicyonians* is well governed and its integrity is upheld by the low and the high together. In regard to this outcome, then, it seems less important, at least in the play as we have it, that Stratophanes and Moschion turn out despite their skirmishing to become brothers, than that Smikrines and Blepes, who see their differences so clearly, are able nevertheless to abide effectively by one set of laws, a common political process, and by a similar ethical instinct that seems not to be conditioned exclusively by wealth or family background.

Polis and *Oikoumenê*

Aristotle was the last major philosopher to construe man as a political animal, arguing that "the *polis* is both natural and prior to the individual." The new philosophy which emerged in Menander's generation put the individual first. Epicurus, Menander's exact contemporary, construed individuals as freely moving social atoms who bind themselves to others in order to secure individual happiness. The Stoics stressed the need for individuals to attune their souls to the law of nature, universal law not political law. These philosophical changes have an obvious political context in the hegemony of Macedon, and the declining autonomy of the Greek city-state. Menander's comedy marks the point of transition from Aristotelian to post-Aristotelian thinking, and could be said to dramatize the emergence of the autonomous individual. Autonomy is symbolized by the decision to marry for love. Fifth-century tragedy characteristically asked its audience to consider the question: "who are you first—a member of your *oikos* or a member of your *polis*?" New Comedy posed a rather different question: "who are you—a member of your *polis* or a member of humanity?" Sophocles expected his audience to understand and appreciate Creon's argument that the needs of the state must often override family responsibilities. By the time of Menander, the requirements of the state have become alien and almost incomprehensible. The legal requirement, for instance, that heiresses marry their nearest male relative in order to prevent the concentration of wealth was a theme for tragedy in Aeschylus' *Danaid* trilogy, but becomes an arbitrary and ludicrous piece of legislation in Menander's *The Shield*. Where classical tragedy dealt always with two equal and opposite moral forces, New Comedy dealt with the struggle of an individual moral agent against impersonal and arbitrary forces.[69]

In this excerpt from his recent book, David Wiles treats the relation of Menander and the polis according to the tendency I noted at the outset of this essay: as the polis weakens, specifically vis-à-vis Macedon, and loses its autonomy, so New Comedy concentrates instead on the individual person, who still has autonomy; thus the polis disappears from Menander.

I focus on two objections to Wiles' formulation. First, the chronology of Wiles' argument is arguable. Epicurus and Menander were, perhaps, *sunepheboi*. But by the time Epicurus' κῆπος was established and his ideas known and disseminated within Athens—likely not before the end of the last decade of the third century—Menander was already roughly halfway through his career as a comic playwright. Likewise, Stoic ideas were not current, nor was Zeno even philosophically active in Athens, until Menander's career was well advanced.[70]

Second, it seems premature to portray Menander as "post-Aristotelian." I have already demonstrated that in his drama Menander engages ideas that resemble discussions of similar issues in the works of Aristotle. Indeed elsewhere in his stimulating book Wiles himself seeks to illustrate Menander's interest in Aristotelian ethical and aesthetic issues.[71] So I doubt that even Wiles would insist that the term "post-Aristotelian" applies to Menander in its basic sense. The more particular sense suggested by Wiles, as describing one who holds the classical polis to be a form of community that has been superseded, fits Menander even less. This we will attempt to show in the final section, though conceding that Menander may have suffered doubt over the survivability of the traditional polis.

In Menander the question "oikos or polis?" has not been superseded by that of "polis or humanity?" In fact, it is not even clear that Menander has given up on the autonomy of the polis. This autonomy is no longer measured by the city's capacity to effect x or y in its relations with another Greek polis. Attention fastens instead on the ability of the polis to maintain proper conditions within itself: to assure that its citizens possess what is essential for a civilized life, that is, a relatively harmonious, rationally self-governing community. I have already demonstrated in discussions of *Samia* and *Sicyonian* Menander's deep concern for the integrity of the polis in these terms. Returning to *Samia* briefly, I might review Wiles' suggestion that Menander emphasizes the individual and disregards the concerns of the polis. In my analysis Moschion's dilemma took second place to the conflict between the two citizens, Demeas and Nikeratos; by this approach, interests of the polis overshadow those of the young Moschion. Even yielding place to Moschion momentarily, however, one does not make the polis disappear.

Moschion never mentions Eros in his prologue, when he embarrassedly confesses the rape that obligated him to Plangon's family. He only says that he swore to the mother that he would marry the girl. In the final act, when Moschion lists the considerations that render impossible his running away to punish Demeas, he first names this "oath" (ὅρκος). He does then go on to say that Eros is now master of his thinking (γνώμη), yet this eros is a consequence of Moschion's sense of duty, not the other way around. Obligations to his father as well as to the girl and her family demanded that he "do the right thing." Whatever Moschion's other failings, this sense of honor is what makes him capable of becoming κόσμιος (a *gentleman*, for lack of an equivalent in English).[72] The term κόσμιος relates to a constellation of personal qualities, all of which have social implications. Moschion will not gain his autonomy if he can "marry for love." On the contrary, Moschion will have his "autonomy" only if the relationship of trust he has built up with his father, and the significant social role to which his father has helped him (which now must include keeping his pledge to Plangon and her mother), will not be destroyed by his (moment of) thoughtlessness. The social context is central to Moschion's experience.

To resolve the issue of whether or not the polis held its place in Menander's dramaturgy over against a new interest in "humanity," I look finally at *Epitrepontes*, since this play, considered by many to be Menander's most mature drama, contains some highly pertinent evidence on the question.

The main plot of *Epitrepontes* involves the separation of Charisios and Pamphile, while the return of their child, whom Pamphile had abandoned in desperate hope of mollifying Charisios, to parents and oikos constitutes the chief subplot. Both plot lines reflect how *Epitrepontes* assumes that the integrity of the polis relies on the oikos, its basic constituent, in this instance specifically a newly formed household.

Let us examine these plots in reverse order. First, even a brief inspection of the subplot, the struggle to restore the child, reveals the presence of the polis. The arbitration scene that secures the baby's fortune constitutes most of act 2, and is undertaken by two men, Daos and Syros. These two have come into possession of the baby (Daos first, by chance, then Syros by Daos' gift) by virtue of their living on the margins of the polis. It is Daos who articulates how their "location" figured in the recent fortunes of the disputed infant: "I was herding my sheep about a month ago in the scrub land that's just beyond these farms [ἐν τῶι δασεῖ τῶι πλησίον τῶν χωρίων]. I was alone that day, and I found the infant boy . . ." (*Ep.* 242–45).

Sandbach describes the *choria* as farms located within the agricultural territory of the polis, obviously outside the urban center;[73] this area of settlement therefore represents a second tier of civilization, as it were. Beyond it is the less cultivated, less traveled, *dasus*. It is here that the two primitives, Daos and Syros pursue their marginal economic activities, in an area still further removed from the focal point of the polis, its urban center. The urban center itself is the third term of the equation, and is represented in this scene by Smikrines. If one puts aside the ironies with which Smikrines is laden, it becomes clear how Smikrines represents the urban aspect of the polis. It is not just that he provides judgment (grudgingly at first) in the dispute of Daos and Syros. Smikrines represents the town in this play, not by his sophistication, of course, but by his coming and going to and from the town throughout, as he is in fact doing at the very moment when he meets up with the two "litigants." (Cf. 370 with 577–79; also see 752–53, where he imagines Charisios setting himself up in Piraeus, an "urban" fantasy out of keeping with Charisios' actual state of mind.) Moreover, although Smikrines is unappealing in many ways, he nevertheless names the rustics for what they are—οἱ διφθέρας ἔχοντες ("fellows in overalls")—and thus is implicitly contrasted with them. Finally, obtuse or not, Smikrines is still the infant's grandfather and thereby source of the child's eventual citizenship.

Thus the entire polis is mapped out in the scene by means of a combination of setting, characters, and narrative. In that way the polis forms the background of the "choice" being enacted on behalf of the helpless child. The baby has been forced out into the margins of the polis, yet belongs in its center; though the full citizenship is his by birthright, that simple fact has been obscured by chance. Menander dramatizes how this existence as a citizen has been threatened by that chance as well as the temper of Charisios through an imaginative recreation of the space whereby the infant is alienated from its proper oikos. We do not need to have seen the child exposed, owing to the economy of Menander's dramatic technique. Within the "extended" setting,

Daos' narration of the child's adventitious disposal into strange hands high-lights the fragility of the citizenship dispensation, and likewise underscores its value, touching once again on that basic anxiety of the polis dweller, namely, the loss of one's place within the polis.

To move in the other direction, the tendentious remarks of Syros might seem to represent a brand of humanism. His dependence on human resources to remedy the miscues of fortune appears as "humanistic," and more importantly Syros even declares concern for fellow humans in general, without specifying, for example, one's fellow citizens (although it is true that otherwise Syros would have little reason as a noncitizen to concern himself with a strange infant, or anyone else).[74] In this manner Syros might seem to answer of his own accord what is effectively the "postclassical question": who are you—a member of your polis or a member of humanity? But does Syros in fact serve a more "humanistic" ideal, in place of the polis, namely, one that recognizes a com-monality and fundamental responsibility among men who are not *sympolitai*?

To the contrary, Syros bases his behavior on a fundamental role embedded in the structure of oikos and polis; namely, the role of the *kurios*. We have already seen the importance of the function of *kuria* through its deployment within Stratophanes' oration in the *Sicyonians*. Syros himself stresses nothing so much as his function as *kurios* of the child, until the discovery of its parents and thus a rightful guardian. Citing this responsibility in lines 306–7, Syros reiterates it in 315–17. In this second instance Syros answers his own imagined question, "Why did you not ask for the child's trinkets at that time when you first took the child?" The obvious response to this question is actually something like "because I did not know the child had any possessions or tokens; otherwise I would have asked." Syros instead responds as he does because he has focused so strongly on his "legal" role as the child's guardian, as *kurios*. And the role of the *kurios* is, once again, embedded in the single structure which comprises oikos and polis. It is one of "the requirements of the state" which has not in the least become "alien or incomprehensible." In this sense Syros is parochial still, and therefore compromised as the advocate of a new humanistic attitude.

Turning to the main plot, one might see Charisios himself as evidence for the shift in thinking that Wiles discusses. Charisios' characterization is clearly a central feature of the play; perhaps the emphasis on the developing conscience within Charisios fairly embodies the "emergence of the autonomous individ-ual." The way Charisios overcomes the lack of faith (as well as charity) he shows toward Pamphile, although he is beset by the uncomprehending Smik-rines, might again be seen as the "struggle of an individual moral agent against impersonal and arbitrary forces." Only one might object that, as for these "forces," the unestimable Smikrines simply does not answer. Any fearsomeness is circumscribed by a consistent irony, best shown, for example, in the way Smikrines acts as judge for his own grandson without a faint inkling of the significance of what he is doing.[75]

It is true, however, that Charisios' moral development, that is, his confrontation with the fact and consequences of his "error" (cf. *Ep.* 908), involves a struggle that takes place largely within himself. This locates a share of the dramatic interest where Wiles would wish it. The objection here is that Charisios' transformation is itself inextricably wrapped up in the restored relation with Pamphile, a point obscured by the damaged state of the text. The focus shifts to Charisios at the end of act 4, but it had been trained decidedly upon Pamphile just before, in her scenes first with her father, then with Habrotonon. If the first half of act 4 were not in such a lamentable state of preservation, then the mutuality of the fortunes of this pair would be much clearer; there would be less emphasis on Charisios' scene at the conclusion of the act. By presenting the pair thus in act 4, with Pamphile initiating the reversal of their situation in the scene with her father, Menander affirms that the salvation of their marriage is the triumphant result of the action of the play. This is not a valuable outcome, furthermore, only because it will delight a sentimental audience; rather, the outcome is satisfying because thereby the principals conform happily to their necessary social roles (of husband and wife within a new oikos) despite the momentary interference of chance and misunderstanding.[76]

In the *Epitrepontes*, then, Menander's concern for the polis is still apparent. There is one passage—Onesimos' teasing of Smikrines in act 5—in another part of the play, however, in which the paradigm of the world seems indeed to have shifted. The relevant text is as follows:

Sm.   πρὸς θεῶν καὶ δαιμόνων—

On.   οἴει τοσαύτην τοὺς θεοὺς ἄγειν σχολὴν
        ὥστε τὸ κακὸν καὶ τἀγαθὸν καθ' ἡμέραν
        νέμειν ἑκάστωι, Σμικρίνη;

Sm.   λέγεις δὲ τί;

On.   σαφῶς διδάξω σ'. εἰσὶν αἱ πᾶσαι πόλεις,
        ὁμοῖον εἰπεῖν, χίλιαι· τριμύριοι
        οἰκοῦσ' ἑκάστην. καθ' ἕνα τούτων οἱ θεοὶ
        ἕκαστον ἐπιτρίβουσιν ἢ σώζουσι;

Sm.   πῶς;
        λέγεις γὰρ ἐπίπονόν τιν' αὐτοὺς ζῆν [βίον.

On.   οὐκ ἄρα φροντίζουσιν ἡμῶν οἱ θεοί,
        φήσεις; ἑκάστωι τὸν τρόπον συν[ῴκισαν
        φρούαρχον· οὗτος ἔνδο[ν] ἐπ[

ἐπέτριψεν, ἂν αὐτῶι κακῶς χρη[σώμεθα,
ἕτερον δ' ἔσωσεν. οὗτος ἐσθ' ἡμῖν θεὸς
ὅ τ' αἴτιος καὶ τοῦ καλῶς καὶ τοῦ κακῶς
πράττειν ἑκάστωι· τοῦτον ἱλάσκου ποῶν
μηδὲν ἄτοπον μηδ' ἀμαθές, ἵνα πράττῃς καλῶς.

Sm.   εἶθ' οὑμός, ἱερόσυλε, νῦν τρόπος ποεῖ
ἀμαθές τι;

On.   συντρίβει σε.

Sm.   τῆς παρρησίας.

(*Ep.* 1083–1101)

Sm.   By all the gods great and small!

On.   Do you think the gods have such leisure that they take care of everyone's fortunes, good and bad, every single day, Smikrines?

Sm.   What are you trying to say?

On.   I will make it as clear to you as I can. All together there are, one might
as well say, a thousand cities. Each one has thirty thousand citizens.
For every single one of these men do the gods bring on afflictions or
salvation?

Sm.   How could you say that? They would have a pretty rough life.

On.   So then the gods do not care for us, you would say? No, they set up in
each of us a character—a garrison, as it were. This afflicts us if we treat
it poorly, but someone else's character may preserve him. This is our
god, and it is the cause of each man's doing well or doing badly.
Propitiate this god by doing nothing out of the ordinary, or just plain
stupid, and you will do just fine.

Sm.   Are you saying that my "character" is doing something stupid, then,
you disgusting wretch!

On.   It's wearing you out cruelly.

Sm.   . . . with this outrageous talk of yours!

This opening of Onesimos' elaborate spoof of Smikrines clearly implies the
transcendence of a new world order over that of the polis. Onesimos' vision
subverts the order of the traditional polis in two fundamental ways. First, in
terms of religion, the gods of the polis and their cults become obsolete. Without rejecting their existence, Onesimos cuts the city loose from any necessary
ties to the Olympian gods. These are all replaced by surrogate *daimones*; each
single citizen has, residing in the citadel of his being, a conscience. The gods no
longer insure the moral order by their oversight and active intervention, since
instead the agency of good or ill is implanted in each human being.[77] Consequently a person's fortune is more than ever a matter of personal responsibility.

Onesimos has unwrapped the weave of personal and communal religion, which is one of the central features of the polis.

In addition, Onesimos' phrasing assigns no special place to the native polis, in this case, Athens. The autonomous polis no longer serves as the standard of reference, for it has yielded to a larger, more impressive entity, the *oikoumenê gê* of the Hellenistic age—the world reshaped by Alexander's conquests and augmented by his city foundations and those of his marshals after his death. Perhaps the greatest change entailed in this transformation is that the political significance of the individual polis is erased in a world that contains so many cities. The designation of the personal gods as phrouarchs has a touch of bitter and highly pertinent humor, besides, since it alludes to the Macedonian hegemony that dictated the real shape of political significance in this post-polis world—large territorial blocs, or "kingdoms," the true counters now, within each of which many Greek poleis are subsumed.

Onesimos' number of inhabitants seems exaggerated, but suits the new *oikoumenê*, whose magnitude Onesimos thus reflects in its subordinate parts, the cities. At the same time, this *oikoumenê* is not so impossibly large that we cannot conceive its extent; though of great size, it conforms to a rational accounting.[78] Along similar lines, this new world is remarkably homogeneous. Every polis has the same number of inhabitants, and thus looks and feels the same. In this detail of Onesimos' vision of the world, more than in any other, the polis has sacrificed its most essential characteristic, that is, the sense of itself as unique. In Onesimos' vision of a world of identically sized, uniform poleis, no longer is any one polis distinctive, or independent in the sense of owning its own peculiar set of cults and customs, landscape, and material culture.[79]

Thus Onesimos paints the incipient Hellenistic world in a few brief strokes. The emblematic quality of his characterization of the *oikoumenê* recalls the one implied in Stasicrates' offer to Alexander of a gargantuan portrait monument:

> It was Stasicrates who had remarked to Alexander at an earlier interview that of all mountains it was Mount Athos which could most easily be carved into the form and shape of a man and that if it pleased Alexander to command him, he would shape the mountain into the most superb and durable statue of him in the world: its left hand would enfold a city of ten thousand inhabitants, while out of its right would flow the abundant waters of a river which would pour, like a libation, into the sea. Alexander declined this proposal. (Plut. *Alex.* 72, trans. Scott-Kilvert)

If the anecdote refers to a real event, Alexander might have refused out of a desire not to offend the Greeks, many of whom would have seen the display when they traveled to the Chalcidice or en route to the Black Sea. The scale alone would cause affront, Alexander would have realized, a Xerxes-like imposition on nature. Alexander would also have perceived the offense in the ambiguous message of the monument, since it could suggest either that Alexander had fulfilled the destiny of the Greek polis by overturning the Persian Empire, imaginably its antithesis, and carrying the polis ideal through the rest of the world, or to the contrary that the world created by Alexander now dwarfed the polis, reducing it to insignificance before its absorption within a system of petty states dominated by a hegemonic Macedon. Stasicrates must have conceived of the colossus mostly in terms of the latter, the symbol of Alexander as *oikistês* of a new world order incorporating the polis, yet also clearly transcending the polis as a political unit.

If Alexander did in fact hesitate to broach this idea publicly, what might Menander have had in mind in foisting it on his Athenian audience in the last act of the *Epitrepontes*? Since we claim in this essay that Menander was committed to the ideals of the traditional polis, we would expect Menander to have suggested that a new-fashioned *oikoumenê* had superseded the polis only for the purpose of subjecting such a view to a subtle ridicule. Indeed it can be shown on both internal and external grounds that Menander, by making Onesimos a spokesman for this notion of the replacement of the polis, thereby looks to exercise the minds of his audience on the idea in order to undercut it.

I add nothing to what I said already about the interdependence of oikos and polis in the *Epitrepontes*, except that the concern shown their interrelationship argues a priori against Onesimos' vision of a world which does not know the primacy of the polis. Beyond that, the internal grounds for rejecting Onesimos' perspective consist first in the placement of Onesimos' scene within the play, and then in the nature of Onesimos' character itself.

Under the first heading (of Onesimos' scene viewed in structural terms), the very fact that his gambit comes in act 5 of *Epitrepontes* itself puts his "teaching" inside inverted commas. In Menander's plays basic conflicts may appear resolved by the end of the fourth act; the fifth act therefore often seems subsidiary to the fourth act in relation to the important issues of a given play.[80] In the *Dyskolos*, for example, after Sostratos' engagement has been achieved, and in addition Gorgias' to Sostratos' sister, all in act 4, the action then transfers in act 5 to the "low characters," Getas and Sikon, who take revenge (for themselves, as well as everyone else) on Knemon by tormenting him with requests for the loan of absurdly expensive items. This scene suits the festive ending of the play, and ushers in the mood of the κῶμος ("revel").[81] The dramatic tension has been broken already—by Knemon's rescue and "apology," and then by Kallipedes' acquiescence in Sostratos' plan for himself and his new friend, Gorgias. The fifth act dispels any lingering tension by providing another sort of confrontation, with its separate and appropriate tone and a more raucous sort of resolution.[82]

The final act of *Dyskolos* thus affords a comparison to *Epitrepontes* because in the latter's final fifth act Smikrines likewise is tied into the resolution that, in the fourth act, has already been achieved for the characters who are of real concern to the ethical and social themes of the play. As the text stands, it is unclear if the action issued into a κῶμος-type celebration; however, the parallel with *Dyskolos* is maintained insofar as Onesimos introduces into his play the same mood of absurdity and hilarity that Getas generates at the close of his. If this is Onesimos' function in the last act of the play, then the specific content of his speech ought to matter less than its subservience to a conventional strategy of boisterous good humor. This is not the place one would expect to find Menander's considered endorsement of the *oikoumenē* and the new world order of the *diadochoi*.

There is also the matter of Onesimos himself. His characterization through the rest of the play must impinge on his quality as a spokesman at the end of it. Without making Onesimos out as unsympathetic, one might claim nonetheless that he is singularly unadapted to speak with any authority to an audience of citizens concerning the shape of their world. A comparison with two other characters in the play, both of whom share with Onesimos the disadvantages of low status, may clarify the point.

As odd as Syros' performance in act 2 may seem, it nevertheless distinguishes him from Onesimos, without flattering Onesimos. Frequently in the play Onesimos appears helpless to act, in terror at what he expects will happen. Syros, on the other hand, when his opportunity presents itself, displays an outlandish competence, as a sort of skin-clad ombudsman—μέτριος ῥήτωρ: "a regular speechmaker."[83] Syros makes excellent use of his case to win the verdict and obtain custody of the child as well as the disputed property.

Onesimos by contrast falls into a pattern of feeling overwhelmed and of simply wishing himself out of the way (e.g., at 580–81, 901–7). In perhaps the best example of this tendency, at the beginning of act 3, Onesimos is caught flat-footed by Charisios' changing of heart, and cannot use the ring he has found, a critical token in the play, to any advantage. When Onesimos cannot decide what to do with this ring, just obtained from Syros, it is another character equally disadvantaged by her status, Habrotonon, who conceives the plan to turn the ring into a useful instrument for Charisios, the child, and Habrotonon herself—for all, that is, but Onesimos. Onesimos' speech at 557–62 praises Habrotonon's cleverness and attests his own failure to make any improvements in his lot. In comparison with both of these characters, who act in a manner more suggestive of the freeborn (in Syros' case, perhaps for the sake of an incongruous humor), Onesimos seems to suit himself to being a slave. In this way he least qualifies as a serious spokesman in act 5, since he is the least free of the players in the drama.

When Onesimos finally "finds his tongue," and produces his own kind of eloquence, it is at a time in the play when nothing is at stake. The pressure is off, and it is almost in direct reaction to that release of pressure that Onesimos suddenly flies off the handle. Only a short time before Onesimos was praying to Zeus "to save him, if it is possible" (907). Now in act 5, his neck out of the noose, Onesimos does away with Zeus, posting his semidivine phrouarchs in Zeus' stead. His gambit in the final act seems more than anything like "blowing off steam." Indeed Smikrines, humorously enough, is the one person than whom Onesimos is better-informed, to whom Onesimos is fully superior in his understanding of events. Onesimos' joy at finally feeling not only safe, but also superior, in this sense, gives rise to the exuberance that issues in his cosmopolitan vision of a homogenized world of a thousand altarless cities. Given this context, Onesimos' allusion to the *oikoumenê* is self-critiquing: this is the kind of thing such a slave might think, and say, but not a good *politês*, "citizen."

The external grounds that militate against Menander's apostasy from the polis belong in two categories. For the first category, I need to examine briefly the way Onesimos' passage has figured in discussions of Menander's place within the evolution of an ancient Greek belief in the "unity of mankind." Finally, I will conclude this essay by adducing the small group of ancient testimonia that depict Menander as *philopolis*, and even, one is tempted to say, as something of a homebody—recalling Socrates himself.

We may begin with H. C. Baldry's discussion of Menander's so-called humanism. In his book *The Unity of Mankind in Greek Thought*, Baldry took note of Onesimos' speech: "These lines are certainly an advance on the limited outlook of local city-state patriotism. They may seem to present a picture of the whole Hellenistic world, at once cosmopolitan and individual, the other barriers that divide men forgotten."[84] It is surprising that Baldry takes Onesimos this seriously since he himself notes within this same section that "deciding how far opinions expressed by particular characters can be taken as the author's own" is a "difficulty in drama."[85] Nevertheless, here Baldry ignores the dramatic context of Onesimos' remarks to consider them as evidence for a cosmopolitan spirit in Menander. My discussion of Onesimos' speech, of course, depends heavily upon context, and this context, consisting of the scene's placement in the structure of the play and also of the characterization of Onesimos, undercuts Onesimos' "argument." To read the scene in light of these dramatic circumstances convinces one that Onesimos' view of the world ought not to be taken seriously.

It is difficult for Baldry to determine precisely how cosmopolitan Menander had become. Baldry rightly insists that a belief in the "unity of mankind" does not manifest itself suddenly in the writings of ancient Greeks, but that most evidence for what appears to be such a belief in fact is suspect when examined closely—something Baldry does throughout his book. Yet in Menander's case he seems to wish to mark some degree of advance: once the Greeks considered *tropos*, or "character," a common possession of men, then any man of good character, whatever his race or origins, could achieve "merit," or "excellence of character," that is, by assimilating to a Greek ideal.

> Where others—notably the Cynics—had talked of the universal worth of wisdom, Menander sets up merit as a universal standard: a Greek standard primarily, but one to which others, even Ethiopians or Scythians, may conform. The true division of the human race, it is implied, is between the good and the bad, not between riches and poverty or between Greek and foreign blood. Thus Menander may be seen as taking his place alongside Alexander in rejecting the Aristotelian point of view, and in this sense, that there is one standard for all, he repeatedly emphasises the idea of the unity of mankind; but his conception of it seems to have arisen as a natural development out of earlier Greek thought rather than a result of sudden awareness of the wider horizons opened up by Alexander.[86]

Baldry is careful to qualify Menander's humanism as less than fully universal— "a Greek standard primarily"—yet still desires to mark Menander off from the long-standing ethnocentric biases of the Greeks. Baldry's suspicion may be right. The problem is that no clear-cut evidence of any such "universal standard of merit" for Menander exists. In certain fragments a speaker may seem to suggest a generous attitude toward others, and not simply fellow demesmen; Baldry quotes fragment 602 K:

> For me no man who's good
> Is foreign. The same nature have we all,
> And it is character that makes men kin.

Without context, however, we are not in a favorable position to analyze the fragment, and we certainly cannot use it, in all fairness, to build a case for what lay in Menander's own mind.[87]

At the end of the paragraph quoted above, moreover, Baldry places Menander side by side with Alexander, in order to contrast both with Aristotle, but then distinguishes Menander from Alexander. If the urge to set up Menander (and Alexander, for that matter) as "post-Aristotelian" is again premature, at least that last added qualification reasserts Baldry's sensible doubts. For Baldry clearly saw that Menander's willingness to understand "character," or "merit," as other than purely a function of race does not distinguish him sharply from certain other earlier Greek writers; it is a common motif in Greek literature to divide mankind, in a general way, among the "good" and the "bad," as Baldry himself shows.[88] For Baldry, in the end, Menander is more traditional than "progressive"; Baldry hesitates—rightly, it seems—to attribute to Menander any special enthusiasm for "the wider horizons opened up by Alexander." This caution is more in keeping with the tone of his study as a whole, and harmonizes with the cardinal point he makes earlier in this chapter, arguing against Tarn:

> "Man as a political animal," wrote Tarn, "a fraction of the polis or self-governing city state, had ended with Aristotle; with Alexander begins man as an individual." The statement is striking, but hardly true to the facts. It is all too easy to dramatise the impact of so dramatic a figure. . . . Perhaps even the change of label, from the Hellenic to the Hellenistic period, tempts us to imagine a sudden shift in the climate of thought. . . . The truth lies not in a sudden change to a "Hellenistic" world, but in a complicated sequence of developments whereby trends already at work, stimulated and given fresh scope by the achievements of Alexander, grew in strength and had a cumulative effect over the next century or more.[89]

To explain the origin of the pressure on Baldry to assess the attitude of Menander differently, one may note an anachronistic assumption that appears at the beginning of Baldry's appraisal of Menander's "cosmopolitanism." The bias is clear in what Baldry writes of Menander's audience:

> Although Menander probably mirrors the ideas of the more prosperous and better educated section of his audience, this only means that he represents those to whom the new circumstances offered the greatest opportunity, those most likely to be alive to the potentialities of the world around them.[90]

Yet it is unwarranted to assume that money, status, and a higher education always and everywhere produce this kind of attitude, a cosmopolitan spirit suspiciously alike in certain respects to the supranationalist instinct of modern liberalism. A wealthy, upper-class Athenian might instead have had little enthusiasm for the changing world order of the late fourth century and the accompanying decline of his native polis. Such a person might have considered the newly emergent *oikoumenê* with unease or disgust, skepticism or bemusement. Assuming such a range of responses in his audience, one should not expect a simple response on Menander's part.

Menander might have sympathized with those spectators to whom the "potentialities of the world around them" held no great appeal. The scene that closes *Samia* may illustrate this disinclination. Moschion is unhappy in act 5 because he feels his father should not have assumed his guilt. It would serve Demeas right if Moschion were to go far away, to Bactria or Caria, that is, to serve as a mercenary—"he would not have me around to blame" (626–27). It is crucial to note that Moschion expresses his "resolve" to leave contrafactually (623–29; see *Sam.* 623 G.-S.), marking the idea as an impossibility in his mind; this is at least not the most forceful way to phrase a threat. In fact, Moschion finally admits within the monologue that he does not intend to leave (633–38). When the realization strikes, however, that Demeas may not object to his leaving, suddenly for Moschion departure from home becomes a frightening and wholly unpleasant possibility.

This scene contains a hint of Menander's attitudes toward the "cosmopolitanism" of his day.[91] If we put aside the foolish aspects of his behavior here, Moschion's threat to leave the polis (ἀποφθαρεὶς / ἐκ τῆς πόλεως, 627–28) for the eastern rim of the Greek world seems at first to reflect the opportunities open to enterprising Greeks (such as mercenaries) since Alexander's Bactrian and Indian campaigns.[92] That Moschion in reality has no interest in going, however, colors this concept of opportunity: the experiences "out there" are mostly unpleasant and the supposed benefits are mostly illusory.[93] In fact, instead of pursuing such adventures, Moschion through the play becomes the gentleman his father, Demeas, wants him to be, and therefore also the good citizen—ἄνθρωπος ὁ κόσμιος. He will be comfortable financially, have many friends around him, hence a standing in society, and also a respectable wife. What more could any young Athenian want, or what, at the least, that one is more likely to find in the steppes of Bactria or among the slavish inhabitants of the Carian coastlands than in one's native polis? Menander inserts the geographical detail into Moschion's speech to deflate the idea that any great benefits adhere to the now widely spread Greek world, or supra-polis.

One might object that it is dangerous to assume Menander to be as prescriptive as this implies. There may be more ambiguity in his approach than this reading allows. The following passage from the *Perikeiromene* suggests how Menander might embody the conflict of polis and *oikoumenê* in a dramatic situation so that the determination of "sympathies" is almost impossible.

Mo. What sort of life would you like best, Daos? Think it over, then say.

Da. Working a mill isn't the acme, then?

Mo. This one will go to a mill, all right—with our help!

Da. Don't suggest anything too hard.

Mo. I would make you a chief of Hellenic affairs, and a superintendent of army camps.

Da.   I wouldn't want to be responsible for foreign troops who might cut my throat if, by some chance, I were caught stealing.

Mo.   But you could steal, and get away with it, if you were providing a loan, and took a little off the top.

Da.   I'd rather just sit in the market, Moschion, and sell things, cheese maybe—I don't care to be rich—that's what I'd do, it would suit me much better.

(Peric. 275–86)

Moschion asks the question of Daos in order to arrive at a suitable reward for his services; they begin to dispute over the good life, however, since for one it involves operating outside the polis and for the other working very intimately within it. For Moschion, fortune attends on those who attach themselves to what is basically the Macedonian-dominated supra-polis; Daos, on the other hand, looks no further than the agora. If this is not simply a scene in which Menander pokes fun at a slave's lack of imagination, then Daos represents, mutatis mutandis, the citizen of the polis to whom the *oikoumenê* is distinctly uninviting. Even if this be granted, though, it is still very difficult to know whether the question of "sympathy" is appropriate. Is Menander making fun of either Moschion, the "globalist," or Daos, the *Kleinbürger*? Or is he merely putting their conflict into play, so to speak? The issue may have struck Menander as an urgent one for his age, after all, regardless of his having formed a preference of his own.[94]

Yet, considering the momentous changes which the polis was undergoing at this time, it would seem to have been difficult for Menander to remain aloof, to have not formed some personal and partisan opinion on the viability of the polis, and the likely shape of the world, as his generation grew older. Surely Menander saw the frailty of the polis as a form of autonomous community, especially after the wars among the Successors ground on toward Ipsus without a sign that the poleis would regain their former prominence, or even their independence. Perhaps Menander even perceived in the polis, as Nicholas Purcell has recently described it, a form of community which contradicted the historical norm in Greece, that is, less dedicated to a high degree of mobility and also less permeable to the outside world. The polis, Purcell writes, obsessed with self-sufficiency and inviolability of boundaries, drew an antagonistic line between itself and the outside:

But in the end involution and exclusiveness of this kind, which was alien to the dominant patterns of Mediterranean social and economic life, alien and actually structurally antagonistic, made it impossible for Athenian institutions to form the basis for really wide social and political institutions. The polis in general, we might say, was a cul-de-sac, an unhelpful response to the challenges of the Mediterranean reality, if building large and relatively harmonious and inclusive societies is considered a worthwhile goal.[95]

Whether he was ever aware of this contradiction of the polis form of community or not, the ancient testimonia lead us to believe that Menander resisted the changes through which he must have seen the city-state passing. One reads in Pliny (*NH* VII.111) that Menander turned down an invitation to the court of Ptolemy, which represents just the sort of advantage the new alignment of power would have produced for the talented or well placed. Alciphron's fanciful exchange of letters between Menander and Glycera dramatizes this moment in the poet's life. According to Alciphron, the seed of Menander's ultimate refusal lay in these sentiments:

> May it be my lot to find a mound of earth and a grave in my own country! O King Ptolemy, may it be my lot always to be crowned with a wreath of Attic ivy and every year to raise my voice in honour of Dionysus of the Hearth, to perform the rites of the Mysteries, and to bring out a new play at the annual scenic contests, laughing, rejoicing, eagerly contending, fearing defeat, and coming out the victor! Let Philemon go to Egypt and enjoy my blessing there along with his own! He hasn't any Glycera, and perhaps he was not worthy of such a treasure. (4.18.16–17, trans. Benner and Fobes [Loeb ed.])

Despite the many absurdities here there may be a grain of truth in Alciphron's conceit of a love of *res Atticas* which animated Menander. "Coming out the victor!" would not have been the first thing out of Menander's mouth, for example, based on what we know of his success at the Dionysia. (Admittedly this *nostalgia Atheniensis* in Alciphron's fiction [cf. 4.18.10–11] may be mainly his own and may therefore postdate Menander.)[96] Menander's more than ninety-seven plays could not all have been produced at Athens during the thirty years in which he wrote them; a good hypothesis regarding the venue of the "extra" plays would have many of them produced in the various regional theaters located around Attica.[97] It may be that life in Athens and its environs was ample enough to consume Menander, or that in fact his remaining so near to home was a kind of life-long response to the alternative gesture of treating everywhere, and nowhere, as one's true homeland.[98] In Alciphron's version of Glycera's response to the letter cited above, she imagines Menander considering the invitation to Alexandria at his property in Piraeus (see 4.19.21). It was while swimming at Piraeus, after all, that Menander died by drowning, according to a scholium on the *Ibis*.

Whatever difficulties remain in assessing Menander's views on the polis after

332 TIMOTHY P. HOFMEISTER

these observations, one hopes that henceforward a discussion of Menander and the polis will at least be regarded as possible and worthwhile. In that event, the discussion ought to focus on the kinds of fundamental questions explored in this essay: How did Menander view the inherent problems of the polis? In what ways did he see the life of the polis endangered (or transformed) by the expanded Greek world of his time, the *oikoumenê*? Based on what has been offered here, the idea that the polis had disappeared in Menander ought not be so easily allowed.

Notes

1. Arnott 1972, 67, writes: "The material of comedy, for example, grew less chauvinistically Athenian and more cosmopolitan. . . . To use Professor R. Cantarella's pungent phrasè, the *polis* has been dissolved."

2. See Slater 1987, 5–6.

3. Mossé 1973, 117 expresses a typical attitude: "Whereas in the days of Aristophanes the problems of war and peace and the excesses of democracy were at the core of comic drama and often provided its plots (*Peace, Acharnians, Lysistrata, Ekklesiazusae* [*sic*]), in the New Comedy, although we occasionally find political allusions, they play no part in the development of the plot, which is essentially a love story." The terms of this description are not inaccurate so much as partial and inelastic. Barigazzi 1965, 18, writes more sweepingly: "tramontava la polis, ma nasceva l'ecumene; il polites si ritirava a vita privata, ma diventava cosmopolites, cittadino del mondo: mentre sembrava rimpicciolirsi, grandeggiava fino ai confini del mondo. Questo il frutto incommensurabile del sacrificio della libertà di Atene." One encounters a different tone in the introduction to the commentary of Gomme and Sandbach 1973, 21–22: "There are other schol- ars who imagine that political activity at Athens had dwindled away, and that Menander repre- sents the predominant interests of an unpolitical, philistine bourgeoisie. . . . Such criticisms are misguided." Compare Hunter 1985, 12–13, but see esp. Treu 1981, a brief yet potent essay that has reinforced my own views. David Konstan's new book *Greek Comedy and Ideology* (1995) also treats seriously the political ramifications of Menander's comedy, and its essential kinship with Aristophanes': "For all the differences between the forms of Old and New Comedy, the contradic- tions that they manifest in lapses of narrative coherence and the multiply determined motivations of characters are symptomatic of a shared problematic. Ancient comedy enacts the strains inher- ent in the corporate identity of the classical city-state" (167).

Despite all this, however, even very recent work on Menander exhibits the reflex whereby Menander is focused not on a public sphere, but on the private: "But Menander's interests lie ultimately in human natures rather than human societies, and what seems to attract him most in this scenario is not the [class] barriers themselves but the characters' willingness to accept and even to reinforce them." (For this see Lowe 1987, 137.) This view takes its extreme form, one might say, in Green 1990, 66–67, 71–79.

4. See Scolnicov 1987, 14–15. Cf. Webster 1963, 240: "We shall find that Menander imagines places and objects with great clarity and that we can reconstruct his imagination from our knowledge of Greek scenery and archaeological remains, and this precise and particular imagina- tion not only goes far beyond what can be produced on stage but may also conflict with the limited possibilities of production. The conflict may be solved by theatrical convention and the convention become an accepted theatrical reality"; and Handley 1970, 20: "Menandrean drama has means for conveying the character of a setting, and for distracting from its fixity by action and words."

5. One should not imagine, however, that Aristophanes had much more in the way of physical resources than Menander, the *mechanē* notwithstanding (cf. Arnott 1962, 91–106, esp. 101ff.); for Aristophanes' use of "imaginative space," see Slater 1987, 3–4. One might also compare A. M. Dale's case for the "daring simplicity" of fifth-century tragic stagecraft in "Seen and Unseen" (1956).

6. Menander's physical theater has received more sympathetic attention, partly owing to increased study of the stagecraft of ancient drama in general. Naturally *Dyskolos* has received a number of extended treatments: Webster 1963, 235–72, esp. 241–42 and 249–50; Hoffmann 1986, 269–80; Lowe 1987, 128ff. On the shape of the theater, see Winter 1983, 38–47. For a discussion of Menander's physical theater within a semiology of the theatrical production as a whole, see Wiles 1991, 36–67.

7. See the qualifications, however, that Padel 1990, 343 n. 34, suggests regarding the application of Scolnicov's conception to the Greek conception of theatrical space.

8. Henderson, unlike Sommerstein in his translation, takes this woman to be Demostratus' wife (believing that the article in 392 is possessive, and also because of the μὲν . . . δέ, one assumes): see Henderson 1987, 120 (ad *Lys.* 392).

9. Vaio 1973, 372, illustrates how public and private spaces merge beginning with the staging of the prologue.

10. On this Demostratus, see Henderson's (1987) note ad 391.

11. Henderson 1987, 117–21, contends that the proboulos' "thesis" is "that failure to control wives brings disaster to husbands" and that therefore he has failed to assess the situation at all acutely, a satiric twist on the Athenians' expectations of his real-life counterparts. Cf. Vaio 1973, 372–73.

12. Foley 1982, 12, writes: "The 'female intruder' of the *Lysistrata*, then, moves in response to male violation of those ideal values of domestic and inter-Greek relations that encourage the survival of the oikos and of Greece as a whole without exercising illegitimate powers or dissolving the values and boundaries of her enclosed domestic world. The apparent collapse of boundaries between domestic and political spheres in the language and action of the play serves ultimately to maintain and to reinforce limits and to prevent the female from endangering exclusively male social and political structures in her apparent movement into the outside world." Though its context is different (preindustrial Europe) there is a good discussion of whether such sexual inversion aims at renewal or subversion of the status quo in Davis 1978, 147–90.

13. Henderson comments that the passage "does allow a glimpse of the popular mood of scapegoating and recrimination that followed the disaster" but feels that "by the time of the *Lysistrata* much of the initial shock had passed." (See Henderson 1987, 119, and also introduction xvi–xviii.)

14. For a demonstration that Menander could at times be overtly "political" in his plays, see Burstein 1980, 69–78: "occasionally Menander used his art to influence Athenian opinion on a political issue which interested him" (69). See also fr. 264 (319 K) for the joke on Kallimedon.

15. We should not overemphasize this contrast between the two comic poets and thus stereotype Aristophanes. In fact, Aristophanes' and Menander's polis are much the same, if one treats the polis of comic discourse in the way suggested by the essays of Ober and Strauss, Henderson, and Redfield in *Nothing to Do with Dionysos?* (Winkler and Zeitlin 1990). As argued by Ober and Strauss 1990, "Political rhetoric and drama can be seen, and analyzed, as closely related forms of public speech" (237–38). Drama then becomes one forum among many in which the "dynamic, interactive, and symbolic process" of "public communication" (249) may take place. Though Ober and Strauss correlate mostly the evidence of fifth-century drama and fourth-century oratory, and Henderson and Redfield deal respectively with Old Comedy and Tragedy and Old Comedy, nevertheless on a general level these essays redefine the idea of the "political," especially in connection with what the ancient Athenian community experienced in the theatrical perfor-

mances of the Dionysia. The influence of this perspective will be apparent in my discussion of the polis in Menander's drama.

16. Murray wrote this for the *Oxford History of the Classical World*, quoted in "Cities of Reason" (1990b, 23).

17. Murray may have in mind *NE* 1160a8–30, in which Aristotle mentions various "associations" subsumed in the κοινωνία πολιτική ("association of the polis"). Cf. *Pol.* 1325b23–28.

18. Frost 1988, 103 n. 5, provides bibliography on the *parodoi*. For the ancient evidence see Pollux 4.126–27. (Cf. Lowe 1987, 127 n. 6.)

19. See Blume 1974, 199 n. 48; Goldberg 1980, 95–96.

20. Demeas is characterized by Nikeratos himself as ἡδύς (412); Demeas says of Nikeratos at 550: τραχὺς ἄνθρωπος, σκατοφάγος, αὐθέκαστος τῶι τρόπῳ/ (cf. 1974, 43). Demeas' remarks are not wholly dependent on the dramatic context, but seem generally true of Nikeratos. Nikeratos is blunt, impulsive, and easily provoked. Menander characterizes him by contrast with Demeas throughout; e.g., ironically, just before exploding, Nikeratos calls Demeas "insensitive" and "gauche"; characteristically, his disapproval issues in a crude threat: οἰμώξεται σκαιὸς ὤν (426–28). Though in 416–20 Nikeratos had been calm, a few minutes inside the house (αἱ γυναῖκες τεθορύβηνται) are sufficient to rile him. For Demeas' "violence" at this stage, based on "error" and hence corrigible, see Goldberg 1980, 100.

21. The evidence for Demeas' fetish of secrecy: 20–21. Demeas had kept Chrysis "secret"; 351–52: "cover up as much as can be done" (cf. 355 ἐμφανίσῃς γὰρ ἄλλο μηδὲ ἕν); 371–74: Demeas divulges nothing (though perhaps tempted to?) to Chrysis; 454–55: Demeas' choice not to "level" with Moschion (οὐχὶ σόν . . . τοὖργον ἐστίν ἀλλὰ παντελ[ὼς ἐμὸν) allows his confusion to compound; 488: δή σ' ἐρωτῶ ἐναντίον τῶν πάροντων (here revealed in its opposite, a passionate disclosure; cf. Gomme and Sandbach 1973, 598 [ad *Sam.* 488] on οἱ πάροντες); 500: διὰ σε . . . καταφανῆ (Demeas to Moschion); 706: οὐχὶ τοῖς ἐχθροῖς ἔθηκα φανερὸν ἐπιχαίρειν κτλ.

22. See Blume 1974, 200–203 (esp. 201 n. 51); cf. Ar. *Wealth* 337–39.

23. Nikeratos' complaints of poverty (see note 35) may be disingenuous or exaggerated. If Demeas is (somewhat) wealthier than Nikeratos, for some reason he has become his neighbor's benefactor; perhaps owing to his generous nature (shown in 13–16 and 381–82): see Dedoussi 1970, 177–78. In his review of Ober's *Mass and Elite*, Yunis (1991, 73) speaks of "economic cooperation between mass and elite," though at the macrocosmic level (in reference to liturgies, etc.). Perhaps these two neighbors in *Samia* may be thought of in such terms, literally or symbolically, at the microlevel; yet Nikeratos' status (social and economic status identical?) remains problematical.

24. See Gomme and Sandbach 1973, 597 (ad *Sam.* 475): τις = Moschion.

25. So in *NE* 1155a6–12: "Rich men and those who hold office and power are, above all others, regarded as requiring friends. . . . How could prosperity be safeguarded and preserved without friends? The greater it is the greater are the risks it brings with it." This implies that by rising in society one naturally acquires enemies. As Gomme and Sandbach remark (ad *Sam.* 474), "For ancient Greeks both friends and enemies loomed larger than they do to us." The citation of Plutarch's Chilon adumbrates the point.

26. Demeas' "eavesdropping" from the storeroom/pantry (*tamieion*) illustrates the emphasis in this play on his "interiority." True, his disclosure outside the house (beginning of act 3) of what he has just seen within is standard: Sostratus enacts the same device (*Dyskolos* 666–67); likewise Onesimos in *Epitrepontes* 878–79. In these other examples, however, the space within is not described per se, or delineated, as in Demeas' case (see esp. *Sam.* 232–36). Demeas' hearing from the *tamieion* is a thematically significant detail, therefore, and represents Menander's variation of a conventional device for a specific effect. (See Blume 1974, 85–87. Cf., however, Turner's discussion following Handley 1970, 37. Frost 1988, 57, 75, and 106, treats the above scenes not as *Lauscherszenen* but as "entrance speeches.")

27. See Blume 1974, 170–71.

28. See Kraus 1934, 68. Consider also 487–88 (ἐναντίον δὴ σ᾽ ἐρωτῶ τῶν πάροντων G.-S. 488· οἱ πάροντες = audience), a striking variation of audience address and a gesture of confidence. Goldberg 1980, 98, discusses Demeas' rapport with the audience. Blundell 1980, 41–42, notes the irony inherent in Demeas' relation with an audience that can view his situation more comprehensively than he himself can. For general discussion of the device, see Gomme and Sandbach 1973, 14–15; Bain 1977, 190–94, 205–7.

29. See Gaiser 1968, 193–219.

30. The speaker of the fragment talks of near extinction; he couches his experience in imagery relating to the Asklepeion: fr. Didot. b 3–4, 9–11.

31. According to Gaiser 1968, 214, this "Gefühl der besonderen Verbundenheit" is grounded in the audience and speaker's sharing citizenship in the city of Athens, whose "greatness" makes such an experience as he has had possible. Blume 1974, 46–48, sees this short passage as an intense expression of fellow feeling between Menander himself and the Athenian audience.

32. Attached to the progress from dark into light is a parallel progress in terms of *dianoia*. In this manner the fragment celebrates not only the city's beauty, including its rarefied atmosphere, but also its intellectual attainments and heritage, providing a context conducive to the praise of Athenian theater. (See Gaiser 1968, 206–8, 210–12.)

33. On this, see Gaiser 1968, 210–11; yet he offers the potential for irony in the dramatic context (see 216).

34. This oath with Dionysos' name is used elsewhere in *Samia*: by Moschion at 139, 668; by Parmenon at 309.

35. The following comic bits mark Nikeratos' poverty, or his tendency to feel impoverished: the skinny beast: 399–404; his leaky roof: 592–93; death before dowry: 727–28.

36. This is developed in 1970, 167–68.

37. Likewise one wonders whether 181 πρὶν εἰπεῖν τοῖς φίλοις refers exclusively to Nikeratos' φίλοι, or to mutual "friends."

38. Gomme and Sandbach 1973 (ad 518) is helpful on the sense of ὡς ἄν in this usage.

39. "As Finley, Ste. Croix, and Meier (among others) saw, a key feature of the Athenian democracy was the use of political power by political equals to counterbalance various social inequalities—especially the unequal distribution of wealth." (See Ober 1989, 336–37.) For a brief response to the claim that ancient Greek society was not highly differentiated, see Ober 1991, 132–33.

40. So Gomme and Sandbach 1973, 556 (ad *Sam.* 101).

41. See Webster 1974, 4. Treu 241, quoted by Blume 1974, 46 n. 91, discusses grounds for a date very soon after the Lamian War (322 B.C.).

42. The fate of Phokion, with the grotesque proceedings at his "trial" (held in the theater), testifies to these tensions: see Plut. *Phok.* 34–36.

43. For a dating of the *Samia* later than Webster's (or Treu's), see the discussion in Dedoussi 1970, 159–60 and 173–74.

44. *Pace* Blume 1974, 45. Casson 1976 argues for a mostly upper-class audience. See Hunter 1985, 10 and 154 n. 23 on this thesis. On the *theorika*: Ferguson 1911, 23, 58, 73; *contra* Blanchard 1983, 388 n. 27: "Aucun document ne vient appuyer l'affirmation de Ferguson concernant l'abolition du théorique . . ."

45. See, e.g., *Dyskolos* 129–31, 284–86, 295–98.

46. Mette 1969, 432–39, addresses the theme of κοσμιότης.

47. Menander underscores this point by echoing μὴ παροξύνου (612) in μὴ παροξύνῃς (721). Likewise, Nikeratos' δοκεῖ; (723) seems to echo 117–18, and perhaps means to pay Demeas back, since in that prior passage he had spoken to Nikeratos somewhat overbearingly: (Δη.) δέδοκται ταῦτα; (Νι.) ἐμοὶ γοῦν. (Δη.) ἀλλὰ μὴν/κἀμοὶ προτέρωι σου. ("Does this seem alright?" "Sure." "But to *me* before you!")

It is possible, of course, to see these difficulties which Menander has evoked not as symptoms of a sustainable tension, but instead as arising from unnegotiable social and economic differences; so, e.g., Hoffmann 1986, 290 (apropos *Dyskolos*): "Or, par les armes du rire, que sont l'ironie et la dérision, Ménandre vient de prouver que le consensus civique n'est plus de ce lieu ni de ce temps."

48. See the discussion in Sinclair 1988, 24–27, and n. 2. For an attempt to gauge the depth of concerns over the issue of citizenship during the classical period, see Davies 1977, 105–21.

49. See esp. Arnott 1986, 1–9; also Katsouris 1975. A new survey of the relation of Menander and tragedy overall is now available in Hurst 1990.

50. Willink 1986, xxv, writes: "We may certainly see in *Or.* a reflection (among other things) of the diverse ethos of Athens in 409/8 B.C." See Burkert's exploration 1974, 106–9, of the *Orestes*' "Zeitbedingtheit"; at the heart of his assessment is "Die Polarisierung der sozialen Klassen," which reached a peak at the end of Euripides' life, signaling in fact the end of a class of aristocrats who "hatten, seit Kleisthenes, Athen zu seiner großartigen, historisch einmaligen Entfaltung geführt." Dissent: Zuntz 1968 urges caution in attempting to connect works of dramatic fiction to their historical milieu.

51. Arnott 1986, 6–8, concentrates on Menander's relationship to previous dramatic models, arguing that the influences of late tragedy and earlier comedy (i.e., Aristophanes) upon Menander are not easily separable. Regarding Menander's other purpose(s), Arnott seems to prefer agnosticism (6): "Katsouris' study of the two speeches closes with the considered judgment that 'Menander did not copy, but adapted the *Orestes* speech to his needs.' But what were these needs?" Still more salutary, if not chilling, is Gomme and Sandbach 1973, 651: "There is a parallel between this speech [Blepes'] and that of the *Orestes*. . . . The likeness was no doubt intended to catch the notice of a literary spectator, but it is fleeting and its importance not to be exaggerated."

52. If this profile is accurate, the αὐτουργός resembles the type underlying the propaganda for the "constitution of the 5000," which Thucydides discusses in his narrative of the events in 411 B.C.: see Thuc. 8.67, 72, 86, 89, but esp. 97. (On [χωρεῖν] ὁμόσε see Willink 1986 note ad 921; cf. LSJ s.v.; Ar. *Eccl.* 863; Thuc. 2.62.)

53. Arnott 1986, 9 n. 19, feels that Smikrines speaks line 150, ὄχλος εἶ φλυάρου μεστός, to Blepes, and so prefers δημο]. See also Gomme and Sandbach 1973, 651 (ad *Sic.* 182).

54. See, e.g., Procleon's juridical bloodlust in *Wasps* 320–22: ἐπεὶ βούλομαί γε πάλαι μεθ' ὑμῶν ἐλθὼν ἐπὶ τοὺς καδίσκους κακόν τι ποιῆσαι. MacDowell 1971, 8: "To him condemning is not only a duty but a pleasure too."

55. On the difficulty of assigning *Sic.* 150–68, see Gomme and Sandbach 1973, 646–47, and 650 (ad *Sic.* 169).

56. Kolb 1981, 5–15, deals with the occurrences and significance of this phrase.

57. "Ein Vertreter der sophistischen Kairos-Lehre" is used in apposition to Menelaus by Biehl (quoted in Schein 1975, 57 n. 27). Willink 1986, 191–92, summarizes other critical opinion on Menelaus, then effects a nice balance: "We should not complain because E. rejected both the 'virtuous' and the 'villainous' postures in favour of something more subtle (requiring us to attend closely to a blend of self-revealing candour and disingenuousness), according to a *persona* in line at once with a traditional 'negative' view of Menelaus (whose 'heroism' had always been somewhat suspect . . .) and with the topical analogy of political 'trimmers' like Theramenes . . ."

58. Willink 1986, 224, calls the view of the "'admired' αὐτουργός" "repugnant"; he essentially writes this character off, emphasizing Diomedes' role instead, particularly in the way, according to Willink, Diomedes' proposal offers a decent alternative to the extreme views of the demagogue and the αὐτουργός (cf. Schein 1975, 61). Lloyd 1992, 127, rightly objects to this interpretation: "Diomedes' proposal of exile has been treated by some scholars as being clearly correct, but if this were so it would be very surprising that it should be so unemphatically presented (898–902). Exile seems here to be no more than a compromise solution, which may preserve the city's εὐσέβεια, but which evades the important issues." Lloyd emphasizes the corruption of the assembly; this helps explain the misogyny and violence that some critics have pointed to in the

speech of the αὐτουργός: "The whole description of the Argive assembly makes it clear that no serious discussion of Orestes' case can take place there, and that even sympathetic characters must express their arguments in crude terms" (128). This view would accord well, I think, with what Menander himself took away from the Euripidean scene.

59. In unflattering depictions of democratic processes, "noise" is a common element and has a double source: the crowd (e.g., *Apol.* 30c2 μὴ θορυβεῖτε, ἄνδρες Ἀθηναῖοι); and the speaker's platform (Ar. *Knights* 218 [Agoracritos' φωνὴ μιαρά]; *Wasps* 34–36). For a modern appraisal of the role of *thorubos*, in the context of the Athenian jury courts, for the most part, see Bers 1985.

60. Arnott 1986, 4 (also 9 n. 16), points out that Euripides' *Orestes* was extremely popular, and so would have been well known to Menander's audience. See also Willink 1986, lxiii.

61. Katsouris 1975, 47–48, draws a parallel between Moschion and the ἀνὴρ ἀθυρόγλωσσος based on structural criteria. Yet Moschion is forced into the debate by the crowd of Eleusinians, who will not tolerate his apparent behind-the-scene manipulations (he is seen whispering to Dromon). This treatment brings Moschion into line with Smikrines (*Sic.* 154–55: οὐ κρίνεθ' ἀλήθεια τοῦτον τὸν τρόπον,/ἀλλ' ἐν ὀλίγωι πολλῶι γε μᾶ[λλον συνεδρίωι. [cf. Thuc. 4.22]), Smikrines being his father and, until the disclosure of Stratophanes' identity, perhaps his cohort: see Gomme and Sandbach 1973, 634–36, 647. Therefore Menander disassociates Moschion and the demagogue in *Orestes*, in line with the ideological shift through which Menander puts Euripides' play. Stratophanes, a man of natural virtue and politically a moderate, thus has two opponents: (1) Moschion, a spoiled oligarchic youth, and (2) the rhetorical challenge of guiding the mass toward an understanding of its own best interest (in the immediate context a just verdict).

62. Ober 1989, 304.

63. Ibid., 305.

64. Ibid., 306.

65. Ibid., 307.

66. Ober (ibid.) invokes a metaphor of the theater in a very interesting way in the presentation of his conclusions. In explaining why jurors, e.g., chose not to call attention to the "transparent fictions" in which an elite litigant portrayed himself as an average Athenian, he suggests that "the juror's experience as a member of a mass audience in the theater, watching and hearing actors play their parts, reinforced the useful process of suspension of disbelief that he employed when sitting as a member of a mass jury, listening to the elite litigant plead his case."

If we subscribe to the reality behind this metaphor, that Athenians in the theater participated in an essentially political exercise (the thesis of the articles in *Nothing to Do with Dionysos?* already mentioned [see note 15]), then we gain an important perspective on the political discourse within Menander's comedy: even without the benefit of a precise historical context for the plays, we may nonetheless read them on a different level, as exercises within an inherited system of "social communication," and furthermore as Menander's own contribution to "a vocabulary of social mediation which defined the nature of mass-elite interaction for the Athenians and legitimated both the power of the masses and the special privileges of the elites" (Ober 1989, 306). But whether, or to what extent, the needs to which this "vocabulary" was meant to respond were pressing when Menander wrote a given play again represents the sort of question that lack of more specific historical data makes unanswerable.

One of the readers for this press, besides making a number of helpful observations, brought to my attention a new book by Adele Scafuro *The Forensic Stage* (Cambridge, 1995), which I would have liked to consult, yet I was unable to do so before completion of this essay.

67. Ober 1991, 129–31, discusses Aristotle's attempt "to balance elitist and egalitarian principles."

68. On the imperfection of friendship among bad men, see *NE* 1157a16–20, 1157b1–4. An inconsistency remains, or else the *philia politikē* itself, being imperfect from the start because the participants cannot enjoy each other for the sake of virtue alone, is simply accepted as such.

Inconsistency in Aristotle's political philosophy is far from unlikely, of course; one prime source of such inconsistency resides in the tension there between the ideal of a virtuous community and the reality of mixed, or democratic, governments. As *Rhetoric* 3.1.4 1403b illustrates (for one example), Aristotle was pessimistic about Athenian-style democracy; yet at several points in the *Politics* he discusses democracy (in a variety of shapes and sizes) as a practicable form of government: cf. note 67 above. (For a good discussion of Aristotle's pessimistic view of the democracy at Athens, see Strauss 1991.)

69. See Wiles 1991, 30.

70. Epicurus' early years were spent on Samos, then Teos, before he spent his ephebic year (323 B.C.) in Attica; if Epicurus and Menander did become acquainted through their *sunephebeia*, then that acquaintance must have been interrupted by Epicurus' further residence abroad (Colophon, Mytilene, Lampsacus), for he did not return to Athens until 306 B.C. (see "Epikuros (4)," *RE* XI.133–35). Though Zeno's chronology is difficult, it is likely that he did not arrive in Athens until 312 B.C., and then perhaps did not begin teaching for another ten years. (See "Zeno (2) von Kition," *RE* XIX.83–85.)

71. For an example, Brown, *CR* 92 (1992), 273, criticizes the following statement by Wiles: "The intellectual project behind Menander's plays is the search to define the good citizen, not merely the good human being"—yet here Wiles has proposed the opposite of what I have criticized him for stating elsewhere in his book. In this connection Brown's counterexample of *theoria* as discussed in *NE* X is not convincing, unless the point is simply that one cannot treat Aristotle as though he were not alive to contradictions.

The relation of Menander and Aristotle is much argued over. In this essay I have operated on the premise that, just as it is wrong to assume a necessary or causal connection between Aristotelian teaching and the ideas in Menander's plays (as several scholars have shown: see Gaiser 1967, 8–40; cf. Hunter 1985, 147–51), it is equally wrong to ignore any resemblances that some Menandrian motifs may bear to specific Aristotelian concepts; though the resemblances may not be definitive in themselves, they provide a hermeneutic tool, thanks to which the critic comes away with more of the potential meaning contained in Menander's text. For good examples of the application of Aristotle's philosophy to Menander's plays, see Fortenbaugh 1974 and Lord 1977. Cf. Fantham 1977.

72. Zagagi 1988, 194–97, has shown how this final scene presents special problems. However, as she points out, there is a "gap" between Moschion's image through the rest of the play and the "somewhat devious stance" he takes here: "The very idea of faking a departure stands in sharp contrast to Moschion's previous κοσμιότης" (196). Without denying Moschion's "passion," one wants to emphasize that it has more to do with Menander's dramatic strategy than with the emotion per se. Moschion acts as he does in act 5 not to express anything to Plangon, after all, but to make a point to Demeas by hurting him. That Menander alters Moschion for this final scene in order to lay "the strongest stress on the problematic nature of the father-son relationship" (195) does not indicate a sudden interest in Eros in the play, but in itself reaffirms the centrality of the father-son bond and its importance for the social order. (For κόσμιος as "contrasted with doing what one likes," see Seager 1973, 19.)

Concerning the opening of the play, Demeas does say later in act 2 ἐγὼ γὰρ οὐκ εἰδὼς ἔχον[τα τουτονὶ/ἐρωτικῶς (165–66); however, he says this without understanding Moschion's motivation. Demeas is in fact forecasting his own susceptibility to error here.

73. See Gomme and Sandbach 1973, 307 (ad *Ep.* 242). Such farms, or the "villages"/demes of which they are part, provide the setting of several plays, e.g., *Dyskolos, Heros* (?), as well as here. (On the importance of the demes in the residential pattern of Attica, and for its political map as well, see Osborne 1985.)

74. Syros may hope for his freedom as a reward; or he takes himself seriously as a kind of *therapōn* to his heroic foundling (*Ep.* 326–33).

75. Gomme and Sandbach 1973 point out this Smikrines' similarity to Smikrines in the *Sicyonian*, who without knowing what he is doing complains of the assembly that initiates the restoration of his own son's citizenship. The Smikrines character often belongs to a miser type: cf. *Aspis*; Wiles 1991, 92–93: "The mask of Smikrines does not create a money-hoarder so much as a man of the type who tends to hoard money."

76. In his scene in act 5 Onesimos abruptly cuts off the joking with the question ἀλλ᾽ ἀπαγαγεῖν παρ᾽ ἀνδρὸς αὑτοῦ θυγατέρα/ἀγαθὸν σὺ κρίνεις, Σμικρίνη; (*Ep.* 1102–3), and in doing so identifies the issue at the core of the play. (Cf. Gomme and Sandbach 1973 on 1102: "The absence of the article with ἀνδρός emphasizes the relationship of husband and wife.")

77. On the echoes of philosophical doctrine in Onesimos' speech, see Gomme and Sandbach 1973, 377–78. Barigazzi 1965, 198–212, attempts to derive Onesimos' position from Aristotle.

78. Onesimos' accounting here may be a satire of Smikrines' penchant for *logismos*, which was ridiculed earlier by Chairestratos at 140: εὖ λελόγισται.

79. For an eloquent statement of this aspect of the identity of the traditional polis, see Fine 1983, 52–53.

80. Gomme and Sandbach 1973, 618 (on *Samia*): "Once again at the end of Act IV all seems arranged for the best, and the audience would wonder during the interval, if not entirely absorbed by the dancing of the chorus, how the play could continue. The new Act brings the answer." (Cf. Holzberg 1974, esp. 136–41, and Hunter 1985, 40–42.) For some additional comment on this discussion, see Brown 1990, 39–48, and the comments of Thomas, *CP* 87 (1992), 165.

81. See Lloyd-Jones 1987, 314. Lowe 1987, 134 n. 26, points out the uniqueness of this ending in respect to the νίκη-motif.

82. In an interesting reading of this last scene in the *Dyskolos*, Wiles 1984, 176–78, suggests on the contrary that Menander in the finale does not aim at "hilarity" but at a "treatment of authoritarianism and anarchy."

83. Wiles 1991, 170–71, emphasizes the cleverness of Syros in connection with his views on the "Syrian (slave-)mask."

84. See Baldry 1965, 137.

85. Ibid., 138–39.

86. Ibid., 40.

87. Ibid., 136. Long 1986, 152–56, displays much of the same material, though with some additions, and seems also to want to show some advance in the attitudes of New Comedy, e.g., "a conception of Atticism that is embracing rather than excluding, that makes of the Greek ideal an entree by which many can enter" (153). One can accumulate fragments according to *sententia*; however, Long too recognizes that without context the fragments are difficult to interpret.

88. See, e.g., Baldry 1965, 58 (on Democritus).

89. Ibid., 133–34.

90. Ibid., 135.

91. In discussing the convention that underlies Moschion's performance here, Zagagi 1988, 194–97, stresses the originality of Menander's use of the exile motif. The effect we argue for must occur, if at all, in addition to those described by Zagagi.

92. For the comical effect of Moschion's geography, see Blume 1974, 250. Goldberg 1980, 105–6, discusses "the absurdity of Moschion's plan." On its "heroic" flourishes, see Gomme and Sandbach 1973, 620.

93. See Blume 1974, 251 n. 7, on the ample opportunities for mercenary soldiers. For others the sense of opportunity may not have been much greater than before. Scholars have questioned recently the solidity of the Greek presence in many of the "new" areas opened up by Alexander's campaigns: see, e.g., Briant 1978; cf. Will 1985. Holt 1988, 99, writes: "Except in isolated cases of expedience or exploitation, there was never a union of Central Asia and Macedonia even in the marriage of Alexander to Roxane. The Greeks left in the east made their way as best they could

according to local conditions, just as the Sogdian Roxane and her son did for a much shorter time in the west." The eastern situation remained thus, until the renewed campaigning and colonization of Seleucus, after 293 B.C. (see Holt 1988, 99–103), i.e., toward the end of Menander's life.

94. According to Schneider 1967, 60–61, one of the "tensions" that helped to define "der hellenistische Mensch und das hellenistische Menschenbild" was indeed "Die Spannung zwischen dem Menschen der Weltweite und dem Kleinbürger." (Cf. also 128–29.)

95. See Purcell 1990, 58.

96. Lefkowitz 1981, 113–14, is skeptical not just of Alciphron, but the whole tradition of Menander, which other scholars, however, take seriously: see, e.g., Blanchard 1983, 407.

97. Gomme and Sandbach 1973, 1–2; see also 470 on the "non-Attic first performance" of some plays. For an account of theaters and productions in the demes: Pickard-Cambridge 1968, 42–52.

98. Diog. Laer. II.7 tells how Anaxagoras, when asked, "Have you no concern for your native land (τῆς πατρίδος)?" answered yes while pointing into the sky; Schneider 1967, 61, takes the whole as "eine hellenistische Anekdote."

Bibliography

Arnott, P. 1962. *Greek Scenic Conventions*. Oxford.

Arnott, W. G. 1972. "From Aristophanes to Menander." *G&R* 19.65–80.

——. 1986. "Menander and Earlier Drama." In *Studies in Honour of T. B. L. Webster*, edited by J. H. Betts, J. T. Hooker, and J. R. Green, 1.1–9. Bristol.

Bain, D. 1977. *Actors and Audience: A Study of Asides and Related Conventions in Greek Drama*. Oxford.

Baldry, H. C. 1965. *The Unity of Mankind in Greek Thought*. Cambridge.

Barigazzi, A. 1965. *La Formazione Spirituale di Menandro*. Lezioni "Augusto Rostagni." Vol. 2. Istituto di Filologia Classica Facoltà di Lettere e Filosofia Università Torino. Turin.

Bers, Victor. 1985. "Dikastic *Thorubos*." In *Crux: Essays presented to G. E. M. de Ste. Croix*, edited by P. A. Cartledge and F. D. Harvey, 1–15. London.

Blanchard, Alain. 1983. *Essai sur la composition des comédies de Ménandre*. Paris.

Blume, H.-D. 1974. *Menanders Samia: Eine Interpretation*. Impulse der Forschung 15. Darmstadt.

Blundell, J. 1980. *Menander and the Monologue, Hypomnemata, Untersuchungen zur Antike und zu ihrem Nachleben, h. 59*. Göttingen.

Briant, Pierre. 1978. "Colonisation hellénistique et populations indigènes: La phase d'installation." *Klio* 60.57–92.

Brown, P. G. MacC. 1990. "The Bodmer Codex of Menander and the Endings of Terence's Eunuchus and Other Roman Comedies." In *Relire Ménandre*, edited by Handley and Hurst, 37–61.

Burkert, Walter. 1974. "Die Absurdität der Gewalt." *A&A* 20.97–109.

Burstein, Stanley M. 1980. "Menander and Politics: The Fragments of the *Halieis*." In *Panhellenica: Essays in Honor of Truesdell S. Brown*, edited by Stanley M. Burstein and Louis A. Okin, 69–78. Lawrence, Kans.

Casson, L. 1976. "The Athenian Upper Class and New Comedy." *TAPA* 106.29–59.

Dale, A. M. 1956. "Seen and Unseen on the Greek Stage: A Study in Scenic Conventions." *Wiener Studien*. 69.96–106. Reprinted in *Classical Papers*, 119–29. Cambridge, 1969.

Davies, J. K. 1977. "Athenian Citizenship: The Descent Groups and the Alternatives." *CJ* 73.105–21.

Davis, Natalie Z. 1978. "Women on Top: Symbolic Sexual Inversion and Political Disorder in Early Modern Europe." In *The Reversible World: Symbolic Inversion in Art and Society*, edited by Barbara A. Babcock, 147–90. Ithaca.

Dedoussi, C. 1970. "The Samia." *Fondation Hardt Entretiens* 16.159–80.

Fantham, E. 1977. "Philemon's *Thesauros* as a Dramatization of Peripatean Ethics." *Hermes* 105.406–21.

Ferguson, W. S. 1911. *Hellenistic Athens*. London.

Fine, John V. A. 1983. *The Ancient Greeks: A Critical History*. Cambridge, Mass.

Foley, Helene P. 1982. "The Female Intruder Reconsidered: Women in Aristophanes' *Lysistrata* and *Ecclesiazusae*." *CP* 77.1.1–21.

Fortenbaugh, W. W. 1974. "Menander's *Perikeiromene*: Misfortune, Vehemence, and Polemon." *Phoenix* 28.430–43.

Frost, K. B. 1988. *Exits and Entrances in Menander*. Oxford.

Gaiser, Konrad. 1967. "Menander und der Peripatos." *A&A* 13.8–40.

———. 1968. "Ein Lob Athens in der Komödie." *Gymnasium* 75.193–219.

Goldberg, S. 1980. *The Making of Menander's Comedy*. Berkeley.

Gomme, A. W., and F. H. Sandbach. 1973. *Menander: A Commentary*. Oxford.

Green, Peter. 1990. *Alexander to Actium: The Historical Evolution of the Hellenistic Age*. Berkeley.

Handley, E. W. 1970. "Conventions of the Comic Stage." *Fondation Hardt Entretiens* 16.3–42.

Handley, E. W., and A. Hurst. 1990. *Relire Ménandre. Recherches et rencontres: Publications de la Faculté de Genève*. Geneva.

Henderson, J. 1987. *Aristophanes Lysistrata*. Oxford.

Hoffmann, Geneviève. 1986. "L'espace théâtral et social du *Dyscolos* de Menandre." *Metis* 1.269–90.

Holt, Frank L. 1988. *Alexander the Great and Bactria: The Formation of a Greek Frontier in Central Asia*. Mnemosyne Suppl. 104. Leiden.

Holzberg, N. 1974. *Menander: Untersuchungen zur dramatischen Technik, Erlanger Beiträge zur Sprach- und Kunstwissenschaft, b. 50*. Nürnberg.

Hunter, R. L. 1985. *The New Comedy of Greece and Rome*. Cambridge.

Hurst, A. 1990. "Ménandre et la tragédie." In *Relire Ménandre*, edited by Handley and Hurst, 93–122.

Katsouris, A. G. 1975. "Tragic Patterns in Menander." *Hellenic Society for Humanistic Studies, International Center for Classical Research, Studies and Researches*, 2d ser., 28.29–54. Athens.

Kolb, Frank. 1981. *Agora und Theater, Volks- und Festversammlung*. Deutsches Archäologisches Institut, Archäologische Forschungen. Berlin.

Konstan, David. 1995. *Greek Comedy and Ideology*. New York.

Kraus, Walther. 1934. "'Ad spectatores' in der römischen Komödie." *Wiener Studien* 52.66–83.

Lefkowitz, Mary. 1981. *The Lives of the Greek Poets*. Baltimore.

Lloyd, M. 1992. *The Agon in Euripides*. Oxford.

Lloyd-Jones, Hugh. 1987. "The Structure of Menander's Comedies." *Dioniso* 57.313–21.

Long, Timothy. 1986. *Barbarians in Greek Comedy*. Carbondale, Ill.

Lord, Carnes. 1977. "Aristotle, Menander and the *Adelphoe* of Terence." *TAPA* 107.183–202.

Lord, Carnes, and David O'Connor, eds. 1991. *Essays on the Foundations of Aristotelian Political Science*. Berkeley.

Lowe, N. J. 1987. "Tragic Space and Comic Timing in Menander's *Dyskolos*." *Bulletin of the Institute of Classical Studies* 34.126–38.

MacDowell, Douglas M. 1971. *Aristophanes Wasps*. Oxford.

Mette, H. J. 1969. "Moschion ὁ κόσμιος." *Hermes* 97.432–39.

Mossé, C. 1973. *Athens in Decline: 404–86 BC*. Translated by Jean Stewart. London.

Murray, O. 1990. "Cities of Reason." In *The Greek City*, edited by Murray and Price, 1–23.

Murray, O., and S. Price, eds. 1990. *The Greek City: From Homer to Alexander*. Oxford.

Ober, J. 1989. *Mass and Elite in Democratic Athens: Rhetoric, Ideology, and the Power of the People*. Princeton.

———. 1991. "Aristotle's Political Sociology: Class, Status, and Order in the *Politics*." In *Essays*, edited by Lord and O'Connor, 112–35.

Ober, J., and Barry Strauss. 1990. "Drama, Political Rhetoric, and the Discourse of Athenian Democracy." In *Dionysos*, edited by Winkler and Zeitlin, 237–70.

Osborne, R. 1985. *Demos: The Discovery of Classical Attika*. Cambridge.

Padel, Ruth. 1990. "Making Space Speak." In *Dionysos*, edited by Winkler and Zeitlin, 336–65.

Pickard-Cambridge, Arthur W. 1968. *The Dramatic Festivals of Athens*. Revised by J. Gould and D. M. Lewis. Oxford.

Purcell, Nicholas. 1990. "Mobility and the *Polis*." In *The Greek City*, edited by Murray and Price, 29–58.

Schein, Seth L. 1975. "Mythical Illusion and Historical Reality in Euripides' *Orestes*." *Wiener Studien* 9.49–66.

Schneider, Carl. 1967. *Kulturgeschichte des Hellenismus*. Munich.

Scolnicov, Hanna. 1987. "Theatre Space, Theatrical Space, and the Theatrical Space Without." *Themes in Drama 9: The Theatrical Space*, 11–26. Cambridge.

Seager, Robin. 1973. "Elitism and Democracy in Classical Athens." In *The Rich, the Well Born, and the Powerful*, edited by F. C. Jaher, 7–26. Urbana, Ill.

Sinclair, R. K. 1988. *Democracy and Participation in Athens*. Cambridge.

Slater, Niall W. 1987. "Transformations of Space in New Comedy." *Themes in Drama 9: The Theatrical Space*, 1–10. Cambridge.

Strauss, B. 1991. "On Aristotle's Critique of Athenian Democracy." In *Essays*, edited by Lord and O'Connor, 212–33.

Treu, Max. 1969. "Humane Handlungsmotive in der *Samia* Menanders." *RhM* 112.230–54.

———. 1981. "Menanders Menschen als Polisbürger." *Philologus* 125.211–14.

Vaio, John. 1973. "The Manipulation of Theme and Action in Aristophanes' *Lysistrata*." *GRBS* 14.369–80.

Webster, T. B. L. 1963. "Menander: Production and Imagination." *Bulletin of the John Rylands Library*, 45.235–72.

———. 1974. *Introduction to Menander*. Manchester.

Wiles, David. 1984. "Menander's *Dyskolos* and Demetrius of Phaleron's Dilemma." *G&R* 31.2.170–79.

———. 1991. *The Masks of Menander: Sign and Meaning in Greek and Roman Performance*. Cambridge.

Will, Edouard. 1985. "Pour une 'anthropologie coloniale' du monde hellénistique." In *The Craft of the Ancient Historian: Essays in Honor of C. G. Starr*, edited by J. W. Eadie and J. Ober, 273–301. Lanham, Md.

Willink, C. W. 1986. *Euripides Orestes*. Oxford.

Winkler, John J., and Froma I. Zeitlin. 1990. *Nothing to Do with Dionysos? Athenian Drama in Its Social Context*. Princeton.

Winter, F. E. 1983. "The Stage of New Comedy." *Phoenix* 37.38–47.

Yunis, H. 1991. Review of Ober, *Mass and Elite*. *CP* 86.1.67–74.

Zagagi, Netta. 1988. "Exilium Amoris in New Comedy." *Hermes* 116.193–209.

Zuntz, G. 1968. "Euripides und die Politik seiner Zeit." *Wege der Forschung: Euripides* 89.417–27. Darmstadt.

CONTRIBUTORS

Elizabeth Bobrick is a writer and classical scholar who teaches at Wesleyan University in Middletown, Connecticut. Her fiction and articles have appeared in magazines, newspapers, and scholarly journals, and she is the author of a commentary on Theophrastus' *Characters*.

Gregory Crane, Associate Professor of Classics at Tufts University, teaches courses on Greek literature and on the impact of electronic technologies on literary texts. He has published widely on Greek literature and computing in the humanities. His newest book, *The Ancient Simplicity: Thucydides and Political Realism*, is being published by the University of California Press.

Gregory W. Dobrov is Assistant Professor of Greek and Latin at the University of Michigan where he teaches in classical studies and comparative literature. His publications include *Figures of Play: Greek Drama and Metafictional Poetics* (1998), *Beyond Aristophanes* (1995), and articles on linguistics, drama, and Byzantine literature. He is currently at work on *A Companion to the Study of Greek Comedy* (forthcoming) and a book on Greek literature of the Imperial period.

Malcolm Heath, Reader in Greek at the University of Leeds, has teaching and research interests in Greek drama, and in ancient literary criticism and rhetorical theory. His publications include *The Poetics of Greek Tragedy* (1987), *Political Comedy in Aristophanes* (1987), *Unity in Greek Poetics* (1989), and numerous articles. Current projects include an investigation of Menander Rhetor's commentary on Demonsthenes, and studies of aspects of ancient Homeric scholarship.

Jeffrey Henderson, Professor and Chairman of Classical Studies at Boston University, is the author of many works on Greek comedy and its historical context, including *The Maculate Muse: Obscene Language in Attic Comedy*, and an edition with commentary of Aristophanes' *Lysistrata*. He is currently at work on an edition with commentary of Aristophanes' *Knights*, and a new Loeb edition of Aristophanes.

Timothy P. Hofmeister is Associate Professor and Chair of the Department of Classical Studies at Denison University in Granville, Ohio, where he teaches courses primarily in Greek and Latin languages and literature. In 1995–96 he was Blegen Research Fellow in Classics at Vassar College. He has published articles on Homer, and also on the poetry of Derek Walcott. Current projects include a study of Homeric genealogy, and a book, *Walcott's Classics*, dealing with Walcott's relation to the classical tradition.

Thomas K. Hubbard is Associate Professor of Classics in the University of Texas at Austin. He has published numerous articles on Greek and Latin literature. His books include *The Pindaric Mind* (1985), *The Mask of Comedy: Aristophanes and the Intertextual Parabasis* (1991), and *The Pipes of Pan: Intertextuality and Literary Filiation in the Pastoral Tradition from Theocritus to Milton* (1998).

David Konstan is the John Rowe Workman Professor of Classics and Comparative Literature at Brown University. He has published books on Greek and Roman comedy, Epicurean philosophy, Catullus, the ancient novel, and, most recently, on friendship in the classical world. He is currently working on a book on revenge in Greek antiquity.

Heiz-Guenther Nesselrath, Full Professor of Classical Studies at the University of Bern, Switzerland, teaches Greek and Roman literature. His major publications, which include the books *Lukains Parasitendialog* (1985), *Die attische Mittlere Komödie* (1990), and *Ungeschehenes Geschehen* (1992), deal with Greek literature of Imperial times, Greek comedy, Greek and Roman epic, and

Herodotus. His current projects include a German translation (with commentary) of Plato's *Critias* and an edition and translation, with commentary, of the Church historian Socrates.

F. E. Romer, Associate Professor of Classics at the University of Arizona, teaches Greek and Roman literature, history, and religion. His articles and book, *Pomponius Mela's Description of the World* (1997), reflect his interests in cultural, literary, and intellectual history. He also does historical research for the university's excavations in Italy at Lugnano and Chianciano Terme (both directed by David Soren). At Arizona he has been recognized twice for excellence in teaching.

Ralph M. Rosen is Associate Professor of Classical Studies at the University of Pennsylvania. He is especially interested in Greek and Roman comic and satirical genres, as well as in archaic lyric and epic. He is the author of *Old Comedy and the Iambographic Tradition* (1988) and numerous articles on Greek comedy and related genres. Currently he is writing a book that attempts to articulate the unifying structures of Greco-Roman genres of poetic mockery and abuse.

Lacking the fortitude to be a starving actor, **Niall W. Slater** opted for the leisure of the theoried class and is now Professor of Classics at Emory University, specializing in drama and the novel. His publications include *Plautus in Performance* (1985; revised edition forthcoming) and *Reading Petronius* (1990). He is currently completing a book on metatheatre in Aristophanes, tentatively entitled *Spectator Politics*.

John Wilkins, Senior Lecturer in Classics in the Department of Classics and Ancient History at Exeter University, teaches courses on comedy, the place of food in Greek culture and on Greek literature. His books include *Euripides: Heraclidae* (1993), *Food in Antiquity* (edited with D. Harvey and M. Dobson, 1995), and *Archestratus: The Life of Luxury* (with S. Hill, 1994). Current projects include a monograph on food in Greek comedy and a study of Athenaeus.

INDEX

Index